BLACK FIRSTS

2,000 YEARS OF EXTRAORDINARY ACHIEVEMENT

BLACK FIRSTS

2,000 YEARS OF EXTRAORDINARY ACHIEVEMENT

EDITED BY
JESSIE CARNEY SMITH

WITH
CASPER L. JORDAN, ROBERT L. JOHNS

FOREWORD BY
JOHNNETTA B. COLE
PRESIDENT, SPELMAN COLLEGE

VISIBLE
INK
PRESS

BLACK FIRSTS

Visible Ink Press®
43311 Joy Road #414
Canton, MI 48187-2075

Visible Ink Press is a trademark of Visible Ink Press LLC.

Most Visible Ink Press books are available at special quantity discounts when purchased in bulk by corporations, organizations, or groups. Customized printings, special imprints, messages, and excerpts can be produced to meet your needs.
For more information, contact Special Markets Director, Visible Ink Press, at www.visibleink.com.

Cover and Page Design: Sean Deason and Pamela Galbreath

ISBN 1-57859-117-1

CONTENTS

~~~~~~

Foreword, by Johnnetta B. Cole VII

Preface IX

Acknowledgments XIII

Photo Credits XV

Calendar of Firsts XVII

Timeline XXV

Arts & Entertainment: From Obscurity to Celebrityhood................ 1

Business: New Enterprises & Corporate Advancement 49

Civil Rights & Protest: 400 Years of Struggle........................ 67

Education: Overcoming Racial Bias................................... 79

Government: County & State Pioneers 115

Government: Federal Firsts... 153

Government: Local Heroes.. 189

Journalism: Firsts in the Fourth Estate 219

Military: Marching Up the Ranks.................................... 237

Miscellaneous: A Variety of Milestones............................. 255

Organizations: Group Firsts... 271

Religion: Reaching New Spiritual Levels 299

Science & Medicine: Groundbreaking Breakthroughs................ 341

Sports: First, Best, & Enduring 363

Writers: Published & Prizewinning.................................. 409

Index by Year... 423

Keyword Index.. 473

FOREWORD

We all have our heroes and our sheroes. For people who have been systematically excluded from the mainstream of a society, it is especially important to remember and celebrate those who have won personal victories against the forces arrayed against them. This remembrance can take different forms. One is the folk tale. From Africa came tales of an animal—spider or rabbit—who, though cunning, triumphed over stronger predatory and dangerous animals. But apparent meekness was not the only strategy. Black people also celebrated, as openly as they dared, the bold rebel who broke the bonds. Black folklore is a way of remembering in order to struggle against oppression and in the interest of building a community.

For many African Americans the first person to achieve a goal and gain recognition is ever so important as a symbol of hope and a beacon for the future. These women and men become living proof that it is possible to crack what seems to be a monolithic system of oppression. P. B. S. Pinchback and L. Douglas Wilder are shining examples of men who joined the ranks of our heroes because they were the first to do what had never been done before by black Americans. Pinchback was the first black state governor and held the appointed position in Louisiana from December 1872 to January 1873. More than a century would pass before Wilder became the first black elected governor—for the state of Virginia—in 1990. *Black Firsts* records and celebrates the pioneers who displayed and continue to display great courage and perseverance in the face of odds that would discourage lesser souls.

Not all of the trailblazers encountered in *Black Firsts* set out to challenge the system directly. Many used their guile and courage to build and sustain the black community. And as a community, African Americans, no matter how oppressed, have always nurtured positive values that are then passed on to subsequent generations. *Black Firsts* records the names of African-American women and men known to history who first formed the churches and built the schools and performed a myriad of other tasks without which black folks as a people could not have survived. In doing this, the book offers a sense of the richness of black history and will perhaps inspire the ignorant or the forgetful to explore the past to gain insight for the present and strength for the future.

Johnnetta B. Cole
President, Spelman College

PREFACE

^^

Black history can be told in many ways. The historian writes books; the musician plays and sings; the artist draws and paints; and the writer creates novels and poetry. But people have a great interest in the historical firsts—the pioneers. Utilizing the lens of the firsts, we can focus on a version of history that reveals the depth and richness of the black experience in this country and worldwide. As educator Geraldine Rickman says, 'Firsts' are always difficult. We don't know that things can be done, that dreams can be fulfilled, that great accomplishments can be realized, until somebody takes that first step and shows the way."

Black Firsts represents a ground-breaking collection of the most significant firsts achieved by blacks, with an emphasis on African-American efforts. Nearly 3,000 instances of firsts ranging from science to education to sports and entertainment are described, supplemented by tables, illustrations, and photographs. While the length of the description is generally linked to the level of importance of the achievement or of the person involved, the limitations of sources and space also play a role. Some very prominent persons do not figure at all in this work since their substantial achievements follow in the footsteps of other pioneers.

We cast the net widely in trying to locate and establish firsts. Our research started with the gathering of earlier lists and with the perusal of the last 20 years of *Jet* magazine. *Jet* was a major source for the more recent milestones, and it and other magazines and newspapers have brought the timeliness of *Black Firsts* as close to the moment of publication as possible. In the process of writing, more firsts were garnered as we widened our reading, but we have no illusions that we have found all that should be here. The criteria for selection grew clearer as the work progressed, focusing on the earlier firsts as primary. For instance, township clerk John Mercer Langston had to be included. After all, this is the earliest record of the election of an African American to any public office. We have also made a deliberate attempt not to overlook firsts by women.

We have made our best efforts to be complete and accurate. History is occasionally skewed by the modesty and reluctance of some pioneers to call attention to themselves and their achievements. It likewise suffers, at a more pronounced rate, when others triumphantly trumpet word of their pioneering while maintaining only a passing familiarity with accuracy. Inevitably some seemingly well-established firsts have vanished in the light of recent study.

In other cases, we were convinced of a probable first which we could not include for lack of the final bits of proof. Occasionally, the bias of established sources may have led to attributing some firsts to significant national figures in African-American history rather than to the real pioneers on the local or regional level. Since information on these pioneers too often remains local and difficult to access, we welcome receiving news on these achievers.

Many of the remaining discrepancies may come from unrecognized inaccuracies in our sources. Overall, dates seem especially troublesome. Some errors in dates are obvious failures in transcription (1954 for 1945), and others are simply wrong. In some cases we have rejected dates while still referring the reader to a readily available source. Our choice of a different date is more often a deliberate choice rather than a mistake. Yet another source of error is the uncertainty about the exact day of an event mentioned in newspapers or of the year in magazines like *Jet,* where an early January number can refer to an event as happening recently—but without always clearly indicating late December or in early January.

Even where no question exists about the date intended by a source, there may be uncertainty about the date to use. Does a politician achieve a first in the year of the election or the year of the inauguration? The resolution of some cases depends on more information than we have immediately at hand. For example, Carl Stokes and Richard G. Hatcher were both elected mayors on the same day. Without the additional information that Stokes was sworn in on November 13, 1967, and Hatcher, on January 1, 1968, we would have assigned both men equal status as firsts. Even when the year is certain and we have enough information to fix an exact date, persons may legitimately differ about which to use. Did Laurian Rugambwa become the first black Roman Catholic cardinal in modern times when the pope named him, when the College of Cardinals concurred, or when he was officially raised to the rank?

The date is not the only problem in the choice of priority. Three black women were the first to earn Ph.D.'s in 1921. One finished her requirements first, but another's graduation ceremony was earlier. Who was the first? (We choose to list all three.) Was the first basketball player in the National Basketball Association Chuck Cooper, who was the first drafted, or Earl Lloyd, who was the first to actually suit up and play in a game?

We are further misled by information in sources that is sometimes quite simply wrong. Once published, however, the errors tend to persist. Alexander Bouchet is not the first identifiable black member of Phi Beta

Kappa, as so many sources allege. (The first is George Washington Henderson.) Michael R. Winston established this fact clearly in the *Dictionary of American Negro Biography* in 1982, with little effect on subsequent publications. While this reflects the persistence of published error, more creative and difficult to investigate are events that seem to have sprung only from the active imaginations of writers. Sometimes we were able to follow a misspelled name accompanied by probably fictitious information from source to source.

Not all mistakes are due to conscious fabrication. For example, some people genuinely believe that they are the first to do something, overlooking an earlier claim about which they know nothing. Their beliefs creep into interviews and so into biographies. Other errors arise from careless writing. Is the "first black woman to serve on a city's board of education," also the first black and the first woman? In other cases, the claim has appeared due to distortion of real information. Martin Delany was one of the blacks admitted very early to the Harvard Medical School. Due to the complaints of the white students, the black students were asked to leave after a semester. On the basis that he was a physician and did attend Harvard, we later find the claim that Delany is the first black to earn an M.D. at Harvard.

We have tried to be as careful as possible to avoid these pitfalls. While we cannot claim to be exempt from perpetuating the occasional error, we have tried to deal with our sources critically and honestly. Our goal is to present the fullest and most accurate list of firsts by blacks possible. *Black Firsts* is the end result of that endeavor.

Jessie Carney Smith, Editor
Casper L. Jordan, Associate Editor
Robert L. Johns, Associate Editor

ACKNOWLEDGMENTS

Black Firsts was created through the combined efforts of many, and we deeply appreciate their support. Research assistance was provided by Vallie Pursley of Tennessee State University, Rick Smith and Sharon Williams of Fisk University, and Vando Rogers of Nashville. Betty Gubert identified photographs in the Schomburg Collection for Research in Black Culture; Daniella Olibrice at the Schomburg Collection expedited the processing of photographs. Charles L. Blockson at Temple University suggested entries and identified and provided photographs. Marcia Lein identified and quickly supplied the photographs from AP/Wide World Photos. We thank others who contributed to the making of this book through research in libraries and archives, submission of a photograph, or in other ways.

To our editors we give special thanks: Christine Nasso for introducing us to the project; David Salamie for his early work on the project; Lawrence W. Baker for trying to keep us on schedule and remaining calm when we were not; Jane Hoehner for her extra end-of-production efforts; and the collective undertakings of Peg Bessette, Christa Brelin, Judy Galens, Kelly Hill, Allison McNeill, Jennifer Mast, Kelle Sisung, and Julie Winklepleck.

PHOTO CREDITS

Photographs appearing in *Black Firsts* were received from the following sources:

ABC Television 231; **American Library Association** 278; **AP/Wide World Photos** 14, 17, 21, 26, 28, 36, 72, 127, 130, 138, 140, 144, 166, 168, 176, 182 (both), 186, 191, 194, 200, 203 (both), 204, 209, 212, 225, 232, 233, 234, 235, 257, 258, 265, 315, 326, 364 (both), 365, 380, 389, 390, 394, 399, 406; **Atlanta History Center, The Atlanta Historical Society** 123; **Bennett College Library** 287; **Cardiss Collins** 181; **Contemporary Forum** 420; **Drew University** 328; **Episcopal Center** 323, 325; **Sharon Farmer** 217; **Fisk University Library** 8 (both), 10, 11 (both), 12, 15, 18, 29, 36, 41, 42, 46, 50, 54, 58, 72, 75, 76, 79, 93, 94, 95, 96, 106, 107 (both), 129, 133, 142 (both), 143, 146, 156, 160, 167, 170 (both), 173, 177, 198, 206, 207, 219, 224, 228, 239, 242, 245, 250, 251, 259, 262, 263, 273, 274, 285 (both), 287, 299, 300, 301, 308, 309, 316, 344 (both), 345, 349, 351, 352, 353, 355, 359, 368, 384, 386, 393, 397, 398, 406, 412, 414, 418; **Lincoln University** 85; **Helen Marcus** 413; **Meharry** 350; **Moorland-Springarn Research Center, Howard University** 159, 175, 199; **NASA** 360; **Negro Leagues Baseball Museum** 366; **Carrie Saxon Perry** 194; **Rick Reinhard** 83; **Van Do Rogers** 172; **Schomberg Center for Research in Black Culture** 2, 5, 6, 7, 22, 27, 32, 37, 39, 44, 60, 62, 64, 74, 76, 161, 168, 207, 216, 245, 252, 255, 263, 266, 272, 275, 286, 292, 320, 345, 347, 354, 358 (both), 372, 404; **Seaver Center for Western History Research, Natural History Museum of Los Angeles County** 61; **Spelman College** 85; **Joan Vitale Strong** 208; **Temple University** 145, 178, 220; **United Methodist Communications** 333; **United Press Photo** 376; **UPI** 381; **Walker Collection of A'Lelia Perry Bundles** 57; **Jean Weisinger** 416; ***Women in Congress*, Raymond W. Smock, Historian** 179, 180

CALENDAR OF FIRSTS

JANUARY

1 first black college football bowl game 386
   first black mayor of Gary, Indiana 211
   first black to score a Rose Bowl touchdown 386
   first blacks to play in the Cotton Bowl 387
   first meeting of the Catholic Afro-American Lay Congress 314
   Lincoln University was incorporated 99

6 first black Catholic bishop to serve in the United States in
      this century 315
   first black member of the Tennessee state house
      of representatives 147
   first black Pennsylvania state supreme court justice 145

8 first woman ordained a priest in the Protestant
      Episcopal Church 324

11 first black Supreme Court judge 135

13 first black elected governor (Virginia) 151

16 first black sheriff in the South since Reconstruction 115

18 first black professional hockey player 392
   first black to head a congressional standing committee
      in recent times 177

20 first black radio network 35
   first black astronaut killed during a space mission 362
   first black U.S. senator 174

23 first black Baptist missionary to Africa 307

25 first female priest of the Protestant Episcopal Church in the
      New York City Archdiocese 324

26   first black Protestant Episcopal bishop in the West 325

29   first black woman lawyer admitted to practice before the U.S.
        Supreme Court 125

31   first meeting of black Masonic lodge recognized by
        white Masonry...294

FEBRUARY

1   first black to speak in the House of Representatives as a
        congressman 175

2   first black lawyer to argue a case before the Supreme Court 186

3   first black student admitted to the University of Alabama 103

4   first black judge in Florida since Reconstruction 122

8   first black reporter to attend White House press conference 223

11   first black secretary of the army 162

12   first black man to preach in the rotunda of the Capitol to
        the House of Representatives 170
        first female Anglican bishop in the world 324

13   first successful black professional baseball league organized 366

21   first black to receive an honorary degree from a white college......104

26   first black middleweight champion of the world 380

27   first black to speak on the floor of the House 173

MARCH

1   first black minister appointed to Liberia 154

3   first black to receive a patent 343
        first university open to all races...102

4   first black assistant secretary of labor...156
        first black congressman elected from the state of Florida 173

8   first black boxers to draw a multimillion dollar gate........................382
     first act passed forbidding the importation of black slaves 132

12   New York established a Fair Employment
     Practices Commission 138

13   first black daily newspaper in modern times...................................222

20   patenting of the first successful shoe lasting machine.....................345

21   first black woman to complete the requirements for a Ph.D. 93

28   first black team on record to win a professional world's
     basketball championship...374

29   railroad brake patent 346

31   first black cardinal in the Catholic church.......................................315
     first black man to hold an American title in any sport 380
     first black votes as a result of the ratification of the Fifteenth
     Amendment 71

APRIL

3   first black to patent an improved window ventilator for
     railroad cars...345

7   first black American depicted on U.S. postage stamp.......................259
     first major slave revolt in New York City...74

9   African Orthodox Church was organized 303
     Civil Rights Bill of 1866 passed..70
     Daniel Coker elected first AME bishop..300
     Richard Allen became first AME bishop...300

10   first black to play in the Masters Tournament..................................391

11   first institution of higher education established to educate
     black women...100

12   Free African Society organized in Philadelphia 329

14   first influential revival to emphasize the centrality of speaking in
     tongues..334

15   first black in major league baseball 367

18   first black coach in the National Basketball Association 376
first black to coach a major, predominantly white professional
basketball team 376

22   first black bishop consecrated in the United States 315

23   first black woman admitted to practice before the district Supreme
Court (Washington, D.C.)...153

24   United Negro College Fund established...101

25   patent on a paper bag manufacturing device....................................345

26   first white church to give money in response to James Forman's
demand for reparations 332

28   first black nominated director of the Office of National
Drug Policy..213

MAY

2   first black student at Vanderbilt University.......................................103

5   first black bishop in the state of Tennessee 318

12   first American-born black to win a world boxing crown 380
first black to pitch a no-hitter 370

13   African-American Catholic Church established 303
first black mayor of Fayette, Mississippi 135

17   first black blues musician on postage stamp....................................260
first black moderator of the Presbyterian Church...........................338

18   first law passed regulating black servitude (General Court of
Election, Rhode Island) 146
Supreme Court decision in *Plessy v. Ferguson* affirmed the doctrine
of "separate but equal" 71

21   first black moderator of the United Presbyterian Church...............338
first black to be ordained by an American bishop 313

24   first black to address a joint session of the (Alabama state)
legislature in this century 116

26   first black to win a major tennis title 405

30   first black student to graduate from the University of Alabama 104
      Vesey revolt in Charleston...75

JUNE

10   first American black to be ordained in the Catholic church............313

14   first black woman to receive a Ph.D.....................................93

15   first black American to receive a Ph.D. in economics........................93
      first woman jockey..394

17   first black elected bishop of the Evangelical Lutheran
         Church in America...328
      patenting of the first cost-efficient method for producing
         carbon filaments for electric lights 345

22   first black national sports hero...381
      first black of his rank to score a one-round knock-out...................381

27   first black world champion in boxing.....................................380

JULY

1   first black superintendent of schools in Atlanta, Georgia.................111

2   patenting of lubricator for steam engines................................344
      first state to abolish slavery in its constitution (Vermont)..............150
      first permanent order of black Catholic nuns..............................312

3   first black Protestant Episcopal church in New York City 321

5   first black player in the American League (major league) 367

6   first black to win a Wimbledon championship...............................405
      first state legislative body with a black majority 146

7   first widely known black priest to celebrate mass.........................314

8   first black in Olympic history to win an individual gold medal.......396

9   world's first successful heart operation..................................353

10   first black National Basketball Association team owners 378

12   patenting of a practical refrigeration system for trucks
       and railroad cars 347

13   Continental Congress prohibited slavery in the Northwest
       Territories 142

14   first patent of the first known black woman inventor.....................346

17   first black Protestant Episcopal church 321

18   railroad brake patent 346

20   first woman bishop of the United Methodist Church......................333

28   first pitcher of any race to lose twenty-seven consecutive
       games in major league baseball 374

AUGUST

3   First issue of *Atlanta Daily World* newspaper...................................222

7   first black permanent member of the delegation to the
      United Nations 156

11   first African Methodist Episcopal Conference started 302

22   first black college founded in Tennessee, and still in existence 99

25   first black candidate certified to run for a U.S. Senate seat.............115
      first meeting of the American National Baptist Convention............309

26   first black pitcher in the major leagues..367

30   first black American astronaut to make a space flight 362

SEPTEMBER

8   first black to win a major United States national championship 405

15   first black prizefight to gross more than five-million dollars...........382
      first boxer to win the heavyweight title three times........................383

16   first black to rush for 250 yards in one NFL game............................388

24   first black bishop of the Episcopal Church in the diocese
        of Washington 324
      first black fighter to draw a million-dollar gate 381

25   first black to win a national boxing crown...379

27   first and only black Catholic college 100

28   National Baptist Convention, USA, held its first meeting
        in Atlanta..309

OCTOBER

10   first exclusively black parish in the United States............................313

16   first black director of physical culture at Harvard University 384

21   first black to play in the National Basketball Association................375

24   opening of first play by a black author to be a long-run
        Broadway hit..45

NOVEMBER

1   first free secular school in New York City...105

3   first black elected to the General Assembly (Tennessee)
        in this century..147

6   first black mayors of Detroit and Los Angeles elected 203

7   first black mayor of New York City elected...208

8   first black to win a statewide election since Reconstruction 134

10   first black presidential press secretary 157
      first black to win a major professional golf tournament....................391

11   first black to patent an image converter for detecting
        electromagnetic radiation 349

24   Baptist Foreign Mission Convention of the United States of America
        formed 308

26   first black appointed to a sub-Cabinet post...155

29   first two known black converts (one being a woman) to the
           Methodism movement baptized..328

DECEMBER

2   telephone transmitter patent 345

3   first black Catholic association whose documentation has
           been preserved...313

5   first televised heavyweight boxing championship bout...................381

9   first black elected to the National Rodeo Cowboy
           Hall of Fame 403
           first black state governor of Louisiana began his office...................129

12   first black elected to Congress to represent South Carolina...........173

18   first black welterweight champion..380

26   first black heavyweight boxing champion 380
           first black to sing with the Chicago Civic Opera Company
           during the regular season..19

BLACK FIRSTS

2,000 YEARS OF EXTRAORDINARY ACHIEVEMENT

ARTS & ENTERTAINMENT: FROM OBSCURITY TO CELEBRITYHOOD

ARCHITECTURE

1908 • Vertner W. Tandy, Sr., (1885–1949) was the first black American architect registered in New York State. He designed Villa Lewaro, on the Hudson River, the mansion of hair care magnate Madame C. J. Walker. Tandy is also known for founding Alpha Phi Alpha fraternity at Cornell University.

Sources: Who's Who In Colored America, 1929, p. 352; Garrett, Famous First Facts About Negroes, p. 72.

1953 • Paul Revere Williams (1894–1980), was the first black architect to become a fellow of the American Institute of Architects. Certified in California in 1915, he designed homes and buildings for Hollywood luminaries. In addition to designing more than three thousand homes, ranging in value from ten thousand to six hundred thousand dollars, Williams served as associate architect for the fifty-million dollar Los Angeles International Airport.

Sources: Cederholm, Afro-American Artists, p. 307; Negro Almanac, 1989, p. 1092; Robinson, Historical Negro Biographies, pp. 262–63.

1954 • Norma Merrick Sklarek (1928–) was the first black woman registered architect. Registered in New York State and later in California (1962), she was also the first black woman fellow of the American Institute of Architects in 1980.

Sources: Black Women in America, pp. 1042–43; Lanker, I Dream a World, p. 41; Notable Black American Women, p. 1027.

CARTOONS

1910 • George Herriman (1880–1944) was the first black to achieve fame as a syndicated cartoonist. On July 26, 1910, the prototype of Ignatz Mouse

E. SIMMS CAMPBELL.

hit the prototype of Krazy Kat with a brick. The strip *Krazy Kat* was extremely popular in the 1920s, especially with intellectuals, and continued with somewhat diminished success until July 25, 1944. Herriman was born in New Orleans in a family classified as black, and the family moved to Los Angeles to escape racial labeling. Some of his friends called him "The Greek," but he never openly divulged his background.

Source: McDonnell, O'Connell, and de Havenon, *Krazy Kat,* p. 30–31, 55.

1933 • E[lmer] Simms Campbell (1906–1971) was the first black cartoonist to work for national publications. The St. Louis–born artist contributed cartoons and other art work to *Esquire* (he was in nearly every issue from 1933 to 1958), *Cosmopolitan, Redbook,* the *New Yorker, Opportunity,* and syndicated features in 145 newspapers. Campbell created the character "Esky," the pop-eyed mascot who appeared on the cover of *Esquire.*

Sources: Dictionary of Black Culture, p. 81; *Encyclopedia of Black America,* 214; *Who's Who in Colored America, 1950,* p. 592.

1964 • Morrie (Morris) Turner (1923–), cartoonist and educator, created "Wee Pals," the first integrated comic strip in the world. Influenced by Charles Schultz's "Peanuts" and inspired by Dick Gregory, "Wee Pals" became nationally syndicated and appeared in all of the large daily and Sunday comics. "Nippie," the main character in "Wee Pals," is named for the comedian Nipsey Russell.

Sources: Contemporary Authors, vol. 29–32, p. 646; *Ebony Success Library,* vol. 1, p. 311; *Essence* 5 (July 1974), pp. 58–59, 64, 67.

1991 • Barbara Brandon (1958–) became the first black woman cartoonist nationally syndicated in the white press. Her comic strip, "Where I'm Coming From," appeared first in the *Detroit Free Press,* and was acquired by Universal Press Syndicate in 1991. Brandon was born in Brooklyn, New York, and her father, Brumsic Brandon, Jr., was creator of the "Luther" comic strip which first appeared in the late 1960s.

Sources: Black Women in America, pp. 161–62; *Contemporary Black Biography,* vol. 3, pp. 16–17.

CIRCUS

1966 • The first black showgirl with Ringling Brothers Circus was Toni Williams (1943–) of Reading, Pennsylvania. Since then she has formed a trapeze act on her own.

Sources: Alford, *Famous First Blacks,* p. 71; *Essence* 8 (March 1978), pp. 56, 58, 60.

1977 • Bernice Collins (1957–) was the first black woman clown with Ringling Brothers. The Kansas City native decided to become a clown when she was fourteen years old.

Source: Essence 8 (March 1978), p. 58.

DANCE

1845 • William Henry Lane (c. 1825–52), "Master Juba," was the first black dance star. He took his stage name from the African dance, the juba. In 1845, Lane won the title "King of All Dancers" after three challenge contests. He toured with three white minstrels, receiving top billing, and garnered acclaim for his 1848 performance in London. Lane died in 1852, without ever returning to the United States.

Sources: Emery, *Black Dance,* pp. 185–90; Thorpe, *Black Dance,* pp. 42–44.

1923 • In October, 1923, *Running Wild* was the first black show to introduce the Charleston to nonblack audiences. After its appropriation by a white show in 1926, the dance achieved a world-wide popularity second only to the black-inspired Tango, which came to Europe and America from Argentina. A third black dance to achieve wide success in the 1920s was the Black Bottom, which reached New York in *Dinah* at Harlem's Lafayette Theater in 1924. Both the Charleston and the Black Bottom were theatrical adaptations of dances known to blacks in the South for a decade or more.

Sources: Emery, *Black Dance,* pp. 226–28; Johnson, *Black Manhattan,* pp. 189–90.

1932 • Buddy (Clarence) Bradley was the first black to choreograph a show of white dancers. He was hired to prepare the London production of *Evergreen* for which he was in charge of sixty-four dancers. Bradley received full-credit in the program. His career from this time on was mainly in Europe, where he was an important figure in popular dance.

Source: Thorpe, *Black Dance,* pp. 106–7.

Hemsley Winfield (1906–1934) was the first black dancer to be involved in ballet. He choreographed and performed with his own company in the Metropolitan Opera's production of Louis Gruenberg's *The Emperor Jones.* This was a one-time exception to the rules—management did not list the dancers in the program. The next black dancer did not appear with the company until 1951. Winfield's mother was a playwright, and he made his debut in one of her plays, *Wade in the Water* (1926). He became a dancer and a pioneer in black concert dance, organizing the Negro Art Theater Dance Group. This group gave its first concert on April 29, 1931, and appeared in Hall Johnson's *Run Little Chillun* in 1933.

Sources: Emery, *Black Dance,* pp. 242–43, 320; Thorpe, *Black Dance,* pp. 112–14.

1951 • Janet Collins (1923–) was the first black prima ballerina at the Metropolitan Opera Company, a position that she held for three years. She made her debut in *Aida.* Collins was born in New Orleans on March 2, 1923, and her family later settled in Los Angeles. A graduate of Los Angeles City College and Arts Center School, Collins is known for her choreography and her dance instruction.

Sources: Emery, *Black Dance,* pp. 320–22; *Encyclopedia of Black America,* p. 279; *Negro Almanac, 1989,* p. 1429; *Notable Black American Women,* pp. 210–11.

1958 • The first black dancer in the country to become a member of a classical ballet company, the New York City Ballet, was Arthur Mitchell (1934–). Born in New York City, Mitchell studied at the city's High School of Performing Arts and at the School of American Ballet. He founded the Dance Theatre of Harlem as a school of dance—especially classical ballet—for children, regardless of race. The first black classical ballet company in the United States, it made its debut at the Guggenheim Museum of Art in New York City. In 1988 the company became the first black cultural group to tour the Soviet Union under the renewed cultural exchange program.

Sources: Emery, *Black Dance,* pp. 279–84; *Encyclopedia of Black America,* p. 564; Garrett, *Famous First Facts About Negroes,* p. 44; *Jet* 74 (23 May 1988), p. 56.

1963 • Katherine Dunham (1910–) was the first black choreographer to work at the Metropolitan Opera House. A dancer, choreographer, school founder, and anthropologist, she was born in Glen Ellyn, Illinois, and graduated from the University of Chicago and Northwestern University. Dunham incorporated her training in anthropology and her study of African and West Indian dances into her own techniques and dance instruction.

Sources: Emery, *Black Dance,* pp. 251–60; *Notable Black American Women,* pp. 296–301; Thorpe, *Black Dance,* pp. 124–30.

1984 • The Alvin Ailey Dance Theater was the first black modern dance troupe to perform in the Metropolitan Opera House. Founded in 1958 by Alvin Ailey (1931–89), the troupe has performed before more than an estimated fifteen million people throughout the world. Ailey's best known work, "Revelations," based on his childhood experiences in black Baptist churches, was created in 1961. The dancer and choreographer was born in Rogers, Texas.

Sources: Emery, *Black Dance,* pp. 272–79; Hornsby, *Milestones in 20th-Century African-American History,* pp. 432–33; *Jet* 66 (23 July 1984), p. 13; Thorpe, *Black Dance,* pp. 131–35.

DRAMATISTS

1970 • Maya Angelou (Marguerite Johnson, 1928–), actress, dancer, and writer, was the first black woman to have an original screenplay produced, *Georgia, Georgia,* which she directed. Angelou was also the first black woman to have a non-fiction work on the best-seller list. Her autobiographical *I Know Why the Caged Bird Sings* (1970) evoked images of a black girl's childhood in the South, and was nominated for a 1970 National Book Award and aired as a television movie in 1979. An artist of wide-ranging talents, she was nominated for a Tony award for acting and a Pulitzer Prize for poetry. (*See also* **Writers: Poetry, 1993.**)

Sources: Current Biography, 1974, pp. 12–15; *Jet* (8 February 1993), pp. 4–10; Lanker, *I Dream a World,* p. 162; *Notable Black American Women,* pp. 23–27.

MAYA ANGELOU

Charles Gardone (1925–), playwright, was the first black dramatist to win the Pulitzer Prize for drama, for the play *No Place to be Somebody.*

Sources: Black Writers, pp. 224–26; *Dictionary of Black Culture,* p. 187.

FESTIVALS

1949 • (Daniel) Louis "Satchmo" Armstrong (1900–71), jazz trumpeter, was the first black to preside over the New Orleans Mardi Gras. Born in New Orleans, he learned to play the coronet and read music while in the Negro Waifs Home for Boys. Armstrong moved to Chicago and became one of the most influential jazz artists. A superb showman, he was known for his gravelly, growling vocal style. He acquired the nickname "Satchmo" in 1932 from an editor of *The Melody Maker.*

Sources: Cantor, *Historical Landmarks of Black America,* pp. 165–66; *Encyclopedia of Black America,* p. 118; Southern, *Biographical Directory,* pp. 17–18; Southern, *The Music of Black Americans,* pp. 373–77.

LOUIS ARMSTRONG

1988 • The first National Black Arts Festival in the United States was held in Atlanta.

Source: Jet 74 (25 April 1988), p. 51.

FILM

1902 • The first appearance of blacks in film came in *Off to Bloomingdale Asylum.* The slapstick comedy was made in France, and produced by George Méliès. The black characters were probably played by white actors.

Sources: Bergman, *The Chronological History of the Negro in America,* p. 338; *Negro Almanac, 1989,* p. 1234.

1905 • *The Wooing and Wedding of a Coon* is the earliest known American-made film with an all-black cast. A derogatory one-reeler, the film presented undisguised mockery of a black couple.

Sources: Bergman, *The Chronological History of the American Negro in America,* p. 347; Klotman, *Frame by Frame,* p. 585; *Negro Almanac, 1989,* p. 1234.

1914 • Sam Lucas (Samuel Milady, 1840–1916) was the first black to play the title role in *Uncle Tom's Cabin* on film. He had been the first black man to play Uncle Tom on stage in 1878. Born in Washington, Ohio, Lucas performed with major minstrel troupes, wrote one of the most popular minstrel songs of the 1870s (*Carve dat 'Possum*) appeared in vaudeville, and starred in musical comedies, including *A Trip to Coontown* (1898). He is also known as the first black composer of popular ballads.

Sources: Emery, *Black Dance,* pp. 205, 209; Johnson, *Black Manhattan,* pp. 90–92, 102, 113; Southern, *The Music of Black Americans,* p. 237.

1915 • Madame Sul-Te-Wan (1873–1959) was the first black American to be hired by a major movie producer on a continuing basis. D. W. Griffith hired her after she worked on *Birth of a Nation*.

Sources: Beasley, *The Negro Trail Blazers of California*, p. 237; *Black Women in America*, pp. 1129–32; *Our World* 9 (February 1954), 80–82; *Notable Black American Women*, pp. 1093–94.

1926 • Stepin Fetchit (Lincoln Theodore Monroe Andrew Perry, 1902–1985) and Carolynne Snowden played in the first on-screen black romance in the movie, *In Old Kentucky*. Fetchit, an actor and comedian, was the first black actor to receive feature billing in movies, and the first black to appear in films with stars like Will Rogers and Shirley Temple. He appeared in films in the 1920s and 1930s. The Key West, Florida, native took his stage name from a race horse on which he had bet in Oklahoma, before he left for Hollywood in the 1920s.

Sources: Encyclopedia of Black America, p. 38; Hornsby, *Milestones in Twentieth-Century African-American History*, pp. 345–46; *Split Image*, p. 138.

1928 • The first black sound film was *Melancholy Dame*, a comedy two-reeler, starring Evelyn Preer, Roberta Hyson, Edward Thompson, and Spencer Williamson.

Source: Klotman, *Frame by Frame*, p. 347.

1929 • The first two full-length films with all-black casts were *Hearts in Dixie*, starring Daniel Haynes, Nina Mae McKinney, and Victoria Spivey; and *Hallelujah*, starring Clarence Muse, Stepin Fetchit, and Mildred Washington. *Hearts in Dixie* was also the first black-oriented all-talking, all-singing film from a major company.

Sources: Bergman, *The Chronological History of the Negro in America*, p. 447; Kane, *Famous First Facts*, p. 401; Klotman, *Frame by Frame*, pp. 217–18, 227; Southern, *The Music of Black Americans*, pp. 436–37.

1940 • Hattie McDaniel (1895–1952), singer, vaudeville performer, and actress, was the first black to win an Oscar. She was named best supporting actress for her portrayal of Mammy in *Gone with the Wind*. McDaniel made her radio debut in 1915, and is said to be the first black American woman to sing on radio. Often called "Hi-Hat Hattie," she was born in Wichita, Kansas, and moved to Hollywood in 1931. She made her movie debut in *The Golden West* in 1932, and appeared in more than three hundred films during the next two decades. Her career was built on the "Mammy" image, a role she played with dignity. In 1947, she continued the role in "Beulah" on the radio.

Sources: Dictionary of American Negro Biography, pp. 414–15; Hornsby, *Milestones in 20th-Century African-American History*, p. 35; *Negro Almanac,1989*, p. 1426; *Notable Black American Women*, pp. 703–5.

HATTIE MCDANIEL

1944 • The first United States Army training film favorably depicting blacks was made. It was designed to introduce black and white soldiers to the contributions of blacks in military history. Frank Capra (the producer), Carlton Moss (a black writer), and a large group of black soldiers were among those who created *The Negro Soldier.*
Source: *Split Image,* p. 150.

1955 • Dorothy Dandridge (1922–65) was the first black woman nominated for an Oscar in a leading role for her portrayal of Carmen in *Carmen Jones,* a role she acted while someone else sang for her.

    She was born on November 9, 1922, in Cleveland, and later moved to Los Angeles. From 1937 to 1964, Dandridge appeared in a number of films, often typecast in the stereotypical roles commonly given to black actresses. In 1951 she was the first black to perform in the Empire Room of New York's Waldorf Astoria. *Island in the Sun,* a 1957 film in which she appeared opposite white actor John Justin, marked the first time the theme of interracial love was explored in the movies. Harry Belafonte and Joan Fontaine were also paired in this film. Dandridge returned to night club performances when her film career ended.

HARRY BELAFONTE

Sources: *Dictionary of American Negro Biography,* pp. 157–58; Lee, *Interesting People,* p. 129; *Notable Black American Women,* pp. 248–49.

SIDNEY POITIER

1958 • The first black male nominated for an Academy Award for best actor was Sidney Poitier (1924–) for his performance in *The Defiant Ones.* He was born on February 20, 1924, in Miami, and later moved to the Bahamas with his family. At age fifteen, Poitier returned to Miami, then went to New York City. He made his Hollywood debut in 1950 and won an Oscar for best actor in the film *Lilies of the Field* in 1963, becoming the first black to win an Oscar for a starring role. In 1967 Poitier became the first black to have his hand and foot prints placed in front of Grauman's Chinese Theater.
Sources: *Encyclopedia of Black America,* p. 697; Kane, *Famous First Facts,* p. 405; *Negro Almanac, 1989,* pp. 191, 1153.

1971 • Richard Roundtree (1942–) became the first black private detective and superhero in a motion picture role in the trend-setting movie, *Shaft.* Born in New Rochelle, New York, he attended Southern Illinois University on a football scholarship, but became interested in acting in campus theater. In 1967 he was a model for the Ebony Fashion Fair and later advertised hair care products for black men in *Ebony* magazine. After Bill Cosby advised him to study dramatic arts in New York, Roundtree joined the Negro Ensemble Company and appeared in three of their productions.
Source: *Ebony Success Library,* vol. 2, pp. 224–27.

1989 • Euzham Palcy was the first black woman director of a full-length film, *A Dry White Season,* for a major United States studio. Starring Donald Sutherland and Susan Sarandon, the film deals with apartheid in South Africa. Palcy was born in Martinique.

Sources: Jet 81 (18 November 1991), p.62; *Movies on TV and Videocassette, 1993–1994,* p. 295.

1992 • Julie Dash (1952–) became the first black woman writer and director to have a feature-length film in national distribution. The film, *Daughters of the Dust,* is the story of one day in the lives of a black family living on Ibo Island, South Carolina.

Sources: Black Women in America, pp. 301–2; *Essence* 22 (February 1992), pp. 38.

John Singleton was the first black film director nominated for an Academy Award for the box office hit *Boys N the Hood,* starring rap artist Ice Cube, Cuba Gooding, Jr., Larry Fishburne, and Morris Chesnut. Although the film presents an anti-drug and anti-violent message, it sparked violence when it opened in several cities in the United Sates on July 12, 1991.

Sources: Hornsby, *Milestones in 20th-Century African-American History,* p. 479; *Time* 139 (23 March 1992).

1993 • Woody Strode, known for his groundbreaking roles in films, was the first black inducted into the Walk of Western Stars at a ceremony held at the California Institute of the Arts in Valencia, California. Strode acted in such films as *Sergeant Rutledge* and *Posse.*

Source: Jet 84 (3 May 1993), p. 34.

MUSIC

1764 • Newport Gardner (Occramer Marycoo, 1746–1826) was the first black American to compose in the European tradition. An African, he was sold into slavery in Newport, Rhode Island, when he was fourteen years old. He began to write music in 1764, and it is likely that Gardner became one of the first black music teachers in the new nation in 1783. In 1791 he purchased freedom for himself and his family, and established a singing school in Newport. "Crooked Shanks," one of his compositions, was probably the first musical composition by an American black to be published, in 1803. The text of *Promise Anthem,* one of his choral pieces performed in Newport and Boston, still exists.

Sources: Detroit Free Press (9 February 1992); Hornsby, *Chronology of African-American History,* p. 10; Southern, *Music of Black Americans,* pp. 69–70; Southern, *Readings in Black American Music,* pp. 36–40.

1770s • The Chevalier de Saint-Georges (Joseph Boulogne) (c. 1739–99) was the first black classical composer of note. Between 1772 and 1779 he published most of his instrumental music, and made his debut as an operatic composer in 1777. Although little is known about his musical training, it is said that he had some violin lessons with his father's plantation manager and studied composition with Gossec in France. One of the finest swordsmen in Europe, Saint-Georges also excelled in dancing, swimming, skating, and riding. He was born of racially mixed parents near Basse Terre, Guadeloupe.

Sources: Black Perspective in Music 7 (Fall 1979), p. 143; Detroit Free Press (9 February 1992); New Grove Dictionary of Music and Musicians, pp. 391–92; Phillips, Piano Music by Black Composers, p. 218.

1818 • Frank (Francis) Johnson (1792–1844), composer and band leader, was the first black American musician to publish sheet music. This is perhaps the earliest of a long series of firsts: he was also the first black to win wide acclaim as a musician in the United States and in England, the first to give formal band concerts, and the first to tour widely in the United States. In the 1843–44 season, Johnson produced the first racially integrated concerts in United States history. He was the first American musician of any race to take a musical group abroad to perform in Europe, and he introduced the promenade concert to the United States. Said to have been born in Martinique, he migrated to the United States in 1809 and settled in Philadelphia.

Sources: Black Perspective in Music 5 (Spring 1977), pp. 3–29; Southern, Biographical Dictionary of Afro-American and African Musicians, pp. 205–7; Southern, The Music of Black Americans, pp. 107–10, 112–16.

ELIZABETH GREENFIELD

1853 • Elizabeth Taylor Greenfield (c. 1819–76), the nation's first black concert singer, became the first black singer to give a command performance before royalty when she appeared before Queen Victoria on May 10, 1853. Born in Natchez, Mississippi, she was called "The Black Swan" because of her sweet tones and wide vocal compass. Greenfield toured the United States and Canada extensively during her career and became the best-known black concert artist of her time. In the 1860s, she organized and directed the "Black Swan Opera Troupe."

Sources: Dictionary of American Negro Biography, pp. 268–70; Notable Black American Women, pp. 412–16; Southern, The Music of Black Americans, pp. 103–4.

1858 • The first black pianist to win national fame was Thomas Greene Bethune, or "Blind Tom" (1849–1909). Born a blind slave near Columbus, Georgia, his talent as a composer and a pianist was soon recognized by Colonel Bethune, who had purchased him in 1850. The child prodigy made his debut in Savannah, Georgia, and for over forty years amazed his audiences "with his artistry and his gift for total recall" of the more than seven hundred pieces that he played. Bethune had sporadic formal training and is said to have composed over a hundred works. The most celebrated of the early black pianists, he began a tour of Europe in 1866 that netted $100,000.

Sources: Dictionary of American Negro Biography, pp. 43–44; *Encyclopedia of Black America,* p. 174; Southern, *The Music of Black Americans,* pp. 246–47; Garrett, *Famous First Facts About Negroes,* pp. 122–23.

THOMAS BETHUNE

1873 • The first black opera troupe organized to present complete operas in the United States was the Colored American Opera Company of Washington, D.C. They received critical acclaim for the production of Julius Eichberg's *The Doctor of Alcantara,* but the company was short lived. The first lasting black opera company was the Theodore Drury Colored Opera Company, which began in Brooklyn, New York, in 1889. Drury (1860s–1940s), singer and music teacher, achieved a series of nine consecutive annual performances from 1900 to 1908. His last production was *Carmen,* in Philadelphia, in 1938.

Sources: Garrett, Famous First Facts about Negroes, p. 125; Moses, *Alexander Crummell,* p. 202; Southern, *The Music of Black Americans,* pp. 256, 288.

1878 • James Bland (1854–1911), composer and minstrel entertainer, was the first black to compose a song that became an official state song. "Carry Me Back to Old Virginny" was adopted by the state in April 1940, although few knew that it was by a black composer. Bland wrote approximately seven hundred songs in his career, including "Oh, Dem Golden Slippers" and "In the Evening by the Moonlight." Born in Flushing, New York, he attended Howard University Law School but gave up his law studies to join the entertainment world.

Sources: Dictionary of American Negro Biography, pp. 46–47; *Encyclopedia of Black America,* p. 184; Southern, *The Music of Black Americans,* pp. 234–37.

JAMES BLAND

1891 • Charles (Buddy) Bolden (1877–1931) was the first black to form what may have been a real jazz band, in New Orleans. He has been called the patriarch of jazz, and because of his fierce, driving tone, he became "King Bolden." His band incorporated blues and ragtime. A plasterer by trade, Bolden developed a coronet style that influenced musicians such as King Oliver and Dizzy Gillespie. Diagnosed as paranoid in 1907, he was committed to East Louisiana State Hospital, where he spent the rest of his life.

Sources: Encyclopedia of Black America, p. 603; *Negro Almanac, 1989,* p. 1204; Southern, *The Music of Black Americans,* pp. 340–41, 375; Williams, *Jazz Masters of New Orleans,* pp. 2–25.

1897 • In December, 1897, the first piano rag by a black, "Harlem Rag," was published. Its composer, Thomas Million Turpin (1873–1922), was a bar owner in St. Louis's tenderloin district and eventually became the owner of the Booker T. Washington Theater in that city.

Source: Southern, *The Music of Black America,* pp. 291, 316, 323.

WILLIAMS & WALKER.

1901 • Bert (Egbert Austin) Williams (1873–1922) was the first black to record with Victor Talking Machine Company. Between 1901 and 1903 he recorded fifteen titles, primarily show tunes or comedy routines that he had done on stage. In 1910, he was the first black to receive feature billing in the Ziegfield Follies, and remained with them until 1919. Williams was born in Antigua, British West Indies, and moved with his family to New York and California. He studied civil engineering for a period, then entered show business. He and George Nash Walker formed a successful vaudeville team that reached New York City in 1896. *In Dahomey* opened in a Times Square theater in 1902 and had a command performance during a tour abroad in 1903. The team became known for their characterizations: Walker as a citified dandy, and Williams as a blackface comic, wearing an outlandish costume and using black dialect. In 1914, Williams became the first black to star in a movie, *Darktown Jubilee.* The film is said to have caused a race riot when it was shown in Brooklyn. It was Williams's only movie. Williams's trademark was the song "Nobody," which he wrote and sang. He is regarded by many as the greatest black vaudeville performer in American history.

Sources: Dictionary of American Negro Biography, pp. 653–54; Emery, Black Dance, pp. 211–13; Encyclopedia of Black America, p. 857; Johnson, Black Manhattan, pp. 104–8.

1902 • Ma (Gertrude) Rainey (1886–1939), of the Rabbit Foot Minstrels, was the first black to sing the blues in a professional show. She learned a blues song from a local woman in Missouri, and audience response was such that she began to specialize in blues.

Sources: Bergman, The Chronological History of the Negro in America, p. 336; Notable Black American Women, pp. 913–16; Southern, The Music of Black Americans, p. 330.

1903 • Wilbur Sweatman (1882–1961) and his band were the first black dance band to record. They played Scott Joplin's "Maple Leaf Rag" in a music store in Minneapolis, Minnesota. Sweatman was noted for playing three clarinets at the same time.

Source: Southern, The Music of Black Americans, pp. 305–6.

1905 • The Memphis Students, a vaudeville act organized by Ernest Hogan (1865–1909), a multi-talented black entertainer, presented the world's first syncopated music show. The group had no students and no one from Memphis, but did include twenty talented, experienced performers such as Abbie Mitchell (singer) and Ida Forsyne (dancer). New Yorkers were the first exposed to syncopated music played by a group of instrumentalists, including saxophonists. New Yorkers also witnessed the first singing band, the first dancing conductor, and the first drummer (Buddy Gilmore) to perform stunts while drumming. The Memphis Students' initial two-week engagement lasted five months. Will Marion Cook later led the group on a European tour lasting several months.

Sources: Bergman, The Chronological History of the Negro in America, p. 346; Johnson, Black Manhattan, pp. 120–22; Southern, The Music of Black Americans, pp. 297, 343–44.

W. C. HANDY

1909 • "Memphis Blues," by W[illiam] C[hristopher] Handy (1873–1958), composer, cornetist, band leader, and publisher, was the first written blues composition. It was also the first popular song to use a jazz break. Written in 1909 as a campaign song for legendary "Boss" Edward H. Crump when he ran for mayor of Memphis, it was published in 1912. The song was the third blues song published; black songwriter Artie Matthews published the first, "Baby Seals Blues" in August 1912, a white composer published the second in September 1912, and Handy's song came three weeks later. Handy led the way in the adaptation of Southern black folk blues into popular music. His "St. Louis Blues," published two years later, carried the blues all over the world. Handy was born in a log cabin in Florence, Alabama, and began playing in a minstrel band at a young age. He was bandmaster and director of a dance orchestra in the Mississippi Delta, then returned to Memphis where he continued band activities. In 1918, he established himself in New York City, where he made his first recordings and co-founded a music company. Handy lost his sight after World War I, partially regained it, but became totally blind in 1943. Over the years he continued to write music, arrange spirituals and blues, and compose marches and hymns. One of the most celebrated musicians of his time, Handy is known as the "Father of the Blues."

Sources: Bergman, *The Chronological History of the Negro In America,* pp. 273–74; Cantor, *Historic Landmarks of Black America,* pp. 127–28; *Dictionary of American Negro Biography,* pp. 282–83; *Encyclopedia of Black America,* p. 415; Southern, *Biographical Dictionary of African-American and African Musicians,* pp. 165–66; Southern, *The Music of Black Americans,* pp. 336–38.

1915 • "Jelly Roll Blues," by Jelly Roll Morton (Ferdinand Joseph La Menthe, 1885–1941) was the first published jazz arrangement. Morton was the first true jazz composer and the first to notate his jazz arrangements. Born in Gulfport, Mississippi, he soon became immersed in the music world of New Orleans.

Sources: Dictionary of American Negro Biography, pp. 445–56; Southern, *The Music of Black Americans,* pp, 376–77.

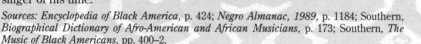

1917 • Roland Hayes (1887–1976) became the first black to sing in Symphony Hall in Boston. Born in Curryville, Georgia, the son of former slaves, Hayes studied at Fisk University where he was a member of the Fisk Jubilee Singers. He left Fisk to study voice in Boston, then traveled and studied in Europe. The 1917 concert did not attract much public attention, but another in the same venue on December 2, 1923, was a triumph. It was the beginning of a major career for Hayes. In 1923, he sang with the Boston Symphony, and may have been the first black to sing with a major orchestra. Hayes became the first black to give a recital at Carnegie Hall in 1924. He was known in the United States for his interpretation of classical lieder and Negro spirituals, and was the leading black singer of his time.

Sources: Encyclopedia of Black America, p. 424; *Negro Almanac, 1989,* p. 1184; Southern, *Biographical Dictionary of Afro-American and African Musicians,* p. 173; Southern, *The Music of Black Americans,* pp. 400–2.

ROLAND HAYES

1921 • The Pace Phonograph Company, which used the Black Swan label, was the first black owned and operated record company. It was established in January, 1921, by Henry Pace (1897–1943), who had been owner of a music publishing company with W. C. Handy. Two former workers for the Pace-Handy Company joined him: Fletcher Henderson (1897–1952) as a recording manager, and William Grant Still (1895–1978) as an arranger. In spring 1921, Ethel Waters (1896–1977) recorded the company's first hit, "Down Home Blues/Oh, Daddy." During its first six months the company reportedly sold over half a million records. It went broke in 1923, and was sold to Paramount Records the following year.

Source: Southern, *The Music of Black Americans,* pp. 366–67.

1922 • Kid (Edward) Ory (1886–1973), jazz trombonist, and his Sunshine Orchestra made the first instrumental jazz recording for the Nordskog label in Los Angeles in June 1922. King (Joseph) Oliver (1885–1938) and his band, often cited as the first to record, did not actually make their first record until April 6, 1923. George Morrison (1891–1974), who headed big bands operating out of Denver, Colorado, made recordings in March and April 1920, but they were never released.

Sources: Garrett, *Famous First Facts About Negroes,* p. 129; Southern, *Biographical Dictionary,* pp. 295–96; Southern, *The Music of Black Americans,* pp. 373, 379.

1923 • The record "Downhearted Blues/Gulf Coast Blues" was the first by a black to sell over a million copies. The singer Bessie Smith (1894–1937) became one of the most important women in the history of American music, both as a stage performer and recording star. From 1923 to 1933 she gave us such works as "Backwater Blues" and "Do Your Duty," which became twentieth-century landmarks. Born in Chattanooga, Tennessee, Smith first performed on the city streets. She eventually performed with Ma (Gertrude) Rainey, the first professional to sing blues, in the Rabbit Foot Minstrels. Smith's only movie appearance was in the first film short featuring black musicians, Saint Louis Blues, later retitled Best of the Blues, in 1929.

Sources: Dictionary of American Negro Biography, pp. 561–62; *Encyclopedia of Black America,* p. 797; *Notable Black American Women,* pp. 1041–45; Southern, *Biographical Dictionary,* p. 343; Southern, *The Music of Black Americans,* pp. 368–69, 437.

In October the first male to record the blues guitar, either as solo or accompaniment, was Sylvester Weaver (1897–1960). However, the first to achieve success was "Papa" Charlie Jackson (?–1938), who recorded "Lawdy, Lawdy Blues" and "Airy Man Blues" in August 1924. These men represented the down-home blues as opposed to the classic city blues of the great women blues singers.

Source: Southern, *The Music of Black Americans,* p. 369.

1924 • Sidney Bechet (1897?–1959), an outstanding representative of the New Orleans tradition, became the first black to achieve recognition on the soprano saxophone. He was also one of the first blacks recognized in classical music circles as a serious musician. Born in New Orleans, he was playing the clarinet by the age of six. In his early teens he played professionally, working with famous bands and orchestras such as King Oliver's and Jack Carey's, and made his first recording in 1924. A statue of Bechet was erected in Antibes in honor of his work in France.

Sources: Dictionary of American Negro Biography, p. 36; Garrett, *Famous First Facts About Negroes,* p. 129; *Negro Almanac, 1989,* p. 1203.

DeFord Bailey, Sr., (1899–1982), a harmonica player, became the first black musician to perform on the Grand Ole Opry in Nashville, Tennessee, on December 26, 1924. Originally called "The Barn Dance," the show's name was changed to "The Grand Ole Opry" in the autumn of 1927. Bailey was perhaps the first black heard on nationwide radio. The next year, he was the first black to have a recording session in Nashville, Tennessee. Bailey recorded eight sides for RCA. Known for his train sounds, he was one of the most influential harmonica players in blues and country music, and one of the most popular performers in the first fifteen years of the Opry, the longest-running radio show in the country. Bailey was fired in 1941 as a by-result of the dispute between ASCAP and the newly formed BMI over payment for music played on the radio. In 1991, a memorial marker was erected near his birth site in Wilson County, Tennessee.

DEFORD BAILEY, SR.

Sources: Essence 7 (September 1977), pp. 154–55; Morton, *DeFord Bailey; Split Image,* p. 176; (Nashville) *Tennessean* (18 December 1991).

1926 • Eva Jessye (1895–1992), composer, musician, choral director, educator, writer, and actress, became the first black woman to achieve acclaim as director of a professional choral group. The Eva Jessye Choir performed regularly at the Capital Theater in New York City, from 1926 to 1929. Jessye directed the choir in Hollywood's first black musical, *Hallelujah,* in 1929. She was born in Coffeyville, Kansas, graduated from Western University (Quindaro, Kansas), and later attended Langston University in Oklahoma. In 1935 Jessye became choral director of the premier of Gershwin's *Porgy and Bess.*

Sources: Black Women in America, pp. 635–36; *Notable Black American Women,* pp. 573–75; Southern, *Music of Black Americans,* pp. 429–35.

1927 • Lillian Evanti (1890–1967), a singer and composer, was the first black American to sing opera with an organized European opera company, singing *Lakmé* in Nice, France. She was born Annie Lillian Evans in Washington, D.C., and attended Howard University. Novelist Jessie Fauset suggested the name Evanti, a contraction of her maiden name and her married name. She was a founder of the Negro Opera Company in Washington, D.C.

Sources: Dictionary of American Negro Biography, pp. 215–16; *Notable Black American Women,* pp. 329–31; Southern, *The Music of Black Americans,* p. 406.

1930 • The first woman to lead an all-male band was Blanche Calloway (1902–1973), one of the most successful bandleaders of the 1930s. For a while, she and her brother, Cab, had their own act. (*See* **Arts & Entertainment: Music, 1988.**) Born in Baltimore, Maryland, she studied at Morgan State College, and later moved to Miami, Florida, where she became the first woman disk jockey on American radio. Calloway toured from 1931 to 1944 with "The 12 Clouds of Joy" as singer, dancer, and conducter.

Sources: Black Women in America, p. 216; Encyclopedia of Black America, p. 212; Notable Black American Women, pp. 152–53.

The National Baptist Convention, U.S.A., was the first major religious group to publicly endorse gospel music. From this endorsement followed the first choruses, the first publishing houses, the first professional organizations, and the first paid gospel concerts. Thomas Dorsey (1899–1993), the "Father of Gospel," founded the first gospel choir in the world with Theodore Frye at Chicago's Ebenezer Baptist Church in 1931. He established the first music publishing firm dedicated only to gospel music in 1932. The action of the Baptist convention, which had been carried away by Dorsey's "If You See My Savior," called public attention to a major change that had been taking place in the music of black churches, and is often considered the starting point for the history of gospel music.

Sources: The New Grove Dictionary of Music and Musicians, pp. 391–92; Southern, The Music of Black Americans, pp. 451–53, 472.

WILLIAM GRANT STILL

1931 • William Grant Still (1895–1978) was the first black to compose a symphony performed by a major orchestra, the Rochester Philharmonic Orchestra, which presented the Afro-American Symphony, his first symphony, on October 29. Born in Woodville, Mississippi, he studied at Wilberforce University, Oberlin Conservatory of Music, and the New England Conservatory of Music. Still worked in a great variety of musical settings, from playing in dance and theater orchestras, to supplying arrangements of popular music for black show people, and was a prolific composer in the art-music tradition. In 1936 he was the first black to conduct a major symphony orchestra, the Los Angeles Philharmonic, and became the first black American to have an opera performed by a major opera company in 1949, when New York City Opera put on Troubled Island.

Sources: Abdul, Blacks in Classical Music, pp. 29–32; Bergman, The Chronological History of the Negro in America, p. 316; Encyclopedia of Black America, p. 809; Southern, Biographical Dictionary, pp. 359–61; Southern, The Music of Black Americans, pp. 406, 423–27.

1932 • Don (Donald Matthew) Redman (1900–64), jazz saxophonist, bandleader, and arranger, was the first orchestra leader to have a sponsored radio series. He was a pioneer jazz arranger-composer and contributed significantly to the development of the big-band sound of the 1920s and 1930s. A child prodigy, Redman was born in Piedmont, West Virginia, and studied at music conservatories in Boston and Detroit.

Sources: Chilton, *Who's Who of Jazz,* pp. 313–14; *Encyclopedia of Black America,* p. 729; Southern, *Biographical Dictionary,* p. 318.

1933 • Caterina Jarboro (1903–1986) was the first black to sing with the Chicago Opera Company. She sang the title role in *Aida* with the company in New York City. Born Catherine Yarboro in Wilmington, North Carolina, she began her career in Broadway musicals, including *Shuffle Along* (1921) and *Running Wild* (1923).

Sources: *Encyclopedia of Black America,* p. 469; Southern, *Biographical Dictionary of African-American and African Musicians,* pp. 200–1; Southern, *The Music of Black Americans,* p. 407.

Florence Price (1888–1953) was the first black woman to compose a symphony performed by a major symphony orchestra. The Chicago Symphony, under Frederick Stock, first played her Symphony in E minor at the Chicago World Fair. The first black woman to achieve distinction as a composer, Price was a graduate of the New England Conservatory of Music in 1906, and won her first Harmon prize for composition in 1925.

Sources: *Black Women in America,* pp. 940–41; *Notable Black American Women,* pp. 872–74; Southern, *The Music of Black Americans,* pp. 416–19.

1934 • Opening on February 22, 1934, *Four Saints in Three Acts,* by Vergil Thompson, was the first black-performed opera on Broadway. The opera had nothing to do with black folk life; it is a nonlogical presentation of European saints.

Source: Southern, *The Music of Black Americans,* pp. 439–41.

On November 14, 1934, William Levi Dawson's (1899–1990) Symphony No. 1, *Negro Folk Symphony,* was the first symphony on black folk themes by a black composer to be performed by a major orchestra. The symphony was substantially revised in 1952, after a visit to West Africa. Born in Anniston, Alabama, Dawson began to compose when he was sixteen years old. Under his leadership, the Tuskegee Choir became internationally renowned.

Sources: *Encyclopedia of Black America,* p. 305; *Famous First Facts,* pp. 72, 630; Southern, *Biographical Directory,* pp. 98–99; Southern, *The Music of Black Americans,* pp. 418–19.

1937 • La Julia Rhea (1908–) was the first black to sing with the Chicago Civic Opera Company during the regular season. She opened December 26, 1937, in the title role of Verdi's *Aida.*

Sources: Lee, *Interesting People,* p. 69; Southern, *Biographical Directory,* pp. 319–20; Southern, *The Music of Black Americans,* pp. 407–8.

1938 • "Sister" Rosetta Tharpe (1921–73) was the first black to take gospel music into a secular setting, when she sang on a Cab Calloway show from the Cotton Club. When she signed with Decca, she became the first gospel singer to record for a major company. Born in Cotton Plant, Arkansas, and raised in the Holiness Church, Tharpe began touring as a professional when she was six. She took the lead in bringing gospel music to the mainstream. Tharpe was the first to tour extensively in Europe, and in 1943 she was the first to sing gospel at the Apollo Theater in New York City.

Sources: Notable Black American Women, pp. 1120–21; Southern, *The Music of Black Americans,* pp. 456, 472.

1940 • "Surely God is Able," written by W. Herbert Brewster, Sr., (1897–1987) a Memphis Baptist minister, and recorded by the Ward Singers, is said to be the first gospel recording by a black singing group to sell more than one million copies. Principal singers in the group were organizer Gertrude Ward (1901–83) and Clara Mae Ward (1924–73). In 1957 the group was the first to perform at the Newport Jazz Festival. They were also the first to appear in nightclubs in 1961, and the first to sing at Radio City Music Hall in New York City in 1963.

Sources: Ebony (December 1950), p. 95; *Encyclopedia of Black America,* p. 832; Heilbut, *Gospel Sound,* pp. 137–43; *Notable Black American Women,* pp. 1202–5; Southern, *The Music of Black Americans,* pp. 468–69.

1941 • The first black electric guitarist to use single-string solos was Charlie Christian (1919–42). He was also a pioneer in the development of the jazz revolution later named Bop. Christian was one of a group of musicians meeting after hours at Minton's Playhouse, a night club in Harlem. The group usually included Thelonius Monk, Kenny Clarke, and Dizzy Gillespie. From 1939 to 1941, he played in Benny Goodman's band.

Sources: Chilton, *Who's Who of Jazz,* p. 72; *Encyclopedia of Black America,* p. 226; Southern, *The Music of Black Americans,* pp. 474–75.

Dean Charles Dixon (1915–76) was the first black to conduct the New York Philharmonic and was possibly the first black American recognized as a symphonic conductor of international stature. He was the first to hold permanent positions for long periods with symphony orchestras, and toured worldwide as a guest conductor. Born in New York City, Dixon was educated at Juilliard School of Music and Columbia University Teachers College. In 1949 he settled in Europe, where he remained until 1970.

Sources: Ebony Success Library, vol. 1, p. 96; *Encyclopedia of Black America,* 318; Garrett, *Famous First Facts about Negroes,* pp. 131–32; Southern, *Biographical Dictionary of African-American and African Musicians,* pp. 107–8; Southern, *The Music of Black Americans,* p. 510.

1943 • Muddy Waters (McKinley Morganfield, 1915–) was the first person to combine blues and amplified guitar to create urban blues. A guitarist and singer, he was born in Rolling Fork, Mississippi, and grew up in Clarksdale, Mississippi. Waters was discovered by folklorist Alan Lomax. In 1943 he moved to Chicago, where he adopted the electric guitar. Waters signed with a recording company in 1948 and became known as the "King of the Delta (or Country) Blues."

Sources: Encyclopedia of Black America, p. 847; Lee, *Interesting People,* p. 95; Southern, *The Music of Black Americans,* pp. 493–94.

MUDDY WATERS

1945 • Robert Todd Duncan (1903–) appeared as Tonio in I *Pagliacci* with the New York City Opera Company in September, becoming the first black to sing with a major American operatic company. He was the original Porgy in Gershwin's *Porgy and Bess,* and played the role more than 1,800 times. The baritone was born in Danville, Kentucky, and graduated from Butler University and Columbia University. He later became a voice instructor and coach in Washington, D.C.

Sources: Ebony Success Library, vol. 1, p. 100; *Encyclopedia of Black America,* p. 329; Southern, *The Music of Black Americans,* pp. 406–7.

As soloist for the New Orleans Symphony in 1945, Orrin Clayton Suthern (1912–), a college professor and organist, was the first black to perform with a white Southern orchestra. He was also the first black organist to perform on the CBS network. Born in Renovo, Pennsylvania, Suthern studied at Case Western Reserve, Cleveland Institute of Music, Northwestern University, and Columbia University.

Sources: Encyclopedia of Black America, p. 812; *Negro Yearbook, 1952,* p. 63; Southern, *Biographical Dictionary of Afro-American and African Musicians,* pp. 363–64.

Camilla Williams (1925–) was the first black woman to sing with the New York City Opera when she performed the title role in Puccini's *Madam Butterfly.* In 1954 she was the first black singer to appear on the stage of the Vienna State Opera. Born in Danville, Virginia, Williams graduated from Virginia State College, studied voice in Philadelphia, and became known as an interpreter of lieder.

Sources: Current Biography, 1952, pp. 632–34; *Encyclopedia of Black America,* p. 857; Southern, *Biographical Dictionary,* p. 403; Story, *And So I Sing,* pp. 72–75.

1950 • Joe Bostic, the "Dean of Gospel Disc Jockeys," produced the first Negro Gospel and Religious Music Festival at Carnegie Hall in New York.

MARIAN ANDERSON
SINGING WITH THE
BOMBAY CITY
ORCHESTRA, 1955.

Mahalia Jackson (1911?–72), whose recording of "Move On Up a Little Higher" (1946), was the second gospel recording to sell more than a million copies in a year, was the star. Through her recording she became the first to bring gospel singing to the general public. Acclaimed as America's greatest gospel singer, Jackson was the first gospel singer to appear on the "Ed Sullivan Show," and became the first gospel artist to sing at the Newport Jazz Festival in 1958. Born in New Orleans, she moved to Chicago at age sixteen, and met Thomas A. Dorsey, her musical advisor and accompanist.

Sources: Encyclopedia of Black America, p. 467; *Notable Black American Women,* pp. 557–59; Southern, *The Music of Black Americans,* pp. 467–68, 472–73.

1953 • Mattiwilda Dobbs (1925–), who sang at all of the major opera houses in Europe, was the first black to sing a principal role at La Scala, in Milan, Italy, where she played Elvira in Rossini's *L'Italiana in Algieri.* On November 9, 1956, she became the third black to sing at the Metropolitan Opera in New York City, and as Gilda in *Rigoletto,* the first black to sing a romantic lead there. Born in Atlanta, she graduated from Spelman College and studied at Columbia University.

Sources: Ebony Success Library, vol. 1, p. 96; *Encyclopedia of Black America,* p. 318; *Negro Almanac, 1989,* 1181; *Notable Black American Women,* pp. 280–83.

Dorothy Maynor (1910–), opera singer, choral director, and school founder, became the first black to sing at a presidential inauguration when she sang "The Star Spangled Banner" at Dwight D. Eisenhower's inauguration. Born Dorothy Leigh Mainor, in Norfolk, Virginia, on September 3,

1910, she graduated from Hampton Institute (now Hampton University). In 1965 she founded the Harlem School of the Arts.

Sources: Encyclopedia of Black America, p. 548; Notable Black American Women, pp. 739–40; Southern, The Music of Black Americans, p. 405.

1954 • "Sh-Boom" was the first rock 'n' roll record. Recorded by a black male rhythm blues group, it went to the top of that chart and then went to the top of the pop chart. At first, most of the records of this kind were covers of black recordings by white groups and soloists. It was some time before nonblack consumers began to seek out records cut by blacks.

Source: Southern, The Music of Black Americans, pp. 504–5.

1955 • Marian Anderson (c.1896–1993), one of the twentieth century's most celebrated singers, was the first black to sing a principal role with the Metropolitan Opera. She made her debut as Ulrica in Verdi's *Un Ballo in Maschera* on January 7, and remained with the Met for seven performances. In October 1930 Anderson received critical acclaim for her concert in the Bach Saal in Berlin and then embarked on an extensive tour of Europe. She made national news in 1939 when the Daughters of the American Revolution refused to allow her appearance in their Constitution Hall. Anderson continued to tour until her farewell trip in the 1964–65 season. (*See also* **Miscellaneous: Honors and Awards, 1963.**)

Sources: Black Women in America, pp. 29–33; Current Biography Yearbook, 1940, pp. 17–19; Current Biography Yearbook, 1950, pp. 8–10; Notable Black American Women, pp. 14–20; Story, And So I Sing, pp. 37–58.

Robert McFerrin (1921–) made his debut as the first black man to join the Metropolitan Opera Company and the first black singer to have a permanent position with the Met on January 27. Born in Marianna, Arkansas, he was a graduate of Chicago Music College, and sang with the National Negro Opera from 1949 to 1952.

Sources: New Grove Dictionary of American Music, p. 147; New York (24 February 1992); Southern, Biographical Directory of African-American and African Musicians, p. 258; Southern, Music of Black Americans, pp. 513–24.

1956 • Dizzy (John Birks) Gillespie (1917–93) was the first black to make an overseas tour sponsored by the United States Department of State. The jazz trumpeter and bandleader was born in Cheraw, South Carolina, and studied harmony and theory at Laurinburg Institute in North Carolina. He played in Cab Calloway's band from 1939 to 1941 and, along with Oscar Pettiford and Charlie "Bird" Parker, pioneered the formation of the jazz style called Bop.

Sources: Bergman, The Chronological History of the Negro in America, pp. 383, 493, 515; Encyclopedia of Black America, p. 405; Southern, The Music of Black Americans, pp. 475–78.

1958 • Errol Louis Gardner (1921–77) was the first black pianist to give a jazz concert in Carnegie Hall. Born in Pittsburgh, Pennsylvania, he had no formal music training, but became one of the most important jazz pianists.

Sources: Encyclopedia of Black America, p. 402; Southern, *Biographical Dictionary of Afro-American and African Musicians,* p. 143; Thorpe, *Black Dance,* pp. 162–65.

1959 • Count (William) Basie (1904–84) was the first black man to win a Grammy. He was also the first black from the United States to have a band give a command performance before Queen Elizabeth. Born in Red Bank, New Jersey, he began playing the piano while a young teenager and studied with Fats Waller. Basie's own band, formed in 1935 in Kansas City, Missouri, took the flowering of that city's style to Chicago and New York City. The band established itself as one of the leaders in jazz.

Sources: Encyclopedia of Black America, p. 168; *Jet* 81 (18 November 1991), p. 12; Southern, *Biographical Dictionary of African-American and African Musicians,* pp. 29–30; Southern, *The Music of Black Americans,* pp. 384–85.

Ella Fitzgerald (1918–) was the first black woman to win a Grammy. Fitzgerald was born April 25, 1918, in Newport News, Virginia, and moved to Yonkers, New York. She began her career at age fifteen, at the Apollo Theater in Harlem, and was later hired by Chick Webb's band. Fitzgerald recorded the well-known "A Tisket-A-Tasket" in 1938 and developed her famous skat singing on a tour with Dizzy Gillespie. Known as the "first lady of jazz," she is one of the most celebrated singers of the century.

Sources: Notable Black American Women, pp. 346–49; *Jet* 81 (18 November 1991), p. 12; Southern, *Biographical Dictionary of African-American and African Musicians,* pp. 133–34.

1960 • Chubby Checker (Ernest Evans, 1941–), rock singer, became well known for his recording of "The Twist," which remains the first and only record to reach number one on the pop charts twice, in 1960 and 1962. He introduced a dance by the same title, and set off the greatest dance craze since the Charleston of the 1920s.

Sources: Split Image, p.85; Southern, *Biographical Directory,* p. 129; *Ebony* 16 (January 1961), pp. 40–44.

1961 • The first black to perform at the Wagner Bayreuth Festival was Grace Ann Bumbry (1937–) as Venus in *Tannhäuser* on July 23, 1961. Her selection by Wieland Wagner, the composer's grandson, caused an international stir. Greatly influenced by Marian Anderson, Bumbry won critical acclaim for her lieder and other art songs. She was born in St. Louis and studied at Northwestern University, where she became a protégée of Lotte Lehmann.

Source: Current Biography, 1964, pp. 60–62; *Notable Black American Women,* pp. 126–28; Southern, *Biographical Dictionary of African-American and African Musicians,* p. 55.

Quincy (Delight) Jones, Jr., (1934–) composer, was the first black vice-president of a white record company, Mercury. By 1991 he had become the first black to win six Grammy awards in one year, for "Back on the Block," and won a total of twenty-five awards, second only to Georg Solti, the orchestra and opera conductor, who has twenty-eight. Born in Chicago, he grew up in Seattle and attended Berklee College of Music. Jones also composes in large forms, such as his Black Requiem, performed by the Houston Symphony and an eighty-voice choir, with Ray Charles as a soloist.

Sources: Negro Almanac, 1989, pp. 1147–48; Southern, *Biographical Dictionary of African-American and African Musicians,* p. 219; Southern, *The Music of Black Americans,* pp. 543, 544.

1964 • Jimmy (James Oscar) Smith was the first black to win the *Downbeat* magazine award for jazz when a category for organ was first included. He won *Playboy* magazine's Jazz Poll in 1969, the year in which it too added a category for organ. Smith won recognition from both jazz polls for a number of years. Born in Norristown, Pennsylvania, he studied piano at the Ornstein School of Music and formed his own jazz trio by 1954.

Source: Ebony Success Library, vol. 1, p. 284.

1966 • On September 16, 1966, Leontyne (Mary Violet Leontine) Price (1927–) was the first black to open a Metropolitan Opera season and to sing the title role at the opening of new Metropolitan Opera house. Samuel Barber wrote the role in his new opera *Anthony and Cleopatra* for her; unfortunately, the opera did not enjoy great success. In 1955, she was Flora Tosca in Puccini's *Tosca* shown on NBC-TV's nationally televised "Opera Workshop," becoming the first black to appear in opera on television. Emerging in the 1950s as a major artist, Price was the first black lyric soprano to achieve international diva status in our time. Born in Laurel, Mississippi, she graduated from Juilliard School of Music.

Sources: Encyclopedia of Black America, p. 707; Lee, *Interesting People,* p. 142; *Notable Black American Women,* pp. 874–78; Story, *And So I Sing,* pp. 100–14.

1967 • Charley Pride (1939–), singer and guitarist, became the first black singer with the Grand Ole Opry. His interest at first was in baseball; at age sixteen he left his home state of Mississippi to seek employment with the now-defunct Negro American Baseball League. He was pitcher-outfielder with the Memphis Red Sox, later played with the Birmingham Black Barons, and in 1961 played in the majors with the Los Angeles Angels. Opry star Red Foley heard Pride sing country music in 1963, and encouraged him to go to Nashville, where he charmed RCA Records and entered the country music field. The white audience at his first major concert in 1967 did not know his race until he appeared on stage. His recording "Just Between Me and You" launched him into super-stardom and made him a number one country music attraction. In 1971 Pride was the first black named Entertainer of the Year and Male Vocalist of the Year in the field of country music.

Sources: Current Biography, 1975, pp. 329–32; *Ebony Success Library,* vol. 2, pp. 212–15; Southern, *Biographical Dictionary of African-American and African Musicians,* p. 314.

CHARLIE PRIDE SINGS
THE NATIONAL
ANTHEM AT THE 1984
DEMOCRATIC NATIONAL
CONVENTION.

1968 • Henry Lewis (1932–) joined the New Jersey Symphony Orchestra, becoming the first black conductor of a leading American symphony orchestra. In 1972 he was engaged by the Metropolitan Opera to conduct *La Bohème* and became the first black to conduct in that house.

Sources: *Encyclopedia of Black America,* p. 505; Southern, *Biographical Dictionary of African-American and African Musicians,* pp. 244–45.

1977 • Chuck Berry's song "Johnny B. Goode," and Blind Willie Johnson's 1927 recording, "Dark Was the Night, Cold Was the Ground," were the first by blacks to be sent out of the solar system. The space ship Voyager I was sent into outer space with a copper phonograph record containing greetings in a hundred languages, Bach's Concerto No. 2, "Johnny B. Goode," and "Dark Was the Night, Cold Was the Ground" on the chance that aliens might find it. Chuck (Charles Edward Anderson) Berry (1926–) was the first black to receive four Special Commendation Awards from Broadcast Music, Inc. (BMI) in 1981. His first song, "Mabelline," received wide attention, and "Roll Over Beethoven" became one of his best known songs. Blind Willie Johnson (1902?–1950?), gospel singer and guitarist, was born in Marlin, Texas, and blinded at age seven. He sang at Baptist Association meetings and rural churches near Hearne, Texas, accompanying himself on the guitar. He made several recordings of exceptionally high quality between 1927 and 1930 and strongly influenced other gospel singers. After the depression, Johnson returned to street singing.

Sources: Cohn, et al, *Nothing But the Blues,* pp. 119–26; *Current Biography, 1977,* pp. 57–60; *Essence* 24 (May 1993), p. 40; *Jet* 60 (21 May 1981), p. 62; *New Grove Dictionary of American Music,* vol. 2, p. 577; Southern, *Biographical Dictionary of African-American and African Musicians,* p. 33.

1977 • Alberta Hunter (1895–1985) was the first black to record a best-selling album at age eighty-three. Born in Memphis, Tennessee, she moved to Chicago where her singing career began. She appeared on the vaudeville circuit, stage, screen, and radio. Hunter worked as a practical nurse for twenty years, then returned to music after she was forced to retire. She recorded extensively, appeared on radio and television, sang on film tracks, and performed in night clubs.

Sources: Lee, *Interesting People,* p. 47; *Notable Black American Women,* pp. 524–29; Southern, *Biographical Dictionary of African-American and African Musicians,* pp. 190–91.

ALBERTA HUNTER

1978 • Simon Lamont Estes (1938–), bass-baritone and opera singer, was the first black man to sing at the Bayreuth Festival when he appeared in the title role of *Der Fliegende Hollander.* He also won the first International Tchaikovsky Vocal Competition in Moscow. Born in Centerville, Iowa, Estes attended the University of Iowa and Juilliard School of Music.

Sources: Abdul, *Blacks in Classical Music,* pp. 118–19; *Ebony Success Library,* vol. 1, p. 107; Southern, *The Music of Black Americans,* pp. 516–17.

1979 • Ray Charles (Ray Charles Robinson, 1930–) was the first person of any race to perform before the Georgia Assembly. Born in Albany, Georgia, he moved to Florida as a young child and was blinded by glaucoma when he was about six. Charles formed a trio in 1950, but the next year he formed a larger and more successful rhythm and blues group. He made a number of records, including "Georgia on My Mind," which set new sales records in 1959. It is said that Charles developed the concept of soul, merging gospel, rhythm and blues, and popular music into a musical entity.

Sources: Current Biography, 1965, pp. 59–62; Southern, *Biographical Dictionary of African-American and African Musicians,* p. 68.

The first two rap records were "King Tim III (Personality Jock)," record-ed by the Fatback Band, a Brooklyn group, and "Rapper's Delight," by the Sugar Hill Gang, with a New Jersey-based label. Bronx-style rapping began in 1976, but was not recorded until 1979.

Source: Split Image, p. 112.

1981 • James Cleveland (1931–91), minister, gospel singer, pianist, com-poser, arranger, choir director, and recording artist, was the first black gospel artist to receive a star on Hollywood's Walk of Fame. He was accom-panist for the Caravans and the Roberta Martin Singers and later formed

THE ENERGETIC
MICHAEL JACKSON IN
CONCERT.

the James Cleveland Singers and the Southern California Community
Choir. In 1968 Cleveland founded and was national president of Gospel
Music Workshop of America. Known as the "Crown Prince of Gospel," he
received four Grammy awards. He was born in Chicago, and attended
Roosevelt University.

Sources: Ebony Success Library, vol. 1, p. 71; Heilbut, *Gospel Sound,* pp. 233–47; *Who's Who
Among Black Americans, 1992-93,* p. 1595.

1982 • Max (Maxwell Lemuel) Roach (1924–), was the first black percussionist inducted into the Percussive Art Society. A founding member of
Bebop, and a member of Dizzy Gillespie's 1945 quintet which gave the
name to the music, he pioneered in exploiting the drums as melodic as well
as rhythmic instruments.

Sources: Jet 63 (20 December 1982), p. 21; Feather, *Encyclopedia of Jazz,* p. 398; Southern,
Biographical Dictionary of African-American and African Musicians, p. 322; Southern, *The
Music of Black Americans,* pp. 476–77.

1983 • Michael Jackson's album *Thriller* was the first to produce five top
singles: "The Girl is Mine," "Billie Jean," "Beat It," "Wanna Be Startin'
Somethin'," and "Human Nature." In 1984 the *Guinness Book of Records* certified *Thriller,* for which Jackson won eight Grammy Awards, as the best-
selling album of all time. *Guinness* also cites Jackson for winning the most
awards (seven) at the American Music Awards in 1984.

Sources: Jet 81 (November 18, 1991), p. 60; *Who's Who Among Black Americans, 1992–93,* p. 724.

1984 • Wynton Marsalis (1961–), trumpeter and band leader, was the first
black instrumentalist to simultaneously receive Grammy awards as best

classical and jazz soloist. Born in New Orleans into a musical family, Marsalis was trained in both jazz and classical traditions. He made his first LP in 1981.

Sources: Hornsby, *Milestones in 20th-Century African-American History,* p. 343; *Negro Almanac,* p. 1217.

1986 • Aretha Franklin (1942–), the "Queen of Soul," was the first black woman selected for induction into the Rock 'n' Roll Hall of Fame and Museum. Born in Memphis, she and her family soon moved to Detroit. As a child she sang gospel in the church pastored by her father, a noted evangelist and singer, and later joined the quartet directed by James Cleveland. She turned to blues in the 1960s, and in 1967 two of her albums sold more than a million copies each. Franklin won four Grammy awards between 1967 and 1969.

Sources: Encyclopedia of Black America, p. 393; *Jet* 71 (13 October 1986), p. 54; *Notable Black American Women,* pp. 364–68.

Isaiah Jackson (1945–) was the first black to be appointed conductor of the Royal Ballet Company, Covent Garden. He founded the Juilliard String Ensemble, toured widely as guest conductor, and appeared with major symphony orchestras.

Sources: Encore (December 1974), p. 37; *Jet* 70 (16 June 1986), p. 54; Southern, *Biographical Dictionary of African-American and African Musicians,* p. 196.

1988 • Cab (Cabell) Calloway III (1907–), jazz band leader, singer, and entertainer, was the first black winner of the ASCAP Duke Award. He was an important big-band leader of the 1930s and 1940s, and played the role of Sportin' Life in *Porgy and Bess* in 1952. Born in Rochester, New York, Calloway moved to Chicago with his family and studied at Crane College.

Sources: Bogle, *Toms, Coons, Mulattoes, Mammies, and Bucks,* pp. 131–32; *Jet* 74 (30 May 1988), p. 36; Southern, *Biographical Dictionary of African-American and African Musicians,* pp. 61–62.

CAB CALLOWAY

1989 • The first black woman vice-president of a major record company, Atlantic Records, was Sylvia Rhone (1952–). In 1991, she was named co-president and chief executive officer of East-West Records America, her own Atlantic label. Born in Philadelphia, Pennsylvania, Rhone graduated from the Wharton School of Finance and Commerce at the University of Pennsylvania.

Source: Contemporary Black Biography, vol. 2, pp. 194–95.

The first black Rockette at Radio City Music Hall was Jennifer Jones.

Source: Jet 73 (18 January 1988), p. 8.

1992 • Boyz II Men, of Philadelphia, was the first black group to have a record at the top of *Billboard's* Hot One Hundred chart. For twelve consecutive weeks, "End of the Road" was the longest-running pop-single, breaking the record set by their debut album, *Cooleyhighharmony,* which went quadruple platinum. They also broke a record set by Elvis Presley to have the longest-running pop single of the rock era.

Source: Time 140 (2 November 1992), 77.

RuPaul Andre Charles became the first drag queen recording star. His "Supermodel (You Better Work!)" made its debut in November at designer Todd Oldham's spring showing to become one of the videos most asked for on MTV.

Source: New Yorker (22 March 1993), p. 49.

The first black pianist to win the Naumburg Competition for young musicians was Awadagin Pratt. A student at Peabody Institute in Baltimore, Maryland, Pratt received a five thousand dollar prize, two major residencies with national arts organizations, and forty concerto and recital appearances.

Source: Jet 82 (1 June 1992), p. 22.

PAINTING

1798 • Joshua Johnston (1765–1830) was the first black portrait painter to win recognition in America. Born a slave, he lived and worked in the Baltimore, Maryland, area. A highly accomplished craftsman, Johnston was probably the first black in America to become a professional artist. An advertisement in the *Baltimore Intelligencer* on December 19, 1798, stated that Johnston was a "self-taught genius." He painted many prominent citizens, and his works are in many museum collections.

Sources: Dictionary of American Negro Biography, p. 362; *Encyclopedia of Black America,* p. 118; Garrett, *Famous First Facts About Negroes,* p. 17.

1842 • Robert Scott Duncanson (1817–72) was the first black American painter to win acclaim at home and abroad as a serious landscape artist and muralist. Born in New York, he received his early education in Canada and moved to Ohio in 1841 or 1842. Duncan traveled in the northern United States and made three trips to Europe.

Sources: Cederholm, *Afro-American Artists,* pp. 83–85; *Dictionary of American Negro Biography,* p. 203; Dwight, *Negro History Bulletin* 18 (December 1954), p. 53.

1876 • Edward Mitchell Bannister (1828–1901) was the first black to achieve full recognition in America as a painter. The most renowned black artist of the nineteenth century, he specialized in landscapes. Bannister received the gold medal in the Philadelphia Centennial Exhibition of 1876 for his huge landscape *Under the Oaks.* He was one of the founders of the Providence Art Club, which developed into the Rhode Island School of Design.

Sources: Cederholm, *Afro-American Artists,* pp. 15–16; *Dictionary of American Negro Biography,* p. 25–26; Garrett, *Famous First Facts About Negroes,* p. 18.

1927 • Henry Ossawa Tanner (1859–1937), painter of biblical, landscape and genre subjects, was the first black artist elected to full membership in the National Academy. Pennsylvania-born, Tanner studied at the Pennsylvania Academy of the Fine Arts, and in France, where he settled. He developed a fine reputation, based principally on his biblical paintings, on both sides of the Atlantic.

Sources: Cederholm, *Afro-American Artists,* pp. 272–75; *Dictionary of American Negro Biography,* p. 577; Garrett, *Famous First Facts About Negroes,* p.18.

Laura Wheeler Waring (1887–1948) was the first black woman to receive the Harmon Award for her painting. She painted prominent persons in the struggle for black culture and taught for more than thirty years at Cheyney Training School for Teachers in Philadelphia.

Sources: Black Women in America, pp. 1124–25; *Dictionary of American Negro Biography,* p. 632; *Jet* 65 (6 February 1984), p. 67; *Notable Black American Women,* pp. 1205–6.

1970 • Jacob Lawrence, Jr., (1917–) was the first black artist to receive the NAACP's Spingarn Award. Considered one of America's premier artists, he is represented in many museum collections. Lawrence depicted Toussaint L'Ouverture, John Brown, Harriet Tubman, the struggles of the Revolutionary heroes, and Harlem settings in his paintings.

Sources: Encyclopedia of Black America, p. 498; *Negro Almanac, 1989,* pp. 1050–51; Robinson, *Historic Negro Biographies,* p. 222.

PHOTOGRAPHY

1884 • James Conway Farley (1854–1910) of Richmond, Virginia, was the first black American to gain recognition as a photographer. He won first prize at the Colored Industrial Fair in Richmond in 1884 and a premium at the New Orleans World Exposition in 1885, where he exhibited with white photographers. Of the many photographs he made, only one remains that is attributed to him.

Sources: Dictionary of American Negro Biography, p. 219; Richings, *Evidences of Progress Among Colored People,* p. 495; Simmons, *Men of Mark,* pp. 801–4.

RADIO

1922 • Jack L. Cooper (1889–), black radio pioneer and ventriloquist, emulated vaudevillian Bert Williams's comedy routine, which enabled him to claim that he was "the first four Negroes on radio." He moved to Chicago in 1926, and in 1927 originated a community news broadcast about black Americans, "The Negro Hour," a pioneering achievement that set precedents in black radio history. Cooper, the only broadcaster who played pop-

HENRY TANNER.

ular black music on race labels, built up a loyal black audience and gathered news from black publications to develop the first regular black newscast. He created a missing persons bureau to help itinerant black migrants locate relatives who had moved to Chicago. By 1949, Cooper owned his own broadcast studio and advertising agency, and had become a millionaire.
Sources: Ebony 3 (December 1947), p. 47; *Ebony* 7 (July 1952), p. 14; *Ebony* 12 (July 1957), p. 5; Garrett, *Famous First Facts About Negroes,* p. 166; *Negro Digest* 3 (February 1945), pp. 11–12; *Split Image,* pp. 182, 185–86.

1929 • The Harlem Broadcasting Corporation was established, becoming the first black radio venture of its kind. It operated its own radio studios at Lenox Avenue and 125th Street in Harlem, leased time on local radio outlet WRNY, and operated an artist bureau for black radio talent.
Source: Split Image, p. 185.

1929 • The Mills Brothers were the first black group to have commercial sponsorship on a national network, CBS. They first broadcast over WLW in Chicago in 1929. The longest-lived group of modern times, the Mills Brothers performed from about 1922 to 1982. During this period, there were two changes in personnel: bassist John, Jr., died in 1936, and was replaced by his father, who retired in 1954. The quartet then became a trio.
Source: Southern, *The Music of Black Americans,* pp. 437, 498.

1933 • The first black hero to be heard on network radio was Juano Hernandez's depiction of "John Henry: Black River Giant," which he performed in a series broadcast on CBS.
Source: Split Image, p. 187.

1943 • "King Biscuit Time" was the first live black country blues program. The program was heard on KFFA in Helena, Arkansas, until 1981, although the music was not always live. Harmonica-player Rice (Willie) Miller (1899–1965), also known as "Sonny Boy Williamson, No. 2," and guitarist Junior (Robert) Lockwood (1915–) began the program in November. For the first time, black Americans in the South developed their own radio programs.
Sources: Split Image, p. 208; Southern, *The Music of Black Americans,* pp. 492–93.

1945 • WSM, located in Nashville, Tennessee, provided the first clear-channel broadcasting oriented to blacks in the South. The success of this format was a stimulus to the growth of radio programming aimed at black audiences in the South. The late-night programs had white announcers.
Source: (Nashville) *Tennessean* (20 February 1992).

1948 • Nat King Cole (Nathaniel Coles, 1919–65) led the first black jazz group to have its own sponsored program on radio. Cole soon began to concentrate his attention on his singing, and by 1952 he was one of the most successful singers of popular music. In 1956 and 1957 he was the second black to host a nationwide network television show. Born in Montgomery, Alabama, his family moved to Chicago, and by 1936 he was piano player for the touring black revue, *Shuffle Along.* He formed the King Cole Trio, which toured the country and made recordings. "Straighten Up and Fly Right," his first record, sold more than five hundred thousand copies. "Nature Boy" (1948), "Mona Lisa" (1949), and "Too Young" (1951) are among his most successful hits.

Sources: Dictionary of American Negro Biography, pp. 120–21; *Encyclopedia of Black America,* p. 277; Southern, *Biographical Dictionary of Afro-American and African Musicians,* p. 76; Southern, *The Music of Black Americans,* pp. 497–98.

Hal Jackson (1922–) was the first black announcer and disc jockey on WOOK, in Washington, D.C., when the station changed to a black format. Known as the dean of broadcasting, he was also the first black master of ceremonies of a network jazz show, the first black to host an interracial network jazz show, the first black host of an international network television presentation, and the first minority person inducted into the National Association of Broadcasters' Hall of Fame. Jackson founded the Miss Black Teenage America Pageant (now the Miss United States Talented Teen Pageant).

Sources: Split Image, p. 212–13; Tenth Anniversary, Candace Awards (program), 22 June 1992.

1949 • WDIA in Memphis, Tennessee, a white-owned radio station, became the first to have all black-oriented programming. The station hired Nat D. Williams (?–1983), who became the first black disk jockey in the South, and the first black announcer in the South to play popular rhythm and blues records on the air. On October 21, 1948, the station launched "Tan Town Jamboree," its first black show. Memphis became a center for blues broadcasting. Blues Boy "B. B." (Riley) King (1925–) was on WDIA with his band, and in 1949 KWEM in West Memphis, Arkansas, featured Howlin Wolf (Chester Burnett, 1910–75) and his band.

Sources: Jet 65 (5 December 1983), p. 18; Southern, *The Music of Black Americans,* p. 493; *Split Image,* pp. 209–10; (Nashville) *Tennessean* (29 February 1992).

The first black-owned radio station, in Atlanta, Georgia, was WERD, purchased on October 4, 1949, by J. B. Blayton. Broadcast began on October 7. Jack Gibson was the first black program director and oriented programming to black Atlantans. In 1955 he was an organizer of the National Association of Radio Announcers. The station signed off the air, was sold, and relocated in 1957.

Sources: Alford, *Famous First Blacks,* p. 76; Bergman, *The Chronological History of the Negro in America,* p. 521; *Going Against the Wind,* pp. 123, 161; *Split Image,* p. 213.

1954 • W. Leonard Evans, Jr., (1915–) publisher of the black radio trade magazine *Tuesday,* a Sunday magazine supplement appearing in twenty papers, founded the National Negro Network. The first black radio network, it began programming on January 20, 1954, and was carried on forty stations. Juanita Hall starred in the first program, "The Story of Ruby Valentine," a soap opera.

Sources: Encyclopedia of Black America, p. 378; Negro Almanac, 1989, p. 1429; Split Image, p. 226.

1955 • The National Association of Radio Announcers (NARA) was the first black disc jockey trade organization. It was organized and controlled by a group known as the "Original Thirteen." By 1967 NARA faced an internal crisis that destroyed it as a viable organization. A militant new breed of disc jockeys made a number of angry demands and tried to change its name to NARTA, to include television announcers. The organization was unable to overcome this conflict.

Source: Split Image, pp. 216, 226.

1972 • The first black controlled station of the National Federation of Community Broadcasters was KPOO-FM, in San Francisco. Called "Poor People's Radio," it was founded by Lorenzo Milam to serve the inner-city poor and predominantly black people.

Source: Split Image, p. 233.

John H. Johnson, publisher and editor, purchased Chicago radio station WGRT and became the first black in the city to own a broadcasting outlet. (*See also* **Business: Miscellaneous Industries, 1972** and **Publishing, 1938; Journalism: Periodicals, 1942** and **1944.**)

Source: Ebony Success Library, vol. 2, pp. 132–37.

RECORDING

1920 • On February 14, 1920, Mamie Smith (1883–1946) was the first black woman to make a record. She recorded "You Can't Keep a Good Man Down" and "This Thing Called Love." These songs were written by her black manager, Perry Bradford, who also wrote the next two songs she recorded, "It's Right Here for You" and "Crazy Blues." The first blues song ever recorded, "Crazy Blues" sold 790,000 copies in the first year. Its success led OKeh Records to establish its series "Original Race Records" under black musical director Clarence Williams (1893–1965).

Sources: Encyclopedia of Black America, p. 599; Notable Black American Women, pp. 1048–49; Southern, Biographical Dictionary of African-American and African Musicians, p. 347; Southern, The Music of Black Americans, p. 365.

1960 • Moms (Jackie) Mabley (1894–1974) became the first black comedienne to have a best selling record. For many years she was the only black woman comedienne in the country, and was the first to become widely recognized. Born Loretta Mary Aiken in Brevard, South Carolina, she moved to Cleveland at age fourteen. Mabley travelled on the vaudeville circuit, was a regular at the Apollo in Harlem, made several recordings, and appeared in Broadway shows, on television, and in films.

Sources: Current Biography, 1975, pp. 216–64; Lee, *Interesting People,* p. 56; *Notable Black American Women,* pp. 688–90.

**MOMS
MABLEY**

SCULPTURE

1870 • [Mary] Edmonia Lewis (1845–c.1890) was the first black American sculptor to study abroad, and in 1871 was the first black artist to exhibit in Rome. After studying at Oberlin College, Ohio, she opened a studio in Boston and earned enough money to move to Europe. Lewis received many commissions for her neoclassical sculptures from eminent and wealthy persons in the United States. She received national recognition at Philadelphia's Centennial Exhibition in 1876.

Sources: Cederholm, *Afro-American Artists,* pp. 176–78; *Dictionary of American Negro Biography,* pp. 393–95; *Notable Black American Women,* pp. 663–66.

1934 • Augusta [Fells] Savage (1892–1962), a sculptor and educator, was the first black member of the National Association of Women Painters and Sculptors. One of her major commissions was the creation of sculpture for New York World's Fair 1939–40, *Lift Every Voice and Sing,* a sculptural group symbolizing blacks' contribution to music, which became Savage's best known and most widely recognized work. Another of her most successful works was *The Negro Urchin.*

Sources: Black Women in America, pp. 1010–13; *Encyclopedia of Black Culture,* p. 741; *Notable Black American Women,* pp. 979–83.

1943 • Selma [Hortense] Burke (1900–), sculptor, educator, and school founder, was the first black sculptor to design a United States coin. She won a competition to design the portrait of President Franklin D. Roosevelt that appeared on the dime.

Sources: Black Women in America, pp. 190–95; Cederholm, *Afro-American Artists,* p. 41; *Notable Black American Women,* pp. 128–30; *Who's Who in Colored America, 1950,* p. 77.

RICHMOND BARTHÉ.

1945 • Richmond Barthé (1901–89) was the first black sculptor elected to the National Academy of Arts and Letters. In 1946 he was commissioned to sculpt the bust of Booker T. Washington, to be placed in the American Hall of Fame of New York University. He is noted for his sensitive small bronzes and monumental statues.

Sources: Cederholm, *Afro-American Artists*, pp. 17–18; *Encyclopedia Americana, 1988*, vol. 3, p. 278; Garrett, *Famous First Facts About Negroes*, p. 175.

AUGUSTA SAVAGE.

TELEVISION

1948 • Timmie Rogers, entertainer, comedian, dancer, singer, composer, and musician, launched the first all-black show, "Sugar Hill Times," on CBS television. Known for his famous "Oh, Yeah!" trademark, he is sometimes called the "dean of black comedians," and has inspired such black entertainers as Red Foxx, Dick Gregory, Nipsey Russell, and Slappy White. He also wrote songs for Nat King Cole and Sarah Vaughan.
Source: Ebony Success Library, vol. 1, p. 268.

Hazel Dorothy Scott (1920–81) was the first black performer to have her own network television program, from 1948 to 1950. The musician, singer, actress, social activist, and child prodigy was born in Port-of-Spain, Trinidad, and moved to the United States at about age four. She studied at the Juilliard School of Music.
Sources: Feather, *Encyclopedia of Jazz,* p. 412; *Notable Black American Women,* pp. 997–98.

1949 • "Happy Pappy" was the first black variety talent show series with an all-black cast. First televised on April 1, 1949, on WENR-TV in Chicago, the show featured the Four Vagabonds and the Modern Modes. Ray Grant was master of ceremonies.
Source: Kane, *Famous First Facts,* p. 657.

1957 • The first black producer of network television programs at NBC was George E. Norford (1918–). He was the only black correspondent on the staff of the army weekly magazine *Yank* during World War II. Born in New York City, Norford studied journalism and playwriting at Columbia University and attended the New School for Social Research.
Source: Ebony Success Library, vol. 1, p. 237.

1959 • Harry (Harold George) Belafonte, Jr., (1927–) singer, actor, and civil rights crusader, was the first black to have an hour-long special on television. Born in New York City, he lived in Jamaica from 1935 to 1940. He received a Tony Award in 1954 for a supporting role in *John Murray Anderson's Almanac.* In 1966, Belafonte was the first black to produce a major show for television. During President John F. Kennedy's administration, he became the first cultural advisor to the Peace Corps. In 1990, he was the first person to receive the Nelson Mandela Courage Award of TransAfrica Forum.
Sources: Current Biography, 1956, pp. 45–47; *Ebony Success Library,* vol. 2, pp. 6–9; *Encyclopedia of Black America,* p. 170; Garrett, *Famous First Facts About Negroes,* p. 189; *Jet* 78 (23 April 1990), p. 6; *Jet* 81 (18 November 1991), pp. 6, 8.

1963 • Cicely Tyson (1942–), actress, won a regular feature role in "East Side, West Side" and became the first black to appear in a key part on a television series. Born in East Harlem, New York, and raised in poverty, she studied acting at the Actors Playhouse, and made her Broadway debut with a hit role in *The Dark of the Moon.* Tyson had successful roles in a number of films, including black films, and was universally hailed by critics for her portrayal of a sharecropper's wife in *Sounder.* She is regarded as one of the most gifted actresses in Hollywood.

Sources: Current Biography, 1975, pp. 422–25; *Ebony Success Library,* vol. 2, pp. 264–67; *Notable Black American Women,* pp. 1160–64.

1965 • Bill Cosby (1937–) broke the color barrier in television and became the first black in a non-traditional role when he costarred in a network television series, "I Spy." In 1966 and 1967 he became the first black actor to win Emmy awards for best actor in a running series. Cosby was also the first black star in a television series that excluded racial themes. Born in Germantown, Pennsylvania, he began comedy routines when he was in the fifth grade. Cosby entered Temple University on a track and football scholarship, dropped out in his sophomore year to perform in Philadelphia coffee houses, and later completed his doctorate degree there. The outspoken critic of black images in television made a bid to purchase the National Broadcasting Company on October 28, 1992.

BILL COSBY

Sources: Ebony Success Library, vol. 1, p, 80; *Encyclopedia of Black America,* pp. 289, 724; Lee, *Interesting People,* p. 154; *Tennessean Showcase* (26 April 1992).

1968 • Diahann Carroll (1935–) was the first black woman to have her own television series in a nonstereotypical role in the weekly NBC series "Julia." Born Carol Diahann Johnson in the Bronx, New York City, she graduated from the High School of Music and Art. She began singing at age six in Adam Clayton Powell's Abyssinian Baptist Church in Harlem.

Sources: Ebony Success Library, vol. 1, p. 59; *Current Biography, 1962,* pp. 74–76; *Notable Black American Women,* pp. 160–63.

Charles Hobson, broadcast journalist and educator, wrote what may have been the nation's first black-produced community program on television, "Inside Bedford-Stuyvesant," while he was with WNEW-TV in New York City. He has also served as writer-producer for the National Educational Television series, "Black Journal."

Source: Ebony Success Library, vol. 1, p. 153.

1969 • The first black actress to receive an Emmy award was Gail Fisher (1935–). She was also the first black to have a speaking part in a nationally televised commercial in 1961 and is the only black woman to receive the Duse Award from the Lee Strasberg Actors Studio.

Sources: Ebony (November 1974), p. 77; *Ebony* (November 1975), p. 158; *Ebony* (October 1978), p. 40; *Negro Almanac, 1989,* pp. 1137–38; *Who's Who among Black Americans, 1992–93,* p. 458.

Della Reese (1932–) was the first black woman to host a television variety show, "The Della Reese Show." The show was broadcast five days a week in the 1969–70 season. Reese also appeared in the television shows "Chico and the Man" (1976–78) and "The Royal Family" (1991–92). Born Deloreese Patricia Early in Detroit, she attended Wayne State University. Reese sang with Mahalia Jackson's chorus and also appeared with Erskine Hawkins' band.

Sources: Black Women in America, p. 967; Current Biography, 1971, pp. 338–40; Encyclopedia of Black America, p. 729; Southern, Biographical Dictionary of African-American and African Musicians, p. 319.

1970 • Flip (Clerow) Wilson (1933–), a comedian, was the first black man to have a weekly prime time comedy television show in his own name. He created the character "Geraldine," a black woman impersonation character. Born in Jersey City, New Jersey, Wilson spent some of his early years in a reformatory. He served in the United States Air Force and became a regular at the Apollo Theater in Harlem.

Sources: Current Biography, 1969, pp. 454–56; Ebony 25 (December 1970), pp. 176–82; Ebony 27 (December 1971), p. 67; Encyclopedia of Black America, p. 860.

1972 • The first black television show sponsored by a black business was "Soul Train." Johnson Products, Inc., supported the show, which began locally in Chicago and then spread nationwide.

Source: Alford, Famous First Blacks, p. 76.

1975 • "The Jeffersons," the first black show to run eleven seasons, made its debut. Starring Isabel Sanford, Sherman Hemsley, and Marla Gibbs, the show became the longest-running black series.

Source: Jet 81 (18 November 1991), p. 45.

WGPR-TV (Detroit) was the first television station owned and operated by blacks.

Source: Encyclopedia of Black America, p. 725.

1977 • Alex Haley (Alexander Murray Palmer Haley, 1921–92) became the first black to win a Pulitzer Prize for *Roots*. When he was six weeks old, Haley and his mother moved to Henning, Tennessee, where they lived at her family home. In 1939, after two years of college, he volunteered in the United States Coast Guard. Haley devoted much of his free time to reading, writing letters, and writing adventure stories. The Coast Guard created the position of chief journalist for him in 1949, and he retired ten years later to become a full-time writer. In 1962 *Playboy* magazine retained Haley to write a series of interviews, including an interview with Malcolm X, which in 1964 led him to write *The Autobiography of Malcolm X,* a bestseller that outsold *Roots*. Haley launched upon a twelve-year venture to track the ancestry of his mother's family. His search eventually took him to Gambia in West Africa, where his fourth great-grandfather, Kunte Kinte, had been born. Blending fiction with fact, Haley wrote *Roots: The Saga of an American Family.* Published in the fall of 1976, the work brought him prompt renown. Haley received a Pulitzer Prize, a National Book Award, and numerous other honors. The book was translated into thirty languages. The ABC television network telecast of "Roots" in an eight-episode miniseries was one of the most watched television events ever.

ALEX HALEY

Sources: Current Biography, 1977, pp. 184–87; Ebony Success Library, vol. 1, p. 136; Funeral Program, February 1992; Encyclopedia of Black America, pp. 411–12; Hornsby, Milestones in 20th-Century African-American History, pp. 283, 488; Jet 81 (18 November 1991), p. 46.

1980 • Robert L. Johnson was the first black to found and own a black-oriented cable television network, Black Entertainment Television (BET). BET premiered on January 25, 1980, and marked the first time that viewers had access to quality programming that reflected the needs, interests, and lifestyles of black Americans.

Sources: Hornsby, Milestones in 20th-Century African-American History, p. 494; Jet 77 (16 October 1989), p. 40.

1986 • WLBT-TV, in Jackson, Mississippi, was the first black-owned network affiliate; the owner was the Civic Communications Corporation.

Source: Jet 71 (13 October 1986), p. 17.

1989 • Arsenio Hall (1960–) was the first black man to host a nationally broadcast television talk show. He was born in Cleveland and began his career as a standup comic. Hall starred with Eddie Murphy in the film *Coming to America.*

Sources: Negro Almanac, 1989, p. 1142; Who's Who Among Black Americans, 1992–93, p. 581.

Jennifer Karen Lawson (1946–), became the first black executive vice-president of programming for Public Broadcasting Service (PBS) in Washington, D.C. The highest-ranking black woman to serve in public television, she oversees the creation, promotion, and scheduling of national programming for 330 stations. For the first time, her appointment centralizes national program decision-making in one executive. *The Civil War,* which was aired under her administration, drew over fifty million viewers and became the most-watched show in PBS history. Lawson was born in Fairfield, Alabama, and graduated from Columbia University.

Sources: Contemporary Black Biography, vol. 1, pp. 137–38; *Essence 21* (August 1966), p. 37.

THEATER

1821 • The African Company was the first black theatrical company, performing in the African Grove, at the corner of Beeker and Mercer Streets in New York City. Henry Brown formed the group, which lasted until at least 1823. The company's building was destroyed by white rowdies in that same year.

Sources: Bergman, *The Chronological History of the Negro in America,* pp. 117–18; Emery, *Black Dance,* p. 180; Johnson, *Black Manhattan,* pp. 78–80; Southern, *Biographical Dictionary of African-American and African Musicians,* p. 178.

1823 • In June 1823, *The Drama of King Shotaway* was the first play by a black to be produced in the United States. Written by Henry Brown and produced by the African Company, it dealt with the insurrection of the Caravs on Saint Vincent and featured James Hewlett, an actor and singer. The text is not extant, but the play may have been founded on personal experiences of the author, who came to New York from the West Indies.

Source: Southern, *The Music of Black Americans,* p. 120.

1826 • The first black actor to attain international renown was Ira Frederick Aldridge (1805–67), one of the leading Shakespearean actors of the century. He attended the African Free School No. 2, in New York City, until he was about sixteen years old and then left home. From 1821 to 1824 Aldridge worked with the African Theater company in New York City, and later moved to Europe, where he studied briefly at the University of Glasgow in Scotland. His first professional engagement in London was in October 1825 with the Coburg Theater. For three decades his fame on the continent exceeded his high standing in England. Aldridge won acclaim for his portrayal of tragic, melodramatic, and comic roles, but was best known for his portrayal of Othello.

Sources: Dictionary of American Negro Biography, pp. 8–9; *Encyclopedia of Black America,* pp. 96–97; Johnson, *Black Manhattan,* pp. 80–87.

IRA ALDRIDGE

1858 • William Wells Brown (c. 1814–44), abolitionist, author, and reformer, wrote *The Escape, or A Leap to Freedom,* the first play written by a black American. (Henry Brown, the author of *The Drama of King Shotaway,* was from the West Indies.) The play was published in Boston, but probably not produced, although Brown gave lyceum readings from it. (*See also* **Writers: Novels, 1853.**)

Sources: Abramson, *Negro Playwrights,* pp. 8–14; *Dictionary of American Negro Biography,* pp. 71–72; *Encyclopedia of Black America,* p. 532.

1865 • Charles "Barney" Hicks, a black showman, organized the first permanent black minstrel company, the Georgia Minstrels. Black entertainers had appeared in troupes as early as the 1840s, and an all-black company, Lew Johnson's "Plantation Minstrel Company," was formed in the early 1860s. Organized in Indianapolis, Indiana, the celebrated Georgia Minstrels' tours included performances in Germany and Great Britain. Hicks faced great difficulties in dealing with white theater managers, and sold his rights in 1872 to Charles Callender. The troupe was then known as "Callender's Georgia Minstrels."

Sources: Johnson, *Black Manhattan,* pp. 89–93; Southern, *The Music of Black Americans,* p. 229; Thorpe, *Black Dance,* p. 48.

1891 • *The Creole Show,* an all-black production in New York City with a white promoter, John Isham, was the first minstrel show to introduce black women into the cast. In the finale Dora Dean and Charles Johnson introduced the first theatrical cake walk, derived from the old plantation chalk-line walk. It also is one of the first shows in which black performers did not wear black face.

Sources: Emery, *Black Dance,* pp. 207–9; Johnson, *Black Manhattan,* pp. 95–96; Thorpe, *Black Dance,* pp. 28–29, 53.

1897 • *Oriental America* was the first show to play on Broadway and the first to break away from playing in burlesque theaters. The production followed the minstrel pattern, but the after-piece was a medley of operatic selections. It did not enjoy a long run.

Sources: Emery, *Black Dance,* pp. 208–9; Johnson, *Black Manhattan,* pp. 96–97; Thorpe, *Black Dance,* p. 55.

1898 • *A Trip to Coontown* was the first black musical comedy. In a break with the minstrel tradition, it had a cast of characters involved in a story from beginning to end. The show was written and produced by Robert "Bob" Cole (1863?–1911), a composer, dancer, singer, musician, and actor. The first black show to be organized, produced, and managed by blacks, it ran for three seasons after its April 1898 debut in New York.

Sources: Dictionary of American Negro Biography, pp. 121–22; *Encyclopedia of Black America,* p. 530; Johnson, *Black Manhattan,* p. 102; Southern, *The Music of Black Americans,* p. 297.

The operetta *Clorindy—The Origin of the Cake-Walk,* based on Paul Laurence Dunbar's book with the same title, was the first show to introduce syncopated ragtime music to New York City theatergoers. It opened after *A Trip to Coontown* and ran the summer season at the Casino Roof Garden. The composer, Will Marion Cook (1869–1944), was composer-in-chief and musical director for the George Walker–Bert Williams company.

Sources: Emery, *Black Dance,* pp. 209–10; *Encyclopedia of Black America,* p. 530; Johnson, *Black Manhattan,* pp. 102–3; *Negro Almanac, 1989,* p. 1118; Southern, *The Music of Black Americans,* pp. 268–69.

1905 • The Pekin Theater in Chicago was the first black-owned theater in the United States. Founded by Robert Mott (?–1911), the theater was important not only for stage productions, but also for its concert series. The Pekin Stock Company was the first black repertory company in this century. The theater ceased operation in 1916.

Sources: Dictionary of American Negro Biography, p. 261; Southern, *The Music of Black Americans,* p. 291.

ANITA BUSH.

1915 • Anita Bush (1883–1974), dancer and actress, organized the Anita Bush Players and became the first black woman to organize a professional black stock dramatic company in the United States. Her company was also the first stock company in New York since the African Players of 1821. The players opened at the Lincoln Theater, in New York City, on November 15, 1915, with *The Girl at the Fort.* They had a short but successful run, and by December 27, 1915, had transferred to the larger Lafayette Theatre, where they became the Lafayette Players.

Sources: Black Women in America, pp. 205–6; Kellner, *The Harlem Renaissance,* p. 63; *Notable Black American Women,* pp. 142–43.

1916 • *Rachel,* a play by Angelina Grimké (1880–1958), was the first known play written by a black American and presented on stage by black actors in this century. It portrays a respectable black family destroyed by prejudice. The play was first produced by the Drama Committee of the NAACP at Myrtilla Miner Normal School, in Washington, D.C. Grimké, a poet, was born in Boston and taught school in Washington, D.C.

Sources: Encyclopedia of Black America, p. 532; *Notable Black American Women,* pp. 416–21.

1917 • Black actors in serious drama first won the attention of mainstream audiences and critics on April 5, 1917, when three one-act plays written for blacks were presented at the Garden City Theater. The author, Ridley Torrence, was white, but this production marked the first serious use of black life on a commercial stage. A folk comedy, a tragedy, and a religious play broke stereotypes that had imprisoned black actors.

Sources: Bergman, The Chronological History of the Negro in America, p. 384; *Encyclopedia of Black America,* p. 532; Johnson, *Black Manhattan,* pp. 175–78.

1920 • Charles Sidney Gilpin (1878–1930) was the first black to star in a major American play, Eugene O'Neill's *The Emperor Jones.* He has been called "the first modern American Negro to establish himself as a serious actor of first quality." Born in Richmond, Virginia, he received little education. In 1896 Gilpin began travelling with vaudeville troupes, a practice which he followed for two years. In 1907 he joined the Pekin Stock Company of Chicago as a dramatic actor, and in 1916 joined the Lafayette Theater Company in Harlem. Gilpin played the lead in The *Emperor Jones* from 1920 to 1924, winning the Spingarn Award in 1921 for his theatrical accomplishment.

Sources: Bergman, *The Chronological History of the Negro in America,* pp. 284, 400; *Dictionary of American Negro Biography,* pp. 261–62; Johnson, *Black Manhattan,* pp. 182–85; Kellner, *The Harlem Renaissance,* pp. 137–38; *Negro Almanac, 1989,* p. 1140.

1923 • The first nonmusical play by a serious black writer to reach Broadway was *Chip Woman's Fortune,* a one-act play presented by the Ethiopian Art Players on May 7, 1923, along with Oscar Wilde's *Salome* and an interpretation of Shakespeare's *The Comedy of Errors.* Written by Willis Richardson (1889–1977), it was presented at the Frazee Theater and was the only play on the bill to be fully approved by the critics. The North Carolina native wrote and published several other plays, but he had little commercial success.

Sources: Brawley, *Negro Genius,* pp. 282–84; Johnson, *Black Manhattan,* pp. 190–91; Kellner, *The Harlem Renaissance,* p. 302; Rush, *Black American Writers,* vol. 2, pp. 629–30; *Who's Who in Colored America, 1927,* pp. 167–68.

1933 • The first folk opera by a black to reach Broadway was *Run, Little Children,* by (Francis) Hall Johnson (1888–1970). It ran 126 performances. Johnson was one of the most successful choral directors of his time and had been choral director of *Green Pastures* in 1930.

Sources: Robinson, *Historical Negro Biographies,* pp. 211–12; Southern, *Biographical Dictionary,* pp. 207–8; Southern, *The Music of Black Americans,* pp. 411–13.

1935 • *Mulatto,* by Langston Hughes (1902–1967), was the first play by a black author to be a long-run Broadway hit. It opened at the Vanderbilt Theatre on October 24, 1935, and played continuously until December 9, 1937. The poet and author was born James Mercer Langston Hughes in Joplin, Missouri, and graduated from Lincoln University, Pennsylvania. He published ten volumes of poetry; more than sixty short stories; a number of dramas, operas, and anthologies; as well as two autobiographies, *The Big Sea* (1940) and *I Wonder as I Wander* (1956). Hughes created the black folk character Jesse B. Simple, and wrote about him in *Simple Speaks His Mind* (1950), and *Simple Stakes a Claim* (1957).

Sources: Bontemps, *Harlem Renaissance Remembered,* pp. 90–102; *Dictionary of American Negro Biography,* pp. 331–34; *Encyclopedia of Black America,* p. 456.

1939 • Ethel Waters (1896–1977), as Hagar in *Mamba's Daughters,* became the first black woman to perform the leading role in a dramatic play on Broadway. She made her first public appearance when she was five years old as a singer in a church program. Waters appeared in nightclubs and vaude-ville, and in 1927 made her Broadway debut in *Africana.* When she toured in *As Thousands Cheer* (1934), she became the first black person to co-star with white players below the Mason-Dixon line. Her greatest role came in 1940 when she appeared on stage in *Cabin in the Sky;* she also appeared in the movie version in 1943. From 1957 to 1976 she toured with evangelist Billy Graham and achieved wide recognition for the gospel hymn "His Eye is on the Sparrow." In 1950 Waters was the first black to star in a scheduled comedy program on television. She appeared in "Beulah" on ABC on October 3, taking over the role played by Hattie McDaniel (1895–1952) on the radio. Waters' health only allowed her to film a few episodes.

Source: Encyclopedia of Black America, p. 724; Negro Almanac, 1989, p. 1162; Notable Black American Women, p. 1225; Southern, Biographical Dictionary of African-American and African Musicians, p. 393.

PAUL ROBESON

1943 • Paul Robeson (1898–1976) was the first black to play Othello on an American stage with a white cast. The son of a former slave, he was born in Princeton, New Jersey, and graduated from Rutgers University and Columbia University School of Law. At Rutgers, he was an All-American athlete and elected to Phi Beta Kappa. Robeson developed an international career on stage and in film, as well as in concert, and became a recording star. His work with the Progressive Party, the Council on African Affairs, the National Negro Congress, the left-wing unions of the CIO, and his early call for a militant black movement made him a hero in Communist and Third-World countries, and led the U.S. State Department to revoke his passport.

Sources: Duberman, Paul Robeson; Hornsby, Milestones of 20th-Century African-American History, pp. 263–66; Encyclopedia of Black America, p. 732; Lee, Interesting People, p. 57.

1959 • Lorraine Hansberry (1930–65) was the first black to win the New York Drama Critics Award, for *A Raisin in the Sun,* in May 1959. The play was the first on Broadway written by a black woman, and the first serious black drama to impact the dominant culture. In 1973 the musical *Raisin,* a revival of her play, won the Tony Award for best musical. Born in Chicago on May 19, 1930, she studied at the University of Wisconsin and the Art Institute of Chicago. In addition to plays, Hansberry's works included poems, articles, and books.

Sources: Abramson, Negro Playwrights in the American Theatre, pp. 239–54; Black Women in America, pp. 524–29; Encyclopedia of Black America, p. 425; Notable Black American Women, pp. 452–57.

Lloyd Richards, who directed Lorraine Hansberry's *Raisin in the Sun,* was the first black director of a straight play on Broadway. He was dean of the Yale School of Drama from 1979 to 1991.

Sources: Bergman, *The Chronological History of the Negro in America,* p. 562; Hornsby, *Milestones in 20th-Century African-American History,* p. 62; *Jet* 81 (18 November 1991), p. 12.

1964 • Frederick Douglass O'Neal (1905–92), stage, movie, and radio actor, was the first black president of Actor's Equity Association (1964–73), and later the first black international president of the Associated Actors and Artists of America. The actor and director was born in Brookville, Missisippi, and studied at the New Theatre School and the American Theatre Wing in New York City.

Sources: Current Biography, 1946, pp. 438–40; *Encyclopedia of Black America,* pp. 655–56; *State of Black America, 1993,* p. 295.

1965 • Ruby Dee (1924–) was the first black actress to play major parts at the American Shakespeare Festival in Stratford, Connecticut, where she played Kate in *The Taming of the Shrew* and Cordelia in *King Lear.* Born Ruby Ann Wallace in Cleveland, Ohio, she is a graduate of Hunter College. Dee is known for her appearances in Broadway performances, including *A Raisin in the Sun* (1959) and *Purlie Victorious* (1961). She and her husband, Ossie Davis, share careers in television, stage, screen, and other public appearances, and have been active in civil rights.

Sources: Black Women in America, pp. 313–15; *Current Biography, 1970,* pp. 107–10; *Encyclopedia of Black America,* p. 30; *Notable Black American Women,* pp. 260–62.

BUSINESS: NEW ENTER-PRISES & CORPORATE ADVANCEMENT

ADVERTISING

1893 • Nancy Green (1831–98), a former slave from Montgomery County, Kentucky, was the first Aunt Jemima and the world's first living trademark. She made her debut at age fifty-nine at the Columbian Exposition in Chicago, where she served pancakes in a booth. The Aunt Jemima Mills Company distributed a souvenir lapel button which bore her photograph and the caption, "I'se in town honey." The slogan later became the slogan on the company's promotional campaign. Green was the official trademark for three decades.

Sources: Black Ethnic Collectibles, p. 18; *They Had a Dream,* vol. 3, p. 29.

1956 • Vince Cullers Advertising, Inc., was the first black advertising agency in the United States. It was founded by Vincent T. Cullers.

Sources: Black Enterprise 1 (February 1971), pp. 15–22; *Ebony Success Library,* vol. 1, p. 82; *Who's Who Among Black Americans, 1992–93,* p. 329.

1977 • Richard A. Guilmenot III (1948–) was the first black vice-president of BBDO Advertising, New York.

Sources: Jet 52 (21 April 1977), p. 19; *Who's Who Among Black Americans, 1992–93,* p. 573.

AUTOMOBILE INDUSTRY

1916 • Frederick Douglass Patterson (?–1932) was the first black to manufacture cars. Between 1916 and 1919 Patterson built some thirty Greenfield-Patterson cars in Greenfield, Ohio.

Source: Reasons, They Had a Dream, vol. 3, p. 48.

1967 • Albert William Johnson (1921–) was the first black to be awarded an Oldsmobile dealership. A native of St. Louis, Missouri, Jackson gained the franchise in a predominantly black area of Chicago. In less than four years, his success led to a Cadillac dealership.

Sources: Ebony Success Library, vol. 1, p. 175; Black Enterprise 8 (June 1978), pp. 98–102; Who's Who Among Black Americans, 1992–93, pp. 747–48.

1987 • Barbara J. Wilson (1940–) was the first black woman to be an automobile dealer. She received the Candace Award as Businesswoman of the Year in 1987. Wilson is president of Ferndale Honda, Ferndale, Michigan, (1984–) and Porterfield's Marina Village, Detroit (1989–).

Sources: Jet 72 (6 July 1987), p. 51; Who's Who Among Black Americans, 1992–93, p. 1543.

1990 • Sheleme S. Sendaba was the first black vice-president of Nissan Motor Corporation in the United States. Born in Ethiopia, Sendaba holds an M.B.A. from the Walter Heller Graduate School of Business (1977). He had long worked at General Motors before going to Nissan.

Sources: Jet 79 (22 October 1990), p. 29; Who's Who Among Black Americans, 1992–93, p. 1259.

BANKING

1888 • The True Reformers' Bank of Richmond, Virginia, and the Capital Savings Banks of Washington, D.C., were the first black-created and black-run banks. The True Reformers' Bank was chartered on March 2 and opened for business on April 3. The Capital Savings Bank was organized on October 17, and it is the first black bank with no fraternal connections.

Source: Kane, Famous First Facts, p. 93; Negro Year Book, 1913, p. 230.

1889 • The Mutual Bank and Trust Company of Chattanooga, Tennessee, was the first black bank in the state. It failed during the panic of 1893.

Sources: Negro Year Book, 1913, p. 230.

1890 • The Alabama Penny Savings Bank was the first black-owned bank in Alabama. It opened in Birmingham on October 15 and was in business until 1915.

Source: Negro Year Book, 1913, p. 230.

1903 • Maggie Lena Walker (1865–1934) was the first black woman to be a bank president. She founded the Saint Luke Penny Savings Bank in Richmond, Virginia. The bank began as an insurance society in which Walker became active at the time of her marriage in 1886. When she retired because of ill-health in 1933, the bank was strong enough to survive the Depression, and is still in existence.

Sources: Encyclopedia of Black America, pp. 152, 830; Negro Almanac, pp. 231, 1394; Notable Black American Women, pp. 1188–93.

MAGGIE LENA WALKER
FOUNDED A VIRGINIA
BANK MORE THAN 100
YEARS AGO.

1908 • Jesse Binga (1865–1950) was the founder of the first black-owned bank in Chicago, Binga State Bank. Beginning as a private bank, the institution received a state charter in 1920. It closed during the Depression in 1932.

Sources: Encyclopedia of Black America, p. 180; Gosnell, Negro Politicians, p. 107; Hornsby, Chronology of African-American History, p. 53.

1913 • The Atlanta State Savings Bank was the first chartered black banking institution in Georgia. Atlanta Mutual, North Carolina Mutual, Pilgrim Health and Life, and Standard Life insurance companies were among its depositors.

Source: Going Against the Wind, p. 53.

1953 • James Del Rio (1924–) was the first black licensed mortgage banker in the United States, and established one of the first black mortgage companies in the country. Del Rio was a successful real estate broker in Detroit. Later he served eight years in the Michigan legislature until 1973 when he became a Detroit Recorder's Court judge.

Sources: Ebony 18 (February 1963), pp. 55–60; Ebony 29 (June 1974), pp. 90–92; Ebony Success Library, vol. 1, p. 93.

The Sivart Mortgage Company, Chicago, Illinois, was the first black mortgage banking firm. The firm was established by Dempsey J. Travis (1920–), a Chicago businessman. In 1961, the company was the first black-owned firm approved by the Federal Housing Administration and the Veterans Administration.

Sources: Alford, Famous First Blacks, p. 16; Ebony Success Library, vol. 2, pp. 256–59; Who's Who Among Black Americans, 1992–93, p. 1411.

1965 • The Freedom National Bank was the first black-chartered and black-operated bank in Harlem. It was in business until November 5, 1990, when it was closed by federal regulators amid considerable controversy.

Sources: Hornsby, Milestones in 20th-Century African-American History, p. 459; Negro Almanac, 1989, p. 219.

1970 • Thomas A. Wood (1926–) was the first black to serve on the board of a major bank not run by blacks, Chase Manhattan. Wood took a B.S. degree in electrical engineering at the University of Michigan, and in 1968 founded TAW International Leasing, a New York-based firm operating principally in Africa.

Sources: Ebony 27 (March 1972), pp. 88–96; Ebony Success Library, vol. 2, pp. 302–5; Encyclopedia of Black America, p. 867.

1982 • Mildred Glenn was the first black woman bank president in Pennsylvania. She became president of the New World National Bank, the only minority bank in the state.

Source: Jet 62 (14 June 1982), p. 47.

INSURANCE

1810 • The African Insurance Company of Philadelphia is the first known black insurance company. It was not incorporated, but had capital stock in the amount of five thousand dollars. Its president was Joseph Randolph; treasurer, Carey Porter; and secretary, William Coleman.

Sources: Kane, *Famous First Facts,* p. 322; *Negro Year Book, 1913,* p. 300; *Negro Year Book, 1916–17,* p. 318.

1893 • The North Carolina Mutual Life Insurance Company, founded in this year in Durham, North Carolina, was the first black insurance company to attain one hundred million dollars in assets. It is still the largest black-owned insurance company. The success of the company was largely due to the abilities of Charles Clinton Spaulding (1874–1952), who became general manager of the company in 1900 and was president from 1923 until his death.

Sources: Alford, *Famous First Blacks,* p. 16; *Dictionary of American Negro Biography,* pp. 567–68; *Encyclopedia of Black America,* p. 207, 806.

1931 • Alexander and Company General Insurance Agency of Atlanta, Georgia, established by Theodore Martin Alexander, Sr., (1909–) was the first black-owned and black-controlled general insurance brokerage and risk management agency in the South. Eventually, it grew to be the largest.

Sources: Jet 61 (24 September 1981), p. 16; *Jet* 77 (19 March 1990), pp. 15–16; *Who's Who Among Black Americans, 1992–93,* p. 18.

1932 • Asa T. Spaulding (1902–90) was the first black actuary in the United States. After earning a magna cum laude degree in accounting from New York University in 1930, and an M.A. from the University of Michigan in 1932, Spaulding went to work for the North Carolina Mutual Life Insurance Company of Durham, North Carolina. He became president of the company in 1959 and retired in 1968. He was also the first black to serve on the board of directors of a major non-black corporation, W. T. Grant (1964), and the first black elected to the Durham County Board of Commissioners. He is a member of the state Business Hall of Fame.

Sources: Ebony Success Library, vol. 1, p. 289; *Encyclopedia of Black America,* p. 806; *Jet* 78 (24 September 1990), p. 15; *Who's Who Among Black Americans, 1992–93,* p. 1610.

1957 • Cirilo A. McSween (1929–) was the first black to represent a major white-owned insurance company, New York Life Insurance Company, and the first black to sell a million dollars worth of life insurance for any company in one year. McSween went on to surpass this feat in later years: he was the first black to sell a million dollars of insurance in one month. Born in Panama City, Panama, he was a varsity letterman at the University of Illinois, where he took his B.A. in 1954. In 1984, he was the first black elected to the State Street Council (Chicago).

Sources: Ebony 20 (May 1965), pp. 207–8; *Ebony Success Library,* vol. 1, p. 213; *Who's Who Among Black Americans, 1992–93,* p. 974.

1977 • The E. G. Bowman Company was the first major American black-owned commercial insurance brokerage firm on Wall Street. It was founded in 1953 by Ernesta G. Procope. She named it for her husband, who had died the previous year, and led it as it grew. Her present husband is editor and publisher of the *Amsterdam News*.

Sources: Notable Black American Women, pp. 885–86; Who's Who Among Black Americans, 1992–93, p. 1152.

LABOR UNIONS

1850 • In July of 1850 in New York, Samuel Ringgold Ward (1817–64) was the first president of the American League of Colored Workers; Frederick Douglass was a vice-president. Ward is primarily known as a lecturer and the author of *The Autobiography of a Fugitive Negro* (1855). The league was primarily interested in industrial education rather than trade unionism.

Sources: Dictionary of American Negro Biography, pp. 631–32; Foner, Organized Labor and the Black Worker, p. 11; Negro Almanac, 1989, pp. 13, 1017.

1858 • In July, 1858, the Association of Black Caulkers in Baltimore, Maryland, became the first black labor organization on record. Earlier organizations were more mutual aid societies and fraternal organizations than labor unions. The Association of Black Caulkers was formed to resist the efforts of white workers to drive blacks from a line of work blacks had traditionally controlled.

Sources: Encyclopedia of Black America, p. 491; Foner, Organized Labor and the Black Worker, p. 11.

1862 • The American Seamen's Protective Association was the first seaman's organization in the United States. (Some half of the 25,000 American seamen on American ships in 1850 were black.) Its founder was William M. Powell, born in New York City of slave parents. In 1870 he reported that 3,500 black seamen were headquartered in the city.

Source: Foner, Organized Labor and the Black Worker, pp. 14–15.

1869 • The Colored National Labor Union was the first attempt to build a black labor organization parallel to the National Labor Union, established in 1866. Almost all of the affiliates of the National Labor Union, a forerunner of the Knights of Labor, excluded blacks. The moving spirit in the black organization was Isaac Myers. The continued hostility of white workers undermined attempts to develop black labor organizations.

Sources: Dictionary of American Negro Biography, pp. 468–69; Encyclopedia of Black America, p. 491; Foner, Organized Labor and the Black Worker, pp. 30–46.

1925 • A. Philip Randolph (1889–1979) founded the Brotherhood of Sleeping Car Porters, the first major nationwide black union. It would take

LABOR UNION LEADER
A. PHILIP RANDOLPH.

ten years of struggle and new federal labor legislation before the union established a collective bargaining agreement with the Pullman Palace Car Company. Thus the union became the first official bargaining agent for black workers on October 1, 1935. In 1957, Randolph became the first black vice-president of the AFL-CIO; he served until 1968.

Sources: Bennett, *Before the Mayflower,* pp. 366, 525, 532; *Encyclopedia of Black America,* pp. 727–28; Foner, *Organized Labor and the Black Worker,* pp. 177–87; *Jet* 81 (13 April 1992), p. 32; *Negro Almanac, 1989,* p. 560.

1936 • The opening of the National Negro Congress, the first attempt at a united front organization to try to better the conditions of black workers, was on February 14, 1936. A. Philip Randolph was its first president. It supported the unionization efforts of the CIO. The organization ran into trouble as a Communist front in 1940, and ceased to exist around 1950.

Sources: Bennett, *Before the Mayflower,* pp. 361, 531; Foner, *Organized Labor and the Black Worker,* pp. 213–14.

1938 • Ferdinand C. Smith (1894–1961) was a founder of the National Maritime Union, and in 1938 became the first black vice-president. When that office was abolished in 1939, he became the first black national secretary. In 1943, he became the first black member of the National CIO Executive Board. He was influential in recruiting the mixed crew for Hugh Mulzac, who set sail as the first black captain of a merchant ship on October 20, 1942. (*See also* **Miscellaneous: Miscellaneous Topics, 1942.**) A native of Jamaica, and an alleged subversive because of his Communist ties, in 1948 he was arrested and deported as an undesirable alien.

Sources: Dictionary of American Negro Biography, pp. 562–64; Foner, *Organized Labor and the Black Worker,* pp. 227, 231, 285.

1962 • Nelson Jack Edwards (1917–74) was the first black member of the International Executive Board of the United Auto Workers. Born in Lowndes County, Alabama, Edwards moved to Detroit in 1937, and found work in a Dodge plant. In 1970 he became the first black vice-president of the union.

Sources: Ebony Success Library, vol. 2, pp. 68–71; *Encyclopedia of Black America,* p. 352; *Negro Almanac, 1989,* pp. 1405–6.

1974 • William E. Pollard (1915–) was the first black to head the AFL-CIO civil rights department in Washington, D.C. Pollard began his union career as secretary-treasurer of Dining Car Employees #582 in 1941. He held the civil rights post until 1986, when he joined the NAACP as deputy executive director.

Sources: Ebony 29 (October 1974), p. 32; *Jet* 62 (12 April 1982), p. 16; *Jet* 70 (21 April 1986), p. 4; *Who's Who Among Black Americans, 1992–93,* p. 1135.

1976 • As vice-president, Leon Lynch (1935–) was the first black national officer of the AFL-CIO Steel Workers Union. Lynch began to work for the

Youngstown Sheet and Tube Company as a loader in 1956. In 1967, he took a B.S. at Roosevelt University in Chicago, Illinois, and began to work as a union staff representative in 1968.

Sources: Jet 56 (26 July 1979), p. 10; *Who's Who Among Black Americans, 1992–93,* p. 897.

As a member of the National Executive Board of the Amalgamated Meat Cutters and Butcher Workmen, Addie Wyatt (1924–) was the first black woman labor executive.

Sources: Ebony 32 (August 1977), p. 70; 39 (March 1984), p. 104; Lee, *Interesting People,* p. 196; *Who's Who Among Black Americans, 1992–93,* p. 1577.

1978 • Vallorie Harris O'Neil was the first black woman engineer for the Burlington-Northern Railroad. Harris worked in the Cicero, Illinois, yard.

Source: Jet 53 (5 January 1978), p. 28.

1979 • Audrey Neal was the first woman of any ethnic group to become a longshoreman on the Eastern seaboard.

Source: Negro Almanac, 1989, p. 1432.

1981 • Barbara B. Hutchinson was the first black woman member of the AFL-CIO Executive Council. Hutchinson was director of women's affairs for the American Federation of Government Employees. Her choice as director was the occasion of some controversy.

Sources: Jet 61 (10 December 1981), p. 8; *Jet* 64 (21 March 1983), p. 9.

1984 • Michelle V. Agins (1956–) was the first black woman still photographer admitted to the International Photographers of the Motion Picture and Television Industries union. She was personal photographer to Chicago mayor Harold Washington at the time.

Sources: Jet 66 (9 April 1984), p. 8; *Negro Almanac, 1989,* p. 1067.

Jacqueline Barbara Vaughn (1935–) was the first black woman president of the Chicago Teachers Union. Vaughn began to teach in the Chicago schools in 1956, and was a vice-president of the Illinois Federation of Teachers in 1969.

Sources: Jet 66 (30 July 1984), p. 21; *Jet* 67 (19 November 1984), p. 40; *Who's Who Among Black Americans, 1992–93,* p. 1432.

Althea Williams was the first black woman president of the Michigan State Employees Union. Williams was a 1981 graduate of Wayne State University, Detroit, where she earned her degree in psychology.

Source: Jet 66 (27 August 1984), p. 12.

1988 • Edgar O. Romney (1943–) was the first black vice-president of the International Ladies' Garment Workers Union. A native of New York City, Romney has worked for the union since 1966.

Sources: Jet 76 (17 July 1989), p. 38; *Who's Who Among Black Americans, 1992–93,* p. 1221.

John Nathan Sturdivant (1938–) was the first black president of the American Federation of Government Employees and so the first black to head a major mixed ethnic group of the AFL-CIO. A native of Philadelphia, and a 1980 graduate of Antioch College, Ohio, Sturdivant has worked for the union since 1962.

Sources: Jet 75 (3 October, 1988), p. 10; *Who's Who Among Black Americans, 1992–93,* p. 1351.

1990 • Lee Jackson was the first black to head the Kentucky Association of State Employees/FSE. Jackson was program supervisor at the Department For Employment Services, Lexington, Kentucky.

Source: Jet 78 (22 October 1990), p. 20.

MANUFACTURING

1798 • James Forten, Sr., (1766–1842) established the first major black-owned sailmaking shop in Philadelphia. (*See also* **Science & Medicine: Inventions, c. 1798.**) His financial worth soon reached $100,000. Forten was a leader in the radical abolitionist movement. An organizer of the American Antislavery Society (1833), he also supported women's suffrage and temperance. He inspired his daughters Margaretta, Sarah, and Harriet, and his granddaughter Charlotte Forten Grimké, in their efforts on behalf of blacks.

Sources: Dictionary of American Negro Biography, pp. 234–35; *Encyclopedia of Black America,* p. 391–92; *Negro Almanac, 1989,* p. 808.

1818 • Thomas Day (c. 1800–60?) was the first widely recognized black furniture maker in the deep South. He worked in Milton, North Carolina, and his workshop, the Yellow Tavern, is a National Historical Landmark.

Sources: Cantor, *Historic Landmarks of Black America,* p. 231; *Dictionary of American Negro Biography,* pp. 162–63; *Negro Almanac, 1989,* pp. 221–22.

1885 • D. Watson Onley built the first steam saw and planing mill owned and operated entirely by blacks in Jacksonville, Florida. After the mill was destroyed by fire set by an incendiary, Onley worked for Florida State Normal and Industrial College, attended Howard University School of Dentistry, and established a practice in Washington, D.C.

Sources: Culp, *Twentieth Century Negro Literature,* opposite p. 347.

1910 • Madame C. J. Walker (1867–1919) is believed by some to be the first black woman to become a millionaire. This is disputed by supporters of Annie Turnbo Malone (1869–1957). Both women produced hair care products for black women and were developing their businesses at the same time; it is asserted that Walker worked as a salesperson for Malone products. Both became very wealthy by around 1910, but Malone's business began to run into difficulties due to poor management after 1927.

Sources: Dictionary of American Negro Biography, p. 621 (Walker); *Encyclopedia of Black America,* p. 545 (Malone); p. 830 (Walker); *Negro Almanac, 1989,* pp. 1393–94 (Walker); *Notable Black American Women,* pp. 724–27 (Malone); 1184–93 (Walker).

1962 • Harvey Clarence Russell, Jr., (1918–) was the first black vice-president in a leading national corporation, Pepsico. This Louisville native

MADAME C. J. WALKER MADE A FORTUNE IN HAIR CARE PRODUCTS AT THE TURN OF THE CENTURY.

ANNIE TURNBO
MALONE WAS A MIL-
LIONAIRE, BUT WAS SHE
THE FIRST?

became vice-president in charge of special markets in 1962, vice-president in charge of planning in 1965, and vice-president for community affairs in 1969.

Sources: Black Enterprise 2 (September 1971), pp. 15–18; *Ebony* 17 (June 1962), pp. 25–32; *Encyclopedia of Black America,* p. 737; *Who's Who Among Black Americans, 1992–93,* p. 1232.

1963 • James Phillip McQuay (1924–) was the first and only black in wholesale-retail fur manufacturing. McQuay, who operated his fur business in New York City, won fur designer awards in 1970, 1975, and 1976. He was born in White Plains, New York.

Sources: Ebony 24 (July 1969), p. 38; *Encyclopedia of Black America,* p. 552; *Negro Almanac, 1989,* pp. 1412–13; *Who's Who Among Black Americans, 1992–93,* p. 973.

1970 • Clarence C. Finley (1922–) was the first black president of a major white firm, Charm-Tred-Monticello, a division of Burlington Industries. Finley had begun to work for Charm-Tred Company as a file clerk in 1942.

Sources: Alford, *Famous First Blacks,* pp. 16–17; *Ebony* 26 (February 1971), pp. 58–65; *Ebony Success Library,* vol. 2, pp. 72–75.

1971 • Melvin R. Wade (1936–) purchased the Eastern Rubber Reclaiming Company, Chester, Pennsylvania. He became the first (and only) black to own a rubber recycling plant. Wade had worked as a technician at General Electric before this purchase.

Source: Ebony Success Library, vol. 1, p. 314.

1986 • William R. Harvey (1941–) was the first black to be the sole owner of a major soft-drink bottling franchise, a Pepsi plant in Houghton,

Michigan. A native of Alabama, Harvey holds his Ed.D. from Harvard University (1971), and became president of Hampton University in 1978.

Sources: Jet 70 (7 April 1986), p. 8; *Who's Who Among Black Americans, 1992–93,* p. 620.

1990 • Bertram M. Lee (1939–) was the first black member of the board of directors of Reebok International. Lee has a B.A. from North Central College. He is president of Kellee Communications Group (1986–) and the Denver Nuggets Corporation, Denver, Colorado, and is active in many other businesses. Lee and Peter Bynoe became minority partners in owning the Denver Nuggets in 1989.

Sources: Jet 78 (1 October 1990), p. 35; *Who's Who Among Black Americans, 1992–93,* p. 855.

MISCELLANEOUS INDUSTRIES

1846 • William Leidesdorff (1810–48) opened the first hotel in San Francisco. He is also credited with organizing the first horse race and operating the first steamboat (1847). In April 1848, he was the chair of the board of education, which opened California's first public school. Leidesdorff was born in the Virgin Islands, the son of a Danish man and an African woman. He came to California in 1841, and became a Mexican citizen in 1846 in order to acquire extensive land holdings. When he became a United States subconsul in 1845, he was probably the first black to hold a diplomatic post in United States history.

Sources: Cantor, *Historic Landmarks of Black America,* p. 294; *Dictionary of American Negro Biography,* pp. 392–93; Katz, *The Black West,* pp. 117–19.

1959 • Ruth J. Bowen (1930–) was the first black woman to establish a successful booking and talent agency in New York City. She had done personal relations work for Dinah Washington, and her firm has represented such artists as Sammy Davis, Jr., Aretha Franklin, and Ray Charles. Bowen began in 1959 with an initial five hundred dollar investment, and within ten years her firm became the largest black-owned agency in the world.

Sources: Black Women in White America, p. 151; *Encyclopedia of Black America,* p. 188; *Negro Almanac, 1989,* pp. 1375–76; *Who's Who Among Black Americans, 1992–93,* p. 135.

1972 • On May 16, 1972, the Johnson Publishing Company headquarters was dedicated. The eleven-story edifice was the first building built by blacks in downtown Chicago since the time of Jean Baptiste Point Du Sable.

Source: Ebony Success Library, vol. 2, p. 1355.

1977 • Harambee House, Washington, D.C., was the first large hotel designed and built by blacks. The hotel was designed by Sulton-Campbell and Associates, and was owned by the Peoples Involvement Corporation, a local citizens group. The hotel is now owned by Howard University and operates as the Howard Inn.

Source: Jet 52 (24 March 1977), p. 13.

JOHN H. JOHNSON'S
COMPANY, JOHNSON
PUBLISHING COMPANY
INC., IS ONE OF THE
LARGEST PRIVATELY
OWNED COMPANIES IN
THE U.S.

Kenwood Commercial Furniture was the first black-owned company to sign a million-dollar contract with Consolidated Edison. The firm, established by Kenneth N. Sherwood (1930–), was to furnish and install carpet in all the utility company's offices in New York City and Westchester County.

Sources: Ebony 28 (August 1973), pp. 168–73; Ebony Success Library, vol. 2, pp. 236–39.

1990 • Errol B. Davis, Jr., was the first black to head a major utility company, Wisconsin Power and Light.

Source: Jet 78 (30 July 1990), p. 16.

1992 • Roberta Palm Bradley was the first woman to head a major public utility, Seattle City Light. A native of Frederick, Maryland, she took a degree in English at Morgan State University.

Source: Ebony 47 (September 1992), p. 10.

1993 • Pearline Motley was the first black honored as American Business Woman of the Year. She received the award from the American Business Women's Association for 1993. Motley was the manager of the Federal Women's Program of the Agricultural Stabilization and Conservation Service in Kansas City, Missouri.

Source: Jet 83 (December 28, 1992), p. 20.

PUBLISHING

1938 • John H. Johnson, the founder of *Ebony* (1945) and *Jet* (1951), was the first black named as one of the country's "Ten Outstanding Young Men" by the United States Junior Chamber of Commerce. This was the first of many awards won by Johnson for his success in publishing. In 1972, he became the first black to receive the Henry Johnson Fisher Award of the Magazine Publishers Association, the most prestigious honor in that field.

Sources: Ebony Success Library, vol. 2, p. 132–37; The Negro Almanac, 1989, pp. 1261–62; Who's Who Among Black Americans, 1992–93, p. 760.

1960 • Charles F. Harris (1935–), as editor at Doubleday, established Zenith Books, the first series to present minority histories for the general and educational markets. A graduate of Virginia State College (1955), Harris worked for Doubleday and Random House before joining the Howard University Press in 1971.

Sources: Ebony 20 (March 1965), p. 6; Ebony Success Library, vol. 1, p. 143; Who's Who Among Black Americans, 1992–93, p. 605.

1979 • Dolores Wharton (1927–) was the first black woman on the board of Gannett Company. Wharton is the founder and president of the Fund for Corporate Initiatives.

Sources: Blackbook, 1984, p. 79; Jet 56 (12 April 1979), p. 21; Who's Who Among Black Americans, 1992–93, p. 1488.

REAL ESTATE

1866 • Biddy Mason (1818–91) was the first known black woman property owner in Los Angeles, California. Born into slavery in Georgia or Mississippi, she and her master went first to the Utah Territory and then to California, where Mason legally gained her freedom on January 21, 1856. She worked as nurse and midwife, and her savings and careful investment became the foundation that enabled her grandson Robert to be called the richest black in Los Angeles around 1900. A very religious and charitable woman, Mason opened her house for the establishment of the first African Methodist Episcopal church in the city in 1872. She is also said to have opened the first day care nursery for homeless community children.

Sources: Katz, The Black West, pp. 129–30; Notable Black American Women, pp. 732–34; Sepia (April 1960), p. 71.

BIDDY MASON

1890 • Thomy Lafon (1810–93) was the first black man reputed to be a millionaire. He was a New Orleans real estate speculator and moneylender. His estate was valued at nearly half a million dollars. Lafon was noted for philanthropy, and he left the bulk of his estate to charity.

Sources: Dictionary of American Negro Biography, pp. 379–80; Dictionary of Black Culture, p. 261; Efforts for Social Betterment Among Negro Americans, pp. 40–41.

1905 • Phillip A. Payton, Jr., (1876–?) was the first black to open Harlem to black residents. He persuaded persons who had overbuilt apartments to rent to blacks. By 1908, Payton controlled more than half a million dollars worth of property in New York City. Unfortunately, he spent money as quickly as he made it, and he went broke in 1908.

Sources: Black Enterprise 6 (June 1976), pp. 126–27; Encyclopedia of Black America, p. 417; Lewis, When Harlem Was in Vogue, pp. 25–26.

RETAILING

1834 • David Ruggles (1810–49) was the first known black bookseller. His New York City shop was burned out by a white mob in September 1835. An active abolitionist and worker on the Underground Railroad, Ruggles was also noted as the first black hydrotherapist. (*See also* **Science & Medicine: Medicine, 1846.**)

Source: Dictionary of American Negro Autobiography, pp. 536–38.

1968 • Leon Howard Sullivan (1922–) developed the first major black-sponsored shopping center, Progress Plaza, in Philadelphia, Pennsylvania. This Baptist minister was very active in developing black business. On January 4, 1971, he became the first black selected to sit on the board of General Motors.

Sources: Current Biography, 1969, pp. 419–21; Ebony Success Library, vol. 2, pp. 248–51; Encyclopedia of Black America, p. 811; Hornsby, Chronology of African-American History, pp. 158, 250–51; Negro Almanac, 1989, pp. 61, 618, 1417; Who's Who Among Black Americans, 1992–93, p. 1353.

Frederick D. Wilson, Jr., (1921–) was the first black vice-president of Macy's. Wilson had joined the retail chain in 1948, after distinguished service in the wartime army, followed by an M.A. in business administration from Harvard University.

LEON HOWARD
SULLIVAN IS A
MINISTER AS WELL
AS A BUSINESSMAN.

Source: Ebony Success Library, vol. 2, pp. 288–91.

1975 • Wally "Famous" Amos (1937–) was the first black to open a cookie-only retail store. He went from mail clerk to executive vice-president at the William Morris Agency, which made him their first black talent agent. Two years after he founded Famous Amos Chocolate Chip Cookies, the company was grossing two million dollars a year.

Sources: Jet 72 (30 March 1987), p. 6; Sepia 27 (June 1978), pp. 22–28; Time 109 (13 June 1977), pp. 72, 76; Who's Who Among Black Americans, 1992–93, p. 29.

1982 • Sybil Collins Mobley (1925–) was the first black woman member of the board of Sears, Roebuck and Company. An educator with a Ph.D. from the University of Illinois, she taught in the business school of Florida Agricultural and Mechanical University, where she became a dean in 1974.

Sources: Jet 62 (30 August 1982), p. 38; *Who's Who Among Black Americans, 1992–93,* p. 1005.

1983 • Ben F. Branch (1924–87) was the president of the nation's first black-owned soft drink company, Dr. Branch Products, in Chicago, Illinois. Branch was also a civil-rights activist and a musician. He combined these interests by organizing the SCLC-Operation Breadbox Orchestra, the world's only gospel orchestra.

Source: Jet 72 (14 September 1987), p. 55.

1986 • Eldo Perry was the first black vice-president/region manager in St. Louis, Missouri, for Church's Fried Chicken.

Source: Jet 69 (24 February 1986), p. 20.

STOCK BROKERAGE

1970 • On February 13, 1970, Joseph L. Searles III (1940–) was the first black member of the New York Stock Exchange.

Sources: Black Enterprise 1 (October 1970), p. 19; *Negro Almanac, 1989,* p. 1430; *Jet* 37 (19 February 1970), p. 20; *Jet* 69 (17 February 1986), p. 22; *Statistical Record of Black America,* p. 474.

1971 • On June 24, 1971, the firm of Daniels and Bell was the first black company to become a member of the New York Stock Exchange. The firm was founded by Willie L. Daniels (1937–), and Travers Bell, Jr.

Sources: Ebony Success Library, vol. 1, p. 86; *Negro Almanac, 1976,* p. 1024; *Sepia* 21 (June 1972), pp. 67–70.

Johnson Products became the first black firm to be listed on a major stock exchange when it was listed on the American Stock Exchange in 1971. The firm was founded by George Ellis Johnson (1927–) in 1954.

Sources: Ebony Success Library, vol. 2, pp. 126–31; *Encyclopedia of Black America,* p. 473; *Jet* 69 (18 November 1985), p. 16; *Who's Who Among Black Americans, 1992–93,* p. 757.

1972 • Jerome Heartwell Holland (1916–85) was the first black to serve on the board of the New York Stock Exchange. Holland was an all-American football player at Cornell University, New York, where he took his B.S. (1939), and M.S. (1941) degrees. He was the first black player on the Cornell football team. After receiving a Ph.D. from the University of Pennsylvania in 1950, Holland served as president of Delaware State College from 1953 to 1960, and of Hampton Institute from 1960 to 1970, when he became ambassador to Sweden.

Sources: Ebony Success Library, vol. 2, pp. 104–7; *Encyclopedia of Black America,* p. 443; *Jet* 68 (6 May 1985), p. 54.

1984 • Christine Bell was the first black woman financial futures specialist for Prudential-Bache Securities in Chicago.

Source: Jet 66 (26 March 1984), pp. 38–39.

TRANSPORTATION, SHIPPING & SAILING

1784 • Paul Cuffe (1759–1817) was the first black to sail as master of his own ship. Born near Bedford, Massachusetts, Cuffe went to sea at a young age and became involved in the coastwide trade. He later developed trade with Sierra Leone, where he encouraged missionary work and colonization. His name is sometimes given as Cuffee. (*See also* **Miscellaneous: Pioneers, 1811.**)

Sources: Dictionary of American Negro Biography, pp. 147–48; *Encyclopedia of Black America,* pp. 280, 296; *Negro Almanac, 1989,* pp. 9, 209, 234.

1831 • John Mashow was the first black to establish a prominent ship-building firm. He was active in South Dartmouth, Massachusetts, until shortly before the Civil War.

Source: James, *The Real McCoy,* p. 33.

1840S • A. F. Boston was the first known black to command an American whaling ship, the *Loper.* The officers and most of the ship's crew were black, and the ship made at least one successful trip.

Source: James, *The Real McCoy,* p. 35.

1866 • On February 12, the Chesapeake Marine Railway and Drydock Company of Baltimore, Maryland, was the first major black shipfitting company. Organized by Isaac Myers, it was in business until 1884. The company was formed by and for black workers driven from longshoremen and caulkers jobs by white strikers.

Sources: Dictionary of American Negro Biography, pp. 468–69; *Encyclopedia of Black America,* p. 201; Foner, *Organized Labor and the Black Worker,* pp. 22–23.

AIRLINE EXECUTIVE
JAMES O. PLINTON, JR.,
GOT HIS START IN THE
MILITARY.

1971 • James O. Plinton, Jr., (1914–) was the first black top executive of a major airline, Eastern Airlines. A graduate of Lincoln University in Pennsylvania, Plinton became a pilot instructor for the United States Army Air Corps in 1935, and was the first black to complete the Air Corps' Central Instructors School, in 1944. He was the first black to co-organize an airline outside the United States; Quisqueya Lte. in Port-au-Prince, Haiti, was established in 1948. He joined Trans World Airlines in 1950, and became vice-president for marketing affairs for Eastern in 1971.

Sources: Black Enterprise 10 (September 1979), pp. 59–60; *Ebony Success Library,* vol. 1, p. 250; *Encyclopedia of Black America,* pp. 146, 678; *Who's Who Among Black Americans, 1992–93,* pp. 1130–31.

1979 • The Kent-Barry-Eaton Connection Railway Company was the first minority-owned company to operate a railroad. The line ran forty-two miles between Grand Rapids and Vermontville, Michigan.

Source: Jet 56 (23 August 1979), p. 24.

1985 • Robert J. Brown (1935–) was the first black member of the board of directors of the Norfolk Southern Railroad Company. Brown was also recognized as the "Most Outstanding Young Man in America" by the Junior Chamber of Commerce in 1985.

Sources: Jet 69 (2 December 1985), p. 18; *Who's Who Among Black Americans, 1992–93,* p. 179.

1987 • Vander Brown, Jr., was the first black to head a division of Greyhound Lines, Western Greyhound, one of the four regional divisions. The thirty-nine-year-old Brown was born in Bakersfield, California, and had worked for the company for eighteen years.

Source: Jet 72 (29 June 1987), pp. 38–39.

CIVIL RIGHTS AND PROTEST: 400 YEARS OF STRUGGLE

~~~~~~

ABOLITION

1688 • The Mennonite Quakers at Germantown, Pennsylvania, adopted and signed the first formal abolitionist document in United States history. After the Society of Friends declared that slavery violated the rights of man and was in opposition to Christianity, the Mennonite Antislavery Resolution was approved by the group on February 18.

Sources: Garrett, Famous First Facts About Negroes, p. 1; Hornsby, Chronology of African-American History, p. 4; Kane, Famous First Facts, p. 598; Negro Almanac, 1989, p. 3.

1777 • Vermont became the first colony to abolish slavery on July 2, 1777. Although the results were gradual, by 1804, all states north of Delaware had taken action to abolish slavery.

Sources: Bennett, Before the Mayflower, p. 446; Hornsby, Chronology of African-American History, p. 8.

1797 • On January 30, 1797, the first recorded antislavery petition was presented to Congress, but rejected. The petition by North Carolina blacks sought "redress against a North Carolina law which requires that slaves, although freed by their Quaker masters, be returned to the state and to their former condition."

Sources: Hornsby, Chronology of African-American History, p. 12; Negro Almanac, 1989, p. 8.

1832 • A group of "females of color" in Salem, Massachusetts, formed the first black women's antislavery society in the United States on February 22, 1832. The abolitionist press documents the existence of a variety of women's antislavery societies during this period. Free black women actively participated in the racially mixed societies.

Sources: Black Women in America, vol. 1, p. 8; Salem, We Are Your Sisters, p. 113; Yee, Black Women Abolitionists, pp. 6, 87.

Maria W. Stewart (1803–79), women's rights activist, journalist, and educator, was the first American-born woman to speak publicly on political

DATES OF EMANCIPATION IN THE NORTHERN STATES

1777	Vermont
1780	Pennsylvania[1]
1783	Massachusetts
1783	New Hampshire
1784	Rhode Island
1799	New York[1]
1804	New Jersey[2]

[1] Gradually instituted.
[2] Gradually instituted; abolition completed by statute in 1846.
Source: Hornsby, *Chronology of African-American History,* p. 8.

themes to a mixed audience of men and women. On September 21, 1833, she was perhaps the first black woman to lecture in defense of women's rights. Her public speeches, delivered in Boston during a two-year period, also made her the first black woman to lecture on antislavery issues. Abolitionist William Lloyd Garrison published the text of her four public speeches in 1835.

Sources: Black Women in America, vol. 2, pp. 1113–14; *Notable Black American Women,* pp. 1083–87; Yee, *Black Women Abolitionists,* p. 26.

1838 • The first known black regular lecturer in the antislavery cause and the first major black abolitionist was Charles Lenox Remond (1810–73). After a triumphant tour of England, his fame soared. He became one of the seventeen members of the New England Anti-Slavery Society.

Sources: Bennett, *Before the Mayflower,* pp. 161–62; *Dictionary of American Negro Biography,* pp. 520–22; Robinson, *Historical Negro Biographies,* pp. 115–16.

1846 • The first known black organization in St. Louis dedicated to the overthrow of slavery, the Knights of Liberty, was formed by Moses Dickson and eleven other free blacks. After a decade, the organization turned its primary attention to helping slaves escape to freedom. Dickson established the Knights and Daughters of Tabor Society, in 1871, as a memorial of this group.

Source: Negro Year Book, 1921–22, p. 158.

1862 • Slavery was abolished in the District of Columbia when "an act for the release of certain persons held to service or labor in the District of Columbia," was enacted April 16, 1862. The law stated that persons held "by reason of African descent are hereby discharged and freed from all claim to such service or labor" and "neither slavery nor involuntary servitude …

ANTISLAVERY LAWS

August 6, 1861	The congressional confiscation bill freed slaves who were forced to fight against the United States government, or to work in support of the rebellion.
July 22, 1862	The District of Columbia passes a law abolishing slavery.
January 1, 1863	Emancipation Proclamation.
June 19, 1863	West Virginia admitted as a state with a constitution forbidding slavery.
January 11, 1864	Missouri amends constitution, forbidding slavery.
March 14, 1864	Arkansas amends constitution, forbidding slavery.
May 11, 1864	Louisiana amends constitution, forbidding slavery.
June 28, 1864	Fugitive Slave Acts of 1793 and 1850 repealed.
July 6, 1864	Maryland amends constitution, forbidding slavery.
June 19, 1865	Texas slaves are informed by proclamation that they are free.
July 13, 1865	The provisional governor of Georgia abolishes slavery by proclamation.
July 20, 1865	The provisional governor of Arkansas abolishes slavery by proclamation.
July 21, 1865	Mississippi amends constitution, forbidding slavery.
August 3, 1865	The provisional governor of Florida abolishes slavery by proclamation.
September 28, 1865	South Carolina amends constitution, forbidding slavery.
October 2, 1865	North Carolina amends constitution, forbidding slavery.
December 18, 1865	The Thirteenth Amendment, which abolished slavery in the United States, was adopted.

Sources: Bennett, *Before the Mayflower,* p. 463; Hornsby, *Chronology of African-American History,* p. 39; *Negro Almanac, 1989,* p. 16; *Negro Year Book, 1921–22,* pp. 134–35.

shall hereafter exist in said district." Slave owners were compensated, and $100,000 was appropriated to support emigration of former slaves from the United States. A law passed on April 2, 1862, offering compensated emancipation to the border slave states found no takers.

Sources: Hornsby, *Chronology of African-American History,* p. 34; Kane, *Famous First Facts,* p. 598; *Negro Year Book 1921–22,* p. 134.

GOVERNMENT ACTION

1854 • The first successful suit to end segregation in street cars was won this year. Until that time blacks in New York were restricted to certain cars marked "Colored People Allowed in This Car." A black woman, who was a public school teacher and protester, was dragged out of her seat. She took her case to court, with Chester A. Arthur as one of her lawyers.

Source: Johnson, *Black Manhattan,* p. 46.

1857 • Dred Scott (1795–1858), a Virginia slave, sued for his freedom after becoming a resident living on free soil in Missouri. The Dred Scott decision (*Dred Scott v. Sanford*) rendered this year was the first unequivocal decision by the Supreme Court denying blacks citizenship, saying that blacks could not be citizens of the United States, even though they might be citizens of their states. The doctrine of dual citizenship remained important as it resurfaced in the post–Civil War attack on black rights. The Supreme Court in 1873 affirmed again the doctrine of dual citizenship, federal and state, and suggested that most civil rights fell under state citizenship, and so were not protected under the Fourteenth Amendment.

Sources: Bennett, *Before the Mayflower,* pp. 178, 262, 463; *Dictionary of American Negro Biography,* pp. 548–49; *Negro Almanac, 1989,* pp. 332–33.

1866 • Citizenship was first conferred upon blacks by the Civil Rights Bill, an "Act to Protect all Persons in the United States in their Civil Rights and Furnish the Means of Their Vindication." The bill also gave blacks "the same right, in every State and territory… as is enjoyed by white citizens." Enacted during the first session of the thirty-ninth Congress on April 9, 1866, the bill passed over the president's veto.

Sources: Bennett, *Before the Mayflower,* p. 476; Hornsby, *Chronology of African-American History,* p. 41; Kane, *Famous First Facts,* p. 170.

1867 • Black males were first granted the right to vote by the act of January 8, 1867, which was "to regulate the elective franchise in the District of Columbia." The right was given to every male person twenty-one years of age, except those who were paupers, under guardianship, convicted of infamous crimes, or who had voluntarily comforted rebels. President Andrew Johnson vetoed the bill on January 5, 1867, but both the Senate and the

House of Representatives voted to override the veto, and the bill became law.

Sources: Clayton, *The Negro Politician,* pp. 23–24; Kane, *Famous First Facts,* p. 234; Hornsby, *Chronology of African-American History,* p. 40; *Negro Almanac, 1989,* p. 17.

1868 • Black Americans were granted citizenship and equal protection under the law for the first time with the passage of the Fourteenth Amendment on July 28, 1868. (*See also* **Civil Rights: Government Action, 1857.**)

Sources: Bennett, *Before the Mayflower,* pp. 260–61, 483; Hornsby, *Chronology of African-American History,* p. 42; *Negro Almanac, 1989,* p. 17.

1870 • Thomas Mundy Petersen (Petersen-Munday), a school custodian of Perth Amboy, New Jersey, became the first black person to vote as a result of the adoption of the Fifteenth Amendment on March 31, 1870, one day after the ratification of the amendment to the United States Constitution. The special election was held to ratify or reject a city charter. Petersen was appointed to the committee to revise the charter, which was adopted in the election. He later became a delegate to the country's Republican convention.

Sources: Cantor, *Historic Landmarks of Black America,* p. 87; Kane, *Famous First Facts,* p. 233; *Jet* 58 (3 April 1980), p. 20; 72 (6 April 1987).

1881 • Tennessee was the first state to require the separation of the races in railway cars. This is usually taken as the beginning of the increasingly onerous burden of "Jim Crow" legislation that changed a largely *de facto* system of segregation into a legally defined system in the South. The test of a similar 1890 law in Louisiana led to the United States Supreme Court decision in *Plessy v. Ferguson* on May 18, 1896. The court's doctrine of "separate but equal" became the legal underpinning of segregation for the next sixty years.

Sources: Bennett, *Before the Mayflower,* p. 267; Hornsby, *Chronology of African-American History,* pp. 50, 55; *Negro Almanac, 1989,* pp. 150–52; *Negro Year Book,* 1921–22, p. 171.

1989 • The first memorial to the civil rights movement of the 1960s was dedicated in Montgomery, Alabama, in 1989. This is perhaps the first wide recognition of little-known martyrs of the civil rights movement, along with the famous. The memorial consists of two simple black granite pieces, a circular stone which lists forty civil rights martyrs, and a wall of rushing water.

Source: Cantor, *Historic Landmarks of Black America,* pp. 132–33.

GROUP ACTION

1830 • The first National Negro Convention met at Mother Bethel Church in Philadelphia on September 20–24, 1830, "to devise ways and means for bettering of our condition," to fight oppression, to promote universal education, and inspire other pursuits. Richard Allen presided. After the Civil War, the conventions focused on voting, fair employment, education, citizenship rights, and the repeal of discriminatory laws.

Sources: Baer and Singer, *African-American Religion in the Twentieth Century,* p. 26; *Encyclopedia of Black America,* p. 834; Hornsby, *Chronology of African-American History,* p. 18.

MARCUS GARVEY

1914 • Marcus (Mozian Manasseth) Garvey (1887–1940), black nationalist, orator, and organizer, formed the first black mass movement organization, the United Negro Improvement Association (UNIA), which aimed to unite blacks under the motto "One God! One Aim! One Destiny!" UNIA's divisions and subsidiaries later included the African Legion and the Black Cross Nurses. Garvey was born in St. Ann's Bay, Jamaica, traveled to England in 1912, and returned to Jamaica in 1914. He came to America on March 23, 1916, and one year later established a branch of UNIA in Harlem. This branch immediately became the headquarters of Garvey's international movement. He founded a weekly newspaper, *Negro World,* in 1918, which spread his word. By mid 1919, he had launched the Black Star Shipping Line to help create economic opportunities for blacks, who bought stock in the line. Later, Garvey and his stockholders expanded the business to form a cross-continent steamship trade. In 1923, he was convicted and jailed for mail fraud. He was pardoned and deported in 1927, when he moved to London. He wrote extensively about his movement and race philosophy, and with more than a million followers, he had built the largest and most powerful black mass movement in American history.

Sources: Black Leaders of the Twentieth Century, pp. 104–38; *Contemporary Black Biography,* vol. 1, pp. 75–78; *Dictionary of American Negro Biography,* pp. 254–56; Garrett, *Famous First Facts About Negroes,* p. 167; Katz, *Eyewitness: The Negro in American History,* pp. 399–400.

CHARLES HAMILTON HOUSTON

1935 • Charles Hamilton Houston (1895–1950), lawyer and educator, became the first full-time paid special counsel for the NAACP. He devised a strategy at the NAACP which led to school desegregation. The campaign against discrimination in education ended two decades later, after Houston's death, when the *Brown v. Board of Education* decision of 1954 declared segregation in public schools unconstitutional. During his career, Houston helped prepare civil rights cases in lower federal and state courts, and argued such cases before the United States Supreme Court. Houston was born in Washington, D.C., and graduated from Amherst College and Harvard Law School, where he studied under Supreme Court Justice Felix Frankfurter. He was the first black to serve on the editorial board of the *Harvard Law Review.* In 1929, he became dean of Howard

University Law School, Washington, D.C., and led the school into full accreditation by the American Bar Association. Civil rights and civil libertarian groups acknowleged him for his work at Howard and his philosophy of social engineering. For his pioneering work in developing the NAACP legal campaign, he was posthumously awarded the Spingarn Medal on September 27, 1950.

Sources: Bennett, *Before the Mayflower,* pp. 363, 546; *Black Leaders of the Twentieth Century,* pp. 220–40; *Dictionary of American Negro Biography,* pp. 328–30.

1947 • The first known freedom ride occurred April 9, 1947, when the Congress of Racial Equality (CORE) and the Fellowship of Reconciliation tested the South's compliance with the court's decision of June 3, 1946, which banned segregation on interstate buses. CORE sent twenty-three black and white riders through the South. This was the first challenge to segregation on interstate buses. The freedom rides of May 1961 were more widely publicized. They led to a firm policy on desegregation of interstate travel.

Sources: Bennett, *Before the Mayflower,* p. 542; Hornsby, *Milestones in 20th-Century African-American History,* p. 44; *Negro Almanac, 1989,* p. 27.

1957 • The first organization to coordinate the work of nonviolent groups devoted to racial integration and improved life for black Americans was the Southern Christian Leadership Conference (SCLC), formed in 1957. Prominent in the Southern civil rights movement as a nonviolent, direct-action organization, SCLC was formed by Martin Luther King, Jr., Bayard Rustin, and Stanley Levinson and grew out of the 1955–56 Montgomery bus boycott.

Sources: Alford, *Famous First Blacks,* p. 26; *Contemporary Black Biography,* vol. 1, pp. 132–33; *Encyclopedia of Black America,* pp. 804–5; *Negro Almanac, 1989,* p. 30.

1958 • The first sit-ins to win concessions in a Southern state in modern times occurred in restaurants in Oklahoma City, on August 19, 1958. The NAACP Youth Council members sat at lunch counters and were served without incident or publicity.

Sources: Alford, *Famous First Blacks,* p. 25; Bennett, *Before the Mayflower,* p. 556.

1960 • The first sit-in movement to achieve major results began February 1, 1960, when four students from North Carolina Agricultural and Technical College sought service at a F. W. Woolworth store's lunch counter reserved for whites. The students were Ezell Blair, Franklin McCain, David Richmond, and Joseph McNeil. The movement, patterned after the passive resistance techniques of Mahatma Ghandi, gained momentum, and by February 10, 1960, had spread to fifteen southern cities in five states. On

March 16, 1960, San Antonio, Texas, became the first city to integrate its lunch counters as result of the movement.

Sources: Alford, Famous First Blacks, p. 25; Bennett, Before the Mayflower, pp. 383–84, 557; Cantor, Historic Landmarks of Black America, pp. 229–31; Hornsby, Milestones in 20th-Century African-American History, pp. 63, 66.

Marion Barry (1936–) was the first national chairman of the Student Nonviolent Coordinating Committee (SNCC). A native of Itta Bena, Mississippi, Barry would become mayor of Washington, D.C., in 1979.

Sources: Ebony 23 (December 1976), pp. 82–89; Ebony Success Library, vol. 1, p. 21; Who's Who Among Black Americans, 1992–93, p. 77.

1964 • The first wave of large riots in a black urban neighborhood of the sixties occurred in the Harlem section of New York July 18-22. The riots then spread to the Bedford-Stuyvesant section of Brooklyn, Rochester, New York, and Jersey City and Paterson, New Jersey.

Sources: Bennett, Before the Mayflower, p. 571; Hornsby, Milestones in 20th-Century African-American History, p. 78; Negro Almanac, 1989, p. 32.

MARION BARRY HAS BEEN IN THE PUBLIC EYE FOR MORE THAN 30 YEARS.

Civil rights activist Stokely Carmichael (1941–) was the first person to popularize the phrase "Black Power" as a slogan during James Meredith's voter registration drive through Mississippi. In 1966, he became head of the Student Nonviolent Coordinating Committee and altered its orientation from nonviolent orientation to black liberation. Carmichael was born in Trinidad, came to the United States when he was eleven years old, and later graduated from Howard University.

Sources: Alford, Famous First Blacks, p. 24; Encyclopedia of Black America, p. 215; Negro Almanac, 1989, pp. 240–42, 284.

1984 • The first Black Family Summit was held at Fisk University, Tennessee, in May 1984. This was in response to Benjamin Hooks's and the NAACP's call to bring together organizations and other resources to map plans for family survival.

Source: Negro Almanac, 1989, pp. 258–59.

SLAVE REVOLTS

1663 • The first major conspiracy between black slaves and indentured servants occurred in Gloucester County, Virginia, September 13, 1663. The conspiracy was betrayed by an indentured servant.

Sources: Alford, Famous First Blacks, p. 27; Hornsby, Chronology of African-American History, p. 3; Negro Almanac, 1989, p. 3.

1712 • The first major slave revolt occurred in New York City on April 7, 1712. As a result, twenty-one blacks were executed, and six others committed suicide. The men had met about midnight, April 6, to take revenge for their masters' abuse. Some were armed with firearms, swords, knives, and hatchets. Paul Cuffe set fire to his master's house, which attracted a crowd of townspeople. The revolt grew as the insurgents opened fire on the crowd, killing nine whites and wounding five or six more.

Sources: Hornsby, *Chronology of African-American History,* p. 4; Johnson, *Black Manhattan,* pp. 7–8; *Negro Almanac, 1989,* p. 4; *Negro Year Book,* 1921–22, p. 149.

1720 • The first insurrection of slaves in South Carolina occurred in 1720, when whites were attacked on the streets and in their houses in Charleston. Twenty-three slaves were arrested, six convicted, and three executed.

Source: Negro Yearbook, 1921–22, p. 149.

1739 • The first serious slave revolt took place in South Carolina, when a slave named Cato led an uprising at Stono, about twenty miles west of Charleston. After killing two warehouse guards and securing arms and ammunition, the slaves headed south, hoping to reach Florida. As they marched to drum beats, they killed about twenty to thirty whites who attempted to interfere. Armed whites captured all but a dozen slaves, and more than thirty blacks, who were alleged participants, were killed.

Sources: Hornsby, *Chronology of African-American History,* p. 4.

1791 • Toussaint L'Ouverture (François Dominique Toussaint Breda), (1743–1803) led the first slave revolt against the French in Haiti to liberate the colony. A self-educated slave, this insurgent, soldier, statesman, and martyr was imprisoned by Napoleon. He is ultimately responsible for making Haiti the first independent, black-ruled country in the Western Hemisphere.

Sources: Bennett, *Before the Mayflower,* pp. 117, 118, 120–23; *Negro Almanac, 1989,* p. 7; *Negro History Bulletin 15* (November 1951), pp. 38, 40–41.

1822 • The first revolt leader of note was Denmark Vesey, who on May 30, 1822, organized a slave revolt in Charleston, South Carolina. Vesey and nearly fifty others were executed after the revolt, one of the most elaborate on record. Vesey, a sailor and carpenter, had been free since 1800. His uprising had been planned over several years and involved carefully chosen collaborators. As many as five thousand blacks were prepared to participate in the revolt, originally set for July that year, but authorities thwarted the insurrection. After the insurrection, South Carolina and other states passed laws to control free blacks and to tighten the reins on slaves. The prominent leader of the African Methodist Episcopal (AME) Church in South Carolina, Morris Brown, became suspect and fled to the North, where he succeeded Richard Allen as AME bishop. Another well-known leader of a

TOUSSAINT L'OUVERTURE IS HAILED AS THE LIBERATOR OF HAITI.

Nat Turner

by **PAUL PETERS**

Opening **November 21**

PEOPLE'S DRAMA THEATRE
212 Eldridge Street

Tickets: Tues.-Wed.-Thurs. $1.20 & $1.80

THE STORY OF NAT
TURNER'S REVOLT BEARS
RETELLING.

slave revolt was Gabriel Prosser (c.1775–1800), who planned a revolt for August 30, 1800, which subsequently failed.

Sources: Bennett, *Before the Mayflower,* pp. 127–31; Hornsby, *Chronology of African-American History,* pp. 15–16; *The Negro Almanac, 1989,* p. 10.

1831 • In Southampton County, Virginia, on August 21–22, 1831, Nat Turner, a brilliant minister and moody slave, led the first slave revolt of magnitude. The revolt was crushed, but only after Turner and his band had killed some sixty whites and threw the South into panic. After hiding out, Turner was captured on October 30, 1831, and hanged in Jerusalem, Virginia, on November 11. Thirty other blacks were also implicated and executed. It was not until John Brown's raid on Harpers Ferry, Virginia, in 1859 that another slave revolt or conspiracy became known.

Sources: Bennett, *Before the Mayflower,* pp. 131–39; Hornsby, *Chronology of African-American History,* p. 18; *Negro Almanac, 1989,* p. 11.

CINQUE AND HIS
FOLLOWERS FOUGHT TO
AVOID SLAVERY, AND
WON.

1839 • A group of Africans launched the first revolt at sea that resulted in the legal freedom of the rebels. They seized the slaveship *Amistad* and brought it into Montauk, Long Island, New York. The ship came into American custody on August 26, 1839. Cinque, the young African leader, and his followers were tried in court, defended by former President John Quincy Adams. The Supreme Court decision to free them was handed down on March 9, 1840. The thirty-five surviving Africans were returned to Africa on November 25, 1841.

Sources: Bennett, *Before the Mayflower,* p. 457; Hornsby, *Chronology of African-American History,* p. 1838; *Negro Almanac, 1989,* p. 12.

SLAVERY

1619 • Twenty unnamed persons of African extraction were the first blacks in Virginia. They arrived in Jamestown in August, transported by a Dutchman who sold them to the planter colonists as indentured servants.
Sources: Bennett, *Before the Mayflower,* p. 441; Kane, *Famous First Facts,* p. 598; *Negro Almanac, 1989,* p. 2.

1622 • Anthony and Mary Johnson and family were the first known free blacks. They lived in Old Accomack, later Northampton County, in the Virginia colony. In 1651, Anthony Johnson, John Johnson, and John Johnson, Sr., were the first black landowners in Virginia, receiving grants totaling 850 acres, and in the same year, Richard Johnson appears to be the first black to enter Virginia as a free man. Anthony Johnson and his wife were among the twenty-three black servants in the 1624–25 census of the colony. In 1653, Anthony Johnson became the first black on record as a slave owner. The hardening of caste lines was proceeding, however, and in 1662 slavery was made hereditary in the colony by a decree assigning freedom or slavery according to the condition of the mother. Still, free blacks in Virginia did not lose the right to vote until 1723. (*See also* **Religion: Church of England, 1623.**)
Sources: Bennett, *Before the Mayflower,* pp. 35–38; *Encyclopedia of Black America,* p. 37; *Negro Year Book, 1921–22,* pp. 126–27.

1640 • The first known black "servant for life," or more plainly, slave, was John Punch, who had run away with two fellow white servants. All three were whipped, and the indentures of the whites were extended five years— while Punch was bound for life.
Source: Negro Year Book, 1921–22, p. 126.

1641 • The first colony to legalize slavery, and to forbid use of "unjust violence" in the capture of slaves, was Massachusetts.
Sources: Hornsby, *Chronology of African-American History,* p. 3; *Negro Year Book,* 1921–22, p. 126.

1642 • The colony of Virginia was the first to pass a fugitive slave law. After a second escape attempt, slaves were branded. The law probably applied to servants. Seven years later there were only four hundred blacks in the colony, and the first formal recognition of slavery is 1661.
Sources: Negro Almanac, 1989, p. 2; *Negro Year Book, 1921–22,* p. 127.

1643 • The first intercolony agreement about fugitive slaves was made in the New England Confederation. Certification by a magistrate would convict an escaped slave.
Source: Negro Almanac, 1989, p. 2.

1664 • The lower house of Maryland asked the upper house to draft an act declaring that baptism of slaves did not lead to their freedom. At least six of the colonies had laws making this specific declaration by 1710. This is the first known attempt to resolve the question by statute.
Source: Raboteau, *Slave Religion,* p. 99.

1786 • The first evidence of the existence of an "underground railroad," in the sense of people organized to help fugitive slaves escape, refers to a group of Quakers in Philadelphia. Between 1812 and the Civil War, the necessarily clandestine organizations became more widespread and more effective. From 1830 to 1860, it is estimated that some nine thousand fugitives passed through Philadelphia, and some forty thousand through Ohio. One of the most famous conductors was Harriet Tubman (c.1820–1913), who within a ten-year period made at least ten trips from the North into Southern states and led over two hundred slaves into free states of the North.
Sources: Negro Year Book, 1921–22, pp. 153–54; *Notable Black American Women,* pp. 1151–55.

1842 • Frederick Douglass made his first appearance in print as he agitated for the freedom of George Latimer, an escaped slave. Latimer had been captured, leading to the first of several famous fugitive slave cases. Later, Latimer's freedom was purchased by the Boston abolitionists. George Latimer is the father of Lewis H. Latimer, the inventor. (*See also* **Science and Medicine: Inventions, 1882; Writers: Short Stories, 1853.**)
Sources: Dictionary of American Negro Biography, p. 385; *Negro Almanac, 1989,* p. 12; *The Real McCoy,* pp. 96–97.

EDUCATION: OVER–COMING RACIAL BIAS

AWARDS AND HONORS

1907 • Alain Leroy Locke (1885–1954), educator, interpreter, and promoter of black culture, was the first black Rhodes scholar. From 1907 to 1910 he studied at Oxford (England), and from 1910 to 1911 at the University of Berlin (Germany). It was not until 1960 that the second black Rhodes scholar, Joseph Stanley Sanders, was selected.

Sources: Alford, *Famous First Blacks,* p. 35; Bennett, *Before the Mayflower,* p. 642; *Dictionary of American Negro Biography,* pp. 398–404; Hornsby, *Milestones in 20th-Century African-American History,* pp. 8–9.

ALAIN LOCKE, FIRST BLACK RHODES SCHOLAR RECIPIENT.

**CHARLOTTE
H. BROWN**

1928 • Charlotte Hawkins Brown (1883–1961) became the first black member of the 20th Century Club of Boston. Membership in the club included persons distinguished in education, art, science, and religion. Brown was born in Henderson, North Carolina, and educated at State Normal School (Salem, Massachusetts), Harvard University (Cambridge, Massachusetts), and Simmons College (Boston, Massachusetts). On October 10, 1902, she founded Alice Freeman Palmer Institute in Sedalia, North Carolina. On November 23, 1907, the school was renamed and incorporated as Palmer Memorial Institute.

Sources: Encyclopedia of Black America, p. 194; *Notable Black American Women,* pp. 109–14; Robinson, *Historical Negro Biographies,* pp. 167–68; *Who's Who Among Black Americans, 1927,* pp. 25–26.

1990 • The first building named in honor of a black at Louisiana State University, Baton Rouge, was Alexander Pierre Tureaud, Sr., Hall. Tureaud was the only black practicing attorney in the state from 1938 to 1947. He initiated students' suits to enter LSU's law school, medical school, and graduate school, and filed suits at other public colleges and universities in the state. He initiated more than thirty public school district desegregation cases and filed suits to desegregate buses, parks, playgrounds, and public facilities before the 1964 Civil Rights Act.

Source: Jet 78 (28 May 1990), p. 24.

COLLEGE ADMINISTRATORS

**DANIEL A.
PAYNE**

1863 • Historian, educator, and AME minister Daniel A. Payne (1811–93) was the first black president of a black college in the Western world—Wilberforce University (Ohio). He was president for sixteen years. He spent most of his life working in education, and promoting expansion of the black church. On Payne's advice, the AME Church purchased Wilberforce University, which in 1856 had been founded by the Methodist Episcopal Church. The university was officially transferred on March 30, 1863. Payne turned to writing in his later years and produced several works. His most important works were The History of the African Methodist Episcopal Church (1891), and Recollections of Seventy Years (1888).

Sources: Dictionary of American Negro Biography, pp. 484–85; Bennett, *Before the Mayflower,* pp. 173, 463; *Negro Almanac, 1989,* p. 1010; Simmons, *Men of Mark,* pp. 1078–85.

FIRST BLACK PRESIDENTS OF SELECTED BLACK COLLEGES

YEAR	NAME	COLLEGE	YEAR FOUNDED
1863	Daniel A. Payne	Wilberforce College (Wilberforce, Ohio)	1854
1871	Hiram Rhodes Revels	Alcorn College (Lorman, Mississippi)	1871
1882	John Mercer Langston	Virginia State College	1882
1926	Mordecai Wyatt	Howard University (Washington, DC)	1867
1937	Dwight Oliver Wendell Holmes	Morgan State College (Baltimore, Maryland)	1867
1947	Charles Spurgeon Johnson	Fisk University (Nashville, Tennessee)	1866
1945	Horace Mann Bond	Lincoln University (Lincoln University, Pennsylvania)	1854
1946	Harold L. Trigg	Saint Augustine's College (Raleigh, North Carolina)	1867
1949	Alonzo G. Morón	Hampton University (Hampton, Virginia)	1868
1952	Arthur D. Gray	Talladega College (Talladega, Alabama)	1867
1953	Albert Edward Manley	Spelman College (Atlanta, Georgia)	1881

1906 • Scholar-minister John Wesley Edward Bowen, Sr., (1855–1933) was the first black president of Gammon Theological Seminary, Atlanta, Georgia. He was also the first black to teach at the school. In 1904 he founded and edited *The Voice of the Negro,* a publication appealing to the black middle class in the South.

Sources: Dictionary of American Negro Biography, pp. 52–53; *Encyclopedia of Black America,* pp. 187–88; *Heritage and Hope,* p. 92.

1926 • Mordecai Wyatt Johnson (1890–1976), clergyman, educator, administrator, and public speaker, became the first black president of Howard University, Washington, D.C., on June 20, 1926. Martin Luther King, Jr., heard Johnson lecture on a trip to India, in which Johnson spoke of Mahatma Ghandi's life and teachings. This led King to purchase books on Ghandi's life and works, and to become committed to nonviolent resistance.

Sources: Bennett, *Before the Mayflower,* p. 526; *Encyclopedia of Black America,* p. 475; Katz, *Eyewitness,* pp. 507–8.

1937 • Dwight Oliver Wendell Holmes (1877-1963), educator and writer, became the first black president of Morgan State College (now University), where he guided the transition of the school from Methodist control to state control. He served until 1948, when he retired. He is known also for his book *Evolution of the Negro College,* published in 1934. Through his career and his writings, he significantly influenced black higher education.

Sources: Dictionary of American Negro Biography, pp. 320–21; *Encyclopedia of Black America,* p. 443; *Who's Who in America, 1946-1947,* p. 1106.

CHARLES SPURGEON JOHNSON

1946 • Charles Spurgeon Johnson (1893–1956), socologist, editor, writer, and educational statesman, became the first black president of Fisk University, Nashville, Tennessee, on September 1, 1946. He graduated from Virginia Union University then went to the University of Chicago for his Ph.D. degree. He became a close associate of sociologist Robert E. Park, and later directed research and records at the Chicago Urban League while Park was president. In 1923 he edited the Urban League's *Opportunity* magazine and throughout the 1920s the magazine became an outlet for works by the Harlem Renaissance literary and artistic figures.

Sources: Dictionary of American Negro Biography, pp. 347–49; Hornsby, *Milestones in 20th-Century African-American History,* pp. 45–46.

The first black president of Saint Augustine's College, Raleigh, North Carolina, was Harold L. Trigg. The college was founded in 1867 by the Freedman's Commission of the Protestant Episcopal Church, a group including clergy and laymen of North Carolina's episcopal diocese.

Source: Encyclopedia of Black America, p. 739.

1949 • The first black president of Hampton Institute (now University) was Alonzo Graseano Morón (1909–71). Born in Saint Thomas, he graduated from Brown University in 1932, where he was elected to Phi Beta Kappa. He graduated from Harvard Law School in 1947.

Sources: Current Biography, 1949, pp. 435–36; Hornsby, *Milestones in 20th-Century African-American History,* p. 157.

1953 • Albert Edward Manley (1908–) became the first black president of Spelman College. He served until 1976, when he became president emeritus. Born in San Pedro Sula, Spanish Honduras, he graduated from Johnson C. Smith University (North Carolina), Columbia Teachers College, and Stanford University (California).

Sources: Ebony Success Library, vol. 1, p. 215; *Who's Who Among Black Americans, 1992-1993,* p. 909.

1965 • James Madison Nabrit, Jr., (1900–) and Samuel Milton Nabrit (1905–) became the first black brothers to hold simultaneously the presidencies of two of the largest black universities. James Nabrit, lawyer, educator, and civil rights advocate, was president of Howard University, Washington, D.C., from 1960 to 1969, while educator Samuel Nabrit was president of Texas Southern University, Houston, Texas, from 1955 to 1966.

Sources: Encyclopedia of Black America, pp. 611–12; Who's Who among Black Americans, 1992–93, p. 1045; Wormley, Many Shades of Black, pp. 61, 159.

1966 • James Colston (1909–82) became the first black to head a college in New York State when he was appointed president of Bronx Community College, where he worked through 1976. He graduated from Morehouse College (Georgia) and obtained his Ph.D. degree from New York University. He was president of Knoxville College, Knoxville, Tennessee, from 1951 until his new appointment in 1966.

Sources: Jet 61 (11 February 1982), p. 54; Negro Almanac, 1976, p. 1023; Who's Who Among Black Americans, 1980–81, p. 165.

1969 • William M. Boyd III (1942–) was the first black on the board of trustees of Williams College (Massachusetts), where he served from 1969 to 1972. The Tuskegee, Alabama, native graduated from Williams College and the University of California, Berkeley, and was a Peace Corps volunteer in Cameroun from 1963 to 1965.

Source: Ebony Success Library, vol. 1, p. 38.

Leon A. Higginbotham, Jr., (1928–) lawyer, judge, and graduate of the Yale Law School, was the first black elected to the university's board of trustees, the Yale University Corporation. He defeated five other candidates in the April and May nationwide balloting. In 1970 he became the youngest person and the first black to serve on the Federal Trade Commission.

Source: Encyclopedia of Black America, pp. 436–37; Garrett, Famous First Facts about Negroes, pp. 162–63; Negro Almanac, 1989, pp. 342–43, 1430; Who's Who in America, 1982–83, vol. l, p. 1332.

1970 • The first black president of a major American university in the twentieth century was Clifton Reginald Wharton, Jr., (1926–) who on January 2, 1970, became president of Michigan State University in East Lansing. He was named chancellor of the State University of New York in 1977. (*See also* **Government—Federal Firsts: Federal Appointees, 1993.**)

Sources: Encyclopedia of Black America, pp. 851–52; Garrett, Famous First Facts About Negroes, pp. 61–62; Who's Who Among Black Americans, 1992–93, p. 650.

1972 • The first black woman elected to the Yale University Corporation was Marian Wright Edelman (1939–), lawyer, children's rights activist, and head of the agency that she founded in 1973, the Children's Defense Fund. In 1980 she became the first black (and the second woman) to head the Spelman College Board of Trustees.

Source: Black Women in America, vol. 1, pp. 377–78; Encyclopedia of Black America, p. 331; Notable Black American Women, vol. 1, pp. 309–12.

CHILDREN'S DEFENSE FUND FOUNDER MARIAN WRIGHT EDELMAN.

1974 • Charles Shelby Rooks (1924–) was named the first black president of Chicago Theological Seminary on April 8, 1974, and remained in the position until January 1984. He left to become executive vice president of the United Church Board for Homeland Ministries in New York City.

Sources: Hornsby, *Chronology of African-American History,* pp. 218–19; *Jet* 66 (18 June 1984), p. 26; *Who's Who Among Black Americans, 1992–93,* p. 1222.

1977 • Wenda Weekes Moore (1941–), Minneapolis civic leader, was the first black chairperson of the University of Minnesota Board of Regents.

Sources: Jet 53 (29 September 1977), p. 24; *Who's Who Among Black Americans, 1992–93,* p. 1018.

1980 • Benjamin Lelon McGee (1943–) became the first black chairperson of the Arkansas State University Board of Trustees—the first in the South to attain that position at a predominantly white institution.

Sources: Jet 59 (18 September 1980), p. 30; *Who's Who Among Black Americans, 1992–93,* p. 954.

1981 • Jewell Plummer Cobb (1924–) became president of California State University at Fullerton. She was the first black woman appointed in the system and believed to be the first to head a major public university on the West Coast. A cell biologist, Cobb has concentrated on cell research, specifically melanin, a brown or black pigment that colors the skin. Cobb was born in Chicago and received her Ph.D. degree from New York University.

Sources: Black Women in America, vol. 1, pp. 257–58; *Jet* 60 (13 August 1981), p. 25; *Notable Black American Women,* pp. 195–98; *Who's Who Among Black Americans, 1992–93,* p. 279.

Walter J. Kamba was installed as the first black president of the University of Zimbabwe. The Yale Law School graduate taught at several European universities before locating in Zimbabwe.

Source: Jet 61 (22 October 1981), p. 22.

Yvonne Kennedy (1945–) became the first black woman junior college president in Alabama in 1981, when she took the position at S. D. State Junior College (now Bishop State Community College) in Mobile. She received her Ph.D. degree from the University of Alabama, and also served as a member of the Alabama house of representatives, where she chaired the Black Caucus.

Sources: Jet 61 (19 November 1981), p. 24; *Who's Who Among Black Americans, 1992–93,* p. 815.

The first black rector of James Madison University (Virginia) was James H. Taylor, Jr., former assistant superintendent of the Lynchburg, Virginia, city schools. The Tuskegee University graduate received his doctorate from Duke University.

Source: Jet 62 (6 September 1982), p. 22.

1984 • The first woman of any race to become president of Wilberforce University was Yvonne Walker-Taylor. Her father, D. Ormond Walker, was president there for nearly a half-century. Walker had served as provost and interim president of Wilberforce, and she is now presidential professor at Central State University (Oklahoma).

Sources: Jet 66 (12 March 1984), p. 23; *Who's Who Among Black Americans, 1992–93,* p. 1448.

1985 • Elridge W. McMillan, prominent Atlanta, Georgia, educator and executive director of the Southern Education Foundation, became the first black vice-chairperson of the Board of Regents of the University System of Georgia. He served as the first black chairperson of the Board of Regents in 1986–87.

Sources: Jet 68 (12 August 1985), p. 22; *Jet* 74 (11 July 1988), p. 15.

The first black chancellor of California's 106 community colleges was Joshua L. Smith (1934–), former president of Manhattan Borough Community College.

Sources: Jet 69 (13 January 1986), p. 11; *Who's Who Among Black Americans, 1992–93,* p. 1305.

1986 • Niara Sudarkasa (1938–), educator and anthropologist, became the first black woman president of Lincoln University, Lincoln, Pennsylvania. A native of Fort Lauderdale, Florida, she received her Ph.D. from Columbia University (New York).

Sources: Black Women in America, vol. 2, pp. 1123–24; *Jet* 71 (27 October 1986), p. 22; *Notable Black American Women,* pp. 1089–93; *Who's Who Among Black Americans, 1992–93,* p. 1352.

LINCOLN UNIVERSITY'S FIRST BLACK WOMAN PRESIDENT, NIARA SUDARKASA.

1987 • Educator and anthropologist Johnnetta Betsch Cole (Robinson) (1936–) became the first black woman president of Spelman College, Atlanta, Georgia. She is affectionately called "sister president," a label which she gave herself in 1987. Born in Jacksonville, Florida, Cole received her Ph.D. degree from Northwestern University. Her landmark book, *All American Women,* published in 1986, broke new ground in women's studies for its emphasis on ethnicity, race, and class.

Sources: Black Women in America, vol. 1, pp. 260–61; *Negro Almanac, 1989,* pp. 97, 1081; *Notable Black American Women,* pp. 198–201; *Who's Who Among Black Americans, 1992–93,* p. 203.

Marilyn Yarbrough (1945–) became the first black law school dean in the South, and the only black woman law school dean in the country, when she was hired at the University of Tennessee at Knoxville. She is a graduate of Virginia State University and received her law degree from the University of California, Los Angeles.

Sources: Black Issues in Higher Education 7 (28 February 1991), p. 25; *Jet* 73 (5 October 1987), p. 39; *Who's Who Among Black Americans, 1992–93,* p. 1580.

SPELMAN COLLEGE "SISTER PRESIDENT" JOHNNETTA BETSCH COLE.

1988 • Clark University and Atlanta University, both in Atlanta, merged in July 1988, to become Clark Atlanta University. Thomas W. Cole, Jr., became the first president. A native of Vernon, Texas, he received his Ph.D. degree from the University of Chicago, and served as chancellor of the West Virginia Board of Regents.

Sources: Jet 77 (16 October 1989), p. 16; *Who's Who Among Black Americans, 1992–93,* p. 283.

1989 • The first black chancellor of Los Angeles Community Colleges was Donald Gayton Phelps (1929–). He was inaugurated in May, 1989 to head the nine-campus system, the largest community college system in the world.

Sources: Jet 76 (17 April 1989), p. 37; *Who's Who Among Black Americans, 1992–93,* p. 1119.

1990 • Marguerite Ross Barnett (1942–92), took office as the first woman and first black president of the University of Houston on September 1, 1990. In 1968 she had been the first black woman president of the University of Missouri, St. Louis. The Charlottesville, Virginia, native received her Ph.D. degree from the University of Chicago.

Sources: Black Women in America, vol. 1, pp. 89–90; *Jet* 78 (21 May 1990), p. 36; *Notable Black American Women,* pp. 55–56.

Dolores E. Cross (1938–) was the first black woman president of Chicago State University. She was also the first woman to head a college in the Illinois system of public higher education. She was appointed in May and took office on September 1, 1990. Cross received her Ph.D. degree from the University of Michigan.

Sources: Jet 78 (18 June 1990), p. 22; *Jet* 79 (15 April 1991), p. 22; *Who's Who Among Black Americans, 1992–93,* p. 325.

Otis L. Floyd (1928–93) became chancellor of the Board of Regents in Tennessee on June 29, 1990. He was the first black person ever to head a university system in Tennessee. He served as president of Tennessee State University, in Nashville, from 1987 until his new appointment. Born in Selmer, McNairy County, Tennessee, he began his career as a teacher in a one-room school in Purdy. He received his doctorate in education from Memphis State University.

Sources: Nashville Banner 19 May 1993; (Nashville) *Tennessean* 20 May 1993.

1991 • The first black president of Andover Newton Theological School, Newton Centre, Massachusetts, the oldest theological school in the nation, was David T. Shannon (1934–). He is an Old Testament scholar.

Source: Jet 80 (14 October 1991), p. 36.

James Walker (1941–) became the first black president of Middle Tennessee State University in Murfreesboro, and the first head of a majority white state college in Tennessee. A native of Phenix City, Alabama, he holds a doctorate from Pennsylvania State University.

Source: Jet 80 (27 May 1991), p. 38.

1992 • Blenda J. Wilson (1941–) became the first black woman to head a public university in Michigan when she was appointed president of University of Michigan, Dearborn. She is now president of California State University, Northridge.

Sources: Detroit Free Press, 21 May 1992; *Who's Who Among Black Americans, 1992–93,* p. 1543.

1993 • Barbara Ross-Lee, practicing family physician, Naval officer, and medical educator, was named dean of Ohio University College of Osteopathic Medicine in East Lansing, Michigan. She assumed the position on August 1, 1993, to become the first black woman to head a medical school in the United States. She is a 1973 graduate of Michigan State University College of Osteopathic Medicine in East Lansing and for ten years had a private practice. Ross-Lee is the sister of singer and actress Diana Ross.

Source: Jet 84 (31 May 1993), p. 20; *Jet* 84 (8 November 1993), p. 18; (Nashville) *Tennessean* (28 September 1993).

Condoleeza Rice (1954–), political scientist and Sovietologist, became the youngest and first black chief academic and budget officer at Stanford University, Stanford, California, on September 1, 1993. From 1989 to 1991 Rice was director of Soviet and East European Affairs of the National Security Council, under President George Bush.

Sources: Contemporary Black Biography, vol. 3, pp. 206–8; *Jet* 84 (7 June 1993), p. 22.

COLLEGE BUILDINGS

1881 • Allen Hall, located on the Huston-Tillotson College campus in Austin, Texas, is believed to be the first building in Texas (and the first west of the Mississippi) built to educate blacks. The college was founded in 1876, when Sam Houston College and Tillotson College merged.

Source: Encyclopedia of Black America, p. 457–58.

1887 • The first gymnasium erected on a black college campus was at Fisk University, Nashville, Tennessee. The building is now known as the Van Vechten Gallery of Art.

Source: Fisk University, *Mission and Management,* part 6, p. 60.

COLLEGE DEGREES

1734 • Anthony William Amo (c. 1700–?), an African born in Guinea, was the first known black to obtain a European medical doctorate. He attended the University of Wittenberg, and eventually returned to Africa after a thirty year's stay in Europe.

Source: Simmons, *Men of Mark,* pp. 617–19.

1823 • Alexander Lucius Twilight (1795–1857), educator, preacher, and legislator, became the first known black to graduate from an American college, when he received his B.A. degree from Middlebury College (Vermont). Other blacks who graduated from college during this early period were: Edward A. Jones, who received his degree from Amherst College (Massachusetts); and John Brown Russwurm, first black graduate from Bowdoin College (Maine). Both graduated in 1826, with Jones some few days ahead of Russworm. By 1860, only about twenty-eight blacks had received baccalaureate degrees from American colleges.

Sources: Bennett, *Before the Mayflower,* p. 172; Bowles and DeCosta, *Between Two Worlds,* pp. 12–13; *Dictionary of American Negro Biography,* p. 613.

1844 • George Boyer Vashon (1824–78), lawyer, educator, and writer, was the first black to receive a bachelor's degree from Oberlin College in Ohio. He was admitted to the New York bar in 1847.

Sources: Dictionary of American Negro Biography, p. 617; Bennett, *Before the Mayflower,* p. 460, 172; *Encyclopedia of Black America,* p. 826.

1850 • The first woman to graduate from college was Lucy Ann Stanton (Mrs. Levi N. Sessions, d. 1910). She completed the two-year ladies' course and received the Bachelor of Literature degree from Oberlin College (Ohio) on December 8, 1850. She taught school in the South during Reconstruction. Two other women have been called the first black woman college graduate. Grace A. Mapps was the first black woman to obtain a degree from a four-year college in the United States—Central College, McGrawville, New York. Apparently she finished in 1852, and joined Charles L. Reason, then recently named head, at the Institute for Colored Youth in Pennsylvania. Mary Jane Patterson (1840–94) was the first black woman to earn a B.A. degree from the four-year gentleman's course at Oberlin College (Ohio), in 1862.

Sources: Dictionary of Black Culture, p. 399; Jackson-Coppin, *Reminiscences of School Life, and Hints on Teaching,* p. 149; Kane, *Famous First Facts,* p. 118; Lane, *William Dorsey's Philadelphia and Ours,* pp. 137, 139; *Women in American Protest and Religion, 1800–1930,* p. 202.

1865 • Patrick Francis Healy (1834–1910), a Jesuit theologian, passed his final examination on July 26, 1865, and received a Ph.D. degree from Louvain University, Belgium, to become the first black American to receive an earned doctorate. He became America's first black president of a predominantly white university when he was inaugurated on July 31, 1871, as president of Georgetown University, Washington, D.C., the oldest Catholic university in America. He resigned the position in 1884. (*See also* **Religion: Catholics, 1854.**)

Sources: Bennett, *Before the Mayflower,* pp. 474, 641; *Dictionary of American Negro Biography,* pp. 304–5; *Encyclopedia of Black America,* p. 433.

1869 • George Lewis Ruffin (1834–86) was the first black to graduate from Harvard University Law School, and perhaps the first black American to graduate from a university law school and obtain a law degree. Also in 1869, he became one of the first blacks to practice law in Boston. He became judge of the District Court of Charlestown, Massachusetts, November 19, 1883, and was a member of the Common Council of Boston in 1875 and 1876. He married Josephine St. Pierre Ruffin (1842–1924), a leader in the black women's club movement.

Sources: Dictionary of American Negro Biography, p. 535; Simmons, *Men of Mark,* pp. 740–43.

1870 • Richard Theodore Greener (1844–1922), educator, lawyer, consular officer, and reformer, was the first black to graduate from Harvard University. In October 1873, he became professor of metaphysics at the University of South Carolina. In addition to his primary teaching duties, he assisted in the departments of Latin, Greek, mathematics, and constitutional history. He was acting librarian, arranging the university's rare book collection of 27,000 volumes, and beginning preparation of a catalog. During this same time, Greener studied law. In 1876, he graduated from the university's law school. He was admitted to the Supreme Court of South Carolina in 1877, and the next year practiced at the District of Columbia bar. He remained at South Carolina until March 1877, when the Wade Hampton legislature abruptly closed the door of the university to black students. He headed the law school at Howard University and developed a considerable reputation as a speaker and writer. Greener became active in the foreign service, serving in Bombay and Vladivostok. He retired in 1905.

RICHARD THEODORE GREENER

Sources: Bennett, *Before the Mayflower,* p. 642; *Blacks at Harvard,* pp. 36–41; *Dictionary of American Negro Biography,* pp. 267–68; Garrett, *Famous First Facts About Negroes,* p. 52; Robinson, *Historical Negro Biographies,* pp. 83–84; Simmons, *Men of Mark,* pp. 326–35.

1874 • Edward Alexander Bouchet (1825–1918) became the first black to receive a doctorate from an American university when he graduated from Yale in November of 1874. His graduate work in physics was supported by the Institute for Colored Youth of Philadelphia, the institution with which he was associated for twenty-six years as a teacher of chemistry and physics. (*See also* **Organizations: Academic and Intellectual Societies, 1877.**)

Sources: Dictionary of American Negro Biography, pp. 50–51; *Encyclopedia of Black America,* p. 187; Lane, William Dorsey's *Philadelphia and Ours,* p. 144.

1883 • In 1879, William Adger (1857–85) was the first black to enter the college department of the University of Pennsylvania. In 1883, he was the first to graduate with a B.A. degree. A native of Philadelphia and a graduate of the Institute for Colored Youth, he died during his senior year at the Episcopal seminary.

Source: Coppin, *Reminiscences of School Life,* pp. 150–51.

1888 • Aaron Albert Mossell, Jr., (1863–?) was the first black American to graduate from the University of Pennsylvania Law School (Philadelphia). He became a member of the bar in 1895. He later served as attorney for the Frederick Douglass Memorial Hospital in Philadelphia, where his brother, Nathan Francis Mossell, was superintendent. Aaron Mossell was the father of Sadie Tanner Mossell, one of the first three black women to earn a Ph.D. degree (*See* **Education: College Degrees, 1921**).

Sources: Dictionary of American Negro Biography, p. 458; Lane, William Dorsey's Philadelphia and Ours, pp. 172–73, 181–82; Notable Black American Women, p. 5.

FIRST BLACK HOLDERS OF DOCTORATES IN BIOLOGICAL SCIENCES

YEAR	RECIPIENT	GRANTING INSTITUTION
1889	Alfred O. Coffin	Illinois Wesleyan University, Bloomington, IL (Biology)
1916	Ernest E. Just	University of Chicago, Chicago, IL (Physiology and Zoology)
1940	Roger Arliner Young	University of Pennsylvania, Philadelphia, PA (Zoology)

Source: Greene, Holders of Doctorates Among American Negroes, pp. 182–83.

1893 • Harriet (Hattie) Aletha Gibbs Marshall (1869–1941), concert artist, pianist, and educator, was the first black graduate of the Oberlin Conservatory of Music (Ohio). In 1903 she established the Washington Conservatory of Music in Washington, D.C., which she directed until 1923. She moved to Haiti with her husband that year, where she founded an industrial school and collected folk music. She returned to the United States in 1936, and established a National Negro Music Center in association with the Washington, D.C. conservatory. Born in Vancouver, British Columbia, the daughter of Mifflin Gibbs, she was a pioneer in her efforts to bring black concert artists from all over the nation to Washington, D.C.

Sources: Dictionary of American Negro Biography, p. 426; Encyclopedia of Black America, p. 546; Southern, Biographical Dictionary of Afro-American and African Musicians, pp. 264–65.

1895 • The first black to receive a Ph.D. from Harvard University was William Edward Burghardt (W. E. B.) DuBois (1868–1963), educator, author, writer, Pan-Africanist. He was also the first black to earn a Ph.D. in history. (*See also* **Writers: History, 1896.**)

1897 • Anita Hemmings was the first black to graduate from Vassar College, Poughkeepsie, New York. Since she was very light-skinned, her declaration of her racial identity upon graduation attracted the sensational press and caused "dismay" for the college administration.

Source: Lane, *William Dorsey's Philadelphia and Ours,* p. 273.

1900 • The first black woman to graduate from Smith College (Northampton, MA) was Otelia Cromwell (1873–1972), educator and author. She received an honorary LL.D. degree from Smith in 1950.

Sources: Encyclopedia of Black America, pp. 295–96; *Notable Black American Women,* pp. 241–43.

WILLIAM EDWARD BURGHARDT (W. E. B.) DUBOIS.

FIRST BLACK HOLDERS OF DOCTORATES IN LANGUAGES AND LITERATURE

YEAR	RECIPIENT	GRANTING INSTITUTION
1893	William L. Bulkley	Syracuse University, Syracuse, NY (Latin)
1896	Lewis B. Moore	University of Pennsylvania, Philadelphia, PA (Greek and Latin)
1920	Harry S. Blackiston	University of Pennsylvania, Philadelphia, PA (German)
1921	Georgianna Rose Simpson (first woman in German)	University of Chicago, Chicago, IL (German)
1921	Eva Beatrice Dykes	Radcliffe College, Cambridge, MA (English)
1925	Anna Haywood Cooper	University of Paris, France (French)
1931	Valaurez B. Spratlin	Middlebury College, Middlebury, VT (Spanish)

Source: Greene, *Holders of Doctorates Among American Negroes,* pp. 163–64.

FIRST BLACK HOLDERS OF DOCTORATES IN SOCIAL SCIENCES

YEAR	RECIPIENT	GRANTING INSTITUTION
1895	W. E. B. DuBois	Harvard University, Cambridge, MA (Social Science)
1906	R. L. Diggs	Illinois Wesleyan, Bloomington, IL (Sociology)
1911	Richard Robert Wright, Jr.	University of Pennsylvania, Philadelphia, PA (Sociology) (first from organized graduate school)
1921	Sadie T. Mossell Alexander	University of Pennsylvania, Philadelphia, PA (Economics)
1925	Charles H. Wesley	Harvard University, Cambridge, MA (concentration in History)
1931	Laurence Foster	University of Pennsylvania, Philadelphia, PA (Anthropology)
1934	Ralph J. Bunche	Harvard University, Cambridge, MA (Political Science)
1937	Anna Johnson Julian	University of Pennsylvania, Philadelphia, PA (Sociology)
1941	Merle Johnson	State University of Iowa, Ames, IA (History)
1941	Merze Tate	Radcliffe College, Cambridge, MA (Political Science and International Relations)

Source: Greene, *Holders of Doctorates Among American Negroes,* pp. 46–47.

FIRST BLACK HOLDERS OF DOCTORATES IN PSYCHOLOGY AND PHILOSOPHY

YEAR	RECIPIENT	GRANTING INSTITUTION
1903	T. Nelson Baker, Sr.	Yale University, (New Haven, CT) (Philosophy)
1920	Francis Cecil Sumner	Clark College (Atlanta, GA) (Psychology)
1934	Ruth Howard Beckham	University of Minnesota (Child Welfare and Psychology)

Source: Greene, *Holders of Doctorates Among American Negroes,* pp. 199–200.

1909 • Gilbert H. Jones received a Ph.D. in German from the University of Jena and reportedly became the first black American to receive this degree from a German University.
Source: Negro Year Book, 1921–22, p. 27.

1921 • Eva Beatrice Dykes (1893–1986), Sadie Tanner Mossell Alexander (1898–1989), and Georgianna R. Simpson (1866–1944) were the first three black American women to earn a Ph.D. degree. They all received the degree in 1921. Dykes was the first to complete the requirements, in English, at Radcliffe College (Massachusetts) on March 21, 1921, yet her June 22 commencement was the latest. Simpson's degree, in German, was awarded June 14, by the University of Chicago, making her the first ever to receive the degree. The University of Pennsylvania awarded Alexander's degree on June 15, when she became the first black American to receive a Ph.D. in economics.
Sources: Bennett, *Before the Mayflower,* p. 523; *Black Women in America,* vol. 2, pp. 1038–39; *Notable Black American Women,* pp. 5–8, 304–6.

EVA BEATRICE DYKES WAS THE FIRST BLACK AMERICAN WOMAN TO COMPLETE REQUIREMENTS FOR A PH.D.

1927 • Sadie Tanner Mossell Alexander (1898–1989) was the first black woman to receive a law degree from the School of Law at the University of Pennsylvania. Later in 1927, she became the first black woman to enter the bar and practice law in Pennsylvania. (*See also* **Education: College Degrees, 1921.**)
Sources: Black Women in America, vol. 1, pp. 17–19; *Encyclopedia of Black America,* p. 98; Lee, *Interesting People,* p. 59; *Notable Black American Women,* pp. 5–8.

1950 • Juanita E. Jackson Mitchell (1913–92) was the first black woman to graduate from the University of Maryland law school. Denied admission to the university in 1927, she later challenged the university's racial barriers. She also became the first black woman to practice law in Maryland.
Sources: Black Women in America, pp. 804–5; *Ebony* 12 (October 1957), pp. 17–24; *Notable Black American Women,* p. 758.

FIRST BLACK HOLDERS OF THE DOCTOR OF EDUCATION (ED.D.) DEGREE

YEAR	RECIPIENT	GRANTING INSTITUTION
1933	Howard H. Long	Harvard University, Cambridge, MA
1933	Edgerton Hall	Rutgers University, New Brunswick, NJ
1939	Rose Butler Browne	Harvard University (first black woman to receive a doctorate from Harvard)

Source: Greene, *Holders of Doctorates Among American Negroes,* p. 83.

1952 • Floyd Bixler McKissick (1922–91) was the first black to graduate from the University of North Carolina Law School. He became active in the civil rights movement. He served as legal counsel for the Congress of Racial Equality (CORE), and in 1966 succeeded James Farmer as its national chairperson. He formed a company that organized Soul City, a new town in North Carolina.

Sources: Current Biography, 1968, pp. 238–41; Hornsby, *Milestones in 20th-Century African-American History,* pp. 82, 471; Robinson, *Historical Negro Biographies,* p. 225.

1954 • The first black woman to receive a doctorate in political science was Jewel Limar Prestage (1931–). She is now dean and professor of political science in the Benjamin Banneker Honor College, at Prairie View Agricultural and Mechanical University (Texas).

Sources: Black Women in America, vol. 2, p. 940; *Jet* 61 (31 December 1981), p. 23; *Who's Who Among Black Americans, 1992–93,* p. 1146.

PROMINENT PENNSYLVANIA LAWYER SADIE ALEXANDER.

1973 • Shirley Ann Jackson (1946–) received the Ph.D. in physics, and became the first black woman in the United States to receive a doctorate from Massachusetts Institute of Technology. Since 1976 she has been at AT & T Bell Laboratories, where she conducts research on topics relating to theoretical material sciences.

Sources: Negro Almanac, 1989, pp. 106, 1084; *Notable Black American Women,* pp. 565–66; *Who's Who Among Black Americans, 1992–93,* p. 725.

1981 • The first black woman to earn the doctor of science (Sc.D.) in chemical engineering was Jennie Patrick-Yeboah, of Gadsden, Alabama. She received her degree from Massachusetts Institute of Technology. She was inspired by her mother, who worked as a maid, and her father, who worked as a janitor.

Sources: Jet 57 (6 December 1979), p. 21; *Who's Who Among Black Americans, 1992–93,* p. 1093.

OPPOSITE PAGE: GEORGIANNA R. SIMPSON WAS THE FIRST BLACK AMERICAN WOMAN TO RECEIVE A PH.D. DEGREE.

FIRST BLACK HOLDERS OF DOCTORATES IN PHYSICAL SCIENCES

YEAR	RECIPIENT	GRANTING INSTITUTION
1916	Saint Elmo Brady	University of Illinois, Urbana, IL (Chemistry)
1925	Elbert Cox	Cornell University, Ithaca, NY (Mathematics)
1942	Marguerite Thomas Williams	Catholic University of America, Washington, DC (first woman in the field of geology) (Geology)

Source: Greene, *Holders of Doctorates Among American Negroes,* p. 140.

COLLEGE FACULTY

CHARLES LEWIS REASON.

1849 • The first black faculty member on a white college campus was at Central College, McGrawville, New York. Charles Lewis Reason (1818–93), reformer and writer, was named professor of mathematics, belles lettres, and French in October 1849. In 1852, he became principal of the Institute for Colored Youth in Philadelphia. Another early black faculty member was William G. Allen, professor of Greek and German languages, rhetoric, and belles lettres. Allen married one of his white students, and later was forced to flee with her to England. The third black in this early group was George Boyer Vashon (1824–78), who joined the McGrawville faculty in 1854.

Sources: Dictionary of American Negro Biography, pp. 516–517; Jackson, *A History of Afro-American Literature,* vol. 1, p. 126; Lane, *William Dorsey's Philadelphia and Ours,* p. 137; Woodson, *The Education of the Negro Prior to 1861,* p. 280.

1870 • The first black teacher to be engaged by the Freedmen's Aid Society to teach at Claflin College (South Carolina), was William Henry Crogman (1841–1931), a scholar and writer. He was president of Clark College, in Atlanta, Georgia, from 1903 to 1910. He is known for his early histories of blacks, *Progress of a Race* and *Citizenship, Intelligence, Affluence, Honor and Trust.* The last work was revised and published as *The Colored American.*

Sources: Dictionary of American Negro Biography, pp. 140–41; *Heritage and Hope,* pp. 91–92.

The first black to teach white college students in Kentucky was Julia Britton Hooks (1852–1942), who was instructor of instrumental music at Berea College, Berea, Kentucky. She was one of the first black women in the country to attend Berea.

Sources: Black Women in America, pp. 572–73; *Notable Black American Women,* pp. 511–13.

1932 • James Weldon Johnson (1871–1938), educator, lyricist, consul, author, editor, poet, and civil rights activist, was appointed in January 1932 to teach creative writing at Fisk University, Nashville, Tennessee, where he held the Adam K. Spence Chair of Creative Literature and Writing, becoming the first poet to teach creative writing at a black college.

Sources: Dictionary of American Negro Biography, pp. 353–57; Kane, *Famous First Facts,* p. 476.

1946 • Allison Davis (1902–83), psychologist and educator, was the first black professor at the University of Chicago, where in 1970 he became the first John Dewey Distinguished Service Professor of Education. He was the first in education from any race to become a fellow in the American Academy of Arts and Sciences, and one of the first to challenge the accuracy of the IQ test for "measuring accurately the educational potential of children from low-income families."

Sources: Encyclopedia of Black America, p. 302; Garrett, *Famous First Facts about Negroes,* pp. 62, 185; *Jet* 65 (12 December 1983), p. 15; *Who's Who in America, 1982–1983,* p. 766.

The first black woman instructor in New York University's department of nursing education was Estelle Massey Riddle Osborne (1901–1981). She received a master's degree in nursing education in 1931, becoming the first black to do so. In 1943, she became consultant to the National Nursing Council for War Service and was the first black consultant on the staff of any national nursing organization.

Sources: Black Women in America, pp. 903–5; *Negro Almanac, 1989,* pp. 1389, 1426; *Who's Who Among Black Americans, 1980–81,* p. 607.

1968 • Jacquelyne Johnson Jackson (1932–), sociologist and civil rights activist, became the first full-time black faculty member (and in 1971 the first black tenured faculty member) at Duke University Medical School (North Carolina). She was also the first woman chair of the Association of Black Sociologists. The Winston-Salem native received her Ph.D. in 1960, becoming the first black woman to earn the degree in sociology from Ohio State University.

Sources: Notable Black American Women, pp. 554–56; *Ebony Success Library,* vol. 1, p. 167; *Who's Who Among Black Americans, 1992–93,* p. 721.

1969 • Derrick Bell (1930–), a constitutional law scholar, became the first black law professor at Harvard Law School (Massachusetts) and in 1971 became the first black tenured professor. After twenty-three years, he began an unpaid leave of absence to protest Harvard's hiring policies. He was dismissed in 1992, when he exceeded his two-year maximum leave.

Sources: Blacks at Harvard, pp. 467–73; *Jet* 72 (29 June 1982), p. 28; *Jet* 78 (14 May 1990), p. 25; *Jet* 82 (20 July 1992), p. 22; *Jet* 82 (27 July 1992), p. 56.

The first chairperson of Harvard University's Department of Afro-American Studies was Ewart Guinier (1911–90). His daughter, Lani Guinier, gained national recognition in 1993, when President Bill Clinton picked her to head the United States Department of Justice's civil rights division. He later withdrew the nomination.

Sources: Jet 84 (21 June 1993), pp. 4–7; *Who's Who Among Black Americans, 1988,* p. 282.

Kelly Miller Smith, Sr., (1920–84), clergyman and writer, became the first black faculty member in the Vanderbilt University Divinity School (Tennessee), and later became assistant dean. The Mound Bayou, Mississippi, native was Martin Luther King's associate in Nashville, Tennessee, during the civil rights struggle of the 1960s.

Source: Ebony Success Library, vol. 1, p. 285.

1985 • The first black tenured professor at Harvard Business School was James Ireland Cash, Jr. (1947–). He is a specialist in the management of information systems technology in large corporations.

Sources: Jet 68 (22 July 1985), p. 21; *Who's Who Among Black Americans, 1992–93,* p. 245.

COLLEGE FOUNDINGS

1833 • The first college in the United States founded with a mission to educate blacks was Oberlin College (Ohio). One of the elements creating the institution was Lane Seminary in Cincinnati, Ohio. When many of the students converted to abolitionism, it became expedient to move to northern Ohio and join the nucleus of students and instruction already established there. By the time of the Civil War, one-third of the student body was black.

Sources: Negro Almanac, 1989, p. 11; Woodson, *The Education of the Negro Prior to 1861,* pp. 275–76, 300.

1839 • Cheyney State College, sometimes referred to as the oldest black college in the United States, had its beginning in 1832. Richard Humphreys, a Philadelphia Quaker, willed $10,000 to a board of trustees to establish a school for blacks. A school for black boys was eventually established in 1839, and incorporated in 1842. The school became known as the Institute for Colored Youth in 1852. It reorganized in 1902 and moved to Cheyney, Pennsylvania. Here it was renamed, and became a teacher training school in 1914, and a normal school in 1921, when it was purchased by the state. Since 1932 Cheyney State College has been a degree-granting institution.

Sources: American Colleges and Universities, 1983, p. 1565; Bowles and DeCosta, *Between Two Worlds,* pp. 23–24; Lane, *William Dorsey's Philadelphia and Ours,* p. 338; Woodson, *The Education of the Negro Prior to 1861,* pp. 268–70.

1854 • Lincoln University (Pennsylvania) and Wilberforce University (Ohio) are the oldest historically black colleges established in America. Unlike Cheyney State, which had its origin in 1832, these institutions were the first to remain in their original location, indicate their aim to award baccalaureate degrees, and develop fully into degree-granting institutions. Lincoln University, the outgrowth of Ashmun Institute, was incorporated January 1, 1854, and opened its doors to young black men on August 30, 1856. Wilberforce University was incorporated in 1856, and awarded its first baccalaureate degree in 1857. Beginning in 1862, the college came under black control, making it the oldest college controlled by blacks.

Sources: Bennett, *Before the Mayflower,* pp. 457, 462–63, 641; Bowles and DeCosta, *Between Two Worlds,* p. 20; Woodson, *The Education of the Negro Prior to 1861,* pp. 268–72.

1858 • Berea College, Berea, Kentucky, is the first college still existing south of the Ohio river that was established specifically to educate blacks and whites together. Activities of the college were suspended during the Civil War in 1865, but it later reopened. The integrated school received numerous threats of violence, but also experienced periods without friction. The legislature of Kentucky passed a law forbidding the racial mix, which ended the biracial experiment abruptly in 1904.

Source: Holmes, *Evolution of the Negro College,* pp. 81–82.

1866 • Edward Waters College, Jacksonville, Florida, became the first institution of higher learning for blacks in Florida. It was founded in Live Oak, Florida, by the African Methodist Episcopal Church. It was renamed Brown University, and moved to Jacksonville. In 1892 it was incorporated under its present name of Edward Waters College.

Source: Encyclopedia of Black America, pp. 352–53.

The first institution of higher learning for blacks in Mississippi was Rust College, in Holly Springs. Founded by the Methodist Episcopal Church, the original name, Shaw University, was changed in 1890, presumably to avoid confusion with the school in Raleigh, North Carolina. The school was then named for Richard Rust, a white antislavery advocate who supported the Freedmen's Aid Society of the church.

Sources: Cantor, *Historical Landmarks of Black America,* p. 172; *Encyclopedia of Black America,* p. 737.

1867 • The first black college founded in Tennessee, and still in existence, is Fisk University. Although work on the founding of the school was begun in October 1865, it did not become incorporated under the laws of the State of Tennessee until August 22, 1867, under the auspices of the American Missionary Association. The institution opened on January 9, 1866. It was named in honor of General Clinton B. Fisk of the Freedmen's Bureau.

Sources: Fisk University Bulletin, 1986–89, p. 4; Richardson, *A History of Fisk University 1865–1946.*

On January 8, 1867 Howard Theological Seminary changed its name to Howard University. On that date the university became the first black school to establish undergraduate, graduate, and professional schools. The school was established under the auspices of the Freedmen's Bureau, and named in honor of General Oliver O. Howard, who headed the Bureau.

Sources: Encyclopedia of Black America, p. 455; Hornsby, *Chronology of African-American History,* p. 40; *Jet* 81 (13 January 1992), p. 38.

The first college open to blacks in Alabama was Talladega College. Founded by the American Missionary Association as a primary school, the first college program was published in the 1890 catalogue, and the first class graduated in 1895.

Source: Encyclopedia of Black America, p. 813.

1871 • The first college founded as a land grant college for blacks was Alcorn Agricultural and Mechanical College, Lorman, Mississippi. This was made possible under the Morrill Act of 1862. Ironically, the college was named in honor of James I. Alcorn, a Reconstruction governor of the state who led the white branch of the Republican Party, and who opposed black legislators during his term of office. Hiram Rhoades (Rhodes) Revels (1822–1901) was the first president. The college maintained, for a considerable period, a liberal arts curriculum, in spite of the disapproval of the legislature.

Sources: Cantor, *Historic Landmarks of Black America,* pp. 168–69; *Encyclopedia of Black America,* p. 96; *The Negro Almanac, 1976,* p. 532.

1874 • Alabama State University was founded at Salem, as the State Normal School and University for Colored Students and Teachers. It was the first state-supported institution in the United States to train black teachers. The institution moved to its present site, in Montgomery, in 1887.

Sources: Bowles and DeCosta, *Between Two Worlds,* p. 292; *Encyclopedia of Black America,* p. 95.

1877 • The first regular school for blacks in North Carolina was Fayetteville State. Until 1960, the only major was education. The first four-year class was graduated in 1939. The school graduated its first white student in 1969.

Sources: Cantor, *Historical Landmarks of Black America,* p. 350; *Encyclopedia of Black America,* p. 384.

1881 • Spelman College, Atlanta, Georgia, was the first institution of higher education established to educate black women. Sponsored by philanthopist John D. Rockefeller, the school opened on April 11, 1881, as the Atlanta Baptist Female Seminary. In 1884, the name Spelman was adopted in honor of Mrs. John D. Rockefeller's parents. (*See also* **Education: College Fund-Raising, 1992.**)

Sources: Black Women in America, pp. 1091–95; *Encyclopedia of Black America,* p. 807; Hornsby, *Chronology of African-American History,* p. 50; Read, *The Story of Spelman College.*

1915 • Xavier University in New Orleans was the first (and remains the only) black Catholic college. It was founded by Katherine Drexel and the

Sisters of the Blessed Sacrament; it opened on September 27, 1915, as a high school. The College Department was added in 1925.

Sources: Alford, *Famous First Blacks in the United States,* p. 32; Davis, *The History of Black Catholics,* p. 254; *Encyclopedia of Black America,* p. 871.

1925 • The first black state-supported liberal arts college was North Carolina Central University in Durham. Founded in 1910 by James E. Shepard, the school was first chartered as the National Religious Training School and Chautauqua. It later became a state normal school. Then in 1925, as North Carolina College for Negroes, it became a liberal arts college.

Source: Encyclopedia of Black America, p. 651.

1929 • The first and only black college consortium, the Atlanta University System, was founded in 1929. John Hope (1868–1936) became the first president of the system when Atlanta University (a co-educational institution), Spelman College (an undergraduate college for women), and Morehouse College (an undergraduate college for men), entered a consortial arrangement. Later Clark and Morris Brown colleges and the Interdenominational Theological Seminary (all co-educational) joined to form the largest educational center in the world for blacks. Atlanta and Clark merged in 1988, to become Clark Atlanta University, which remains a part of the Center.

Sources: Encyclopedia of Black America, p. 144; Hornsby, *Chronology of African-American History,* p. 82; Hornsby, *Milestones in 20th-Century African-American History,* p. 30; *Jet* 52 (2 June 1977), p. 15.

1991 • The United Methodist Church established its first higher education institution in Zimbabwe, the United Methodist Africa University. Groundbreaking ceremonies were planned for April 6 with the opening scheduled for 1992.

Sources: Jet 79 (21 January 1991), p. 36.

COLLEGE FUND-RAISING

1981 • Lou Rawls' Parade of Stars, a national fundraiser to benefit the United Negro College Fund, had begun five years earlier, and in 1981 became the first nationally televised benefit for education. Co-hosted with Marilyn McCoo, the show received pledges from all over the country to support the forty-two historically black member institutions. UNCF was founded on April 24, 1944, to coordinate fundraising efforts of private black colleges. (*See also* **Organizations: Charitable and Civic Organizations, 1944.**)

Sources: Hornsby, *Milestones in 20th-Century African-American History,* pp. 41, 340; *Jet* 67 (21 January 1985), p. 22.

1992 • Spelman College, Atlanta, Georgia, became the first black college to receive a single gift of $37 million, the largest gift ever made to a historically black college. The gift from the DeWitt Wallace/Spelman College fund was established in the New York Community Trust by the Reader's Digest Association. The funds will be used for scholarships, and to build a curriculum development program within the honors program.

Source: Jet 82 (25 May 1992), p. 22.

FIRST BLACK HOLDERS OF DOCTORATES IN PROFESSIONAL AND VOCATIONAL FIELDS

YEAR	RECIPIENT	GRANTING INSTITUTION
1887	John Wesley E. Bowen, Sr.	Boston University, Boston, MA (Religion)
1915	Julian H. Lewis	University of Chicago, Chicago, IL (Medicine)
1923	Charles Hamilton Houston	Harvard University, Cambridge, MA (Law)
1932	Frederick Douglas Patterson	Cornell University, Ithaca, NY (Agricultural Science)
1934	George M. Jones	University of Michigan, Ann Arbor, MI (Engineering)
1936	Flemmie P. Kittrell	Cornell University, Ithaca, NY (Home Economics)
1939	Maurice W. Lee	University of Chicago, Chicago, IL (Business)
1940	Eliza Atkins Gleason	University of Chicago, Chicago, IL (Library Science)
1941	Alfred B. Turner	Pennsylvania State University, University Park, PA (Industrial Education)
1942	Oscar A. Fuller	University of Iowa (Music)

Source: Greene, *Holders of Doctorates Among American Negroes,* p. 115.

COLLEGE INTEGRATION

1868 • The University of South Carolina was first opened to all races on March 3, 1868. Elected to the Board of Trustees were B. A. Boseman and Francis L. Cardoza. The integrated student body seems to have ended with Wade Hampton's 'redemption' of the state in 1876. There was a long series of disturbances between July 8 and October 26, 1876, and federal troops were sent in. During this period, Democratic as well as Republican state governments were established in South Carolina. The deal that elected Rutherford B. Hayes president of the United States was struck on February 26, 1877. Democrats took over South Carolina on April 10, 1877, when federal troops were withdrawn.

Source: Bennett, *Before the Mayflower,* p. 485.

1953 • Joseph A. Johnson, Jr., (1914–) became the first black student at Vanderbilt University, Nashville, Tennessee, on May 2, 1953. By vote of the Board of Trustees, who said that "Christianity is not the exclusive possession of any one nation or race," he was admitted to the Divinity School. He was also the first black to graduate and receive a Ph.D. from Vanderbilt, in 1958. He has since served on the school's board of trustees. The Shreveport native later became a presiding bishop in the Christian Methodist Church.

Sources: Ebony Success Library, vol. 1, p. 178; *Jet* 60 (7 May 1981), p. 18; *Jet* 84 (3 May 1983), p. 32; *Who's Who Among Black Americans, 1980–81,* p. 431.

1956 • After three and a half years of legal efforts, Autherine Juanita Lucy (Foster) (1929–) was the first black student admitted to the University of Alabama, on February 3, 1956. A riot followed, and she was suspended that evening. She was expelled February 29 for making "false" and "outrageous" statements about the school. In 1989, she entered the university's graduate program in elementary education. She and her daughter, Grazia, graduated in the spring of 1992.

Sources: Bennett, *Before the Mayflower,* p. 552; *Black Women in America,* pp. 448–49; *Ebony* 11 (June 1956), p. 93; 12 (March 1957), pp. 51–54; Hornsby, *Milestones in 20th-Century African-American History,* p. 59; *Jet* 81 (18 November 1991), p. 10.

1961 • Charlayne Hunter (Gault) (1942–) and Hamilton Earl Holmes (1941–) were the first black students to enroll at the University of Georgia. Students rioted in protest of their admission, and they were temporarily suspended. Both students graduated from the school in 1963. Holmes became the first black medical student at Emory University (Georgia) in 1967. Hunter Gault received the George Foster Peabody Award from the University of Georgia's School of Journalism in 1986. In 1961, Holmes became the first black trustee of the University of Georgia Foundation.

Sources: Black Women in America, vol. 1, pp. 595–96; *Ebony Success Library,* vol. 1, p. 122; *Notable Black American Women,* pp. 535–36; *Who's Who Among Black Americans, 1992–93,* p. 674 (Holmes); p. 704 (Hunter Gault).

The first black admitted to the University of Mississippi was Air Force veteran James Howard Meredith (1933–), after being denied admission three times. Although the United States Supreme Court ordered Meredith's admission, Governor Ross R. Barnett defied the court's decision. United States marshalls were called to escort him to classes on October 1. Federal troops were called out to quell campus disturbances. Meredith graduated in 1963.

Sources: Crisis 70 (January 1963), pp. 5–11; *Encyclopedia of Black America,* p. 553; Hornsby, *Milestones in 20th-Century African-American History,* p. 71; *Jet* 71 (1 December 1986), p. 8. Katz, *Eyewitness,* pp. 483, 496–97.

1963 • Harvey Bernard Gantt (1943–) was the first black student admitted to Clemson University (South Carolina), where he studied architecture, graduating in 1965. (*See also* **Government—Local Heroes: Charlotte, 1983.**)

Sources: *Contemporary Black Biography,* vol. 1, pp. 72–74; *Who's Who Among Black Americans, 1992–93,* p. 502.

1965 • The first black student to graduate from the University of Alabama, on May 30, 1965, was Vivian Malone (1942–). She and another black student, James Hood, upstaged Governor George Wallace, who defied their admission by standing in a doorway. National Guard troops escorted them through registration. Hood dropped out on the first day, but Malone continued and graduated.

Sources: *Negro Almanac, 1976,* p. 39; *Notable Black American Women,* pp. 727–28.

HONORARY DEGREES

1804 • Lemuel Haynes (1753–1833) was the first black to receive an honorary degree in the United States. Middlebury College (Vermont) at its second commencement in 1804, awarded Haynes an M.A. (*See also* **Religion: Congregationalists, 1785; Military: Revolutionary War, 1775.**)

Source: *Dictionary of American Negro Biography,* pp. 300–1.

1896 • Educator, school founder, and race leader Booker T. Washington was the first black recipient of an honorary degree from Harvard University. He received an M.A. in 1896. (*See also* **Miscellaneous: Commemoratives and Monuments, 1940** and **1946.**)

Sources: Alford, *Famous First Blacks,* p. 35; *Dictionary of American Negro Biography,* pp. 633–38; Hornsby, *Chronology of African-American History,* p. 55.

1946 • On February 21, 1946, Mary McLeod Bethune (1875–1955), educator and civic leader, became the first black to receive an honorary degree from a white college in the South; she received the degree from Rollins College, Winter Park, Florida. (*See also* **Government—Federal Firsts: Federal Appointees, 1936; Miscellaneous: Commemoratives and Monuments, 1974;** and **Organizations: Civil Rights and Political Organizations, 1935.**)

Sources: Garrett, *Famous First Facts about Negroes,* pp. 59, 122–23, 161; *Jet* 82 (6 July 1992), p. 32; Kane, *Famous First Facts,* p. 216.

1973 • B. B. (Riley B.) King (1925–) received a doctorate of humanities from Tougaloo College (Mississippi), the first black musician to receive an honorary degree for work in the blues. He was born in Indianola, Mississippi, and moved to Memphis, Tennessee, where he had his own radio show and in 1950–51 was a disc jockey. By the 1960s and 1970s he had become a successful performer. In 1979 he was the first black blues artist to perform in the USSR. The recordings of such musicians as Blind Lemon Jefferson (1897–1929) influenced his early style. (*See also* **Arts and Entertainment: Radio, 1949.**)

Sources: Current Biography, 1970, pp. 226–27; *Encyclopedia of Black America,* p. 489; Southern, *Biographical Dictionary of Afro-American and African Musicians,* p. 232.

LAW SCHOOLS

In October, 1868, John Mercer Langston (1829–97) founded and organized the Law Department at Howard University, the first in a black school. He headed the department when classes formally began on January 6, 1869, and was its dean from 1870 to 1873. From 1873 to 1875 he was vice-president and acting president of the university. (*See also* **Government— County Seats & State Capitols: Ohio, 1855.**)

Sources: Dictionary of American Negro Biography, pp. 382–83; Logan, *Howard University,* pp. 55–62, 67.

1990 • The first black student to become editor of the *Harvard Law Review* was Obama Barack. He noted that his election did not signal that social barriers had broken down. A second-year law student and a native of Hawaii, Barack was employed in social work on Chicago's South Side before entering law school.

Source: Jet 77 (26 February 1990), p. 10.

SCHOOLS

1750 • Anthony Benezet led the Philadelphia Quakers in opening the first free school for blacks. It was an evening school taught by Moses Patterson. Benezet left money at his death to continue the school.

Sources: Garrett, *Famous First Facts About Negroes,* p. 48; *Negro Almanac, 1976,* pp. 528–29.

1787 • The African Free School was the first free secular school in New York City. The free school for blacks was opened on November 1, 1787, before any free school for whites, by the Manumission Society. It began as a one-room school, and the first permanent building was erected in 1796. After this building burned, African School No. 2 was opened in 1815, with room for five hundred pupils. There were seven African Free Schools by 1834, and they were eventually incorporated into the public school system.

Sources: Hornsby, *Chronology of African-American History,* pp. 8–9; Horton, *Free People of Color,* pp. 59, 153; Johnson, *Black Manhattan,* pp. 20–23; *Negro Almanac, 1976,* p. 429.

1829 • Saint Francis Academy, Baltimore, Maryland, was the first boarding school for black girls. The school was established by the Oblate Sisters of Providence, and opened with twenty-four girls.

Sources: Black Women in America, p. 382; Garrett, *Famous First Facts About Negroes,* p. 49; *Notable Black American Women,* pp. 813–14.

NOVEMBER 1, 1787, MARKED THE OPENING OF THE AFRICAN FREE SCHOOL, NEW YORK CITY'S FIRST FREE SECULAR SCHOOL.

1849 • Benjamin Roberts filed the first petition to abolish segregated schools. Roberts filed the school integration suit on behalf of his daughter, against the city of Boston, which had a local ordinance requiring separate schools. The Massachusetts Supreme Court in *Roberts v. Boston* rejected the suit. Separate schools were abolished by state law in 1855, which resulted in Boston being the first major city to eliminate segregated schools.

Sources: Cantor, *Historic Landmarks of Black America*, p. 70; Garrett, *Famous First Facts About Negroes*, p. 49; *Negro Almanac, 1976*, p. 531.

1861 • Mary Smith Kelsick Peake (1823–62) a free woman of color, was the first teacher supported by the American Missionary Association for freed slaves. She began teaching children at Fort Monroe, Virginia, and on September 17, 1861, she opened a school in Hampton, Virginia, marking the beginning of the general education of blacks in the South. The school started as a day school, giving elementary education to children. A night school for adults was soon added. Hampton Institute (later University) has its roots in this school. Peake's health gave out shortly after the establishment of the school, and she died of tuberculosis on February 22, 1862.

Sources: Cantor, *Historic Landmarks of Black America*, pp. 253–54; *Dictionary of American Negro Biography*, p. 486; *Negro Yearbook, 1921–22*, pp. 230–31; *Notable Black American Women*, pp. 834–35.

NEW YORK EDUCATION PIONEER SARAH GARNET.

1863 • Sarah J. (Smith) Thompson Garnet (1831–1911) was the first black woman to be appointed principal in the New York public school system. Her second marriage, about 1879, was to the prominent abolitionist and Presbyterian minister Henry Highland Garnet (1815–82). In 1892, Sarah

Garnet and a number of prominent black women raised funds to replace the destroyed presses of Ida B. Wells's Memphis newspaper. Garnet was superintendent of the Suffrage Department of the National Association of Colored Women. Her sister was the pioneer woman physician Susan Maria Smith McKinney Steward (1847–1918).

Sources: Black Women in America, vol. 1, p. 479; Dictionary of American Negro Biography, pp. 253–54; Notable Black American Women, pp. 388–91.

1865 • Francis Louis Cardoza (1837–1903) was the first black principal of Avery Normal Institute, Charleston, South Carolina. Avery was an agent of the American Missionary Association and performed pioneer work in the education of the newly-freed slaves. Born in Charleston of a Jewish father and a mother of mixed ancestry, Cardoza was educated abroad and was very active in Reconstruction politics. He served in several high governmental positions, including secretary of state in South Carolina; he later was principal of the Colored Prepatory High School, and its successor, the M Street High School, in Washington, D.C.

FANNY JACKSON (COPPIN) WAS THE FIRST BLACK WOMAN TO HEAD A MAJOR EDUCATIONAL INSTITUTION FOR BLACKS.

Sources: Dictionary of American Negro Biography, pp. 89–90; Dictionary of Black Culture, p. 81; Encyclopedia of Black America, p. 102.

1869 • Fanny Jackson (Coppin) (1837–1913) became the first black woman to head a major educational institution for blacks, the Institute for Colored Youth of Philadelphia. The Society of Friends founded the school in 1837, and when Coppin graduated from Oberlin College (Ohio) in 1865, she became principal of the Institute's female department. She was promoted to principal of the entire school in 1869. The Institute was a prestigious school, with a faculty comprising some of the most highly educated blacks of the period. She retired in 1902.

Sources: Black Women in America, vol. 1, pp. 281–83; Lane, William Dorsey's Philadelphia and Ours, pp. 135, 142–47; Notable Black American Women, pp. 224–28.

1870 • Snowden School, Virginia, was the first state school for blacks. The school was short-lived.

Source: Kane, Famous First Facts, p. 563.

1879 • Josephine Silone Yates (1859–1912), teacher, journalist and club woman, was the first black American certified to teach in the public schools of Rhode Island. In 1877, she had been the first black to graduate from Rogers High School in Newport, Rhode Island. She later became an outstanding teacher at Lincoln Institute in Jefferson, Missouri, and president of the National Association of Colored Women.

Sources: Black Women in America, vol. 2, pp. 1297–98; Notable Black American Women, p. 1286–87.

JOSEPHINE SILONE YATES WAS THE FIRST CERTIFIED BLACK AMERICAN TEACHER IN RHODE ISLAND.

1895 • Mary Church Terrell (1863–1954) was the first black woman to serve on the Washington, D.C., Board of Education. She served from 1895 to 1901, and again from 1906 to 1911. (*See also* **Organizations: Civil Rights and Political Organizations, 1895.**)

Sources: Black Women in America, pp. 1157–59; Hornsby, *Milestones in 20th-Century African-American History,* pp. 49, 55; *Notable Black American Women,* pp. 1115–19.

1908 • Virginia Estelle Randolph (1870–1958) was the first black Jeanes teacher. Anna T. Jeanes, a Philadelphia Quaker, provided one million dollars to initiate a fund for teachers who worked with other teachers to encourage improvements in small black rural schools. Randolph was one of the most effective educators of her day. The Jeanes teacher program was fashioned after her notable practices in Henrico County, Virginia. Through the Jeanes movement that covered the period 1908 to 1969, Randolph was instrumental in bringing about improvements in the lives of thousands of teachers, children, and community residents.

Sources: Black Women in America, vol. 2, pp. 962–63; *Notable Black American Women,* pp. 918–21; *Who's Who in Colored America, 1937,* p. 429.

**VIRGINIA
ESTELLE
RANDOLPH**

1922 • Bessye Jeanne Banks Bearden (1888–1943), political and civic worker, was the first black woman member of the New York City Board of Education. Bearden was very dynamic in Democratic party politics; she founded and was the first president of the Colored Women's Democratic League. Bearden had a major role in political, civic, and social activities both in her community of Harlem and nationwide. Romare Bearden, renowned African-American artist, was her son.

Sources: Black Women in America, pp. 97–98; *Encyclopedia of Black America,* p. 169; *Notable Black American Women,* pp. 70–72.

FIRST BLACK HOLDERS OF DOCTORATES IN EDUCATION

YEAR	RECIPIENT	GRANTING INSTITUTION
1925	Charles H. Thompson	University of Chicago, Chicago, IL
1928	Althea Washington	Ohio State University, Columbus, OH
1928	Jennie Porter	University of Cincinnati, Cincinnati, OH
1931	Ambrose Caliver	Columbia University, New York City, NY (with special reference to college administration)

Source: Greene, *Holders of Doctorates Among American Negroes,* pp. 82–83.

1935 • Alvin D. Loving, Sr., (1907–) educator, was the first black high school teacher in the Detroit public schools. He later was a professor at the University of Michigan, and also worked in government.
Source: Who's Who Among Black Americans, 1978, p. 566.

1936 • Gertrude Elise McDougald Ayer (1884–1971), activist, educator, and writer, was the first black woman to have a full-time principalship in a New York City public school after the desegregation of the school system. (Sarah Garnet was the first black woman principal in 1863, in a black school.) Ayer had a strong commitment to the education and training of African-Americans. She wrote a number of articles and a chapter on women in Alain LeRoy Locke's *The New Negro,* the seminal work on the Harlem Renaissance.
Sources: Notable Black American Women, pp. 29–31; Who's Who in Colored America, 1950, p. 585.

WASHINGTON, D.C., BOARD MEMBER MARY CHURCH TERRELL.

1939 • Midian Othello Bousfield (1885–1948) was the first black to serve as a member of the Chicago Board of Education. During World War II, Bousfield, along with thirty-five other black officers, organized a hospital at Fort Huachuca, in the Arizona desert, for the all-black Ninety-third Division.
Sources: Dictionary of American Negro Biography, pp. 51–52; Dictionary of Black Culture, p. 61; Journal of the National Medical Association 49 (May 1948), p. 20.

1944 • Ruth Wright Hayre (1910–) was the first black to become a regular high school teacher in Philadelphia, at William Penn High School. She was the daughter of African Methodist Episcopal Bishop Robert Richard Wright, Jr., and the granddaughter of the pioneer black banker and entrepreneur R. R. Wright, Sr. She coedited, with her father, an edition of the poetry of Phillis Wheatley. In 1985 she was elected to the Philadelphia Board of Education, and in 1990 she was the first black (and the first woman) elected president of the board.
Sources: Encyclopedia of African Methodism, p.136.; Marketing (14 April 1992), p. 7; Who's Who Among Black Americans, 1992–93, p. 630.

1953 • Rufus Early Clement (1900–67) was the first black elected to a school board in the deep South since Reconstruction. Clement was elected to the Atlanta Public School board by black and white citizens. In 1925 he was the youngest academic dean in America, at Livingstone College in Salisbury, North Carolina. He later became dean of Louisville Municipal College in Kentucky. In 1936, he became president of Atlanta University and was instrumental in fostering their newly formed graduate school (1929), as well as enlarging the influence of the Atlanta University Center. In 1966, *Time* magazine chose Clement as one of the fourteen most influential university presidents in America. He was always identified with organizations in the South directed toward the healing of race relations, and the eradication of all forms of discrimination.

Sources: Bacote, *The Story of Atlanta University,* pp. 316–30, 344–82; *Dictionary of American Negro Biography,* p. 117; *Encyclopedia of Black America,* p. 275; Hornsby, *Chronology of African-American History,* p. 99; *Time* 87 (11 February 1966), p. 64.

1956 • John Henrik Clarke (1915–), editor, writer, teacher, and historian, was the first black licensed to teach African and African-American history in New York State public schools. He is best known as a critic, anthologist, and editor; he has also written short stories and poetry. He was the co-founder of the *Harlem Quarterly,* book review editor of the *Negro History Bulletin,* and associate editor of *Freedomways: A Quarterly Review of the Negro Freedom Movement.*

Sources: Encyclopedia of Black America, p. 273; *Negro Almanac, 1989,* p. 985; *Who's Who Among Black Americans, 1992–93,* p. 269.

1958 • Ernest Gideon Green (1941–), investment banker and government worker, was the first black graduate from the Little Rock, Arkansas, Central High School. Green was one of the "Little Rock Nine," the black students who integrated the Little Rock public schools under the watch of the federal troops called out by President Dwight D. Eisenhower in 1957. Along with the other students and advisor Daisy Bates, Green was the recipient of the Spingarn Medal in 1958.

Sources: Cantor, *Historic Landmarks of Black America,* pp. 147–48; Hornsby, *Chronology of African-American History,* p. 106; *Who's Who Among Black Americans, 1992–93,* p. 556.

1964 • Harlem School of the Arts was the first school in the state of New York founded to offer preprofessional training to mostly black and Latino children. The noted soprano, opera singer, and school founder Dorothy Maynor (1910–) was the first executive director of the school. The school provided performing arts instruction for underprivileged community children. Maynor served as its director until 1979, culminating a forty year career which began with her historic Town Hall voice recital in 1939. She was internationally acclaimed as a leading soprano and an interpreter of German lieder.

Sources: Black Women in America, pp. 761–62; *Notable Black American Women,* pp. 739–40; *Who's Who Among Black Americans, 1978,* p. 593.

1967 • Benjamin Elijah Mays (1895–1984), college president, clergyman, and educational administrator, was elected the first black president of the Atlanta Public School Board of Education. He had retired as president of Morehouse College (Georgia) in 1967. He was born in South Carolina to tenant farmers, and he was educated in New England and at the University of Chicago. Before becoming president of Morehouse, Mays taught at Howard University (Washington, D.C.) and held a number of Baptist church pastorates. He was a militant civil rights advocate. Martin Luther King, Jr., was a student at Morehouse during Mays's tenure, and Mays delivered the eulogy at King's funeral. In January 1984, Mays was inducted into the South Carolina Hall of Fame, and cited for his long career in education and civil rights.

BENJAMIN ELIJAH MAYS

Sources: Black Enterprise 7 (May 1977), p. 26–29; *Ebony* 33 (December 1977), p. 72–80; Hornsby, *Chronology of African-American History,* pp. 131, 142, 327, 329.

1969 • John W. Porter (1931–), educator, was the first black state superintendent of public instruction since Reconstruction. Porter was appointed to the position by Michigan Governor William G. Millikin.

Sources: Ebony 14 (February 1959), p. 6; Garrett, *Famous First Facts About Negroes,* p. 61; *Who's Who Among Black Americans, 1978,* p. 723.

1970 • Elbert E. Allen (1921–), a dentistry graduate of Meharry Medical College (1947), was the first black since Reconstruction to hold office in Shreveport, Louisiana, when he was elected to the Caddo Parish School Board. In the same year of his election to the school board, Allen also became head of the American Woodmen, a fraternal organization with some forty thousand members.

Sources: Ebony Success Library, vol 1, p. 9; *Who's Who Among Black Americans, 1992–93,* p. 22.

Wilson Camanza Riles (1917–) was the first black elected to a statewide office in California. He was state superintendent of education from 1971 to 1983. Riles was educated at Northern Arizona University. From 1958 to 1970 he served in the California State Department of Education.

Sources: Current Biography, 1971, pp. 348–50; *Ebony Success Library,* vol. 2, pp. 216–19; *Who's Who Among Black Americans, 1992–93,* p. 1194.

1971 • Roland Nathaniel Patterson (1928–) was the first black appointed superintendent of schools in Baltimore, Maryland. Patterson came from the Seattle, Washington, school system.

Source: Who's Who Among Black Americans, 1977–78, p. 697.

1973 • On July 1, 1973, Alonzo A. Crim (1928–) became the first black superintendent of schools in Atlanta, Georgia. A native of Chicago, Illinois,

Crim held the position until 1988, when he became a professor at Georgia State University.

Sources: Hornsby, *Chronology of African-American History,* pp. 207–28; *Negro Almanac, 1989,* p. 69; *Who's Who Among Black Americans, 1992–93,* p. 322.

Marianna White Davis (1929–) was the first black woman member of the South Carolina Board of Education, on which she served from 1973 to 1976. This educator was acting president of Denmark Technical College in 1985–86.

Sources: Encore 8 (20 November 1979), p. 7; *Jet* 50 (8 April 1976), p. 55; *Sepia* 28 (November 1979), p. 72–76; *Who's Who Among Black Americans, 1992–93,* p. 358.

1977 • John D. O'Bryant (1931–92) was the first black member of the Boston School Committee. The Boston-born educator began his career in the Boston schools in 1956 after earning a M.Ed. degree from Boston University.

Sources: Jet 82 (27 July 1992), p. 22; *Who's Who Among Black Americans, 1992–93,* p. 1069.

1979 • Willie W. Herenton (1940–) became the first black superintendent of the Memphis City School System, Tennessee, in 1979. Herenton had begun his teaching career in the elementary schools of Memphis. He was elected the first black mayor of that city in 1992. (*See also* **Government— Local Heroes: Memphis, 1992.**)

Sources: Ebony 47 (March 1992), pp. 106, 108; *State of Black America, 1992,* pp. 383–84; *Who's Who Among Black Americans, 1992–93,* p. 644.

1981 • Ruth Burnett Love (Holloway) (1935–) was the first black and the first woman to serve as superintendent of the Chicago school system. She served from 1981 to 1984 and was faced with an extremely difficult situation for a newcomer to the state and the system. Her school administrative work began in California, where she had been superintendent of the Oakland Unified School District. She subsequently opened a consulting firm in California.

Sources: Notable Black American Women, pp. 685–87; *Who's Who Among Black Americans, 1990–91,* p. 1157.

1982 • Bettye Davis (1938–), state representative, was the first black woman elected to the Anchorage, Alaska, Board of Education. Born in Louisiana, Davis was elected to the Alaska legislature in 1991.

Source: Who's Who Among Black Americans, 1992–93, p. 349.

Charles Albert Highsmith (1921–) was the first black superintendent of the Philadelphia, Pennsylvania, public schools.

Source: Who's Who Among Black Americans, 1992–93, p. 652.

1985 • Laval S. Wilson (1935–) was the first black superintendent of schools in the Boston public school system.

Source: Who's Who Among Black Americans, 1992–93, p. 1548.

1986 • Ethel Harris Hall (1928–) and Willie Paul were the first blacks elected to the Alabama Board of Education. Hall became an associate professor at the University of Alabama in 1978. Paul headed the Montgomery Head Start Program.

Sources: Jet 70 (14 July 1986), p. 16; Who's Who Among Black Americans, 1992–93, p. 582, (Hall).

1988 • Marvin E. Edwards (1943–) was named the first general superintendent of the Dallas, Texas, Independent School District.

Source: Who's Who Among Black Americans, 1992–93, p. 422.

Richard R. Green was named the first black chancellor of the New York City school system, the largest in the country.

Source: Jet 73 (18 January 1988), p. 8; Jet 74 (8 August 1988), p. 12.

1990 • Gwendolyn Calvert Baker (1931–) was the first black woman president of the New York City Board of Education. She is national executive director of the YWCA of America and president of the United States Committee for UNICEF Children's Fund.

Sources: Chicago Defender 13 July 1993; Jet 79 (1 April 1991), p. 31; Who's Who Among Black Americans, 1992–93, p. 60.

GOVERNMENT: COUNTY & STATE PIONEERS

∧∧∧∧∧∧∧∧∧∧∧∧∧∧∧∧∧∧∧∧∧∧∧∧∧∧∧∧∧∧∧∧∧

ALABAMA

1967 • On January 16, 1967, Lucius D. Amerson became the first black sheriff in the South since Reconstruction. Amerson was sheriff of Macon County.

Sources: Alford, *Famous First Blacks,* p. 48; Bennett, *Before the Mayflower,* p. 578; Hornsby, *Chronology of African-American History,* pp. 131, 164, 172; *Negro Almanac, 1989,* p. 44.

1970 • Fred Davis Gray and Thomas J. Reed (1927–) were the first blacks in the Alabama legislature in modern times. Gray is an attorney and an evangelist. He was Rosa Parks's lawyer during the Montgomery Bus Boycott, and the first civil rights lawyer for Martin Luther King, Jr. Gray was in the legislature for four years. Reed took degrees in economics at Tuskegee Institute. Also a civil rights activist, he was instrumental in getting the legislature to hire the first black page.

Sources: Ebony Success Library, vol. 1, pp. 131 (Gray), 260 (Reed); *Jet* 38 (18 June 1970), p. 10; *Jet* 43 (16 November, 1972), p. 5; *Jet* 46 (17 July 1974), pp. 1416; *Who's Who Among Black Americans, 1992–93,* p. 550 (Gray), 1175 (Reed).

1972 • On August 25, 1972, John L. LeFlore (1911–76) became the first black candidate officially certified to run for a United States Senate seat. He ran as a National Democratic Party of Alabama candidate. LeFlore was an active civil rights worker, for many years executive secretary of the Mobile branch of the NAACP.

Sources: Crisis 83 (April 1976), 141–42; Hornsby, *Chronology of African-American History,* pp. 200, 272.

1974 • Jesse J. Lewis (1925–) was the first black cabinet officer in Alabama in modern times as head of the Office of Highway Traffic Safety, a position he held until 1978. Lewis was named to his position by Governor George

Wallace. He is, at present, president of Lawson State Community College, Birmingham, Alabama.

Sources: Hornsby, *Chronology of Black America,* p. 248; *Who's Who Among Black Americans, 1992–93,* p. 871.

1977 • John T. Porter was the first black member of the Pardon and Parole Board. Porter was a first-term legislator at the time of his appointment. He had served the Sixth Avenue Baptist Church, Birmingham, for fourteen years.

Source: Jet 52 (28 April 1977), p. 9.

1979 • Cain James Kennedy (1937–) was the first black appointed circuit judge in Alabama in this century. Kennedy was born in Thomaston, Alabama, and took his law degree at George Washington University in 1971.

Sources: Jet 57 (20 December 1979), p. 55; *Who's Who Among Black Americans, 1992–93,* p. 813–14.

1981 • Oscar W. Adams, Jr., (1925–) was the first black on the state Supreme Court. A 1947 graduate of Howard Law School, Adams was a prominent Birmingham lawyer.

Source: Who's Who Among Black Americans, 1992–93, p. 8.

1983 • On May 24, 1983, Jesse L. Jackson (1941–) was the first black to address a joint session of the legislature in this century.

Source: Negro Almanac, 1989, p. 86.

1984 • Jackie Walker was the first black woman tax collector in Dallas County.

Source: Jet 67 (29 October 1984), p. 18.

ALABAMA-MISSISSIPPI

1977 • Howard A. Gunn was the first black member of the Tenn-Tom Waterway Board of Directors. Gunn is president of the Ministerial Institute and College, West Point, Mississippi.

Source: Jet 53 (10 November 1977), p. 28.

ALASKA

1960 • Blanche Preston McSmith was the first black state legislator.

Sources: Ebony 16 (March 1961), p. 148; *Ebony* 25 (November 1969), p. 132; Garrett, *Famous First Facts About Negroes,* p. 186.

1982 • Walt Furnace was the first black elected to public office in the state as a Republican. He was elected to the state legislature.

Source: Jet 64 (23 May 1983), p. 21.

ARIZONA

1967 • Cloves C. Campbell (1931–) was the first black elected to the state senate.

Source: Encyclopedia of Black America, p. 234.

1980 • Cecil Booker Patterson, Jr., (1941–) was the first black to sit on a court of record, the Maricopa County Superior Court. Patterson was born in Newport News, Virginia, and took his law degree at Arizona State University in 1971.

Sources: Jet 59 (4 December 1980), p. 4; *Who's Who Among Black Americans, 1992–93,* p. 1094.

ARKANSAS

1919 • Scipio Africanus Jones (1863?–1943) was the first black lawyer in charge of an important case for the NAACP in a Southern state; previously, in an effort to mollify white sensibilities, blacks had only assisted white lawyers. Jones handled the appeal process of twelve blacks sentenced to death for the Elaine, Arkansas, riot of October 1919 and helped take the case to the Supreme Court. An attempt to organize sharecroppers in Phillips County had resulted in violence. Twelve of the seventy-nine blacks tried for murder and insurrection as a result were sentenced to death; fifty-six of the others received long prison terms after a mere semblance of a trial. Black witnesses were beaten to compel testimony, a mob surrounded the courthouse calling for convictions, court-appointed counsel called no defense witnesses, and the jury deliberated five minutes. In the United States Supreme Court, *Moore v. Dempsey* resulted in overturning the verdicts in 1923.

Sources: Dictionary of American Negro Biography, pp. 368–69; *Encyclopedia of Black America,* pp. 500, 618; *Negro Almanac, 1989,* pp. 314–15; *Negro Year Book, 1921–22,* pp. 78–79.

1987 • George Hammons was the first black appointed to the state racing commission. Hammons is a professor at Philander Smith College, Little Rock. The state position is unsalaried, and has a five-year term.

Source: Jet 71 (16 February 1987), p. 17.

1988 • Kathleen Bell, Jesse Kearney, and Joyce Williams Warren (1949–) were the first blacks appointed to circuit chancery judgeships to oversee the juvenile division. These were newly established positions. Thus Warren was the first black woman judge in Pulaski County, and Bell was the first black in the First Judicial District.

Sources: Jet 77 (9 October 1989), p. 22; *Who's Who Among Black Americans, 1992–93,* p. 1459 (Warren).

Tommy Sproles was the first black chair of the state Game and Fish Commission. The Little Rock businessman became the first black on the commission when he was appointed to a seven-year term in 1983.

Source: Jet 76 (11 September 1989), p. 47.

Joyce Williams-Warren (1949–) was the first black to chair the state board of law examiners. Williams-Warren became a county judge in 1983, and a state judge in 1989. She took all of her degrees at the University of Arkansas at Little Rock (J.D. 1976), and was an administrative assistant to Governor Bill Clinton in 1979–81.

Sources: Jet 77 (15 January 1990), p. 38; *Who's Who Among Black Americans, 1992–93,* p. 1459.

1990 • Lottie H. Shackelford (1941–) was the first black chair of the state Democratic Party. A native of Little Rock, Shackelford had been executive director of the Urban League of Greater Little Rock (1973–78), and served on the Arkansas Regional Minority Council (1982–) at the time of her selection. She was also the first woman elected mayor of Little Rock, in 1987.

Sources: Jet 71 (9 February 1987), p. 57; *Jet* 78 (30 April 1990), p. 33; *Who's Who Among Black Americans, 1992–93,* pp. 1261–62.

1991 • Daniel Terry Blue, Jr., (1949–) was the first black speaker of the state house of representatives, and thus the first black speaker in any Southern state since Reconstruction. Born in Dillon, South Carolina, Blue was organizer of the first successful effort to desegregate Woolworth's, the bus depot, and other facilities in Orangeburg in 1959–60.

Sources: Jet 79 (21 January 1991), p. 27; *State of Black America, 1992,* p. 364; *Who's Who Among Black Americans, 1992–93,* p. 121.

1993 • Jerry Donal Jewell (1930–) was the first black to serve as governor of Arkansas. A dentist, and the president *pro tem* of the state senate, Jewell held the post for three days, as Governor Jim Guy Tucker attended the Presidential inauguration of former Governor Bill Clinton.

Source: Jet 83 (8 February 1993), pp. 22–23.

CALIFORNIA

1919 • Frederick Madison Roberts (1880–1952) was the first black to serve in the California legislature. Reputedly a great-grandson of Thomas Jefferson and Sally Hemings, Roberts was born in Ohio and moved to

California while young. He became a mortician, and the publisher of the *New Age*. He held his seat until he was defeated in 1934 by a black Democrat, Augustus F. Hawkins.

Sources: Dictionary of American Negro Biography, pp. 526–27; *Encyclopedia of Black America*, p. 83.

1944 • Doris E. Spears was the first black woman deputy sheriff in the United States.

Source: Lee, Interesting People, p. 19.

1946 • In January 1946, Pauli Murray was the first black deputy attorney general of California. Due to illness, she held the position only briefly.

Sources: Black Women in America, pp. 825–26; *Encyclopedia of Black America*, p, 584; Lee, *Interesting People*, p. 83; *Notable Black American Women*, pp. 783–88.

1967 • Yvonne Watson Braithwaite Burke (1932–) was the first black woman elected to the state assembly. (*See also* **Government—Federal Firsts: U.S. House of Representatives, 1966.**)

Sources: Encyclopedia of Black America, pp. 199–200; *Notable Black American Women*, pp. 130–32; *Who's Who Among Black Americans, 1992–93*, p. 199.

1974 • Mervyn M. Dymally (1926–) was the first black to be elected lieutenant governor of California on November 5, 1974. Dymally was an educator who had served in the assembly and senate since 1963. He was the first black to serve in the California legislature. In 1980, he was elected to the United States house of representatives.

Sources: Ebony 29 (January 1974), p. 37; *Ebony* 30 (March 1975), p. 128; *Ebony Success Library*, vol. 1, p. 102; *Who's Who Among Black Americans, 1992–93*, p. 411.

1977 • Wiley E. Manuel (1928–) was the first black state supreme court judge.

Sources: Ebony 33 (March 1978), p. 25; *Jet* 51 (10 March 1977), p. 45.

1978 • Florence Stroud was the first black, the first woman, and the first non-physician to head the California Board of Medical Quality.

Source: Jet 53 (9 February 1978), p. 18.

Diane Edith Watson (1933–) was the first black woman elected to the state senate. She holds a Ph.D. in educational administration from Clairmont College (1976), and worked in the Los Angeles United School District from 1956 to 1975, when she became a member of the Board of Education.

Sources: Jet 59 (19 February 1981), p. 21; *Who's Who Among Black Americans, 1992–93*, p. 1472.

WILLIE LEWIS BROWN, JR.

1980 • Willie Lewis Brown, Jr., (1934–) became the first black speaker of the California State Assembly. Brown was born in Texas and took his law degree in 1958. He was first elected to the assembly in 1964. He has been active in both state and national politics.

Sources: Ebony Success Library, vol. 1, p. 47; Jet 59 (18 December 1980), p. 5; Who's Who Among Black Americans, 1992–93, p. 184.

1982 • Thomas Bradley (1917–) was the first black nominated by a major party (Democratic) as a candidate for governor.

Sources: Negro Almanac, 1989, p. 428; Who's Who Among Black Americans, 1992–93, p. 144.

1983 • Raymond L. Johnson (1936–) was the first black chief of the southern district of the California Highway Patrol. Before joining the highway patrol, he worked in the Bakersfield police department, and he is currently chief of the Inglewood police department.

Sources: Jet 64 (27 June 1983), p. 21; Who's Who Among Black Americans, 1992–93, p. 768.

COLORADO

1956 • George L. Brown (1925–) was the first black elected to the state senate. In 1969, Brown became the first executive director of the Metro-Denver Urban Coalition, and in 1974, he became the first black elected lieutenant governor of the state. After 1979, his career was primarily as a business executive for the Grumman Corporation. George L. Brown and Mervyn Dymally of California were both elected lieutenant governor of their states on the same day in 1974. (*See* **Government—County & State Pioneers: California, 1974.**)

Sources: Ebony 30 (March 1975), p. 129; Ebony 33 (October 1978), p. 91; Ebony Success Library, vol. 1, p. 44; Encyclopedia of Black America, p. 194; Who's Who Among Black Americans, 1992–93, p. 170.

1991 • Gregory K. Scott was the first black named to the Colorado supreme court, a post he assumed in January 1993. A native of California, and holder of a law degree from Indiana University, Scott was a law professor at the University of Denver.

Source: Jet 82 (5 Oct. 1992), p. 28.

CONNECTICUT

1980 • Carrie Saxon Perry (1931–) was the first black woman elected to the state legislature. (*See also* **Government—Local Heroes: Connecticut, 1986—Hartford.**)

Sources: Negro Almanac, 1989, pp. 430–31; Notable Black American Women, pp. 837–40; Who's Who Among Black Americans, 1992–93, p. 1110–11.

1991 • Joseph Perry, Jr., became the first black commander of the Connecticut State Police.
Source: State of Black America, 1993, p. 275.

DELAWARE

1964 • Herman M. Holloway, Sr., (1922–) was the first black to serve in the Delaware senate. A native of Wilmington, Holloway was a building inspector and had long been active in politics. In 1963, he served in the house, filling an unexpired term.
Sources: Ebony Success Library, vol. 1, p. 154; *Who's Who Among Black Americans, 1992–93,* p. 672.

FLORIDA

1968 • In November 1968, Joe Lang Kershaw became the first black elected to the Florida legislature in this century.
Source: Hornsby, *Chronology of African-American History,* p. 134.

1970 • Gwendolyn Sawyer Cherry (1923–79) was the first black woman in the state legislature. Cherry taught in the Dade County schools for eighteen years. When the University of Miami's law school opened to blacks, she attended and became a lawyer. She then worked for the Coast Guard. Cherry was killed in an automobile accident during her fourth term.
Sources: Ebony Success Library, vol. 1, p. 65; *Essence* 4 (March 1974), p. 20; *Jet* 55 (1 March 1979), p. 18; Lee, *Interesting People,* p. 130.

1979 • Wallace E. Orr was the first black secretary of labor in the state. He had served as president of the Florida Education Association.
Source: Jet 56 (26 April 1979), p. 11.

1982 • Carrie Meek was the first black state senator since Reconstruction. A graduate of Florida Agricultural and Mechanical University, Meek served in the state house for three years.
Source: Jet 62 (23 August 1982), p. 27.

Cynthia Reese, a resident of Riviera Beach, was the first black woman state trooper.
Source: Jet 61 (15 February 1982), p. 39.

By gaining the position of county judge in Miami, Leah Simms became the first black woman state judge. Simms holds a law degree from Willamette University Law School, and has served as assistant state's attorney and assistant United States attorney for Southern Florida.
Source: Jet 61 (4 February 1982), p. 22.

1990 • Leander J. Shaw, Jr., (1930–) was the first black state supreme court chief justice, and the first black to head any branch of government in the state. Shaw was appointed to the court in 1983. Shaw was born in Salem, Virginia, and took his law degree at Howard University in 1957. He had wide experience in governmental service, and private practice, at the time of his selection.

Sources: *Jet* 77 (2 April 1990), p. 8; *Jet* 78 (23 July 1990), p. 33; *Who's Who Among Black Americans, 1992–93*, p. 1265.

GEORGIA

1962 • Leroy Reginald Johnson (1928–) was the first black elected to a Southern legislature since Reconstruction. He served for twelve years.

Sources: *Encyclopedia of Black America*, p. 475; Hornsby, *Chronology of African-American History*, pp. 113, 249; *Ebony* 18 (March 1963), pp. 25–28; *Ebony* 30 (January 1975), p. 35; *Who's Who Among Black Americans, 1992–93*, p. 763.

1964 • On February 4, 1964, Austin T. Walden (1885–1965) became the first black judge in the state since Reconstruction. He was a municipal judge in Atlanta. Walden obtained a law degree from the University of Michigan in 1911, and was admitted to the Georgia bar the following year. He began his law practice in Atlanta in 1919.

Sources: *Chronology of African-American History*, p. 117; *Negro Digest* 8 (August 1950), pp. 65–69. *Who's Who in America, 1966–1967*, p. 2214.

1967 • Grace Towns Hamilton (1907–92) was the first black woman in the state legislature. A native of Atlanta, Georgia, she was active in social work, and from 1943 to 1960 was executive director of the Atlanta Urban League.

Sources: *Encyclopedia of Black America*, p. 413; *Notable Black American Women*, pp. 444–48; *Who's Who Among Black Americans, 1992–93*, p. 587.

1969 • Edith Jacqueline Ingram-Grant (1942–) was the first black woman judge in the state, when she became a judge of the Hancock County Court of Ordinary.

Sources: *Encyclopedia of Black America*, p. 463; *Notable Black American Women*, p. 553; *Who's Who Among Black Americans, 1992–93*, p. 710.

1977 • Horace T. Ward (1927–) was the first black to serve on the Fulton County Superior Court. Ward earned his law degree from Northwestern University in 1959, and was elected to the Georgia state senate in 1964. In 1979, he became a United States District Court judge.

Sources: *Ebony* 20 (September 1965), p. 50; *Jet* 46 (30 May 1974), p. 5; Hornsby, *Chronology of Black-American History*, pp. 296–97; *Who's Who Among Black Americans, 1992–93*, p. 1456.

1982 • Charles S. Johnson was the first black member of the Georgia Board of Bar Examiners. In 1987, Johnson became the first black chair of the organization.

Sources: *Jet* 63 (20 December 1982), p. 46; *Jet* 72 (13 July 1987), p. 20.

1984 • Robert Benham (1946–) was the first black named to the state court of appeals. In 1989, Benham was the first black supreme court justice. A

GRACE TOWNS
HAMILTON

native of Cartersville, Georgia, he graduated from Tuskegee in 1967, and took his law degree at the University of Georgia in 1970.

Sources: Jet 66 (23 April 1984), p. 12; *Jet* 77 (25 December 1989), p. 6; *Who's Who Among Black Americans, 1992–93,* p. 99.

1985 • Gloria Butler was the first black and first woman to chair the state Campaign and Financial Disclosure Commission. Butler was executive director of Augusta Opportunities Industrialization Center. Before her election, she had served as vice-chair of the state commission.

Source: Jet 69 (30 September 1985), p. 37.

Clarence Cooper (1942–) was the first black to serve on the state supreme court in this century when he temporarily filled in for a sitting judge who recused himself. Cooper became associate judge of the Atlanta Municipal Court in 1979, and is now judge on the Fulton County Superior Court.

Sources: Jet 68 (29 April 1985), p. 4; *Who's Who Among Black Americans, 1992–93,* p. 303.

Thelma Laverne Wyatt-Cummings (1945–) was the first black woman appointed judge in the State Court of Fulton County. She was born in Amarillo, Texas, and took her law degree at the Emory Institution School of Law in 1971. She had become a judge on the Municipal Court of Atlanta in 1977, a position she held until 1980.

Sources: Jet 68 (8 July 1985), p. 37; *Who's Who Among Black Americans, 1992–93,* p. 1578.

1988 • Thomas Edison Brown, Jr., (1952–) was the first black director of public safety in DeKalb County, the location of Decatur. Brown began his career with the Atlanta Fire Bureau in 1972, and became fire chief of DeKalb County in 1985.

Source: Who's Who Among Black Americans, 1992–93, p. 181.

1991 • Jackie Barrett was the first black woman elected sheriff, winning the post of Fulton County sheriff. Barrett has sixteen years' experience in law enforcement, and as sheriff she supervises more than seven hundred employees.

Source: Jet 83 (23 November 1992), pp. 58–59; (11 January 1993), p. 18.

Paul L. Howard, Jr., was the first black to be elected Fulton County solicitor. Fulton County includes Atlanta. Howard is a graduate of Morehouse College, and holds a law degree from Emory University.

Source: Jet 83 (27 December 1992), p. 28.

ILLINOIS

1871 • John Jones (1816–79) was the first black elected to any public office in Cook County. A native of North Carolina and the son of a free black mother and a white father, Jones had been apprenticed to a tailor in Tennessee, and came to Chicago in 1845. He was elected to a one-year term on the county board in 1871, to a three-year term in 1872, and defeated in 1875. No other black was elected to the board until Theodore W. Jones won in 1894.

Sources: Dictionary of American Negro Biography, pp. 366–67; Gosnell, *Negro Politicians,* pp. 81–82; Hornsby, *Chronology of African-American History,* pp. 37–38; Katz, *The Black West,* pp. 67–70.

1889 • E. H. Wright was the first black to be appointed to a major state job when he became a bookkeeper and railroad incorporation clerk in the office of the secretary of state. In 1920, he would become the first black ward committeeman in Chicago.

Sources: Clayton, *The Negro Politician,* pp. 46–48; Gosnell, *Negro Politicians,* pp. 153, 213.

1917 • James G. Cotter was the first black assistant attorney-general in Illinois. Cotter was a graduate of Fisk University and the Illinois College of Law and entered private practice in 1919.

Source: Gosnell, *Negro Politicians,* p. 213.

1920 • Violette N. Anderson (1882–?) was the first black woman admitted to the Illinois bar. Born in London, England, Anderson received her law degree from the University of Chicago in 1920, and became the first woman assistant prosecutor in Chicago in 1922. She was the first black woman lawyer admitted to practice before the United States Supreme Court on January 29, 1926.

Sources: Garrett, *Famous First Facts About Negroes,* p. 94; *Opportunity* 4 (March 1926), p. 107; *Who's Who in Colored America,* pp. 13–14.

1924 • Adelbert H. Roberts was the first black elected to the Illinois Senate. Roberts was a native of Michigan who came to Chicago early in the 1890s. After taking a law degree, he became a clerk for the municipal court. He took office on January 10, 1925, and held his senate position until 1934.

Sources: Clayton, *The Negro Politician,* p. 46; Gosnell, *Negro Politicians,* pp. 69–71; Hornsby, *Chronology of African-American History,* p. 75.

1958 • Floy Clements was the first woman elected to the Illinois legislature.

Source: Clayton, *The Negro Politician,* p. 147.

1970 • Ronald Townsel (1934–) was the first black superintendent of adult parole in Illinois. A native of Chicago, Townsel was a twelve-year veteran of the parole system at the time of his appointment.

Sources: Ebony Success Library, vol. 1, p. 308; *Who's Who Among Black Americans, 1992–93,* p. 1409.

1971 • Dora B. Somerville (1920–) was the first black woman to hold the position of correctional programs administrator for the Illinois Department of Corrections. Somerville had a distinguished career in juvenile work and corrections, and is co-author of *The Delinquent Girl* (1970). Before assuming the position with the Department of Corrections, she had been the first woman member of the Illinois Parole and Pardon Board.

Sources: Ebony Success Library, vol. 1, p. 228; Who's Who Among Black Americans, 1992–93, p. 1319.

Cecil A. Partee (1921–) was the first black to head a chamber of a legislature since Reconstruction, when he became president *pro-tem* of the senate. Partee, a Chicago lawyer, was elected to the house of representatives in 1956. In 1971, he was also the first black governor in the nation since Reconstruction, and the first ever in Illinois, when he briefly held the position from 9:15 A.M. to 11:00 P.M.

Sources: Ebony 27 (April 1972), p. 195; Encyclopedia of Black America, p. 665; Who's Who Among Black Americans, 1992–93, p. 1092.

1978 • Roland W. Burris (1937–) was the first black elected to statewide office as comptroller of the state. In 1987, Burris was the first person elected to three consecutive terms as comptroller. He held the office until 1991, when he became state attorney general, the second black to hold such a position, and the first black Democrat. In 1963, he had also been the first black hired by the United States Treasury Department as a bank examiner. In 1991, he became the first black attorney general of the state.

Sources: Jet 55 (25 January 1979), p. 6; Jet 71 (2 February 1987), p. 4; Jet 76 (21 August 1989), p. 5; Sepia 29 (May 1980), pp. 60–62; State of Black America, 1992, pp. 360–61; Who's Who Among Black Americans, 1992–93, p. 203.

1980 • Joyce Tucker was the first black woman to serve in the state cabinet, as director of the Department of Human Rights. A graduate of the University of Illinois, a Chicago lawyer, and a judge on the U.S. Court of Appeals, in Washington, D.C., Tucker was nominated in 1990 to the United States Equal Employment Opportunity Commission by President George Bush.

Sources: Jet 58 (10 July 1980), p. 30; Jet 78 (30 July 1990), p. 14.

INDIANA

1881 • James Sidney Hinton (1834–?) was the first black elected to Indiana's house of representatives.

Source: Encyclopedia of Black America, p. 439.

OPPOSITE PAGE: ROLAND W. BURRIS ANNOUNCES HIS RUN FOR THE SENATE.

1990 • Robert D. Rucker, Jr., was the first black appointed to the Indiana Court of Appeals. Rucker was born in East Chicago, Indiana, and took his law degree at the Valparaiso University School of Law.

Sources: Jet 78 (8 October 1990), p. 31; Who's Who Among Black Americans, 1992–93, p. 1229.

1991 • Pamela Carter was the first black woman in the United States to be elected state attorney general, and the first woman to be elected to the position in the state. Carter was the second black elected to a statewide office. Dwayne Brown, elected state clerk of the courts in 1990, was the first.
Source: Jet 83 (23 November 1992), p. 58.

IOWA

1918 • Gertrude E. Durden Rush (1880–?) was the first black woman admitted to the Iowa bar. She was born in Navasota, Texas, and in 1924 served as attorney for the Women's Auxiliary of the National Baptist Convention.
Sources: Jet 52 (4 August 1977), p. 18; *Jet* 60 (6 August 1981), p. 23.

1977 • Shirley Creenard Steele was the first black woman assistant attorney general of the state.
Source: Hornsby, *Chronology of African-American History,* pp. 280–81; *Jet* 52 (12 May 1977), p. 26.

1983 • Thomas J. Mann, Jr., (1949–) was the first black state senator. He took his law degree at the University of Iowa Law School in 1974, and served as an assistant state attorney general from 1974 to 1976, and from 1980 to 1982. From 1978 to 1979, he was executive director of the Iowa Civil Rights Commission.
Sources: Jet 63 (10 January 1983), p. 6; *Who's Who Among Black Americans, 1992–93,* p. 909.

KANSAS

1882 • Edward (sometimes Edwin) P. McCabe (1850–1920) was the first black elected to state office outside the deep South when he became state auditor. McCabe moved to Oklahoma in 1889, and was one of the founders of Langston City, Oklahoma.
Sources: Dictionary of American Negro Biography, pp. 410–13; *Encyclopedia of Black America,* p. 83; Katz, *The Black West,* pp. 254–61.

KENTUCKY

1936 • Charles W. Anderson (1907–60) was the first black elected to the Kentucky state legislature, in which he served six consecutive terms. He helped dismantle legal segregation in the state when his bill allowing black and white nurses to go to the same school was passed in 1948. The bill further allowed black physicians to take residencies at white hospitals.
Sources: Jet 51 (6 January 1977), p. 25; Clayton, *The Negro Politician,* pp. 118–19; *Encyclopedia of Black America,* p. 265.

1969 • Georgia M. Davis Powers (1923–) was the first black, and the first woman, elected to the Kentucky state senate. Prior to the election, she was a Louisville businesswoman and civil rights worker.

Sources: Ebony Success Library, vol. 1, p. 88; Notable Black American Women, pp. 867–69; Who's Who Among Black Americans, 1992–93, p. 1144.

1980 • William Eugene McAnulty was the first black in the state cabinet as secretary of the Department of Justice.

Source: Jet 57 (28 February 1980), p. 53.

1988 • Gary D. Payne (1948–) was the first black judge in Fayette County, the location of Lexington. A native of Paducah, Kentucky, Payne took his law degree from the University of Kentucky in 1978. Before becoming a judge, he was staff attorney for the Kentucky Corrections Cabinet in Frankfort.

Sources: Jet 76 (10 April 1989), p. 22; Who's Who Among Black Americans, 1992–93, p. 1099.

1991 • Janice R. Martin was the first elected black woman judge in the state. The thirty-six-year-old graduate of the University of Louisville Law School is a Jefferson District judge in Louisville, Kentucky.

Source: Jet 83 (1 February 1993), p. 18.

LOUISIANA

1868 • Oscar James Dunn (c. 1821–71) was the first black lieutenant governor. He was elected on April 22, 1868, and took office on June 13. Dunn may have been freeborn, and was a music teacher before the Civil War. During his term as lieutenant governor, he won a reputation for integrity. His sudden death after a violent two days' illness came at a moment when it seemed that he might become the Republican nominee for governor. The first black state treasurer, Antoine Dubuclet, was also named in the same election.

Sources: Bennett, Before the Mayflower, p. 481; Dictionary of American Negro Biography, pp. 204–5; Kane, Famous First Facts, p. 352; Hornsby, Chronology of African-American History, pp. 41–42.

1872 • Pinckney Benton Stewart Pinchback (1837–1921) was the first black state governor. He served from December 9, 1872, to January 13, 1873, while Governor Henry Clay Warmoth faced impeachment proceedings. Born of a white father and a freed slave mother in Mississippi, Pinchback had been sent to Ohio for an education. He became active in Louisiana politics; his election to the United States House of Representatives in 1872 was disputed, as was his election to the United States Senate in 1873. He became surveyor of customs in New Orleans about 1883. In the 1890s, he moved permanently to Washington, D.C.

Sources: Dictionary of American Negro Biography, pp. 493–94; Encyclopedia of Black America, p. 677; Hornsby, Chronology of African-American History, p. 45; Kane, Famous First Facts, p. 290.

PINCKNEY BENTON STEWART PINCHBACK

1951 • Kermit Parker was the first black to qualify as a Democratic party primary candidate for the nomination for governor.
Source: Jet 65 (17 October 1983), p. 22.

1967 • Ernest Nathan Morial (1929–89) was the first black elected to the state legislature since Reconstruction. (*See* **Government—Local Heroes: Louisiana, 1970—New Orleans** and **1977—New Orleans.**)
Sources: Encyclopedia of Black America, p. 568; *Who's Who Among Black Americans, 1992–93,* p. 1605.

1971 • Dorothy Mae Taylor was the first black woman elected to the Louisiana legislature. In 1986, she was elected the first councilwoman-at-large of New Orleans, and was also the first woman to serve as acting mayor of the city.
Source: Jet 70 (28 July 1986), p. 20.

SIDNEY BARTHELEMY

1974 • Sidney John Barthelemy (1942–) was the first black elected to the state senate in this century. In 1986, he became mayor of New Orleans. From 1974 until the year of his election as mayor, Barthelemy was associate professor of sociology at Xavier University.
Sources: Negro Almanac, 1989, p. 427; *Who's Who Among Black Americans, 1992–93,* p. 77.

1976 • James D. Wilson (1937–) was the first black appointed to the state Board of Pharmacy. Wilson was a 1963 graduate of the Xavier University College of Pharmacy. He has received an award for being the first black owner of a surgical supplies company.
Sources: Jet 51 (16 December 1977), p. 24; *Who's Who Among Black Americans, 1992–93,* p. 1547.

1984 • Joan B. Armstrong became the first black woman state judge when she was appointed to the state court of appeal. Armstrong took her law degree at Loyola University School of Law in 1967, and she served as New Orleans Parish Juvenile Court judge from 1974–84.
Sources: Jet 67 (24 September 1984), p. 32; *Who's Who Among Black Americans, 1992–93,* p. 42.

MAINE

1971 • Gerald Edgerton Talbot (1931–) was the first black member of the Maine legislature. He introduced into the congress legislation for a Martin Luther King, Jr., holiday. At the time of his election this Maine native was a newspaper compositor. Among his numerous other achievements, he served as chair of the Maine Board of Education in 1983–84.
Sources: Crisis 80 (February 1973), p. 69; *Ebony Success Library,* vol. 1, p. 298; *Who's Who Among Black Americans, 1992–93,* p. 1361.

MARYLAND

1958 • Irma Dixon and Verda Freeman Welcome (?–1990) were the first black women elected to the Maryland House of Delegates. The two represented bitterly opposed factions in the Democratic Party. In 1962, Welcome became the first black woman elected to the state senate.

Sources: Black Women in America, pp. 1241–42 (Welcome); Clayton, The Negro Politician, pp. 145–47; Ebony 19 (June 1964), p. 139 (Dixon); Ebony 20 (April 1965), p. 195 (Dixon); Ebony Success Library, vol. 1, p. 324 (Welcome); Sepia 13 (October 1964), pp. 8–12 (Welcome); Who's Who Among Black Americans, 1992–93, p. 1613 (Welcome).

1977 • Claudia H. Payne was the first black to head 4-H home economics activities in the state. She was a state 4-H program leader for the United States Department of Agriculture.

Source: Jet 53 (29 December 1977), p. 20.

1978 • Aris Allen (1910–91) was the first black to run for statewide office in Maryland. A Republican, Allen ran for the office of lieutenant governor. A physician with an M.D. from Howard University Medical College (1944), he entered the Maryland legislature in 1966. He served in 1977 as the first black chair of the state Republican party.

Sources: Encyclopedia of Black America, p. 99; State of Black America 1992, p. 367; Who's Who Among Black Americans, 1988, p. 1591.

1982 • Delawrence Beard was the first black superior court judge in Montgomery County. Beard holds law degrees from the University of Maryland and Georgetown Law School, and spent three years as head of the Public Defender's Office before his appointment.

Source: Jet 62 (10 May 1982), p. 40.

1984 • Julia Davidson-Randall was the first black woman state registrar of vital records in the United States.

Source: Jet 66 (21 May 1984), p. 14.

1991 • Vera Hall, a member of the Baltimore City Council, was the first black woman chair of the Democratic Party of Maryland.

Sources: Jet 82 (17 August 1992), p. 7; State of Black America, 1993, p. 291.

MASSACHUSETTS

1630 • Massachusetts passed the first law protecting slaves who fled brutal treatment by their masters.

Source: Negro Almanac, 1989, p. 2.

1641 • Massachusetts was the first colony to legalize slavery. The second was Connecticut, in 1650; the third, Virginia, in 1661.

Sources: Bennett, Before the Mayflower, p. 441; Negro Almanac, 1989, p. 2.

1774 • On March 8, 1774, the General Assembly passed the first act forbidding the importation of black slaves. It was suspended by the governor the following day. Rhode Island passed similar legislation on June 13. Slaves brought into the colony were to gain their freedom immediately.

Sources: Kane, Famous First Facts, p. 598; Negro Almanac, 1989, p. 811.

1783 • Paul Cuffe and his brother John were the leaders in a law suit that gave blacks civil equality in the state by permitting them to vote. In 1780, they were the first blacks to protest the denial of suffrage by refusing to pay taxes. This protest developed into a petition drive and a court case. The courts decided in 1783 in their favor.

Source: Dictionary of American Negro Biography, p. 147.

1845 • Macon B. Allen (1816–94) of Worcester was the first black formally admitted to the bar in any state on May 3, 1845. He had been allowed to practice in Maine two years earlier. Born in Indiana, Allen had been a businessman in Portland, Maine. He moved to Massachusetts to practice law. By 1870, he had moved to South Carolina, where he entered politics, and in 1873, became one of the first black judges, as a judge of the Inferior Court. (Miflin W. Gibbs was the first black judge that year in the municipal court of Little Rock.) Little is known of his life after the 1870s; in 1894, he died in Washington, D.C.

Sources: Dictionary of American Negro Biography, pp. 11–12; Garrett, Famous First Facts about Negroes, p. 93; Negro Almanac, 1989, p. 13.

1866 • Charles Lewis Mitchell (1829–1912) and Edward Garrison Walker (1831?–1910) were the first blacks elected to a state legislature. Walker would jokingly claim to be the first on the grounds that the polls in his ward closed a few hours earlier than those in Mitchell's. Mitchell, who had lost his foot during war service, served as the first black inspector of customs in Boston. He retired in 1909. Walker became a prominent Boston lawyer and a Democrat, a surprising switch at this time. (Walker was the son of David Walker, who issued the inflammatory tract David Walker's Appeal.) (*See* **Writers: Pamphlets, 1829.**)

Sources: Bennett, Before the Mayflower, p. 477; Dictionary of American Negro Biography, pp. 443–44 (Mitchell), 623 (Walker); Negro Almanac, 1989, pp. 16, 1425.

1960 • Edward William Brooke (1919–) was the first black to be nominated to run for statewide office in Massachusetts. He lost this election, but in 1962, he was the first black to be elected Massachusetts attorney general. (*See also* **Government—Federal Firsts: U.S. Senate, 1966.**)

Sources: Current Biography Yearbook, 1967, pp. 40–43; Ebony Success Library, vol. 2, pp. 16–21; Who's Who Among Black Americans, 1992–93, p. 158.

1988 • Henry Tomes, Jr., (1932–) was the first black commissioner of the Department of Mental Health. A native of San Antonio, Texas, Tomes took

EDWARD WILLIAM
BROOKE

his B.A. at Fisk University, and his Ph.D. at the Pennsylvania State College (1963). He had a distinguished career in teaching, and as an administrator in field of mental health.

Sources: Jet 76 (7 August 1989), p. 20; Who's Who Among Black Americans, 1992–93, p. 1406.

MICHIGAN

1950 • Charline White (1920–59) was the first black woman elected to the Michigan legislature.

Sources: Clayton, The Negro Politician, pp. 138–39; Ebony 11 (August 1956), p. 82; Ebony 21 (August 1966), p. 97.

1951 • Charles C. Diggs, Jr., (1922–) was the first black state senator in Michigan. He was elected in a special election held to replace his father, Charles C. Diggs, Sr., who was the first black elected, but who was denied his seat because he had been convicted of accepting a $150 bribe. (*See also* **Government—Federal Firsts: U.S. House of Representatives, 1954.**)

Source: Clayton, The Negro Politician, p. 87.

1952 • Cora M. Brown (1914–72) was the first black woman in the United States to be elected to a state senate. Since the only previous woman senator in Michigan had been appointed, she was the first woman of any race elected to the Michigan senate. After supporting Eisenhower in the 1956 election, she was appointed special associate general counsel of the United

CORA M. BROWN

States Post Office Department on August 15, 1957, becoming the first black woman member of the department's legal staff.

Sources: Alford, *Famous First Blacks,* p. 45; Clayton, *The Negro Politician,* pp. 139–43; *Ebony* 22 (September 1967), pp. 27–28.

1960 • On November 8, 1960, Otis M. Smith (1922–) became the first black to win a statewide election since Reconstruction when he was elected auditor general of Michigan. He also was a Michigan State Supreme Court justice from 1961 to 1966. He was the first black to serve in this capacity in any state since Reconstruction. Becoming a lawyer for General Motors in 1967, Smith was named head of the firm's legal staff in 1977. He held this post until his retirement in 1983.

Sources: Ebony 16 (March 1961), pp. 75–80; *Ebony* 33 (December 1977), pp. 33–42; *Ebony* 37 (March 1982), p. 130; *Ebony Success Library,* vol. 1, p. 286; *Encyclopedia of Black America,* p. 798; *Who's Who Among Black Americans, 1992–93,* p. 1309.

1970 • Richard H. Austin (1913–) became the first black secretary of state in modern times when he assumed that position in Michigan. He was also the first licensed certified public accountant in the state in 1941. He worked in the private arena before his election.

Sources: Alford, *Famous First Blacks,* p. 48; *Ebony* 26 (January 1971), p. 94; *Ebony Success Library,* vol. 1., p. 15; *Who's Who Among Black Americans, 1992–93,* p. 51.

1979 • Loren Eugene Monroe was the first black state treasurer.

Source: Negro Almanac, 1989, p. 1432.

MINNESOTA

1991 • Alan Cedric Page (1945–) was the first black elected to the state supreme court. Page had played professional football as a member of the Minnesota Vikings. He was inducted into the National Football League Hall of Fame in 1988. He graduated from Notre Dame University in 1967, and took his law degree at the University of Minnesota Law School in 1978. (*See also* **Sports: Football, 1971.**)

Sources: Jet 83 (23 November 1992), pp. 58–59; *Jet* (1 February 1993), p. 22; *Who's Who Among Black Americans, 1992–93,* p. 1082.

MISSISSIPPI

1868 • Charles Caldwell (?–1875) was the first black in the state to be accused of the murder of a white man and found "not guilty" by an all-white jury. While he was attending the state constitutional convention, Caldwell killed the son of a white judge in self-defense. In 1870, Caldwell was elected to the state senate, and on December 25, 1875, he was assassinated in Clinton, Mississippi.

Sources: Bennett, *Before the Mayflower,* pp. 245, 497; *Encyclopedia of Black America,* p. 221.

1968 • Robert G. Clark (1931–) was the first black elected to the state legislature since Reconstruction. A native of Ebenezer, Mississippi, Clark was a graduate of Jackson State College (1953). In addition to his legislative duties, he runs a furniture store.

Sources: Ebony 23 (February 1968), p. 26; *Ebony Success Library,* vol. 1, p. 68; *Jet* 62 (9 August 1982), p. 12; *Who's Who Among Black Americans, 1992–93,* p. 267.

1971 • (James) Charles Evers (1922–), who had become the first black mayor of Fayette, Mississippi, on May 13, 1969, was the first black candidate for governor in modern times. A 1951 graduate of Alcorn State University, this civil rights activist is the brother of the slain Medgar Evers.

Sources: Alford, *Famous First Blacks,* p. 39; *Current Biography, 1969,* pp. 134–36; Fax, *Contemporary Black Leaders,* pp. 131–48; *Negro Almanac, 1989,* p. 51; *Who's Who Among Black Americans, 1992–93,* p. 443.

1981 • Reuben Vincent Anderson (1942–) was the first black circuit court judge in the state. On January 11, 1985, Anderson became the first black supreme court judge. Born in Mississippi, he took his law degree at the University of Mississippi Law School in 1967, becoming a municipal judge in 1975, and a county judge in 1977.

Sources: Hornsby, *Chronology of African-American History,* p. 336; *Jet* 61 (19 November 1981), p. 22; *Jet* 67 (28 January 1985), p. 23; *Who's Who Among Black Americans, 1992–93,* p. 35.

1985 • Alyce Griffin Clarke (1939–) was the first black woman member of the state house of representatives. She was appointed to fill the term of Fred Banks, who had been appointed a circuit judge. Born in Yazoo, Clarke was educated in Mississippi schools, taking four M.S. degrees, each at a different school. She worked as a public school teacher and as a nutritionist.

Sources: Jet 68 (22 April 1985), p. 5; *Who's Who Among Black Americans, 1992–93,* p. 269.

1987 • Beverly Wade Hogan (1951–) was the first black and the first woman commissioner of the state's Workers' Compensation Commission. A native of Louisiana, Hogan took a B.A. at Dillard University, and an M.A. at Fisk University. At the time of her appointment she was executive director of federal-state programs in the governor's office.

Sources: Jet 72 (24 August 1987), p. 20; *Who's Who Among Black Americans, 1992–93,* p. 667.

Rosie S. Simmons was the first black elected in a countywide election since Reconstruction, when she was elected to the position of Bolivar County circuit clerk. A 1967 graduate of Tuskegee, Simmons had been deputy circuit clerk for seven years at the time of her election.

Source: Jet 72 (14 September 1987), p. 6.

MISSOURI

1920 • Walthall M. Moore was the first black elected to the Missouri legislature in modern times.

Source: Garrett, *Famous First Facts About Negroes*, p. 186.

1962 • Deverne Lee Calloway (1916–) was the first black woman to be elected to state office in Missouri, when she became a member of the state house of representatives. Calloway held the legislative position for nine consecutive terms.

Sources: Ebony 20 (April 1965), p. 196; *Ebony Success Library,* vol. 1., p. 57; *Encyclopedia of Black America,* p. 231; *Who's Who Among Black Americans, 1992–93,* p. 221.

1977 • Gwen B. Giles (1933?–86) was the first black woman elected to the state senate. She served as city assessor in St. Louis from 1981 until her death.

Source: Jet 70 (14 April 1986), p. 18.

1983 • Evelyn Marie Baker was the first black woman circuit court judge in the state. She was the third woman, and the second black, to be a judge in St. Louis.

Source: Jet 64 (2 May 1983), p. 30.

Cheryl Holland was the first black in the state to hold the position of clerk of the Superior Court, in Gates Country.

Source: Jet 63 (24 January 1983), p. 21.

1991 • Alexis Otis-Lewis was the first black woman judge in St. Clair County. A forty-year-old graduate of Washington University School of Law (St. Louis), she served as assistant state's attorney in the county before entering private practice.

Source: Jet 82 (10 August 1992), p. 27.

MONTANA

1974 • Geraldine Travis was the first black elected to the Montana legislature. She was the wife of an Air Force Sergeant.

Source: Negro Almanac, 1989, p. 331.

NEBRASKA

1892 • Matthew O. Ricketts, an ex-slave, was the first black elected to the state legislature from Omaha. A physician who graduated from the

University of Nebraska College of Medicine in 1884, the Omaha resident served two terms.

Sources: Katz, *The Black West,* p. 177; *Jet* 58 (3 April 1980), p. 20.

NEW HAMPSHIRE

1974 • Henry B. Richardson (?–1981) was the first black state representative. Richardson was a retired U.S. Army major.

Source: Jet 60 (2 April 1981), p. 14.

NEW JERSEY

1920 • Walter Gilbert Alexander (1880–1953) was the first black elected to the New Jersey legislature. Alexander was a physician who first practiced medicine for a year in his native West Virginia, and then established himself in Orange, New Jersey in 1904.

Sources: Garrett, *Famous First Facts About Negroes,* p. 186; *Encyclopedia of Black America,* p. 98.

1957 • Madaline A. Williams (1895–1968) was the first black woman to serve in the state assembly. Williams became a member of the state Migrant Labor Board in 1952. She served two terms in the legislature and then became Essex County Registrar, a position she held at the time of her death.

Sources: Crisis 65 (June/July 1958), pp. 364–67; *Ebony* 21 (August 1966), p. 97; *Jet* 61 (17 December 1981), p. 28.

1960 • Roger M. Yancey (1904–72) was the first black county court judge in the state.

Source: Encyclopedia of Black America, p. 871.

1970 • James Rankin Cowan (1916–) was the first black in the United States appointed to a governor's cabinet as commissioner of health. A very distinguished physician, Cowan earned his M.D. degree from Meharry Medical College in 1944. He held the cabinet position from 1970 to 1974.

Source: Ebony 27 (April 1972), p. 96; *Ebony Success Library,* vol. 2, p. 81; *Who's Who Among Black Americans, 1992–93,* p. 313.

1971 • Leonard (Bud) Simmons (1920–) was the first black to serve on the New Jersey Civil Service Commission. A native of Goldsboro, North Carolina, Simmons had been active in politics in the Roselle borough, serving as city councilman and member of the board of education, as well as being commissioner of police. Earlier he had been the first black policeman in Roselle, and later he would become the first (and only) black to serve on the original New Jersey Lottery Commission.

Sources: Ebony Success Library, vol. 1, p. 282; *Who's Who Among Black Americans, 1992–93,* p. 1280.

1986 • Herbert Holmes Tate, Jr., (1953–) was the first black prosecutor for Essex County, which is the location of the city of Newark. Tate took his law degree at Rutgers University School of Law in 1978, and had extensive experience in both government and private practice.

Sources: Jet 70 (1 Sept. 1986), p. 12; Who's Who Among Black Americans, 1992–93, p. 1364.

NEW YORK

1855 • Frederick Douglass (1817–95) was the first black candidate for state office. The Liberty Party nominated him for secretary of state. (*See also* **Civil Rights and Protest: Slavery, 1842; Writers: Short Stories, 1853.**)

Source: Negro Almanac, 1989, p. 14.

1917 • Edward A. Johnson (1860–1944) was the first black elected to the New York assembly. Before becoming interested in politics, Johnson was an educator who, in 1890, published *A School History of the Negro Race in America from 1619 to 1890.* In 1891, Johnson became a lawyer. A native of Raleigh, North Carolina, a city where he was elected alderman in 1897, Johnson moved to New York City in 1907.

Sources: Clayton, The Negro Politician, p. 62; Dictionary of American Negro Biography, pp. 349–50; Hamilton, Adam Clayton Powell, Jr., p. 112.

1922 • Henry W. Shields was elected to the state legislature as a Democrat. He was the first black Democrat elected to any political office.

Source: Work, The Negro Yearbook, 1925–26, p. 63.

1945 • On March 12, 1945, New York was the first state to establish a Fair Employment Practices Commission.

Source: Hornsby, Chronology of African-American History, p. 92.

1952 • Julius A. Archibald was the first black elected to the state senate. Born in Trinidad, Archibald was a school teacher.

Source: Jet 57 (8 November 1979), p. 18.

1954 • Bessie Allison Buchanan (1902?–80) was the first black woman elected to the state legislature. Before her marriage in 1929 to Charles P. Buchanan, the owner of the Savoy Ballroom, she had been a singer and dancer at the Cotton Club. Buchanan served with distinction for eight years.

Sources: Clayton, The Black Politician, pp. 143–45; Ebony 11 (August 1956), cover and p. 80; Jet 59 (25 September 1980), p. 58.

OPPOSITE PAGE: BESSIE ALLISON BUCHANAN ON THE FLOOR OF THE NEW YORK STATE LEGISLATURE.

1955 • Robert Clifton Weaver (1907–) became New York State rent commissioner, the first black to hold cabinet rank in the state. The following

year, Weaver became the first black to hold federal government cabinet rank as secretary of housing and urban development. (*See also* **Government—Federal Firsts: Federal Appointees, 1961.**)

Sources: Dictionary of Black Culture, p. 464; Encyclopedia of Black America, p. 849; Who's Who Among Black Americans, 1992–93, p. 1478.

1964 • Constance Baker Motley (1921–) was the first black woman to win a seat in the state senate. (She had been appointed to fill an unexpired term the previous year.) Before becoming the first black woman federal judge, Motley was also the first woman New York City borough head in 1965. (*See also* **Government—Federal Firsts: Judiciary, 1966.**)

Sources: Encyclopedia of Black America, p. 582; Negro Almanac, 1989, pp. 344–55; Notable Black American Women, pp. 779–82; Who's Who Among Black Americans, 1992–93, p. 1035.

ERSA HINES POSTON

1967 • Ersa Hines Poston (1921–) was the first black president of the New York State Civil Service Commission. A native of Kentucky, Poston took an M.A. in social work from Atlanta University in 1946, and went to work for the Tuberculosis and Health Association in Connecticut. When she moved to New York City, her rise in government service was rapid. In 1977, she became vice-chair of the United States Merit Systems Protection Board.

Sources: Ebony Success Library, vol. 2, pp. 198–201; Encyclopedia of Black America, p. 697; Negro Almanac, 1989, pp. 1389, 1413; Notable Black American Women, pp. 864–65; Who's Who Among Black Americans, 1992–93, p. 1139.

1971 • Carmel Carrington Marr (1921–) became the first woman (of any race) to serve on the New York State Public Service Commission when she was named its commissioner in 1971. From 1953 to 1971, Marr, a graduate of the Columbia University Law School (1948), served as a lawyer on the staff of the United Nations, and in New York state government. She served on the Public Service Commission until her retirement in 1986.

Sources: Christmas, Negroes in Public Affairs and Government, p. 33; Crisis 78 (March 1971), pp. 48–52; Encyclopedia of Black America, p. 546; Who's Who Among Black Americans, 1992–93, p. 914.

1981 • Lillian Roberts (1928–) was the first black woman to head the New York State Department of Labor.

Sources: Black Enterprise 13 (August 1983), p. 92; Negro Almanac, 1989, p. 1390; Who's Who Among Black Americans, 1992–93, p. 1201.

1984 • John W. Heritage III was the first black captain in the New York State Police. He had entered the State Police Academy in 1967. In 1986, he became the first black major in the force.

Sources: Jet 67 (22 October 1984), p. 4; *Jet* 70 (1 September 1986), p. 22.

1985 • Fritz W. Alexander II (1926–) was the first black to serve full-time on the state court of appeals. Alexander had become a municipal district judge in 1970, and an associate justice of the appellate division in 1977. A native of Florida, he was educated at Dartmouth and the New York University School of Law (J.D. 1952).

Sources: Jet 67 (28 January 1985), p. 23; *Who's Who Among Black Americans, 1992–93,* p. 15.

NORTH CAROLINA

1969 • Henry E. Frye was the first black member of the state legislature in modern times. He earned his J.D. in 1959 from the University of Carolina Law School. In 1983, Frye became the first black on the state supreme court.

Source: Ebony Success Library, vol. 1, p. 119; Hornsby, *Chronology of African-American History,* p. 134; *Jet* 71 (27 October 1986), p. 20; *Who's Who Among Black Americans, 1992–93,* p. 493.

1971 • As superior court judge, Sammie Chess, Jr., (1934–) was the first black judge in North Carolina. He served from 1971 to 1975. A native of Allendale, South Carolina, Chess took a law degree at North Carolina Central University. His appointment also made him the first black superior court judge in the South in modern times.

Sources: Ebony Success Library, vol. 1, p. 65; *Encyclopedia of Black America,* p. 225; *Who's Who Among Black Americans, 1992–93,* p. 259.

In November, 1971, Elizabeth Bias Cofield (1920–) was the first black, and the first woman, elected to the Wake County, North Carolina, Board of Commissioners. She was director of student life at Shaw University at the time of her election, and had previously been elected to a four-year term on the Raleigh school board in 1969.

Sources: Ebony Success Library, vol. 1, p. 74; *Who's Who Among Black Americans, 1992–93,* p. 281.

On October 6, 1971, John A. Wilkinson was the first black man in North Carolina to legally marry a white woman, Lorraine Mary Turner.

Source: Hornsby, *Chronology of African-American History,* p. 190.

1988 • Everett Blair Ward (1958–) was the first black executive director of the state Democratic party. A native of North Carolina, and a graduate of Saint Augustine's College (1982), Ward had served since 1983 as political director of the party by the time of his selection.

Sources: Jet 77 (20 November 1989), p. 20; *Who's Who Among Black Americans, 1992–93,* p. 1455.

1991 • Ralph Campbell, Jr., was the first black elected to a statewide position, when he won the race for state auditor. Campbell had served on the Raleigh City Council for six years.

Source: Jet 83 (23 November 1992), p. 58.

NORTHWEST TERRITORY

1787 • On July 13, 1787, the Continental Congress prohibited slavery in the Northwest Territory, the area north of the Ohio River and east of the Mississippi River. This was the first law forbidding slavery in territories.

Sources: Bennett, *Before the Mayflower,* p. 448; Kane, *Famous First Facts,* p. 598; *Negro Almanac, 1989,* p. 6.

OHIO

1855 • John M. Langston (1829–97), who had been admitted to the Ohio bar in the previous year, became the first black elected to office in the United States. He was elected clerk of Brownhelm Township in Lorain County. Among his other achievements were election to Congress from Virginia in 1888. (*See also* **Education: Law School, 1868.**)

Sources: Bennett, *Before the Mayflower,* p. 462; Cantor, *Historic Landmarks of Black America,* p. 40; *Dictionary of American Negro Biography,* pp. 382–84; Hornsby, *Chronology of African-American History,* pp. 27–28.

**JOHN M.
LANGSTON**

1885 • Benjamin William Arnett was the first black to represent a majority white constituency in a state house of representatives. A bishop of the AME church, he represented Green County in 1885–87. In 1864, Arnett was the first and, for a period, the only black teacher in Fayette County, Pennsylvania. As a legislator, Arnett helped abolish discriminatory laws in Ohio. In addition to his purely religious work, he remained influential in many fraternal organizations and in politics, especially through his friendship with William McKinley, Jr., who became president in 1897.

Sources: Dictionary of American Negro Biography, pp. 17–18; Kane, *Famous First Facts,* p. 347; *Negro Almanac, 1989,* p. 1425.

1960 • Merle M. McCurdy (1912–68) was the first black public defender in Cuyahoga County, the county where Cleveland is located.

Sources: Christian, *Negroes in Public Affairs and Government,* p. 150; *Jet* 36 (17 July 1969), p. 11; *Encyclopedia of Black America,* p. 550.

BENJAMIN WILLIAM
ARNETT

1963 • As director of industrial relations, William O. Walker (1896–1981) was the first black cabinet member in the state. A 1916 graduate of Wilberforce, Walker became a journalist. In 1932, he founded the *Call and Post* newspaper in Cleveland, Ohio. He was elected to the Cleveland City Council in 1939.

Sources: Ebony 5 (September 1950), p. 49; *Ebony Success Library,* vol. 1, p. 317; Hill, *Who's Who in the Negro Press,* pp. 31–33; Lee, *Interesting People,* p. 51.

OKLAHOMA

1964 • E. Melvin Porter (1930–) was the first black elected to the Oklahoma senate. Porter had a law degree from the Vanderbilt School of Law (1959), and was co-owner and publisher of *Black Voices* magazine.

Sources: Ebony Success Library, vol. 1, p. 252; *Who's Who Among Black Americans, 1992–93,* p. 1137.

1968 • Hannah Diggs Atkins (1923–) was the first black woman elected to the state house of representatives. With a B.L.S. from the University of Chicago Graduate Library School in 1949, Atkins worked primarily as a librarian until her election to the legislature. Since then, she has served as assistant director of the state Department of Human Services (1983–87), and as secretary of state/cabinet secretary of human resources (1987–91). The appointment was the first time a black had occupied a cabinet position in Oklahoma.

Sources: Ebony Success Library, vol. 1, p. 14; *Homecoming,* 9 (No. 1: Spring 1992), p. 6; *Jet* 73 (14 March 1988), p. 10; (21 March 1988), p. 48; *Jet* 76 (19 June 1989), p. 10; *Who's Who Among Black Americans, 1992–93,* p. 48.

1986 • Vickie Miles LaGrange was the first black woman elected to the state senate. She was the third black elected; the first was E. Melvin Porter, whom she defeated in a run-off election. LaGrange is a native of Oklahoma City, and an attorney.

Source: Jet 71 (10 November 1986), p. 5.

PENNSYLVANIA

1938 • Crystal Bird Fauset (1893–1965) was the first black woman elected to a state legislature in the United States. Born in Maryland, Fauset worked for the Young Women's Christian Society, the American Friends Service Committee, and the Works Progress Administration (WPA) before going into politics. She resigned from the legislature after a year to return to the WPA. She continued a career of government service and active involvement in politics.

Sources: Black Women in America, pp. 410–11; *Negro Almanac, 1989,* pp. 25, 1426; *Notable Black American Women,* pp. 333–36.

CRYSTAL BIRD FAUSET

JUANITA KIDD STOUT IS
SWORN IN AS A JUSTICE
TO THE PENNSYLVANIA
SUPREME COURT.

JUANITA KIDD STOUT IS SWORN IN AS A JUSTICE TO THE PENNSYLVANIA SUPREME COURT.

1955 • Andrew M. Bradley (1906–) was the first black to hold cabinet rank in the state. An accountant, Bradley became secretary of property and supplies.
Sources: Ebony 13 (May 1958), pp. 79–84; Encyclopedia of Black America, p. 189.

1959 • Juanita Kidd Stout (1919–) was the first woman judge in the state. Stout was appointed to the Philadelphia Municipal Court in September, and won election to a ten-year term in November of 1959. Born in Oklahoma, she taught grade school in the state until the outbreak of World War II, when she went to Washington. In 1954, she passed the Pennsylvania bar examination. After ten years on the municipal court, she spent twenty years on the court of common pleas. In January 1988, Stout became the first black woman to serve on any state supreme court.
Sources: Encyclopedia of Black America, p. 811; Negro Almanac, 1989, p. 1392; Notable Black American Women, pp. 1087–89.

1967 • Herbert Arlene (1917–) was the first black state senator. Arlene had long been active in Philadelphia Democratic politics and had served in the state house from 1958 to 1966.
Sources: Ebony Success Library, vol. 1, p. 13; Who's Who Among Black Americans, 1992–93, p. 41.

1969 • K. Leroy Irvis (1919–) was the first black majority leader in the Pennsylvania house of representatives. In 1977 he was elected the first black speaker of the house, a first for the state and for the nation. He held the position until his retirement in 1988. A native of New York state, he took his law degree at the University of Pittsburgh Law School, and was first elected to the Pennsylvania house in 1958.

Sources: Ebony, April 1972, p. 95; Hornsby, *Chronology of African-American History,* p. 197; *Negro Almanac* (1976), pp. 360–61; *Who's Who Among Black Americans, 1992–93,* p. 712.

1971 • [Cynthia] Dolores Nottage Tucker (1927–) became the first black woman cabinet member in Pennsylvania when she was appointed secretary of state in 1971. She held the position until 1977. Tucker was very active in politics on the state and national level, and in 1989 she became a newspaper executive on the *Philadelphia Tribune.*

Sources: Ebony Success Library, vol. 2, pp. 260–63; *Encyclopedia of Black America,* p. 820; *Notable Black American Women,* pp. 1155–57; *Who's Who Among Black Americans, 1992–93,* p. 1415.

1977 • Ethel S. Barnett (1929–) was the first black woman member of the state Civil Service Commission. Born in Macon, Georgia, Barnett was, from 1961 to 1971, a police officer in the City of Philadelphia Police Department.

Sources: Jet 51 (3 March 1977), p, 26; *Who's Who Among Black Americans, 1992–93,* p. 75.

1984 • On January 6, 1984, Robert N. C. Nix, Jr., (1928–) became the first black state supreme court justice. Nix had become a judge in the common pleas court of Philadelphia County in 1968. In 1984, he became the chief justice of the state supreme court. Nix is a 1955 graduate of the University of Pennsylvania School of Law.

Sources: Hornsby, *Chronology of African-American History,* p. 327; *Jet* 65 (30 January 1984), p. 4; *Jet* 78 (23 July 1990), p. 33; *Who's Who Among Black Americans, 1992–93,* p. 1061.

1986 • Therese L. Mitchell was the first black chair of the state Civil Service Commission. Mitchell had served as deputy press secretary to Governor Dick Thornburgh.

Source: Jet 71 (29 September 1986), p. 64.

ROBERT C. NIX, JR.

1987 • Ronald M. Sharpe (1940–) was the first black commissioner of the state police. Sharpe started his career with this law enforcement agency in 1962. He had served as acting commissioner for several months.

Sources: Jet 73 (2 November 1987), p. 47; *Who's Who Among Black Americans, 1992–93,* p. 1264.

1990 • Cynthia A. Baldwin (1945–) was the first black woman elected to the Allegheny County bench. The county is the location of Pittsburgh. Baldwin was also the first black woman installed as president of the Penn State Alumni Association. A native of Mckeesport, Pennsylvania, she took her law degree at the Duquesne University School of Law in 1980.

Sources: Jet 78 (30 April 1990), p. 5; *Who's Who Among Black Americans, 1992–93,* p. 62.

RHODE ISLAND

1652 • The first law regulating black servitude was passed by the General Court of Election, on May 18, 1652. This law placed blacks on the same footing as white bondservants; they were to be free after completing their term of service of ten years.

Source: Kane, *Famous First Facts,* p. 598.

SOUTH CAROLINA

1868 • The South Carolina General Assembly was the first state legislative body with a black majority, when it met on July 6, 1868. There were eighty-seven blacks and forty whites in the lower house. The whites, however, had a majority in the state senate, and in 1874 there was again a white majority in the house.

Sources: Bennett, *Before the Mayflower,* p. 629; Hornsby, *Chronology of African-American History,* p. 42.

FRANCIS L. CARDOZA

Francis L. Cardoza (1837–1903) was the first black South Carolina secretary of state. He served for four years in the position, and became the secretary of the treasury; he was elected to two terms in 1872 and 1874, and claimed the election in 1876, but did not try to maintain his position after the downfall of the Republican regime in 1877. During the last fourteen months of his tenure as secretary of state, Cardoza employed a deputy in South Carolina, while he served as professor of Latin at Howard University. A free-born native of Charleston, he pursued an education in Scotland. From 1884 to 1896 he was principal of the Colored Preparatory High School, Washington, D.C., and its successor, the M Street High School.

Sources: Bennett, *Before the Mayflower,* p. 629; Clayton, *The Negro Politician,* pp. 26–27; *Dictionary of American Negro Biography,* pp. 89–90.

1870 • Jonathan Jasper Wright (1840–85) was the first black state supreme court justice in the United States. Born in Pennsylvania, Wright had studied law in that state, where he was the first black admitted to the bar in 1866. He was elected on February 1, 1870, to fill an unexpired term, and re-elected to a full term in November. After the overthrow of the Reconstruction government, Wright resigned December 1, 1877, and died in obscurity of tuberculosis.

Sources: Bennett, *Before the Mayflower,* pp. 233, 487, 639; *Dictionary of American Negro Biography,* pp. 669–70; Hornsby, *Chronology of African-American History,* p. 43; *Negro Almanac, 1989,* p. 1425.

1966 • Herbert Ulysses Fielding (1923–) was the first black elected to the state house since Reconstruction. A native of Charleston, he took a B.S. in business administration at West Virginia State College in 1948. In 1985, he was elected to the state senate.

Sources: Ebony Success Library, vol. 1, p. 111; Who's Who Among Black Americans, 1992–93, p. 454.

1976 • Ernest A. Finney, Jr., (1931–) was the first black circuit court judge in the state. In 1979, he was the first black chairman of the South Carolina Commission on Aging, and in 1985 he became the first black justice on the state supreme court. A 1954 graduate of the New York University School of Law, Finney is a native of Smithfield, Virginia.

Sources: Jet 68 (22 April 1985), p. 5; Negro Almanac, 1989, p. 1431; Who's Who Among Black Americans, 1992–93, p. 457.

1978 • Aletha Morgan was the first black woman trooper in the state highway patrol. A graduate of Howard University, Morgan lived in Orangeburg.

Source: Jet 71 (22 December 1986), p. 8.

1986 • Lucille Simmons Whipper (1928–) was the first black woman member of the state legislature from Charleston County. She took her undergraduate degree at Talledega in 1948. She worked in the Charleston County Schools, in the county Office of Economic Opportunity, and at the College of Charleston, from which she retired.

Sources: Jet 70 (8 September 1986), p. 36; Who's Who Among Black Americans, 1992–93, p. 1490.

TENNESSEE

1873 • When the Tennessee legislature convened on January 6, 1873, Sampson W. Keeble (c. 1833–?) became the first black member of the state house of representatives. Born a slave, prior to the Civil War he had worked as roller boy and pressman for newspapers in Murfreesboro, Tennessee, and at the time of his election was a barber in Nashville.

Sources: Scott, The Negro in Tennessee Politics, pp. 28–29; Taylor, The Negro in Tennessee, 1865–80, pp. 247–48; (Nashville) Tennessean 9 February 1992.

1881 • The state of Tennessee passed the first Jim Crow law to require that railroads be segregated. This initiated a period of statutory, rather than customary, segregation in the South. The state laws were buttressed by the United States Supreme Court decision in *Plessy v. Ferguson* (1896). The dismantling of legal segregation took a major effort during the second half of the twentieth century.

Sources: Bennett, Before the Mayflower, p. 500; Negro Almanac, 1989, pp. 19, 150–52.

1964 • On November 3, 1964, A. W. Willis, Jr., (1925–88) was the first black elected to the General Assembly in this century, taking his seat on the first

Monday in January 1965. A native of Memphis, Tennessee, and a lawyer, Willis had served as chief counsel for James Meredith when Meredith sought to enter the University of Mississippi in 1962.

Source: Scott, *The Negro in Tennessee Politics,* pp. 195–98.

1965 • Benjamin Lawson Hooks (1925–) was the first black criminal court judge in the state. (*See also* **Government—Federal Firsts: Federal Appointees, 1972.**)

Sources: Ebony Success Library, vol. 1, p. 158; *Encyclopedia of Black America,* p. 443–44; *Negro Almanac, 1989,* pp. 276–77; *Who's Who Among Black Americans, 1992–93,* p. 679.

1967 • Dorothy Lavinia Brown (1919–) was the first black woman to serve in the state legislature. (*See also* **Science & Medicine: Medicine, 1948.**)

Sources: Encyclopedia of Black America, p. 194; (Nashville) *Tennessean* 9 February 1992; *Notable Black American Women,* pp. 114–16; *Who's Who Among Black Americans, 1992–93,* p. 169.

1969 • Avon Nyanza Williams, Jr., (1921–) of Nashville, and J. O. Patterson, Jr., (1935–) of Memphis, were the first blacks elected to the state senate. With law degrees from the University of Boston (1947, 1948), Williams has been a leading Nashville lawyer, and he was much in the public eye for his major role in the Nashville school desegregation case. Patterson is a lawyer and a bishop of the Church of God in Christ. Running as a Democrat in August 1972, Patterson was the first black to win a major party nomination for a congressional seat.

Sources: Biographical Dictionary of African-American Holiness Pentecostals 1880–1990, pp. 210–11 (Patterson); Hornsby, *Chronology of African-American History,* pp. 134, 199; (Nashville) *Tennessean* 9 February 1992; *Who's Who Among Black Americans, 1992–93,* p. 1512 (Williams).

1980 • Memphis attorney George Brown was the first black on the Tennessee Supreme Court. Appointed in June, 1980, he lost to the Democratic nominee in the August election.

Source: (Nashville) *Tennessean* 22 August 1993.

1982 • Bernice Bouie Donald (1951–) was the first elected black woman judge in the state of Tennessee as general sessions court judge in Shelby County. In 1988, Donald became the first black woman to serve on a United States Bankruptcy Court. She took her law degree from the Memphis State University School of Law in 1979.

Source: Who's Who Among Black Americans, 1992–93, p. 388.

1987 • A. A. Birch, Jr., was the first black member of the state court of appeals. Birch was a criminal court judge in Nashville at the time of his appointment.

Source: Jet 72 (1 June 1987), p. 20.

Lois Marie Deberry (1945–) was the first black woman speaker *pro tem* of the house. Deberry was first elected to the house in 1972.

Sources: Jet 71 (16 February 1987), p. 8; *Jet* 79 (14 January 1991), p. 12; *Who's Who Among Black Americans, 1992–93,* p. 368.

1991 • Thelma Marie Harper (1940–) was the first black woman elected to the state senate. A graduate of Tennessee State University, Harper was a noted entrepreneur and leading member of the Nashville City Council at the time of her election.

Sources: (Nashville) *Tennessean* 9 February 1992; *Who's Who Among Black Americans, 1992–93,* p. 602.

TEXAS

1967 • Barbara Charline Jordan (1936–) was the first black to sit in the Texas senate since 1883. In 1972, she became president *pro tem* of the senate, the first black woman to preside over a legislative body in the United States, and the first acting black governor of the state. Later that year, she was elected to the United States House of Representatives. (*See also* **Government—Federal Firsts: U.S. House of Representatives, 1972.**)

Sources: Encyclopedia of Black America, p. 480; *Negro Almanac, 1989,* p. 449; *Notable Black American Women,* pp. 609–12; *Who's Who Among Black Americans, 1992–93,* p. 800.

1973 • Albert Hopkins, Sr., (1928–) of Houston, was the first black in the South to serve as a member of the Texas State Board of Pharmacy. A 1949 graduate of Xavier University, he served until 1992.

Sources: Jet 82 (24 August 1992), p. 13; *Who's Who Among Black Americans, 1992–93,* p. 680.

1984 • Donald Joseph Floyd was the first judge and first black appointed to the newly created County Court-At-Law No. 3. Floyd had served as a municipal court judge in Port Arthur.

Source: Jet 65 (9 January 1984), p. 26.

El Franco Lee was the first black to win a seat on the Harris County Commissioners Court, the governing body of the county. Harris County was formed in 1836.

Source: Jet 66 (25 June 1984), p. 5.

1988 • Lee Roy Young was the first black Texas Ranger. A graduate of the University of Texas, he was a Navy veteran and a resident of Del Rio.

Sources: Jet 75 (15 August 1988), p. 8; (26 September 1988), p. 22; *Negro Almanac, 1989,* p. 1432.

UTAH

1984 • Tyrone E. Medley was the first black judge in the state, serving on the Fifth Circuit Court. He is a 1977 graduate of the University of Utah Law School.

Source: Jet 66 (2 July 1984), p. 31.

VERMONT

1777 • Vermont was the first state to abolish slavery in its constitution on July 2, 1777. Massachusetts did not formally abolish slavery until later, although Caesar Hendricks successfully brought suit for his freedom in state courts in November 1773.

Sources: Bennett, *Before the Mayflower,* p. 446; Kane, *Famous First Facts,* p. 598; *Negro Almanac, 1989,* pp. 811, 815.

VIRGIN ISLANDS

1970 • Melvin H. Evans (1918–) was the first elected governor of the Virgin Islands. Evans had been appointed governor in mid-1969. He was the first native-born governor. He was a physician who had served as assistant commissioner of health of the islands.

Sources: Alford, *Famous First Blacks,* p. 39; *Ebony* 26 (March 1971), pp. 105–8; *Ebony* 34 (March 1979), pp. 26; *Negro Almanac, 1989,* p. 1556.

VIRGINIA

1968 • William Ferguson Reid (1925–) was the first black in the House of Delegates in this century. Reid obtained his M.D. from Howard University School of Medicine in 1948, and was a staff surgeon in Richmond hospitals.

Source: Encyclopedia of Black America, p. 730.

1978 • Jean Louise Harris (1931–) was the first black named to the state cabinet as secretary of the Department of Human Resources (1978–82). She holds an M.D. from the Medical College of Virginia (1955), of which she was the first black graduate. At the time of the appointment to the state post, she was professor of family practice at the Medical College of Virginia.

Sources: Crisis 57 (April 1950), p. 228; *Ebony* 10 (July 1955), cover, pp. 76–81; *Jet* 53 (19 January 1978), p. 16; *Who's Who Among Black Americans, 1992–93,* p. 608.

1983 • John Charles Thomas was the first black member of the state supreme court. Thomas is a native of Norfolk.

Source: Jet 64 (2 May 1983), p. 30.

1984 • Yvonne Bond Miller (1934–) was the first black woman member of the General Assembly. In 1988, Miller became a member of the state senate. She has been a professor at Norfolk State University since 1976.

Sources: Jet 65 (27 February 1984), p. 20; *Who's Who Among Black Americans, 1992–93*, p. 993.

1986 • Lawrence Douglas Wilder (1931–) was the first black lieutenant governor of Virginia. In 1969, Wilder had become the first black state senator since Reconstruction, and on January 13, 1990, he became the first black governor of the state. A native of Richmond, he took his B.S. at Virginia Union University in 1951, and his law degree at the Howard University School of Law in 1959.

Sources: Hornsby, *Chronology of African-American History,* pp. 412, 420–21; *Negro Almanac, 1989,* p. 416; *Who's Who Among Black Americans, 1992–93,* p. 1505.

1987 • Marcus Doyle Williams (1952–) was the first black state judge in Fairfax County, and also the youngest—at the age of thirty-four. A 1973 Fisk graduate, Williams took his law degree at the Catholic University of America School of Law in 1977. In 1990, he became a circuit court judge.

Sources: Jet 72 (17 August 1987), p. 36; *Who's Who Among Black Americans, 1992–93,* p. 1529.

1988 • Leroy Rountree Hassell, Sr., (1955–) was the first black state supreme court justice. Hassell took his law degree at Harvard University in 1980. He was in private practice between his graduation and his appointment to the court, and he had served for three and a half years as chair of the Richmond School Board.

Sources: Jet 77 (8 January 1990), p. 8; *Who's Who Among Black Americans, 1992–93,* p. 622.

WASHINGTON

1889 • William Owen Bush (1832–1907) was the first black elected to the Washington legislature. The son of the pioneer George Washington Bush (1790?–1863), William Owen Bush was a master farmer, who won a gold medal for his wheat in the 1876 Centennial Exposition in Philadelphia. He was elected to a second term in the legislature.

Sources: Black World 19 (July 1970), pp. 90–98; *Dictionary of American Negro Biography,* p. 83; Katz, *The Black West,* pp. 74, 75, 77.

WEST VIRGINIA

1962 • Mildred Mitchell-Bateman (1922–) was the first woman in the United States to head a state Mental Health Department; she was also the first black to have cabinet rank in West Virginia government.

Sources: Ebony Success Library, vol. 1, p. 224; *Negro Almanac, 1989,* pp. 1387–88; *Who's Who Among Black Americans, 1992–93,* p. 1004.

WISCONSIN

1978 • Vel R. Phillips (1924–) was the first woman, and the first black, to be elected to a statewide constitutional office, secretary of state. Her law degree from the University of Wisconsin in 1951 was also a first. She was the first black elected to the Milwaukee Common Council (1956–71), the first black elected to serve on the National Convention Committee of either party (1958), and the first black woman judge in the state (1972).

Sources: Clayton, *The Negro Politician,* pp. 132–37; *Ebony Success Library,* vol. 1, p. 246; Lee, *Interesting People,* p. 136; *Notable Black American Women,* pp. 848–51; *Who's Who Among Black Americans, 1992–93,* p. 1122.

GOVERNMENT: FEDERAL FIRSTS

DISTRICT OF COLUMBIA BAR

1872 • The first black woman lawyer in the United States, and the third woman admitted to law practice in this country, was Charlotte E. Ray (1850–1911). As a graduate of Howard Law School (Washington, D.C.), she was automatically admitted to practice in the lower courts of the district, and on April 23, 1872, she became the first black woman admitted to practice before the district Supreme Court. She was born in New York City. Hampered by her gender in trying to establish a practice, she eventually became a teacher in the Brooklyn schools. Her father, Charles Bennett Ray (1807–86), was a notable abolitionist, minister, and editor. Her sister, Florence T. Ray (1849–1916), was an accomplished poet.

Sources: Black Women in America, pp. 965–66; *Encyclopedia of Black America,* p. 500; *Notable Black American Women,* pp. 922–24.

FEDERAL APPOINTEES

1861 • William Cooper Nell (1816–74), historian and antislavery leader, was the first black to hold a federal position. He was a Boston postal clerk. In 1855, Nell published *The Colored Patriots of the American Revolution,* which was the first substantial historical work by a black man in America. (*See also* **Writers: History, 1855.**)

Sources: Dictionary of American Negro Biography, pp. 472–73; Jackson, *A History of Afro-American Literature,* pp. 201–2; Robinson, *Historical Negro Biographies,* p. 104.

1865 • James Lewis (1832–1914), hero and public official, was active in Reconstruction politics and was the first black to receive an appointment from the federal government as inspector of customs for the Port of New Orleans. When the Union troops occupied New Orleans in 1862, Lewis abandoned the Confederate ship on which he was serving as a steward, raised two companies of black soldiers, and led the First Regiment of the Louisiana National Guard during the battle for Port Hudson. He was active in Louisiana politics and received several federal appointments.

Source: Dictionary of Black Culture, p. 270.

1869 • Ebenezer Don Carlos Bassett (1833–1908) was the first black diplomat when he became minister resident to Haiti. Since 1857, prior to the appointment, he had served as principal of Philadelphia's Institute for Colored Youth. After completing his Haitian assignment (1877), he served for ten years as a general consul from Haiti to the United States.

Sources: Dictionary of American Negro Biography, p. 32; Garrett, *Famous First Facts About Negroes,* pp. 46, 158; Robinson, *Historical Negro Biographies,* p. 49.

Henry McNeal Turner (1833–1915) was the first black to serve as a United States postmaster. He served as postmaster for Macon, Georgia. Turner resigned after serving for only a few months, because white racism prevented him from performing his duties. (*See also* **Military: United States Army, 1863; Religion: African Methodist Episcopal Church, 1898.**)

Sources: Dictionary of American Negro Biography, pp. 608–10; Garrett, *Famous First Facts About Negroes,* pp. 156, 158; Robinson, *Historical Negro Biographies,* p. 132.

1871 • Daniel Alexander Payne Murray (1852–1925), librarian, bibliographer and bibliophile, was the first black to hold a professional position at the Library of Congress. Under the mentorship of the librarian of Congress, Ainsworth R. Spofford, Murray became proficient in several languages and acquired invaluable research skills. In 1881, he was advanced to assistant librarian, a position he held until his retirement in 1923. He was asked to prepare an exhibit on black achievements for the 1900 Paris Exposition, and an accompanying bibliography was a cornerstone for future black bibliographies by him and others.

Sources: Dictionary of American Negro Biography, pp. 463–56; Garrett, *Famous First Facts About Negroes,* p. 97.

James Milton Turner (1840–1915), educator and diplomat, was the first black minister to Liberia. In 1866, he was appointed to teach in Missouri's first tax-supported school for blacks. He was active in politics, and his support of Ulysses S. Grant resulted in an appointment as minister resident and consul-general in Liberia. He was named on March 1, 1871. He was the actually the *second* black named, since James W. Mason, nominated in March 1870, never took his post.

Sources: Bennett, Before the Mayflower, pp. 489, 625; *Dictionary of American Negro Biography,* p. 611; *Dictionary of Black Culture,* p. 441.

1890 • Minnie Cox was the first black postmistress in the United States. Cox was appointed to serve in the town of Indianola, Mississippi.

Source: Garrett, Famous First Facts About Negroes, p. 156.

1893 • C. H. J. Taylor (?–1898) was the first black diplomat to be appointed to a white republic. President Grover Cleveland appointed him to serve as minister to Bolivia; however, the Senate refused to confirm his nomination. Later he accepted the post of recorder of deeds for the District of Columbia.

Source: Garrett, *Famous First Facts About Negroes,* p. 161.

1905 • Charles W. Anderson (1866–1938) was the first black appointed by a president to hold office north of the Mason-Dixon line. He was appointed Collector of Internal Revenue for the Second District of New York. Ohio-born, Anderson received his training in business in Cleveland, Ohio. In the late 1880s, he received his first appointment in New York City as United States gauger in the Second District, where he inspected bulk goods subject to duty. He received other presidential appointments until his retirement in 1934.

Sources: Alexander's Magazine 2 (15 September 1906), pp. 19–20; *Dictionary of American Negro Biography,* pp. 14–15.

1911 • William Henry Lewis (1868–1949), football player and coach, lawyer, and public official, was the first black appointed to a sub-Cabinet post. President William Howard Taft appointed him an assistant attorney general of the United States on November 26, 1911. (*See also* **Sports: Football, 1889.**)

Sources: Bennett, *Before the Mayflower,* pp. 266, 515; *Dictionary of American Negro Biography,* pp. 396–97; Garrett, *Famous First Facts About Negroes,* p. 161.

1924 • Clifton Reginald Wharton, Sr., (1899–1990) was the first black American to pass the foreign service examination. Wharton received a law degree from Boston University (Massachusetts) in 1923, and entered the United States Foreign Service in 1925, functioning as third secretary to Monrovia, Liberia. Over the next thirty years he held posts in the Malagasy Republic, Portugal, and Rumania; in 1958 he was the first black to head a United States delegation to a European country, as minister to Rumania.

Sources: Current Biography, 1990, p. 665; Garrett, *Famous First Facts About Negroes,* p. 7; Robinson, *Historical Negro Biographies,* p. 259.

1936 • Mary Jane McLeod Bethune (1875–1955), educator, civil rights leader, advisor to presidents, and government official, was the first black woman to head a federal office. President Franklin D. Roosevelt appointed Bethune to serve as director of the division of Minority Affairs of the New Deal's National Youth Administration (NYA). The NYA was founded in 1935 to provide job-training for unemployed youths, and part-time work for needy students. (*See also* **Education: Honorary Degrees, 1946; Organizations: Civil Rights and Political Organizations, 1935.**)

Sources: Dictionary of American Negro Biography, pp. 41–43; *Notable Black American Women,* pp. 86–92; Robinson, *Historical Negro Biographies,* p. 163.

1939 • George W. Crockett, Jr., (1909–) was the first black lawyer with the U.S. Department of Labor. Florida-born, Crockett was educated at Morehouse College (Atlanta, Georgia) in 1931, and the University of Michigan in 1934. He was senior attorney, U.S. Department of Labor, from 1939 to 1943.

Sources: Negro Almanac, 1976, p. 1024; Who's Who in Colored America, 1950, p. 127.

RALPH BUNCHE

1944 • Ralph Johnson Bunche (1904–71) was the first black nondiplomatic official in the United States Department of State. Bunche was made divisional assistant, Division of Political Studies. In 1947, he transferred to the United Nations. He headed various divisions of the United Nations and mediated the end of the Arab-Israeli War in 1949—he was the highest ranking American at the United Nations. In 1950, he became the first black American to win the Nobel Peace Prize. (*See also* **Miscellaneous: Honors and Awards, 1950** and **1963.**)

Sources: Dictionary of Black Culture, p. 74; Garrett, Famous First Facts About Negroes, p. 185; Robinson, Historical Negro Biographies, p. 170.

1948 • Edward R. Dudley (1911–) was the first black diplomat to receive the designation of ambassador. He was appointed ambassador to Liberia where he served until 1953. Born in Virginia, he studied at Johnson C. Smith and Howard universities and earned his law degree at St. John's University in Brooklyn (1941). (It was not until 1948 that the post at Liberia was raised from a ministership to an ambassadorship—the policy of the State Department until this period was to limit the appointment of blacks in the foreign service to ministerships, consulates, and vice-consulates.)

Sources: Dictionary of Black Culture, p. 144; Garrett, Famous First Facts About Negroes, p. 7; Robinson, Historical Negro Biographies, p. 186.

1954 • On March 4, 1954, James Ernest Wilkins, Sr. (1894–1959) was appointed as the first black assistant secretary of labor. President Dwight D. Eisenhower appointed him to this subcabinet post—the first such appointment since 1911, when William Henry Lewis was named assistant attorney general. Wilkins was the top-ranking black in the executive branch. His son James Ernest Wilkins, Jr., (1923–) had the distinction of obtaining a Ph.D. in mathematics from the University of Chicago, when he was nineteen, in 1942.

Sources: Bennett, Before the Mayflower, p. 549; Dictionary of Black Culture, p. 471; Hornsby, Milestones in 20th-Century African-American History, p. 55.

On August 7, 1954, Charles H. Mahoney (1886–1966), lawyer, was confirmed by the Senate as the first black permanent member of the delegation to the United Nations. Born in Michigan, Mahoney was educated at Fisk University and the University of Michigan.

Sources: Bennett, Before the Mayflower, pp. 550, 625; Garrett, Famous First Facts About Negroes, p. 192; Who's Who in Colored America, 1950, p. 350.

1955 • Jewel Stradford Lafontant (1928–) was the first black woman named assistant U.S. attorney for the Northern Illinois district. Chicago-born Lafontant, who received her education at Oberlin College and the University of Chicago, was a trial lawyer with the Legal Aid Bureau. She served in the Illinois office until 1958. In 1973, Lafontant was the first black woman deputy United States solicitor general. In 1989, she was appointed by President George Bush as an ambassador-at-large and United States coordinator for refugee affairs.

Sources: Black Women In America, pp. 689–90; Notable Black American Women, p. 644.

E. Frederic Morrow (c. 1909–) was the first black man to serve as White House aide. President Dwight D. Eisenhower appointed him administrative assistant. New Jersey–born, Morrow was educated at Bowdoin College and Rutgers University. He wrote *Black Man in the White House* (1963).

Sources: Who's Who Among Black Americans, 1977, p. 651; Who's Who in Colored America, 1950, p. 385.

1957 • Archibald J. Carey, Jr., (1908–), clergyman and public official, was the first black American to head the President's Committee on Government Employment Policy. Appointed by President Dwight D. Eisenhower, Chicago lawyer Carey was a graduate of John Marshall Law School, and a two-term Chicago alderman. From 1953 to 1956 he was an alternate delegate to the United Nations.

Sources: Dictionary of Black Culture, p. 82; Garrett, Famous First Facts About Negroes, p. 162; Jet 84 (9 August 1993), p. 24.

Clinton Everett Knox (1908–) was the first black secretary to the United States Mission to the North Atlantic Treaty Organization (NATO). Born in Massachusetts, Knox was educated at Williams College, and Brown and Harvard universities. A career foreign service officer, he held posts in Haiti, Dahomey, Honduras, and France.

Sources: Dictionary of Black Culture, p. 258; Who's Who Among Black Americans, 1977, p. 530.

1960 • Andrew T. Hatcher (1923–92) was the first black presidential press secretary. President John Kennedy named Hatcher as associate press secretary, on November 10, 1960, and for a time he was the highest-ranking black appointee in the executive branch of the federal government.

Sources: Hornsby, Chronology of African-American History, p. 111; Hornsby, Milestones in 20th-Century African-American History, p. 67.

1961 • Mercer Cook (1903–), scholar, author and diplomat, was the first black American ambassador to Nigeria. Born in Washington, D.C., Cook was educated at Amherst College, the Sorbonne, and Brown University. He had a distinguished teaching career at Howard and Atlanta universities. He published a number of books and edited several scholarly journals. His diplomatic career included appointments in Nigeria (1961–64) and Senegal and Gambia (1964–66).

Sources: Dictionary of Black Culture, p. 117; Robinson, Historical Negro Biographies, p. 175; Who's Who in Colored America, 1950, p. 119.

Cecil Francis Poole (1907–) was the first black U.S. attorney in the continental United States. He was appointed to the San Francisco office. The Alabama-born attorney received his legal training at the University of Michigan and Harvard University. He was a practicing lawyer in California, and taught at the University of California, Berkeley. In 1976, he became a U.S. district judge.

Sources: Dictionary of Black Culture, p.354; Kane, Famous First Facts, p. 49; Who's Who Among Black Americans, 1992–93, p. 1135.

Robert Clifton Weaver (1907–) was the first black administrator of the Federal Housing and Home Finance Administration—at that time the highest federal post ever held by an African-American. In 1966, he was named Secretary of Housing and Urban Development by President Lyndon B. Johnson, becoming the first black to serve in the cabinet of a president. The Harvard-trained Ph.D. wrote several books.

Sources: Hornsby, Chronology of African-American History, pp. 111, 126; Garrett, Famous First Facts About Negroes, p. 113; Robinson, Historical Negro Biographies, pp. 257–58.

1962 • Henry M. Michaux, Jr., (1930–) was the first black federal assistant district attorney in the South. Born in North Carolina, Michaux was educated at North Carolina Central University and Rutgers University. He was later a member of the North Carolina legislature and a United States attorney.

Sources: Paths Toward Freedom, p. 65; Who's Who Among Black Americans, 1992–93, p. 983.

1963 • Leslie N. Shaw (1922–85) was the first black postmaster to head a postal unit of a major city. Ohio-born Shaw was appointed postmaster of Los Angeles, California—the world's third largest postal operation. He supervised over ten thousand employees, and handled more than eighty-four million dollars of stamps and services. He was educated at Ohio State University, and the University of California, Los Angeles. He began his career in the post office as a janitor.

Sources: Dictionary of Black Culture, p. 400; Garrett, Famous First Facts About Negroes, p. 156; Who's Who Among Black Americans, 1977, p. 804.

1964 • Charlotte Moton Hubbard was the first black deputy assistant secretary of state for public affairs. This was the highest permanent position held by a woman. Hubbard was later the first black appointed to an important position with a television station.

Source: Negro Almanac, 1976, p. 1008.

Carl Thomas Rowan (1925–) was the first black to head the United States Information Agency (1964–65). He was deputy assistant secretary of state for public affairs (1961–63), and from 1963 to 1964 he was ambassador to Finland. Tennessee-born, Rowan is a successful nationally syndicated columnist and journalist. He was the first black to ever attend a meeting of the National Security Council.

Sources: Contemporary Black Biography, vol. 1, pp. 208–12; *Dictionary of Black Culture,* p. 385; Robinson, *Historical Negro Biographies,* p. 246.

1965 • Andrew Felton Brimmer (1926–), economist and educator, became the first black member of the governing body of the Federal Reserve System. He was educated at the University of Washington, and Harvard University, and then taught at Michigan State University. He joined government service as an assistant secretary for economic affairs at the Commerce Department.

Sources: Contemporary Black Biography, vol. 2, pp. 37–39; Garrett, *Famous First Facts About Negroes,* p. 163; *Negro Almanac, 1976,* pp. 345–46.

Patricia Roberts Harris (1924–85), lawyer and diplomat, was the first black woman ambassador appointed to an overseas post. A graduate of Howard and George Washington universities, Illinois-born Harris was appointed ambassador to Luxembourg by President Lyndon B. Johnson. Two years later, she was named an alternate delegate to the United Nations. In 1971, she was elected to the boards of directors of International Business Machines and Chase National Bank. The same year, she was also elected to head the credentials committee at a meeting of the Democratic National Committee—the first black to chair the committee. President Jimmy Carter appointed her secretary of Housing and Urban Development in 1976—the first black woman cabinet member.

Sources: Garrett, *Famous First Facts About Negroes,* p. 7; Hornsby, *Chronology of African-American History,* p. 280; Kane, *Famous First Facts,* pp. 31, 50; *Notable Black American Women,* pp. 468–72.

PATRICIA HARRIS WAS THE FIRST BLACK WOMAN CABINET MEMBER.

**THURGOOD
MARSHALL**

Thurgood Marshall (1908–93) was named the first black American U.S. Solicitor General. Baltimore-born Marshall graduated from Lincoln University in Pennsylvania, and Howard University to become the nation's foremost civil rights lawyer. He served for many years as NAACP counsel (1938–61). Marshall represented the plaintiff in the *Brown v. Board of Education* before the Supreme Court, which ruled that racial segregation in the public schools was unconstitutional in 1954. President John F. Kennedy appointed Marshall judge of the Second Circuit Court of Appeals (1962); and President Lyndon B. Johnson appointed him solicitor general—this was, at the time, the highest law enforcement position ever held by an African-American. In 1967, President Johnson named Marshall the first black associate justice of the Supreme Court. He was the recipient of the coveted NAACP Spingarn Medal in 1946.

Sources: Kane, *Famous First Facts,* p. 624; Robinson, *Historical Negro Biographies,* p. 226; Hornsby, *Chronology of African-American History,* pp. 101, 112, 125.

James Madison Nabrit, Jr., (1900–) educator and civil rights lawyer, was the first black American ambassador to the United Nations. Atlanta-born Nabrit was educated at Morehouse College and Northwestern University. President Lyndon B. Johnson appointed him United States deputy representative to the United Nations Security Council, where he served from 1965 to 1967. (*See also* **Education: College Administrators, 1965.**)

Sources: Bennett, *Before the Mayflower,* p. 574; Hornsby, *Chronology of African-American History,* p. 105; *Who's Who Among Black American, 1992–93,* p. 1045.

Robert B. Pitts (1909-1982), business executive, was the first black appointed to a federal regional administrative post with the United States Department of Housing and Urban Development, in Region VI (San Francisco). Born in Georgia, he was educated at Howard University and the University of Washington.

Source: Who's Who Among Black Americans, 1977, p. 718.

1968 • Barbara M. Watson (1918–83), administrator, was the first black woman to serve as an assistant secretary of state. Born in New York City, Watson received her education at Barnard College, and New York Law School. She began her career in the State Department in 1966.

Sources: Garrett, *Famous First Facts About Negroes,* pp. 163, 197; *Jet* 63 (7 March 1983), p. 12.

1970 • Samuel Riley Pierce, Jr., (1922–) was the first black to serve as a general counsel to the United States Treasury Department. In 1980, President-elect Ronald Reagan named Pierce secretary of Housing and Urban Development. He was the first and only black cabinet member in the Reagan administration. Pierce was born in New York state and educated at

Cornell University. He held a number of governmental offices in New York prior to his entry into federal service.

Sources: Hornsby, *Chronology of African-American History*, p. 307; Hornsby, *Milestones in 20th-Century African-American History*, pp. 182, 307, 418; *Who's Who Among Black Americans, 1992–93*, p. 1124.

As human resources development officer for the Bureau of Latin America, Gloria Gaston was the first black to hold a major post in the Agency for International Development.

Source: Negro Almanac, 1976, p. 1005.

1972 • As economic and commercial officer, James Estes Baker (1935–), diplomat, was the first black assigned to serve in South Africa. Virginia-born, Baker was educated at the Fletcher School and Haverford College. He entered the State Department in 1961.

Sources: Alford, *Famous First Blacks,* pp. 29–30; Hornsby, *Milestones in 20th-Century African-American History*, p. 164; *Who's Who Among Black Americans, 1992–93*, p. 60.

Benjamin Lawson Hooks (1925–) was the first black commissioner of the Federal Communications Commission. Born in Tennessee, Hooks received his law degree from DePaul University (Chicago, Illinois) in 1948, after studying at Le Moyne College (Syracuse, New York) and Howard University (Washington, D.C.). He was a Baptist church minister and a founding member of the Southern Christian Leadership Council, and was the executive secretary of the National Association for the Advancement of Colored People (1977–92). He was the 1986 NAACP

BENJAMIN HOOKS
STEPPED DOWN AS THE
NAACP EXECUTIVE
SECRETARY IN 1992.

Spingarn medalist. (*See also* **Government—County & State Pioneers: Tennessee, 1965.**)

Sources: Hornsby, *Milestones in 20th-Century African-American History,* pp. 215, 489; *Who's Who Among Black Americans, 1992–93,* p. 679.

1973 • Henry Minton Frances (1922–) was the first black deputy assistant secretary of defense. Born in Washington, D.C., Frances was educated at the University of Pennsylvania, United States Military Academy, and Syracuse University. He was deputy assistant secretary from 1973 to 1977.

Source: Who's Who Among Black Americans, 1992–93, p. 480.

1977 • On February 11, 1977, Clifford Alexander, Jr., (1933–) was confirmed as the first black secretary of the army. Born in New York City, Clifford took a law degree from Yale in 1958. He combined public and private law practice in his career, and at present heads his own law firm in Washington, D.C. He held the army position until 1980.

Sources: Bennett, *Before the Mayflower,* p. 603; Hornsby, *Milestones in 20th-Century African-American History,* pp. 276–77; *Who's Who Among Black Americans, 1992–93,* p. 14.

Drew Saunders Days III (1941–), government official, was the first black director of the United States Justice Department's Civil Rights Division. A graduate of Yale University Law School (1966), he was an attorney with the NAACP Legal Defense Fund.

Sources: Hornsby, *Chronology of African-American History,* p. 281; *Who's Who Among Black Americans, 1977,* p. 228.

Emma Daniels McFarlin (1921–), government official, was the first black woman to head the western region of the U.S. Department of Housing and Urban Development. Born in Arkansas, she was educated at Philander Smith College and the University of Wisconsin.

Source: Who's Who Among Black Americans, 1992–93, p. 954.

Terence A. Todman (1926–), diplomat, was the first black named assistant secretary of state for Latin America. Todman was born in the United States Virgin Islands, and educated in Puerto Rico and America. He began his diplomatic career in 1952, and held positions in India, Africa, Costa Rica, Spain, the United Nations, and Latin America.

Source: Who's Who Among Black Americans, 1977, p. 1404.

Azie B. Taylor Morton (1936–), public official, was the first black American treasurer of the United States. Texas-born, Morton was educated at Huston-Tillotson College.

Sources: Kane, *Famous First Facts,* p. 675; *Who's Who Among Black Americans, 1992–93,* p. 1030.

Joan Scott Wallace (1930–), educator, was the first black assistant secretary for administration in the United States Department of Agriculture.

The Illinois-born public official was closely affiliated with the National Urban League, Howard University, and social work organizations.

Sources: Notable Black American Women, pp. 1195–97; Who's Who Among Black Americans, 1977, p. 922.

Togo Dennis West, Jr., (1942–), business executive and attorney, was the first black Navy general counsel. Born in North Carolina, West was educated at Howard University, and was active in legal circles.

Source: Who's Who Among Black Americans, 1992–93, p. 1486.

1978 • Carolyn Robertson Payton (1925–), educator, was the first woman and black to head the Peace Corps. A graduate of Bennett College, the University of Wisconsin (Madison), and Columbia University, Payton was prominent in the field of education.

Sources: Notable Black American Women, pp. 833–34; Who's Who Among Black Americans, 1992–93, p. 1100.

1979 • Marcus Alexis (1932–), bank official, was the first black American to chair a federal regulatory commission. Brooklyn-born, Alexis was chairman of the United States Interstate Commerce Commission. He received his education at Brooklyn College and the University of Michigan.

Source: Who's Who Among Black Americans, 1992–93, p. 19.

John D. Glover was the first black Federal Bureau of Investigations field office chief and headed the FBI's operations in Milwaukee, Wisconsin. He was also the first African-American inspector at FBI headquarters. In 1986, at FBI headquarters, Glover became the highest-ranking black in the bureau, as the first black executive assistant director in charge of administration.

Source: Negro Almanac, 1989, p. 1432.

1980 • George Albert Dalley (1941–), attorney, was the first black member of the United States Civil Aeronautics Board. Born in Havana, Cuba, Dalley received his education at Columbus College and Columbia University. He worked for Congressman Charles Rangel, the State Department, and was a campaign manager for the "Mondale for President" effort.

Sources: Who's Who Among Black Americans, 1992–93, p. 337; Who's Who in American Politics, 1987–88, p. 251.

1981 • Clarence M. Pendleton, Jr., (1930–88) was the first African-American to chair the United States Civil Rights Commission. He was born in Kentucky and was educated at Howard University. Following President Reagan's desires, he led the commission toward a "color-blind" approach to matters of civil rights.

Sources: Hornsby, Chronology of African-American History, p. 369; Hornsby, Milestones in African-American History, pp. 308, 379; Negro Almanac, 1989, p. 101; Who's Who in American Politics, 1987–88, p. 136.

Lennie Marie Pickens Tolliver (1928–) was appointed as the first black to head the U.S. Commission on Aging. Born in Cleveland, Ohio, she was educated at Hampton University and the University of Chicago. She had a long and distinguished career in social services prior to her appointment by President Ronald Reagan. She resigned in 1984.

Source: Who's Who Among Black Americans, 1992–93, p. 1406.

Carlos Cardozo Campbell (1937–), banking executive, was the first black assistant secretary of commerce. Born in New York City, Campbell was educated at Michigan State University and the Catholic University of America. He was the assistant secretary for economic development and affiliated with the Inter-American Development Bank.

Sources: Who's Who Among Black Americans, 1992–93, p. 223; Who's Who in American Politics, 1987–88, p. 1524.

Gloria E. A. Toote (1931–), attorney, was the first black chair of the Merit System Protection Board (former Civil Service Commission). Born in New York City, Toote was educated at Howard and Columbia universities. She worked for the National Affairs section of Time and for HUD.

Source: Who's Who Among Black Americans, 1992–93, p. 1407.

1982 • Harold E. Doley, Jr., (1947–) was the first person of any race to serve as director of the Mineral Management Service of the United States Department of the Interior. Born in New Orleans, Doley was educated at Xavier and Harvard universities. He is an investment counselor with a long career in minority and African counseling. Doley, in 1983, was the first black United States executive director for the African Development Bank and Fund.

Sources: Who's Who Among Black Americans, 1992–93, p. 388; Who's Who in American Politics, 1987–88 p. 586.

1983 • Barbara J. Mahone, automobile executive, was the first black woman to chair the United States Federal Labor Relations Authority. Born in Alabama, Mahone was educated at Ohio State University, the University of Michigan, and Harvard University. She has held a variety of positions in the automotive industry.

Source: Who's Who Among Black Americans, 1992–93, p. 904.

1984 • Aulana Louise Peters (1941–), attorney, was the first black woman appointed to the Securities and Exchange Commission. Born in Louisiana, Peters was educated at the College of New Rochelle and the University of Southern California.

Source: Who's Who Among Black Americans, 1992–93, p. 1114.

1985 • Julius Wesley Becton, Jr., (1929–) was the first black director of the Federal Emergency Management Agency. A retired army officer, Becton was born in Pennsylvania, and educated at Prairie View Agricultural and Mechanical College, the University of Maryland, and the National War College.

Sources: Negro Almanac, 1989, pp. 892–93; *Who's Who Among Black Americans, 1992–93,* p. 90.

1986 • Edward Joseph Perkins, diplomat, was the first black American ambassador to South Africa—a class A post. A veteran foreign service professional, Perkins was serving as Ambassador to Liberia, when President Ronald Reagan made the appointment.

Sources: Hornsby, Chronology of African-American History, p. 342; Hornsby, *Milestones in 20th-Century African-American History,* p. 349.

1989 • Gwendolyn Stewart King was the first black woman to serve as Commissioner of Social Security. A U.S. government career woman, King was employed by the U.S. Department of Health and Human Services in 1971.

Source: Who's Who Among Black Americans, 1992–93, p. 823.

Audrey Forbes Manley (1934–), federal health officer, was the first black female assistant secretary in the U.S. Health and Human Services Department. Born in Mississippi, Manley was educated at Spelman and Meharry Medical College, and held a number of health-related administrative offices in Georgia and Washington, D.C.

Source: Who's Who Among Black Americans, 1992–93, p. 909.

Roscoe Michael Moore, Jr., (1944–) was the first chief veterinary officer for the U.S. Public Health Service. Moore took a D.M.V. at Tuskegee in 1969, and a Ph.D. in health services at Johns Hopkins in 1985. His career has been mostly with federal government health organizations.

Sources: Jet 77 (30 October 1989), p. 20; *Who's Who Among Black Americans, 1992–93,* p. 1018.

Constance Berry Newman (1935–), government official, was the first black administrator of the Office of Personnel Management. South Carolina–born, Newman was educated at Bates College, and the University of Minnesota. Active in Republican politics, she was part of the Bush-Quayle transition team at the end of the Reagan administration.

Source: Who's Who Among Black Americans, 1992–93, p. 1055.

Louis Wade Sullivan (1933–), physician, was the first black cabinet member in President George Bush's administration, as Secretary of the United States Department of Health and Human Services. Sullivan was born in Georgia, and educated at Morehouse College and Boston University. He was engaged in medical education at Harvard University, New Jersey

LOUIS SULLIVAN College of Medicine, and Boston University. He was the first dean and president of the Morehouse School of Medicine (1974–89).

Sources: Hornsby, *Chronology of African-American History,* p. 385; *Who's Who Among Black Americans, 1992–93,* p. 1353.

1990 • George Williford Boyce Haley (1925–), attorney, was the first black American to chair the United States Postal Rate Commission. Born in Tennessee, Haley was educated at Morehouse College and the University of Arkansas. He was active in legal circles in Kansas, and served as a state senator before entering the federal service.

Source: Who's Who Among Black Americans, 1992–93, p. 580.

1993 • Jesse Brown (1944–) was the first black ever confirmed to the cabinet as head of Veterans Affairs. Brown, executive director of the Disabled American Veterans, for more than twenty-five years, had been an advocate for those who served in America's armed forces. He was educated at Chicago City College, after serving as a marine in the Vietnam conflict, where he lost the use of his right arm.

Sources: Atlanta Constitution 18 December 1992; *Crisis* 100 (March 1993), p. 16; *Ebony* 48 (May 1993), p.64.

M. Joycelyn Elders (1933–) became the first black and the first woman United States Surgeon General, in August. The outspoken advocate of the immunization of children, quality health care for all American citizens, and the elimination of diseases had been opposed by politicians for her liberal views on health care issues. She was also the first woman and the first black to hold the position of Arkansas health director. The Schaal, Arkansas, native graduated from Philander Smith College in Little Rock, Arkansas, and received an M.D. degree from the University of Arkansas Medical School.

Sources: (Nashville) *Tennessean* (8 September 1993); *Who's Who Among Black Americans, 1992–93,* p. 426.

Sharon Farmer was one of four and the first black woman to serve as White House photographer, covering President Bill Clinton and the first family. Her assignments took her throughout the United States and foreign countries.

Sources: Jet 84 (20 September 1993), p. 10.

Hazel O'Leary (1938–) was the first black (and the first woman) Secretary of Energy. Born in Newport News, Virginia, she graduated from Fisk University, and Rutgers Law School. She acquired governmental experience in the Ford and Carter administrations, and was executive vice-president of Northern States Power Company of Minnesota at the time of her appointment.

Source: Ebony 48 (May 1993), p. 64.

Rodney Slater (1955–) was the first black to head the Federal Highway Administration. A native of Mississippi, Slater took his law degree at the University of Arkansas in 1980. He was closely associated with the Bill Clinton state administration and the presidential campaign.

Sources: Jet 84 (11 July 1993), pp. 26–27; *Who's Who Among Black Americans, 1992–93,* p. 1290.

HAZEL O'LEARY, U.S. SECRETARY OF ENERGY.

Clifton Reginald Wharton, Jr., was the first black named deputy secretary of state. (*See also* **Education: College Administrators, 1970.**)

Source: Ebony 48 (May 1993), p. 62.

FEDERAL EMPLOYEES

1976 • Johnnie Mae M. Gibson (1949–) was the first black woman agent with the Federal Bureau of Investigation. Born in Florida and educated in Georgia and Florida, Gibson was a high school teacher and policewoman before becoming an agent in Florida.

Source: Who's Who Among Black Americans, 1992–93, p. 518.

JUDICIARY

1865 • John Sweat Rock (1825–66), lawyer, was the first black man admitted to practice before the U.S. Supreme Court, but not the first to argue a

JAMES BENTON
PARSONS

case. Following his admission to the court, he may have been the first black lawyer received on the floor of the House of Representatives. A native of Salem, New Jersey, Rock practiced both dentistry and medicine before his health forced him to give up his practice and study law.

Sources: Dictionary of American Negro Biography, pp. 529–31; Garrett, *Famous First Facts About Negroes,* p. 23, 93; *Journal of Negro History* 52 (July 1967), pp. 169–75; Kane, *Famous First Facts,* p. 345.

1937 • William Henry Hastie (1904–76) was the first black appointed to the federal bench. He was appointed United States district judge in the Virgin Islands. He was also the first black governor of the Virgin Islands in 1944, and became judge of the circuit court of appeals in 1949. Hastie served as civilian aide to the Secretary of War (1941–43)—he resigned to protest the lack of a positive commitment to recruit black pilots. In 1939, he resigned his judgeship to teach at Howard University's School of Law (Washington, D.C.), where he later also served as dean.

Sources: Garrett, Famous First Facts About Negroes, p. 86; *Negro Almanac, 1976,* p. 281; Robinson, *Historical Negro Biographies,* p. 199.

1945 • Irving Charles Mollison (1899-1962) was the first black judge of a U.S. Customs Court. This was the first time that a black served as a federal judge in the United States. He served in New York City. The Mississippi-born jurist was educated at Oberlin College and the University of Chicago.

Sources: Garrett, Famous First Facts About Negroes, p. 87; *Negro Almanac, 1976,* p. 1045; *Negro Year Book, 1941-46,* p. 285.

1961 • James Benton Parsons (1911–93) was the first black appointed judge of a U.S. district court in the continental United States. Chicago attorney Parsons was appointed judge of the U.S. District Court of Northern Illinois. In 1975, Parsons became the first black to serve as chief of a U.S. district court.

Sources: Hornsby, Chronology of African-American History, p. 112; Kane, *Famous First Facts,* p. 333; *Negro Almanac, 1976,* p. 284.

CONSTANCE MOTLEY

1966 • Constance Baker Motley (1921–) was the first black woman federal judge. She was elected to the New York state senate in 1964, and in 1965, she became president of the Borough of Manhattan. Her appointment as a judge of the U.S. Circuit Court of the Southern District of New York made her the highest-paid black woman in government. The Connecticut-born jurist received her education at New York and Columbia universities. Motley worked with the NAACP as legal assistant and associate counsel and won many difficult civil rights cases—her most famous victory was the case of James Meredith against the University of Mississippi. The case broke the barriers of segregation in southern universities. (*See also* **Government—County & State Pioneers: New York, 1964.**)

Sources: Black Women in America, vol. 2, pp. 822–24; *Notable Black American Women,* pp. 779–82; Robinson, *Historical Negro Biographies,* p. 230.

1978 • Robert Frederick Collins (1931–) was the first black federal judge in the deep south in modern times. Active in legal services in Louisiana, Collins was appointed a U.S. District Court judge in 1978. In 1991, he was also the first federal judge to be found guilty of taking a bribe.

Sources: Negro Almanac, p. 341; Who's Who Among Black Americans, 1992–93, p. 293.

1979 • Joyce London Alexander, judge, was the first black American U.S. judge in the District of Massachusetts. Alexander was educated at Howard University and the New England Law School.

Source: Who's Who Among Black Americans, 1992–93, p. 16.

Amalya Lyle Kearse (1937–) was the first black woman judge on the U.S. Court of Appeals, Second District of New York. New Jersey–born, Kearse was educated at Wellesley College and the University of Michigan Law School. She was active in legal circles, the National Urban League, and the NAACP Legal Defense Fund.

Sources: Kane, Famous First Facts, p. 333; Who's Who Among Black Americans, 1992–93, p. 809.

1980 • Odell Horton (1929–) was the first black federal judge in the state of Tennessee. A native of Tennessee, Horton was educated at Morehouse College and Howard University; and he was president of Le Moyne-Owen College (1970–74) before his appointment to the U.S. District Court in Tennessee.

Source: Who's Who Among Black Americans, 1992–93, p. 685.

1982 • Reginald Walker Gibson (1927–) was the first African-American to sit on the bench of the U.S. Claims Court. Born in Virginia, Gibson was educated at Virginia Union University, Howard University, and the University of Pennsylvania.

Source: Who's Who Among Black Americans, 1992–93, p. 518.

1984 • Ann Claire Williams (1949–), judge, was the first black woman nominated to the federal bench in Chicago. Born in Michigan, Williams was educated at Wayne State University, the University of Michigan, and Notre Dame University. Prior to her appointment to the U.S. District Court, Williams was a U.S. attorney and an adjunct professor at Northwestern University.

Source: Who's Who Among Black Americans, 1992–93, p. 1511.

1990 • Thelton Eugene Henderson (1933–) was the first black chief judge of the Northern California U.S. District Court. Henderson was born in Louisiana, and received his education at the University of California, Berkeley.

Source: Who's Who Among Black Americans, 1992–93, p. 639.

LABOR RELATIONS

1963 • Howard Jenkins, Jr., (1915–) was the first black to serve on the National Labor Relations Board. A native of Denver, Colorado, Jenkins was a law professor, when he was first appointed by President John F. Kennedy. He was reappointed in 1968, by President Lyndon B. Johnson, in 1973 by President Richard M. Nixon, and in 1978 by President Jimmy Carter.

Sources: Christmas, *Negroes in Public Affairs and Government,* p. 323; *Ebony Success Library,* vol. 1, p. 174; *Who's Who Among Black Americans, 1992-1993,* p. 742.

POLITICAL PARTIES

1843 • Henry Highland Garnet, Samuel Ringgold Ward, and Charles B. Ray were the first blacks to participate in a national political gathering, the convention of the Liberty Party. Garnet (1815–82) pastored a New York Presbyterian church and preached a social gospel. At a Lincoln's birthday memorial, February 12, 1865, he became the first black man to preach in the rotunda of the Capitol to the House of Representatives. In 1843, at the Convention of Free Men in Buffalo, New York, he outlined a brilliant plan for a general slave strike. Ray (1807–86), one of the convention's secretaries, was a minister best known for his work as publisher of *The Colored American,* and president of the New York Society for the Promotion of Education Among Colored Children. Ward (1817–66), who led a prayer at the convention, was the leading black abolitionist before Frederick Douglass. His autobiography, *Autobiography of a Fugitive Negro,* was published in 1855.

PREACHER AND ABOLITIONIST HENRY GARNET.

Sources: Dictionary of American Negro Biography, pp. 252–53 (Garnet), 515–16 (Ray), 631-632 (Ward); *Dictionary of Black Culture,* pp. 181, 370, 460; Robinson, *Historical Negro Biographies,* pp. 82, 140.

1866 • Frederick Douglass (1817–95) was the first black delegate to a national political convention, that of the National Loyalists' Union party. Born a slave, and named Frederick Augustus Bailey, Douglass's talent as an orator won him employment as a lecturer by the Anti-Slavery Society. His freedom was bought while he was on a lecture tour in England. From 1847 until his death, he was a fearless leader of his race. In 1872, Frederick Douglass was the first black to be nominated as a vice-presidential candidate, by the Woman Suffrage Association convention. During Reconstruction he demanded the vote for the freedman. He moved to the nation's capital and became the first black to serve as recorder of deeds in 1881, and U.S. minister to Haiti in 1889. He published his classic autobiography in 1845, a second version appeared in 1855, and this work was again revised and enlarged under the title *The Life and Times of Frederick Douglass* in 1882. In 1888 Frederick Douglass was the first black to be nominated as a presi-

FREDERICK
DOUGLASS

dential candidate, at the Republican convention. He received one vote. (*See also* **Writers: Short Stories, 1853.**)

Sources: Dictionary of American Negro Biography, p. 181; Garrett, Famous First Facts About Negroes, p. 160; Negro Almanac, 1989, p. 290.

1952 • Charlotta A. Spears Bass (1880–1961), journalist and political activist, was the first black woman to run for vice-president. She was the nominee of the Progressive Party. Bass, born in South Carolina, moved to New England and began a career as a journalist. In 1912, she became editor of the *California Eagle* in Los Angeles. She was educated at Brown and Columbia universities and the University of California.

Sources: Black Women in America, vol. 1, p. 93; Notable Black American Women, p. 61–64; Who's Who in Colored America, 1928, p. 23.

1968 • Julian Bond (1940–) and Channing E. Phillips (1928–87), civil rights leaders, were the first blacks proposed for president and vice-president at the same convention. Bond was an early member of the Student Nonviolent Coordinating Committee (SNCC) and communications director of the organization. At the Democratic convention he was the first black to be nominated from the floor of a major convention for the office of vice-president. After a few states voted, he withdrew, as he was too young to accept the nomination. Phillips was the first black nominated for president at a major political convention in modern times. Born in Brooklyn, New York, Phillips was educated at Virginia Union University, and Colgate Rochester Divinity School. He was a Congregationalist minister and active in Democratic politics. As favorite son of the Washington, D.C., delegation, he received 67 ½ votes.

Source: Contemporary Black Biography, vol. 2, pp. 22–27 (Bond); Dictionary of Black Culture, p. 59 (Bond); Dictionary of Black Culture, p. 351 (Phillips); Garrett, Famous First Facts About Negroes, p. 163 (Phillips); Kane, Famous First Facts, p. 479 (Bond); Who's Who Among Black Americans, 1977, p. 710 (Phillips).

1976 • Aris T. Allen, at Detroit, Michigan, was the first black man to call the roll at a Republican Party national convention. In 1977, Allen was the first black to serve as Republican state chairman in Maryland. The Texas-born physician was educated at Howard University. (*See also* **Government—County & State Pioneers: Maryland, 1978.**)

Source: Who's Who Among Black Americans, 1977, p. 12.

1984 • Julian Dixon (1934–), public official, was the first black to chair the rules committee for the Democratic National Convention. Born in Washington, D.C., Dixon was educated at California State University at Los Angeles and Southwestern University. He was elected to Congress in 1978.

He was the first black member to chair an appropriations subcommittee on the District of Columbia.

Sources: Negro Almanac, 1989, 387–88; Who's Who Among Black Americans, 1992–93, p. 384; Who's Who in American Politics, 1987–88, p. 103.

JESSE JACKSON

Jesse Louis Jackson (1941–) was the first black American to be a nonsymbolic candidate for the presidential nomination. Founder of People United to Serve Humanity (Operation PUSH), Jackson was born in South Carolina and educated at the University of Illinois and North Carolina Agricultural and Technical College. He was ordained a Baptist minister in 1968, after studying at the Chicago Theological Seminary. He was a field director for the Congress of Racial Equality (CORE), and in 1967 was named by the Southern Christian Leadership Conference (SCLC) to head its Operation Breadbasket, which he had helped found. A close associate of Martin Luther King, Jr., Jackson left the SCLC in 1971, and in Chicago founded Operation PUSH. In 1983, Jackson launched a major voter-registration drive among black Americans and toward the end of the year declared his candidacy for the Democratic presidential nomination. Jackson ran in a large number of Democratic primary elections in 1984, finishing a strong third to former Vice-President Walter Mondale and Senator Gary Hart. In 1987, Jackson again entered the race for the Democratic presidential nomination.

Sources: Contemporary Black Biography, vol. 1, pp. 108–12; Hornsby, Milestones in 20th-Century African-American History, pp. 122, 185, 247; Negro Almanac, 1989, 278–79; Who's Who Among Black Americans, 1992–93, p. 722.

1985 • Sharon Pratt Dixon—now Sharon Pratt Kelley—(1944–) was the first black (and woman) treasurer of the Democratic National Committee. Born and educated in the nation's capital, Dixon is active in political affairs. (*See* **Government—Local Heroes: Washington, D.C., 1990.**)

Sources: Black Women in America, vol. 1, pp. 675–76; Hornsby, Milestones in 20th-Century African-American History, p. 456; Notable Black American Women, p. 278.

1988 • Lenora Fulani was the first black American woman to qualify for federal matching funds in a presidential election—and the first African-American (and woman) to appear on the presidential ballot in all fifty states. Fulani, a social psychologist, was running on the National Alliance Party ticket. She was on the ballot in forty-five states in 1992.

Source: Emerge 4 (October 1992), p. 59.

U.S. HOUSE OF REPRESENTATIVES

1868 • John Willis Menard (1839–93), public official, was the first black elected to Congress. He was awarded his full salary but never seated. The

committee on elections ruled that it was too early to admit a black to Congress. He was appointed inspector of customs of the port of New Orleans. Born of French creole parents living in Illinois, Menard moved to Louisiana after the Civil War to work for the Republican party. When he was allowed to plead his own case on February 27, 1969, he became the first black to speak on the floor of the House.

Sources: Bennett, *Before the Mayflower,* p. 626; Garrett, *Famous First Facts About Negroes,* p. 29; Robinson, *Historical Negro Biographies,* pp. 99–100.

THE FIRST BLACK SENATOR AND REPRESENTATIVES ELECTED TO THE U.S. CONGRESS, 1872 (LEFT TO RIGHT): SEN. HIRAM R. REVELS AND REPS. BENJAMIN S. TURNER, ROBERT C. DELARGE, JOSIAH T. WELLS, JEFFERSON F. LONG, JOSEPH H. RAINEY, AND ROBERT B. ELLIOTT.

1870 • Joseph Hayne Rainey (1831–87) was the first black elected to Congress to represent South Carolina. He was sworn in on December 12, 1870, since he was elected to fill an unexpired term. He was a delegate to the state constitutional convention in 1868 and to the state senate in 1870. In 1874, Rainey was the first black ever to preside over the House. He served in Washington, D.C., for four consecutive terms until 1879. For a chronological listing of blacks elected to the House of Representatives in the nineteenth century, see the following table.

Sources: Bennett, *Before the Mayflower,* p. 488; Christopher, *America's Black Congressmen,* p. 33; *Dictionary of American Negro Biography,* p. 510; Garrett, *Famous First Facts About Negroes,* p. 32; Robinson, *Historical Negro Biographies,* p. 112.

1871 • Josiah Thomas Walls (1842–1905?) was the first black congressman ever elected from the state of Florida, taking office on March 4, 1871. Born in Winchester, Virginia, Walls had limited education and became a prosperous farmer in Florida after serving as a soldier during the civil war. He was elected a Republican congressman-at-large in 1870 and re-elected

BLACKS ELECTED TO THE HOUSE OF REPRESENTATIVES IN THE NINETEENTH CENTURY

REPRESENTATIVE	STATE	YEARS OF SERVICE
Joseph H. Rainey	South Carolina	1869–79
Jefferson F. Long	Georgia	1870–71
Robert C. Delarge	South Carolina	1871–73
Benjamin S. Turner	Alabama	1871–73
Robert B. Elliott	South Carolina	1871–75
Josiah T. Walls	Florida	1871–77
Alonzo J. Ransier	South Carolina	1873–75
James T. Rapier	Alabama	1873–75
Richard H. Cain	South Carolina	1873–75, 1877–79
John R. Lynch	Mississippi	1873–77, 1881–83
Jeremiah Haralson	Alabama	1875–77
John A. Hyman	North Carolina	1875–77
Charles E. Nash	Louisiana	1875–77
Robert Smalls	South Carolina	1875–79, 1881–87
James E. O'Hara	North Carolina	1883–87
John Mercer Langston	Virginia	1889–91
Thomas E. Miller	South Carolina	1889–91
Henry P. Cheatham	North Carolina	1889–93
George Washington Murray	South Carolina	1893–97
George H. White	North Carolina	1897–1901

Source: Negro Almanac, 1976, pp. 318–31.

twice, serving until 1876, when he was unseated for the second time. He served for a while in the post of superintendent of a farm on the campus of Tallahassee State College (later Florida Agricultural and Mechanical University).

Sources: Dictionary of American Negro Biography, pp. 629–30; Garrett, *Famous First Facts About Negroes,* p. 33; Robinson, *Historical Negro Biographies,* p. 139.

U.S. SENATE

1870 • Hiram Rhoades (Rhodes) Revels (1822–1901), was the first black U.S. senator. He was elected to fill the vacated seat of Confederate President Jefferson Davis on January 20, 1870. He was born of free parents in North Carolina, and educated by Quakers in North Carolina, and at Knox College in Illinois. He became a minister in the African Methodist Episcopal

BLACKS ELECTED TO THE SENATE IN THE NINETEENTH CENTURY

SENATOR	STATE	YEARS SERVED
Hiram Rhoades Revels	Mississippi	1870–71
Blanche K. Bruce	Mississippi	1875–81

Source: Negro Almanac, 1976, pp. 318–31.

Church, a teacher, and a Freedman's Bureau worker in Mississippi. He was elected to the Mississippi state senate in 1869, and elected U.S. Senator by the legislature. He served from February 21, 1870, to March 3, 1871. After serving in the Senate, he served as the first president of the newly founded Alcorn College for Negroes. He remained active in the powerful circles of his church. For a chronological listing of blacks elected to the Senate in the nineteenth century, see the following table.

Sources: Bennett, *Before the Mayflower,* p. 487; *Dictionary of American Negro Biography,* pp. 523–24; Garrett, *Famous First Facts About Negroes,* p. 30; Robinson, *Historical Negro Biographies,* p. 116.

1871 • On February 1, 1871, Jefferson Franklin Long (1836–1900) was the first black to speak in the House of Representatives as a congressman. Long was the second black elected, and the first (and only) one from Georgia during Reconstruction. He served from January 1871 to the end of the session on March 3, 1871.

Sources: Bennett, *Before the Mayflower,* p. 489; *Dictionary of American Negro Biography,* p. 405.

1873 • John Roy Lynch (1847–1939) was the first black congressman from Mississippi. Son of a slave mother and a white Louisiana planter, Lynch attended night school, worked as a photographer's assistant, began to dabble in politics, and at the age of twenty-four became speaker of the Mississippi House. He was elected U.S. congressman three times, and served with distinction from 1873–77. He served the Republican party as state chairman of the executive committee (1881–89) and received federal appointments (1898–1911) as a reward. In 1884, Lynch was the first black to preside over a national nominating convention held by a major political party. He was named temporary chairman of the Republican Party meeting in Chicago. He wrote an authoritative account of post Civil War period, *The Facts of Reconstruction,* in 1913.

Sources: Dictionary of American Negro Biography, pp. 407–409; Garrett, *Famous First Facts About Negroes,* pp. 19, 33–34, 43, 53; Robinson, *Historical Negro Biographies,* p. 98.

1874 • Blanche Kelso Bruce (1841–98) was the first black elected to a full term in the U.S. Senate. Mississippi's second black senator, Bruce took his

BLANCHE K. BRUCE

seat in 1875. He is the only black senator to serve a full term, until the mid-twentieth century. He was born a slave in Virginia, and later obtained an education at Oberlin College in Ohio. He was a wealthy Mississippi farmer and a successful banker. In 1878, Bruce presided over the Senate, the first black to do so. In 1881, President Ulysses S. Grant appointed him register of the treasury.

Sources: Dictionary of American Negro Biography, pp. 74–76; Hornsby, Chronology of African-American History, p. 45, 50, 56; Robinson, Historical Negro Biographies, pp. 56–57.

1875 • John A. Hyman (1840–91) was the first black to serve the state of North Carolina as a U.S. congressman. He was born a slave in North Carolina, and was sold and sent to Alabama where he remained until after the Civil War. He was self-educated. He was elected to the Forty-fourth Congress. During his term, he served on the Committee of Manufacturers. He held several federal appointments in North Carolina.

Sources: Garrett, Famous First Facts About Negroes, p. 35; Paths Toward Freedom, p. 160.

1888 • John Mercer Langston (1829–97), educator and public official, was the first black Virginian elected to the House of Representatives. Langston was also the first black to win an elective office, as a member of the city council of Brownhelm, Ohio in 1855. An active leader in the convention movement before the Civil War, he helped to organize the freedmen in the Negro National Labor Union. In 1868, President Andrew Johnson appointed him Inspector General of the Freedmen's Bureau. From 1869 to 1876, he was associated with Howard University (Washington, D.C.). President Rutherford B. Hayes appointed him minister to Haiti in 1877. Later, Langston served as president of Virginia Normal and Collegiate Institute at Petersburg, Virginia (now Virginia State College). Elected to the U.S. Congress as a Republican in 1888, he was not seated until 1890 because the election was contested. He published a collection of addresses, *Freedom and Citizenship* in 1883, and his autobiography, *From the Virginia Plantation to the National Capitol in 1894. (See also* **Education: Law Schools, 1868; Government—County & State Pioneers: Ohio, 1855.**)

Sources: Christopher, America's Black Congressmen, p. 139; Dictionary of American Negro Biography, pp. 382–84; Garrett, Famous First Facts About Negroes, pp. 36–37, 63, 91; Hornsby, Chronology of African-American History, pp. 27–28, 55.

1929 • Oscar Stanton DePriest (1871–1951) was the first black congressman elected in the twentieth century and also the first from a northern state. He served three terms from the Twenty-first Congressional District of Illinois. Born in Florence, Alabama, and reared in Kansas, he moved to Chicago and became active in real estate before entering politics. He blazed the trail for the return of blacks to Congress.

Sources: Dictionary of American Negro Biography, pp. 173–74; Garrett, Famous First Facts About Negroes, p. 37; Hornsby, Chronology of African-American History, p. 76.

1934 • Arthur W. Mitchell (1883–1968) was the first black Democratic congressman. He defeated Republican congressman Oscar DePriest of Illinois. He was born in Alabama and attended Tuskegee Institute (Alabama), Columbia (New York), and Harvard (Massachusetts) universities. Mitchell was active in rural industrial education in Alabama, before studying law and moving to Washington, D.C., and Chicago to practice as a lawyer and real estate broker. He served from the Seventy-fourth to the Seven-seventh Congress. He was an ardent civil rights advocate and won a significant Supreme Court case in 1941 involving interstate travel.

Sources: Clayton, *The Negro Politician,* pp. 54–55; Garrett, *Famous First Facts About Negroes,* p. 37; Gosnell, *Negro Politicians,* pp. 90–91; Hornsby, *Chronology of African-American History,* p. 89.

1944 • Adam Clayton Powell, Jr., (1908–72) was elected to Congress from Harlem, becoming the first black member of the House of Representatives from the East. He was one of the most flamboyant and controversial politicians of the twentieth century. In 1961, Powell was the first black to chair the powerful Education and Labor Committee. (*See also* **Government— Local Heroes: New York City: 1941.**)

Sources: Hornsby, *Chronology of African-American History,* pp. 92, 194, 224; *Negro Almanac, 1976,* pp. 326–27; Robinson, *Historical Negro Biographies,* pp. 238–39.

ADAM CLAYTON POWELL, JR., WAS HARLEM'S REPRESENTATIVE IN CONGRESS.

1949 • On January 18, 1949, William L. Dawson (1886–1970) became the first black to head a congressional standing committee in recent times, as chair of the House Expenditutes Committee. Born in Albany, Georgia, he studied at Fisk University, Kent College of Law, and Northwestern University. He won election to Congress in 1942—the third northern black, and the second black Democrat, in the U.S. Congress. He served longer than any other black (1941–70). In 1944, he was the first black to be the vice-president of a major political party.

Sources: Bennett, *Before the Mayflower,* p. 627; Clayton, *The Negro Politician,* pp. 67–85; Hornsby, *Chronology of African-American History,* p. 91; Robinson, *Historical Negro Biographies,* p. 181.

1954 • Charles C. Diggs, Jr., (1922–) was elected to the House, becoming the first black federal legislator from Michigan. His election marked the first time in the twentieth century that as many as three blacks served in the House. Detroit-born, Diggs was educated at Wayne State University (1946), and Detroit College of Law (1952). Diggs was a founder and first head of the Congressional Black Caucus. In 1969, Congressman Diggs was the first black to chair the Foreign Relations Subcommittee on Africa. In 1973, he became the first black congressman to head the Committee for the District of Columbia. He resigned his seat in 1980, after being convicted of mail and payroll fraud in 1978.

Sources: Garrett, *Famous First Facts About Negroes,* p. 40; Hornsby, *Chronology of African-American History,* p. 102; *Negro Almanac, 1989,* pp. 74, 77; *Who's Who Among Black Americans, 1977,* p. 238.

CHARLES C. DIGGS, JR.,
WAS THE FIRST
BLACK TO CHAIR THE
FOREIGN RELATIONS
SUBCOMMITTEE ON
AFRICA. HERE, HE
CONFERS WITH ARTHUR
ASHE, LEFT, ABOUT THE
DENIAL OF ASHE'S VISA
TO TRAVEL TO SOUTH
AFRICA.

1958 • Robert Nelson C. Nix (1905–) was the first black congressman from Pennsylvania. Elected congressman from the Second District of Pennsylvania to fill an unexpired term, he won re-election to each subsequent Congress. He held membership on the foreign affairs, post office, and civil service committees. Born in South Carolina, Nix studied in New York and Pennsylvania (Lincoln University and University of Pennsylvania Law School). He was one of the first congressmen to speak out in support of the Montgomery bus boycott. Nix's son, Robert N. C. Nix, Jr, was the first black to sit on a state Supreme Court bench since Reconstruction; he was inaugurated as chief justice of the Pennsylvania Supreme Court in 1984. (*See* **Government—County & State Pioneers: Pennsylvania, 1984.**)

Sources: Dictionary of Black Culture, p. 331; Garrett, *Famous First Facts About Negroes,* p. 40; Hornsby, *Chronology of African-American History,* p. 327.

1962 • Augustus Freeman Hawkins (1907–) was the first black elected to the House from California. Born in Louisiana and educated in California, Hawkins was active in real estate and youth work before entering state politics. He ran for Congress from the Twenty-first District and won by an overwhelming majority. He chaired the House Rules Committee.

Sources: Garrett, *Famous First Facts About Negroes,* p. 41; Robinson, *Historical Black Biographies,* pp. 200–1; *Negro Almanac, 1989,* pp. 391–92; *Who's Who Among Black Americans, 1992–93,* p. 624.

1966 • Edward W. Brooke (1919–), attorney, was the first black to be elected to the U.S. Senate since Reconstruction, and the first ever elected by popular vote. A graduate of Howard University and Boston University,

Brooke served in World War II as a captain. He moved to Massachusetts, where he served as attorney general for the state. He was elected to the U.S. Senate on the Republican ticket. (*See also* **Government—County & State Pioneers: Massachusetts, 1960.**)

Sources: Contemporary Biography, 1967, pp. 40–43; Hornsby, *Chronology of African-American History,* pp. 113, 129, 264; Robinson, *Historic Negro Biographies,* p. 166.

ROBERT N. C. NIX, SR., A CONGRESSMAN FROM PENNSYLVANIA, WAS ONE OF THE FIRST CONGRESSMEN TO PUBLICLY SUPPORT THE MONTGOMERY BUS BOYCOTT.

1968 • Shirley Chisholm (1924–) was the first African-American woman elected to the House of Representatives. Born in Brooklyn, New York, Chisholm graduated from Brooklyn College and Columbia University. In 1964, she was elected to the New York state legislature, and upon her entry into national politics, she won a committee assignment on the veterans affairs committee. In 1972, Chisholm was the first black woman to seek nomination as the Democrats' presidential candidate.

Sources: Black Women in America, vol. 1, pp. 236–38; Garrett, Famous First Facts About Negroes, p. 42; Hornsby, Chronology of African-American History, p. 133; Notable Black American Women, pp. 185–89.

1970 • William L. Clay (1931–) was the first black elected to represent Missouri in Congress. Born in St. Louis, Missouri, Clay was the firebrand of black demonstrations in St. Louis, while he served as alderman. In 1968, Clay defeated his Republican opponent and assumed his place in Congress. He was educated at St. Louis University.

Sources: Garrett, Famous First Facts About Negroes, p. 41; Negro Almanac, 1989, pp. 383–84; Who's Who Among Black Americans, 1992–93, p. 272.

Walter E. Fauntroy (1933–), public official, was the first black nonvoting delegate to Congress from the District of Columbia. He worked long with Martin Luther King, Jr., and he was a coordinator of the 1963 civil rights march on Washington, and the Poor People's Campaign of 1968. A graduate of the Yale Divinity School, he pastors a Baptist church in Washington, D.C.

Sources: Encyclopedia of Black America, p. 384; Negro Almanac, 1989, p. 389; Who's Who Among Black Americans, 1992–93. p. 448.

1971 • Louis Stokes (1925–) was the first black member of the Appropriations Committee. Elected U.S. congressman from Ohio in 1968, Stokes received his legal training at John Marshall School of Law in Cleveland, and had a private practice until his entry into politics. In 1983, Representative Stokes became the first black member of the House Select Committee on Intelligence; and in 1985, the first black congressman to head the Program and Budget Authorization subcommittee, of the House Permanent Select Committee on Intelligence.

Sources: Contemporary Black Biography, vol. 3, pp. 237–39; Hornsby, Milestones in 20th-Century African-American History, pp. 103, 493; Negro Almanac, 1989, p. 395.

The Congressional Black Caucus of the House of Representatives was the first concerted effort on the part of black representatives to influence congressional party politics. An affiliation of black members of Congress, the all-Democratic group, representing mainly Northern big-city districts, was permanently headquartered on Capitol Hill with a director and staff. It maintained political liaison with other black groups and projected a black agenda to influence and promote economic, social, and political goals favored by black Americans. It was formally organized in 1971, and later included Republican members. Michigan congressman Charles C. Diggs, Jr., was founder and first head of the caucus.

Sources: Dictionary of Black Culture, p. 46; Hornsby, *Milestones in 20th-Century African-American History,* pp. 360, 404; *Negro Almanac, 1989,* pp. 380–82.

1972 • Yvonne Braithwaite Burke (1932–) was the first black congresswoman from the West. A California Democrat, Burke was educated in the University of California system. She was victorious in a 1966 campaign to become the first black California assemblywoman. She was the first black woman vicechair of the Democratic National Convention in 1972. She entered national congressional politics and went to Washington in 1972. In 1973, she became the first member of Congress to give birth while serving in office. She resigned in 1978 to run for a local office in California. (*See also* **Government—County & State Pioneers: California, 1967.**)

Sources: Black Women in America, vol. 1, p. 195; Hornsby, *Chronology of African-American History,* p. 211; *Notable Black American Women,* pp. 130–32.

Barbara Charline Jordan (1936–) was the first southern black woman elected to the House. Texas-born Jordan gained recognition from a nationwide television audience as the House Judiciary committee considered articles of impeachment against President Richard Nixon. She received her education at Texas Southern University (Houston) and Boston University Law School. She was elected to the Texas legislature in 1965. Her reputation as one of the twentieth century's great orators was sustained by her keynote address to the 1976 Democratic Convention. Jordan decided in 1978 to retire from Congress. She became the Lyndon B. Johnson Centennial Chair in National Policy professor at the University of Texas at Austin. (*See also* **Government—County & State Pioneers: Texas, 1967.**)

Sources: Black Women in America, pp. 658–59; *Negro Almanac, 1976,* p. 313–14; *Notable Black American Women,* pp. 609–12.

BARBARA JORDAN

Andrew Jackson Young, Jr., (1932–) was the first black member of the House from Georgia since 1870. Born in New Orleans, Young was educated at Howard University and the Hartford Theological Seminary. He was a leader in the civil rights movement and a close associate of Martin Luther King, Jr. Young won re-election to Congress in 1974 and 1976. In 1977, President Jimmy Carter announced the nomination of Young as U.S. Ambassador to the United Nations—marking the first time an African-American led the American delegation (the position carried cabinet-level status). He later served as mayor of Atlanta (1982–90), and ran unsuccessfully for governor of the state of Georgia. He is now co-chair of the Atlanta Committee for the Olympic Games.

Sources: Contemporary Black Biography, vol. 3, pp. 263–67; Hornsby, *Chronology of African-American History,* pp. 280, 282, 290, 305, 349, 409, 428; *Who's Who Among Black Americans, 1992–93,* p. 1583.

1973 • Cardiss Hortense Robertson Collins (1932–) was the first black congresswoman from Illinois and the fourth black woman to serve in the Congress. In 1975, she became the first black to chair the House Government Operations Subcommittee on Manpower and Housing. Born in Missouri, and educated in Michigan and Illinois, Collins was elected to the House of Representatives to fill the seat left vacant by the death of her husband. She was the first woman to chair the Congressional Black Caucus. She was also the first black whip-at-large (1975).

Sources: Black Women in America, vol. 1, pp. 264–65; Notable Black American Women, p. 204; Who's Who Among Black Americans, 1992–93, p. 290.

1974 • Harold Eugene Ford (1945–) was the first black congressman from the state of Tennessee. He was educated at John Gupton College and Tennessee State and Howard universities. He served in the Tennessee state legislature before being chosen to represent his state in Congress.

Sources: Hornsby, Milestones in 20th-Century African-American History, pp. 221, 405; Negro Almanac, 1989, p. 390; Who's Who Among Black Americans, 1992–93, p. 470.

Charles Bernard Rangel (1930–) was the first black member of the House Ways and Means Committee. A native of New York City, Rangel was educated at New York University and St. John's University Law School. In 1983, Rangel was the first black deputy whip in the House. This was a prestigious role in floor leadership. Rangel had been elected to Congress in 1970, after a successful legislative career in New York state.

Sources: Hornsby, Milestones in 20th-Century African-American History, pp. 44, 103; Negro Almanac, 1989, pp. 393–94; Who's Who Among Black Americans, 1992–93, p. 1164.

1980 • Ronald (Ron) H. Brown (1941–), political party executive, was the first black American chief counsel of the Senate Judiciary Committee. Born in Washington, D.C., Brown was educated at Middlebury College and St. John's University Law School. He was spokesperson and deputy director of the Urban League's Washington operations, and worked in the offices of Senator Edward Kennedy. In 1989 he was named chairman of the National Democratic Party—the first black to hold this office. In 1993, Brown was confirmed as the first black to hold the cabinet post of Secretary of Commerce.

Sources: Atlanta Constitution (18 December 1992); *Crisis* 100 (March 1993), p. 16; *Ebony* 48 (May 1993), p. 62; *Who's Who Among Black Americans, 1992–93,* p. 180.

1983 • Trudi Michelle Morrison (1950–), attorney and presidential aid, was the first black woman assistant sergeant-at-arms of the Senate. Born in Colorado, Morrison was educated in Colorado and Washington, D.C.

Source: Who's Who Among Black Americans, 1992–93, p. 1029.

1984 • William H. Gray III (1941–) was the first black congressman to chair the House Budget Committee. Born in Louisiana, Gray was an ordained Baptist minister and was elected to Congress from 1978 to 1991. He served on the Democratic Congressional Steering Committee, the Congressional Black Caucus, and the House Committees on Foreign Affairs, Budget and District of Columbia. In 1989, Gray was the first black to serve as a majority whip in the House. In 1991, he gave up his congressional career to head the United Negro College Fund.

Sources: Contemporary Black Biography, vol. 3, pp. 77–80; Hornsby, *Milestones in 20th-Century African-American History,* p. 501; *Who's Who Among Black Americans, 1992–93,* p. 552.

1986 • Alphonso Michael "Mike" Espy (1953–) was the first black congressman elected from Mississippi since Reconstruction. Born in Mississippi, Espy was educated at Howard University and Santa Clara Law School. He was active in legal services in Mississippi. In 1993, he was confirmed as the first black Secretary of Agriculture.

Sources: Crisis 100 (March 1993), p. 16; *Ebony* 48 (May 1993), p. 62; *Negro Almanac, 1989,* 388–89; *Who's Who Among Black Americans, 1992–93,* p. 439.

1988 • Donald M. Payne (1934–), teacher and businessman, was the first black congressman elected from the state of New Jersey. Born in New Jersey, Payne was educated at Seton Hall University, and taught school in the urban areas of New Jersey. He was a local legislator prior to his election to the U.S. Congress.

Sources: Negro Almanac, 1989, p. 393; *Who's Who Among Black Americans, 1992–93,* p. 1099.

1992 • Alcee Lamar Hastings (1936–) was the first impeached federal officer to be elected to another federal post. In 1979, Hastings was the first

black federal judge in Florida. Hastings was born in Florida and educated at Fisk, Howard, and Florida Agricultural and Mechanical universities. He was impeached by a committee of the U.S. Senate in 1989—the impeachment was nullified by a Supreme Court decision, because according to constitutional procedures the whole Senate must rule in an impeachment. He was elected in 1992 to the House of Representatives.

Sources: Atlanta Constitution 5 November 1992; Hornsby, *Milestones in 20th-Century African-American History,* pp. 400, 424; *Who's Who Among Black Americans, 1992–93,* p. 622.

Carol E. Moseley Braun (1947–) was the nation's first black woman senator. The Chicago-born attorney was educated at the University of Chicago. She was active in Chicago legal circles and the state legislature, and served as Cook County (Illinois) recorder of deeds/registrar of titles.

Sources: Black Women in America, vol. 1, pp. 162–64; *Crisis* 100 (March 1993), p. 7; *Jet* 83 (23 November 1992), p. 8; *Who's Who Among Black Americans, 1992–93,* p. 1032.

Carrie Meek (1926–) was the first black woman to represent Florida in Congress. Meek was born in Florida, and she came under the influence of Mary McLeod Bethune of Bethune-Cookman College, a school at which she served as physical education director, after graduating from Florida Agricultural and Mechanical University—where she was legend in athletics. She was a Florida state senator, and as a legislator sponsored more than thirty major bills and programs—ranging from education to small business to women's rights. (*See also* **Government—County Seats & State Capitals: Florida, 1982.**)

Sources: Ebony 48 (January 1993), p. 32; *Jet* 82 (28 September 1992), p. 34; *Jet* 83 (23 November 1992), pp. 15, 52; *Who's Who in American Politics, 1987–88,* p. 318.

Cynthia McKinney (1955–) was the first black woman elected to the U.S. House from Georgia. Georgia-born and a two-term state representative, McKinney was victorious in a new congressional district mandated by the 1990 census. McKinney was educated at the University of Southern California, and taught at Agnes Scott College in Atlanta, Georgia.

CAROL MOSELEY BRAUN WAS THE FIRST BLACK WOMAN ELECTED TO THE U.S. SENATE.

Sources: Ebony 48 (January 1993), p. 32; *Jet* 82 (31 August 1992), p. 4; *Jet* 83 (23 November 1992), pp. 15, 52.

Eva Clayton (1935–) and Melvin Watt (1945–) were the first black representatives from North Carolina in the twentieth century. Clayton was also the first black woman. She is the owner of her own development company in North Carolina, and a former county official. She took office in November immediately after the election to fill an unexpired term, and so has two month's seniority over other freshman congress members. A Phi Beta Kappa graduate of the University of North Carolina, Watt received his legal training from the Yale University Law School. He was active in local politics and part owner of an elder-care facility. His Twelfth Congressional District, which stretches 170 miles from Gastonia to Durham (and at one place includes only the northbound lanes of Interstate 85) may be challenged as the result of a historic U.S. Supreme Court decision—*Shaw v. Reno*—in the closing days of the term that ended June 23, 1993.

Sources: Atlanta Constitution 4 (November 1992); *Ebony* 48 (January 1993), pp. 34, 52; *Jet* 83 (23 November 1992), pp. 15, 52; *Washington Post* National Weekly Edition, 19–25 July 1993, p. 14; *Who's Who in American Politics,* 1987–88, p. 1127 (Watts).

Earl Frederick Hilliard (1942–) was the first black elected to represent Alabama in the House since Reconstruction. An Alabama native, Hilliard was educated at Morehouse College, Atlanta, and Howard universities. Hilliard was a state senator in his fourth term at the time of his election.

Sources: Atlanta Constitution 4 November 1992; *Ebony* 48 (January 1993), p. 27; *Jet* 83 (23 November 1992), pp. 15, 52; *Who's Who Among Black Americans, 1992–93*, p. 661.

Jim Clyburn (1940–), activist, was South Carolina's first black U.S. Congressman in modern times. Involved in the civil rights movement, Clyburn was a student activist at South Carolina State College where he was educated. He is a former school teacher and community leader.

Sources: Ebony 48 (January 1993), p. 52; *Jet* 83 (23 November 1992), pp. 15, 52.

Robert C. (Bobby) Scott (1947–), attorney, became the first black Virginian elected to Congress in the twentieth century. Scott is a graduate of Harvard University and Boston College of Law School. He was active in local and state politics.

Sources: Ebony 48 (January 1993), p. 54; *Jet* 83 (23 November 1992), pp. 15, 52.

1993 • Ronald V. Dellums (1935–) is the first black chair of the House Armed Services Committee; in 1977 he had been the first black member. A native of Oakland, California, he represents a district which includes Oakland and Berkeley, the starting places for both the student movement and the Black Panther party of the 1960s. When he was elected to the House in 1970, the district was only twenty-two percent black, but he forged a firm coalition by 1974, and his length of service has underpinned his leadership role in Congress. A notable opponent of major military spending, he is nonetheless respected by the military establishment, and by more conservative members of the committee.

Sources: Ebony 48 (May 1993), p. 66; *Negro Almanac*, pp. 386–87; *Who's Who Among Black Americans, 1992–93*, p. 372; *Who's Who in American Politics, 1987–88*, p. 102.

U.S. SUPREME COURT

1880 • Samuel R. Lowery (1832–c. 1900) on February 2, 1880, was the first black lawyer to argue a case before the Supreme Court. This first is distinct from John Sweat Rock's first in 1865—Rock was admitted to practice before the court, a recognition of standing as a lawyer obtained by many more lawyers than ever actually appear before the court to argue a case.

Sources: Encyclopedia of Black America, p. 499; *Leaders of Afro-American Nashville;* Simmons, *Men of Mark*, pp. 144–48.

1948 • William Thaddeus Coleman, Jr., (1920–) was the first black clerk in the Supreme Court. Born in Philadelphia, Coleman was educated at the University of Pennsylvania and Harvard University. He was an honor graduate and law review editor and recipient of a number of academic honors. He was selected to serve as law secretary to Justice Felix Frankfurter.

Sources: Kane, *Famous First Facts,* p. 625; *Who's Who in Colored America, 1950,* p. 116.

1954 • Charles Vernon Bush (1939–) was the first black Supreme Court page. Bush was born in Florida, and was educated at the U.S. Air Force Academy, Georgetown University, and Harvard Business School.

Sources: Alford, *Famous First Blacks,* p. 56; Kane, *Famous First Facts,* p. 626; *Who's Who Among Black Americans, 1992–93,* p. 207.

GOVERNMENT: LOCAL HEROES

∿∿∿∿∿∿∿∿∿∿∿∿∿∿∿∿∿∿∿∿∿∿∿∿∿

ALABAMA

1964—TUSKEGEE • Kenneth L. Buford (1917–) and Stanley Hugh Smith were the first blacks elected with white opponents in the state of Alabama in this century, when they won election to the city council. Buford was a minister, and Smith was a professor at Tuskegee Institute.

Sources: Jet 59 (18 September 1980), p. 18; *Who's Who Among Black Americans, 1992–93*, p. 193 (Buford).

1972—PRICHARD • Algernon J. Cooper (1944–) was the first black to defeat a white incumbent in a sizable Alabama city since Reconstruction, when he won the race for mayor in September, 1972. A 1969 graduate of the New York University School of Law, Cooper had returned to Mobile, Alabama, his native city, as an NAACP Legal Defense Fund lawyer.

Sources: Ebony (December 1972), pp. 163–68; *Ebony Success Library*, vol. 2, pp. 52–55; *The Negro Almanac, 1976*, p. 73.

1979—BIRMINGHAM • On October 30, 1979, Richard Arrington, Jr., (1934–) was the first black mayor of the city. Arrington earned a Ph.D. in invertebrate zoology at the University of Oklahoma (1966), and was executive director of fundraising for the Alabama Center for Higher Education. Active in civic affairs, he decided to run for mayor after a young black woman, Bonita Carter, was shot three times in the back by a white policeman. In 1971, he had been the first black elected to the Birmingham city council.

Sources: Jet 57 (15 November 1979), pp. 6–8; *Negro Almanac*, pp. 425–26; *Who's Who Among Black Americans, 1992–93*, p. 44.

1984—UNION SPRINGS • John McGowan was the first black mayor of Union Springs. The same election day also saw Nathanial Torian, of Hillsboro, and Mary Stoval, of Hurtsboro, as the first black mayors of their towns.

Source: Jet 66 (20 August 1984), p. 34.

1986—BIRMINGHAM • Johnny Johnson was the first black lieutenant in the Birmingham Police Department.

Source: Jet 70 (5 May 1986), p. 20.

ARIZONA

1965—PHOENIX • Hayzel Burton Daniels (1907–) was the first black judge in Arizona when he was appointed one of the ten city magistrates. Daniels's entire education was at the University of Arizona (B.A. 1939, J.D. 1948). He served in the U.S. Air Force, in the Far East, between 1943 and 1945.

Source: Ebony Success Library, vol. 1, p. 85.

ARKANSAS

1873—LITTLE ROCK • Mifflin Wister Gibbs (1823–1915) was the first black elected municipal court judge. Earlier, on November 26, 1872, Macon B. Allen was chosen as a judge of the Inferior Court of Charleston, South Carolina, by the state General Assembly. Gibbs was also an owner and the editor of the first black newspaper in California, *Mirror of the Times,* in 1855. In 1866, Gibbs was elected to the city council of Victoria, British Columbia. Gibbs began to complete his law studies at Oberlin (Ohio) in 1869, and after his service as municipal judge, he held several offices in the Federal government, including that of United States consul in Madagascar. In 1902, he published a biography, *Shadow and Light.*

Sources: Bennett, *Before the Mayflower,* p. 639; *Dictionary of American Negro Biography,* pp. 258–59; *Negro Almanac,* p. 1425; *Encyclopedia of Black America,* p. 403; Katz, *The Black West,* pp. 139–42.

1986—LITTLE ROCK • Lottie H. Shackelford (1941–) was the first woman mayor of Little Rock. Shackelford had served for eight years on the city's Board of Directors. (*See also* **Government—County & State Pioneers: Arkansas, 1990.**)

Sources: Jet 71 (9 February 1987), p. 57; *Who's Who Among Black Americans, 1992–93,* pp. 1261–62.

CALIFORNIA

1781—LOS ANGELES • Los Angeles is the first major city founded with a majority black population. In the eleven founding families, more than half the adults were black, two were white, and the rest Native Americans.

Source: Davis, *The History of Black Catholics in the United States,* pp. 33–34.

1953—BAKERSFIELD • Henry Holton Collins was the first black elected to a city council in California, when he won his election in Bakersfield, California. Collins was pastor of St. Paul Christian Methodist Episcopal Church. He easily won re-election in 1957.

Sources: Jet (16 April 1970), p. 11; *Sepia* 8 (May 1960), p. 23.

THOMAS BRADLEY SERVED THE CITY OF LOS ANGELES FOR THIRTY YEARS.

1961—LOS ANGELES • Vaino Hassen Spencer was the first black municipal court judge in California. She served on the Los Angeles Municipal Court. She was also the first black president of the National Association of Women Judges.

Sources: Clayton, *The Negro Politician,* p. 125; *Ebony* 20 (August 1966), p. 97; *Jet* 77 (4 December 1989), p. 6; *Sepia* (January 1963), pp. 52–55.

1963—LOS ANGELES • Thomas Bradley (1917–) was the first black elected official in the city upon his election to the Los Angeles city council. Between 1940 and 1961 he was a member of the police department, becoming the first black to hold the rank of lieutenant. Bradley studied law at night, and was admitted to the bar in 1956. In 1973, he would become the first black mayor of the city at a time when only fifteen percent of the voters were black. He announced his retirement as mayor in 1992.

Sources: Encyclopedia of Black America, p. 189; *Contemporary Black Biography,* vol. 2, pp. 33–36; *Jet* 82 (12 October 1992), pp. 4–5; *Negro Almanac,* p. 478; *Who's Who Among Black Americans, 1992–93,* p. 144.

1971—BERKELEY • Warren Hamilton Widener (1938–) was the first black elected mayor of Berkeley, in a very close election in April, 1971. A native of California and an attorney, Widener was perceived to be part of the radical coalition that was trying to take control of the city. He held the office until 1979.

Sources: Ebony (October 1971), pp. 74–82; Hornsby, *Chronology of African-American History,* p. 168; *Who's Who Among Black Americans,* 1992–93, p. 1503.

1977—BERKELEY • Odell H. Sylvester, Jr., (1924–) was the first black police chief in the city. Sylvester began as a patrolman in the department in 1947, and he retired in 1981.

Sources: Jet 53 (6 October 1977), p. 4; *Who's Who Among Black Americans, 1992–93,* p. 1360.

1977—OAKLAND • Lionel J. Wilson (1915–)was the first black mayor of Oakland, California. In 1960, Wilson had also been the first black judge in Alameda County. He had a distinguished career as a judge before his election, and he was re-elected mayor in 1981.

Sources: Black Enterprise 8 (August 1977), p. 37; *Negro Almanac,* p. 433; *Who's Who Among Black Americans, 1992–93,* p. 1549.

1978—LOS ANGELES • Yvonne Braithwaite Burke (1932–) was the first black member of the Los Angeles County Board of Supervisors. (*See also* **Government—Federal Firsts: United States House of Representatives, 1968; Government—County & State Pioneers: California, 1967.**)

Sources: Jet 56 (5 July 1979), p. 9; *Notable Black American Women,* pp. 130–32.

1982—PASADENA • On May 6, 1982, Loretta Thompson Glickman became the first woman mayor of a city of more than 100,000. She was elected by the city's board of directors.

Sources: Hornsby, *Chronology of African-American History,* p. 311; *Jet* 62 (24 May 1982), p. 13; *Jet* 63 (31 January 1983), p. 38.

1986—LOS ANGELES • Paul A. Orduna was the first black assistant chief in the Los Angeles City Fire Department. Orduna joined the department in 1957.

Source: Jet 70 (5 May 1986), p. 20.

Maxine F. Thomas (1947–) was the first black woman presiding judge in the Los Angeles Municipal Court. She had been a member of the court since 1980.

Sources: Jet 70 (14 July 1986), p. 14; *Who's Who Among Black Americans, 1992–93,* p. 1385.

1986—OAKLAND • Jayne Williams was the first black woman city attorney in the state of California when she was appointed to the post in Oakland. Williams was thirty-eight years old at the time, and held a law degree from the University of California Hastings College of Law.

Source: Jet 72 (15 June 1987), p. 36.

1988—LOS ANGELES • Jesse A. Brewer was the first black assistant chief in the Los Angeles Police Department. In 1981, Brewer had also been the first black deputy chief.

Source: Jet 73 (11 January 1988),p. 30.

1991—LOS ANGELES • Rita Walters was the first black woman to serve on the Los Angeles City Council.

Source: Jet 80 (8 July 1991), p. 23.

COLORADO

1983—DENVER • Norman S. Early, Jr., was the first black district attorney in Denver. A native of Washington, D.C., Early took his law degree at the Illinois University College of Law, and was thirty-seven at the time of his appointment.

Source: Jet 63 (28 February 1983), p. 15.

1991—DENVER • Wellington E. Webb (1941–) was the first black mayor of Denver. Active in both local and national politics, Webb was a state representative from 1973–77, and was auditor of the city at the time of his election. He took office on June 30, 1991.

Sources: Jet 81 (18 November 1991) p. 66; *State of Black America 1992,* pp. 375, 377; *Who's Who Among Black Americans, 1992–93,* p. 1479.

CONNECTICUT

1978—NEW LONDON • Leo Edwin Jackson (1925–) was the first black mayor of the city and the first black mayor in New England. He was elected by the City Council. In 1975 Jackson had become the first black elected to the council.

Sources: Jet 57 (27 December 1979), p. 5; *Who's Who Among Black Americans, 1992–93,* p. 723.

1981—HARTFORD • Thirman L. Milner (1933–) was the first popularly elected black mayor in any of the six New England states. This businessman held the position until 1987. At the time of his election, he had served two terms in the state legislature.

Sources: Jet 61 (26 November 1981), p. 9; *Jet* 69 (13 January 1986), p. 7; *Who's Who Among Black Americans, 1992–93,* p. 995.

1986—HARTFORD • As mayor of Hartford, Carrie Saxon Perry (1931–) was the first black woman mayor of a major northeastern city. Perry had been an administrator in health care and government agencies. She won re-election in 1989.

Sources: Jet 77 (27 November 1989), pp. 15, 18; *Notable Black American Women,* pp. 837–40; *Who's Who Among Black Americans, 1992–93,* pp. 1110–11.

CARRIE SAXON PERRY,
MAYOR OF HARTFORD,
CONNECTICUT.

DELAWARE

1981—SMYRNA • George C. Wright, Jr., (1932–) was the first black mayor of Smyrna, and the first black mayor in the state. Wright was chief of staffing for civilian personnel at Dover Air Force Base. Over twenty-five percent of the small town's population is black.

Sources: Jet 60 (21 May 1981); *Jet* 60 (6 August 1981), p. 21; *Who's Who Among Black Americans, 1992–93,* p. 1573.

FLORIDA

1565—ST. AUGUSTINE • This city, the center of the Spanish Florida colony, is the first permanent dwelling place for blacks in the present territory of the United States. It had both slaves and free blacks from its beginning.

Source: Davis, *The History of Black Catholics in the United States,* p. 30.

C. 1700—ST. AUGUSTINE • Until 1763, escaped slaves formed the first settlement of free blacks, a *palenque* in Spanish, just north and east of St. Augustine, Florida.

Source: Davis, *The History of Black Catholics in the United States,* p. 30.

OPPOSITE PAGE:
MAYNARD JACKSON
MET WITH
PRESIDENT JIMMY
CARTER IN 1980 TO
DISCUSS FEDERAL AID
TO CITIES.

1883—EATONVILLE • Eatonville was the first all-black incorporated town.

Source: Garrett, *Famous First Facts About Negroes,* p. 191.

1958—MIAMI • Blanche Calloway (1902–73) was the first black woman to vote in the city. (*See also* **Arts & Entertainment: Music, 1930.**)

Sources: Encyclopedia of Black America, p. 212; *Notable Black American Women,* pp. 152–53.

1981—MIAMI • Howard Gary was the first black city manager of Miami. Gary was ousted in 1984.

Source: Jet 67 (12 November 1984), p. 6.

1985—MIAMI • In January 1985, Clarence Dickson was the first black police chief of Miami. He resigned in 1988, citing mistreatment by the city commissioners. At the time of his resignation, Dickson was fifty-four, and a twenty-nine-year veteran on the police force.

Source: Jet 75 (8 August 1988), p. 33.

GEORGIA

1947—SAVANNAH • In April, 1947, John White was the first black police officer in the state of Georgia. He retired from the force on November 1, 1984, at the age of fifty-nine, with the rank of sergeant.

Source: Jet 67 (8 October 1984), p. 5.

1964—ATLANTA • On February 23, 1964, Austin T. Walden became the first black judge in Georgia since Reconstruction, when he became a municipal judge in Atlanta.

Source: Hornsby, *Chronology of African-American History,* p. 117.

1970—SAVANNAH • Bowles C. Ford (1911–) was the first black elected to the Savannah city council. At the time of his election he was executive vice president and secretary of the Guaranty Life Insurance Company.

Sources: Ebony Success Library, vol. 1, p. 114; *Who's Who Among Black Americans, 1992–93,* p. 469.

1973—ATLANTA • On October 16, 1973, Maynard Holbrook Jackson (1938–) was elected the first black mayor of the city; he was inaugurated the following year. Jackson was admitted to the Georgia bar in 1965, and ran for the United States Senate against Herman Talmadge in 1968. He lost by a small margin. Not only was Jackson the first black mayor of a major Southeastern city, he was also the youngest person ever elected mayor of Atlanta.

Sources: Current Biography Yearbook, 1976, pp. 193–96; *Ebony Success Library,* vol. 1, p. 169; *Encyclopedia of Black America,* p. 467; Hornsby, *Chronology of African-American History,* p. 209; *Who's Who Among Black Americans, 1992–93,* p. 724.

1975—ATLANTA • Edward L. Baety became the first full-time Municipal Traffic Judge, and Mary Welcome became the first black Municipal Court Solicitor.

Source: Hornsby, *Chronology of African-American History,* p. 249.

1976—ATLANTA • Mary Hall was the first woman of any race on the Special Weapons and Tactics Team of the Atlanta Police Department. At the time, she was twenty-two-years-old and mother of a two-year-old son.

Source: Jet 50 (15 April 1976), pp. 28–29.

1981—AUGUSTA • Edward M. McIntyre was elected the first black mayor of Augusta on October 28, 1981. McIntyre was a graduate of Morehouse College (Atlanta, Georgia), and an insurance executive. He was forty-nine years old at the time of his election.

Sources: Jet 61 (19 November 1981), p. 9; *Jet* 62 (22 March 1982), p. 32; (30 August 1982), p. 30; *Jet* 81 (18 November 1991), p. 50.

ILLINOIS

1872—CHICAGO • Mayor Joseph Medill appointed the first black fire company of nine men. This is believed to be a first in Northern cities. The first black police officer was also appointed in this year; he served for three years.

Sources: Cantor, *Historic Landmarks of Black America,* p. 5; Gosnell, *Negro Politicians,* pp. 198, 247.

1891—CHICAGO • The first black appointed to Chicago's law department was Franklin A. Denison (1862–?), who served for six years under two mayors as assistant city prosecuting attorney. Neither Denison nor his law partner, S. A. T. Watkins, would receive appointments to the city government until 1911. In 1915 Denison would become commander of the Eighth Illinois Infantry, which he led in a Mexican expedition in 1916 and in France during the American intervention in World War I.

Sources: Barbeau, *Unknown Soldiers of World War I,* pp. 75–77; Gosnell, *Negro Politicians,* pp. 112, 198–99.

1915—CHICAGO • Oscar DePriest was the first black alderman in Chicago. (*See also* **Government—Federal Firsts: United States House of Representatives, 1929** and **1934.**)

Sources: Clayton, *The Negro Politician,* p. 45; *Dictionary of American Negro Biography,* pp. 173–74; Gosnell, *Negro Politicians,* pp. 170–72.

FANNIE BARRIER WILLIAMS

1924—CHICAGO • Fannie Barrier Williams (1855–1944), lecturer, civic leader, clubwoman, and journalist, was the first black—and the first woman—to serve on the Library Board of Chicago. She held the position for two years. In 1895, she had been the first black member of the Chicago Women's Club, a position she held for thirty years. In 1891, she also assisted Daniel Hale Williams in the founding of Provident Hospital and Training School for Nurses, one of the first black-controlled medical centers in the country.

Sources: Dictionary of American Negro Biography, pp. 656–57; *Notable Black American Women,* pp. 1251–54.

1946—CHICAGO • Doris Evans Saunders (1921–) was the first black reference librarian in the Chicago library system. A Chicago native, Saunders became librarian for the Johnson Publishing Company in 1949, and head of the company's book division in 1961, a position she held until 1966.

Sources: Ebony Success Library, vol. 1, p. 274; *Notable Black American Women,* pp. 977–78; *Who's Who Among Black Americans, 1992–93,* p. 1244.

1962—CHICAGO • Edith Spurlock Sampson (1901–79) was the first black woman elected judge to the municipal court. In 1927, Sampson was the first woman to receive a law degree from Loyola University. She was also the first black appointed to serve on the United States delegation to the United Nations in 1950.

Sources: Black Women in America, pp. 1002–3; *Encyclopedia of Black America,* p. 740; *Notable Black American Women,* pp. 969–72.

1968—CHICAGO • Winston E. Moore (1929–) was the first black to head a major jail, the Cook County Jail. Moore was born in New Orleans, and did extensive graduate work in psychology.

Sources: Ebony (July 1969), pp. 60–68.; *Ebony Success Library,* vol. 2, pp. 170–73; *Who's Who Among Black Americans, 1992–93,* p. 1018.

1971—CHICAGO • Joseph G. Bertrand (1931–) was the first black elected to a major city office when he was elected city treasurer in April, 1971. At the University of Notre Dame, where he took an A.B. in economics in 1954, Bertrand was the school's first black basketball All-American. He had been engaged in banking before his election to city treasurer.

Source: Ebony Success Library, vol. 1, p. 26.

Anna R. Langford (1910–) was the first black woman elected alderman in Chicago. A native of Springfield, Ohio, Langford was a prominent criminal lawyer.

Sources: Ebony 24 (March 1969), pp. 57–64; Ebony Success Library, vol. 1, p. 196; Who's Who Among Black Americans, 1992–93, pp. 842–43.

1971—EAST ST. LOUIS • On April 6, 1971, James E. Williams, Sr., became the first black mayor of East St. Louis.

Source: Hornsby, Chronology of African-American History, p. 168.

1978—ROCK ISLAND • Jim Davis was the first black mayor of this city. Davis was an elementary school principal in the city and served as acting mayor before his election to a four-year term.

Source: Jet 56 (10 May 1979), p. 14.

1983—CHICAGO • Fred Rice (1926–) was the first black police superintendent. His career with the Chicago Police Department began in 1955.

Sources: Jet 65 (12 September 1983), p. 8; Who's Who Among Black Americans, 1992–93, p. 1185.

Harold Washington (1922–87) was the first black mayor of Chicago. He was re-elected in 1987, but died of a massive heart attack on November 25. Washington had been a member of the House of Representatives since 1980 before he challenged the Democratic machine to win the mayoralty.

Sources: Bennett, Before the Mayflower, pp. 613, 618–19; Hornsby, Chronology of African-American History, p. 318–19, 354; Jet 64 (21 March 1983), p. 12; Who's Who Among Black Americans, 1988, p. 721.

1988—CHICAGO • Jacqueline Murray was the first black woman commander on the Chicago police force. She had served on the force for twenty-one years.

Source: Jet 75 (10 October 1988), p. 20.

1992—CAIRO • Harold E. Nelson was the first black chief of police of Cairo, Illinois. The sixty-year-old Nelson was a thirty-two-year veteran of the Illinois State Police, retiring in 1987.

Source: Jet 82, (17 August 1992), p. 38.

1993—EVANSTON • Lorraine H. Morton (c. 1919–) was the first black, and the first Democrat, elected mayor of this Illinois city. Evanston, an upscale suburb of Chicago, has a population of 73,000, of whom twenty-three percent are black. Morton was born in North Carolina, and taught in Evanston schools from 1953 to 1989.

Source: Ebony 48 (July 1993), pp. 39, 42.

KENTUCKY

1945—LOUISVILLE • Eugene S. Clayton was the first black elected to a seat on a city council since Reconstruction.

Source: Clayton, *The Negro Politician*, p. 119.

LOUISIANA

1970—NEW ORLEANS • Ernest Nathan Morial (1929–89) was the first black judge on the Juvenile Court of the city. In 1972, he was the first black elected to the Louisiana Fourth Circuit Court of Appeals. He was the first black mayor of New Orleans and served from 1977 until 1986. (*See* **Government—Local Heroes: Louisiana, 1977.**) In 1954, Morial became the first black graduate of the Louisiana State University School of Law, and in 1965 he was the first black lawyer to work in the United States Attorney's office in Louisiana. In 1967, he became the first black elected to the state legislature in this century, and the first ever elected as a Democrat.

Sources: Ebony Success Library, vol. 1, p. 228; *Encyclopedia of Black America,* p. 568; Hornsby, *Chronology of African-American History,* p. 418; *Jet* 77 (15 January 1990), pp. 12–13; *Who's Who Among Black Americans, 1992–93,* p. 1605.

ERNEST NATHAN
MORIAL LEFT A LEGACY
OF FIRSTS IN NEW
ORLEANS AND
LOUISIANA.

1975—NEW ORLEANS • Abraham Lincoln Davis (c. 1915–78) became the first black member of the New Orleans City Council in January 1975. Davis was one of the founders, and the first vice-president, of the Southern Christian Leadership Conference.

Source: Hornsby, *Chronology of African-American History,* p. 301.

1977—NEW ORLEANS • On November 12, 1977, Ernest Nathan Morial (1929–89) was elected the first black mayor of New Orleans. (*See also* **Government—Local Heroes: Louisiana, 1970.**)

Source: Hornsby, *Chronology of African-American History,* p. 418.

1983—BATON ROUGE • Freddie Pitcher was the first black municipal judge in Baton Rouge. A native of the city, Pitcher was thirty-eight years old.

Source: Jet 64 (30 May 1983), p. 6.

1985—NEW ORLEANS • Warren G. Woodfork, Sr., was the first black police superintendent of New Orleans. Woodfork had been named deputy police chief in 1981. In 1985, he was forty-seven years old, and a twenty-year veteran of the force.

Source: Jet 67 (21 January 1985), p. 30.

1993—NEW ORLEANS • Warren E. McDaniels became the first black fire department superintendent in the New Orleans Fire Department. McDaniels had served in the department for twenty-four years.

Source: Jet 84 (3 May 1993), p. 52.

MAINE

1988—AUGUSTA • William D. Burney, Jr., (1951–) was the first black mayor of Augusta, and the first in the state. Burney received his law degree from the University of Maine in 1977, and worked for the Maine State Housing Authority in Augusta beginning in 1981.

Sources: Negro Almanac, p. 428; *Who's Who Among Black Americans, 1992–93,* p. 200.

MARYLAND

1970—BALTIMORE • Milton B. Allen (1917–) was the first black elected state's attorney for the city of Baltimore. He was the first black to be public prosecutor in any major American city. A member of the Maryland bar since 1948, and a 1949 graduate of the University of Maryland Law School, Allen had tried more than seven thousand cases and built a very prosperous law practice before he ran for elected office. He became a judge of the Supreme Bench of Baltimore in 1976.

Sources: Ebony Success Library, vol. 2, pp. 2–5; *The Negro Almanac,* p. 1397; *Who's Who Among Black Americans, 1992–93,* p. 23.

1984—BALTIMORE • Bishop Robinson was the first black commissioner of the Baltimore police. Robinson was fifty-seven, and a thirty-two-year veteran of the force at the time of his appointment. Born in Baltimore,

Robinson holds a bachelor's degree in police administration from Coppin State College. He is a founder, and a past president, of the National Organization of Black Law Enforcement Executives.

Source: Jet 66 (9 July 1984), p. 37.

1986—BALTIMORE • On December 8, 1987, Kurt Lidell Schmoke (1936–) was the first elected black mayor of Baltimore. The first black mayor was Clarence Du Burns, president of the City Council; in January, 1987, Du Burns succeeded Mayor William Donald Schaeffer, who had been elected governor of the state. Du Burns had been a high school locker attendant until his election to the city council in 1971. Schmoke was a Rhodes scholar at Oxford after his graduation from Yale; he earned a law degree at Harvard in 1976. Schmoke worked as an assistant United States attorney and as state's attorney for Baltimore before his election.

Sources: Hornsby, *Chronology of African-American History,* p. 353; *Jet* 71 (26 January 1987), p. 10; *Jet* 71 (9 February 1987), p. 54; *Negro Almanac,* pp. 431–32; *Who's Who Among Black Americans, 1992–93,* p. 201 (Du Burns), p. 1247 (Schmoke).

MASSACHUSETTS

1969—BOSTON • Thomas I. Atkins (1939–) was the first black elected to the Boston City Council. Atkins holds a law degree from Harvard University (1969) and served in the governor's cabinet from 1971 to 1975. At present he is in private law practice.

Sources: Ebony Success Library, vol. 1, p. 14; *Who's Who Among Black Americans,* 1992–93, p. 14.

1986—BOSTON • Bruce C. Bolling was the first black president of the Boston City Council. The council had been in existence for 166 years, being established in 1820.

Sources: Jet 69 (27 January 1986), p. 4; *Who's Who Among Black Americans, 1992–93,* p. 126.

MICHIGAN

1945—YPSILANTI • Frank M. Seymour (1916–) was the first black official elected in Washtenaw County when he won a seat on the Ypsilanti city council. In 1965, he founded Seymour and Lundy Associates, a public relations firm in Detroit.

Source: Ebony Success Library, vol. 1, p. 278.

1967—FLINT • Floyd McCree was elected the first black mayor of Flint.

Source: Hornsby, *Chronology of African-American History,* p. 131.

1973—DETROIT • Coleman Young (1918–) was elected the first black mayor of Detroit on November 6, 1973. Young and Thomas Bradley, elected at the same time, were the first black mayors of cities with populations over one million. In 1968, Young was the first black to serve on the Democratic National Committee.

Sources: Encyclopedia of Black America, p. 873; *Negro Almanac,* pp. 434–35; Hornsby, *Chronology of African-American History,* p. 211; *Who's Who Among Black Americans, 1992–93,* p. 1584.

1981—DETROIT • Billie Ann Willis was the first woman of any race to become a police precinct commander in Detroit. A graduate of West Virginia State College, Willis had served on the force for twenty-three years.

Sources: Jet 60 (21 May 1981), p. 13; *Jet* 61 (17 September 1981), p. 21.

COLEMAN YOUNG SPENT TWENTY YEARS IN OFFICE BEFORE RETIRING AFTER FIVE TERMS.

MINNESOTA

1992—ST. PAUL • William K. Finney was the first black police chief in St. Paul, Minnesota. The forty-three-year-old Finney was a native of St. Paul, and a twenty-one-year veteran on the force.

Source: Jet 82 (3 August 1992), p. 56.

MISSISSIPPI

1870—NATCHEZ • In December, 1870, Robert H. Wood was elected mayor; he may be the first black mayor in the United States.

Sources: Bennett, *Before the Mayflower,* pp. 489, 629; *Ebony* (March 1982), p. 130.

1887—MOUND BAYOU • Sam Bass was the first black mayor of Mound Bayou, an all-black town incorporated in 1887.

Source: Alford, *Famous First Blacks,* pp. 47, 71.

1964—LAUREL • Simon Shanks, Sr., (?–1982) was the first black patrolman in the police department. Shanks eventually became a captain.

Source: Jet 62 (14 June 1982), p. 9.

1969—FAYETTE • On May 13, 1969, James Charles Evers (1922–) was elected the first black mayor of a racially mixed Mississippi town. Fayette is the county seat of Jefferson County and has a population of about 2,000. In June 1971, he became the first black in this century to seek the governor's office.

Sources: Ebony Success Library, vol. 1, p. 109; *Encyclopedia of Black America,* p. 378; Hornsby, *Chronology of African-American History,* pp. 137, 176, 191, 262; *Negro Almanac,* p. 51; *Who's Who Among Black Americans, 1992–93,* p. 443.

JAMES CHARLES EVERS HAS ALSO LENT HIS SUPPORT TO THE POOR AND ELDERLY IN MISSISSIPPI.

1976—MEYERSVILLE • Unita Blackwell was the first black woman mayor in Mississippi. She was a leading figure in the civil rights struggle, and in the organization of the Mississippi Freedom Democratic Party in 1964. She became the first female president of the National Conference of Black Mayors in 1990. Blackwell was awarded a MacArthur Fellowship in 1992.

Sources: Jet 82 (6 July 1992), pp. 34–35; Lanker, *I Dream a World*, p. 50; (Nashville) *Tennessean*, (16 June 1992).

1986—GREENVILLE • Malcolm Wynn (1940–) was the first black chief of police, a position he held until his retirement from police work in 1989. In 1977, Wynn had been the first black captain on the force.

Sources: Who's Who Among Black Americans, 1992–93, pp. 1578–79.

1988—NATCHEZ • Eddie Jones was the first black chief of the police department of Natchez. Jones was forty-five years old, and had served on the police force for nineteen years.

Source: Jet 75 (17 October 1988), p. 28.

1989—TCHULA • Jessie Banks was the first black mayor of Tchula. Now sixty-seven years old, Banks had been elected the first black alderman of the city in 1977.

Source: Jet 76 (7 August 1989), p. 8.

MISSOURI

1982—PAGEDALE • As mayor of Pagedale, Mary Hall was head of the reputed first all-black, and all-woman, city administration.

Source: Jet 82 (24 May 1982), p. 13.

1991—KANSAS CITY • Emanuel Cleaver II (1944–) was the first black mayor of Kansas City, Missouri. A native of Waxahachie, Texas, Cleaver was pastor of St. James United Methodist Church at the time of his election.

Sources: Jet 81 (18 November 1991), p. 66; *Heritage and Hope*, p. 284; *Who's Who Among Black Americans, 1992–93*, p. 274.

1993—ST. LOUIS • Freeman Bosley, Jr. (1954–) was elected the first black mayor of St. Louis. An attorney with a degree from St. Louis University (1979), Bosley became clerk of the circuit court in 1983. His father, Freeman Bosley, Sr., a longtime city alderman, had tried to become mayor twice. The final tally gave Bosley, Jr., 66.55 percent of the votes.

Sources: Ebony 48 (July 1993), pp. 38, 40; *Jet* 83 (26 April 1993), p. 8; *Who's Who Among Black Americans, 1992–93*, p. 132.

NEW JERSEY

1966—PATERSON • William H. Hicks (1925–) was the first black alderman in Paterson. Hicks was a very successful car salesman. In 1971, he would be elected to the New Jersey legislature.

Sources: Ebony Success Library, vol. 1, p. 151; *Who's Who Among Black Americans, 1992–93,* p. 650.

1970—NEWARK • On June 16, 1970, Kenneth Allen Gibson (1932–) was elected the first black mayor of a major Eastern city, becoming mayor on July 1. A 1963 graduate of the Newark College of Engineering, he worked on Urban Renewal projects of the Newark Housing Authority before his election as mayor. He was also the first black president of the United States Conference of Mayors, in July 1976.

Sources: Current Biography Yearbook, 1971, pp. 149–52; *Ebony Success Library,* vol. 1, p. 125; *Encyclopedia of Black America,* p. 404; Hornsby, *Chronology of African-American History,* p. 145; *Who's Who Among Black Americans, 1992–93,* p. 518.

1971—PRINCETON • On January 1, 1971, James A. Floyd was elected the first black mayor of Princeton Township by the five-member township committee. In December, 1971, Frederick M. Porter became the first black police chief.

Sources: Hornsby, *Chronology of African-American History,* p. 158; *Negro Almanac,* p. 61.

1972—ENGLEWOOD • Walter Scott Taylor (1916–) was the first black mayor of Englewood. This Mississippi-born United Methodist minister held the office until 1975.

Sources: Jet 66 (30 July 1984), p. 33; *Who's Who Among Black Americans, 1992–93,* p. 1374.

1984—ATLANTIC CITY • James Leroy Usry (1922–) was the first black mayor of Atlantic City. The former member of the Harlem Globetrotters became an educator before entering politics. He was mayor until 1990.

Sources: Jet 66 (2 April 1984), p. 30; *Jet* 70 (30 June 1986), p. 4; *Jet* 78 (2 July 1990), p. 6; *Who's Who Among Black Americans, 1992–93,* p. 1427.

NEW YORK

1626—NEW YORK CITY • There were eleven blacks in New Amsterdam, now New York City, in the year of its founding, 1626. Four are the first named blacks there: Paul d'Angola, Simon Congo, Anthony Portuguese, and John Franciso.

Source: Johnson, *Black Manhattan,* p. 4.

1935—NEW YORK CITY • Eunice Hunton Carter (1900–70) was the first black woman assistant district attorney. She held the post for ten years, and she served as the only black on Thomas E. Dewey's staff in his investigation of the rackets.

Sources: Jet 84 (19 July 1993), p. 39; Lerner, Black Women in White America, p. 322; Notable Black American Women, pp. 165–66.

**JANE M.
BOLIN**

1939—NEW YORK CITY • Jane M. Bolin (1908–) became the first black woman judge in the United States when she was appointed to the Domestic Relations Court of New York City. Bolin was born in Poughkeepsie, New York. Her father, Gaius C. Bolin, had been the first black graduate of Williams College in 1889. Jane Bolin retired on January 1, 1979, after forty years of service on the bench.

Sources: Encyclopedia of Black America, p. 185; Negro Almanac, p. 1426; Notable Black American Women, pp. 94–95.

1941—NEW YORK CITY • Adam Clayton Powell, Jr., was the first black to serve as a member of the City Council in 1941. (*See also* **Government— Federal Firsts: United States House of Representatives, 1944.**)

Sources: Cantor, Historic Landmarks of Black America, p. 93; Hamilton, Adam Clayton Powell, Jr., p. 116.

1943—BUFFALO • Robert B. Howard, Jr. (1916–) was the first black firefighter in Buffalo. A native of Barnesville, Georgia, Howard became commissioner of the department in 1966.

Sources: Ebony Success Library, vol. 1, p. 160; Who's Who Among Black Americans, 1992–93, p. 690.

1953—NEW YORK CITY • On December 31, 1953, Hulan Jack (1907–) became the first black borough president of Manhattan. A native of St. Lucia, in the British West Indies, Jack was the son of a bishop of the African Orthodox Church. He came to New York City as a very young man, and soon was active in politics. He had served in the state assembly for thirteen years when he became head of Manhattan. He was removed from office in 1959 during his second term.

Sources: Clayton, *The Negro Politician*, pp. 57–61; Hornsby, *Chronology of African-American History*, p. 99; *Encyclopedia of Black America*, p. 465; *Negro Almanac*, p. 28.

HULAN JACK

1954—NEW YORK CITY • Anna Arnold Hedgeman (1899–1990) was the first black woman member of the cabinet of a mayor, Robert F. Wagner. In 1922, she was the first African-American graduate of Hamline University (St. Paul, Minnesota). After working at Rust College in Mississippi, she went to work for the Young Women's Christian Association (YWCA) in Springfield, Ohio, (1924) eventually moving to the Harlem branch in New York City. She worked for local and federal governments, and for religious and civic organizations throughout her life. She was a major organizer of the March on Washington in 1963.

Sources: *Encyclopedia of Black America*, p. 435; *Negro Almanac*, pp. 1381–82; *Notable Black American Women*, pp. 483–89.

ANNA ARNOLD HEDGEMAN

1966—NEW YORK CITY • On January 1, 1966, Robert O. Lowery (1916–) was the first black fire commissioner of a major city. Lowery had joined the department as a fireman in 1941.

Sources: *Ebony Success Library*, vol. 2, pp. 154–57; *Negro Almanac*, p. 1412; *Who's Who Among Black Americans, 1992–93*, p. 893.

Constance Baker Motley (1921–) was the first black woman president of the Borough of Manhattan. (*See also* **Government—County & State Pioneers: New York, 1964; Government—Federal Firsts: Judiciary, 1966.**)

Sources: *Negro Almanac*, pp. 344–45; *Ebony Success Library*, vol. 2, pp. 174–77; *Encyclopedia of Black America*, p. 582; *Notable Black American Women*, pp. 779–82; *Who's Who Among Black Americans, 1992–93*, p. 1035.

1972—NEW YORK CITY • Benjamin J. Malcolm (1920–) was the first black appointed commissioner of corrections.

Source: Encyclopedia of Black America, p. 544.

1974—NEW YORK CITY • Paul Gibson (1927–) was the first black deputy mayor of New York. Gibson was in charge of city planning.

Sources: Black Enterprise 2 (September 1971), pp. 15–18; Encyclopedia of Black America, p. 404; Who's Who Among Black Americans, 1992–93, p. 518.

1977—NEW YORK CITY • Lucille Mason Rose (1920?–87) was the first black woman named deputy mayor of the city. Her first efforts were devoted to providing jobs for teenagers. Rose held a degree in economics from Brooklyn College (1963), and had been named New York City Commissioner of Employment in 1972.

Sources: Jet 52 (24 March 1977), p. 6; Jet 72 (7 September 1987), p. 52; The Negro Almanac, pp. 1390–91.

1982—NEW YORK CITY • JoAnn M. Jacobs was the first black woman firefighter in the city. At the time, Jacobs was thirty-one years old, and had been a physical education instructor.

Source: Jet 63 (13 December 1982), p. 44.

1984—NEW YORK CITY • Benjamin Ward (1926–) was the first black police commissioner of New York City. He served until 1989, when he resigned for health reasons. He had joined the department in 1951.

Sources: Jet 77 (16 October 1989), p. 38; Who's Who Among Black Americans, 1992–93, p. 1455.

1985—MOUNT VERNON • As mayor of Mount Vernon, Ronald A. Blackwood (1926–) was the first black elected mayor in the state of New York. A native of Kingston, Jamaica, Blackwood had lived in the city for thirty years. He was chosen in a special election to replace a mayor who died in office.

Sources: Jet 67 (4 March 1985), p. 6; Who's Who Among Black Americans, 1992–93, p. 116.

DAVID DINKINS

1989—NEW YORK CITY • On November 7, 1989, David Dinkins (1927–) was elected the first black mayor of New York; he took office in 1990. Dinkins took his law degree at Brooklyn Law School in 1956. From that year he was active in Democratic Party politics, and was elected to the New York State Assembly in 1966. He held office as president of the city Board of Elections (1972–73), city clerk (1975–85), and Manhattan borough president (1986–90) before he became mayor.

Sources: Hornsby, Chronology of African-American History, pp. 411–12; Jet 79 (22 January 1990), p. 4; Jet 81 (18 November 1991), p. 62; Who's Who Among Black Americans, 1992–93, p. 382.

Janice White was first woman warden of the Manhattan House of Corrections, often called the Tombs, and at the time the only woman warden in the New York penal system. Born in Philadelphia, the forty-nine-year-old White had worked for the state corrections department for some twenty years.

Source: Jet 76 (17 April 1989), pp. 28–31.

HARVEY BERNARD GANTT IS PICTURED AT THE U.S. CONFERENCE OF MAYORS IN 1987.

NORTH CAROLINA

1966—FAIRMONT • Joy Joseph Johnson (1922–) was the first black elected to the town board. The pastor of the First Baptist Church, Johnson would become the second black elected to the state House, since Reconstruction, in 1970. In 1989, he became the first black mayor of Fairmont.

Sources: Ebony Success Library, vol. 1, p. 179; *Who's Who Among Black Americans, 1992–93,* p. 762.

1969—CHAPEL HILL • Howard N. Lee (1934–) was elected mayor of Chapel Hill, becoming the first black elected mayor in a predominantly white Southern city. Lee would hold this office until 1975.

Sources: Ebony Success Library, vol. 1, p. 199; *Encyclopedia of Black America,* p. 503; *Negro Almanac,* p. 51; *Who's Who Among Black Americans, 1992–93,* p. 857.

1983—CHARLOTTE • Harvey Bernard Gantt (1943–) was the first black elected mayor of Charlotte. This architect holds a degree from Clemson in South Carolina (1965), in which he was the first black to enroll, and an M.A. from the Massachusetts Institute of Technology (1970). Gantt had served as mayor pro tempore of Charlotte from 1981 to 1983. On June 6, 1990, he was the first black to win the Democratic nomination for United States Senator.

Sources: Hornsby, Chronology of African-American History, p. 431; *Jet* 65 (20 February 1984), p. 40; *Who's Who Among Black Americans, 1992–93,* p. 502.

OHIO

1942—CLEVELAND • Perry B. Jackson (1896–) was the first black judge in Ohio when he was appointed to the Municipal Court of Cleveland. In 1960, Jackson became judge in the Court of Common Pleas of Cuyahoga County, a position from which he retired in 1972.

Sources: Ebony (April 1947), p. 17; *Ebony* (September 1950), pp. 45–49; *Ebony Success Library,* vol. 1, p. 170; *Encyclopedia of Black America,* p. 468.

1949—CLEVELAND • Jean Murrell Capers (1913–) was the first black woman elected to the city council.

Sources: Clayton, The Negro Politician, pp. 137–38; *Ebony* (September 1950), pp. 45–49; *Ebony* (November 1950), pp. 48–49; *Ebony* (August 1956), p. 82; *Ebony* (August 1966), p. 97.

1966—SPRINGFIELD • On January 3, 1966, Robert Clayton Henry (1923–) was the first black mayor of an integrated Ohio city.

Sources: Alford, Famous First Blacks, p. 46; *Jet* 61 (7 January 1982), p. 24; *Who's Who Among Black Americans, 1992–93,* p. 643.

1967—CLEVELAND • On November 13, 1967, Carl Stokes (1927–) was the first black elected mayor of a major city. Stokes and Richard G. Hatcher

(1933–) were elected on the same day, but Hatcher was not sworn in until January 1, 1968, when he became the first black mayor of Gary, Indiana.

Sources: Ebony Success Library, vol. 1, p. 145 (Hatcher); p. 293 (Stokes); Encyclopedia of Black America, pp. 422–23 (Hatcher); p. 810 (Stokes); Who's Who Among Black Americans, 1992–93, p. 622 (Hatcher) p. 1343 (Stokes).

1969—CLEVELAND • Lillian W. Burke (1917–) was the first black woman elected to the Ohio bench. She was a judge in the municipal court. A native of Thomaston, Georgia, Burke took her law degree at the Cleveland Marshall Law School in 1951.

CARL STOKES, GRANDSON OF A SLAVE, WON THE MAYORAL ELECTION OVER SETH TAFT, GRANDSON OF PRESIDENT WILLIAM H. TAFT.

Sources: Ebony Success Library, vol. 1, p. 51; Encyclopedia of Black America, p. 199; Who's Who Among Black Americans, 1992–93, p. 198.

1972—CINCINNATI • Theodore Moody Berry (1905–) was the first black mayor of the city. He was chosen by the city council, rather than by popular election. He held the office until 1975. Berry had been the first black elected to the city council in 1949. While he served as acting mayor in December 1955, he was long denied the title he had earned through his competence and vote-getting abilities.

Sources: Clayton, The Negro Politician, pp. 62–66; Ebony Success Library, vol. 1, p. 26; Encyclopedia of Black America, p. 173; Who's Who Among Black Americans, 1992–93, p. 105.

1982—AKRON • Janet Purnell was the first black, and the first woman, executive director of the Metropolitan Housing Authority. Purnell was an elementary school principal in the city at the time of her appointment.

Source: Jet 63 (15 November 1982), p. 6.

1982—CLEVELAND • George James was the first black director of the Cuyahoga Metropolitan Housing Authority. James had been director of the Los Angeles County Housing Authority.

Source: Jet 63 (20 December 1982), p. 21.

As deputy police chief, Lloyd Patterson was the first black to hold an executive position in the Cleveland police department.

Source: Who's Who Among Black Americans, 1992–93, p. 1096.

1992—CINCINNATI • Dwight Tillery was the first black popularly elected mayor of Cincinnati. The two blacks who held the office previously had been selected by the City Council.

Source: Ebony (March 1992), pp. 107, 110.

OKLAHOMA

1973—TAFT • On April 16, 1973, Lelia Smith Foley (1942–)was elected the first black woman mayor in the United States when she became mayor of this town of about 500. She was mayor of this town for thirteen years.

Sources: Jet 60 (23 April 1981), pp. 61–62; Lee, Interesting People, p. 93; Negro Almanac, p. 429.

PENNSYLVANIA

FORMER PHILADELPHIA
MAYOR W. WILSON
GOODE.

1984—PHILADELPHIA • On January 2, 1984, W. Wilson Goode (1938–) became the first black mayor of Philadelphia. He won a second term in 1987. His term of service was marked by controversy over the fire bombing of a house occupied by a cult group the police were trying to remove. In 1988, a two-year investigation cleared him of criminal responsibility.

Sources: Hornsby, *Chronology of African-American History,* p. 326; *The Negro Almanac,* pp. 86, 88, 430; *Who's Who Among Black Americans, 1992–93,* p. 535.

1986—PITTSBURGH • William "Mugsy" Moore was the first black police chief in Pittsburgh. The sixty-year-old Moore had joined the force in 1951, become a detective in 1960, and been promoted to inspector in 1969. He resigned in 1987, calling his appointment "window dressing" and saying, "this city will have to find someone else to play the role of token...."

Sources: Jet 70 (12 May 1986), p. 6; *Jet* 72 (1 June 1987), p. 8.

1988—PHILADELPHIA • Willie L. Williams was the first black commissioner of police in Philadelphia. Williams was forty-four years old, and a twenty-four-year veteran of the police force. In 1992, Williams became the first black chief of police in Los Angeles, California.

Sources: Ebony 48 (December 1992), pp. 71–74, 132; *Jet* 74 (20 June 1988), p. 8; (Nashville) *Tennessean,* (1 July 1992).

1989—PHILADELPHIA • Gloria Twine Chisum, psychologist and library administrator, was the first black, and first woman, chair of the Board of Trustees of The Free Library of Philadelphia.

Sources: Jet 77 (5 February 1990), p. 20; *Who's Who Among Black Americans, 1992–93,* p. 261.

RHODE ISLAND

1981—NEWPORT • Paul Laurence Gaines (1932–) was the first black mayor of the city. In 1977, he had also been the first black member of the City Council. The mayor of Newport is designated by the council. Gaines was a forty-eight-year-old administrator at Bridgewater State College in Massachusetts.

Sources: Jet 61 (15 October 1981), p. 16; *Who's Who Among Black Americans, 1992–93,* p. 499

SOUTH CAROLINA

1982—CHARLESTON • Reuben M. Greenberg (1943–) became the first black chief of police in Charleston on March 17, 1982; this also made him the first black police chief in South Carolina in modern times.

Sources: Hornsby, *Chronology of African-American History,* p. 310; *Who's Who Among Black Americans, 1992–93,* p. 558.

TENNESSEE

1982—NASHVILLE • A. A. Birch, Jr., was the first black presiding judge of Nashville-Davidson County's twelve courts.

Source: Jet 62 (12 April 1982), p. 21.

1992—MEMPHIS • Willie W. Herenton (1940–) was elected the first black mayor of Memphis; he took office in 1992. Herenton had begun his teaching career in the elementary schools of the Memphis City School System, and had become the first black superintendent of the system in 1979.

Sources: Ebony 47 (March 1992), pp. 106, 108; *State of Black America 1992,* pp. 383–84; *Who's Who Among Black Americans, 1992–93,* p. 644.

TEXAS

1982—HOUSTON • Lee P. Brown (1937–) became Houston's first black chief of police on March 23, 1982. A native of Oklahoma, Brown holds a Ph.D. in criminology from the University of California at Berkeley (1970). His career included both university teaching and law enforcement, beginning as sheriff of Multnomah County, Oregon. In 1990, he became police commissioner of New York City, a position from which he soon resigned due to illness in the family. On April 28, 1993, President Clinton announced Brown's nomination as director of the Office of National Drug Policy, a position to which Clinton gave cabinet rank.

Sources: Hornsby, *Chronology of African-American History,* p. 311; *Jet* 84 (19 July 1993), p. 10; (Nashville) *Tennessean* (29 April 1993); *US News and World Report* 109 (31 December 1990), p.73; *Who's Who Among Black Americans, 1992–93,* p. 175.

1986—DALLAS • Richard Knight, Jr., (1945–) was the first black city manager of Dallas. Knight had served as assistant city manager from 1982 to 1986, and held the position of city manager until 1990. (*See also* **Organizations: Business and Professional Organizations, 1988.)**

Sources: Jet 75 (17 October 1988), p. 40; *Jet* 78 (30 April 1990), p. 6; *Who's Who Among Black Americans, 1992–93,* p. 831.

1990—AUSTIN • Iris J. Jones became the first black woman city attorney of Austin. Jones is a graduate of the Thurgood Marshall School of Law at Texas Southern University, and had been serving as acting city attorney.

Source: Jet 78 (2 July 1990), p. 20.

VIRGINIA

1948—RICHMOND • On June 9, 1948, Oliver W. Hill (1907–) was the first black elected to the city council in this century.

Sources: Encyclopedia of Black America, p. 438; Hornsby, *Chronology of African-American History,* p. 96; *Who's Who Among Black Americans, 1992–93,* p. 658.

1977—RICHMOND • On March 8, 1977, Henry L. Marsh III (1933–) was the first black mayor of Richmond, Virginia.

Source: Bennett, *Before the Mayflower,* pp. 604, 630.

1986—NEWPORT NEWS • Jessie M. Rattley (1929–) was the first black and first woman mayor of Newport News. Rattley had served on the city council for sixteen years.

Sources: Jet 70 (28 July 1986), p. 33; *Who's Who Among Black Americans, 1992–93,* p. 1166.

WASHINGTON

1871—CENTRALIA • George Washington (1817–1905) was the first black to found a large integrated city in the United States. Born in Virginia, his white mother gave him up for adoption to a white family, which moved to the frontier. In 1850 he moved to the Oregon Territory, and homesteaded in present-day Washington. He established Centralia in 1872, when the Northern Pacific Railroad crossed his land. A city park bears his name.

Sources: Cantor, *Historic Landmarks of Black America,* p. 336; *Dictionary of American Negro Biography,* p. 638; Katz, *The Black West,* pp. 72–73.

1981—SPOKANE • James Chase was the first black mayor of this western city of 172,000, of which 1.6 percent were black. Chase had spent forty years as the manager of an auto body shop, and held the position of mayor until 1985.

Sources: Jet 61 (26 November 1981), p. 8; *Who's Who Among Black Americans, 1992–93,* p. 255.

1988—OLYMPIA • Cora Pinson was the first black city council member, and the first black woman elected to any city post in the state. A native of Memphis and a graduate of Hammond Business College, Indiana, the fifty-three-year-old Pinson had moved to the city from Chicago thirteen years earlier, and had served two terms as commissioner of the Housing Authority of Thurston County.

Source: Jet 73 (25 January 1988), pp. 12–14.

1989—SEATTLE • Norman Blann Rice (1943–) was the first black elected mayor of Seattle. A native of Denver, Colorado, he earned a B.A. and an M.A. degree from the University of Washington (1972, 1974). He was manager of corporate contributions and social policy coordinator for Ranier National Bank at the time of his election to the City Council in 1978.

Sources: Fortune 126 (2 November 1992), cover and p. 43; *Jet* 77 (22 January 1990), p. 4; *Who's Who Among Black Americans, 1992–93,* p. 1185.

WASHINGTON, D.C.

1902 • Robert H. Terrell (1857–1925) was the first black justice of the peace, as judges of the municipal court were then called, which made him the first federal judge at any level. He held this position until his death. An 1884 *magna cum laude* graduate of Harvard, Terrell took his law degree at Howard University Law School in Washington, D.C., in 1889.

Sources: Dictionary of American Negro Biography, pp. 585–86; *Encyclopedia of Black America,* p. 815; *Negro Almanac,* p. 338.

1967 • In September, 1967, Walter E. Washington (1915–) was appointed mayor, the first for the city. In 1974, Washington became the first elected mayor and went on to serve a second term.

Sources: Ebony Success Library, vol. 2, pp. 272–75; *Encyclopedia of Black America,* pp. 846–47; Hornsby, *Chronology of African-American History,* p. 131; *Who's Who Among Black Americans, 1992–93,* p. 1466.

1975 • As the first black woman appointed judge of the District of Columbia Appellate Court, Julia P. Cooper (1921–) became the highest ranking woman in the Federal courts.

Sources: Ebony 12 (February 1957), p. 5; *Negro Almanac,* p. 71.

1976 • Theodore Roosevelt Newman, Jr., (1934–) was named the chief judge of the Washington Court of Appeals; he was the first black in the United States to head a court at this level. At the time of his appointment, there were fewer than a dozen black judges on appeals courts in the various states.

Sources: Jet 51 (9 December 1976), p. 20; *Who's Who Among Black Americans, 1992–93,* p. 1055.

1978 • Burtell Jefferson was the first black chief of police in the District of Columbia. A native Washingtonian, Jefferson was fifty-two years old, and a twenty-year veteran on the force. He was named second-in-command of the department in 1974 by Mayor Walter Washington.

Source: Jet 53 (19 January 1978), p. 5.

1985 • Joyce F. Leland (1941–) was the first woman deputy police chief in the city. A graduate of Howard University, Leland had been on the force for twenty years.

Sources: Jet 67 (28 January 1985), p. 24; *Who's Who Among Black Americans, 1992–93,* p. 863.

1990 • On November 6, 1990, Sharon Pratt Dixon (now Kelly) (1944–) was elected the first black woman mayor of Washington, a first for a woman of any race. In 1966, she took a law degree at Howard University Law School. In 1976, she became the first black, and the first woman, vice-president for consumer affairs of Potomac Electric Power Company.

Sources: Marketing (14 April 1992), p. 47; *Notable Black American Women,* pp. 278–80; *Who's Who Among Black Americans, 1992–93,* p. 385.

SHARON PRATT DIXON (KELLY) (1944–)

1992 • Zinora M. Mitchell (1957–) and Michael L. Rankin were the first husband and wife to serve together on the Superior Court of the District of Columbia. Rankin was appointed in 1985, and Mitchell in 1990. A graduate of Spelman, Mitchell took her law degree at the University of Georgetown Law School. Rankin took his law degree at Howard University School of Law.

Sources: Jet 77 (5 February 1990), p. 32; *Who's Who Among Black Americans, 1992–93,* p. 1004 (Mitchell), p. 1165 (Rankin).

OPPOSITE PAGE:
WALTER E.
WASHINGTON, THE
FIRST MAYOR OF
WASHINGTON, D.C.

JOURNALISM: FIRSTS IN THE FOURTH ESTATE

NEWSPAPERS

1817 • The first abolitionist newspaper was the *Philanthropist,* published and edited by Charles Osborn on August 29, 1817, in Mount Pleasant, Ohio.
Source: Kane, *Famous First Facts,* p. 426.

1827 • *Freedom's Journal,* which advocated the abolition of slavery and attacked anti-black sentiment, appeared on March 30, 1827, in New York. It was the first black newspaper. This newspaper sought to put the black cause before the American public. It was owned and edited by Presbyterian minister Samuel E[li] Cornish (1795–1858) and abolitionist and colonizationist John Brown Russworm (1799–1851). For a listing of other anti-slavey newspapers published by blacks before the Civil War see the table on pg. 221.

1843 • The *Mystery,* the first black newspaper west of the Alleghenies (Pittsburgh), was published by Martin Robinson Delany (1812–85). The four-page weekly was devoted to news of the antislavery movement. In connection with this paper, Delany was the first black editor to be tried for libel and found guilty; the fine was eventually remitted. The paper was suspended after four years.
Sources: Dictionary of American Negro Biography, p. 170; Penn, *The Afro-American Press,* pp. 56–57.

1855 • Mifflin Wistar Gibbs (1823–1915) was owner and editor of the *Mirror of the Times,* an abolitionist newspaper, and California's first black newspaper. (*See also* **Government—Local Heroes: Arkansas, 1873—Little Rock.**)
Sources: Dictionary of American Negro Biography, pp. 258–59; *Encyclopedia of Black America,* p. 403; Penn, *The Afro-American Press,* p. 77.

CALIFORNIA NEWSPAPER-MAN MIFFLIN W. GIBBS.

**THOMAS
MORRIS
CHESTER**

1864 • Thomas Morris Chester (1834–92), was the first and only black correspondent for a major daily, the *Philadelphia Press,* during the Civil War. His dispatches cover the period from August 1864 through June 1865. He was previously editor of the *Star of Liberia.* For eight months he reported on black troop activity around Petersburg (Florida) and the Confederate capital, both before and after Richmond, Virginia, was taken. Chester was born in Harrisburg, Pennsylvania, to abolitionist parents. He studied first at Alexander High School in Monrovia, Liberia, then at the Thetford Academy in Vermont. He read law under a Liberian lawyer, then spent three years at Middle Temple in London, England. In April 1870, he became the first black American barrister admitted to practice before English courts.

Sources: Simmons, *Men of Mark,* pp. 671–76; Spradling, *In Black and White,* vol. 1, p. 182; Blackett, *Thomas Morris Chester.*

La Tribune de la Nouvelle Orléans was the first black daily published in the United States. It began on October 4, 1864.

Source: Dictionary of American Negro Biography, p. 534.

1878 • The *Conservator* was the first black newspaper published in Chicago. Richard De Baptiste assumed editorial control later in 1878.

Source: Penn, *The Afro-American Press,* p. 262.

William Lewis Eagleson (1835–99) published the first black newspaper in Kansas in January, 1878.

Source: Dictionary of American Negro Biography, p. 207.

1885 • The *Philadelphia Tribune,* the oldest continually published non-church newspaper, was first published.

1888 • Edward Elder Cooper (1859–), journalist and editor, established the *Freeman,* at Indianapolis, Indiana. This was the first black newspaper to make a feature of portraits and cartoons. First published July 14, 1888, the newspaper reached national prominence and made a fortune for its owner.

Sources: Alexander's Magazine 6 (15 August 1908), editorial; Penn, *The Afro-American Press,* pp. 334–39.

1905 • Robert Abbott Sengstacke [Robert Sengstake Abbott] (1870–1940) first published the *Chicago Defender* on May 6, 1905, establishing what he called "The World's Greatest Weekly." The *Defender* reached national prominence during the great black migration from the South during World War I, and by his death, he had made it into the most widely circulated black weekly. Abbott was born in St. Simon's Island, Georgia, of former

BLACK ANTI-SLAVERY NEWSPAPERS

TITLE	CITY	ESTABLISHED
Freedom's Journal	New York, New York	March 30, 1827
Rights of All	New York, New York	March 28, 1828
The *Weekly Advocate*	New York, New York	January 1837
Colored American (formerly The *Weekly Advocate*)	New York, New York	March 4, 1837
The *Elevator*	Albany, New York	1842
The *National Watchman*	Troy, New York	1842
The *Clarion*		1842
The *People's Press*	New York, New York	1843
The *Mystery*	Pittsburgh, Pennsylvania	1843
The *Genius of Freedom*		1845
The *Ram's Horn*	New York, New York	January 1, 1847
The *North Star*	Rochester, New York	November 1, 1847
The *Moral Reform Magazine*	Philadelphia, Pennsylvania	1847
The *Impartial Citizen*	Syracuse, New York	1848
The *Christian Herald*	Philadelphia, Pennsylvania	1848
The *Colored Man's Journal*	New York, New York	1851
The *Alienated American*	Cleveland, Ohio	1852
The *Christian Recorder* (formerly The *Christian Herald*)	Philadelphia, Pennsylvania	1852
The *Mirror of the Times*	San Francisco, California	1855
The *Herald of Freedom*	Ohio	1855
The *Anglo African*	New York, New York	July 23, 1859

Sources: *Dictionary of American Negro Biography*, pp. 134–35, 538–39; *Negro Yearbook, 1913*, p. 75; Penn, *The Afro-American Press*.

slave parents. He studied at Claflin University (Orangeburg, South Carolina), Hampton Institute (Hampton, Virginia), and Kent College of Law in Chicago.

Sources: *Dictionary of American Negro Biography*, pp. 1–2; Hornsby, *Milestones in 20th-Century African-American History*, pp. 5–6.

1909 • The *New York Amsterdam News* was first published by James H. Anderson on December 4, 1909. The four-page newspaper sold for a penny a copy. At the peak of its popularity—at the time of and just following the Second World War—the paper claimed a circulation of more than a hundred thousand copies; the paper began to decline in 1971.

Sources: *Encyclopedia of Black America*, p. 647; *Jet* 67 (10 December 1984), p. 37; *Split Image*, p. 362.

THE OLDEST CONTINUALLY PUBLISHED NEWSPAPERS

NAME	ESTABLISHED
Christian Recorder (African Methodist Episcopal)	1846
Star of Zion (AME Zion)	1867
American Baptist	1880
Philadelphia Tribune	1885
Houston Informer	1892
Baltimore Afro-American	1892
Des Moines Bystander	1894
Indianapolis Recorder	1895

Sources: *Encyclopedia of Black America*, p. 642; *Gale Directory of Publication and Broadcast Media*, 1993.

1912 • Carlotta Bass (1880–1969) is thought to be the first woman to own and publish a newspaper in this country. She bought the *California Eagle* in 1912, and ran it for some forty years. Bass was the Progressive party vice-presidential candidate in 1952, another first for a black woman.

Sources: *Black Women in America*, vol. 1, pp. 93, 664; *Notable Black American Women*, pp. 61–64.

1930 • The *New York Times* adopted the captalized spelling of "Negro" and "Negress," becoming the first major newspaper to recognize this proper spelling.

Source: Menken, *The American Language*, p. 379.

1932 • The first black daily newspaper in modern times was the *Atlanta Daily World*, which was published daily beginning March 13, 1932. It was founded on August 3, 1928, by William A. Scott III, (1903–34). In spring 1930, it became a bi-weekly.

Sources: Alford, *Famous First Blacks*, p. 75; *Going Against the Wind*, pp. 79, 101; *Jet* (3 March 1992), p. 29; *Negro Yearbook*, 1947, p. 386.

1935 • Joel Augustus Rogers (1883–1966) became the first black foreign correspondent, when he was sent to Addis Ababa, Ethiopia. From October 1935 through April 21, 1936, he covered the Italian-Ethiopian War for the *Pittsburgh Courier*. Born in Jamaica, Rogers came to the United States in 1906, and was largely self-educated. He traveled extensively in Europe and Africa, and became a journalist, historian, and a prolific writer.

Sources: *Dictionary of American Negro Biography*, pp. 531–32; *Encyclopedia of Black America*, p. 735; Kane, *Famous First Facts*, p. 425.

1944 • Harry S. McAlpin (?–1985) became White House correspondent for the National Negro Press Association and the *Atlanta Daily World,* and was the first black admitted to White House press conferences. He first attended a White House press conference on February 8, 1944. Later, in 1947, the Negro Newspaper Publishers Association and individual newspaper correspondents were accredited to the Congressional Press Galleries and to the State Department. The early journalists accredited at this time were James L. Hicks, accredited to the State Department; and Percival L. Prattis and Louis Lautier, House and Senate press galleries.

Sources: Jet 53 (9 February 1978), p. 58; Kane, *Famous First Facts,* p. 425; *Negro Almanac,* p. 1427; *Negro Year Book,* 1952, pp. 46–48.

Elizabeth B. Murphy Moss (Phillips) (1917–) was the first black woman certified as a war correspondent during World War II. She became ill and had to return without filing reports. Later, Moss became vice-president and treasurer of the Afro-American Company, and publisher of the largest black chain of weekly newspapers in the United States, the *Baltimore Afro-American* group.

Sources: Black Women in America, vol. 1, p. 664; *Encyclopedia of Black America,* p. 570; *Negro Yearbook,* 1947, p. 387.

1947 • On March 18, 1947, the Senate Rules Committee ordered that Louis Lautier be granted access to the congressional press galleries, making him the first black newspaperman to have such a privilege since 1871. Lautier was Bureau Chief of the Negro Newspapers Publishers Association, and had been denied accreditation on the grounds that he did not represent a daily newspaper. He based his appeal of the original decision that barred him in 1946 on the grounds that he did indeed represent a daily, the *Atlanta Daily World.* Shortly before, Percival L. Prattis had gained access to the Periodical Gallery of both House and Senate, as part owner of *Our World* magazine. Prattis was also a newspaperman, being executive editor of the *Pittsburgh Courier,* and was the first black admitted to the National Press Club, on February 5, 1956.

Source: Negro Year Book, 1952, pp. 46–47.

Alice Dunnigan (1906–83) of the Associated Negro Press was the first black woman accredited to the White House and the State Department, and to gain access to the House of Representatives and Senate press galleries. At the State Department, she joined James L. Hicks, assistant chief of the Negro Newspapers Publishers Association, who had been the first black accredited to the department shortly before. Dunnigan was also the first black elected to the Women's National Press Club. In 1948, she became the first black news correspondent to cover a presidential campaign, when she covered Harry S Truman's whistlestop trip. Dunnigan was born on April 27, 1906, near Russellville, Kentucky. She attended Kentucky State College, in Frankfort, and later graduated from West Kentucky Industrial College.

ALICE
DUNNIGAN

Sources: Black Women in America, vol. 1, pp. 368–70; *Jet* 64 (30 May 1983), p. 42; *Notable Black American Women,* pp. 301–3; *Negro Year Book,* 1952, p. 47.

1949 • The first black full-time reporter for the *Mirror-News,* owned by the *Los Angeles Times,* was Chester Lloyd Washington (1902–). He specialized in superior court cases. Originally a reporter for the *Los Angeles Sentinel,* he became its editor in 1961, and its editor-in-chief in 1965. Through purchases and mergers of existing weekly newspapers and the creation of others, he established Central News-Wave Publications in Los Angeles, which became the largest black-owned newspaper operation in any single metropolitan area. Washington was born in Pittsburgh, Pennsylvania, and graduated from Virginia Union University. He served on the Los Angeles County Parks and Recreation Commission, and in 1982, Western Golf Course in Los Angeles was renamed the Chester L. Washington Golf Course.

Sources: Encyclopedia of Black America, pp. 845–46; *Negro Almanac, 1989,* pp. 1256, 1263–64; *Who's Who Among Black Americans, 1988,* p. 721.

1950 • Marvel Jackson Cooke was the first full-time black woman reporter on a mainstream newspaper, the *Daily Compass,* where she was a colleague of I. F. Stone. She had begun her career as an editorial assistant to W. E. B. Du Bois in 1926 at the *Crisis* and became assistant manager of Adam Clayton Powell's *People's Voice* in 1935.

Source: Black Women in America, vol. 1, p. 664.

Albert L. Hinton, representing the Negro Newspaper Association, and James L. Hicks, representing the *Afro-American* group, were the first black war correspondents in the Korean conflict. Hinton died when his plane went down between Japan and Korea, but Hicks was able to carry out his assignment.

Sources: Jet 70 (29 June 1970), p. 9; *Negro Year Book, 1952,* p. 46.

1952 • Journalist Simeon S. Booker (1918–) was the first full-time black reporter for the *Washington Post,* from 1952 to 1954. In 1982, he was the first

black to win the Fourth Estate Award of the National Press Club, Washington, D.C. The Baltimore native later became Washington Bureau Chief of Johnson Publishing Company.

THE OAKLAND TRIBUNE BUILDING RISES BEHIND ROBERT MAYNARD.

Sources: Ebony Success Library, vol. 1, p. 34; Rush, Black American Writers, vol. 1, p. 84; Who's Who Among Black Americans, 1992–93, pp. 129–30.

1964 • Stanley S. Scott (1933–) became the first black full-time general assignment reporter for United Press International (UPI). In 1965, he was nominated for a Pulitzer prize for his eyewitness account of the assassination of Malcolm X. In 1967, he became the first full-time black news anouncer for WINS, an all-news radio station in New York City. Scott won the Russwurm Award for Excellence in Radio News Reporting, as well as the New York Silurians Award.

Sources: Ebony Success Library, vol. 1, p. 277; Who's Who Among Black Americans, 1992–93, p. 1254.

1968 • Kenneth Chow (1947–) founded the *Black Progressive Shopper-News* in Kansas City, Kansas, the first paper of its kind in the Kansas and Missouri area. He received his high school diploma in 1965, while in Terre Haute Federal Penitentiary, Indiana.

Source: Encyclopedia of Black America, pp. 225–26.

1971 • William A. Hilliard was the first black city editor on a mainstream paper, the *Portland Oregonian*. He joined the newspaper in 1952 as a copy aide, and on April 5, 1982, he became the first black executive editor of the news department. In 1993, the American Society of Newspaper Editors elected Hilliard its first black president.

Sources: Jet 62 (5 April 1982), p. 29; Negro Almanac, 1989, p. 1258.

1974 • Hazel Garland (?–1988) editor-in-chief of the *Pittsburgh Courier,* was the first woman head of a nationally circulated black newspaper in the United States.

Sources: Black Women in America, vol. 1, p. 664; Jet 74 (25 April 1988), p. 59.

1979 • Robert C. Maynard (1937–93) was the first black to direct the editorial operations of a major American daily, the *Oakland Tribune* in California. In 1983, he became owner and publisher of the *Oakland Tribune* and the first black to become a majority shareholder in a major metropolitan daily newspaper. Maynard had spent ten years at the *Washington Post* as its first black national correspondent, and later as ombudsman and editorial writer. On October 15, 1992, the name and certain assets of the *Oakland Tribune,* then the nation's only black-owned major daily newspaper, were sold to the Alameda Newspaper Group.

Sources: Hornsby, Milestones in 20th-Century African-American History, pp. 495, 503; Atlanta Journal and Constitution (19 August 1993); Split Image, p. 366; State of Black America, 1993, p. 302; Who's Who Among Black Americans, 1992–93, p. 935.

1982 • Pamela McAllister Johnson (1945–) became the first black woman publisher of a mainstream paper, the *Ithaca Journal* on December 10, 1982, in New York State. The paper has a circulation of 20,000 and is a part of the Gannett chain. In 1987, Johnson received the Candace Award from the National Coalition of 100 Black Women.

Sources: Black Women in America, vol. 2, p. 1450; Split Image, p. 367; Negro Almanac, 1989, p. 1432; Who's Who Among Black Americans, 1989, pp. 766–67.

1987 • Roger Wood Wilkins (1932–) was the first black chair of the National Pulitzer Prize Board (1987–88), on which he served from 1980 to 1989. In 1973 he shared a Pulitzer Prize with the *Washington Post* for his reports on Watergate. His autobiography, *A Man's Life,* was published in 1982. The Kansas City, Missouri, native is the nephew of former NAACP director Roy Wilkins.

Sources: Contemporary Black Biography, vol. 2, pp. 250–53; Jet 72 (18 May 1987), p. 10; Who's Who Among Black Americans, 1992–93, p. 1509.

1989 • Clarence Page (1947–) was the first black columnist to be awarded a Pulitzer Prize. He joined the *Chicago Tribune* staff in 1969, and later became a syndicated columnist and editorial writer for the newspaper.

Sources: Contemporary Black Biography, vol. 4, pp. 187–90; Jet 76 (17 April 1989), p. 23.

1990 • The first black chief of the *Detroit Free Press* City-County Bureau was Constance C. Prater (1963–). A graduate of the Medill School of

Journalism at Northwestern University, she became a reporter for the newspaper in 1989. In 1990 Prater was local president of the National Association of Black Journalists.

Source: Jet 78 (24 September 1990), p. 29.

Cynthia Tucker was the first black woman to edit a major daily newspaper, the *Atlanta Constitution,* with a circulation of over 300,000. She joined the newspaper in 1976, serving as reporter, columnist, and editorial writer.

Source: Jet 81 (27 January 1992), p. 9.

Keith Woods (1958–) was named the first black city editor of the *Times Picayune.* The New Orleans native began his career in the sports department of the newspaper in 1978, became a full-time sports writer for the paper in 1988, and was named assistant city editor in 1989. He graduated from Dillard and Tulane universities.

Sources: Hornsby, *Milestones in 20th-Century African-American History,* p. 465; Jet 79 (7 January 1991), p. 37.

1992 • On December 1, 1992, Pearl Stewart (1951–) became the first black woman editor of the *Oakland Tribune,* which has a circulation of over 100,000.

Source: Jet 82 (5 October 1992), p. 36.

PERIODICALS

1820 • The *Emancipator,* the first anti-slavery magazine, was issued monthly from April 30 to October 31, 1820. It was edited and published by Elihu Embree.

Source: Kane, *Famous First Facts,* p. 456.

1838 • The first black periodical, the *Mirror of Liberty,* was published in June, 1838, by David Ruggles (1810–49). The 16-page quarterly was published in New York City from 1838 to 1841. It strongly protested colonization, segregation, disfranchisement, and slavery. (*See also* **Business: Retailing, 1834; Science & Medicine: Medicine, 1846.**)

Sources: Kane, *Famous First Facts,* p. 456; *Dictionary of American Negro Biography,* pp. 536–38.

1841 • The first issue of the oldest continuously published periodical, now known as the *Christian Recorder,* was published by the African Methodist Episcopal Church. Issued first as the *A.M.E. Church Magazine,* and intended as a weekly, it became a quarterly in its first year. Renamed the *Christian Herald* in 1848, it became a weekly again and was published by Martin Robinson Delany, an author, physician, abolitionist, black nationalist, and army officer. In 1852, it was renamed the Christian Recorder.

Sources: Encyclopedia of Black America, p. 33; Penn, *The Afro-American Press,* pp. 78–81.

1853 • Mary Ann Shadd (Cary) (1823–93) became the first black woman journalist, editor, and publisher, for the *Provincial Freeman.* In 1855 she was also the first woman admitted as a corresponding member of the black convention movement.

Sources: Dictionary of American Negro Biography, pp. 552–53; *The Negro Almanac, 1989,* p. 195; *Notable Black American Women,* pp. 998–1003.

1910 • The first issue of *Crisis* magazine, the official organ of the NAACP, and the vehicle for the dissemination of educational and social programs for blacks, was published in April, 1910. Edited by W. E. B. Du Bois, *Crisis* was first printed in one thousand copies, but by 1920 circulation had increased one-hundred fold.

Sources: Hornsby, *Milestones in 20th-Century African-American History,* p. 9; Joyce, *Gatekeepers of Black Culture,* pp. 37, 84; *The Negro Almanac, 1989,* pp. 21, 260.

1918 • Ralph Waldo Tyler (1860–1921), reporter and government official, was the first (and only) black official war correspondent during World War I.

Sources: Dictionary of American Negro Biography, pp. 613–14.; *Jet* 78 (2 July 1990), p. 23; Scott, *The American Negro in the World War,* pp. 284–99.

1942 • John H. Johnson (1918–) published the *Negro Digest,* the first magazine devoted to summarizing and excerpting articles and news about blacks published in mainstream publications. Immediately successful, the magazine laid the foundation for Johnson Publishing Company's success, which was only increased by magazines like *Ebony* and *Jet. Negro Digest,* published from 1942 through 1976, became *Black World* in 1970. (*See also* **Business: Publishing, 1938.**)

Sources: Contemporary Black Biography, vol. 3, pp. 102–4; *Split Image,* pp. 372–74.

1944 • The first issue of *Ebony* was published in 1944, by Johnson Publishing Company of Chicago, with John H. Johnson (1918–), company founder, as editor. In 1945, the magazine was the first advertising medium owned by blacks to attract advertising from white-owned companies. (*See also* **Business: Publishing, 1938.**)

Sources: Contemporary Black Biography, vol. 3, pp. 102–4; Joyce, *Gatekeepers of Black Culture,* p. 63; *Encyclopedia of Black America,* p. 331.

1963 • Ariel Perry Strong became the first woman to head *Tan* (later *Black Stars*) magazine as managing editor. She is a former proofreader for *Tan, Ebony,* and *Jet* magazines.

Source: Ebony Success Library, vol. 1, p. 295.

Time magazine's first black national correspondent was Wallace Houston Terry II (1938–), whose many assignments included coverage of

the Vietnam War. He was named 1993 holder of the John Seigenthaler Chair of Excellence in First Amendment Studies at Middle Tennessee State University.

Sources: Tennessean (15 October 1992); *Who's Who Among Black Americans, 1992–93,* p. 1237.

PHOTOJOURNALISM

1949 • Gordon A. Parks, Sr. (1912–) became the first black photojournalist on the staff of *Life* magazine. He began his photography in 1937 with a camera purchased in a pawn shop. In 1941 he was the first black to receive a Rosenwald Fellowship for photography; in 1942 he was the first black to work for the United States Farm Security Administration (as a photographer); and in 1943, the first to work for the United States Office of War Information (as a photojournalist and a war correspondent). Parks was named the Magazine Photographer of the Year in 1961. A gifted film director, he was the first black to direct movies for a major studio. Parks directed the feature films *Shaft, Sounder,* and *Cotton Comes to Harlem.* He also gained fame for his autobiographical books, *A Choice of Weapons* and *The Learning Tree.*

Sources: Contemporary Black Biography, vol. 1, pp. 184–88; Lee, *Interesting People,* p. 88; *Split Image,* pp. 161, 163, 376.

1969 • The first black journalist to win a Pulitzer Prize for a feature photograph was Moneta J. Sleet, Jr. (1926–). He won the award for his photograph of Coretta Scott King and her daughter at the funeral of Martin Luther King, Jr. Sleet was born in Owensboro, Kentucky, and graduated from Kentucky State College and New York University.

Sources: Ebony Success Library, vol. 1, p. 283; *Encyclopedia of Black America,* p. 796.

PRESS SECRETARY

1990 • Lynette Moten (1954–) became the first black woman press secretary for a United States senator. She worked with Thad Cochran, a Republican from Mississippi, in his Washington, D.C., office. She is a graduate of Tougaloo College and Columbia University's Graduate School of Journalism.

Source: Jet 78 (13 August 1990), p. 4.

RADIO

1927 • Floyd Joseph Calvin (1902–39), a journalist, had the first radio talk show, which focused on black journalism. Broadcast on WGBS, it was the first show of its kind sponsored by a black newspaper, the *Pittsburgh Courier.*

Sources: Encyclopedia of Black America, p. 213; *Split Image,* p. 184.

1960 • Edmund Stanley Dorsey (1930–) became the first black White House broadcast correspondent, with radio station WWDC. Three years later, while he was news director with radio-television station WOOK, he became the first black television news reporter in Washington, D.C. In 1964, he joined station WIND and was sent to Saigon (South Vietnam) in 1966, where he became the first black bureau chief for the Washington Broadcasting Network. While serving with the United States Army in Tokyo, Japan, in 1949, he became the first black managing editor of the military publication *Stars and Stripes.*

Source: Ebony Success Library, vol. 1, p. 98.

1987 • Adam Clayton Powell III (1946–) was the first black to direct a major national radio news network, National Public Radio. He is now a New York City councilman.

Sources: Jet 73 (26 October 1987), p. 22; *Split Image,* p. 214; *Who's Who Among Black Americans, 1992–93,* p. 1141.

1993 • Delano Eugene Lewis (1938–) was named president of National Public Radio (NPR) and became the first black to head a major public broadcasting organization. NPR provides news and cultural programming to nearly 480 member stations in the United States. The Arkansas City, Kansas, native graduated from the University of Kansas and received a law degree from Washburn School of Law in Topeka. He was president and chief executive officer of C and T Telephone Company in Washington, D.C., before assuming the new position.

Source: Jet 84 (13 September 1993), p. 23; Who's Who Among Black Americans, 1992–93, p. 869.

TELEVISION

1958 • The first black newscaster, for WNTA-TV in New York City, was Louis Emanuel Lomax (1922–70). Lomax, also an author and educator, was born in Valdosta, Georgia, and graduated from Paine College in Augusta, Georgia.

Sources: Dictionary of Black Culture, p. 275; Encyclopedia of Black America, pp. 539–40.

The first major black television news correspondent, for CBS-TV, was Joan Murray (1941–). In 1969, she co-founded Zebra Associates, the first integrated advertising agency with black principals. Murray was born in Ithaca, New York, attended Ithaca College, and later Hunter College and the New School for Social Research, in New York City. She also studied at the French Institute and Harvard University.

Sources: Ebony 21 (October 1966), p. 50; Encyclopedia of Black America, 584; Notable Black American Women, pp. 782–83.

1962 • Malvin (Mal) Russell Goode (1908–), hired by ABC, became the first black network news correspondent. Born in White Plains, Virginia, he

ABC NEWSMAN
MAL GOODE.

became the first black member of the National Association of Radio and Television News Directors in 1971.

Sources: Ebony Success Library, vol. 1, p. 127; The Negro Almanac, 1989, p. 1280; Split Image, p. 389; Who's Who Among Black Americans, 1992–93, p. 534.

1968 • Xernona Clayton (1933–) was the first black woman to host a television show in the South, in Atlanta, in August, 1968. In 1988, she became the first black assistant corporate vice-president of urban affairs at Turner Broadcasting System.

Sources: Clayton, I've Been Marching All the Time; Contemporary Black Biography, vol. 3, pp. 34–36; Encyclopedia of Black America, p. 274; Who's Who Among Black Americans, 1992–93, p. 274.

1969 • Mal Johnson (1924–) was the first black woman television reporter to cover the White House. In 1970, she became the first national correspondent for WKBS-TV.

Sources: Jet 80 (10 June 1991), p. 10; Klever, Women in Television, pp. 134–38; Who's Who Among Black Americans, 1992–93, p. 764.

1978 • Charlayne Hunter-Gault (1942–) was the first black woman to anchor a national newscast, "The MacNeil/Lehrer Report." She was born in Due West, South Carolina. In January 1961, she and Hamilton Homes were the first two black students to attend the University of Georgia. The university awarded her the prestigious George Foster Peabody Award in 1986. (*See also* **Education: College Integration, 1961.**)

Sources: Black Women in America, vol. 1, pp. 595–96; Jet 7 (26 March 1990), p. 33; Current Biography, 1987, pp. 261–64; Notable Black American Women, pp. 535–36.

BERNARD SHAW HOLDS THE ACE AWARD THAT HE WON FOR HIS WORK ON CABLE NEWS NETWORK (CNN).

Max Robinson (1939–88) was the first black network news anchor, with ABC-TV, broadcasting from Chicago, Illinois. He had been the first co-anchor on the midday newscast with WTOP, Washington, D.C., in 1969. Robinson left ABC in 1983 to become the first black anchor for WMAQ-TV in Chicago and won an Emmy Award in 1980 for coverage of the national election. Born in Richmond, Virginia, he attended Oberlin College, Virginia Union University, and Indiana University.

Sources: Contemporary Black Biography, vol. 3, pp. 209–12; Hornsby, *Milestones in 20th-Century African-American History,* p. 390; *Jet* 76 (1 May 1989), p. 25.

1980 • Bernard Shaw (1940–) was appointed chief Washington correspondent and became was the first black anchor at Cable News Network (CNN). In 1987 Shaw joined the major television networks in a nationally televised interview with President Ronald Reagan. The next year, he moderated the second presidential debate in Los Angeles. Born in Chicago, Shaw attended the University of Illinois.

Sources: Contemporary Black Biography, vol. 2, pp. 217–21; *Essence* 21 (November 1990), p. 42; *Negro Almanac, 1989,* p. 1285–86; *Split Image,* p. 389.

1981 • Edward R. (Ed) Bradley (1941–) became the first black co-editor of "Sixty Minutes," a weekly news magazine on CBS-TV. His previous assignments included principal correspondent for "CBS Reports," CBS News White House correspondent, anchor of the "CBS Sunday Night News," and reports broadcaster on "CBS Evening News with Walter Cronkite." He is a native of Pennsylvania and a graduate of Cheyney State College.

Sources: Contemporary Black Biography, vol. 2, pp. 28–32; *Negro Alamanac, 1989,* pp. 1278–79; *Who's Who Among Black Americans,* 1992–93, p. 143.

EDWARD R. BRADLEY

1982 • The first black co-host of the "Today" show was Bryant Charles Gumbel (1948–). Since 1975, he had been co-host for NBC's Rose Bowl Parade. Gumbel worked as chief anchor of NBC's football games and in 1977 was co-host for Super Bowl XI. In 1988, he was NBC's host for the Olympics in Seoul, South Korea. The New Orleans, Louisiana, native is a graduate of Bates College (Maine).

Sources: Jet 61 (12 November 1981), p. 15; *Split Image,* p. 389; *Who's Who Among Black Americans,* 1992–93, p. 573.

THE FIRST FACE THAT
MILLIONS OF PEOPLE SEE
IN THE MORNING IS
THAT OF BRYANT
GUMBEL.

1986 • Valerie Coleman, veteran television reporter in Los Angeles, was named weekday anchor for KCBS-TV in Los Angeles, becoming the first black in that time slot.

Source: Jet 70 (8 September 1986), p. 20.

Oprah Winfrey (1954–) became the first black woman to host a nationally syndicated weekday talk show, "The Oprah Winfrey Show." She moved from WTVF, a CBS local affiliate in Nashville, Tennessee, (where in 1971 she was the first woman co-anchor) to Baltimore, Maryland, and subsequently to Chicago. In 1984, Winfrey took over "A.M. Chicago," which aired opposite Phil Donahue, and later expanded to the one-hour television show. She formed Harpo Productions, which enabled her to develop her own projects, and in 1989 bought her own television and movie production studio.

Sources: Black Women in America, vol. 2, pp. 1274–76; *Contemporary Black Biography,* vol. 2, pp. 262–66; *Notable Black American Women,* pp. 1273–76; *Who's Who Among Black Americans, 1992–93,* p. 1556.

1990 • Dana Tyler and Reggie Harris formed the first black anchor team in a major metropolitan city for WCBS-TV, in New York City. Tyler, who graduated from Boston University, is the great-granddaughter of Ralph Waldo Tyler, the first black war correspondent during World War I. (*See also* **Journalism: Periodicals, 1918.**) Harris, former weekend anchor at the station, graduated from Florida State University.

Source: Jet 78 (2 July 1990), p. 23.

OPPOSITE PAGE:
EMMY AWARD-WIN-
NING TALK SHOW
HOST OPRAH
WINFREY.

MILITARY: MARCHING UP THE RANKS

CIVIL WAR

1861 • Nicholas Biddle was the first black wounded in the Civil War. The sixty-five-year-old former slave shed blood from an injury while he accompanied the first Pennsylvania troops through Baltimore on April 18, 1861.

Sources: Encyclopedia of Black America, p. 62; Garrett, Famous First Facts about Negroes, p. 9.

1865 • The first black Confederate troops were mustered into service for the Southern cause. On March 13, 1865, Confederate President Jefferson Davis signed a bill authorizing the employment of blacks as soldiers, culminating a long period of dispute in the South. General Robert E. Lee recommended the enlistment as "not only expedient but necessary." The action was taken at very end of the war; Lee surrendered at Appomattox Courthouse on April 9, 1865, and the remaining Confederate forces soon followed his example.

Source: Hornsby, Chronology of African-American History, p. 38.

NATIONAL GUARD

1869 • Robert Brown Elliott (1842–84) was the first black commanding general of the South Carolina National Guard. A brilliant lawyer born in Liverpool, England, of West Indian parents, and educated in England, Elliott was elected to the South Carolina legislature in 1868, and served as United States Congressman (1871 and 1874). In March 1869, he was appointed assistant adjutant-general of the state, in which capacity he was charged with the formation and maintenance of a state militia—often called the Black Militia—to protect white and black citizens from the murderous, fast growing Ku Klux Klan.

Sources: Dictionary of American Negro Biography, pp. 210–11; Encyclopedia of Black America, p. 354; Negro Almanac, p. 405.

1917 • Vertner W. Tandy (1885–?) was the first black officer in the New York National Guard. During World War I, he was commissioned first lieutenant, later promoted to captain, and then promoted to major in command of a separate unit in the New York National Guard Fifteenth Infantry. A prominent architect, Tandy designed the house of Madame C. J. Walker, Villa Lewaro. (*See also* **Arts & Entertainment: Architecture, 1908.**)

Sources: *Encyclopedia of Black America,* p. 813; *Who's Who in Colored America, 1929,* p. 352.

REVOLUTIONARY WAR

1775 • The Earl of Dunmore's Ethiopian Regiment was the first regiment made up of slave soldiers promised their freedom in exchange for fighting on the British side. John Murray, Earl of Dunmore (1732–1809), British Royal Governor of Virginia, issued a proclamation promising freedom to slaves who joined the British forces.

Sources: *Encyclopedia Americana, 1988,* vol. 9, p. 475; Hornsby, *Chronology of African-American History,* p. 7.

On April 19, 1775, Lemuel Haynes, Peter Salem, Pomp Blackman, Caesar Ferrit and his son, John Prince Estabrook, and Samuel Craft were the blacks known to have participated in the defense of Concord Bridge, the first encounter in the armed phase of the American Revolution.

Source: *Negro Almanac,* p. 803.

Salem Poor (1758?–?) was the first black soldier to win a battle commendation. A free man of color, Poor enlisted in a Massachusetts militia company, and on June 17, 1775, fought valiantly at the battle of Bunker Hill (fought on Breed's Hill), where he wounded a British officer. Several officers petitioned the Continental Congress to recognize his bravery as "a Brave & gallant Soldier." There is no record that he received such notice. Other blacks at the battle were Barzillai Lew, Cuff Whittemore, Titus Coburn, Charlestown Eads, Peter Salem, Sampson Taylor, and Caesar Brown.

Sources: *Dictionary of American Negro Biography,* p. 500; *Encyclopedia of Black America,* p. 684; *Negro Almanac,* p. 804.

1778 • The First Rhode Island Regiment was the first and only all-black unit to fight in the American Revolution. On February 2, 1778, Rhode Island passed the first slave enlistment act. In August, the regiment of 125 blacks—95 among them slaves—successfully sustained three attacks by the British, allowing the rest of the American army to make a successful retreat at the Battle of Rhode Island.

Sources: Cantor, *Historic Landmarks of Black America,* p. xvii; *Negro Almanac,* pp. 806–7.

UNITED STATES AIR FORCE

1954 • Benjamin Oliver Davis, Jr. (1912–) was the first air force general and the first black man to command an airbase. Davis paralleled his father's career in rising to the rank of general, albeit in another branch of the armed forces. His book, *Autobiography: Benjamin O. Davis, Jr.: American,* was published in 1991.

Sources: Contemporary Black Biographies, vol. 2, pp. 51–53; Hornsby, *Milestones in 20th-Century African-American History,* p. 55; *Negro Almanac,* p. 909.

1975 • Daniel H. "Chappie" James, Jr. (1920–78) became the first black four-star general in the United States Air Force. He was promoted to the rank of brigadier general in 1970, and received many awards and citations. James was born in Florida and educated at Tuskegee University (B.S., 1942).

Sources: Encyclopedia of Black America, pp. 468–69; *Negro Almanac,* p. 911; *Who's Who Among Black Americans, 1977,* p. 466.

1990 • Marcelite J. Harris (1943–) became the first black woman brigadier general in the air force. Born in Houston, Texas, Harris was educated at Spelman College, Central Michigan University, Chapman College, the University of Maryland, and Harvard University. She entered the air force in 1965 and in 1971 she became the first black woman to become an aircraft maintenance officer. In 1978, as commander of a cadet squadron at the United States Air Force Academy, Harris became one of the first two female commanding air officers.

Sources: Black Women in America, vol. 1, pp. 538–39; *Notable Black American Women,* pp. 467–68; *Who's Who Among Black Americans, 1992–93,* p. 610.

UNITED STATES ARMED FORCES

BRIGADIER GENERAL
MARCELITE HARRIS IS
NOTED FOR ACHIEVING
MANY "FIRSTS" IN THE
U.S. AIR FORCE.

1971 • Robert Morton Duncan (1927–) was the first black appointed to the United States Court of Military Appeals. Born in Urbana, Ohio, Duncan was educated at Ohio State University. He was chief justice in 1974.

Source: Who's Who Among Black Americans, 1992–93, p. 404.

1971 • Benjamin L. Hunton (1919–) was the first black army officer to receive a commission as brigadier general in the reserves. Hunton was employed for twenty-two years in the public schools of Washington, D.C., and served at the Departments of Interior and Health, Education, and Welfare.

Source: Encyclopedia of Black America, p. 457.

UNITED STATES ARMY AIR CORPS

1942 • Tuskegee Institute, Alabama, was the first and only training facility for black airmen in World War II. The United States Army established a school for black pilots, in spite of black opposition to the establishment of segregated Air Force facilities. While pilots began their training at Tuskegee, ground crews were prepared at Chanute Field in Illinois. By the end of the year the Ninety-ninth Pursuit Squadron, the first black air unit in the history of the United States, was ready for action. In April 1943, the unit was in French Morocco for training under experienced combat pilots. The following month the leader of the squadron, Captain Benjamin Oliver Davis, Jr., was promoted to major, then lieutenant colonel—all in one day. About six hundred black pilots received their wings during World War II.

Sources: Black Americans in Defense of Our Nation, p. 35; Cantor, Historic Landmarks of Black America, p. 352; Hornsby, Chronology of African-American History, p. 90; Negro Almanac, pp. 847–48.

1943 • Lieutenant Charles B. Hall of Brazil, Indiana, shot down the first German plane officially credited to the Ninty-ninth Pursuit Squadron on July 2, 1943. He was awarded the Distinguished Flying Cross.

Sources: Kane, Famous First Facts, p. 65; Lee, Negro Medal of Honor Men, p. 112.

UNITED STATES ARMY

1861 • James Stone (?–1862), was the first black to fight with the Union forces during the Civil War. He was a very light-complexioned fugitive slave, who enlisted in the First Fight Artillery of Ohio on August 23, 1861, and fought with the unit in Kentucky, the state in which he had been a slave. His racial identity was revealed after his death, which was caused by a service-related illness.

Source: Hornsby, Chronology of African-American History, p. 33.

1862 • The First South Carolina Volunteers was the first regiment of black soldiers raised in the Civil War. They were quickly followed by the First and Second Kansas Colored Volunteers, a group who fought the first skirmish by black troops in the Civil War, in Clay County, Missouri. The First Regiment Louisiana Native Guards were mustered into the army on September 27,

1862. For political reasons, all of the early groups were disavowed by the central government, and officially disbanded. It was not until the late summer of 1862 that the federal government officially enrolled black soldiers.

Sources: Encyclopedia of Black America, p. 63; *Negro Almanac,* p. 833.

1863 • On May 27, 1863, two black Louisiana regiments made charges on the Confederate fortification at Port Hudson, Louisiana. On July 9, 1863, eight black regiments had a prominent part in the siege of Port Hudson, a city whose fall was an important step in the eventual Union control of the Mississippi. These two engagements were the first battles to fully demonstrate the abilities of black troops.

Sources: Encyclopedia of Black America, p. 63; Hornsby, *Chronology of African-American History,* p. 35.

The Fifty-fourth Massachusetts Regiment was the first regiment raised in the North during the Civil War. Black leaders helped to recruit blacks from free states, slave states, and Canada. The regiment fought valiantly at Fort Wagner in July—its commander, Colonel Robert Gould Shaw, was killed and buried with his black soldiers. The attack at Fort Wagner was the first major engagement seen by black troops. The regiment objected to the pay differential between black and white enlisted men and served a year without pay rather than accept discriminatory wages.

Sources: Hughes and Meltzer, *Pictorial History of Black Americans, 1972,* p. 180; Cantor, *Historic Landmarks in Black America,* pp. 73–74; Hornsby, *Chronology of African-American History,* p. 35.

Alexander T. Augusta was the first black commissioned medical officer. (*See also* **Science & Medicine: Medicine, 1863.**)

Source: Dictionary of American Negro Biography, pp. 19–20.

WILLIAM HARVEY CARNEY

William Harvey Carney (1840–1908), sergeant of Company C, Fifty-fourth Massachusetts Colored Infantry, was the first black in the Civil War to earn the Medal of Honor. Born in Norfolk, Virginia, he was educated privately and later settled in New Bedford, Massachusetts, where he became a seaman. Carney enlisted on February 17, 1863, and earned his medal of honor five months later at Fort Wagner, South Carolina. When the color bearer was wounded in the battle, Carney, also hurt, sprang forward and seized the flag before it slipped from the bearer's grasp. By doing so, he prevented the flag from touching the ground. Carney was discharged from the infantry with disabilities caused by the wounds he had received. The medal of honor was not issued until May 23, 1900. Upon Carney's death, the flag on the Massachusetts state house was flown at half mast—an honor formerly restricted to presidents, senators, and governors.

Sources: Alexander's Magazine 7 (15 January 1909), p. 109; *Dictionary of American Negro Biography,* p. 90–91; *Encyclopedia of Black America,* p. 835; Lee, *Negro Medal of Honor Men,* pp. 24–26.

Henry McNeal Turner (1834–1915), clergyman and legislator, was the first black chaplain in the United States Army and the first black commissioned army officer. A minister in the African Methodist Episcopal Church, he was a leader of the post-Civil War expansion of the church in the South. Turner was also a Georgia legislator and a member of the Georgia Constitutional Convention (1867–68). An active churchman, he was elected bishop in 1880. Always active in politics, Turner urged blacks to return to Africa where they could realize their manhood and their human rights. (*See also* **Religion: AME, 1898; Government—Federal Firsts: Federal Appointees, 1869.**)

Sources: Dictionary of American Negro Biography, p. 608; *Encyclopedia of Black America,* p. 820; Kane, *Famous First Facts,* p. 33.

1865 • Martin Robinson Delany (1812–85) was the first black commissioned field officer with the rank of major in the regular infantry. Assigned to Charleston, South Carolina, he recruited two regiments of blacks. (*See also* **Writers: Pamphlets, 1852.**)

Sources: Dictionary of American Negro Biography, pp. 169–72; *Encyclopedia of Black America,* pp. 306–7; Kane, *Famous First Facts,* p. 35.

1867 • Congress approved the first all-black units in the regular army. These soldiers, known as "Buffalo Soldiers," served in the West and comprised the Ninth and Tenth Calvary Regiments as well as the Twenty-fourth and Twenty-fifth Infantry Regiments—United States Colored Troops. Their nickname came from the Indians, who believed their short curly hair was similar to that on the buffalo's neck and that their brave and fierce fighting matched the buffalo. Eleven black soldiers earned the Congressional Medal of Honor in combat against Utes, Apaches, and Comanches. Soldiers served in black regiments until the integration of United States forces in 1952. A monument honoring the Buffalo Soldiers was unveiled at Fort Leavenworth in 1992.

Sources: Black Americans in Defense of Our Nation, pp. 25–27; *Jet* 82 (7 September 1992), p. 34; Katz, *Black Indians,* p. 174.

1870 • Emanuel Stance (c.1848–87), a sergeant of Company F, Ninth United Calvary, Fort Kavett, Texas, was the first black in the Indian Campaigns to earn the Medal of Honor. As a "Buffalo Soldier," he and a small group of soldiers dispersed a band of marauding Indians. It is believed that he was murdered by one of his own men.

Sources: Black Americans in Defense of Our Nation, pp. 26–27; *Dictionary of American Negro Biography,* pp. 568–69; Lee, *Negro Medal of Honor Men,* p. 59.

1884 • Henry Vinson Plummer (1844–1905) was the first black chaplain in the regular army. Appointed on July 8, 1884, he held the rank of captain and was assigned to the Ninth Cavalry. Born a slave in Maryland, Plummer escaped during the Civil War and taught himself to read while serving in the navy. A strong advocate for temperance, he was court-martialed and dismissed from the army on a charge of drunkenness—a charge supported by one witness, who had a ten-year grudge against him.

Sources: Dictionary of American Negro Biography, pp. 498–99; Foner, Blacks and the Military in American History, p. 65.

1898 • Dennis Bell, George H. Tomkins, Fitz Lee, William H. Thompkins, and George H. Wanton, privates in the Tenth Calvary, were the first black soldiers honored with Medals of Honor in the Spanish-American War. They selflessly rescued a stranded group of soldiers in the Cuban province of Puerto Principle—a maneuver that had been thwarted on three previous attempts.

Sources: Black Americans in Defense of Our Nation, pp. 60–61; Lee, Negro Medal of Honor Men, p. 90.

1904 • Charles Young (1864–1922) was the first black military attaché in the history of the United States; he was accredited to Haiti. In 1889, Young was the third man of color to graduate from the United States Military Academy. He was commissioned as second lieutenant in the United States Cavalry. During the Spanish-American War, Young served as a major in charge of the Ninth Ohio Regiment, an all-black volunteer unit. He served in Haiti, the Philippines, and Mexico, and by 1916, he had attained the rank of lieutenant colonel. Young was the first military person to be honored with the NAACP's Spingarn Medal in 1916. In 1917, at the advent of World War I, he was forced to retire for reasons of "physical unfitness for duty." (He was suffering from extremely high blood pressure and Bright's disease.) In response, Young mounted his favorite horse at Wilberforce, Ohio, and rode five hundred miles to Washington, D.C., to prove that he was indeed fit for service. The army reinstated him in 1918, and he was assigned to train black troops at Fort Grant, Illinois. In 1919, Colonel Young was sent as military attaché to Liberia on a second tour of duty. He died in Lagos, Nigeria, during an inspection tour.

Sources: Dictionary of American Negro Biography, pp. 679–80; Foner, Blacks and the Military, pp. 64, 113; Jet 80 (29 July 1991), p. 4; Robinson, Historical Negro Biographies, p. 268.

1906 • Allen Allensworth (1842–1914) was the first black American to hold the rank of lieutenant colonel. Born a slave, he taught under the auspices of the Freedmen's Bureau, operated a number of businesses, and served as a chaplain during the Spanish-American War. At the time of his retirement, he was the senior chaplain in the army. He founded an all-black town named Allensworth in Tulare County, California, in 1908. A town resident named Oscar Over became California's first black justice of the peace in 1914.

Sources: Cantor, Historic Landmarks of Black America, p. 290; Dictionary of American Negro Biography, pp. 13–14; Foner, Blacks and the Military in American History, p. 65, 70.

1909 • Wade Hammond, Alfred Jack Thomas, William Polk, and Egbert Thompson were promoted to the rank of chief musician and became the first black bandmasters in the army. Previously the bands attached to black regiments had been headed by whites.

Source: Southern, *The Music of Black Americans,* p. 301.

1917 • Fort Des Moines, Iowa, was the first army camp for training black officers in World War I. About half (639) of the black officers commissioned during the war were trained there.

Sources: Dictionary of Black Culture, p. 166; Kane, *Famous First Facts,* p. 31.

In December, 1917, the 369th Infantry Regiment was the first group of black combat soldiers to arrive in Europe. Cited for bravery eleven times, the regiment was awarded the *croix de guerre* by the French government. In 1918, they were the first allied regiment to reach the Rhine in an offensive against Germany. The regimental band, conducted by James Reese Europe and Noble Sissle, is credited with the introduction of American jazz abroad.

Sources: Dictionary of Black Culture, p. 432; *Encyclopedia of Black America,* p. 836.

1918 • Henry Johnson (1897–1929) and Needham Roberts were the first black soldiers to be awarded the French *croix de guerre* as individuals. As privates with the 369th Infantry, they were injured in an assault by German soldiers but succeeded in routing their attackers.

Sources: Dictionary of American Negro Biography, p. 351; *Dictionary of Black Culture,* p. 240; Kane, *Famous First Facts,* p. 367.

HENRY JOHNSON WAS HONORED BY THE FRENCH GOVERNMENT FOR HIS SERVICE IN WORLD WAR I.

1940 • Benjamin Oliver Davis, Sr. (1877–1970) was the first black American general in the United States Army. Born and educated in Washington, D.C., he graduated from Howard University in 1898. Davis served in the Eighth United States Volunteers Infantry from 1898 to 1899, then in the Ninth Calvary from 1899 to 1917, and in the United States Army from 1918 to 1948. He was made a brigadier general in 1940 and retired in 1948, having served in the United States armed forces for a half century.

Source: Black Americans in Defense of Our Nation, pp. 106–7; *Encyclopedia of Black America,* pp. 303–4; Hornsby, *Milestones in 20th-Century African-American History,* p. 36; *Who's Who in Colored America, 1950,* p. 139.

1943 • Nine doctors and thirty nurses comprised the first black medical group sent overseas. The group was sent to Liberia.

Source: Black Americans in Defense of Our Nation, p. 95.

BRIGADIER GENERAL BENJAMIN DAVIS, SR., SPENT 50 OF HIS 93 YEARS IN THE MILITARY.

On August 21 Harriet M. West was the first black woman major in the Women's Army Corps (WAC). She was chief of the planning in the Bureau Control Division at the WAC headquarters in Washington, D.C.

Sources: Foner, *Blacks and the Military in American History,* p. 165; Lee, *Interesting People,* p. 44.

1944 • The defense against the attempted German breakthrough in the Ardennes included platoons of blacks assigned to white units—the first and only example of integrated units in World War II.

Source: Black Americans in Defense of Our Nation, p. 35.

1948 • Nancy C. Leftenant was the first black nurse in the regular army. She was a graduate of Lincoln Hospital School for Nurses, and had joined the army reserve nurse corps in February 1945.

Sources: Alford, Famous First Blacks, p. 65; Black Women in America, vol. 1, p. 795.

1951 • William Henry Thompson (1928–50), private first class, Company M, Twenty-fourth Infantry Regiment, became the first black to earn the Medal of Honor in the Korean conflict. He was mortally wounded on August 2, 1951, while manning his machine gun during a surprise attack on his platoon. His actions allowed the unit to withdraw to a more defensible position.

Sources: Black Americans in Defense of Our Nation, p. 62; Kane, Famous First Facts, p. 371; Lee, Negro Medal of Honor Men, pp. 9–12.

1961 • Fred Moore was the first black guard at the Tomb of the Unknown Soldier in Arlington National Cemetery.

Source: Garrett, Famous First Facts About Negroes, p. 16.

1965 • Milton L. Olive III (1946–65) was the first black Medal of Honor winner in the Vietnam War. Private First Class Olive was a member of the Third Platoon of Company B, Second Battalion (Airborne), 503d Infantry on duty in Vietnam. On October 22, 1965, he caught an exploding grenade and died to save his comrades.

Sources: Black Americans in Defense of Our Country, p. 76; Cantor, Historic Landmarks of Black America, p. 8; Lee, Negro Medal of Honor Men, p. 123.

1976 • In 1976 Clara Leach Adams-Ender (1930–) was the first black woman and nurse to graduate with a master's degree from the United States Army Command and General Staff College. In July 1967, she had been the first woman in the army to be awarded the Expert Field Medical Badge, and in 1982 she was the first black Army Nurse Corps officer to graduate from the Army War College. Adams-Ender became the first black nurse appointed chief of nursing at Walter Reed Army Medical Center in Washington, D.C., in 1984. In 1987, Brigadier General Adams-Ender became the first black chief of the United States Army Nurse Corps.

Sources: Black Women in America, vol. 1, pp. 10–11; Jet 63 (15 November 82), p. 16; Notable Black American Women, pp. 1–2.

1982 • Roscoe Robinson, Jr. (1928–93) was the first black four-star general in the United States Army. The St. Louis-born soldier was educated at the

BRIGADIER GENERAL CLARA LEACH ADAMS-ENDER HAS PURSUED A SUCCESSFUL NURSING CAREER IN THE U.S. ARMY.

Military Academy, the University of Pittsburgh, and the National War College.

Sources: *Jet* 84 (9 August 1993), p. 15; (Nashville) *Tennessean* (23 July 1993); *Negro Alamanac*, 1976, p. 656; *Who's Who Among Black Americans, 1992–93*, p. 1214.

1985 • Sherian Grace Cadoria (1940–) was the first black woman to obtain the rank of brigadier general in the regular army. She served as one of the four women army generals. Cadoria's tours of duty included Vietnam and key assignments with the Joint Chiefs of Staff, the Law Enforcement Division, and the Criminal Investigation Command. She retired in 1990.

Sources: *Black Women in America*, vol. 1, p. 214; Lanker, *I Dream a World*, p. 150.

1987 • Colin L. Powell (1937–) was the first black National Security Advisor. Born in New York City, Powell was educated at City College of New York (B.S. 1958), George Washington University (M.B.A. 1971), and the National War College. In 1989 he became the first black chairman of the Joint Chiefs of Staff. Powell was especially prominent in this position because of his highly visible role in the Persian Gulf War of 1991.

Sources: *Contemporary Black Biography*, vol. 1, pp. 195–98; Hornsby, *Milestones in 20th-Century African-American History*, pp. 412, 419, 460; *Who's Who Among Black Americans, 1992–93*, p. 1142.

1989 • Henry Doctor, Jr., was the first black inspector general of the army. A native of Oakley, South Carolina, he took a B.S. in general agriculture from South Carolina State College in 1954, and entered the army through the ROTC program.

Sources: *Jet* 76 (21 August 89), p. 10; *Negro Almanac*, p. 898.

1991 • The Medal of Honor was awarded posthumously to Corporal Freddie Stowers, the first black to earn the Medal of Honor in World War I. Corporal Stowers had been recommended for the medal during World War I, but it was awarded seventy-two years later, following an Army investigation of prejudice in the bestowing of awards. On September 28, 1918, Stowers was a squad leader whose company was trying to capture a hill in the Champagne-Marne section in France. The Germans feigned surrender

COLIN POWELL IS ONE OF TODAY'S MOST WELL-KNOWN MILITARY FIGURES.

to lure the Americans into a trap that killed more than half of the company, including those in command. Stowers took charge, leading a squad that destroyed the German guns. He was mortally wounded, but the company pressed on and captured the hill.

Sources: Atlanta Constitution (8 April 1993); *Jet* 80 (13 May 91), p. 9.

UNITED STATES COAST GUARD

1865 • Michael Augustine Healy (1839–1904) was the first black appointed to the Coast Guard. In 1865, he entered the United States Revenue Service, the forerunner of the Coast Guard. In 1886, he was assigned to command the famous cutter *Bear,* and became the chief federal law enforcement officer in the northern waters around Alaska, making him the first officer. The Healy family also produced the first black Roman Catholic American bishop, James Augustine (1830–1900), and the first black American Jesuit and president of Georgetown University, Patrick Francis (1834–1910). (*See also* **Religion: Catholics, 1854** and **1875.**)

Source: Dictionary of American Negro Biography, pp. 303–4.

1880 • The Pea Island, North Carolina, Lifesaving Station was the first (and only) all-black Coast Guard facility. Richard Etheridge, a former slave, established it. All traces of the station have now been washed away, but the North Carolina Aquarium on Roanoke Island has an exhibit of the original station.

Sources: Black Americans in Defense of Our Nation, pp. 159–60; Cantor, *Historic Landmarks of Black America,* p. 232.

1966 • Merle J. Smith, Jr., was the first black graduate of the Coast Guard Academy.

Sources: Black Americans in Defense of Our Nation, p. 163; Kane, *Famous First Facts,* p. 64.

1989 • Alex Haley (1921–92) was the first person of any race to receive an honorary degree from the Coast Guard Academy. (*See* **Arts & Entertainment: Television, 1977.**)

Source: Jet 76 (12 June 89), p. 17.

UNITED STATES MARINES

1944 • James E. Johnson (1926–) was the first black warrant officer in the Marines.

Source: Encyclopedia of Black America, p. 474.

1952 • Frank E. Peterson, Jr. (1932–) was the first black marine pilot and the first black to win Marine Corps wings. In 1979, he became the first black general in the Marines, and in 1986 he was the first black comman-der of the Quantico, Virginia, facility.

Sources: Jet 70 (14 July 1986), p.28; Negro Almanac, p. 905.

1967 ‣ Private First Class James Anderson, Jr. (1947–67) was the first black Marine to receive the Medal of Honor. On January 22, 1967, in Vietnam, he threw himself on a grenade to save his comrades. Anderson was acknowl-edged by the naming of a military supply ship in his honor.

Source: Black Americans in Defense of Our Nation, p. 63.

UNITED STATES MILITARY ACADEMY

1870 ‣ James Webster Smith was the first black admitted to the military academy at West Point. He left the academy after being subjected to unbearable hazing and ostracism.

Sources: Black Americans in Defense of Our Nation, p. 131; Garrett, Famous First Facts About Negroes, p. 12; Kane, Famous First Facts, p. 36.

HENRY OSSIAN FLIPPER

1877 ‣ Henry Ossian Flipper (1856–1940) was the first black to graduate from the United States Military Academy at West Point, New York. A native of Georgia, and a student at Atlanta University at the time of his appointment, Flipper graduated fiftieth out of a class of seventy-six after suffering four years of exclusion and ostracism by white cadets. He joined the Tenth Cavalry in 1878, serving in Oklahoma and Texas. The only black officer in the army, Flipper was cleared of an embezzlement charge in 1882, but was convicted of conduct unbe-coming an officer and gentleman, and discharged. He remained in the West and, for the next fifty years, engaged in engineering, mining, and survey work. He also lived in Atlanta for a number of years with his equally renowned brother, Josephus Flipper, a bishop in the African Methodist Episcopal Church. In 1976, Flipper was exonerated posthumously by the army, and on May 3, 1977—the centennial of his graduation—a bust was unveiled in his honor at West Point. His *Colored Cadet at West Point* (1878) gives a penetrating insight into his early life.

Sources: Black Americans in Defense of Our Nation, p. 27; Dictionary of American Negro Biography, pp. 227–28; Garrett, Famous First Facts About Negroes, p. 12.

1976 ‣ James H. Stith was the first black faculty member to become a tenured professor. He was an associate professor of physics.

Source: Jet 50 (1 April 76), p. 50.

1979 ‣ Vincent K. Brooks was the first black to serve as first captain and brigade commander of the Corps of Cadets.

Source: Black Americans in Defense of Our Nation, p. 139.

UNITED STATES NAVAL ACADEMY

1872 • James Henry Conyers was the first black appointed to the United States Naval Academy at Annapolis, Maryland, although he did not graduate. He was a native of South Carolina.
Sources: Black Americans in Defense of Our Nation, p. 141; Lee, Negro Medal of Honor Men, p. 50.

1949 • Wesley A. Brown was the first black graduate of the United States Naval Academy at Annapolis.
Sources: Black Americans in Defense of Our Nation, p. 142; Dictionary of Black Culture, p. 70.

1966 • Samuel P. Massie was the first black American faculty member at the United States Naval Academy. A former president of North Carolina Central University, Durham, he was assigned to the chemistry department.
Source: Black Americans in Defense of Our Nation, p. 147–48.

1980 • Janie L. Mines was the first black woman student at the United States Naval Academy, and in 1980, she became the academy's first black woman graduate.
Sources: Black Americans in Defense of Our Nation, p. 142; Jet 50 (27 June 76), p. 16.

1981 • Walter Nobles was the academy's first black brigade commander, the highest ranking midshipman there, showing impressive leadership skills. He was born and raised in New York, and majored in physical science.
Source: Black Americans in Defense of Our Nation, p. 146.

UNITED STATES NAVY

1863 • Robert Smalls (1839–1915) was the first and only black to attain the rank of captain in the navy during the Civil War. He was a skilled pilot in charge of the armed Confederate dispatch boat, *The Planter,* in Charleston, South Carolina. With the help of eight black crewmen, Smalls put his family and other fugitives on board, and sailed it out of the harbor to turn it over as a prize of war to the Union Navy on May 13, 1862. The boat was eventually refitted as a gunboat, and Smalls was made a captain in the Union navy. As a congressman from South Carolina, he served longer than any black during Reconstruction—although not in consecutive terms.
Sources: Dictionary of American Negro Biography, pp. 560–61; Hornsby, Chronology of African-American History, p. 34; Negro Almanac, p. 833.

ROBERT SMALLS PILOTED A BOAT, AND HIS FAMILY, OUT OF THE CONFEDERACY.

1864 • Robert Blake, powder boy aboard the USS *Marblehead,* was the first black awarded the Naval Medal of Honor "for conspicuous gallantry, extraordinary heroism, and intrepidity at the risk of his own life." The heroic action occurred during a victorious battle off the coast of South Carolina on December 23, 1863.

Sources: Bergman, *The Chronological History of the Negro in America*, p. 233; *Black Americans in Defense of Our Nation*, p. 54; Lee, *Negro Medal of Honor Men*, p. 35; *Negro Almanac*, p. 875.

1898 · Robert Penn (1872–?) was the only black seaman during the Spanish-American War to receive the Naval Medal of Honor. On July 20, 1898, the USS *Iowa* was anchored off Santiago, Cuba, when an explosion occurred in the boiler room. Penn saved a coal handler, single-handedly averting an explosion that could have destroyed the *Iowa* and taken the lives of many crewmen. The medal was issued to Penn on December 14, 1898. Born in Virginia, Penn enlisted in the Navy, and by early 1898, he had progressed to Fireman Second Class.

Sources: Lee, *Negro Medal of Honor Men*, p. 53; *Negro Almanac*, p. 876.

1917 · Bandmaster Alton Augustus Adams (1889–?) was the first black bandleader in the United States Navy. Born in the Virgin Islands, he began music study at the age of nine (by correspondence) with Hugh A. Clarke of the University of Pennsylvania. Adams served as assistant director of the municipal band of St. Thomas, bandmaster of the United States Navy band at St. Thomas (the first and only black band in the navy), and supervisor of music of the Virgin Islands' public schools.

Sources: Encyclopedia of Black America, pp. 2–3; *Who's Who in Colored America, 1929*, p. 1.

1941 · Dorie Miller (1919–43) was the first national black hero during World War II and was honored with the Navy Cross. A Navy messman first

PEARL HARBOR HERO DORIE MILLER WAS LATER LOST AT SEA.

class on the battleship *Arizona* at Pearl Harbor when the Japanese attacked on December 7, 1941, he shot down four Japanese planes. As a messman, Miller had not been trained in the use of a weapon. Miller was among the crew of the carrier *Liscome Bay* when it sank at sea after a torpedo struck her on November 24, 1943.

Sources: Dictionary of American Negro Autobiography, pp 434–35; Encyclopedia of Black America, p. 837; Lee, Negro Medal of Honor Men, p. 107.

1943 • The USS *Mason,* a destroyer escort, was the first naval destroyer with a predominately black crew, and at least one black officer.

Source: Black Americans in Defense of Our Nation, p. 35.

PC 1264 was the first submarine chaser with an all-black crew.

Source: Black Americans in Defense of Our Nation, p. 35.

1944 • The USS *Harmon* was the first navy fighting ship named after a black, Leonard Roy Harmon. Harmon (1916–42) was a World War II naval hero who "deliberately exposed himself to hostile gunfire in order to protect a shipmate and as a result...was killed in action." He was awarded the Navy Cross.

Sources: Black Americans in Defense of Our Nation, p. 37; Dictionary of Black Culture, p. 201.

Samuel Lee Gravely, Jr., (1922–) was the first black ensign commissioned during World War II. He was released from active service after the war, but was recalled in 1949. In January 1962, Gravely was given command of the destroyer USS *Falgout.* This was the first time a black officer had been given command of a ship in the modern navy. In 1963, Gravely and George I. Thompson were the first two blacks chosen to attend the Naval College. A veteran of three wars, Gravely was the first black admiral in United States history. His promotion was confirmed by the United States Senate on May 15, 1971.

Sources: Encyclopedia of Black America, p. 408; Garrett, Famous First Facts About Negroes, pp. 15–17; Kane, Famous First Facts, p. 421; Lee, Negro Medal of Honor Men, p. 118.

The first black women were sworn into the Women Accepted for Volunteer Emergency Service (WAVES). The Navy accepted only seventy-two enlisted women and two officers. The WAVES were incorporated into the regular navy in 1948, thirty years before the WACs were incorporated into the regular army.

Sources: Black Americans in Defense of Our Nation, p. 93; Black Women in America, pp. 794–95.

1945 • Phyllis Mae Dailey was the first black woman to serve as a nurse in the United States Navy.

Sources: Black Women in America, vol. 1, pp. 795–96; Dictionary of Black Culture, p. 125.

1949 • Jesse Leroy Brown was the first black pilot in the Naval Reserve and in 1950 was the first black flier killed in Korea. In 1971 he was the first black naval officer to have a frigate named for him.

Sources: Black Americans in Defense of Our Nation, pp. 48–49; Kane, Famous First Facts, pp. 90, 561; Lee, Negro Medal of Honor Men, p. 14.

1966 • Thomas David Parham, Jr., was the first black chaplain in the Navy to attain the rank of captain. Parham, of Newport News, Virginia, was a chaplain assigned to Quonset Point, Rhode Island, Naval Air Station.

Sources: Kane, Famous First Facts, p. 418; Lee, Negro Medal of Honor Men, p. 121.

1968 • Paul Stewart Green, a physician, was the first black captain in the United States Navy Medical Corps.

Source: Kane, Famous First Facts, p. 467.

1972 • Richard E. Williams (1934–) was the first black to command a naval unit in the deep South.

Source: Encyclopedia of Black America, p. 859.

1974 • Vivian McFadden was the first black woman United States Navy chaplain.

Source: Kane, Famous First Facts, p. 419.

MISCELLANEOUS: A VARIETY OF MILESTONES

AVIATION

1921 • Bessie Coleman (1893–1926) was the first black woman to gain a pilot's license. Coleman was also the first black woman stunt pilot, and on Labor Day weekend of 1922 she appeared for the first time as a stunt flyer. Coleman died in an air crash.

Sources: Black Women in America, pp. 262–63; Alford, *Famous First Blacks,* p. 71; *Notable Black American Women,* pp. 202–3.

1933 • Albert Ernest Forsythe and Charles Alfred Anderson were the first black pilots to make a round-trip transcontinental flight. They left Atlantic City on July 17, 1933, in their plane *The Pride of Atlantic City,* arrived in Los Angeles, and completed their round trip on July 28.

Source: Powell, *Black Wings,* pp. 181–88.

1934 • Willa Brown-Chappell (1906–92) was the first black woman in the United States to hold a commercial pilot's license, and the first black woman to gain officer rank (lieutenant) in the Civil Air Patrol Squadron. She also formed the National Airmen's Association of America, the first black aviators' group. In 1938, with her husband Cornelius R. Coffey, she established the first black-owned flying school, the Coffey School of Aeronautics. This school was also the first black-owned school certified by the Civil Aviation Authority. In 1972, Brown-Chappell was the first black member of the Federal Aviation Agency's Women's Advisory Commission.

Sources: Atlanta Constitution 22 July 1992; *Black Women in America,* vol. 1, pp. 184–86; *Nashville Banner* (21 July 1992).

WILLA BROWN-CHAPPELL

1957 • Perry H. Young (1919–) was the first black pilot of a scheduled passenger commercial airline. He flew for New York Airways.

Sources: Alford, *Famous First Blacks*, p. 70; *Who's Who Among Black Americans, 1992–93*, p. 1587.

BESSIE COLEMAN'S LOVE
FOR FLYING LED TO HER
DEATH.

1958 • Ruth Carol Taylor (1933–) was the first black commercial airline stewardess. Taylor was hired by Mohawk Airlines.

Source: Garrett, *Famous First Facts About Negroes*, p. 6.

1970 • Otis B. Young, Jr., was the first black pilot of a 740 jumbo jet.
Sources: Alford, *Famous First Blacks,* p. 70; Lee, *Interesting People,* p. 202.

1978 • Jill Brown was the first black woman pilot on a major airline. Brown was a former naval pilot.
Sources: Encyclopedia of Black America, p. 146; Lee, *Interesting People,* p. 202.

1987 • Erma Chansler Johnson (1942–) was the first black and the first woman to chair the Dallas/Fort Worth International Airport Board of Directors.
Source: Who's Who Among Black Americans, 1992–93, p. 755.

BEAUTY INDUSTRY

1970 • The first black contestant in a Miss America Pageant was Cheryl Adrenne Brown, Miss Iowa.
Source: Alford, *Famous First Facts,* p. 68.

The first black Miss World was Jennifer Josephine Hosten, who won the honor on December 3, 1970. The Grenada native was then an airline flight attendant.
Source: Garrett, *Famous First Facts about Negroes,* p. 23.

1974 • The first black woman to appear on the cover of a major fashion magazine was Beverly Johnson (1952–). The model, actress, and singer

VANESSA WILLIAMS
WAS CROWNED MISS
AMERICA IN 1983.

APRIL
$2.25

GLAMOUR

Special Anniversary Issue!

●

The Happiness Report

Supermodel Gossip

Fabulous Hair

Surprise Shape-ups

Sexual Chemistry

Unforgettable Don'ts

appeared on the August issue of *Vogue* in 1974. In the early 1970s she also became the first black woman to appear on the cover of the French magazine, *Elle,* and by 1992 she would appear on the covers of some five hundred magazines. Born in Buffalo, New York, she studied at Northeastern University in Boston.

Sources: Contemporary Black Biography, vol. 2, pp. 123–24; *Ebony* 47 (September 1992), p. 32; Hornsby, *Milestones in 20th-Century African-American History,* pp. 222–23; *Notable Black American Women,* pp. 575–76.

1977 • Janelle Penny Commissiong (1954–) became the first black Miss Universe. She was also Miss Trinidad Tobago. The former fashion buyer and fashion institute graduate was born in Trinidad.

Sources: Essence 8 (April 1978), p. 32; *Jet* 53 (10 November 1977), p. 30.

1983 • Vanessa Lynn Williams (1963–), representing New York State, became the first black Miss America. She also was the first to resign the title, in 1984. Suzette Charles, the first black Miss New Jersey, and the first black runner-up in the Miss America contest, took Williams' place. Williams later became an actress and singer.

Sources: Black Women in America, pp. 409, 1266–68; 71 *Jet* (2 February 1987), p. 56; and 76 (18 September 1989), p. 27; *The Negro Almanac,* p. 1432; *Who's Who Among Black Americans, 1992–93,* p. 1537.

1990 • The first black Miss USA was Carole Gist (1970?–), who was crowned in Wichita, Kansas, on March 3, 1990. The six-foot tall, twenty-year-old queen from Detroit entered the contest as Miss Michigan. She was also first runner-up in the Miss Universe pageant later that year.

Sources: Contemporary Black Biography, vol. 1, pp. 84–85; Hornsby, *Milestones in 20th-Century African-American History,* p. 441; *Jet* 77 (19 March 1990), p. 59; and (26 March 1990), pp. 58-60.

COMMEMORATIVES AND MONUMENTS

1876 • A monument to Richard Allen, dedicated June 12, 1876, in Philadelphia's Freemont Park, may have been the first erected to a black by blacks.

Source: Dictionary of American Negro Biography, p. 13.

BOOKER T. WASHINGTON, A HIGHLY REGARDED EDUCATOR, FOUNDED ALABAMA'S TUSKEGEE INSTITUTE.

1940 • The first black American depicted on a U.S. postage stamp was Booker Taliaferro Washington (1856–1915). His photograph was reproduced on the ten-cent brown stamp, which became available on April 7, 1940, at Tuskegee Institute in Alabama. The stamp was part of the Famous American Commemorative series issued in 1940. He was honored again on a stamp in 1956, marking the one-hundredth anniversary of his birth. Perhaps the two most important black-related stamps are the Thirteenth Amendment issue of 1940, which celebrated the seventy-fifth anniversary of

OPPOSITE PAGE: BEVERLY JOHNSON ON THE JOB.

BLACKS COMMEMORATED ON POSTAGE STAMPS

DATE	HONOREE	AREA OF CITATION
April 7, 1940	Booker T. Washington	Educator
January 5, 1948	George Washington Carver	First black scientist
February 14, 1967	Frederick Augustus Douglass	First black civil rights leader
May 17, 1969	W. C. Handy	First black blues musician
April 29, 1986	Duke Ellington	First jazz musician
September 10, 1973	Henry O. Tanner	First black painter
May 1, 1975	Paul Laurence Dunbar	First black poet
February 1, 1978	Harriet Tubman	Abolitionist and author; first black woman honored on a stamp
March 5, 1985	Mary McLeod Bethune	First black female educator
May 28, 1986	Matthew Henson	First black explorer
February 20, 1987	Jean Baptiste Pointe Du Sable	First black frontiersman
February 1, 1990	Ida B. Wells (Barnett)	First black woman journalist
September 15, 1991	Jan E. Matseliger	First black inventor
June 22, 1993	Joe Louis	First black boxer

Sources: I Have a Dream; Jet 84 (28 June 1993), pp. 48–51; Kane, *Famous First Facts,* p. 482.

the Constitutional abolition of slavery in the United States, and the Emancipation Proclamation stamp of 1963, which honored the one-hundredth anniversary of the freeing of slaves in federally controlled areas during the Civil War.

1946 • The first coin honoring a black and designed by a black was issued. The fifty-cent piece, which became available on December 16, 1946, contained the bust of Booker T. Washington, the founder of Tuskegee Institute in Alabama. It was designed by Isaac S. Hathaway, who later also designed the George Washington Carver half-dollar.

Sources: Alford, *Famous First Blacks,* p. 68; *Jet* 81 (30 March 1992), p. 32; *Negro Year Book,* 1947, p. 33.

1960 • George Washington Carver (1864–1943), agronomist, scientist, and educator who produced more than four hundred different products from the peanut, potato, and pecan, became the first black scientist memorialized by a federal monument in the United States. In 1953, the United States Congress authorized the establishment of the George Washington Carver National Monument. It was erected on his birth site near Diamond, Missouri, and dedicated July 17, 1960. His scientific work improved the quality of life for millions of people and enhanced agriculture in the South. He took his mule-drawn "movable school" on weekend visits to impoverished farmlands to teach poor farmers to raise, improve, and preserve foods. Carver was born a slave. In 1894, he became the first black to graduate from Iowa State College. He joined the faculty of Tuskegee Institute (now University) in 1896, where he developed a program of research in soil conservation and crop diversification.

GEORGE WASHINGTON CARVER

Sources: Current Biography, 1940, pp. 148–50; *Dictionary of American Negro Biography,* pp. 92–95; *Encyclopedia of Black America,* p. 744; Hornsby, *Milestones in 20th-Century African-American History,* pp. 21, 202.

1963 • Georg (George) Olden (1921–), graphic designer, was the first black artist to design a U.S. postage stamp. The stamp was designed to commemorate the one-hundredth anniversary of the Emancipation Proclamation. It went on sale August 16, 1963.

Sources: Alford, *Famous First Blacks,* p. 9; *I Have A Dream,* p. 60; *Jet* 32 (17 August 1967), p. 11.

1969 • A nuclear-powered submarine named in honor of George Washington Carver was launched and commissioned.

Sources: Garrett, *Famous First Facts About Negroes,* p. 122; Kane, *Famous First Facts,* p. 562.

1974 • A monument honoring the life and contribution of Mary McLeod Bethune (1875–1955) was built in Washington, D.C., becoming the first statue of a black erected on public land. A noted educator, in 1939 she was named director of the National Youth Administration's Division of Negro Affairs and thus became the highest ranking black woman in government. (*See also* **Government—Federal Firsts: Federal Appointees, 1936; Organizations: Civil Rights and Political Organizations, 1935.**)

Sources: Cantor, *Historic Landmarks of Black America,* p. 275; *Notable Black American Women,* pp. 86–92; Robinson, *Historical Negro Biographies,* p. 163.

1987 • The first state-owned and -operated historic site honoring a black in North Carolina was the Charlotte Hawkins Brown Memorial State Historic Site, in Sedalia. In 1983, the Charlotte Hawkins Brown Historical Foundation was incorporated to assist the state in establishing the site—the 40-acre former campus and fourteen buildings of Palmer Memorial Institute, which Brown founded. (*See also* **Education: Club Memberships, 1928.**)

Sources: Greensboro News and Record (3 November 1991); *Jet* 73 (12 October 1987), p. 34; *Notable Black American Women,* p. 113.

1988 • The Black Revolutionary War Patriots Memorial was approved for the Washington, D.C., mall location.

Source: Jet 75 (12 September 1988), p. 12.

EXPLORATION

1536 • Estevanico or Estevan (c.1500–39), probably a native of Azamor, Morocco, was the first black man to traverse the southern portion of the United States, from Florida to Texas, in a journey that lasted eight years. In 1539, he was the first black to explore what is now Arizona and New Mexico. "Little Stephen" guided the expedition that searched for the fabled cities of Cibola, and was leading an advance scouting party when he was killed at Hawikuh Pueblo, New Mexico.

Sources: Cantor, *Historic Landmarks of Black America,* pp. 286, 320–21; *Dictionary of American Negro Biography,* p. 213; Garrett, *Famous First Facts About Negroes,* p. 68; *Negro Almanac,* p. 2.

1804 • York (c. 1770–c. 1832) was the first black to reach the mouth of the Columbia River overland. He was a member of the Lewis and Clark Expedition, which explored the Missouri River and continued on to the mouth of the Columbia. A slave, York excited the admiration of Indians because of his size, strength, and color; he became a valuable member of the expedition, both for his skills and his public relations value. He returned to Kentucky, where he eventually gained his freedom, but he ran into difficulties in his attempts to establish a business.

Sources: Cantor, *Historic Landmarks of Black America,* pp. 313–14, 326–27; *Dictionary of American Negro Biography,* pp. 676–77; Garrett, *Famous First Facts About Negroes,* p. 68.

1859 • Martin Robinson Delany (1812–85), was the first American black explorer in Africa. In the spring of 1859, Delany sailed to Africa and traveled in Liberia and the Niger Valley for nine months. Delany's *Official Report of the Niger Valley Exploring Party* appeared in 1861. (*See also* **Writers: Pamphlets, 1852; Military: United States Army, 1865.**)

Sources: Logan and Winston, *Dictionary of American Negro Biography,* pp. 169–73; Simmons, *Men of Mark,* pp. 1007–15; Jackson, *A History of Afro-American Literature,* vol. 1, pp. 364–69.

MATTHEW HENSON WAS PART OF PEARY'S EXPEDITION TO THE NORTH POLE.

1909 • Matthew Alexander Henson (1866–1955) was the first black man to reach the North Pole, of which he was co-discoverer with Robert E. Peary. There is some debate whether Peary was accurate in his claim to have reached the pole, but Henson went ahead to blaze the trail while Peary, whose toes were frozen, was pulled on the sledge. Hensen planted the flag at the location Peary determined to be the pole, since Peary was unable to stand. In 1961, Maryland erected a monument to honor Henson on the grounds of the state capitol. He recounted his experiences in *A Negro Explorer at the North Pole* (1912).

Sources: Cantor, *Historic Landmarks of Black America,* pp. 62–64; *Dictionary of American Negro Biography,* p. 308; Garrett, *Famous First Facts About Negroes,* p. 68.

HONORS AND AWARDS

1915 • The first black to receive the NAACP's Spingarn Medal was Ernest Everett Just (1883–1941). The award is given annually for the highest or noblest achievement by an American Negro. Ernest Just, zoologist and educator, was born in Charleston, South Carolina, and graduated from Dartmouth College and the University of Chicago. He began teaching at Howard University in Washington, D.C., before he earned his Ph.D. at the University of Chicago in 1916. His career as a distingushed biologist was hampered by racial prejudice, and he increasingly turned to Europe as a base for his research. In 1940, he was interned in France by the Germans, but managed to return to the United States, where he died of pancreatic cancer on October 27, 1941.

Sources: Contemporary Black Biography, vol. 3, pp. 123–25; *Dictionary of American Negro Biography,* pp. 372–75; *Encyclopedia of Black America,* pp. 481, 807.

ERNEST EVERETT JUST

1922 • Mary Burnett Talbert (1866–1923) was the first black woman to receive the NAACP's Spingarn Medal, for her efforts to preserve the home of Frederick Douglass in Anacostia, Virginia. In 1922, the home was dedicated as the Frederick Douglass Museum. In 1920 Talbert had become the first black delegate to be seated at the International Council of Women.

Sources: Brown, *Homespun Heroines,* pp. 217–19; Dannett, *Profiles of Negro Womanhood,* vol. 1, pp. 316–17; *Encyclopedia of Black America,* p. 807; Garrett, *Famous First Facts About Negroes,* p. 196; *Negro Yearbook, 1921–22,* p. 18; *Notable Black American Women,* pp. 1095–1100.

1946 • Emma Clarissa (Williams) Clement of Louisville, Kentucky, was the first black woman named "American Mother of the Year." The Golden Rule Foundation gave her the honor on May 1, 1946. At the time, Clement's son, Rufus, was president of Atlanta University.

Sources: Alford, *Famous First Blacks,* p. 69; *Chronology of African-American History,* p. 93; *Dictionary of American Negro Biography,* p. 117; Hornsby, *Milestones in 20th-Century African-American History,* p. 44; *Negro Year Book,* 1947, p. 33.

MARY BURNETT TALBERT HELPED ESTABLISH THE FREDERICK DOUGLASS MUSEUM.

1950 • The first black awarded the Nobel Peace Prize was Ralph Bunche (1904–71). The award was presented on September 22, 1950, for his peace efforts in the Middle East. Other blacks who have received Nobel Prizes are Martin Luther King, Jr. (1964), Albert J. Luthuli of South Africa (1960), and Desmond Tutu (1984). Born in the slums of Detroit, Bunche received his Ph.D. in political science from Harvard University in 1934, becoming the first black to be awarded the degree. In 1968, he became undersecretary general of the United Nations and was the highest ranking black in the U.N. at that time. (*See also* **Government—Federal Firsts: Federal Appointees, 1944; Organizations: Academic and Intellectual Societies, 1953.**)

Sources: Alford, *Famous First Blacks,* p. 13; *Encyclopedia of Black America,* pp. 198–99; Hornsby, *Milestones in 20th-Century African-American History,* pp. 47, 49, 73, 158.

1963 • Marian Anderson (1902–93) and Ralph Bunche (1904–71) were the first black winners of the Presidential Medal of Freedom.

Source: Alford, *Famous First Blacks,* pp. 13–14.

William Leo Hansberry (1894–1964) was the first recipient of the Hailie Selassie I prize, which he received for his pioneering work in African history and anthropology.

Source: Dictionary of American Negro Biography, p. 386.

1970 • Charlemae Hill Rollins (1897–1979) was the first black winner of the Constance Lindsay Skinner Award (now the WNBA Award) of the Women's National Book Association. She was born in Yazoo City, Mississippi, on June 20, 1897. A graduate of the University of Chicago, she worked to dispel negative images of blacks in books for children and young adults and became an expert on intercultural relations and children's literature.

Sources: Black Writers, p. 494; Garrett, *Famous First Facts about Negroes,* pp. 197–98; Josey, *The Black Librarian in America,* pp. 153–54; *Notable Black American Women,* pp. 949–53.

1979 • Sir Arthur Lewis (W. Arthur Lewis) (1915–) was the first black to win a Nobel Prize in a category other than peace, and the first to win in economics. He was born in the West Indies.

Sources: Jet 57 (1 November 1979), p. 5; Scobie, *Black Britannia,* p. 149.

The first black recipient of the AMC Cancer Research Center Humanitarian Award was Kenneth Gamble (1943–). Born in Philadelphia, Gamble became a businessman and songwriter, and co-founded Philadelphia International Records. He and his partner, Leon Huff, wrote and produced chart-topping songs and records for such artists as Lou Rawls, Teddy Pendergrass, and the O'Jays. He received a Grammy Award in 1976.

Sources: Jet 59 (15 January 1981), p. 29; *Who's Who Among Black Americans, 1992–93,* p. 501.

MISCELLANEOUS TOPICS

C.1850 • A black chef, possibly Hyram S. Thomas Bennett, was reputed to have introduced potato chips in America. It has also been claimed that an

American Indian, George Crum, first made potato chips in 1853; they were called Saratoga Potato Chips. Another claim is made on behalf of a locally famous black cook, Mrs. Catherine A. Wicks (1814–1917). She is said to have introduced them at Moon's Clubhouse in Saratoga Lake, New York.

Sources: Bennett, *Before the Mayflower,* p. 650; Kane, *Famous First Facts,* p. 493; *Negro Year Book, 1921–22,* p. 6.

HUGH MULZAC

PAUL

CUFFEE

CAPTAIN

1812.

1889 • "Nigger Add" (Old Add, Old Negro Ad) (fl. 1889–c.1906) was the first known range boss in the Southwest. He was also a rider and roper. He worked most of his active life with cattleman George W. Littlefield or his outfits in the Texas Panhandle and Eastern Mexico.

Source: Dictionary of American Negro Biography, pp. 5–6.

1892 • Hotel Berry in Athens, Ohio, was the first to provide needles, thread, buttons, and cologne in its guest rooms. Owned by Edwin C. Berry (1854–1931), the hotel had 20 rooms, all of which were restricted to white patrons.

Source: Dictionary of American Negro Biography, p. 40–41.

1905 • George McJunkin (1851–1922), cowboy, bronc buster, Indian arrowhead collector, and explorer, was the first person to recognize bones of extinct bison near Folsom, New Mexico, and try to call them to the attention of other people. The bones themselves were less significant than the spear points found with them. He had discovered the first site that proved people lived in North America over 10,000 years before.

Sources: Dictionary of American Negro Biography, pp. 417-18; Durham, *The Negro Cowboys,* pp. 159–60; *Negro Almanac,* p. 215.

1919 • Southside Settlement House, the first for blacks with a black staff, was founded by Ada S. McKinley (1868–1952), who recognized such a need among those blacks who migrated to Chicago during World War I in search of work. In 1949, with the help of the community, a new home was founded and renamed McKinley House in her honor. She was born in Texas and attended Prairie View College.

Source: Lee, Interesting People, p. 25.

1942 • Hugh Mulzac (1886–1971) was the first black captain of an American merchant marine ship. In 1920 he became the first black to earn a ship master's license, but he couldn't find a position as captain because of racial prejudice. In 1942 he was granted the right to man the liberty ship *Booker T. Washington.* His ship saw anti-aircraft action on a number of occasions.

Sources: Dictionary of Black Culture, p. 311; Hornsby, *Chronology of African-American History,* p. 91; *Negro Almanac,* p. 1426.

1969 • Learie Constantine (Lord Constantine, 1801–1971) was the first black to become a British peer. He was a member of the West Indies Cricket touring team from 1922 to the 1940s. He was knighted in 1962, and from 1962 to 1964 he was high commissioner from Trinidad.

Sources: File, Black Settlers in Britain, pp. 82–83; *Jet* 68 (8 July 1985), p. 4.

Sammy Davis, Jr., (1926–90) became the first black entertainer to sleep in the White House. Known as America's "Ambassador of Goodwill," he

OPPOSITE PAGE:
AN ENGRAVING OF
PAUL CUFFE AND HIS
SHIP, <u>TRAVELLER.</u>

began his career at age three, performing in vaudeville with his father, Sam, Sr., and his uncle, Will Mastin. This singer, dancer, and actor appeared on almost every variety show and comedy series on network television between 1956 and 1980. While he often worked with his friends Frank Sinatra and Dean Martin, he made his last film appearance in 1989 with Gregory Hines in *Tap*.

Sources: Hornsby, *Milestones in 20th-Century African-American History*, p. 447; *Jet* 78 (4 June 1990), pp. 32, 34; Southern, *Biographical Dictionary of Afro-American and African Musicians*, p. 96.

1977 • Carmen Elizabeth Turner (19??–1992) was the first black woman to head a major public transportation network. Turner was named as general manager of the Washington, D.C., transit authority, and served until 1983. Under her administration, Washington's Metropolitan Area Transit Authority grew from forty-two miles and forty-seven stations, to seventy miles and sixty-three stations. In mid-December 1990, Turner became the first black undersecretary at the Smithsonian Institution. Born in Teaneck, New Jersey, she studied for her doctorate at American University.

Sources: Ebony 39 (March 1984), pp. 93–94, 98; *Jet* 79 (29 October 1990), p. 10; *Washington Post* (3 October 1990); *Who's Who Among Black Americans, 1992–93,* p. 1419.

PIONEERS

1811 • Paul Cuffe (1759–1818) led the first group of blacks to investigate resettlement in Sierra Leone. He transported thirty-eight blacks there in the first systematic attempt to repatriate blacks from the United States. (*See also* **Business: Transportation, Shipping & Sailing, 1784.**)

Sources: Dictionary of American Biography, vol. 2, no. 2, p. 585; Robinson, *Historical Negro Biographies,* pp. 12–13; Simmons, *Men of Mark,* pp. 336–39.

1816 • Bob, baptized as Juan Crisobal (1819), was the first black English-speaking settler in California.

Source: Encyclopedia of Black America, p. 78.

1826 • Peter Ranne (or Ranee) was the first black to reach California via overland travel.

Source: Encyclopedia of Black America, p. 78.

1847 • Green Flake, Oscar Crosby, and Hank Lay were the first blacks to settle in Salt Lake Valley, Utah.

Source: Cantor, *Historic Landmarks of Black America,* p. 334.

PONY EXPRESS

1861 • The first black Pony Express riders were stagecoach driver and gold miner George Monroe (1843–86), and William Robinson. Little else is known about their activities, although Monroe became a noted stage driver in whose honor Monroe Meadows in Yosemite National Park is named.

Sources: Katz, *Black West,* pp. 128–29; *Negro Almanac,* p. 213; Reasons, *They Had a Dream,* vol. 2, p. 41.

1861 • George Monroe and William Robinson were the first black riders for the Pony Express. The Pony Express was a fast mail service using a relay of horses between St. Joseph, Missouri, and Sacramento, California.

Source: Katz, *Black West,* pp. 128–29.

ORGANIZATIONS: GROUP FIRSTS

~~~~~~

ACADEMIC AND INTELLECTUAL SOCIETIES

1786 • On August 23, 1786, Jean-Baptiste Lislet-Geoffrey was the first black correspondent of the French Academy of Sciences. Lislet was an artillery officer and in charge of maps on the Isle de France (now Mauritius). He made contributions in cartography and natural science.

Sources: Jet 56 (23 August 1979), p. 18; *Jet* 70 (25 August 1986), p. 24; Simmons, *Men of Mark,* pp. 991–92.

1877 • George Washington Henderson was the first black elected to Phi Beta Kappa. Phi Beta Kappa was founded in 1776 and became the most prestigious honors society in the humanities. He was elected by the University of Vermont, from which he graduated. Edward Alexander Bouchet (1825–1918) was elected on the basis of his work as a member of the Yale class of 1874, but not until 1884, when the Yale chapter was reactivated.

Sources: Black Issues in Higher Education, (27 September 1990), p. 20; *Dictionary of American Negro Biography,* pp. 50–51; *Phi Beta Kappa in American Life,* p. 233.

1897 • The American Negro Academy, founded on March 5, 1897, with the purpose of studying various aspects of black life and establishing a black intellectual tradition, was the first national black learned society. Papers appeared in print until 1924. A leading figure in the establishment of the academy was Alexander Crummell (1819–98). Noted contributors of publications were W. E. B. Du Bois (1868–1963) and Theophylus G. Steward.

Sources: Bennett, *Before the Mayflower,* p. 507; *Dictionary of American Negro Biography,* pp. 145–47; Moses, *Alexander Crummell,* pp. 258–75, 365–66.

1915 • The Association for the Study of Negro Life and History was organized by Carter G. Woodson (1875–1950) as the first learned society specifically devoted to the professional study of black history. Its first meeting was on September 9, 1915, in the office of the Wabash Avenue YMCA,

THE FATHER OF NEGRO HISTORY, CARTER G. WOODSON.

Chicago. Woodson was born in New Canton, Virginia and was educated at Berea College (Kentucky) (Litt.B., 1907), the University of Chicago (B.A., 1907; M.A., 1908) and Harvard (Ph.D., 1912). For both his own research and his encouragement of the research of others, Woodson is known as the Father of Negro History. The first issue of the *Journal of Negro History* appeared in 1916. This organization first sponsored Negro History Week (now Black History Month) in 1926.

Sources: Cantor, *Historic Landmarks of Black America,* p. xxvi; *Dictionary of American Negro Biography,* pp. 665–67; *Ebony* 48 (February 1993), pp. 23–24, 28; *Encyclopedia of Black America,* pp. 867–68; *Negro Almanac, 1989,* pp. 22–24.

1937 • Hugh Morris Gloster (1911–) was the founder and first president of the College Language Association. A native of Brownsville, Tennessee, Gloster took a Ph.D. at New York University in 1943. His distinguished career in education was capped with his presidency of Morehouse College (Atlanta, Georgia) from 1967 to 1987.

Sources: Encyclopedia of Black America, p. 406; Shockley and Chandler, *Living Black American Authors,* pp. 56–57; *Who's Who Among Black Americans, 1992–93,* p. 529.

1943 • On December 22, 1943, W. E. B. Du Bois was the first black elected to the National Institute of Arts and Letters. (*See also* **Education: College Degrees, 1895; Writers: History, 1896.**)

Sources: Dictionary of American Negro Biography, pp. 193–99; *Jet* 65 (27 February 1984), p. 24; Kane, *Famous First Facts,* p. 39.

1946 • Charles Spurgeon Johnson (1893–1956) was the first black to head the Southern Sociological Society. A distinguished sociologist and founder of the

National Urban League's magazine, *Opportunity,* he was also the first black president of Fisk University (Nashville, Tennessee) in 1946. (*See also* **Education: College Administrators, 1946.**)

Sources: Dictionary of American Negro Biography, pp. 347–49; *Encyclopedia of Black America,* pp. 471–72; *Negro Almanac, 1989,* p. 262.

1948 • E. Franklin Frazier (1894–1962) was the first black president of the American Sociological Society. Born in Baltimore, Frazier took his Ph.D. at the University of Chicago in 1931. He spent most of his teaching career, which spanned from 1934 to 1959, at Howard University in Washington, D.C. A prolific author, his most famous work is *Black Bourgeoisie* (1957).

Sources: Dictionary of American Negro Biography, pp. 241–44; *Encyclopedia of Black America,* p. 398; Robinson, *Historical Negro Biographies,* pp. 192–93.

SOCIOLOGIST
E. FRANKLIN FRAZIER.

1953 • Ralph Johnson Bunche (1904–71) was the first black president of the American Political Science Association. (*See also* **Government—Federal Firsts: Federal Appointees, 1944; Miscellaneous: Honors and Awards, 1950** and **1963.**)

Sources: Encyclopedia of Black America, pp. 1298–99; *Who's Who in America,* 1960–61, p. 407.

The first chapter of Phi Beta Kappa at a black university was established at Fisk University (Nashville, Tennessee) on April 4, 1953. The chapter at Howard University (Washington, D.C.) was formed four days later. Phi Beta Kappa, founded in 1775, is the most prestigious honorary society for undergraduate achievement in the humanities.

Sources: Delta of Tennessee, Phi Beta Kappa, Charter; *Famous First Blacks,* p. 35; *Phi Beta Kappa in American Life,* p. 231.

1957 • W. Montague Cobb (1904–90) was the first black president of the American Association of Physical Anthropologists (1957–59). A native of Washington, D.C., Cobb took his Ph.D. at Western Reserve University (now called Case Western Reserve) in 1932. He spent most of his career as professor of anatomy at Howard University. In 1957, he presided over the first Imhotep Conference (March 8–9). The organization's purpose was to eliminate segregation in the field of hospitalization and health care.

Sources: Morais, *The History of the Negro in Medicine,* pp. 142–144; Robinson, *Historical Negro Biographies,* pp. 174–75; *Who's Who Among Black Americans, 1992–93,* p. 1596.

1965 • David H. Blackwell (1919–) was the first black member of the National Academy of Sciences. A mathematician specializing in statistics, he earned a Ph.D. at the University of Illinois in 1941. In 1955, he became president of the Institute of Mathematical Statistics.

Sources: A Common Destiny: Blacks and American Society, p. 68; *Encyclopedia of Black America,* pp. 183, 744; *Who's Who Among Black Americans, 1992–93,* p. 115.

1969 • Kenneth Bancroft Clark (1914–) was the first black president of the American Psychological Association. The achievements of this distinguished psychologist were recognized by the award of the NAACP's Spingarn Medal in 1961.

Sources: Encyclopedia of Black America, p.273; Negro Almanac, 1989, p. 1403; Who's Who Among Black Americans, 1992–93, p. 266.

1973 • John Hope Franklin (1915–) became the first black president of Phi Beta Kappa. Since he held office until 1976, he presided over the two-hundredth anniversary celebrations of this honorary society for the humanities. He was also the first black president of the Southern Historical Association (1970), and of the American Historical Association (1978).

Sources: Current Biography, 1963, pp. 139–41; Encyclopedia of Black America, pp. 393–94; Who's Who Among Black Americans, 1992–93, p. 483.

1977 • Henry Aaron Hill (1915–79) was the first black president of the American Chemical Association.

Sources: Encyclopedia of Black America, p. 437; Who's Who in America, 1978–79, vol. 1, p. 1494.

JOHN HOPE FRANKLIN
PRESIDED OVER SEVERAL
ACADEMIC SOCIETIES.

1980 • James E. Blackwell (1926–) was the first black president of the Society for the Study of Social Problems. Blackwell was born in Anniston, Alabama, and became a sociologist, taking his Ph.D. at Washington State University in 1959.

Sources: Jet 57 (18 October 1979), p. 29; Who's Who Among Black Americans, 1992–93, p. 115.

1986 • Reginald Bess was the first black to chair a session of the International Courtly Literature Society as chairman of the 1986 Special Session. Bess is professor of German and English at Grambling State University (Louisiana).

Source: Jet 70 (8 September 1986), p. 20.

J. Russell George was the first black president of the Harvard Ripon Society. George was a twenty-five-year-old member of the first-year law school class.

Source: Jet 70 (12 May 1986), p. 8.

BUSINESS AND PROFESSIONAL ORGANIZATIONS

1904 • John Robert Edward Lee (1870–1944), director of the Academic Department of Tuskegee Institute (Alabama), was the first president of the National Association of Teachers in Colored Schools. Lee later served as president of Florida Agricultural and Mechanical College (1924–28).

Sources: Encyclopedia of Black America, p. 503; Negro Year Book, 1921–22, p. 410.

John R. Mitchell, Jr., (1863–1929) was the first black member of the American Bankers Association. A native of the outskirts of Richmond, Virginia, Mitchell first won fame as the crusading and militant editor of the *Richmond Planet,* which he took over in 1884. He served on the Richmond City Council from 1888 to 1896, and in 1902 he founded the Mechanics Saving Bank. His bank failed in 1922, and he died without money.

Sources: *Dictionary of American Negro Biography,* pp. 444–45; Penn, *The Afro-American Press,* pp. 183–87; Simmons, *Men of Mark,* pp. 314–32.

1925 • George H. Woodson of Des Moines, Iowa, became the first president of the National Bar Association, an organization formed to forward the concerns of black lawyers.

Sources: *Encyclopedia of Black America,* pp. 129–30; *Negro Almanac, 1989,* p. 1358.

1940 • The National Negro Newspapers Association was founded in 1940. (Negro was dropped from the organization's title in 1956.) In 1989, the association had 148 members. The co-founders were Frank L. Stanley, Sr., (c. 1906–74) and Carter Walker Wesley (1892–1969).

Sources: *Ebony Success Library,* vol. 1, p. 292 (Stanley); *Encyclopedia of Black America,* p. 850 (Wesley); Hornsby, *Chronology of Black America,* pp. 237–38; *Negro Almanac, 1989,* pp. 305, 1288; *Split Image,* p. 355.

1962 • Herman Jerome Russell (1930–) was the first black member of the Atlanta Chamber of Commerce. Russell is an Atlanta builder and land developer, who serves on many business, civic, and religious boards. In 1981, he became the second black president of the chamber.

Sources: *Ebony Success Library,* vol. 1, p. 270; *Jet* 59 (25 January 1981), p. 39; *Who's Who Among Black Americans, 1992–93,* p. 1232.

1968 • Elizabeth Duncan Koontz (1919–89) was the first black president of the National Education Association. Koontz was a classroom teacher in North Carolina until she became president of the department of classroom teachers in the National Education Association in 1965. From 1969 to 1972 she was director of the Women's Bureau of the United States Department of Labor.

Sources: *Black Women in America,* pp. 683–84; *Encyclopedia of Black America,* p. 490; *Notable Black American Women,* pp. 638–43.

**ELIZABETH
DUNCAN
KOONTZ**

1970 • Edward S. Lewis (1901–) was the first black president of the National Cooperative Education Association. A native of Platte City,

Missouri, Lewis was a graduate of the University of Chicago (Ph.B., 1925) and received his Ph.D. from New York University (1961).

Source: Ebony Success Library, vol. 1, p. 201.

1971 • Cleo W. Blackburn (1909–) was the first black director of the United States Chamber of Commerce. Blackburn was an educator who was president of Jarvis Christian College, Hawkins, Texas, from 1953 to 1964.

Source: Encyclopedia of Black America, p. 181.

1972 • Fred M. Crosby (1928–) was the first black elected to the board of the Ohio Council of Retail Merchants Association. Crosby is the president of the Crosby Furniture Company, one of Cleveland's most successful black businesses.

Sources: Ebony Success Library, vol. 2, p. 82; *Who's Who Among Black Americans, 1992–93,* p. 325.

Carl T. Rowan (1925–) was the first black member of the Gridiron Club, an organization of Washington journalists founded in 1885. (*See also* **Government—Federal Firsts: Federal Appointees, 1964.**)

Source: Ebony Success Library, vol. 2, pp. 228–31.

The first and only black executive director of the American Library Association was Robert Wedgeworth, Jr., (1938–).

Sources: American Libraries 41 (July/August 1980), p. 458; Josey and Shockley, *Handbook of Black Librarianship,* p. 22.

1973 • Celestine Strode Cook (1924–) was the first black woman to serve on the National Business Committee for the Arts. Strode was a business-woman in Galveston, Texas, until 1958, when she moved to New Orleans, Louisiana. In 1974, she would be the first black woman selected as one of the ten most outstanding women of New Orleans.

Source: Encyclopedia of Black America, p. 286.

1974 • Lewis Carnegie Dowdy (1917–), president of North Carolina Agricultural and Technical State University (1964–80), was the first black president of the National Association of Universities and Land Grant Colleges.

Sources: Encyclopedia of Black America, p. 325; *Famous First Blacks,* p. 33–34; *Who's Who Among Black Americans, 1992–93,* p. 395.

1976 • Joe Booker became the first black vice president of the National Association of Intercollegiate Athletics Sports Information Directors. At the time of his selection, he was sports publicity director at Prairie View Agricultural and Mechanical University (Texas). He was the only black offi-cer of the association.

Source: Jet 50 (6 May 1976), p. 20.

Mary Hatwood Futrell (1940–) was the first black president of the Virginia Education Association. She would go on to become president of the National Education Association (1980–89).

Sources: Negro Almanac, 1989, pp. 1379–80; *Notable Black American Women,* pp. 376–80; *Who's Who Among Black Americans, 1992–93,* p. 496.

Clara Stanton Jones (1913–) was the first black president of the American Library Association. A graduate of Spelman College, Jones spent most of her professional career with the Detroit Public Libraries, of which she became the first black, and the first woman, director in 1970.

Sources: Encyclopedia of Black America, p. 476; *Jet* 50 (12 August 1976), p. 29; *Notable Black American Women,* pp. 593–97.

As president of the New York City Housing Patrolmen's Benevolent Association, Jack Jordan was the first black to head a police union in the state.

Source: Jet 51 (30 December 1976), p. 46.

1977 • Roslyn Maria (Roz) Abrams (1948–) became the first black vice president of the Atlanta Press Club. Abrams was a news reporter for WXIA-TV at the time.

Sources: Ebony 34 (January 1979), p. 115; *Jet* 52 (2 June 1977), p. 20; *Who's Who Among Black Americans, 1992–93,* p. 3.

Samuel L. Williams was the first black president of the Los Angeles Bar Association. In 1981, Williams was the first black president of the State Bar of California. A Los Angeles attorney, Williams had turned down an offer of an appointment to the state supreme court earlier in 1977.

Source: Jet 61 (12 November 1981), p. 28.

1978 • Jesse Hill, Jr., was the first black president of the Atlanta Chamber of Commerce. Hill was president and chief executive officer of the Atlanta Life Insurance Company.

Sources: Black Enterprise 7 (June 1977), p. 122; *Jet* 53 (12 January 1978), p. 25; *Jet* 59 (15 January 1981), p. 39; *Sepia* 27 (June 1978), pp. 75–80; *Who's Who Among Black Americans, 1992–93,* p. 657.

Marilyn French Hubbard (1946–) was the founder and first president of the National Association of Black Women Entrepreneurs.

Sources: Jet 77 (16 October 1989), p. 40; *Who's Who Among Black Americans, 1992–93,* p. 694.

Milton L. Reynolds (1924–) was the first black president of the New York State School Boards Association. Reynolds was a systems programming manager for International Business Machines (IBM) at the time.

Sources: Jet 53 (17 November 1977), p. 29; *Who's Who Among Black Americans, 1992–93,* p. 1182.

1979 • Jack Bell was the first black president of the Texas Restaurant Association. Bell was a restaurant operator and caterer in Corpus Christi, Texas.
Source: Jet 56 (26 July 1979), p. 22.

Curtis J. Moret was the first black president of the Municipal Court Clerks Association of California. Moret was division chief of the Oakland-Piedmont municipal court.
Source: Jet 57 (27 December 1979), p. 21.

Mack Sewell was the first black president of the Georgia Association of Independent Juvenile Courts. Sewell was a probation officer in Clarke County.
Source: Jet 57 (25 October 1979), p. 21.

1980 • J. Clay Smith, Jr., (1942–) was the first black president of the Federal Bar Association, an organization for federal lawyers. After working for the U.S. Army and the government, Smith became a law professor at the Howard University School of Law (1982), becoming dean of the school in 1986.
Sources: Jet 59 (9 October 1980), p. 6; *Jet* 61 (17 September 1981), p. 6; *Jet* 61 (26 November 1981), p. 11; *Who's Who Among Black Americans, 1992–93,* p. 1303.

Larry W. Whiteside (1937–) was the first black chair of the board of directors of the Baseball Writers Association of America. He was a sportswriter for the *Boston Globe* newspaper.
Sources: Jet 57 (10 January 1980), p. 21; *Who's Who Among Black Americans, 1992–93,* p. 1500.

1981 • Arnette R. Hubbard was the first woman president of the National Bar Association, the national association for black lawyers. A Chicago attorney, Hubbard took her law degree at John Marshall Law School in 1969. She had also been the first woman president of the Cook County (Illinois) Bar Association.
Sources: Ebony 37 (January 1982), p. 32; *Jet* 60 (20 August 1981), p. 21; *Who's Who Among Black Americans, 1992–93,* p. 693.

1982 • Samuel Fredrick Lambert (1928–) was the first black president of the National Association of Power Engineers. A native of Alabama, Lambert served as supervisor of custodians and engineers for the New York City Board of Education.
Sources: Jet 62 (19 July 1982), p. 21; *Who's Who Among Black Americans, 1992–93,* p. 839.

Scott C. Westbrook III (1939–) was the first black president of the Michigan Occupational Education Association. Westbrook is currently

OPPOSITE PAGE: CLARA STANTON JONES IS RECOGNIZED FOR HER WORK IN THE FIELD OF LIBRARIANSHIP.

supervisor of Vocational Specialist Needs for the Pontiac, Michigan, School District.

Sources: Jet 62 (9 August 1982), p. 21; *Who's Who Among Black Americans, 1992–93,* p. 1487.

1983 • Charles R. Smith was the first black president of the North Carolina Watchmakers Association. Smith was a member of the Cape Fear Watchmakers Guild.

Source: Jet 64 (1 August 1983), p. 21.

Betty Lou Thompson (1939–) was the first black president of Women in Municipal Government. Thompson was a councilwoman in University City, Missouri.

Sources: Jet 64 (21 March 1983), p. 24; *Who's Who Among Black Americans, 1992–93,* p. 1390.

Betty Anne Williams (1952–) was the first black president of the Washington Press Club. Williams worked for the Associated Press and left that position to work for the Democrat and Chronicle newspaper, Rochester, New York.

Sources: Crisis 90 (November 1983), p. 38; *Jet* 64 (9 May 1983), p. 13; *Jet* 65 (13 February 1984), p. 13; *Jet* 67 (17 December 1984), p. 10.

1984 • Maxine Young was the first woman of any race to hold the position of executive director of the Gary, Indiana, Chamber of Commerce.

Source: Jet 66 (9 July 1984), p. 21.

1985 • I. S. Leevy Johnson (1942–) was the first black president of the South Carolina Bar Association. This lawyer and funeral director is also one of the first three blacks elected to the South Carolina legislature in this century.

Sources: Jet 68 (22 July 1985), p. 6; *Who's Who Among Black Americans, 1992–93,* p. 759.

1986 • As president of the St. Louis chapter of the National Academy of Television Arts and Sciences, Ava L. Brown was the first black woman to hold a presidential post on either the local or national level. She was public access director for City Cable Television, a black-owned firm.

Source: Jet 70 (8 September 1986), p. 20.

Montez Cornelius Martin, Jr., (1940–) was the first black president of the Trident Chamber of Commerce (Charleston, Dorchester, and Berkeley Counties, South Carolina). Martin was born in Columbia, South Carolina, and is a construction engineer and a realtor.

Sources: Jet 70 (4 August 1986), p. 6; *Who's Who Among Black Americans, 1992–93,* p. 923.

1987 • Barbara Rudd Gross was the first black president of the Women's Advertising Club, Chicago.

Source: Jet 72 (15 June 1987), p. 30.

Sharon B. Hartley was the first black, and the first woman, elected president of the Niagara Frontier Corporate Counsel Association. Hartley was counsel for Delaware North Companies, Buffalo, New York.
Source: Jet 71 (26 January 1987), p. 20.

Elnor B. G. Hickman was the first black president of Professional Secretaries International, Illinois Division. Hickman was executive secretary to the executive director of the Legal Foundation Assistance of Chicago.
Source: Jet 72 (15 June 1987), p. 30.

Ira Jackson was the first black president of the Georgia Municipal Association. Jackson is an Atlanta city councilman.
Source: Jet 72 (3 August 1987), p. 26.

Dolores G. McGhee was the first black president of the Georgia School Boards Association. She had also been the first black elected to the Fulton County Board of Education.
Source: Jet 73 (12 October 1987), p. 20.

Bert Norman Mitchell (1938–) was the first black president of the New York State Society of Certified Public Accountants, a first in the United States. In addition to his work as an accountant and an administrator for various organizations, Mitchell has published more than fifty professional articles.
Sources: Jet 72 (11 May 1987), p. 20; *Who's Who Among Black Americans, 1992–93,* p. 999.

Alan Herbert Peterson (1948–) was the first black member of the national executive board of the National Police Officers' Association of America. A policeman in Newark, New Jersey, Peterson had been totally and permanently disabled by an on-duty explosion in 1983. In recent years, Peterson has been devoting his energies to the investigation of Satanism.
Sources: Jet 73 (7 December 1987), p. 20; *Who's Who Among Black Americans, 1992–93,* p. 1115.

Gregory J. Reed (1948–) was the first black chairman of the Arts, Communication, Entertainment, and Sports Section of the Michigan State Bar Association, the first black to hold such a position in the United States. Reed's specializations as an attorney are corporate, taxation, and entertainment law. He is the author of several books on entertainment and sports law.
Sources: Jet 72 (11 May 1987), p. 22; *Who's Who Among Black Americans, 1992–93,* pp. 1173–74.

Shirley Street was the first black to head Women in Real Estate, Chicago.
Source: Jet 72 (3 August 1987), p. 20.

1988 • Albert Abrams was the first black general manager and vice president for organizational development of the Greater Macon (Georgia)

Chamber of Commerce. He is believed to be the only black to hold such a position in the South.
Source: Jet 75 (21 November 1988), p. 20.

Donald DeHart was the first black state president of the New Jersey Jaycees. DeHart was a probation officer with the Passaic County Probation Department in Paterson, New Jersey.
Source: Jet 75 (31 October 1988), p. 20.

Richard Knight, Jr., (1945–),the first black city manager of Dallas, Texas, was the first black member of the Salesmanship Club. In 1990, he became the first black to hold the position of director of total quality management with Caltex Petroleum Corporation, Irving, Texas.
Sources: Jet 75 (17 October 1988), p. 40; *Jet* 78 (30 April 1990), p. 6; *Who's Who Among Black Americans, 1992–93,* p. 831.

1989 • LaVerne Francis Collins was the first black president of Business and Professional Women/USA. Collins was a human resource specialist for the Federal Aviation Administration in Seattle, Washington.
Source: Jet 76 (4 September 1989), p. 30.

Conrad Kenneth Harper (1940–) was the first black to head the Association of the Bar of the City of New York. Since 1974 Harper has been a partner at Simpson, Thacher, and Bartlett, one of the first black partners in a major law firm.
Sources: Jet 78 (11 June 1990), p. 18; *Who's Who Among Black Americans, 1992–93,* p. 600.

Sandra Cavanaugh Holley (1943–) was the first black president of the American Speech-Language-Hearing Association. Holley was professor of communications disorders at Southern Connecticut State University.
Sources: Jet 75 (19 December 1988), p. 22; *Who's Who Among Black Americans, 1992-93,* p. 670.

1990 • Lee Patrick Brown (1937–), New York City police commissioner (1990–), was the first black president of the International Association of Chiefs of Police. (*See also* **Government—Local Heroes: Texas, 1982—Houston.**)
Source: Who's Who Among Black Americans, 1992–93, p. 175.

Blanton Thandreus Canady (1948–)was the first black president of McDonald's Owners of Chicagoland and Northwest Indiana. A Chicago businessman, Canady is a 1970 graduate of the University of Illinois.
Sources: Jet 78 (3 September 1990), p. 20; *Who's Who Among Black Americans, 1992–93,* p. 225.

1991 • Lois Terrell Mills (1958–) was the first black national president of the American Business Women's Association. With a degree from Stanford

(1980), Mills is currently an industrial engineer with the Ethicon division of Johnson and Johnson in Albuquerque, New Mexico.

Sources: Jet 79 (21 January 1991), p. 20; *Who's Who Among Black Americans, 1992–93,* p. 995.

1992 • Edwyna Anderson, general counsel of the Duquesne Light Company, was the first black, and the first woman, president of the Pennsylvania Electric Association.

Source: Jet 82 (12 October 1992), p. 20.

Hubert Anderson was the first black elected to board of the National Association of the Deaf. Anderson, who was serving as outreach chair for the organization, had also been a basketball coach at Gallaudet University, from which he graduated. He was coach of the gold-medal winning basketball team in the World Games for the Deaf in 1985.

Source: Jet 83 (21 December 1992), p. 26.

Andre L. Dennis was the first black chancellor of the Philadelphia Bar Association, which has some twelve thousand members. Dennis is a 1969 graduate of Howard University School of Law.

Source: Jet 83 (21 December 1992), p. 29.

M. David Lee was the first black president of the Boston Society of Architects.

Source: Jet 81 (16 March 1992), p. 36.

Ben Miles was the first black president of the Virginia Association of Broadcasters. Miles was general manager of WCDX, Richmond, Virginia.

Source: Jet 82 (3 August 1992), p. 35.

Leslie Seymore was the first woman chair of the National Black Police Association. Seymore had served on the Philadelphia police force since 1973.

Source: Jet 81 (16 March 1992), p. 36.

1993 • Connie Perdreau was the first black elected to head Administrators and Teachers of English as a Second Language. Perdreau is a faculty member at the University of Ohio, Athens.

Sources: Jet 83, (26 April 1993), p. 20; *Who's Who Among Black Americans, 1992–93,* p. 1108.

CHARITABLE AND CIVIC ORGANIZATIONS

1780 • Formed on November 10, 1780, the African Union Society of Newport, Rhode Island, was the first attested black mutual aid society. The second, the Free African Society of Philadelphia, was formed in 1787. (*See* *also* **Organizations: Civil Rights and Political Organizations, 1788; Religion: Episcopalians, 1794, and Methodists, 1787 and 1799.**) The African Society of Boston was formed in 1796, and the New York African Society in 1808.

Sources: Dictionary of Black Culture, p. 15; Yee, *Black Women Abolitionists,* p. 74.

1787 • The Free African Society was formed in Philadelphia on April 12, 1787. This society is generally regarded as the first black organization of note in this country because it quickly became the nucleus for two black churches. (*See also* **Religion: Episcopalians, 1794, and Methodists, 1787 and 1799.**) The African Union Society of Newport, Rhode Island, was formed in 1780. Also in Philadelphia, the Female Benevolent Society of Saint Thomas' Episcopal Church was formed in 1793, and the male African Friendly Society of Saint Thomas, in 1795.

Sources: Bennett, *Before the Mayflower,* pp. 55–56, 80–81, 621–22; *Dictionary of American Negro Biography,* p. 147; Hornsby, *Chronology of African-American History,* p. 9; *Negro Almanac, 1989,* pp. 6, 234, 1333; Sterling, *We Are Your Sisters,* p.105.

1790 • The Brown Fellowship of Charleston, South Carolina, is the first known mutual aid society in South Carolina. Limited to fifty free men of color, one of its principal functions was to manage a cemetery for the black members of Saint Philip's Episcopal Church, since they could not be buried in the church's cemetery. The organization survived well into the twentieth century, by which time it had become an exclusive social organization.

Source: Gatewood, *Aristocrats of Color,* pp. 14–15.

1828 • In January, 1828, twenty-one black women, with the advice of male ministers, met in New York to draw up plans for the African Dorcas Society, which was officially organized in February. This was the first black women's charitable group. Its principal object was to aid young blacks in attending schools by supplying them with clothing, hats, and shoes.

Source: Yee, *Black Women Abolitionists,* pp. 75–76.

1853 • The first Colored Young Men's Christian Association was organized in Washington, D.C. Its first president was Anthony Bowen who worked for the patent office.

Sources: Ashe, *A Hard Road to Glory,* vol. 1, p. 12; *Dictionary of American Negro Biography,* p. 449; *Dictionary of Black Culture,* p. 61; *Negro Year Book,* 1925–26, p. 275.

1867 • The first black delegate to an international convention of the Young Men's Christian Association was Edward V. C. Eato (?–1914). Eato was a prominent figure in New York social life as a member of the Ugly Club, Masons, and Society of the Sons of New York. For twenty-five years, he was the president of the African Society.

Sources: Ashe, *A Hard Road to Glory,* vol. 1, p. 12; Gatewood, *Aristocrats of Color,* pp. 213, 224, 233, 252; *Negro Year Book,* 1925–26, p. 275.

1876 • The first student branch of the Young Men's Christian Association (YMCA) at a black school was organized at Howard University, Washington, D.C. By 1911, the number of black student branches was about one hundred.

Sources: Dictionary of American Negro Biography, p. 339; *Negro Year Book, 1921–22,* p. 218.

1888 • William Alphaeus Hunton (1863–1916) became probably the first black employed by the Young Men's Christian Association (YMCA) when he went to the Norfolk, Virginia, branch. In 1893, Hunton became the first colored secretary of the International Young Men's Christian Association. Born in Chatham, Ontario, Canada, he devoted his life to work with the association, particularly in the Colored Men's Department.

Sources: Ashe, A Hard Road to Glory, vol. 1, p. 12; *Dictionary of American Negro Biography,* pp. 338–40; *Notable Black American Women,* pp. 537–38.

1893 • The first black branch of the Young Women's Christian Association (YWCA) was opened in Dayton, Ohio.

Source: Ashe, A Hard Road to Glory, vol. 1, p. 12.

1899 • The Colored Young Men's Christian Association Building in Norfolk, Virginia, was the first YMCA building constructed for blacks.

Source: An Era of Progress and Promise, p. 533 (photograph).

WILLIAM ALPHAEUS HUNTON IS NOTED FOR HIS LIFELONG WORK FOR THE YMCA.

1907 • Addie Hunton (1875–1943) was the first secretary for colored student affairs for the National Board of the Young Women's Christian Association (YWCA). In addition to her work for the YWCA—in the United States and in France during the First World War—Hunton was also very active in the club movement and the women's suffrage movement. In 1889, she had been the first black to graduate from the Spencerian College of Commerce in Philadelphia.

Sources: Ashe, A Hard Road to Glory, vol. 1, p. 12; *Dictionary of American Negro Biography,* pp. 337–38; *Notable Black American Women,* pp. 536–40.

ADDIE HUNTON

MOLLIE MOON,
FOUNDER OF THE
NATIONAL URBAN
LEAGUE GUILD.

1942 • Mollie Moon (1912–90) was the organizer and first president of the National Urban League Guild, a fund-raising organization for the Urban League. She headed the organization until her death.

Sources: Black Women in America, pp. 810–12; Hornsby, *Chronology of African-American History*, p. 436; *Notable Black American Women*, pp. 760–61.

1944 • The United Negro College Fund was first founded on April 24, 1944, to coordinate the fund-raising efforts of forty-one private, accredited, four-year schools. It was chartered in New York. It was the first attempt by private black colleges to establish a cooperative fundraising organization. Its efforts still contribute significantly to the survival of black higher education. The fund's founder was Frederick D. Patterson (1901–), a veterinarian, who also founded the first veterinary school at Tuskegee Institute (Alabama). He later served as president of Tuskegee for twenty-five years, until his retirement. Patterson received the Medal of Freedom on June 23, 1987, when he was eighty-six years old.

Sources: Ebony Success Library, vol. 1, p. 242; *Encyclopedia of Black America*, p. 823; Hornsby, *Chronology of African-American History*, p. 92; *Jet* 72 (11 May 1987), p. 24; *Jet* 72 (27 July 1987), p. 22; *Negro Almanac, 1989*, p. 1369.

1946 • Channing Heggie Tobias (1882–1961) was the first black to head the Phelps–Stokes Fund, an organization founded to further black education. A native of Augusta, Georgia, Tobias was an ordained minister of the Colored (later Christian) Methodist Episcopal Church. In 1911, he began to work for the Young Men's Christian Association (YMCA), where he achieved prominence as senior secretary of the Colored Division of the National Council. In 1950, he was the first black to receive an honorary Doctor of Laws degree from New York University.

Sources: Dictionary of American Negro Biography, pp. 593–95; *Encyclopedia of Black America*, pp. 817–18; Robinson, *Historical Negro Biographies*, pp. 252–53.

1965 • Lois Towles Caesar (1922–) was the first black on the board of directors of the San Francisco Symphony Foundation, and on the board of directors of the San Francisco Symphony Association (1969). In 1976 she became the first black and woman to serve on the Mayor's Criminal Justice Commission of San Francisco, California. In 1978, she became the first minority chair of the commission.

Sources: Handy, Black Women in American Bands and Orchestras, pp. 213–14; *Jet* 41 (2 March 1972), p. 38; *Our World* 8 (May 1953), pp. 28–43; *Who's Who Among Black Americans, 1992–93*, p. 215.

1967 • Mrs. Robert Clayton was the first black president of the national Young Women's Christian Association (YWCA).

Source: Garrett, Famous First Facts About Negroes, pp. 201–2.

1970 • Donald M. Payne (1934–) was the first black to head the National Council of the Young Men's Christian Association (YMCA). In 1989, he was elected as New Jersey's first black congressman.

Sources: Negro Almanac, p 104; Who's Who Among Black Americans, 1992–93, p. 1099.

1975 • Gloria Dean Randle Scott (1938–) was the first black president of the Girl Scouts of America. Scott held this position until 1978. She holds a Ph.D. from Indiana University and has had extensive experience in teaching and academic administration. This educator became president of Bennett College in 1987.

Sources: Black Women in America, pp. 1018–19; Notable Black American Women, pp. 993–97; Who's Who Among Black Americans, 1992–93, p. 1250.

GLORIA DEAN RANDLE SCOTT

1977 • Fredda Witherspoon was the first black president of the Metropolitan St. Louis Young Women's Christian Association (YWCA).

Sources: Jet 54 (15 June 1978), p. 24; Who's Who Among Black Americans, 1992–93, p. 1559.

1978 • Faye Wattleton (1943–) became the first black, and the first woman, president of the Planned Parenthood Federation. A native of St. Louis, Missouri, Wattleton took her nursing degree from the Ohio University School of Nursing in 1964. She was the first person in her family to earn a college degree. She held the post as president until her resignation in 1992.

Sources: Black Women in America, pp. 1239–40; Jet 62 (5 April 1982), p. 41; Notable Black American Women, pp. 1230–32; Who's Who Among Black Americans, 1992–93, p. 1474.

FAYE WATTLETON

1979 • Raymond W. Fannings was the first black director of the Chicago Child Care Society, Chicago's oldest charitable organization.

Source: Jet 56 (10 May 1979), p. 21.

Franklin A. Thomas (1934–) was the first black to head a major foundation, the Ford Foundation. He was born in New York City and attended Columbia University (B.A., 1956), where he was the first black to serve as captain of the basketball team. He became an attorney and worked both in government positions and in private practice.

Sources: Ebony Success Library, vol. 1, p. 302; *Current Biography Yearbook, 1981,* pp. 413–16; *Negro Almanac,* p. 1417; *Who's Who Among Black Americans, 1992–93,* p. 1382.

1981 • The Black Tennis and Sports Foundation was first set up in 1981. Its founder was Augustus Jenkins.

Source: Jet 72 (10 August 1987), p. 9.

1982 • Sherman Jones was the first black vice president of Optimists International, a community service organization. At the time of the election, Jones was a police sergeant on the Kansas City, Missouri, force.

Source: Jet 62 (9 August 1982), p. 21.

1984 • Walter G. Harris, Birmingham (Alabama) city school superintendent, was the first black member of the Birmingham Rotary Club.

Source: Jet 67 (12 November 1984), p. 29.

1985 • Anna F. Jones was the first black woman to head a major community foundation, the Boston Foundation. Jones is the daughter of the first black president of Howard University, Mordecai W. Jones.

Source: Jet 67 (4 March 1985), p. 5.

Archibald Mosley was the first black president of the Pontiac, Michigan, Kiwanis Club. Mosley is Pontiac communications coordinator.

Source: Jet 69 (23 December 1985), p. 20.

1986 • Marie Gasden (1919–) was the first black woman to chair Oxfam America. Gadsden was executive director of the PhelpsStokes Fund (Washington, D.C., office), and later deputy director of the National Association for Equal Opportunity in Higher Education/AID Cooperative Agreement.

Sources: Jet 71 (24 November 1986), p. 20; *Notable Black American Women,* pp. 381–83.

Walter G. Harris was the first black member of the board of directors of the Birmingham, Alabama, Rotary Club. Harris had also been the first black member of the club.

Source: Jet 70 (4 August 1986), p. 31.

1987 • Leria Lowe Jordan was the first black member of the Junior League of Birmingham, Alabama. Jordan was a twenty-nine-year-old auditing analyst.

Source: Jet 72 (18 May 1987), p. 24.

1988 • Madeline Ford was the first woman vice president and corporate secretary of the Young Men's Christian Association (YMCA) of Greater New York. She was thus the highest ranking woman ever in this organization.
Source: Jet 74 (16 May 1988), p. 20.

1989 • Herbert Carter was the first black chairman of the board of directors of United Way. Carter was executive vice chancellor at California State University at Los Angeles.
Sources: Jet 76 (24 July 1989), p. 8; *Jet* 76 (25 September 1989), p. 20.

Gabriel S. Lee, Jr., (1922–) was the first black president of the Cleveland, Ohio, Host Club/Lions Club International. Lee is a clergyman who is very active in civic and social work.
Sources: Jet 77 (18 December 1989), p. 20; *Who's Who Among Black Americans, 1992–93,* p. 857.

Mahlon Martin was the first black to head the Rockefeller Foundation. A native of Arkansas, Martin was the first black city manager in Little Rock in 1980, and the first black director of the state Finance and Administration Department (1983–86).
Source: Jet 76 (22 May 1989), p. 24.

1990 • As president of the Rotary Club of Cheraw, Elmer D. Brooks was the first black president of the organization in the state of South Carolina. Brooks had been a mortician in Cheraw for ten years.
Source: Jet 77 (19 February 1990), p. 20.

Gayleatha Brown, an embassy economic aide in Dar es Salaam, was the first and only woman member of the Rotary Club of Tanzania.
Source: Jet 78 (27 August 1990), p. 11.

Walter G. Sellers (1925–) was the first black trustee of Kiwanis International. This educator has had a long association with Central State University, Wilberforce, Ohio, and in 1990 was special assistant to the university's president.
Sources: Jet 78 (6 August 1990), p. 22; *Who's Who Among Black Americans, 1992–93,* p. 1258.

1992 • Mary Ann Nelson was the first black elected to the national board of the Sierra Club. Nelson was an environmental attorney in Boston.
Source: Jet 82 (13 July 1992), p. 20.

CIVIL RIGHTS AND POLITICAL ORGANIZATIONS

1775 • The Pennsylvania Society for the Abolition of Slavery was the first abolition society. It was organized in Philadelphia on April 14, 1775, and its first president was John Baldwin. After reorganizing and adopting a new constitution, it became incorporated as the Pennsylvania Society for Promoting the Abolition of Slavery, for the Relief of Free Negroes Unlawfully Held in Bondage, and for Improving the Condition of the African Race, on December 8, 1789.

Sources: Encyclopedia of Black America, p. 789; Hornsby, *Chronology of African-American History,* p. 7; Kane, *Famous First Facts,* p. 1; *Negro Almanac, 1989,* pp. 5, 812.

1788 • The African Union Society of Newport, Rhode Island, was the first black organization to advocate black emigration to Africa. This position was challenged by the Free African Society of Philadelphia.

Sources: Bennett, *Before the Mayflower,* p. 145; *Encyclopedia of Black America,* p. 280; *The Negro Almanac, 1989,* p. 6.

1895 • The National Conference of Colored Women met in Boston, Massachusetts, in August, 1895. The leading spirit in organizing the conference was Josephine St. Pierre Ruffin (1842–1924), the founder of the Women's New Era Club. The meeting led to the formation of the National Federation of Afro-American Women, which was merged into the National Association of Colored Women the following year on July 21, 1896. Mary Church Terrell (1863–1954) became the first president of the National Association of Colored Women.

Sources: Bennett, *Before the Mayflower,* p. 507; *Dictionary of American Negro Biography,* pp. 535–36; *Encyclopedia of Black America,* pp. 815, 863; *Notable Black Women,* pp. 961–66 (Ruffin); 1115–19 (Terrell).

1905 • Twenty-nine black intellectuals and activists from fourteen states met near Niagara Falls, New York, on July 11–13 to establish the Niagara Movement. Led by W. E. B. Du Bois and William Monroe Trotter, the organization rejected the accomodationist policies of Booker T. Washington and encouraged blacks to press for immediate civil rights without compromise. In 1909 the movement merged with the National Association for the Advancement of Colored People (NAACP).

Sources: Alford, *Famous First Blacks,* p. 24; Bennett, *Before the Mayflower,* p. 512; Hornsby, *Chronology of African-American History,* p. 61.

1909 • The organizational meeting of the National Association for the Advancement of Colored People (NAACP) was held in New York City on February 12—Abraham Lincoln's birthday. Among those who signed the original charter were Jane Addams, John Dewey, W. E. B. Du Bois, William Dean Howells, and Oswald Garrison Villard. The permanent organization was created May 12–14, 1910; Moorfield Story, a Boston lawyer, was elected president.

Sources: Bennett, *Before the Mayflower,* pp. 337–39, 512; Hornsby, *Chronology of African-American History,* p. 64; *Negro Almanac, 1989,* p. 21.

1911 • The National Urban League was formed in October from the merger of the Committee for Improving the Industrial Conditions of Negroes in New York (1906), the National League for the Protection of Colored Women (1906), and the Committee on Urban Conditions Among Negroes (1910). George Edmund Haynes and Eugene Kinckle Jones were among the cofounders. Edwin R. A. Seligman was president and Eugene Kinckle Jones was executive secretary. The National Urban League became an early leader among black organizations in research when Charles S. Johnson organized the research department in 1920. In addition, Johnson became editor of *Opportunity: A Journal of Negro Life,* a black periodical founded in 1923.

Sources: Bennett, Before the Mayflower, pp. 339, 515; Encyclopedia of Black America, p. 635; Negro Almanac, 1989, pp. 22, 262.

1935 • On December 5, 1935, Mary McLeod Bethune (1875–1955) was instrumental in founding the National Council of Negro Women. She became its first president, a post she held until 1949. This organization had a centralized direction and purpose that Bethune found lacking in the National Association of Colored Women. (*See also* **Education: Honorary Degrees, 1946; Government—Federal Firsts: Federal Appointees, 1936.**)

Sources: Encyclopedia of Black America, pp. 863–64; Negro Almanac, 1989, p. 1360; Notable Black American Women, pp. 86–92.

1960 • Marion S. Barry, Jr., (1936–) was the first national chairman of the Student Nonviolent Coordinating Committee (SNCC). A native of Itta Bena, Mississippi, Barry would become mayor of Washington, D.C., in 1979.

Sources: Ebony Success Library, vol. 1, p. 21; Hornsby, Milestones in 20th-Century African-American History, pp. 352, 450–51, 483; Who's Who Among Black Americans, 1992–93, p. 77.

1972 • Melvin H. Evans, the first popularly elected governor of the Virgin Islands (1970), was the first black vice chairman of the Southern Governors' Conference.

Sources: Alford, Famous First Blacks, p. 39; Negro Almanac, 1989, p. 1556.

FRATERNAL, SOCIAL, AND RELIGIOUS GROUPS

1775 • Prince Hall (1735–1807) and fourteen others joined a Masonic lodge sponsored by British Army officers at Castle William near Boston on March 6. These are the first American black Masons and the origin of the Masonic movement among blacks. On September 29, 1784, the British Grand Lodge approved the formation of African Lodge No. 459, but the notification did not arrive until 1787. The African Grand Lodge was established on June 24, 1791; Prince Hall was the grand master. A second black lodge was formed in Philadelphia in 1797. In 1808, the existing black lodges formed the Prince

MAJOR FRATERNAL ORGANIZATIONS

FOUNDED	NAME	LOCATION
1864	Knights of Pythias	Washington, D.C.
1865	Grand Order of Galilean Fishermen	Baltimore, Maryland
1866	Grand United Order of J. R. Gidding's and Jolliffe Union	Norfolk, Virginia
1867	Independent Order of Saint Luke	
1868	Grand United Order of Brothers and Sisters, Sons and Daughters of Moses	
1871	Knights and Daughters of Tabor	Independence, Missouri
1881	United Order of True Reformers	Richmond, Virginia
1882	National Order of Mosaic Templers of America	Little Rock, Arkansas
1884	Royal Knights of King David	Durham, North Carolina
1886	Colored Brotherhood and Sisterhood of Honor	Franklin, Kentucky
1894	Ancient Order of Gleaners	Cairo, Michigan
1899	Improved Benevolent and Protective Orde of Elks of the World	Cincinnati, Ohio
1900	Grand United Order Sons and Daughters of Peace	Newport News, Virginia
1901	Supreme Camp of American Woodmen	
1909	Royal Circle of Friends of the World	Helena, Arkansas
1915	Woodmen of Union	
1923	African Blood Brotherhood	Louisville, Kentucky
1923	Knights of the Invisible Colored Kingdom	Tennessee

Sources: Encyclopedia of Black America, pp. 395–96; Negro Year Book, 1921–1922, pp. 414–17.

Hall Masons, an organization which declared itself independent from all other Masonic lodges.

Sources: Dictionary of American Negro Biography, pp. 278–80; Encyclopedia of Black America, pp. 394–95, 412–13; Kane, Famous First Facts, p. 276; Negro Almanac, 1989, p. 825.

1843 • The first black Oddfellows lodge, Philomethian Lodge No. 646, was established in New York City by Peter Ogden. He was a ship's steward, who held a card from a lodge in Liverpool, England.

Sources: Dictionary of Black Culture, p. 336; Encyclopedia of Black America, p. 395; Woodson, Negro Makers of History, p. 80.

1854 • The United Brothers of Friendship and Sisters of the Mysterious Ten was formed in Lexington, Kentucky. In 1861 the state granted the organization a charter, so that it became the first chartered and regularly con-

OPPOSITE PAGE:
PRINCE HALL BECAME
GRAND MASTER OF
THE FIRST BLACK
MASONIC LODGE
IN 1791.

stituted black organization south of the Ohio River. Its ancestry lay in the Union Benevolent Society of 1843. The whites who knew of this society, and who supported its charitable goals, did not know that it was also very active in assisting fugitive slaves.

Sources: Encyclopedia of Black America, p. 395; Negro Year Book, 1921–22, pp. 158, 416.

1871 • The first black Masonic lodge recognized by white Masonry in the United States was Alpha Lodge of New Jersey, Number 116, Free and Accepted Masons. The first meeting was held on January 31, 1871, under its first master, Nathan Mingus.

Source: Kane, Famous First Facts, p. 276.

1904 • The first black Greek letter organization, Sigma Pi Phi, was formed at a meeting in the Philadelphia home of physician Henry McKee Minton (1870–1946) on May 4, 1904. This organization was designed to meet the social needs of black professional and business leaders, and to address social issues. Minton became the first grand sire archon.

Sources: Dictionary of American Negro Biography, pp. 440–41; Gatewood, Aristocrats of Color, pp. 234–36; Negro Almanac, 1989, pp. 1366–67.

1906 • Alpha Phi Alpha was the first intercollegiate Greek letter fraternity. It was founded at Cornell University, Ithaca, New York, on December 4, 1906. The first president was George B. Kelley. The first convention, at Howard University, Washington, D.C., was held in 1908. Other black fraternities include Kappa Alpha Psi (founded in 1911), Omega Psi Phi (1911), and Phi Beta Sigma (1914).

Sources: Encyclopedia of Black America, p. 397; Kane, Famous First Facts, p. 275.

1908 • The first black Greek letter sorority was Alpha Kappa Alpha, founded at Howard University, Washington, D.C., in 1908. The prime mover was Ethel Hedgeman Lyle, who became the first vice president. Lucy Slowe (1885–1937) was the first president. Two other early sororities were Delta Sigma Theta (1913) and Zeta Phi Beta (1920).

Sources: Encyclopedia of Black America, p. 397; Kane, Famous First Facts, p. 603; Notable Black American Women, pp. 1031–33.

1909 • The Knights of Peter Claver was founded in Mobile, Alabama. This was the first national Catholic black fraternal order. It embraces some one hundred thousand Catholic families in the United States. There is also a junior auxiliary for boys (established in 1917), a ladies' auxiliary (1922), and a girls' auxiliary (1909).

Sources: Davis, The History of Black Catholics in the United States, pp. 234–37; Directory of African American Religious Bodies, pp. 210–12; Ochs, Desegregating the Altar, p. 182.

1926 • Frederick Williams Seymour of Hartford, Connecticut, was the first black member of the Connecticut Society of the Sons of the American

Revolution. His great-grandfather, Dudley Hayes, was wounded in action on October 19, 1777.

Source: Opportunity 4 (March 1926), p. 107.

1972 • W. Sterling Cary (1927–) became the first black president of the National Council of Churches in America on December 7, 1972. This distinguished Baptist minister was born in Plainfield, New Jersey, and was also a prominent political activist.

Sources: Ebony Success Library, vol. 1, p. 61; *Encyclopedia of Black America,* p. 219; Hornsby, *Chronology of African-American History,* p. 204; *Negro Almanac, 1989,* p. 1326; *Who's Who Among Black Americans, 1992–93,* p. 244.

1977 • Karen Farmer (1951–) was the first known black member of the Daughters of the American Revolution. She traced her ancestry to William Hood, a soldier in the Revolutionary army.

Sources: American Libraries 39 (February 1978), p. 70; *Negro Almanac, 1989,* pp. 73, 1431; *Who's Who Among Black Americans, 1992–93,* p. 446.

1983 • William Watley was the first black national chairman of the National Workshop on Christian Unity. Watley is ordained in the African Methodist Episcopal (AME) Church, and he was associate general secretary of the Consultation Church Union, Princeton, New Jersey.

Source: Jet 65 (10 October 1983), p. 21.

1984 • Philip R. Cousin (1933–) was the first black from a predominantly black denomination to preside over the National Council of Churches. This African Methodist Episcopal (AME) minister has served with distinction as bishop and college president.

Sources: Jet 65 (30 January 1984), p. 24; *Who's Who Among Black Americans, 1992–93,* p. 312.

1985 • As department commander of the Louisiana American Legion, Alvin A. Roche, Sr., was the first black to head a state unit in the deep South. Only six other blacks in the past ten years have occupied a similar post, none in the South. Roche was sixty-nine years old, and a veteran of World War II.

Source: Jet 69 (30 September 1985), p. 37.

1986 • Alpha Kappa Alpha was the first black sorority to have a sorority house on the campus of the University of Alabama.

Source: Jet 71 (29 September 1986), p. 31.

1987 • The Eta Beta chapter of Phi Beta Sigma was the first black fraternity to have a house on fraternity row at the University of Mississippi.

Source: Jet 72 (31 August 1987), p. 24.

1991 • Maryann Coffey was the first black, and the first woman, co-chair of the National Conference of Christians and Jews.

Source: Jet 80 (6 May 1991), p. 37.

MEDICAL AND DENTAL ASSOCIATIONS

1854 • John V. De Grasse was the first black physician to join a medical society. The Massachusetts Medical Society admitted him on August 24, 1854. De Grasse received his M.D. from Bowdoin College (Brunswick, Maine) in 1849, studied further in Europe, and eventually set up practice in Boston. He was one of the eight blacks who were commissioned as surgeons in the United States Army during the Civil War.

Sources: Dictionary of American Negro Autobiography, p. 169; Morais, The History of the Negro in Medicine, p. 38.

1884 • The Medico-Chirugical Society of the District of Columbia is the first black medical society. Its formation was the result of refusal of the white medical society to admit blacks. It would not be until 1952 that black physicians could join the local American Medical Society branch. A national organization for blacks would be formed in 1895, when the Medico-Chirugical Society was reactivated and incorporated. Although the society originally had white members—three of the eight incorporators were white—by 1920 it was entirely black.

Sources: Encyclopedia of Black America, p. 673; Gatewood, Aristocrats of Color, p. 65; Morais, The History of the Negro in Medicine, pp. 57–58.

1895 • The National Medical Association was formed in October, 1895, in Atlanta, Georgia, during the Cotton States and International Exposition. The association was formed in reaction to the practices of predominantly white associations. The American Medical Association would not urge all its local members to remove restrictive provisions until 1950. The first president of the black association was R. F. Boyd of Nashville, Tennessee.

Sources: Dictionary of Black Culture, pp. 320–21; Encyclopedia of Black America, pp. 633–34; Morais, The History of the Negro in Medicine, pp. 68–69.

1913 • Daniel Hale Williams (1856–1931) became the first black elected to the American College of Surgeons, on November 13, 1913. (*See also* **Science & Medicine: Hospitals, 1891,** and **Medicine, 1893.**)

Sources: Dictionary of American Negro Biography, pp. 654–55; Encyclopedia of Black America, p. 857.

1948 • In December, 1948, the Baltimore County Medical Society was the first American Medical Association affiliate in a Southern state to drop the bars against black membership. Oklahoma and Missouri state societies followed in 1949, and the Delaware and Florida societies in 1950.

Sources: Encyclopedia of Black America, p. 674; Morais, The History of the Negro in Medicine, p. 133.

1950 • Peter Marshall Murray (1888–1969) was the first black to serve in the American Medical Society's House of Delegates. Murray had graduated from Howard University School of Medicine in 1914 and went on to become head of obstetrics and gynecology at Harlem Hospital. This gynecologist from Houma, Louisiana, was also the first black to serve on the New York City Board of Hospitals (1958). In 1954, as president of the New York County Medical Society, he was the first black to head an organization that was a component of the American Medical Association.

Sources: *Dictionary of American Negro Biography,* pp. 465–67; *Encyclopedia of Black America,* p. 584; *Jet* 58 (12 June 1980), p. 18; Morais, *The History of the Negro in Medicine,* pp. 119–21, 130, 133–35, 163, 179, 235, 281; *Who's Who in America, 1960–61,* p. 2103.

PETER
MARSHALL
MURRAY

1974 • Richard Caesar was the first black president of the San Francisco Dental Society.

Source: *Jet* 53 (19 January 1978), p. 44.

1979 • John Heartwell Holland (1916–85) was the first black chairman of the board of governors of the American National Red Cross. (*See also* **Business: Stock Brokerage, 1972.**)

Sources: *Encyclopedia of Black America,* p. 443; *Jet* 56 (3 May 1979), p. 28.

Mary Runge was the first black, and first woman, president of the American Pharmaceutical Association. Runge was a pharmacist in Oakland, California.

Source: *Jet* 56 (30 August 1979), p. 6.

1980 • Lonnie R. Bristow was the first black physician elected to the Council on Medical Services of the American Medical Association. In 1981 he would become the first black president of the American Society of Internal Medicine, and in 1985 the first black physician elected to the board of trustees of the American Medical Society. A graduate of the New York University College of Medicine, Bristow was an internist in San Pablo, California.

Sources: *Jet* 57 (7 February 1980), p. 21; *Jet* 61 (5 November 1981), p. 47; *Jet* 68 (8 July 1985), p. 29.

1982 • Colonel William Lofton, Jr., was the first black man named a fellow of the American Occupational Therapy Association. Lofton was director of occupational therapy at the Fitzsimons Army Medical Center, Aurora, Colorado.

Source: *Jet* 62 (16 August 1982), p. 21.

1984 • Charles Warfield Clark (1927–) was the first black president of the Washington, D.C., Urological Society. Clark is a graduate of the Howard University Medical School (1944) and is now a professor of urology at that school in Washington, D.C.

Sources: Jet 65 (19 September 1983), p. 38; *Who's Who Among Black Americans, 1992–93,* p. 265.

Claude H. Organ, Jr., (1928–) was the first black surgeon to chair the American Board of Surgery. Since 1960, Organ has taught at Creighton University School of Medicine (Omaha, Nebraska).

Sources: Jet 69 (17 February 1986), p. 12; *Who's Who Among Black Americans, 1992–93,* p. 1074.

1987 • Henry Cade was the first black president of the National Association of Boards of Pharmacy. Cade was public affairs and professional relations manager for the Walgreen Company in Deerfield, Illinois.

Source: Jet 72 (13 July 1987), p. 14.

Ross M. Miller, Jr., (1939–) was elected the first black president of the Southern California Chapter of the American College of Surgeons. Miller was also the governor of the American College of Surgeons, the first black to hold this national position. Miller is a general surgeon and professor of surgery at the University of California in Los Angeles and Charles R. Drew medical schools.

Sources: Jet 72 (27 April 1987), p. 26; *Who's Who Among Black Americans, 1992–93,* p. 992.

1989 • Jerome C. Scales was the first black president of the Alabama Society of Pediatric Dentistry. Scales had a practice in Birmingham and was associate professor of dentistry at the University of Alabama at Birmingham.

Source: Jet 76 (18 September 1989), p. 20.

1990 • Ezra C. Davidson, Jr., (1933–) was the first black president of the American College of Obstetricians and Gynecologists. Davidson took his medical degree at Meharry Medical College in 1958. He became chair of the obstetrics and gynecology department of Charles Drew University of Medicine and Science, Los Angeles, in 1971.

Sources: Jet 78 (27 August 1990), p. 20; *Who's Who Among Black Americans, 1992–93,* p. 346.

1992 • Juliann Bluitt was the first woman of any race elected president of the Chicago Dental Society. At the time of her selection, Bluitt was an associate dean of the Northwestern University School of Dentistry.

Source: Jet 82 (13 July 1992), p. 15.

Paul A. Stephens (1921–)was the first black president of the Academy of General Dentistry, which is the second-largest dental association in the country. A graduate of Howard University School of Dentistry (1945), Stephens was a long-time practitioner in Gary, Indiana.

Sources: Jet 82 (24 August 1992), p. 36; *Who's Who Among Black Americans, 1992–93,* p. 1335.

RELIGION: REACHING
NEW SPIRITUAL LEVELS

AFRICAN METHODIST EPISCOPAL (AME) CHURCH

1794 • Although friends and collaborators, Richard Allen (1760–1831) refused to follow Absalom Jones into the Episcopal church. He was instrumental in the construction of Bethel Church in Philadelphia, which was founded in this year. Bethel was a Methodist Episcopal church, but in 1816 it became the mother church of the African Methodist Episcopal (AME) Church.

Sources: Dictionary of American Negro Autobiography, pp. 12–13; Lincoln and Mamiya, The Black Church in the African American Experience, pp. 51–52; Smith, Climbing Jacob's Ladder, p. 36.

RICHARD ALLEN

1801 • Richard Allen compiled the first black hymnal, *Collection of Spiritual Songs and Hymns, Selected from Various Authors*. There was another edition in 1807, and this in turn was revised in 1818 with the help of Jacob Tapsico. These hymnals contained only texts that were sung to a limited number of traditional tunes.

Sources: Encyclopedia of Black America, p. 33; Smith, Climbing Jacob's Ladder, p. 60; Southern, The Music of Black Americans, pp. 75–79.

1815 • Methodists in Charleston, South Carolina, secretly began to form their own church when the separate black quarterly conference was abolished. Morris Brown (1770–1849) was one of two persons sent north to be ordained by Richard Allen. Brown became the first pastor of the church when blacks withdrew from the Methodist Episcopal Church. The church was suppressed, and the building demolished, in 1822, due to the involvement of members in the Denmark Vesey plot for a slave uprising. Brown escaped by being smuggled north.

Sources: Dictionary of American Negro Biography, pp. 69–70; Heritage and Hope, p. 31; Raboteau, Slave Religion, pp. 163, 205–6.

1816 · On April 9 representatives of five Methodist congregations assembled at the Bethel Church in Philadelphia. Dissatisfied with the treatment of blacks within the Methodist Episcopal Church, they organized the African Methodist Episcopal Church (AME). The representatives elected Daniel Coker (1780–1846) as their first bishop but he declined, perhaps because his light skin color caused dissension. Richard Allen (1760–1831) then became the first AME bishop. This denomination is currently the largest black Methodist group in the United States, with some 2.2 million members.

Sources: Dictionary of American Negro Biography, pp. 12–13 (Allen); 119–20 (Coker); Encyclopedia of Black America, p. 32; Lincoln and Mamiya, The Black Church in the African American Experience, p. 52; Smith, Climbing Jacob's Ladder, pp. 59–61.

EVANGELIST JARENA LEE.

1817 · Jarena Lee (1783–?) was the first woman to preach in the African Methodist Episcopal (AME) Church. In 1817 she rose in Bethel Church, Philadelphia, to give a spontaneous talk. Although never formally licensed to speak by the church, she began an extraordinary career as an evangelist. Lee, and other women like Juliann Jane Tillman, made a considerable impact on religious life, as well as the growth of their denomination.

Sources: Black Women in America, p. 707; Smith, Climbing Jacob's Ladder, pp. 64–65; Smith, Notable Black American Women, pp. 662–63.

1819 · Daniel Coker (1780–1846) is the first African missionary associated with the African Methodist Episcopal (AME) Church. On April 9, 1816, Coker had declined to become the church's first bishop. Expelled from the church in 1818, but restored in 1819, Coker was sent to Liberia in 1820 by the Maryland Colonization Society, but his group was detained in Sierra Leone because of unfavorable conditions in Liberia. Coker eventually stayed in Freetown, Sierra Leone, where he established a church and spent the rest of his life.

Source: Dictionary of American Negro Biography, pp. 119–20.

1847 · Quinn Chapel was the first African Methodist Episcopal (AME) church in Chicago, Illinois.

Source: Baer and Singer, African-American Religion in the Twentieth Century, p. 74.

1850 · Saint Andrew's AME Church, Sacramento, California, was the first African Methodist Episcopal (AME) church in California. The original affiliation was with the Methodist Episcopal Church, but after failed leadership the congregation joined the AME church. Saint Andrew's was established in a private home, but within four years it had its own building, and in the basement, opened the first school for nonwhites in California.

Sources: Cantor, *Historic Landmarks of Black America*, p. 294; *Heritage and Hope*, p. 309; *Negro Almanac, 1989*, p. 192.

1898 • Henry McNeal Turner (1834–1915) was the first prominent black churchman to declare that God is black. He said: "We had rather believe in no God, or ... believe that all nature is God than to believe in the personality of a God, and not to believe that He is a Negro." Turner was also the first black chaplain in the United States Army in 1863. Later, as a minister and bishop in the African Methodist Episcopal Church, Turner advocated black return to Africa.

Sources: Black Apostles, pp. 227–46; *Encyclopedia of Black America*, p. 820; Hornsby, *Chronology of African-American History*, pp. 66–67; Lincoln, *The Black Church Since Frazier*, p. 148.

**HENRY
MCNEAL
TURNER**

1988 • The Service and Development Agency was the first international development program sponsored by a black church. The first head of this organization was Jonathan L. Weaver.

Source: Jet 75 (15 August 1988), p. 12.

AFRICAN METHODIST EPISCOPAL (AME) ZION CHURCH

1796 • In New York City Peter Williams, Sr., (?–1823), a former slave and sexton of the John Street Methodist Church, organized the first African Chapel for Methodists in a cabinetmaker's shop owned by William Miller, a fellow member of the John Street Methodist Episcopal Church. Services were held there until a black church was completed in 1800. The church was the African Methodist Episcopal Zion Church, which became the mother church of the denomination in 1820. Despite his role in founding the church, Williams remained a member of the John Street Methodist Church, and his son, Peter, Jr., became a Protestant Episcopal priest.

Sources: Dictionary of American Negro Biography, pp. 660–62; Lincoln and Mamiya, *The Black Church in the African American Experience*, pp. 56–57; Smith, *Climbing Jacob's Ladder*, pp. 38–40.

1801 • In New York City the first church of what would become the African Methodist Episcopal Zion Church was incorporated by Peter Williams, Sr., and Francis Jacobs. The building was completed in 1800. The church was initially pastored by a white minister, supplied by the parent John Street Methodist Church. Complete independence would be asserted in 1820.

Sources: Dictionary of American Negro Biography, pp. 660–61; *Encyclopedia of American Religion,* vol. 1, p. 194; Lincoln and Mamiya, *The Black Church in the African American Experience,* pp. 50–52; Smith, *Climbing Jacob's Ladder,* pp. 38–40.

1820 • On August 11 the African Methodist Zion and Asbury African Methodist churches, both of New York City, started their own separate African Methodist Episcopal Conference, still within the Methodist Episcopal Church. The *Discipline* they adopted in September, 1820, included the first and only open anti-slavery declaration by a Methodist church. With four other congregations from Pennsylvania, Connecticut, and New York, the conference held its first annual meeting on June 21, 1821. The denomination uses 1820 as its foundation date, although the breach with the Methodist Episcopal Church did not become complete until 1824. The designation "Zion" was officially added to the name in 1848. It is currently the second largest black Methodist church, with some 1.2 million members in the United States.

Sources: Dictionary of American Negro Biography, pp. 616–17; *Encyclopedia of Black America,* pp. 35–36; Lincoln and Mamiya, *The Black Church in the African American Experience,* pp. 57–58; Smith, *Climbing Jacob's Ladder,* p. 63.

1822 • James Varick (1750–1827) became the first bishop—or superintendent as he was originally called—of the African Methodist Episcopal Zion Church. Born to a slave mother in Newburgh, New York, he became a shoemaker, and joined the John Street Methodist Church. He was active in the Zion Church, and became a deacon in 1806. He was consecrated on July 30, 1822.

Sources: Dictionary of American Negro Biography, pp. 616–17; Lincoln and Mamiya, *The Black Church in the African American Experience,* pp. 57–58; Smith, *Climbing Jacob's Ladder,* p. 63.

1898 • Mary J. Small, wife of Bishop John B. Small, was the first Methodist woman to be ordained an elder. On May 19, 1895, Small became the second woman to be ordained a deacon. The first was Julia A. Foote, who was ordained on May 20, 1894. Foote became the second elder in 1900.

Sources: Black Women in America, pp. 440–41 (Foote); Lincoln and Mamiya, *The Black Church in the African American Experience,* p. 285.

1992 • Samuel Chuka Ekemam was the first non-American black elected to head the Board of Bishops of the African Methodist Episcopal (AME) Zion Church. Ekemam, a Nigerian, was educated at Livingstone College, Yale, and Columbia.

Source: Jet 81 (13 April 1992), p. 7.

AFRICAN ORTHODOX CHURCH

1919 • The movement that became the African Orthodox Church was organized on April 9, 1919, by George Alexander McGuire (1866–1934), who was consecrated its first bishop on September 28, 1921. In 1918, McGuire, an ordained Episcopal priest, had been appointed the first chaplain-general and a spokesperson of the United Negro Improvement Society, by Marcus Garvey. McGuire was disappointed in his hope that the African Orthodox Church would become the official church of the UNIA, but he saw his church spread to Africa and the Caribbean before his death.

Sources: Baer and Singer, *African-American Religion in the Twentieth Century,* pp. 124–25; *Dictionary of American Negro Biography,* pp. 416–17; *Directory of African American Religious Bodies,* p. 126; *Encyclopedia of American Religions,* vol. 1, pp. 109–10.

AFRICAN UNION AMERICAN METHODIST EPISCOPAL CHURCH

1801 • Blacks in Wilmington, Delaware, withdrew from Asbury Methodist Church and—under the leadership of Peter Spencer and William Anderson—established Ezion Church. Because neither leader was ordained, Asbury Church appointed a white minister in 1812. Unable to keep control of the building in the ensuing legal dispute, the blacks again withdrew and built another church, which was dedicated in 1813. Severing all ties with the Methodist Episcopal Church, they formed the Union Church of Africans. The Union Church of Africans was the first all-black independent Methodist Church, and the mother church of one of the smaller black Methodist denominations, the African Union American Methodist Episcopal Church, which had about 6,500 members in 1988. The first annual conference was held in 1814 with three churches. The denomination refused to join the AME church in 1816.

Sources: Directory of African American Religious Bodies, p. 241; *Encyclopedia of American Religions,* vol. 1, pp. 194–95; Lincoln and Mamiya, *The Black Church in the African American Experience,* p. 48; Smith, *Climbing Jacob's Ladder,* pp. 58–59.

AFRICAN-AMERICAN CATHOLICS

1990 • George Augustus Stallings established the African-American Catholic Church on May 13, 1990. He was its first bishop. Stallings broke with the Roman Catholic Church over what he saw as its neglect of the spiritual needs of blacks.

Source: Hornsby, *Chronology of African-American History,* p. 429.

ANTIOCH ASSOCIATION OF METAPHYSICAL SCIENCE

1932 • The Antioch Association of Metaphysical Science seems to be the first predominantly black New Thought church. New Thought grows out of a Christian Science background, emphasizes healing through mental power, and should not be confused with the current New Age movement. The Antioch Association was founded in Detroit by Lewis Johnson.

Sources: Baer and Singer, *African-American Religion in the Twentieth Century,* p. 200; *Encyclopedia of American Religions,* vol. 2, p. 886.

BAPTISM

1641 • The first baptism of a black in New England was performed. The name of the woman is unknown, but she was a slave in Dorchester, Massachusetts.

Source: Raboteau, *Slave Religion,* pp. 108–9.

1664 • The lower house of Maryland asked the upper house to draft an act declaring that baptism of slaves did not lead to their freedom. At least six of the colonies had laws making this specific declaration by 1710.

Source: Raboteau, *Slave Religion,* p. 99.

BAPTISTS

1743 • The first known black Baptist was Quassey, a member of the Newton, Rhode Island, church.

Source: Lincoln and Mamiya, *The Black Church in the African American Experience,* p. 23.

1758 • The first known black Baptist congregation was the "Bluestone" African Baptist Church, located on the William Byrd plantation in Mecklenberg, Virginia. The church's nickname comes from its location near the Bluestone River. (A claim for priority is also advanced for a congregation said to exist at Luneberg in 1756. The evidence is not clear cut, but all claims so far refer to Virginia and the decade of the 1750s.)

Sources: Baer and Singer, *African-American Religion in the Twentieth Century,* p. 16; Lincoln and Mamiya, *The Black Church in the African American Experience,* p. 23; Smith, *Climbing Jacob's Ladder,* p. 33; Wilmore, *Black and Presbyterian,* p. 41.

1773 • The first black Baptist church under black leadership seems to have been formed in Silver Bluff, South Carolina. David George, a slave, became its first black pastor. (*See also* **Religion: Baptists, 1783.**) George Liele and, less probably, Andrew Bryan have also been associated with the church. The congregation seems to have been founded between 1773 and 1775. The present church was remodeled in 1920, and a cornerstone with

EARLY BAPTIST CHURCHES

FOUNDED	NAME	LOCATION
1786	Harrison Street Baptist Church	Petersburg, Virginia
1788	First African Baptist Church	Savannah, Georgia
1790	African Baptist Church	Lexington, Kentucky
1793	First African Baptist Church	Augusta, Georgia
1805	Joy Street Baptist Church	Boston, Massachusetts
1809	African Baptist Church	Philadelphia, Pennsylvania
1809	Abyssinian Baptist Church	New York, New York
1833	First Colored Baptist Church	Washington, D.C.
1835	First Colored Baptist Church	Baltimore, Maryland

Sources: Dictionary of American Negro Biography, p. 287; *Encyclopedia of Black America,* pp. 159–60; Lincoln and Mamiya, *The Black Church in the African American Experience,* pp. 22–23; Raboteau, *Slave Religion,* pp. 139–40; Smith, *Climbing Jacob's Ladder,* pp. 31–33, 45, 46, 47–48, 51–55, 76–77, 79, 81–84.

the founding date of 1750 was put in place. This date appears too early to most historians. In 1793 the congregation of some sixty persons, led by Jesse Galpin, moved to Augusta, Georgia, about twelve miles away.

C. 1775 • George Liele (Leile, Lisle) (c. 1750–1820), the first known black Baptist missionary, was active before the Revolutionary War. Liele was born a slave in Virginia and became a convert after his master moved to Georgia. He was freed a short while before he began to preach. He preached in Savannah, Georgia, during the British occupation of the town from 1779 to 1782. Since British officers had protected him against an attempt to re-enslave him, he accompanied the withdrawal of the British troops to Jamaica. In 1784 he established the first black Baptist church on the island, in Kingston.

Sources: Dictionary of American Negro Biography, p. 397; Lincoln and Mamiya, *The Black Church in the African American Experience,* p. 23–24; Smith, *Climbing Jacob's Ladder,* pp. 32–33.

1783 • David George (c. 1742–1810) established the first black Baptist church in Nova Scotia. Born a slave in Virginia, his attempt to flee and seek freedom in Georgia was foiled when he was captured by the Creek Indians. He was eventually sold to George Gaufin, and sent to a plantation at Silver Bluff, South Carolina, where he became pastor of the first black Baptist con-gregation (1773). During the British occupation of Charleston, South Carolina, Gaufin moved there, and George preached in that city. George and his family were among those who accompanied the British troops when they evacuated the city. In 1792, he and almost all his congregation emigrated to Sierra Leone, where he had a church of nearly two hundred members at the time of his death.

Sources: Dictionary of American Negro Biography, p. 257; Smith, *Climbing Jacob's Ladder,* p. 33.

1791 • The African Baptist Church of Petersburg, Virginia, some five hundred strong, was officially recognized by the Dover Association in 1791. The origin of the church went back to a black man named Moses, who persisted in preaching and holding meetings in spite of whippings. Moses was followed by Gowan Prophet. The church appears to have been in existence before 1786.

Source: Raboteau, *Slave Religion,* pp. 138–39.

1792 • Josiah (or Jacob) Bishop is the first black known to be employed as a preacher by a racially mixed congregation. His congregation in Portsmouth, Virginia, purchased his freedom and that of his family.

Source: Raboteau, *Slave Religion,* p. 134.

Andrew Bryan (1737–1812) began to build the First African Baptist Church building in Savannah, Georgia. The first building built for the purpose of black worship in the city, it was finished in 1794. Bryan was a slave who refused to give up his mission in spite of whipping and imprisonment for preaching. He had formed his church on January 20, 1788. The lot on which the church stood remained in the church's possession until at least 1913. The black Baptist church in Savannah was established before there was a white Baptist church, as was also the case in Petersburg, Virginia.

Sources: Dictionary of American Negro Biography, p. 77; Lincoln and Mamiya, *The Black Church in the African American Experience,* pp. 23–24; Raboteau, *Slave Religion,* pp. 137, 141–42; Smith, *Climbing Jacob's Ladder,* pp. 33, 76.

1806 • The African Meeting House, also known as the Joy Street Baptist Church, Boston, Massachusetts, is the oldest surviving building constructed to serve as a black church. It housed the first black Baptist congregation in Boston, organized in 1805 by Thomas Paul, Sr., (1773–1831) who also founded the Abyssinian Baptist Church in New York City in 1809. On January 6, 1832, William Lloyd Garrison organized the Anti-Slavery Society in the church basement with the participation of prominent church members.

Sources: Baer and Singer, *African-American Religion in the Twentieth Century,* p. 26; Cantor, *Historic Landmarks of Black America,* pp. 70–71; *Dictionary of American Negro Biography,* pp. 482–83; Lincoln and Mamiya, *The Black Church in the African American Experience,* p. 25; Smith, *Climbing Jacob's Ladder,* pp. 48, 51–52.

1812 • Joseph Willis (1762–1854) organized the first black Baptist church west of the Mississippi River in the Bayou Chicot District of Louisiana. Willis was a free black who had begun his missionary efforts in southwest Mississippi and went to Louisiana in 1804. He became the first moderator of the Louisiana Baptist Association, when it was formed in 1818. He was succeeded by his grandson, who was ordained in 1849.

Sources: *Negro Year Book, 1913,* p. 118; Raboteau, *Slave Religion,* pp. 134, 200

1821 • Lott Carey (Cary) (1780–1829) was the first black Baptist missionary to Africa. He established the First Baptist Church in what is now Monrovia, Liberia. Born a slave in Virginia, he underwent conversion in 1807, and then purchased his own, and his two children's, freedom in 1813. On January 23, 1821, Carey, Colin Teague, and twenty-eight others, set sail for Africa. When a group of churches in Virginia; North Carolina; and Washington, D.C., withdrew from the National Baptist Convention, USA, in 1897, they formed the Lott Carey Foreign Mission Convention, which is still in existence today.

Sources: *Dictionary of American Negro Biography,* pp. 95–97; Lincoln and Mamiya, *The Black Church in the African American Experience,* pp. 26, 45; Smith, *Climbing Jacob's Ladder,* p. 92.

1822 • Nathan Paul (1793?–1893) was the first pastor of the African Baptist Church, Albany, New York, the only black church in the city. Nathan, brother of Thomas Paul of Boston, was a prominent abolitionist, and in 1832 the first American black to go to England to further this cause. Paul went to raise money for a school in Wilberforce, Ohio. He was nearly lynched when he came back without any money, and claimed he was owed $1,600 in back salary. The fact that his second wife was an Englishwoman, and probably white, did not improve his situation.

Source: *Dictionary of American Negro Biography,* p. 482.

EARLY BAPTIST ASSOCIATIONS

FOUNDED	NAME	LOCATION
1836	Union Association	Ohio
1839	Colored Baptist Society and Friends to Humanity	Illinois[1]
1840	American Baptist Missionary Convention	New England and Middle Atlantic
1841	Amherstburg Association	Canada and Michigan
1853	Western Colored Baptist Convention	
1864	Northwest and Southern Baptist Convention	
1867	Consolidated American Baptist Missionary Convention	National

[1]This organization split in 1849 to become the Mount Olive Association and the Colored Baptist Association; the latter became the Wood River Colored Baptist Association in 1856.

Sources: *Directory of African American Religious Bodies,* pp. 228–29; *Encyclopedia of Black America,* pp. 161–62; Lincoln and Mamiya, *The Black Church in the African American Experience,* pp. 26–27; Smith, *Climbing Jacob's Ladder,* pp. 63–65.

1834 • The first all-black Baptist association of churches was the Providence Association, in Ohio.

1846 • By this date the first known black Baptist church in Canada, outside the maritime provinces, was in existence. The precise date of its founding in Toronto is not known. (*See also* **Religion: Baptists, 1783.**)
Source: *Encyclopedia of Black America,* p. 161.

1849 • Nelson G. Merry became the first black pastor of the church formed by the separation of some five hundred black members from First Baptist Church of Nashville in 1847; Merry was pastor of the church, presently known as the First Baptist Church, Capitol Hill, until 1884.
Sources: May, *The First Baptist Church of Nashville 1820–1970,* pp. 76–77; Raboteau, *Slave Religion,* p. 204.

1867 • The Consolidated American Baptist Missionary Convention was the first national organization of black Baptists. It was organized in Nashville, Tennessee, in August, 1867, and held its final meeting in 1879.
Sources: *Directory of African American Religious Bodies,* p. 229; *Encyclopedia of Black America,* p. 162; Lincoln and Mamiya, *The Black Church in the African American Experience,* p. 27.

JOHN JASPER

1878 • John Jasper (1812–1901) preached for the first time his famous sermon "De Sun Do Move." He would deliver this sermon 253 times before his death. Born a slave in Virginia and converted in 1837, Jasper became a powerful and very popular preacher. He retained the language of the uneducated, rural black, but his evident sincerity and the power of his oratory impressed even those among his large audiences who came to scoff.
Source: *Dictionary of American Negro Biography,* 343–44; *Encyclopedia of Black America,* pp. 160, 511; Smith, *Climbing Jacob's Ladder,* pp. 110–11.

1880 • The Baptist Foreign Mission Convention of the United States of America was formed at a meeting in Montgomery, Alabama, on November 24, 1880. W. W. Colley became the first corresponding secretary. Not only did the convention support African missions abroad, at home it was an anti-liquor and anti-tobacco organization. Colley had been a missionary sponsored by the Southern Baptist Convention in Africa from 1875 to 1879, and did not agree with that convention's treatment of Africans.
Sources: *Directory of African American Religious Bodies,* p. 229; *Encyclopedia of Black America,* pp. 162–63; Lincoln and Mamiya, *The Black Church in the African American Experience,* pp. 27–28.

1886 • The first meeting of the American National Baptist Convention was held on August 25, 1886, in St. Louis, Missouri. Its first president was William J. Simmons (1849–90). This convention was the largest component of the three bodies that joined to form the National Baptist Convention, USA, in 1895. Simmons had a varied and productive career as a religious and educational leader, but he is most remembered as author of the collection of biographies, *Men of Mark, Eminent, Progressive, and Rising* (1887).

Sources: *Dictionary of American Negro Biography*, pp. 556–57; *Directory of African American Religious Bodies*, p. 229; *Encyclopedia of Black America*, p. 163; Lincoln and Mamiya, *The Black Church in the African American Experience*, p. 28.

1895 • The National Baptist Convention, USA, held its first meeting in Atlanta, Georgia, on September 28, 1895. E. C. Morris was its first president. This remains the largest Baptist organization under the title National Baptist Convention, USA, Inc. The second largest is the National Baptist Convention of America, which split from the parent organization in 1915 in a dispute primarily about the control of the American Baptist Publication Society. The third largest is the Progressive National Baptist Convention, which broke away from the parent organization in 1961 over the issue of the churches' posture on civil rights.

Sources: *Directory of African American Religious Bodies*, pp. 229–32; *Encyclopedia of Black America*, pp. 163–64; Lincoln and Mamiya, *The Black Church in the African American Experience*, p. 28.

1915 • E. P. Jones was the first president of the National Baptist Convention, Unincorporated (now the National Baptist Convention of

America). The split with the National Baptist Convention, Inc., over control of the Baptist Publishing Board, became official on September 9, 1915. The second largest Baptist convention, it now has some 2.4 million members.

Sources: Encyclopedia of American Religions, vol. 2, pp. 89–90; *Encyclopedia of Black America,* pp. 164–65; Lincoln and Mamiya, *The Black Church in the African American Experience,* pp. 33–35.

1962 • L. Venhael Booth was the first president of the Progressive National Baptist Convention, USA. The split in the Baptist convention began in 1957, with a challenge to the renewal of the mandate of J. H. Jackson, the long-standing president of the National Baptist Convention, USA, Inc. It grew to encompass ministers who were ready to follow Martin Luther King, Jr., and undertake activist efforts to secure civil rights. The smallest of the three major Baptist organizations, it had some 1.2 million members in 1989.

Sources: Directory of African American Religious Bodies, pp. 231–32; *Encyclopedia of American Religions,* vol. 2, p. 91; *Encyclopedia of Black America,* pp. 165–66; Lincoln and Mamiya, *The Black Church in the African American Experience,* pp. 36–37.

1969 • Thomas Kilgore, Jr. (1913–) was the first black to become head of the predominantly white American Baptist Convention. Kilgore was senior pastor of Second Baptist Church, Los Angeles, California, which is the oldest black Baptist church in the city.

Sources: Alford, Famous First Blacks, p. 21; *Ebony* (August 1970), p. 106; *Ebony* (March 1982), p. 129; *Ebony Success Library,* vol. 1, p. 191; *Who's Who Among Black Americans, 1992–93,* p. 818.

1983 • As pastor of Mariner's Temple Baptist Church, Manhattan, Suzanne Denise Johnson (1957–) was the first black, and the first female, pastor in the American Baptist Churches in the USA.

Sources: Essence (September 1983), p. 42; *Jet* 64 (13 June 1983), p. 25.

Deborah Partridge Wolfe (1916–) was the first woman Baptist to be president of the Clergy Council of Cranford, New Jersey. Wolfe was a professor of education at Queens College, New York, as well as being a minister.

Sources: Current Biography, 1962, pp. 469–71; *Jet* 64 (4 July 1983), p. 21; *Notable Black American Women,* pp. 1276–78.

The South Carolina Baptist Educational and Missionary Convention authorized the ordination of women. This was the first state organization in the National Baptist Convention to do so.

Source: Jet 64 (30 May 1983), p. 26.

1987 • Leroy Gainey was the first black trustee-elected professor at a Southern Baptist institution, Golden Gate Theological Seminary, Mill Valley, California.

Source: Jet 73 (19 October 1987), p. 20.

1989 • Rodney S. Patterson founded the first all-black church in Vermont, the New Alpha Missionary Baptist Church, located in Burlington.

Source: Negro Almanac, 1989, p. 1432.

1992 • Freedom Baptist Church of Selma, Alabama, was the first black church to be admitted to the Selma Baptist Association, made up of twenty-five white churches affiliated with the Alabama Southern Baptist Convention.

Sources: Jet 83 (9 November 1992), p. 33; *Time 140* (2 November 1992), p. 22.

Frederick J. Streets became the first black and the first Baptist to become university chaplain at Yale University. Streets, a 1975 graduate of Yale Divinity School, was forty-two years old at the time of his appointment.

Source: Jet 82 (11 May 1992), p. 6.

BLACK CHRISTIAN NATIONALIST CHURCH

1966 • Albert B. Cleage, Jr., (1913–) preached a famous sermon at his independent Detroit church, and became the first proponent of Black Theology to attract national attention. He subsequently published two books presenting his position, *The Black Messiah* (1968) and *Black Christian Nationalism* (1972). The activist church maintains that Jesus was a black Messiah and revolutionary sent to liberate blacks. The church building became known as the Shrine of the Black Madonna and the name was added to that of the church which became Shrines of the Black Madonna Pan-African Orthodox Christian Church. In 1970, Cleage renamed himself Jaramogi Abebe Agyeman. By 1972 another name for the group was also in use: the Black Nationalist Church.

Sources: Baer and Singer, *African-American Religion in the Twentieth Century,* pp. 60–61, 126; *Ebony Success Library,* vol. 1, p. 70; *Directory of African American Religious Bodies,* pp. 128–29; *Encyclopedia of American Religions,* vol. 3, p. 156.

BLACK JUDAISM

1896 • William S. Crowdy, a railroad cook, founded the Church of God and Saints of Christ in Lawrence, Kansas. The church mixes Judaism, Christianity, and black nationalism and is sometimes called the first black Jewish group. A principal belief is that blacks are the direct descendants of the lost tribes of Israel. A contemporaneous, and possibly earlier, church with similar views is the Church of God (Black Jews), founded by Prophet F. S. Cherry, but the exact date of founding and current status of this church are unknown. The first black Jewish sect in New York City arose in 1899, when Leon Richelieu (?–1964) established the Moorish Zionist

Temple in Brooklyn. This group emphasized a Jewish ideology rather than nationalism, and seems to have included some white Jewish members.

Sources: Baer and Singer, *African-American Religions in the Twentieth Century,* pp. 50–51, 114–15; *Directory of African American Religious Bodies,* p. 131; *Encyclopedia of American Religions,* vol. 3, pp. 27, 152–53.

1968 • The Original Hebrew Israelite Nation (also known as the Abeta Hebrew Cultural Center) is the first black American Jewish group to migrate to Israel. Formed in the 1960s by Ammi Carter (born G. Parker), the group was at first unsuccessful in establishing itself in Liberia and changed its goal to Israel. Some 1,500 members now live communally in Israel.

Sources: Baer and Singer, *African-American Religion in the Twentieth Century,* pp. 117–18; *Directory of African American Religious Bodies,* p. 133; *Encyclopedia of American Religions,* pp. 1291–92.

CATHOLICS

1730 • The Ursuline nuns of New Orleans, Louisiana, undertook efforts to instruct black Catholics; their efforts persisted until 1824. Catholic instruction for blacks was practically nonexistent in most places, and white Catholics were only somewhat better served.

Source: Raboteau, *Slave Religion,* p. 114.

1794 • The first known Sunday catechism classes for blacks in Baltimore, Maryland, were established in 1794. Louisiana was the only other area with a substantial number of black Catholics. Intermittent efforts to instruct blacks had been made there, with the Ursuline nuns giving instruction to black girls since the 1720s.

Source: Ochs, *Desegregating the Altar,* p. 22.

1824 • The first attempt to build a community of black nuns was the formation of an auxiliary group to the Sisters of Loretto in Loretto, Kentucky. This group consisted of three free black women whose names are not recorded. The attempt did not outlive the stay of the sponsoring priest, who soon left for Missouri.

Source: Davis, *The History of Black Catholics in the United States,* p. 98.

1829 • On July 2, 1829, the first permanent order of black Catholic nuns, the Oblate Sisters of Providence, was founded in Baltimore, Maryland. The order was founded through the efforts of a French priest, James Joubert, and four women of Caribbean origin—Elizabeth Lange, Rosine Boegues, Mary Frances Balas, and Mary Theresa Duchemin. This teaching order was formally recognized October 2, 1831. The sisters opened the first Catholic school for girls, in 1843. The school survives today as Mount

Providence Junior College, established in 1952. The second order founded was the Sisters of the Holy Family. It was founded in New Orleans, in 1842, by Henriette Delille and Juliette Gaudin; that order was not officially recognized until after the Civil War.

Sources: Davis, *The History of Black Catholics in the United States,* pp. 99–105; *Encyclopedia of Black America,* p. 220; *Notable Black American Women,* pp. 813–14; Ochs, *Desegregating the Altar,* pp. 24–25; Smith, *Climbing Jacob's Ladder,* pp. 97–100.

1836 • George Paddington was the first black to be ordained by an American bishop, on May 21, 1836, in Port-au-Prince, Haiti. Bishop John England was a representative of the Holy See at the time. Little is known about Paddington, who was a black from Dublin, Ireland.

Source: Davis, *The History of Black Catholics in the United States,* pp. 93–94.

1843 • The Society of Colored People of Baltimore is the first black Catholic association whose documentation has been preserved. Their notebook began on December 3, 1843, and continued until September 7, 1845, when the society wound up. Besides meeting for worship, the society maintained a library.

Source: Davis, *The History of Black Catholics in the United States,* pp. 86–88.

1854 • On June 10, 1854, James Augustine Healy (1830–1900) was ordained a priest in Paris, France. He is the first American black to be ordained in the Catholic church. Two brothers followed him. All three had to study abroad. James Healy became the first black bishop, of Portland, Maine, in February 1875. Alexander Sherwood was ordained for the diocese of Massachusetts. Patrick Francis (1834–1910) became a Jesuit. He obtained the first Ph.D. earned by a black, from Louvain University, Belgium, and became the first black Jesuit, as well as the first black president of Georgetown University (Washington, D.C.). The three brothers were the sons of an Irish plantation owner in Georgia and a mulatto slave woman. Their sister Eliza (Sister Mary Magdalen, 1846–1918) became a nun and notable school head. Another brother, Michael Alexander (1839–1904), became a captain in the U.S. Revenue Cutter Service (now the U.S. Coast Guard) and the first black to become *de facto* chief law enforcement officer in Alaskan waters. While the racial identity of the Healys was not entirely concealed, it was not widely broadcast, and many of the collateral descendants of the priests and nuns passed as white. (*See also* **Education: College Degrees, 1865 and Military: U.S. Coast Guard, 1865.**)

Sources: Davis, *The History of Black Catholics in the United States,* pp. 147–51; *Dictionary of American Negro Biography,* pp. 301–2 (Eliza); 302–3, (James); 303–4 (Michael); 304–5 (Patrick); *Encyclopedia of Black America,* p. 423 (James); *Notable Black American Women,* pp. 479–81 (Eliza); Ochs, *Desegregating the Altar,* pp. 26–29.

1863 • Saint Francis Xavier Church in Baltimore, Maryland, became the first exclusively black parish in the United States. The Sulpician order of priests had maintained a chapel for blacks earlier in the century, until 1836. Saint Francis Xavier Church grew out of the Chapel of Blessed Peter Claver, which had been established by the Jesuits in 1857. The church was purchased on October 10, 1863, and dedicated on February 21, 1864.

Sources: Kane, *Famous First Facts,* p. 156; Smith, *Climbing Jacob's Ladder,* pp. 97–100.

1875 • James Augustine Healy (1830–1900) became the first black Catholic bishop, of Portland, Maine. He held the position, with distinction, until his death in 1900. (*See also* **Religion: Catholics, 1854.**)

Sources: Davis, *The History of Black Catholics in the United States,* pp. 149–51; *Dictionary of American Negro Biography,* pp. 302–3; *Encyclopedia of Black America,* p. 433; Ochs, *Desegregating the Altar,* pp. 26–28.

1886 • Augustus Tolton (1854–97) celebrated his first mass in the United States at Saint Mary's Hospital in Hoboken, New Jersey, on July 7, 1886. Although Tolton was not the first black priest, he was the first to be widely known and publicized. He seems to have believed himself that he was the first, overlooking the Healy brothers (*See also* **Religion: Catholics, 1854.**) Tolton became a priest on August 24, 1886, and served principally in Quincy, Illinois, and Chicago, Illinois.

Sources: Davis, *The History of Black Catholics in the United States,* pp. 152–62; *Dictionary of American Negro Biography,* pp. 596–97; Ochs, *Desegregating the Altar,* pp. 77–79, 94–95.

1889 • The first meeting of the Catholic Afro-American Lay Congress began on January 1, 1889, in Washington, D.C., under the presidency of William H. Smith. There were five congresses from 1889 to 1894. The most pressing problem for many delegates was the lack of black priests. Only one black priest had been ordained since the Healy brothers were ordained earlier in the century. This priest was Augustine Tolton (1854–97), who took his vows in 1886. (Tolton has sometimes been identified as the first American-born black priest; he was the fourth, as the three Healy brothers were all born in Georgia.) (*See also* **Religion: Catholics, 1854.**)

Sources: Cantor, *Historic Landmarks of Black America,* p. 11; Davis, *The History of Black Catholics in the United States,* pp. 171–94; *Dictionary of American Negro Biography,* pp. 596–97; *Directory of African American Religious Bodies,* pp. 258–60; Ochs, *Desegregating the Altar,* pp. 27–28.

1891 • Charles Randolph Uncles became the first black priest ordained in the United States, on December 19, 1891, in Baltimore, Maryland. (The four previous American blacks had all been ordained in Europe.) He died on July 21, 1933, at the age of seventy-four. He had been a priest for forty-two years.

Source: Ochs, *Desegregating the Altar,* pp. 81–82, 456.

1923 • Saint Augustine's Seminary was established in Bay Saint Louis, Louisiana, by the Society of the Divine Word. This was the first separate and segregated seminary to train black priests. The work of the seminary had begun two years earlier in Greenville, Mississippi. The seminary had a six-year combined high school and college course, a year's novitiate, and a six-year seminary course. The first four missionary priests from the seminary were ordained in 1934.

Sources: Cantor, Historic Landmarks of Black America, p. 169; Davis, The History of Black Catholics in the United States, pp. 234–35; Ochs, Desegregating the Altar, p. 5–6, 271–72.

1953 • On April 22, 1953, Joseph Oliver Bowers (1910–) became the first black bishop consecrated for service in the United States since James A. Healy in 1875. He was from the West Indies, forty-six years old, and a graduate of Saint Augustine's Seminary. He became a priest in 1939. Later in 1953, he became the first black bishop to ordain black priests in the United States.

Sources: Ebony (December 1957), p. 18. Ebony, (August 1953), pp. 25–33; Ochs, Desegregating the Altar, pp. 422–23.

1960 • On March 31, 1960, Laurian Rugambwa (1921–) became the first black cardinal in the Catholic church in modern times. Rugambwa came from Tanganyika, and after attending seminary in Uganda, was ordained in 1943. He became a bishop in 1952.

Sources: Current Biography, 1960, pp. 350–52; Ebony (July 1960), pp. 34–36; Jet 70 (31 March 1986), p. 18.

1962 • Martin de Porres (1579–1639) was the first black canonized a saint by the Catholic Church in modern times. He was born in Peru, the illegitimate son of a Spanish knight and Anna, a freedwoman from Panama. In 1594 he became a Dominican lay brother, and won an exceptional reputation both for his work with the sick and poor and for his holiness.

Sources: Davis, The History of Black Catholics in the United States, pp. 25–27; Delaney, Dictionary of Saints, p. 477.

1966 • On January 6, 1966, Harold Robert Perry (1916–91) became the first black Catholic bishop in the United States in this century to be consecrated for service in Africa. He was named auxiliary bishop of New Orleans, Louisiana. The son of a rice mill worker and a cook, he was ordained in 1944 after completing the course of the Divine Word Seminary in Louisiana. He spent fourteen years in parish work, and then became rector of the seminary in 1958.

BISHOP HAROLD R. PERRY EMERGING FROM THE ST. LOUIS BASILICA FOLLOWING HIS CONSECRATION.

Sources: Current Biography 1966, pp. 311–12; Ebony (February 1966), pp. 62–70; Negro Almanac, 1989, p. 1330; Ochs, Desegregating the Altar, p. 446.

1968 • James P. Lyke (1939–92) was the first black priest in Tennessee, when he served in Saint Thomas Parish, Memphis. At the time of his death from cancer, he was the second black archbishop of Northern Georgia. He was leader in the creation of *Lead Me, Guide Me,* an African American

was leader in the creation of *Lead Me, Guide Me,* an African American Catholic hymnal.

Sources: Jet 83 (18 January 1993), p. 54; Spencer, *Black Hymnody,* pp. 188–89; *The Tennessee Register* (4 January 1993), pp. 1, 11.

1977 • Joseph Lawson Howze (1925–)became the first black to head a diocese in the Catholic Church in this century, when he became diocesan bishop of Biloxi, Mississippi. Howze was born in Daphne, Alabama. After teaching in the public schools of Mobile for some years, he felt a vocation to become a priest. He entered Epiphany Apostolic College, Newburgh, New York. On his graduation from Saint Bonaventure University in New York in 1959, he was ordained, becoming auxiliary bishop of Mississippi in 1973.

Sources: Crisis (April 1973), p. 141; *Ebony Success Library,* vol. 1, p. 160; *Negro Almanac, 1989,* p. 1328.

1981 • Carl Anthony Fisher (1945–1993) was named national coordinator of the Junior Catholic Daughters of the Americas, the first black to hold this position. Ordained in 1974, he became director of vocations for Saint Joseph's Society, and in 1982, the first black parish priest of Saint Francis Xavier Church, Baltimore, Maryland. Saint Francis Xavier was the first black parish, created in 1863. On December 19, 1986, Pope John Paul named him auxiliary bishop of Los Angeles, the first black Catholic bishop in the Western United States.

Sources: Ochs, Desegregating the Altar, pp. 450–51; *Jet 61* (22 October 1981), p. 24; *Jet 63* (6 December 1982), p. 24; *Jet 84* (27 September 1993), p. 12.

1982 • Sergio Carrillo was the first black priest ordained in the Archdiocese of Miami. Carrillo was a member of the failed Bay of Pigs invasion of Cuba in 1960.

Source: Jet 62 (10 May 1982), p. 43.

Emerson J. Moore, Jr., became the first black auxiliary bishop in the Archdiocese of New York. Earlier in 1982, he had been named the first black episcopal vicar of Central Harlem. Moore had been named pastor of Saint Charles Borromeo in Harlem, in 1975, and had served in the archdiocese for eighteen years when he became bishop.

Sources: Negro Almanac, 1989, pp. 1431–32; *Jet 62* (2 August 1982), p. 23.

1983 • Moses Anderson was the first Catholic auxiliary bishop in the Archdiocese of Detroit. Anderson was fifty-four years old and had been a priest for twenty-four years. He graduated from Saint Edmond Seminary, Burlington, Vermont, and did graduate work at the University of Legion, Ghana.

Sources: Jet 63 (17 January 1983), p. 53; *Jet* (14 February 1983), p. 18; *Who's Who Among Black Americans, 1992–93,* p. 34.

OPPOSITE PAGE:
SAINT MARTIN DE
PORRES WAS THE
FIRST BLACK
CANONIZED IN THE
CATHOLIC CHURCH.

1987 • The first National Black Catholic Congress since 1894 met in Washington, D.C.
Source: Jet 72 (15 June 1987), p. 7.

1988 • L. Warren Harvey was the first black priest in the Diocese of Little Rock, thus becoming the first in Arkansas.
Source: Jet 74 (27 June 1988), p. 38.

Eugene Antonio Marino (1934–)became the first black archbishop in the United States, and so only the second ordinary bishop (that is, a bishop who heads a diocese). Marino was a native of Biloxi, Mississippi, and educated at Saint Joseph's Seminary, Washington, D.C. He had served as auxiliary bishop in Washington, D.C., and became archbishop of the Diocese of Atlanta.
Sources: Hornsby, *Chronology of African-American History,* p. 364; *Jet* 81 (18 November 1991), p. 57; *Jet* 83 (5 April 1993), pp. 32–37; *Negro Almanac, 1989,* pp. 100, 1492; *Who's Who Among Black Americans, 1992-93,* p. 913.

Charles and Chester Smith were the first black identical twins ordained priests in the Catholic Church.
Source: Jet 74 (9 May 1988), p. 20.

1993 • On May 5, 1993, J. Terry Steib became the first black bishop in the state of Tennessee, when he was installed as bishop of the diocese of Memphis. The fifty-two-year-old Steib was born in Vacherie, Louisiana, and became a priest in 1967. He was named an auxiliary bishop in St. Louis in 1984, and he is the third black to head a Catholic diocese.
Source: (Nashville) *Tennessean* (24 March 1993).

CHRISTIAN CHURCH (DISCIPLES OF CHRIST)

1853 • Alexander Cross, a former slave from Kentucky, was the first missionary of any race sent to Africa by this denomination.
Source: Encyclopedia of Black America, p. 226.

1982 • Cynthia L. Hale became the first woman president of the predominantly black National Convocation of the Christian Church (Disciples of Christ). Hale was chaplain at the Federal Correctional Institute at Butner, Alabama.
Source: Jet 62 (30 August 1982), p. 24.

CHURCH OF CHRIST

1967 • Joseph H. Evans became the first black national secretary of the United Church of Christ.
Source: Garrett, *Famous First Facts About Negroes,* pp. 191–92.

CHURCH OF ENGLAND

1623 • The first known black child baptized in the colonies was William, the son of Isabella and Anthony Johnson, at Jamestown, Virginia. It is possible that his father is the same Anthony Johnson who owned five servants and was granted five hundred acres of land in 1651.

Sources: Blockson, *Black Geneology,* p. 46; Cantor, *Historic Landmarks of Black America,* p. 255; *Negro Almanac* (1976), p. 1041. Smith, *Ethnic Geneology,* pp. 346–47.

1704 • Elias Neau (?–1722), an agent of the Anglican Society for the Propagation of the Gospel in Foreign Parts, opened a catechism school for blacks in New York City. In 1720 the school had thirty-five women and forty-nine men; all but four women were slaves. It survived after Neau's death until the American Revolution.

Sources: Negro Almanac, 1989, p. 3; Raboteau, *Slave Religion,* pp. 117–18; Smith, *Climbing Jacob's Ladder,* pp. 26, 28.

1743 • The Society for the Propagation of the Gospel in Foreign Parts established in Charleston, South Carolina, the first known school to train black missionaries. Two blacks, Harry and Andrew, were in charge and the school lasted until 1764, when Harry, who was the teacher, died. Andrew had "proved a profligate" some time earlier and been dismissed.

Sources: Raboteau, *Slave Religion,* pp. 116–17; Smith, *Climbing Jacob's Ladder,* p. 28.

1968 • Coretta Scott King was the first woman of any race to preach at Saint Paul's Cathedral, London, England.

Sources: Alford, *Famous First Blacks,* p. 21; *Notable Black American Women,* pp. 631–34.

CONGREGATIONALISTS

1693 • Cotton Mather (1663–1728), the Boston cleric, drew up "Rules for the Society of Negroes" for a group of blacks who were seeking to hold their own prayer meetings on Sunday evenings. These rules are the first known example of this kind of ethnic religious association, which would not, at this date, be a separate church solely under black direction.

Source: Smith, *Climbing Jacob's Ladder,* pp. 26–27.

LEMUEL HAYNES

1785 • Lemuel Haynes (1753–1833) was the first black Congregational minister. Haynes was born in Connecticut. He never knew his black father, and his white mother refused to recognize him. Haynes was very well educated by the man to whom he was bound as a servant. He served in the Revolutionary army. Haynes was ordained in 1785 and became the pastor of a white congregation in Torrington, Connecticut. In 1818, he became pastor in Manchester, New Hampshire. He was the first black to receive an honorary degree, in 1804, when Middlebury College, Vermont, gave him an honorary M.A. Later, in April 1841, the abolitionist Samuel Ringgold Ward (1817–66?) would also become minister of a white Congregationalist congregation located in South Butler, New York—a position he held until 1843, when he resigned because of ill health.

Sources: Dictionary of American Negro Biography, pp. 300–1 (Haynes); pp. 631–32 (Ward); *Negro Year Book, 1913,* p. 115; Smith, *Climbing Jacob's Ladder,* p. 31.

1820 • The Dixwell Congregational Church, New Haven, Connecticut, was the first all-black Congregational church. Francis L. Cardozo, who made a mark in South Carolina politics during Reconstruction, was one of its pastors. The number of black Congregationalists was quite small, but the influence of the denomination as a whole on black life is immense. Through the American Missionary Association, Congregationalists founded, or supported, some five hundred schools in the South after the Civil War. These include surviving black schools of such eminence as Fisk University (Tennessee), Atlanta Christian College (Georgia), Hampton Institute (Virginia), Tougaloo College (Missouri), and Dillard College (Louisiana).

Sources: Encyclopedia of Black America, p. 286; Gatewood, *Aristocrats of Color,* p. 288.

EARLY CHRISTIANS

C. 35 • The first person identified as a black convert to Christianity was the unnamed Nubian eunuch, who was the treasurer of the Candace, either the queen-mother or a queen ruling in her own right. This man was converted by Philip the Deacon.

Source: Acts 8: 26–40.

C. 186 • Saint Victor I was the first pope identified as an African; his racial identity is not clearly established. He reigned until c. 197. Two other early popes are also of African origin: Saint Miltiades (311–14) and Saint Gelasius I (492–96).

Source: Davis, The History of Black Catholics in the United States, p. 13.

410 • Saint Moses the Black is the first saint whose black identity is well established. A rebellious former slave who had become an outlaw in the Egyptian desert, he became a monk and priest and left writings on monastic life. Moses was martyred in 410.

Source: Davis, *The History of Black Catholics in the United States,* pp. 9–10.

EPISCOPALIANS

1794 • On July 17, 1794, the original Free African Society building in Philadelphia was dedicated as Saint Thomas' African Episcopal Church, the first black Protestant Episcopal church. Absalom Jones (1746–1818) was ordained as the first black deacon in the denomination, and became pastor of Saint Thomas. He became the first black American priest in the denomination in 1804.

Sources: Dictionary of American Negro Biography, pp. 262–364; Lincoln and Mamiya, *The Black Church in the African American Experience,* pp. 51–52; Smith, *Climbing Jacob's Ladder,* pp. 36–37.

1819 • On July 3, 1819, Saint Phillip's African Church became the first black Protestant Episcopal church in New York City. Its leader was Peter Williams, Jr., (1780–1840), who became the second black American priest, on July 10, 1826.

Sources: Baer and Singer, *African-American Religion in the Twentieth Century,* p. 104; *Dictionary of American Negro Biography,* 660–61; *Encyclopedia of Black America,* p. 375; Smith, *Climbing Jacob's Ladder,* pp. 47–48, 50.

1828 • The Protestant Episcopal Church of Saint Thomas, Philadelphia, was the first black church to own an organ. This church also introduced the trained choir into services, placing it among the leaders in the development of new musical styles of worship taking place in Protestant churches at the time. The introduction of a trained choir in the AME mother church in Philadelphia, in 1841–42, caused a struggle that split the congregation.

Sources: Smith, *Climbing Jacob's Ladder,* p. 43; Southern, *The Music of Black Americans,* pp. 127–28.

1829 • William Levingston was the first black priest to do missionary work in the South. He established Saint James' Church, Baltimore, Maryland.

Source: Encyclopedia of Black America, p. 375.

1874 • James T. Holly (1829–1911) became the founder and first bishop of the Protestant Episcopal Church in Haiti, a position he held until his death in 1911. As rector of Saint Luke's, New Haven, Connecticut, he baptized W. E. B. Du Bois in 1868. Holly championed black emigration and dreamed of establishing a colony in Haiti. His consecration made him the first black bishop in any Episcopal church. His church was absorbed into the

Episcopal Missionary Diocese in 1913. At present, Lafond Lapointe has been trying to re-establish the church after the fall of the Duvalier regime.

Sources: Dictionary of American Negro Biography, pp. 319–20; *Encyclopedia of American Religions,* vol. 1, p. 70; *Encyclopedia of Black America,* pp. 282, 284, 375–76.

1883 • The Conference of Churchworkers Among Colored People was the first black caucus in the Protestant Episcopal Church. The leader in its foundation was Alexander Crummell (1819–98). (*See also* **Organizations: Academic and Intellectual Societies, 1897.**) The modern successor organization is the Union of Black Episcopalians, formed in 1968.

Sources: Baer and Singer, *African-American Religion in the Twentieth Century,* p. 104; *Dictionary of American Negro Biography,* pp. 145–47.

1885 • Samuel David Ferguson became the first missionary bishop of the Protestant Episcopal Church, and thus the first black to sit in the American House of Bishops. His assignment was Liberia. The first suffragan bishops would not be elected until 1918, and the first diocesan bishop until 1970. (Suffragan bishops are auxiliary bishops who are given special missions.)

Sources: Encyclopedia of Black America, pp. 376–77; *Negro Almanac, 1989,* p. 1425.

1918 • Edward T. Demby and Henry B. Delany were the first black suffragan bishops of the Protestant Episcopal Church. In 1885, Samuel David Ferguson had been a missionary bishop, and the first diocesan bishop would not be consecrated until 1970. (Suffragan bishops are assigned special roles; they do not head dioceses.) American blacks had earlier been named bishops of foreign dioceses: James Theodore Holly, bishop of Haiti (1874); and Samuel David Ferguson, bishop of Liberia (1885). Samuel Crowther, a native African, was made bishop of Nigeria in 1864.

Sources: Encyclopedia of Black America, p. 377; *Negro Year Book, 1918–19,* p. 23.

1969 • John M. Burgess (1909–) was elected presiding bishop of the Protestant Episcopal Church. He was also elected bishop of the Diocese of Massachusetts, becoming the first black to head a diocese. He held that position from 1970 until his retirement in 1976.

Source: Ebony (October 1960), pp. 54–58; *Ebony* (March 1982), p.128; *Ebony Success Library,* vol. 1, p. 50; Toppin, *Biographical History of Blacks,* pp. 261–62; Wormley, *Many Shades of Black,* p. 331; *Negro Almanac, 1989,* p. 1326; *Encyclopedia of Black America,* pp. 199, 377.

Dillard Robinson, with his position as dean of the cathedral in Newark, New Jersey, became the first black dean in an Episcopal cathedral.

Source: Encyclopedia of Black America, p. 377.

1976 • H. Irving Mayson (1926–) was the first Episcopal suffragan bishop in Michigan.

OPPOSITE PAGE:
PAULI MURRAY

Sources: Ebony (March 1956), p. 23; *Jet* 51 (4 November 1976), p. 20.

1977 • On January 8, 1977, Pauli Murray (1910–85) was the first woman ordained a priest in the Protestant Episcopal Church.

Sources: Encyclopedia of Black America, p. 584; Notable Black American Women, pp. 783–88.

John T. Walker (1925–89) was the first black bishop of the Episcopal Church in the diocese of Washington, being installed on September 24, 1977. He had been named coadjutor in 1971. Born in Barnesville, Georgia, he became a priest in 1955, after taking a B.D. degree from Virginia Theological Seminary, where he had been the first black graduate in 1954. Walker's great-grandfather had founded the African Methodist Episcopal (AME) Church in Barnesville.

Sources: Ebony Success Library, vol. 1, p. 316; Encyclopedia of Black America, p. 830; Jet 77 (16 October 1989), p. 7; Negro Almanac, 1989, p. 1418.

1982 • Winnie McKenzie Bolle was the first black, and the first female, priest in the Diocese of Southeast Florida. A fifty-seven-year-old native of Jamaica, Bolle is a graduate of the Divinity School of the Pacific, Berkeley, California.

Source: Jet 62 (12 July 1982), p. 30.

Gayle Elizabeth Harris was the first black female priest in the Diocese of Newark, New Jersey. The fifth woman ordained in the Episcopal Church, Harris is an early black graduate of the Divinity School of the Pacific, Berkeley, California.

Source: Jet 62 (14 June 1982), p. 38.

Sandra Antoinette Wilson became the first female priest of the Protestant Episcopal Church in the New York City Archdiocese on January 25, 1982.

Sources: Negro Almanac, p. 43; Jet 61 (15 February 1982), p. 32.

1984 • As Anglican bishop of Johannesburg, Desmond Tutu became the first black bishop of his church in South Africa.

Source: Jet 67 (3 December 1984), p 31.

1989 • Barbara Harris (1930–) became the first female Anglican bishop in the world. On February 12, 1989, she was consecrated suffragan bishop in the Diocese of Massachusetts. As a woman, her election to a post held only by men from the time of Saint Peter, aroused the same controversy as the ordination of eleven women priests did in 1974. This earlier event encouraged Harris to prepare for the priesthood to which she herself was ordained in 1980.

Sources: Black Women in America, p. 537–38; Hornsby, Chronology of African-American History, p. 382; Negro Almanac, 1989, pp. 105–6; Notable Black American Women, pp. 462–66.

1991 • As suffragan bishop of the Diocese of Los Angeles, Chester Lovelle Talton became the first black Protestant Episcopal bishop in the West on January 26, 1991.

Source: State of Black America 1992, p. 362.

1992 • Nathan D. Baxter became the first black dean of Washington National Cathedral, Washington, D.C.

Source: Jet 81 (2 March 1992), p. 8.

BARBARA HARRIS, THE FIRST FEMALE ANGLICAN BISHOP.

RADIO BROADCASTER
SOLOMON LIGHTFOOT
MICHAUX.

ETHIOPIANS

1920 • The militant claim that blacks were Ethiopians who would fulfill a Biblical prophecy to return to their homeland, first received national attention when Grover Cleveland Redding set an American flag afire during a parade by his movement in Chicago. Whites tried to intervene and the ensuing struggle left two persons dead. Redding's associate in founding the group was R. D. Jonas.

Source: Baer and Singer, *African-American Religion in the Twentieth Century,* p. 113.

HOLINESS

1886 • The United Holy Church, established in Method, North Carolina, is known as the first black holiness church. It grew out of a revival conducted by Isaac Cheshier on the first Sunday in May. Early in this century it became a Pentecostal church.

Sources: Baer and Singer, *African-American Religion in the Twentieth Century,* p. 149; *Directory of African American Religious Bodies,* pp. 114, 250; *Encyclopedia of American Religions,* vol. 1, p. 443.

1929 • Known as the "Happy Am I Evangelist," Solomon Lightfoot Michaux (1885–1968) of the Gospel Spreading Church, Washington, D.C., began radio broadcasts in 1929. After the purchase of a local station by the CBS network, he was the first black to have a national and international audience on a regular basis. In 1934 he broadcast on Saturdays on the CBS radio network, and internationally on shortwave, to reach an audience estimated at twenty-five million people. He preached a mixture of holiness themes and positive thinking, and his church was related to the Church of God, Holiness. By 1941 his radio broadcasts were heard only in a few cities where he had congregations, but the broadcasts continued until his death.

Sources: Baer and Singer, *African-American Religion in the Twentieth Century,* pp. 155–57; *Dictionary of American Negro Biography,* pp. 432–33; *Encyclopedia of American Religions,* vol. 1, p. 223.

INTERCHURCH ORGANIZATIONS

1986 • Christine E. Trigg was the first female president of the New Jersey Council of Churches. Trigg was a member of the Clinton Memorial African Methodist Episcopal Zion Church in Newark, New Jersey.

Source: Jet 70 (9 June 1986), p. 20.

1991 • Vinton R. Anderson was the first black to be one of the seven presidents of the World Council of Churches. Anderson was a bishop of the African Methodist Episcopal (AME) Church and had been active in interchurch work for many years.

Sources: Jet 79 (1 April 1991), p. 29; *Jet* 81 (18 November 1991), p. 66.

ISLAM

622 • Bilal (?–641?) was the first muezzin of Islam. He was a slave of Ethiopian origin and reputed to be the second adult convert, after Abu Bakr. (He suffered much for his faith, but was eventually secured and freed by Abu Bakr.) Bilal emigrated to Medina with the Prophet, who appointed him to call the faithful to prayer. The first to issue the call to prayer from the roof of the Kaaba after the return, he attained high prestige during his lifetime.

Sources: Encyclopaedia of Islam, p. 1215; *Shorter Encyclopaedia of Islam,* pp. 62–63.

1913 • Noble Drew Ali, a name adopted by Timothy Drew (1886–1929), formed the Moorish Science Temple in Newark, New Jersey. This is the first step to the appearance, or the reappearance, of various forms of black Islam. (There is a debate about the survival in the nineteenth century of remnants of Islam coming from Africa.) Noble Drew Ali taught that blacks were not Ethiopians, but the descendants of the Moabites of the Bible, whose homeland was said to be Morocco. He also saw Marcus Garvey as a precursor to his organization. W. D. Fard, the founder of the Nation of Islam in the early 1930s, was originally a member of the Moorish Science Temple.

Sources: Baer and Singer, *African-American Religion in the Twentieth Century,* pp. 51, 60, 118–19; *Directory of African American Religious Bodies,* pp. 141–42; *Encyclopedia of American Religions,* vol. 3. p. 178.

LUTHERANS

1983 • Nelson W. Trout (c. 1921–)was the first black elected bishop of the Evangelical Lutheran Church in America on June 17, 1983. Trout was a professor at Trinity Lutheran Seminary, Columbus, Ohio, when he was named bishop of the South Pacific District in California.

Source: Hornsby, *Chronology of African-American History,* pp. 320–21.

1988 • Sherman G. Hicks became the first black bishop of the Evangelical Lutheran Church in America.

Source: Jet 74 (23 May 1988), p. 12.

METHODISTS

1758 • On November 29 in England John Wesley baptized the first two known black converts (one being a woman) to the Methodism movement. At this time, Methodism had not broken away from the Anglican church. In the United States the split between the Protestant Episcopal Church and the Methodist Episcopal Church would not be complete until 1784.

Sources: Heritage and Hope, p. 27; Lincoln and Mamiya, *The Black Church in the African American Experience,* p. 50.

1764 • A slave named Anne Sweitzer (Aunt Annie) was one of the founding members of the first Methodist society in the colonies, organized in Frederick County, Maryland. Blacks were members of Saint George's Methodist Church in Philadelphia, which dates to 1767. In 1776, a black servant called Betty would be a charter member of the John Street meeting, the first society in New York City.

Sources: Heritage and Hope, p. 24; Lincoln and Mamiya, *The Black Church in the African American Experience,* p. 50; Smith, *Climbing Jacob's Ladder,* pp. 33–35, 39.

PREACHER
HARRY HOSIER.

1781 • The first known black Methodist preacher was "Black" Harry Hosier (c. 1750–1806). His sermon, "Barren Fig Tree," was delivered at Adams Chapel, Fairfax County, Virginia, in 1781, and was the first preached by a black to a congregation of Methodists. His sermon in 1784 at Thomas Chapel, Chapeltown, Delaware, was the first preached by a black to a white congregation.

Sources: Encyclopedia of Black America, pp. 511, 555; *Heritage and Hope,* pp. 50–51, 307; Lincoln and Mamiya, *The Black Church in the African American Experience,* p. 66; Smith, *Climbing Jacob's Ladder,* pp. 34–35.

1785 • The first Methodists in Baltimore met in Lovely Lane and Strawberry Alley beginning in 1772. Blacks began to form their own Colored Methodist Society between 1785 and 1787. This is the origin of the first black Methodist churches in Baltimore, Sharp Street Church (1802), and Bethel African Methodist Episcopal Church.

Sources: Heritage and Hope, p. 43; Smith, *Climbing Jacob's Ladder,* p. 35.

1787 • Richard Allen (1760–1831) and Absalom Jones (1746–1818) organized the Free African Society in Philadelphia on April 12, 1787. This society was originally a mutual aid society. Black members withdrew from Saint George's Methodist Episcopal Church, in Philadelphia, in protest against increased segregation in seating (apparently in November 1787). The Free African Society became the nucleus for the first black Episcopal church, Saint Thomas, in 1794. In the same year, those blacks who wished to remain Methodists formed the Bethel Church, which became the mother church of the African Methodist Episcopal Church in 1816. (The incident in Saint George's is also assigned to the date of 1792. It is possible that the Cumberland Street Methodist Episcopal Church, Charleston, South Carolina, was in fact the first to install a segregated gallery, in 1787, which became a traditional way to separate congregations.) (*See also* **Organizations: Charitable and Civic Organizations, 1787.**)

Sources: Dictionary of American Negro Biography, pp. 12–13 (Allen); 362–64 (Jones); *Heritage and Hope,* p. 29; Lincoln and Mamiya, *The Black Church in the African American Experience,* pp. 50–51; Smith, *Climbing Jacob's Ladder,* pp. 36–37.

EARLY BLACK METHODIST CHURCHES

FOUNDED	NAME	LOCATION
c.1800	Evans Chapel	Fayetteville, North Carolina
1801	Mount Hope	Salem, New Jersey
1802	Sharp Street	Baltimore, Maryland
1805	Ezion	Wilmington, Delaware
1814	Mount Zion	Washington, D.C.
1823	Union	Massachusetts
c. 1824	Calvary	Cincinnati, Ohio
1838	Wesley Chapel	New Orleans, Louisiana
1840	Newnan Station	Newnan, Georgia
1844	Asbury	Lexington, Kentucky
1846	Union Memorial	St. Louis, Missouri
1850	First Colored Methodist[1]	Sacramento, California
1863	Wesley	Little Rock, Arkansas
1866	Clark Memorial	Nashville, Tennessee

[1] Joined the African Methodist Episcopal Church in 1851.

Source: Heritage and Hope, pp. 45, 309.

1794 • African Zoar Church was organized as a mission church in Philadelphia. This was the first all-black church for persons who eventually stayed in the Methodist Episcopal Church. Zoar was incorporated in 1835.

Sources: Encyclopedia of Black America, pp. 32, 555; Heritage and Hope, p. 43; Smith, Climbing Jacob's Ladder, pp. 36, 44.

1799 • Richard Allen (February 14, 1760–March 26, 1831) became the first black ordained deacon in the Methodist Episcopal church in 1799. Born a slave, he became a member of a Methodist society in Delaware about 1780, and by 1783 he was a licensed preacher in New Jersey and Pennsylvania. In 1786, he established prayer meetings for blacks in Philadelphia. Resenting an effort by the white members of Saint George's Methodist Episcopal Church to further segregate black members of the congregation, Allen and Absalom Jones led a walkout of blacks in 1787. The Free African Society, which seems to have been already organized as a mutual aid society, became the center of the congregation's worship. Jones entered the Protestant Episcopal ministry in 1794, but Allen remained a Methodist. When five black churches broke from the parent organization in 1816, Allen became the first bishop of the new African Methodist Episcopal (AME) Church. He is also one of the first black authors of a biography, *The Life Experiences and Gospel Labors of the Right Reverend Richard Allen.*

Sources: Dictionary of American Negro Biography, pp. 12–13; Directory of African American Religious Bodies, p. 242; Smith, Climbing Jacob's Ladder, pp. 35–37.

1800 • Henry Evans (?1810), a free-born shoemaker, established the first Methodist church in Fayetteville, North Carolina. Evans Chapel was dedicated in 1802 and Francis Asbury, the most prominent leader in the establishment of Methodism in the United States, visited it in 1805. The church originally had white members and the numbers increased so that blacks were displaced from their original seating. Evans himself was displaced as minister before his death. The whites withdrew before the Methodist Episcopal Church split into northern and southern parts in 1844. Evans Chapel joined the AME Zion Church in 1866.

Sources: Heritage and Hope, p. 44; Lincoln and Mamiya, The Black Church in the African American Experience, p. 66; Negro Almanac, p. 1301; Raboteau, Slave Religion, p. 135.

1816 • John Stewart (1786–1823) was the first black missionary to the Wyandotte Indians. He was assisted by Jonathan Poynter, a black who had been raised by the Wyandottes. Stewart died one year before his church was completed. In 1960 his grave and missionary church in Upper Sandusky, Ohio, were designated as one of ten official shrines of American Methodism. A monument to him had been established previously on October 19, 1916.

Sources: Dictionary of American Negro Biography, p. 371; Heritage and Hope, pp. 36, 307; Negro Almanac, 1989, p. 223; Negro Year Book, 1918–1919, pp. 23–24.

1858 • Francis Burns (1809–1863) was the first black Methodist Episcopal missionary bishop. A native of Albany, New York, he served in Liberia for twenty-four years. In 1849 he had been the first black to be designated a presiding elder for his work in Liberia. A second missionary bishop, John W. Roberts, was elected in 1866; a third, Isaiah B. Scott, in 1904; and a fourth, Alexander P. Camphor, in 1916. Only in 1920 would a regular bishop be elected. The lack of leadership roles for blacks in the denomination was one of the factors leading to black annual conferences, held officially from 1864 to 1939, and, in effect, dividing the denomination along racial lines.

Sources: Encyclopedia of Black America, pp. 555–57; Heritage and Hope, pp. 54, 67.

1870 • W. H. Miles and Richard H. Vanderhorst were the first bishops of the Colored (now Christian) Methodist Episcopal Church. This denomination was formed by blacks leaving the Methodist Episcopal Church (South).

Sources: Encyclopedia of American Religions, vol. 1, pp. 195–96; Lincoln and Mamiya, The Black Church in the African American Experience, p. 62; Smith, Climbing Jacob's Ladder, pp. 123–24.

1884 • Marshall W. Taylor (1847–87) became the first black editor of the *Southwestern Christian Advocate* of the Methodist Episcopal Church. The periodical was established in 1876, and became the center for both dissemination of news and debate on issues of concern for blacks in the denomination. In 1941 this periodical became the *Central Christian Advocate,* and continued publication until 1968.

Sources: Heritage and Hope, pp. 67, 148–49; Encyclopedia of Black America, p. 558.

1920 • Robert E. Jones (1872–1960) and Matthew W. Clair, Sr., (1865–1943) were the elected bishops by the United Methodist Church for service in the United States. The denomination had elected its first black missionary bishop for service in Liberia in 1858.

Sources: Encyclopedia of Black America, p. 557; Heritage and Hope, pp. 87–88, 308, 314; Negro Year Book, 1921–22, p. 16.

1936 • Laura J. Lange was the first woman ordained a local elder in Methodist Episcopal Church, by the Lexington Conference. Lange had been made a deacon in 1926. It would not be until 1956 (Sallie A. Crenshaw) that a black woman would be ordained an elder and admitted into full connection in an Annual Conference.

Source: Heritage and Hope, pp. 53, 155.

1955 • Simon Peter Montgomery was the first Methodist minister assigned to an all-white congregation, in Old Mystic, Connecticut.

Source: Negro Almanac, 1989, p. 1429.

1958 • Joseph Reed Washington was the first Methodist minister with two all-white churches, the Methodist church in Newfield, Maine, and the

Congregational church in West Newfield, Maine. These places are some three miles apart.

Source: Negro Almanac, 1989, p. 1429.

1964 • Prince A. Taylor (1907–) and James S. Thomas, Jr., (1918–) were the first black bishops of the United Methodist Church appointed to predominantly white jurisdictions. Taylor, a bishop since 1956, was appointed to the New Jersey area on June 25, 1964, and Thomas to Iowa, on July 10, 1964. In 1965–66 Taylor was also the first black president of the Council of Bishops.

Sources: Ebony (February 1965), pp. 54–60; *Ebony* (March 1982), p. 129; *Ebony Success Library,* vol. 1, p. 302 (Thomas); *Heritage and Hope,* pp. 161–63; Wormley and Fenderson, *Many Shades of Black,* pp. 349–50. (Thomas).

1969 • The Washington Square United Methodist Church in New York City was the first white church to give money in response to James Forman's demand for reparations from white churches. Forman (1928–), then leader of the Student Non-Violent Coordinating Committee, had demanded reparations of $500 million from white churches on April 26, 1969, in a surprise appearance in the pulpit of Riverside Church in New York City.

Sources: Baer and Singer, *African-American Religion in the Twentieth Century,* p. 238; *Negro Almanac, 1989,* pp. 1304, 1305.

1971 • Claire Collins Harvey (1916–) became the first black to head Church Women United. Harvey is a Mississippi businesswoman, a civil rights activist, and a church worker.

Sources: Encyclopedia of Black America, p. 560; *Heritage and Hope,* p. 268; *Who's Who Among Black Americans, 1992–93,* p. 619.

1981 • William M. Smith was the first black head of the Ecumenical Committee of the World Methodist Conference. Presiding bishop of the First Episcopal District of the African Methodist Episcopal (AME) Zion Church, he lived in Mobile, Alabama.

Source: Jet 61 (22 October 1981), p. 24.

1984 • Leontine T. C. Kelly (1920–) became the first woman bishop of a major denomination, the United Methodist Church. She was consecrated on July 20, 1984. In addition, she was the first woman of any race to preach on the program National Radio Pulpit of the National Council of Churches. Born in Washington, D.C., Kelly's call to the ministry came after the death of her third husband. Made an elder in 1977, she had experience at both the local and the national level. Upon the retirement of the first (and only) woman bishop in the church, she was elected, and supervised the California and Nevada conferences until her retirement in 1988.

Sources: Black Women in America, pp. 675; Heritage and Hope, p. 280; Notable Black American Women, pp. 621–26.

BISHOP LEONTINE T. C. KELLY

1987 • J. D. Phillips was the first black to head a predominantly white United Methodist church in the Central Texas Conference: Saint Andrew's United Methodist Church, Killeen, Texas.

Source: Jet 72 (13 July 1987), p. 22.

MORMONS

1836 • Elijah Abel (?–1884) was the first black to become an elder (priest) in the Mormon church, in 1836, while the Mormons were headquartered in Nauvoo, Illinois. Abel was an undertaker and had been converted in 1832. He moved with the Mormons to Salt Lake City, Utah, where he became a hotel manager. He was active in the church until his death. After the very early years of the church, a long-standing ban prevented blacks from advancing to the priesthood. This ban was abolished in 1978, and the church has since attracted a number of black members.

Sources: Cantor, Historic Landmarks of Black America, p.334; Encyclopedia of Black America, p. 12.

1978 • Joseph Freeman, Jr., became the first black priest (elder) in this century. Advancement to this rank is normal for all male members of the church, but it had been denied to blacks until a revelation to the presiding elder changed the church's policy in 1978.

Sources: Cantor, Historic Landmarks of Black America, p. 334; Kane, Famous First Facts, p. 167; Negro Almanac, 1989, p. 1325.

MUSLIMS

1991 • Siraj Wahaj was the first Black Muslim to give the invocation in the House of Representatives. The forty-one-year-old Wahaj was from the Bedford-Stuyvesant area of New York City.

Source: Jet 80 (15 July 1991), pp. 30–31.

NATION OF ISLAM

1932 • Elijah Muhammad (Elijah Poole, 1897–1975) established the Nation of Islam's Temple Number Two, the first temple in Chicago. Upon the 1934 disappearance of W. D. Fard, who had founded the movement, Elijah Muhammad became the leader of the movement. The movement grew under his leadership, especially in the late fifties and the sixties, in part due to the charismatic leadership of his principal lieutenant, Malcolm X (1925–65). Malcolm X's suspension from the movement in 1963 marked the first major split in the organization. After Elijah Muhammad's death, Louis Farrakhan formed a new Nation of Islam in 1978. The faction led by Wallace J. Muhammad moved closer to orthodox Islam and renamed itself the American Muslim Mission.

Sources: Directory of African American Religious Bodies, pp. 139–40; *Encyclopedia of American Religions,* pp. 175–76, 179–80; *Negro Almanac, 1989,* pp. 1304–5, 1319.

PEACE MISSION

1914 • It was about this year that Father Divine (George Baker, 1879–1965) first proclaimed himself God as he established his movement, Father Divine's "Kingdom" and Peace Mission. He was tried on a charge of insanity in a Valdosta, Georgia, court on February 27, 1914, on the grounds that his claim to be God was clearly aberrant. He was convicted but not incarcerated.

Sources: Dictionary of American Negro Biography, pp. 178–80; *Directory of African American Religious Bodies,* pp. 122–24; Watts, *God, Harlem U.S.A.,* pp. 31–43.

PENTECOSTALS

1906 • From April 14, 1906, the preaching of William J. Seymour (1870–1922) at the Azusa Street Mission in Los Angeles began one major strand in the diffusion of the Pentecostal movement among both blacks and whites. The first widely influential revival to emphasize the centrality of speaking in tongues as evidence of baptism in the Holy Spirit, it drew both blacks and whites. C. H. Mason's experiences at the Azusa Street Mission in 1907 led him to make the practice central in Church of God in Christ. In 1908,

G. B. Cashwell introduced the practice he had learned from Seymour to the predominantly white Church of God, USA. Pentecostalists soon split along racial lines. C. H. Mason's church was incorporated, however, and some white leaders of segregated congregations continued to be ordained by Mason for a few years so that they would legally be recognized as ministers.

Sources: Baer and Singer, *African-American Religion in the Twentieth Century,* pp. 180–81; *Black Apostles,* pp. 213–25; *Directory of African American Religious Bodies,* pp. 250–51; *Encyclopedia of American Religions,* vol. 1, pp. xxxvii, 43, 45, 226, 231, 243–44; Lincoln and Mamiya, *The Black Church in the African American Experience,* p.79.

PRESBYTERIANS

1757 • Samuel Davis, a white minister in Hanover County, Virginia, reported that he had baptized about 150 blacks after eighteen months of preaching to them. He had begun his activity in 1748. This is the first organized activity of Presbyterians among blacks. Davis would in time become the president of the College of New Jersey (Princeton).

Sources: Raboteau, *Slave Religion,* p. 129–30; Wilmore, *Black and Presbyterian,* p. 40.

1800 • Blacks participated in the Gasper River and Cane Ridge, Kentucky, camp meetings, which were the first to inaugurate the Great Western Revival. The lead given by the Presbyterians was followed by other denominations, and camp meetings became important in the conversion of slaves. Many scholars maintain that the majority of blacks were not converted to Christianity until this second wave of revivalism was taken up by other denominations, principally the Baptists and Methodists, along with new denominations, such as the Campbellites (Disciples of Christ).

Sources: Baer and Singer, *African-American Religion in the Twentieth Century,* p. 6; *Directory of African American Religious Bodies,* pp. 5–6; *Encyclopedia of American Religions,* pp. xxix-xxxi; Raboteau, *Slave Religion,* p. 132.

1801 • John Chavis (1763–1838) became the first black Presbyterian missionary in the South. Chavis was born free in North Carolina. After fighting in the Revolutionary War, he received an education at Washington Academy, Virginia, (now called Washington and Lee University) and at Princeton. He returned to North Carolina after being appointed a Presbyterian missionary to blacks. By 1808, he set up a school where he taught Latin and Greek to both black and white students. The first known black to have taught both races in the South, he was forced to give up his school and pulpit in 1831, after the Nat Turner revolt resulted in laws that barred blacks from teaching and preaching in North Carolina.

Sources: Dictionary of American Negro Biography, pp. 101–2; *Encyclopedia of Black America,* pp. 224, 704; Raboteau, *Slave Religion,* p. 135; Wilmore, *Black and Presbyterian,* p. 64.

1807 • The first all-black Presbyterian church, First African, was organized in Philadelphia. It grew out of the work of John Gloucester, Sr., (c. 1776–1822) a freed slave from Tennessee. The second church, in New York City, would not follow until fifteen years later.

Sources: *Encyclopedia of Black America,* p. 704; Smith, *Climbing Jacob's Ladder,* p. 44.

1818 • George M. Erskine was the first slave in Tennessee to be licensed as a preacher by the Presbyterians. After buying his freedom, and that of his wife and seven children, he went to Africa as a missionary. Only one other southern black is known to have been ordained by the church before the civil war: Harrison W. Ellis, in 1846. He was sent to Liberia as a missionary.

Source: Raboteau, *Slave Religion,* p. 207

1821 • Samuel E. Cornish (1795–1858) established the first black Presbyterian church in New York City: the First Colored Presbyterian Church on New Demeter Street. It was the second in the country. A notable abolitionist, Cornish was also co-editor, with John B. Russworm, of the first black newspaper, *Freedom's Journal,* in 1827. (*See also* **Journalism: Newspapers, 1827.**)

Sources: *Dictionary of American Negro Biography,* pp. 134–35; *Encyclopedia of Black America,* pp. 288–89; Smith, *Climbing Jacob's Ladder,* pp. 48, 51–52; Wilmore, *Black and Presbyterian,* pp. 65–66.

1828 • Theodore Sedgewick Wright (1797–1847) was the first black graduate of Princeton Theological Seminary. Educated at the New York City African Free School and at Princeton, he succeeded Samuel Cornish at the First Colored Presbyterian Church in New York City, and became a noted abolitionist and supporter of rights for blacks.

Sources: *Dictionary of American Negro Biography,* pp. 675–76; *Encyclopedia of Black America,* p. 704; Wilmore, *Black and Presbyterian,* pp. 65–66.

1869 • The Colored Cumberland Presbyterian Church was founded in 1869. This church broke from the white denomination; it was one of the first to split away in the South, as separate black churches became legally possible after the Civil War. Some contact with the parent denomination was maintained, and the separation of the churches was not absolute until 1874. This denomination is now known as the Second Cumberland Presbyterian Church and has some 15,000 communicants.

Sources: *Directory of African American Religious Bodies,* p. 129; *Encyclopedia of American Religions,* vol. 1, p. 170.

1893 • The Afro-Presbyterian Council was the first formal organization for black Presbyterians in the North and West. (Southern Presbyterians were already in segregated synods.) The organization became the Council of the North and West in 1947, and was formally dissolved in 1957. The realization that the dissolution had been premature led to the formation of the Black Presbyterians United in 1968.

Source: Wilmore, *Black and Presbyterian,* pp. 69–71.

REPRESENTATIVE BLACK CHURCHES FOUNDED SINCE 1865

FOUNDED	NAME	FOUNDER
1865	Colored Primitive Baptists	
1867	United Free Will Baptist Church	
1869	Reformed Zion Union Apostolic Church	James R. Howell
1869	Second Cumberland Presbyterian Church	
1870	Colored Methodist Episcopal Church[1]	
1886	United Holy Church of America	
1889	Church of the Living God (Christian Workers for Fellowship)	William Christian
1894	Church of Christ Holiness USA/Church of God in Christ[2]	C. P. Jones and C. H. Mason
1896	Church of God and Saints of Christ	William S. Crowdy
1896	Church of Christ, Holiness, USA	C. P. Jones
1902	Triumph the Church and Kingdom of God in Christ	E. D. Smith
1903	Christ's Sanctified Holy Church	
1905	Free Christian Zion Church of Christ	E. D. Brown
1907	National Primitive Baptist Convention of the USA	
1908	Church of the Living God, the Pillar and the Ground of Truth	Mary L. Tate
1908	Fire Baptized Holiness Church	W. E. Fuller
1920	Apostolic Overcoming Holy Church of God	William Thomas Phillips
1920	National Baptist Evangelical Life and Soul Saving Assembly of USA	A. A. Banks
1921	African Orthodox Church	George Alexander McGuire
1929	Kodesh Church of Immanuel	Frank Russell Killingsworth
1930	Lost-Found Nation of Islam in the West (Black Muslims)	W. D. Fard
1932	The National David Spiritual Temple of Christ Church Union (Inc.), USA	David William Short
1957	Bible Way Church of Our Lord Jesus Christ World Wide	Smallwood E. Williams
1961	Bible Church of Christ	Roy Bryant, Sr.

[1]Now called the Christian Methodist Episcopal Church.

[2]The two churches do not agree about their history, particularly about the date of the adoption of the name Church of God in Christ. See the *Encyclopedia of American Religions,* vol. 1, pp. 222, 272.

Sources: Directory of African American Religious Bodies; Encyclopedia of American Religions; Negro Almanac, pp. 13061325.

1938 • Albert B. McCoy was the first black secretary of the Presbyterian Division of Work with Colored People.
Source: Wilmore, *Black and Presbyterian,* p. 69.

1962 • On May 17, 1962, Marshall Logan Scott was elected the first black moderator of the Presbyterian Church.
Source: Ebony (March 1982), p. 129.

1964 • Edler Garnet Hawkins (1908–77) was elected the first black moderator of the United Presbyterian Church on May 21, 1964. Born in New York City on June 13, 1908, he received his B.D. from Union Theological Seminary in that city in 1938. Hawkins built his church from nine black members to an integrated congregation of more than one thousand. He was also the first moderator of the church to visit the Roman Catholic pope.
Sources: Current Biography 1965, pp. 193–95; *Ebony* (September 1968), p. 66; *Encyclopedia of Black America,* p. 706.

1975 • Lawrence Wendell Bottoms (1908–) was the first black to become moderator of the Presbyterian Church (southern division). After his ordination in 1936, Bottoms was pastor of a Louisville, Kentucky, church until 1949. He served on many church boards and commissions.
Sources: Encyclopedia of Black America, p. 187; Hornsby, *Chronology of African-American History,* p. 226; *Jet* (4 July 1974), p. 44.

1976 • Thelma Davidson Adair (1921–) became the first black woman moderator of the United Presbyterian Church. Adair was a fifty-five year-old professor who specialized in early childhood and elementary education at Queens College in New York. The first black moderator was Edler G. Hawkins. (*See also* **Religion: Presbyterians, 1964.**)
Sources: Afro-American (25 May 1976), p. 1; *Encore* (6 July 1979), p. 41; *Jet* 50 (1 July 1976), p. 9.

1989 • Joan Salmon Campbell was the first black woman to head the Presbyterian Church (USA). A trained singer, Campbell has a degree from the Eastman School of Music.
Sources: Hornsby, *Chronology of African-American History,* p. 392; *Ebony,* (November 1989), pp. 100, 102, 104; *Jet* 77 (26 June 1989), p. 17; (20 November 1989), p. 38.

Sara Brown Cordery was the first black woman moderator of the Presbytery of Baltimore.
Source: Jet 77 (27 November 1989), p. 20.

RASTAFARIANS

1935 • Haile Selassie was crowned emperor of Ethiopia in 1935, the approximate date of the founding of the Rastafarian movement in Jamaica. The coronation of Selassie seemed to fulfill a 1927 prophecy by Marcus Garvey that the crowning of a king in Africa would be a sign that the end of black oppression by whites was near. Since about 1960 the group in the United States has grown to an estimated three to five thousand.

Sources: Directory of African American Religious Bodies, pp. 133–36; Encyclopedia of American Religions, vol. 3, pp. 156–57; Negro Almanac, 1989, p. 1319.

REFORMED DUTCH CHURCH

1954 • James Joshua Thomas became the first black pastor in this denomination. He was given a church in the Bronx, New York City.

Source: Negro Almanac, 1989, p. 1429.

SALVATION ARMY

1970 • B. Barton McIntyre was the first black lieutenant colonel in the Salvation Army in the United States.

Sources: Garrett, Famous First Facts About Negroes, pp. 171–72; Romero, In Black America, p. 140.

SPIRITUAL

1915 • The first verifiable spiritual (formerly referred to as spiritualist) congregation is the Church of the Redemption in Chicago. It is possible that Mother Leafy Anderson had established an earlier one in Chicago before she moved to New Orleans and established the first in that city, Eternal Life Spiritual Church, sometime between 1918 and 1921. (*See also* **Religion: Spiritual, 1922.**)

Source: Baer, The Black Spiritual Movement, p. 2.

1922 • The first black spiritual denomination was the National Colored Spiritualist Association of Churches, formed in 1922 by a breakaway of blacks from the predominantly white National Spiritualist Association. William Frank Taylor and Leviticus Lee Boswell founded the largest present-day association of black spiritual churches, Metropolitan Spiritual Churches of Christ, in 1925.

Sources: Directory of African American Religious Bodies, p. 130; Encyclopedia of American Religions, vol. 2, pp. 270–71.

UNITARIAN-UNIVERSALISTS

1982 • Yvonne Reed Chappelle was the first black woman ordained in the Unitarian-Universalist Church. The forty-four-year-old Chappelle was a graduate of the Howard School of Divinity.

Sources: Black Scholar (January 1970), pp. 36–39; Jet 61 (11 February 1982), p. 32.

UNITED CHURCH AND SCIENCE OF LIVING INSTITUTE

1966 • Frederick J. Eikerenkoetter II (c. 1935–), "The Rev. Ike," first founded his church in 1966. He had begun his ministry in the late 1950s as a Pentecostal, but was shifting away towards a New Thought position, a transition that would be complete by 1968. He rejected sin, taught that salvation must be achieved here and now, and praised monetary and material acquisitiveness.

Sources: Baer and Singer, *African-American Religion in the Twentieth Century,* pp. 64, 200–2; *Directory of African American Religious Bodies,* pp. 124–25; *Encyclopedia of American Religions,* vol. 2, p. 255.

UNITED CHURCH OF CHRIST

1987 • Kwame Osei was the first black to head the Potomac Association Conference of the United Church of Christ in Washington, D.C.

Source: Jet 72 (27 July 1987), p. 38.

1991 • Denise Page Hood became the first black woman to chair the Executive Council of the United Church of Christ.

Source: Jet 80 (5 August 1991), p. 10.

UNITED METHODISTS

1968 • In Cincinnati, Ohio, the First National Conference of Negro Methodists organized a black caucus for the denomination, Black Methodists for Church Renewal.

Sources: Baer and Singer, *African-American Religion in the Twentieth Century,* p. 106; *Directory of African American Religious Bodies,* pp. 204–5, 245; *Heritage and Hope,* pp. 209–10.

UNITED SOCIETY OF BELIEVERS IN CHRIST'S SECOND COMING (SHAKERS)

1859 • Rebecca Cox Jackson (1795–1871) established the first largely black Shaker family in Philadelphia. Its existence in Philadelphia can be traced until at least 1908.

Sources: Black Women in America, pp. 626–27; *Notable Black American Women,* pp. 561–65.

SCIENCE & MEDICINE: GROUNDBREAKING BREAKTHROUGHS

ATOMIC ENERGY COMMISSION

1966 • Samuel M. Nabrit (1905–) was the first black member of the Atomic Energy Commission. A zoologist born in Macon, Georgia, Nabrit received his Ph.D. from Brown University. He became president of Texas Southern University in 1955.

Sources: Current Biography Yearbook, 1963, pp. 295–97; Encyclopedia of Black America, pp. 611–12, 745; Who's Who Among Black Americans, 1992–93, p. 1045.

BUILDINGS

1806 • The African Meeting House, Boston, Massachusetts, is the first major building in Boston to be constructed entirely by blacks. (*See also* **Religion: Baptists, 1806.**)

Sources: Cantor, Historic Landmarks of Black America, pp. 70–71; Dictionary of American Negro Biography, p. 483; Negro Almanac, 1989, p. 208.

CHARITABLE ORGANIZATIONS

1940 • Jesse O. Thomas (1883–1972) was the first black to work for the American Red Cross in a professional and policy-making position. Born and raised in Mississippi, Thomas graduated from Tuskegee Institute in 1911, the New York School of Social Work in 1923, and Chicago School of Research in 1925.

Source: Who's Who in Colored America, 1929, p. 361.

1992 • Anthony Joseph Polk (1941–) was the first black director of transformation operations of the American Red Cross's blood supply. This was the first senior management post held by a black. During his stint in the armed services, Polk was blood supply manager at several army installations.

Source: Who's Who Among Black Americans, 1992–93, p. 1133.

FEDERAL EMPLOYEES

1864 • Solomon G. Brown (1829–1903?) became the first black museum assistant at the Smithsonian Institution. With no formal education, he worked for Samuel F. B. Morse, when the inventor was developing the telegraph system in the 1840s. In 1852, Brown followed Joseph Henry, an associate of Morse, as first secretary to the Smithsonian. He became an indispensable worker who prepared almost all of the illustrations for scientific lectures until 1887. In 1855, he may have been the first American black to deliver a public lecture on science, when he gave a lecture on insects to the Young People's Club of the Israel A.M.E. Church in Washington, D.C.

Sources: Dictionary of American Biography, pp. 70–71; Simmons, Men of Mark, pp. 320–23.

HOSPITALS

1832 • The Georgia Infirmary in Savannah, Georgia, founded by whites, was the first hospital and asylum established for the relief and protection of aged and afflicted blacks. It was chartered in 1832, and an organizational meeting was held at the Exchange, a mercantile building, on January 15, 1833.

Sources: Garrett, Famous First Facts About Negroes, p. 111; Kane, Famous First Facts, p. 309.

1881 • Charles Burleigh Purvis (1842–1929), physician, medical educator, and hospital administrator, was the first black surgeon-in-chief to head a hospital under civilian auspices. He received the appointment to the Freedmen's Hospital in the nation's capital. He was the son of the prosperous abolitionist, Robert Purvis. He attended Oberlin College in Ohio and, wishing to pursue medical training, transferred to Western Reserve Medical School in Cleveland, Ohio, graduating in 1865. He served in the army until 1869, when he became the assistant surgeon at Freedmen's and a faculty member at Howard University in Washington, D.C. When President James A. Garfield was wounded by an assassin's bullet in 1881, he was one of the doctors called to care for the fatally wounded chief executive—the first and only black doctor to serve the president of the United States. He was appointed as the first black to serve on the District of Columbia's Board of Medical Examiners in 1897.

Sources: Dictionary of American Negro Biography, p. 507; Morais, The History of the Negro in Medicine, p. 51.

Good Samaritan Hospital, established in Charlotte, North Carolina, was the first privately run hospital exclusively for blacks in the United States.

Source: Randolph, *An African-American Album,* p. 84.

1891 • Provident Hospital in Chicago, Illinois, was the first American hospital operated by blacks. Founded by Daniel Hale Williams, it spurred blacks to organize comparable hospitals in other cities. Williams's aim was to institute a bi-racial hospital where black doctors and nurses could be prepared, and black patients could receive decorous care without fear of racial bias. (*See also* **Science & Medicine: Medicine, 1893.**)

Sources: Dictionary of Black Culture, p. 362; Morais, *The History of the Negro in Medicine,* p. 75.

1895 • Nathan Francis Mossell (1856–1946) founded Philadelphia's first hospital primarily for blacks, Frederick Douglass Memorial Hospital and Training School for Nurses. The Canadian-born physician was the first black graduate of the University of Pennsylvania when he received his M.D. in 1882 and, after a bitter struggle, was the first black admitted to the Philadelphia Medical Society in 1885. He studied at prestigious hospitals in London, England, before he attacked the problem of founding a hospital. An ardent civil rights activist, Mossell journeyed to Niagara Falls in 1905 with W. E. B. Du Bois as one of the organizers of the Niagara Movement, a forerunner of the NAACP. Paul Robeson, singer, actor, and activist, was his nephew.

Sources: Dictionary of American Negro Biography, pp. 457–58; *Dictionary of Black Culture,* p. 308; Morais, *The History of the Negro in Medicine,* p. 79.

INVENTIONS AND PATENTS

C. 1798 • James Forten, Sr., (1766–1842) was the first black to invent a novel sail-handling device, an invention that brought him considerable affluence. He became owner of a sail loft in 1798, and by 1832 was a wealthy man, employing about forty workers. His fortune enabled him to become one of the leading figures in the abolition movement.

Sources: Dictionary of American Negro Biography, pp. 234–35; *Dictionary of Black Culture,* pp. 166–67; James, *The Real McCoy,* pp. 33–35.

1821 • Thomas L. Jennings (1791–1859) is believed to be the first black to receive a patent, for a dry-cleaning process, on March 3, 1821. He was a tailor and dry cleaner in New York City and, an active abolitionist, the founder and president of the Legal Rights Association. (Henry Blair [c. 1804–60] of Glenross, Maryland, was long believed to be the first black to obtain a patent, for a corn planter, on October 14, 1834.)

Sources: Haskins, *Outward Dreams,* pp. 4–5 (Jennings); James, *The Real McCoy,* p. 31; Katz, *Eyewitness: The Negro in American History,* pp. 98, 99, 139; *Negro Almanac, 1989,* pp. 1079–1424 (Blair).

NORBERT RILLIEUX

1843 • Norbert Rillieux (1806–94) was the first person to apply a multiple vacuum evaporation system to the production of sugar, and by so doing, revolutionized production. This invention helped change the food consumption patterns of the world and determined the nature of colonial dependency for a substantial part of the third world. Born a free black in New Orleans, Rillieux received a thorough education in mechanical engineering at the École Centrale in Paris. After demonstrating the practical effects of his invention in New Orleans and making a good deal of money, Rillieux returned to France in 1854 because of the increasing restrictions on free blacks in Louisiana.

Sources: Dictionary of American Negro Biography, pp. 525–26; Haskins, *Outward Dreams,* pp. 26–33; James, *The Real McCoy,* pp. 41–43.

1848 • Lewis Temple (1800–54), born in Virginia, was the first person to invent an improved model of the whaling harpoon used in the nineteenth century. (In 1845 Temple was running a blacksmith shop in New Bedford, Massachusetts.) He did not patent his new model, which was quickly adopted in the whaling business, but he did enjoy a modest affluence. Unfortunately, his widow and children were left destitute at his death.

Sources: Dictionary of American Negro Biography, pp. 582–83; Haskins, *Outward Dreams,* pp. 20–21; James, *The Real McCoy,* pp. 35–37; *Negro Almanac, 1989,* p. 1090.

ELIJAH McCOY

1872 • On July 2, 1872, Elijah McCoy (1843–1929) patented the first version of his lubricator for steam engines. This was the first in a series of forty-two patents, most of which were designed to facilitate machine lubrication. McCoy was born in Canada, and after an apprenticeship in Edinburgh, Scotland, moved to Michigan. His last patent was granted in 1920 for a graphite lubrication device.

Sources: American Speech 33 (December 1958), pp. 297–98; *Dictionary of American Negro Biography,* pp. 413–14; Flexner, *I Hear America Talking,* p. 291; Haskins, *Outward Dreams,* pp. 40–44; James, *The Real McCoy,* pp. 73–75.

1882 • Lewis H. Latimer (1848–1928) patented the first cost-efficient method for producing carbon filaments for electric lights on June 17, 1882. His father, George, was an escaped slave whose capture precipitated the first of the highly publicized fugitive slave trials in 1842, and provoked Frederick Douglass's first appearance in print. During the Civil War, Lewis Latimer enlisted in the navy as soon as he was old enough. He then became an office boy in a patent office and soon became a patent draftsman. Latimer made patent drawings for many of Alexander Graham Bell's telephone patents, and worked for the United States Electric Lighting Company, where he made many significant innovations in the development of electric lighting, and supervised the installation of electric light plants in New York and Philadelphia. In 1884, he began to work for the Edison Electric Light Company, and entered its legal department in 1890. From 1896 to 1911, he was head draftsman for the Board of Patent Control, and then began to work as a patent consultant.

LEWIS H. LATIMER

Sources: Dictionary of American Negro Biography, pp. 385–86; Haskins, Outward Dreams, pp. 49–52; James, The Real McCoy, pp. 96–99; Negro Almanac, 1989, p. 12.

W. B. Purvis of Philadelphia, Pennsylvania, obtained his first patent on a paper bag device on April 25, 1882. Of the sixteen patents he obtained by 1897, eleven were connected with the manufacture of paper bags. Most of the patents were sold to the Union Paper Bag Company of New York.

Sources: Journal of Negro History 2 (January 1917), p. 33; Twentieth Century Negro Literature, pp. 403, 410; Work, Negro Year Book, 1925–26, pp. 366–67.

1883 • On March 20, 1883, Jan Matzeliger (1852–89) patented the first successful shoe lasting machine. Matzeliger was born in Surinam, of a Dutch father and a black mother. He developed his device while working in a shoe factory in Lynn, Massachusetts. The machine increased productivity from three to fourteen times over hand methods and led to concentration in the industry.

Sources: Dictionary of American Negro Biography, pp. 429–30; James, The Real McCoy, pp. 70–72; Negro Almanac, 1989, pp. 210, 1087.

On April 3, 1883, Humpfrey H. Reynolds was the first black to patent an improved window ventilator for railroad cars, which was adopted on all Pullman cars. Since he received no compensation from the company, Reynolds quit his job as a railroad porter and sued. He won $10,000.

Source: James, The Real McCoy, p. 72.

JAN MATZELIGER PATENTED A SHOE MACHINE THAT INCREASED PRODUCTIVITY.

1884 • Granville T. Woods (1856–1910) patented his first electric device, an improved telephone transmitter on December 2, 1884. By 1900, Woods had received twenty-two patents, most dealing with electricity used in railway telegraphy systems and electric railways. A native of Columbus, Ohio,

Woods worked principally on railroads after an apprenticeship as a machinist and blacksmith, becoming a locomotive engineer before founding the Woods Electric Company in Cincinnati, Ohio, about 1884. He moved to New York in 1890 and patented an automatic air brake purchased by George Westinghouse in 1902. His inventions paved the way for the development of the electric street car. (*See also* **Science & Medicine: Inventions and Patents, 1904.**)

Sources: Dictionary of American Negro Biography, pp. 663–65; Haskins, *Outward Dreams,* pp. 47–49, 95–96; James, *The Real McCoy,* pp. 94–95; *Negro Almanac, 1989,* p. 1092.

1885 • The first known black woman inventor is Sarah E. Goode, who patented a folding cabinet bed on July 14, 1885. Since ethnic identity is not part of a patent application, it is impossible to be sure of absolute priority. Another black woman might be the first, since Ellen F. Eglin of Washington, D.C., invented a clothes wringer before April 1890; however, no patent was issued in her name; she sold the idea to an agent for eighteen dollars since she believed that it would be impossible for a black woman to exploit the device successfully. At the beginning of this century, Miriam E. Benjamin of Massachusetts, who patented a gong signal systems for summoning attendants on July 17, 1888, was believed to be the first; her invention was adopted by the United States House of Representatives to summon pages.

Sources: James, *The Real McCoy,* p. 67; Macdonald, *Feminine Ingenuity,* p. 172; *Twentieth Century Negro Literature,* p. 407.

1895 • The United States Patent Office advertised its first special exhibit of the inventions of blacks.

Source: James, *The Real McCoy,* p. 57.

1897 • Andrew J. Beard (1849–1941), of Alabama, was the first black to patent a coupling device for railroad cars. Although these devices were among the most popular subjects for patents—there were some 6,500 patents by this year—Beard was able to sell his invention for some $50,000.

Sources: Alford, *Famous First Blacks,* p. 54; James, *The Real McCoy,* pp. 72–73; *Journal of Negro History* 2 (January 1917), p. 34.

1904 • Granville T. Woods (1856–1910) and his brother Lyates patented the first of two improvements on railroad brakes on March 29, 1904. The second patent was issued on July 18, 1905. Both were of sufficient importance that the Westinghouse Electric Company purchased them. (*See also* **Science & Medicine: Inventions and Patents, 1884.**)

Source: Journal of Negro History 2 (January 1917), p. 32.

GARRETT A. MORGAN

1912 • Garrett A. Morgan (1875–1963) was the first black to receive a patent for a safety hood and smoke protector. He demonstrated its worth in 1916 by rescuing workers trapped in a smoke-filled tunnel of the Cleveland, Ohio, waterworks. Born on a farm near Paris, Kentucky, Morgan became a very astute businessman and inventor in Cleveland. In 1923 he patented a three-way automatic traffic signal, which he sold to General Electric.

Sources: Cantor, *Historic Landmarks of Black America,* p. 352; *Dictionary of American Negro Biography,* p. 453; *Ebony* 48 (February 1993), p. 182 (portrait); James, *The Real McCoy,* pp. 91–93.

1913 • Henry Edwin Baker (1859–1928), a black assistant examiner in the United States Patent Office, published the first separate list of black inventors, the *Negro Inventor.* Baker used his position in the patent office to discover and publicize the inventions of blacks. (This was quite a formidable task since race is not recorded on applications. Despite this obstacle, Baker was able to reveal the names of some four hundred blacks.)

Source: James, *The Real McCoy,* pp. 77–78.

1928 • Marjorie Stewart Joyner (1896–) was the first black to patent a permanent waving machine. Joyner was an employee of Madame C. J. Walker, to whose company the patent was assigned. She eventually became national supervisor of the Walker organization's chain of beauty schools. In 1945 she was a cofounder of the United Beauty School Owners and Teachers Association. (The graduates of these schools comprise the Alpha Phi Omega sorority and fraternity.)

Sources: Macdonald, *Feminine Ingenuity,* pp. 297–301; *Who's Who Among Black Americans, 1992–93,* p. 806.

1936 • Percy Lavon Julian (1899–1975) was the first black to be hired as a director of research by a major chemical manufacturing company, the Glidden Company of Chicago. He received 105 patents, 66 of which were assigned to this company. In 1954 he established his own company, Julian Laboratories. His name is linked with the synthesis of physostigmine (1935), used in treating glaucoma, and the precursors of cortisone, among many other achievements in chemistry.

Sources: Ebony Success Library, vol. 2, pp. 150–53; Haber, *Black Pioneers of Science and Invention,* pp. 87–101; *Negro Almanac, 1989,* pp. 1084–85.

1940 • Frederick McKinley Jones (1892–1961) was the first man to invent a practical refrigeration system for trucks and railroad cars. He received the patent on July 12, 1940. A native of Cincinnati, Ohio, his formal education ended in the sixth grade, but by 1930 his self-teaching was so effective that

he was manufacturing movie sound equipment. The development of the refrigerating device marked a new direction for his efforts, and its success revolutionized the transportation and marketing of fresh foods. In 1991, he was the first black to receive the National Medal of Technology (posthumously).

Sources: Dictionary of American Negro Biography, p. 366; Jet 82 (20 July 1992), p. 24; Negro Almanac, 1989, p. 1084.

1969 • George R. Carruthers (1940–) was the first black to patent an image converter for detecting electromagnetic radiation on November 11, 1969. With a Ph.D. in physics from the University of Illinois in 1964, Carruthers began working as a researcher for the Navy and then for the National Aeronautics and Space Agency, where he received the NASA Exceptional Scientific Achievement medal for his work as one of the two people responsible for the development of the lunar surface ultraviolet camera/spectrograph placed on the moon in April 1972 during the Apollo 16 mission.

Sources: Ebony 28 (October 1973), pp. 61–63; Haskins, Outward Dreams, pp. 83–84, 88; Negro Almanac, 1989, p. 1080; Who's Who Among Black Americans, 1992–1993, p. 234.

MEDICAL AGENCIES AND SCHOOLS

1876 • Meharry Medical College was the first medical school founded for the sole education of blacks. Situated in Nashville, Tennessee, Meharry was a component of the Central Tennessee College, founded in 1866, and maintained by the Freedmen's Aid Society. The school opened in 1876 with less than a dozen students. The driving spirit behind the school was George W. Hubbard, who administered the school for forty-five years.

Sources: Dictionary of Black Culture, p. 294; Morais, The History of the Negro in Medicine, p. 44.

1945 • The first and only school of veterinary medicine in a black college or university was established at Tuskegee Institute in Alabama. Instruction began September 1, 1945. Frederick D. Patterson (1901–88), veterinarian and then president of Tuskegee, founded the school. (*See also* **Organizations: Charitable and Civic Organizations, 1944.**)

Sources: Bowles and DeCosta, Between Two Worlds, p. 131; Jet 72 (29 June 1987), p. 22; Tuskegee Institute, Sixty-Fifth Annual Catalog, 1946–47, p. 31.

1980 • Maurice C. Clifford (1920–) was inaugurated as the first black president of the Medical College of Pennsylvania—the first at a predominantly white college. Born in Washington, D.C., Clifford took his M.D. degree at Meharry Medical College in 1947.

Source: Who's Who Among Black Americans, 1992–93, p. 276.

OPPOSITE PAGE:
PERCY LAVON JULIAN
WAS A PIONEER IN
THE AREA OF
CHEMICAL RESEARCH.

1993 • David Satcher (1941–) was the first black appointed director of the Centers for Disease Control and Prevention in Atlanta, Georgia. A genetics researcher and president of Meharry Medical College in Nashville, Tennessee, he was born near Anniston, Alabama, and graduated from Morehouse College. He received his M.D. and Ph.D. degrees from Case Western University.

Sources: Atlanta Journal and Constitution (21 August 1993); *Who's Who Among Black Americans, 1992–93,* p. 1243.

**DAVID
SATCHER**

MEDICINE

1667 • Lucas Santomee was the first trained black physician in New Amsterdam.

Source: Encyclopedia of Black America, p. 670.

1706 • Onesimus was the first black to introduce inoculation against small-pox to the American colonies. He revealed the practice to his master, Cotton Mather, the Massachusetts Puritan minister, who promoted the practice during the epidemic of 1721. There was considerable resistance to this life-saving procedure, and several proponents, including Mather, were threatened with mob violence. Inoculation was generally accepted by 1777.

Sources: James, *The Real McCoy,* p. 25; Morais, *The History of the Negro in Medicine,* p. 11.

1773 • James Durham (Derham) (c. 1762–?) was the first regularly recognized black physician in the United States. Born a slave in Philadelphia, his early masters taught him the fundamentals of reading and writing. He was owned by a number of physicians, ending up in New Orleans with a Scottish physician, who hired him to perform many medical services in 1773. He bought his freedom in 1783. Durham moved to Philadelphia, and was lauded by prominent local doctors. He returned to New Orleans and had a flourishing practice until 1801, when the city council restricted him because he was unlicensed and untrained.

Sources: Dictionary of American Negro Biography, pp. 205–6; Garrett, *Famous First Facts About Negroes,* p. 110; Morais, *The History of the Negro in Medicine,* pp. 5, 7–10.

1837 • James McCune Smith (1811–65) was the first black to obtain an M.D. degree. He studied at the African Free School in New York City, where he was so gifted a student that when Lafayette visited the United States in 1824, the young Smith delivered the welcome address. Unable to pursue his education in the United States, Smith studied at the University of Glasgow, in Scotland, where he received his bachelor's, master's, and medical degrees. He was a very successful physician in New York, with a busy practice and two drug stores. He was also an avid abolitionist.

JAMES MCCUNE SMITH

Sources: *Dictionary of Black Culture*, p. 410; Garrett, *Famous First Facts About Negroes*, p. 111; Morais, *The History of the Negro in Medicine*, p. 31.

1846 • David Ruggles (1810–49), hydropathist, journalist, abolitionist, and businessman, erected the first building constructed for hydropathic treatments in the United States. He was a free man of color born in Connecticut. Known as the "water cure doctor," Ruggles operated his successful center in Northampton, Massachusetts, until his death. He was an active abolitionist, supporter of the Underground Railroad movement, and editor and publisher of the *Mirror of Liberty* (1838). (*See also* **Business: Retailing, 1834.**)

Sources: *Dictionary of American Negro Biography,* pp. 536–37; Morais, *The History of the Negro in Medicine,* p. 23; *Negro Almanac, 1989,* p. 1012.

1847 • David J. Peck was the first black to graduate from an American medical school, Rush Medical College in Chicago.

Sources: *Encyclopedia of Black America*, p. 671; Morais, *The History of the Negro in Medicine,* p. 30.

1863 • Alexander Thomas Augusta (1825–90) became the first black surgeon in the United States Army. A free-born Virginian, Augusta served his medical apprenticeship in Philadelphia, graduated from Trinity Medical College in Toronto, Canada (1856), and joined the Union forces in 1863 with the rank of major. In 1865 he became the first black to head any hospital in the United States when the newly created Freedmen Bureau erected buildings on the grounds of Howard University and established the Freedmen's Hospital with Augusta in charge. (Formerly freedmen were treated at Camp Barker.) In 1868 Howard University opened its own medical school, with Augusta as demonstrator of anatomy. He was the first black to receive an honorary degree from Howard University in 1869.

Sources: *Dictionary of American Negro Biography,* pp. 19–20; Garrett, *Famous First Facts About Negroes,* pp. 112–13; Morais, *The History of the Negro in Medicine,* p. 50.

1864 • Rebecca Lee (Crumpler) (1833–?) was the first black woman awarded a medical degree. She completed a seventeen-week course to earn an M.D. degree from the New England Female Medical College in Boston. Lee established a long-lived practice in Richmond, Virginia, at the end of the Civil War.

Sources: Black Women in America, vol. 1, pp. 290–91; Garrett, *Famous First Facts About Negroes,* p. 112; Kane, *Famous First Facts,* p. 467; Morais, *The History of the Negro in Medicine,* p. 43.

SUSAN MCKINNEY STEWARD

1870 • Susan Maria Smith McKinney Steward (1848–1918) was the first black woman to graduate from a New York state medical school. After graduating from New York Medical College for Women, she practiced in Brooklyn for more than twenty years. In 1873 she became the first black woman doctor to be formally certified. Steward undertook postgraduate work at the Long Island Medical School Hospital (1888), the only woman in the entire college. She was a founder of the Women's Loyal Union of New York and Brooklyn and in 1881 she co-founded the Women's Hospital and Dispensary in Brooklyn. Steward married a prominent A.M.E. minister, Theophilus Gould Steward, in 1896, and became the resident physician at Wilberforce University (Ohio).

Sources: Black Women in America, vol. 2, pp. 1109–12; *Dictionary of American Negro Biography,* pp. 569–70; *Notable Black American Women,* pp. 1077–79.

1872 • Rebecca J. Cole (1846–1922) was the first black woman to establish a medical practice in Pennsylvania. Cole, the first black graduate of the Female Medical College of Pennsylvania (1867), practiced medicine for half a century in Philadelphia, Pennsylvania; Columbia, South Carolina; and Washington, D.C.

Sources: Black Women in America, vol. 1, pp. 261–62; Morais, *The History of the Negro in Medicine,* p. 43; *Notable Black American Women,* pp. 201–2.

Henry Fitzbutler (1842–1901) was the first black graduate of the Medical School of the University of Michigan. The Canadian-born doctor moved to Louisville, Kentucky, and became the first black to enter the profession in the state. He was devoted to the cause of black medical education, and in 1888 the Kentucky legislature granted him and his associates permission to establish a school of medicine, the Louisville National Medical College. The school closed in 1911.

Sources: Dictionary of Black Culture, p. 162; Morais, *The History of the Negro in Medicine,* pp. 65–66.

1889 • Monroe Alpheus Majors (1864–1960) was the first black physician to pass the California state boards. Majors had begun practice in Texas, but he was forced to leave the state by segregationist pressures. In 1886, in Texas, Majors had led a group of doctors to establish the Lone Star State Medical Association. An 1886 Meharry College of Medicine graduate, Majors was remarkably versatile as a newspaper editor (*Los Angeles Western News*), a compiler of an indispensable biographical dictionary (*Noted Negro Women: Their Triumphs and Activities, 1893*), politician, poet, and hospital administrator.

Sources: *Dictionary of American Negro Biography*, pp. 421–22; *Dictionary of Black Culture*, p. 282; Morais, *The History of the Negro in Medicine*, p. 58.

1892 • Miles Vandahurst Lynk (1871–?) was the first editor of the first black medical journal in the nation. The *Medical and Surgical Observer* was published in Jackson, Tennessee. The first issue, dated December 1892, was thirty-two pages long. It was published regularly for eighteen months. An 1891 graduate of Meharry Medical College, Lynk organized the Medical Department of the University of West Tennessee, in Memphis, in 1900.

Sources: *Dictionary of Black Culture*, p. 279; Garrett, *Famous First Facts About Negroes*, p. 113; Morais, *The History of the Negro in Medicine*, p. 64.

1893 • Daniel Hale Williams (1856–1931) performed the world's first successful heart operation on July 9, 1893. The open heart surgery was executed at Provident Hospital in Chicago, Illinois, a hospital founded by Dr. Williams. He opened the chest of James Cornish, a laborer who had been stabbed, found the pericardial sac, emptied it of blood, and successfully sutured it. "Doctor Dan" was a founder and first vice-president of the National Medical Association, and the first and only black invited to become a charter member of the American College of Surgeons in 1913. Born in Pennsylvania, Williams graduated in 1883 from the Chicago Medical College. He founded Provident Hospital as an institution to serve all people in 1891. He was the first black on the Illinois State Board of Health in 1889 and in 1893, he was appointed surgeon-in-chief of Freedmen's Hospital, where he reorganized the services and established a nursing school. Williams had two main interests: the NAACP and the construction of hospitals and training schools for African-American doctors and nurses.

DANIEL HALE WILLIAMS

Sources: *Dictionary of American Negro Biography*, p. 654; Garrett, *Famous First Facts About Negroes*, p. 114; Morais, *The History of the Negro in Medicine*, p. 75.

1896 • Austin Maurice Curtis (1868–1939) was the first black on the medical staff of Chicago's Cook County Hospital. (Curtis became the first black to receive such an appointment in a nonsegregated hospital.) An 1891 graduate of Northwestern University, he was the first physician to intern with Daniel Hale Williams. He later succeeded Williams as head of Freedmen's Hospital in Washington, D.C., and taught at Howard University College of Medicine.

Sources: Dictionary of American Negro Biography, pp. 153–54; *Dictionary of Black Culture,* p. 123; *Journal of Negro History* (25 October 1940), p. 502; Morais, *The History of the Negro in Medicine,* p. 78.

LOUIS TOMPKINS WRIGHT

1919 · Louis Tompkins Wright (1891–1952) became the first black appointed to a New York City municipal hospital when he was named clinical assistant in the out-patient department of Harlem Hospital, where he served with distinction for more than thirty years. Georgia-born Wright graduated from Harvard Medical School in 1915, and was an officer in the Army Medical Corps druing World War I. He made significant contributions to the development of his specialty. In 1945, he was the only black member of the American College of Surgeons. Wright was a militant civil rights advocate and a prominent member of the NAACP. As chair of the board of the civil rights organization (1935–52), he was responsible for the establishment of a board committee on health. The association named him its Spingarn Medalist in 1940 for his work as champion of human rights.

Sources: Dictionary of American Negro Biography, pp. 670–71; *Journal of the National Medical Association* 45 (March 1953), p. 130; Morais, *The History of the Negro in Medicine,* p. 106.

1920 · Harold Ellis was the first black to obtain a degree in neurology. He eventually held an appointment with the rank of chief-of-service in neurology at Harlem Hospital.

Source: Morais, *The History of the Negro in Medicine,* p. 120.

1922 · Clilan Bethany Powell (1894–) was the first black roentgenologist in New York City. Virginia-born, Powell was educated at Virginia State College and Howard University College of Medicine. An x-ray specialist, he opened the first laboratory for x-ray diagnosis and treatment in a black community. He served on many government commissions and operated a finance company, insurance company, and the *New York Amsterdam News.*

Source: Who's Who in Colored America, 1950, p. 423.

Joseph H. Ward (1870–1956) was the first black appointed to head a Veterans Administration hospital. In 1922 he was named medical officer-chief of the Veterans Hospital in Tuskegee, Alabama, and had a distinguished twelve-year tenure.

Sources: Garrett, *Famous First Facts About Negroes,* p. 115; Morais, *The History of the Negro in Medicine,* p. 111.

1926 • May Edward Chinn (1896–1980) was the first black woman to intern at Harlem Hospital, and the first black woman to graduate from the University of Bellevue Medical Center.

Sources: Black Women in America, vol. 1, pp. 235–36; Notable Black American Women, pp. 183–85.

1929 • Numa Pompilius Garfield Adams (1885–1940) was the first black dean at the Howard University School of Medicine. Born in Virginia, he moved to Pennsylvania, where he received his early education. A graduate of Howard University and Columbia University, he taught at Howard University (1912–19) before entering Chicago's Rush Medical College, where he received his medical degree in 1924. In June 1929 Adams was appointed dean at Howard University College of Medicine. There he reorganized the curriculum on a more rational basis, establishing the primacy of the school in the teaching functions of Freedmen's Hospital, and recruiting capable young men to study.

Sources: Dictionary of American Negro Biography, p. 5; Dictionary of Black Culture, p. 13; Morais, The History of the Negro in Medicine, pp. 90–92.

1934 • Leonidas H. Berry (1902–) was the first black specialist in the field of digestive diseases and endoscopy. Educated at Wilberforce University (1924), he received his medical training at Rush Medical College in Chicago, and at the University of Illinois. He is a diplomate of the American Board of Internal Medicine. Berry developed one of the early gastroscopes known as the Elder-Berry gastrobiopsy scope and was at the forefront in the movement to increase communications between the black and white medical associations. He wrote *I Wouldn't Take Nothin' for My Journey: Two Centuries of An Afro-American Minister's Family* (1981).

Sources: Berry, I Wouldn't Take Nothin' For My Journey, p. 243; Jet 82 (24 August 1992), p. 32; Who's Who Among Black Americans, 1992–93, p. 64.

1940 • Charles Richard Drew (1904–50) was the first person to set up a blood bank. Born in Washington, D.C., he graduated from Amherst College in 1926, coached and taught at Morgan State College, received his M.D. from McGill University in 1933, and taught pathology at Howard University in 1935. His research at the Columbia Medical Center in New York City led to the discovery that blood plasma could supplant whole blood in transfusions. He set up and administered the British blood bank from 1940 to 1941, then the American Red Cross project, to collect and store blood. Drew was dropped from the American Red Cross project because he differed with the policy of refusing the blood of black donors. He asserted that there was no scientific difference between the blood of blacks and whites. His research was responsible for saving numerous lives during World War II. He was accorded the NAACP's Spingarn Medal, as well as other tributes.

Sources: Bennett, Before the Mayflower, p. 534; Dictionary of American Negro Biography, pp. 190–92; Morais, The History of the Negro in Medicine, pp. 107–9.

CHARLES R. DREW

1948 • Dorothy Lavinia Brown (1919–) was the first black woman appointed to a residency as a general surgeon in the South. Born in Philadelphia, she was educated at Bennett College and Meharry Medical College. She took a residency in general surgery at George Hubbard Hospital in Nashville, Tennessee, from 1949 to 1954. (*See also* **Government—County & State Pioneers: Tennessee, 1967.**)

Sources: *Black Women in America*, vol. 1, pp. 174–75; *Notable Black American Women*, pp. 114–16; *Who's Who Among Black Americans, 1978*, p. 106.

1949 • William Augustus Hinton (1883–1959) was the first black professor at Harvard Medical School. A world-renowned bacteriologist, he developed the Hinton test for syphilis and the Davis-Hinton tests for blood and spinal fluid. His book *Syphilis and Its Treatment* (1936) became an authoritative reference work. Born in Chicago, he received his training at Harvard Medical School. He became an instructor of preventive medicine at Harvard in 1912, and continued there until his retirement in 1950. He was promoted to the rank of clinical professor in 1949. Hinton directed the Massachusetts Department of Public Health's Wassermann Laboratory from its establishment in 1915 until 1954.

Sources: *Dictionary of American Negro Biography*, p. 315–16; Garrett, *Famous First Facts About Negroes*, p. 114; Morais, *The History of the Negro in Medicine*, pp. 103–4.

Jack E. White (1921–) was the first black trained as a cancer surgeon at Sloan Kettering Hospital. A graduate of Florida Agricultural and Mechanical University in 1941, and the Howard University School of Medicine in 1944, White held the directorship of the Howard University Cancer Research Center of Freedman's Hospital in Washington, D.C.

Source: *Who's Who Among Black Americans, 1978*, p. 949.

1956 • Julius Hill (1917–83) was the first black orthopedic surgeon in California. Atlanta-born, Hill was educated at Johnson C. Smith University in 1933, the University of Illinois in 1937, Meharry Medical College in 1951, and completed his orthopedic surgery work at the University of Southern California in 1956.

Source: *Who's Who Among Black Americans, 1978*, p. 419.

1967 • Jane Cooke Wright (1919–) was America's first black woman associate dean of a major medical school, New York Medical College. Wright received her medical degree from New York Medical College in 1945. She had appointments at Harlem Hospital and its Cancer Research Foundation, and began teaching at New York Medical School in 1955. In July 1967 she became associate dean and professor of surgery at her alma mater, retiring in 1987.

Source: *Notable Black American Women*, pp. 1283–85.

1973 • John Lawrence Sullivan Holloman (1919–) was the first black president of the New York City Health and Hospital Corporation. In 1963 Holloman led a physicians' picket line protesting racism within the medical profession. A Washingtonian, Holloman graduated from Virginia Union University and received his medical degree from the University of Michigan.

Sources: Morais, The History of the Negro in Medicine, p. 162; Who's Who Among Black Americans, 1978, p. 427.

1984 • Alexia Irene Canada (1950–) was the first black woman neurosurgeon in the United States. She received her medical education at the University of Michigan, with a specialty in pediatric neurosurgery. She was certified by the American Board of Neurological Surgery in 1984; she has taught at the University of Pennsylvania; the Henry Ford Hospital in Detroit, Michigan; and at Wayne State University in Detroit, Michigan. In 1977 she became the first female (and the first black) neurosurgical resident at the University of Minnesota.

Sources: Lanker, I Dream A World, p. 128; Notable Black American Women, pp. 155–56; Who's Who Among Black Americans, 1978, p. 64.

Levi Watkins, Jr., (1944–) was the first black doctor to establish the surgical implantation of an automatic defibrillator in the human heart. Educated at Tennessee State University (B.S., 1966) and Vanderbilt University School of Medicine (M.D., 1970), Watkins has been a cardiac surgeon at Johns Hopkins University Hospital since 1987.

Source: Who's Who Among Black Americans, 1992–93, p. 1469.

MUSEUMS

1977 • Margaret Santiago was the first black to become registrar of a major scientific museum, the Smithsonian's National Museum of Natural History.

Source: State of Black America 1992, p. 357.

NATIONAL SCIENCE FOUNDATION

1990 • Walter E. Massey (1938–) was the first black to head the National Science Foundation. A graduate of Morehouse College, Massey took his Ph.D. at Washington University, St. Louis, Missouri. A physicist, he has had a distinguished career, including being the first black president of the American Association for the Advancement of Science. In 1993, he was designated vice-president for academic affairs and provost of the University of California system.

Sources: Jet 83 (22 February 1993), p. 22; Negro Almanac, 1989, pp. 1086–87; Scientific American 266 (June 1992), pp. 40–41; Who's Who Among Black Americans, 1992–93, p. 927.

NURSING

SUSIE KING TAYLOR

1863 • Susie King Taylor (1848–1912) was the first black army nurse in United States history, serving with the First Regiment of the South Carolina Volunteers. Her Civil War memoirs, *Reminiscences of My Life in Camp*, which were published in 1902, constitute the first and only continuous written record of activities of black nurses. Taylor was born a slave on a plantation near Savannah, Georgia.

Sources: Dictionary of American Negro Biography, p. 581; Garrett, Famous First Facts About Negroes, p. 147; Notable Black American Women, pp. 1108–13.

MARY ELIZABETH MAHONEY

1879 • Mary Elizabeth Mahoney (1845–1926) was the first black graduate nurse in the United States. She was thirty-three years old in 1878 when she entered the New England Hospital for Women and Children to begin a sixteen-month course. Of the forty applicants in her class, only three remained to receive their diplomas, two white women and Mary Mahoney. Boston-born, Mahoney began as a maid in the hospital, and was later admitted to the nursing program. The Mary Mahoney Medal was named in her honor by the American Nurses' Association, and is given biennially to the person making the most progress toward opening full opportunities in nursing for all, regardless of race, creed, color, or national origin.

Sources: Black Women in America, vol. 2, pp. 743–44; Garrett, Famous First Facts About Negroes, p. 148; Morais, The History of the Negro in Medicine, p. 70; Notable Black American Women, pp. 720–21.

1886 • Spelman Seminary (now Spelman College) in Atlanta, Georgia, began the first nursing school for black women. Blacks were forced to organize schools of their own for the training of nurses. As a result of the founding of all-black training schools, the number of African-American graduate nurses steadily rose. The nursing school flourished until 1921.

Sources: Kane, Famous First Facts, p. 436; Morais, The History of the Negro in Medicine, p. 71.

1891 • The first three schools of nursing for blacks attached to hospitals were established in 1891: Dixie Hospital in Hampton, Virginia; MacVicar Hospital, in connection with Spelman College in Atlanta, Georgia; and

Provident Hospital Training School in Chicago. Alice M. Bacon, founder of the Dixie Hospital, was connected with Hampton Institute, although her hospital was independent.

Sources: Morais, *The History of the Negro in Medicine,* p. 71; *Negro Education,* vol. 1, p. 176.

1936 • Estelle Massey Osborne (1901–81) was the first black director of nursing at City Hospital No. 2 (now the Homer G. Phillips Hospital Training School). Earlier she had been the first black nursing instructor at Harlem Hospital School of Nursing. In 1943, as the first black consultant on the staff of any national organization (in this case the National Nursing Council for War Service), she more than doubled the number of white nursing schools to admit blacks. In 1948 Osborne was the first recipient of an M.A. in nursing education from Teachers College of Columbia University. She was the first black member of the nursing faculty at New York University, and also became the first black to hold office in the American Nurses Association.

Sources: Black Women in America, pp. 903–5; *Encyclopedia of Black America,* p. 90; Morais, *The History of the Negro in Medicine,* p. 255; *Who's Who in Colored America, 1950,* p. 402.

PUBLICATIONS

1792 • Benjamin Banneker (1731–1806) was the first black man to issue an almanac. (The series continued until 1797.) Banneker was born free in Maryland, where he became a tobacco farmer. As a result of his interest in mathematics and mechanics, he constructed a successful striking clock in about 1752. His model for the clock was the mechanism of a watch someone lent to him. The clock was still running at the time of his death. In 1787, a Quaker neighbor lent Banneker some texts on astronomy and instruments, and he taught himself the skills necessary to produce his almanac. Banneker also saw some service in surveying the national capital. Although Banneker was unwell and could not work in the field, he did function as an assistant to George Ellicot in the survey of the ten-mile square of the District of Columbia, from early February to the end of April 1791, when he returned to his farm.

BENJAMIN BANNEKER

Sources: Bedini, *The Life of Benjamin Banneker,* pp. 42–46, 103–36, 137–95; *Dictionary of American Negro Biography,* pp. 22–25; James, *The Real McCoy,* pp. 96–99.

1909 • Charles Victor Roman (1864–1934) was the first editor of the *Journal of the National Medical Association.* The physician, teacher, historian, and author favored support of black institutions, and believed black history should be written by blacks. Born in Williamsport, Pennsylvania, Roman studied at Fisk University and Meharry Medical College, both in

Nashville, Tennessee. He later directed health service at Fisk and taught at Meharry.

Sources: Dictionary of American Negro Biography, p. 532; *Encyclopedia of Black America,* pp. 735–36; Morais, *The History of the Negro in Medicine,* pp. 69–70.

RESEARCH AND DEVELOPMENT

1942 • W. Lincoln Hawkins (1911–) was the first black researcher hired by Bell Telephone Systems, a company from which he retired in 1976. He earned a Ph.D. at McGill University in 1938. In 1992, he became the second black to receive the National Medal of Technology.

Sources: Jet 82 (20 July 1992), p. 24; *Who's Who Among Black Americans, 1992–93,* pp. 626–25.

1971 • Walter McAfee (1914–), ranking scientist at the Army Electronics Research and Development Command, was the first black to attain the civil service rank of GS 16 while working for the army. McAfee was also involved in the first radar contact with the moon in 1946.

Sources: Ebony 13 (May 1958), p. 20; *Negro Almanac, 1989,* p. 1088; *Who's Who Among Black Americans, 1992–93,* p. 937.

SPACE

1963 • On March 31, 1963, Edward Joseph Dwight, Jr., became the first black astronaut candidate. He was dropped from the program in 1965.

Sources: Ebony 18 (June 1963), pp. 74–81; *Ebony* 20 (June 1965), pp. 29–36; *Jet* 68 (1 April 1985), p. 20.

1967 • Robert H. Lawrence, Jr., (1935–67), who had been named the first black astronaut and assigned to the Manned Orbiting Laboratory, died in a plane crash before the start of the mission. Lawrence was a native of Chicago, Illinois, and received his Air Force commission and a B.S. in chemistry from Bradley University in 1956.

Sources: Ebony 23 (February 1968), pp. 90–94; *Jet* 69 (17 February 1986), p. 17; *Negro Almanac, 1989,* pp. 1085–86.

1980 • Arnaldo Tamayo Mendez was the first black astronaut. A Cuban, he participated in a mission launched by the Soviets.

Sources: Class (December 1983), p. 8; *Jet* 59 (9 October 1980), p. 8.

OPPOSITE PAGE:
MAE C. JEMISON, THE
FIRST BLACK WOMAN
ASTRONAUT.

**GUION S.
BLUFORD**

1983 • On August 30, 1983, Guion (Guy) S. Bluford, Jr., (1942–) was the first black American astronaut to make a space flight. He went on to make two more flights, with 314 hours in space, before he retired from the program in 1993. A native of Philadelphia, Pennsylvania, Bluford holds a Ph.D. in aerospace engineering from the Air Force Institute of Technology (1978). He had earned his wings in 1965. He was the second black in space: a black Cuban had previously flown on a Soviet mission.

Sources: Contemporary Black Biography, vol. 2, pp. 19–21; *Ebony* 34 (March 1979), pp. 54–62; *Jet* 64 (22 August 1983), p. 2; (5 September 1983), pp. 20–22, 24; *Negro Almanac, 1989,* p. 1093; *Who's Who Among Black Americans, 1992–93,* pp. 121–22.

1986 • On January 20, 1986, Ronald McNair (1950–86) was the first black astronaut killed during a space mission, when the space shuttle *Challenger* met with disaster. McNair, a Ph.D. from the Massachusetts Institute of Technology, was assigned to the shuttle *Challenger* which blew up shortly after take-off.

Sources: Contemporary Black Biography, vol. 3, pp. 164–66; Hornsby, *Chronology of African-American History,* p. 340; *Negro Almanac, 1989,* p. 1094.

1987 • Frederick Drew Gregory (1941–) was the first black to command a space shuttle. A nephew of the developer of blood plasma storage, Dr. Charles Drew, Gregory was also the first to pilot a space shuttle mission, in 1985.

Sources: Jet 77 (20 November 1989), p. 23; 80 (15 July 1991), p. 26; *Who's Who Among Black Americans, 1992–93,* p. 563.

Mae C. Jemison (1956–) was named the first black woman astronaut. Jemison holds her M.D. from Cornell Medical School (1981). She worked as a staff physician for the Peace Corps for two and a half years in Sierra Leone. In 1992, she became the first black woman in space.

Sources: Contemporary Black Biography, vol. 1, pp. 113–14; *Jet* 82 (14 September 1992), cover, pp. 34–38; *Negro Almanac, 1989,* p. 1064; *Notable Black American Women,* pp. 571–73; *Who's Who Among Black Americans, 1992–93,* p. 739.

SPORTS: FIRST, BEST, & ENDURING

~~~~~~

ADMINISTRATION

1986 • Harriet Hamilton of Fisk University became the first black woman athletic director in the Southern Intercollegiate Athletic Conference.
Source: Jet 70 (14 July 1986), p. 16.

ASSOCIATIONS

1906 • The first black athletic association, the Interscholastic Athletic Association, was organized with the purpose of fostering sports in the Baltimore/Washington, D.C., area. Comprised of colleges and high schools, the first event—a track and field event—was held on May 30 at Howard University in the District of Columbia.
Sources: Ashe, *A Hard Road to Glory,* vol. 1, pp. 13–14, 61, 105; Young, *Negro Firsts in Sports,* pp. 91–92.

AUTOMOBILE RACING

1923 • Rojo Jack became the first black to participate in automobile racing, albeit on a restricted basis. A 245-pound man, Jack was the only black participant in the two Honolulu Chamber of Commerce-sponsored races in early 1954, and drove his 275 horsepower car to victory. Although he lost an eye in a 1938 racing accident, the California resident continued to race beyond the age of sixty.
Sources: Encyclopedia of Black America, p. 139; Young, *Negro Firsts in Sports,* pp. 176–77.

1954 • Berton Groves became the first black to enter the Pikes Peak Hill Climb automobile race.
Sources: Jones and Washington, *Black Champions Challenge American Sports,* p. 114; Young, *Negro Firsts in Sports,* p. 281.

WENDELL OLIVER SCOTT
WAS THE FIRST BLACK
RACE CAR DRIVER TO
WIN THE NASCAR
WINSTON CUP.

1963 ◦ Wendell Oliver Scott (1921?–90) was the first and only black driver to win a NASCAR Winston Cup (then the Grand National) race. He was the first black driver since Rojo Jack (1923) to earn a national following. Scott began racing at Danville Fairgrounds Speedway in Danville, Virginia, and won more than one hundred short-track Sportsman races, as well as several state and track titles. He moved to NASCAR's premier division in 1961 where he made almost five hundred starts. In the summer of 1964 Scott won a short-track race at Jacksonville, Florida. Injuries in a race at Talladega ended his career in 1973. The film *Greased Lightning,* starring Richard Pryor, was based on his life.

Sources: Ashe, *A Hard Road to Glory,* vol. 2, pp. 231–32; *Autoweek* 41 (7 January 1991), p. 55; *Jet* 79 (14 January 1990), p. 51.

1991 ◦ Willy (Willie) T. Ribbs (1956–) became the first black ever to qualify for the Indianapolis 500. He attended the Jim Russell Driving School and began racing in and around San Jose, California. Ribbs has participated in various forms of racing, from Indy cars to IMSA, including a season in NASCAR Winston Cup competition. He has had difficulty in finding sponsors, a perennial problem for unestablished drivers, compounded by his reputation for being outspoken and aggressive. He entered the race again in 1993, but in spite of entertainer Bill Cosby's advice, support, and offers to make free personal endorsements to any major sponsor, no one would share the commitment. In 1987 Ribbs was the first driver ever suspended by IMSA for hitting another driver; he was sidelined for thirty days.

IN 1991, WILLY RIBBS
BECAME THE FIRST
BLACK TO QUALIFY FOR
THE INDIANAPOLIS 500.

Sources: Ashe, *A Hard Road to Glory,* vol. 3, pp. 232–33, 258; *Contemporary Black Biography,* vol. 2, pp. 196–99; *Road and Track* 44 (August 1993), pp. 130–32.

BASEBALL

1867 • Scattered evidence of black baseball begins in this immediate post-Civil War era. In October 1867, the Brooklyn Uniques were hosts to the Excelsiors of Philadelphia in a contest called "the championship of colored clubs." These two teams are among the first known black baseball clubs, and this is the first known intercity contest. The Excelsiors won 37-24.
Source: Total Baseball, p. 548.

1869 • The Philadelphia Pythons were the first black team to play an all-white club. They defeated the Philadelphia City Items, 27-17.
Source: Total Baseball, p. 548.

1878 • The first known black professional player—previous to the present league organization—was pitcher John W. "Bud" Fowler (1858?–?), whose real name was John W. Jackson. In April 1878, playing for a local team from Chelsea, Massachusetts, he defeated the Boston club of the National League in an exhibition game. Fowler later became also a second baseman, and his career as a semi-professional can be traced at least as late as 1891. He was the first of more than seventy black players on interracial teams in organized baseball during the nineteenth century until the last, Bert Jones, of Atchison in the Kansas State League, was forced out in 1899.
Sources: Chalk, Pioneers of Black Sport, pp. 5, 25–27; Total Baseball, pp. 548, 550; Young, Negro Firsts in Sports, pp. 16, 55–56, 206.

1881 • Moses Fleetwood Walker (1857–1924) was the first black college varsity baseball player and a member of the first Oberlin College varsity baseball team. In 1883 the bare-handed catcher signed with the Northwestern League Toledo team. He became the first black in minor league baseball when the team entered the American Association in 1884.
Sources: Ashe, A Hard Road to Glory, vol. 1, pp. 70–72; Kane, Famous First Facts, p. 104; Total Baseball, pp. 548–49; Young, Negro Firsts in Sports, pp. 16, 55, 73.

1889 • In 1885 Frank P. Thompson organized a group of waiters and bellmen at the Argyle Hotel on Long Island, New York, to form the Cuban Giants. Four years later the team joined the Middle States League and became the first black professional baseball team, finishing the season with a 55-17 record. The Cuban Giants made a final minor league appearance in 1891. The last black team in organized interracial baseball was the Acme Colored Giants of the Pennsylvania Iron and Oil League in 1898.

BARE-HANDED CATCHER MOSES FLEETWOOD WALKER WAS THE FIRST BLACK COLLEGE VARSITY BASEBALL PLAYER.

Sources: Ashe, A Hard Road to Glory, vol. 1, pp. 72, 73; Kane, Famous First Blacks, p. 105; Total Baseball, p. 550; Young, Negro Firsts in Sports, pp. 55–58, 206.

1901 • Charles Grant, a second baseman, became the first black player in the American League (not yet a major league) under the name Charles Tokahama, claiming he was a full-bloodied Cherokee. A former member of the black Columbia Giants, he played for the Baltimore Orioles until the deception was exposed.

Sources: Encyclopedia of Black America, p. 125; Kane, *Famous First Facts,* p. 104; *Total Baseball,* p. 550; Young, *Negro Firsts in Sports,* pp. 56–57, 61, 72, 149.

ANDREW "RUBE" FOSTER

1920 • Andrew "Rube" Foster (1879–1930), a former pitcher, organized the first successful black professional baseball league, the National Association of Professional Baseball Clubs, usually called the Negro National League, on February 13. (The International League of Independent Baseball Clubs, with four black and two white teams, lasted one season in 1906, and in 1910 the National Negro Baseball League collapsed before a single game had been played.) The Indianapolis ABC played the Chicago Giants in the league's first game. Foster insisted that all teams in the league should be black controlled with the one exception of the Kansas City Monarchs. The league ran into difficulties in 1926 when Foster became ill and it collapsed in 1931, a year after his death. A new Negro National League was organized in 1933, based on a number of strong teams controlled by men in the numbers racket. Donn Rogosin wrote, "The Negro National League meetings were enclaves of the most powerful black gangsters in the nation."

Sources: Ashe, *A Hard Road to Glory,* vol. 1, pp. 83–84; *Encyclopedia of Black America,* p. 125; *Total Baseball,* p. 552; Young, *Black Firsts in Sports,* pp. 58–62.

PLAYERS FROM BLACK LEAGUES IN BASEBALL HALL OF FAME

YEAR	NAME
1971	Satchel Paige
1972	Josh Gibson
1972	Walter "Buck" Leonard
1973	Monfors "Monte" Irvin
1974	James "Cool Papa" Bell
1975	William "Judy" Johnson
1976	Oscar Charleston
1977	Martin Dihigo
1977	John Henry "Pop" Lloyd
1981	Rube Foster
1987	Ray Dandrige

Source: Total Baseball, pp. 311–12, 322, 329, 338, 331, 341, 352, 354, 361–62, 376–77, 517–23.

1924 • The first world series between Negro league clubs was held this year. Leagues from this period included the National Negro Baseball League, the American Association League, the Mid-Western Baseball League, and the Negro International League.

Sources: Chalk, *Pioneers of Black Sport,* p. 66–67; *Encyclopedia of Black America,* p. 125; Young, *Negro Firsts in Sports,* p. 158.

1933 • Gus Greenlee organized the first annual East-West All-Star Game in Chicago. The event came to outshadow the black World Series, and by 1939 leading players were attracting 500,000 votes.

Source: Total Baseball, p. 552.

1947 • Jackie (John Roosevelt) Robinson (1919–72) joined the Brooklyn Dodgers as a third baseman to become the first black in major leagues of the modern era. He played his first game in this capacity against the Boston Braves at Ebbets Field in Brooklyn on April 15, 1947, and in 1948 shifted to second base. Robinson probably received more racial insults in his career than any other person in history. In 1949 he became the first black batting champion and the first black to receive the National League's Most Valuable Player Award. Robinson became the first black enshrined in the Baseball Hall of Fame in 1952. Other blacks who began playing this year included Larry Doby for Cleveland, Dan Bankhead for Brooklyn, and Hank (Henry Curtis) Thompson and Willard Jessie Brown for St. Louis.

Sources: Bennett, *Before the Mayflower,* p. 633; *Encyclopedia of Black America,* p. 126; Jones and Washington, *Black Champions Challenge American Sports,* pp. 96–101; *Total Baseball,* pp. 383–84, 503, 1412.

The first black player in the American League was Larry (Lawrence Eugene) Doby (1924–), who joined the Cleveland Indians on July 5. In 1948 he became the first black to hit a run in the World Series. The first black home run champion in 1952, with thirty-two homers for the Indians, Doby spent thirteen seasons in major league ball. In 1978 he became manager of the Chicago White Sox.

Sources: Bennett, *Before the Mayflower,* p. 633, 636; *Encyclopedia of Black America,* p. 127; *Total Baseball,* pp. 332, 1072.

Dan (Daniel Robert) Bankhead (1920–76), a member of the Brooklyn Dodgers, became the first black pitcher in the major leagues on August 26. A native of Empire, Alabama, he played in the majors until 1951.

Sources: Ebony, May 1969, p. 110; *Negro Almanac, 1989,* pp. 1427–28; *Total Baseball,* p. 1586; Young, *Negro Firsts in Sports,* p. 207.

The first black players in a World Series were Brooklyn Dodgers players Dan Bankhead and Jackie Robinson. Robinson participated in all seven games against the New York Yankees; Bankhead only played in one.

Sources: Bennett, *Before the Mayflower,* p. 633; *Total Baseball,* p. 157.

1948 • Satchel (Leroy Robert) Paige (1900–82) was the first black pitcher in the American League and the first black to actually pitch in a World Series game. One of the best known players in black baseball, he became the first black elected to the Baseball Hall of Fame for his career in the Negro leagues in 1971. During five seasons in the majors, 1948–53, he won twenty-eight games and lost thirty-two. He appeared in one game in 1965 to pitch three innings for the Kansas City Athletics. At fifty-nine, the oldest man ever to pitch in the majors, he allowed one hit.

Sources: Ashe, *A Hard Road to Glory,* vol. 2, p. 31, 38, 40; *Encyclopedia of Black America,* p. 126; *Total Baseball,* pp. 158, 376–77, 1871; Young, *Negro Firsts in Sports,* p. 207.

1951 • Monte (Monford Merrill) Irvin (1919–), of the New York Giants, was the first black runs-batted-in champion of the National League.

Sources: Ashe, *A Hard Road to Glory,* pp. 14–15, 266; Jones and Washington, *Black Champions Challenge American Sports,* p. 107; Young, *Negro Firsts in Sports,* pp. 209–10.

Don (Donald) "Newk" Newcomb, (1926–) was the first black pitcher to win twenty games in a major league. In 1956 he became the first black winner of the Cy Young Award, with a season record of 27-7. A recovered alcholic, Newcomb counsels other baseball alcholics as a member of the Dodger's front office.

Sources: Current Biography, 1957, pp. 399–401; Jones and Washington, *Black Champions Challenge American Sports,* p. 104; *Total Baseball,* p. 374.

1952 • A member of the Brooklyn Dodgers and the 1952 Rookie of the Year, Joe Black (1924–) became the first black pitcher to win a World Series game. The Dodgers beat the New York Yankees on October 1 by 4-2. Black later became a vice-president of Greyhound Corporation.

Sources: Alford, *Famous First Blacks,* p. 85; *Negro Almanac, 1989,* pp. 1400–1; *Total Baseball,* pp. 162, 508, 1600.

1953 • Roy "Campy" Campanella (1921–93) became the first black catcher to hit twenty or more homers in five successive seasons (22-31-33-22-41). He also had the most put-outs (807) and the most runs batted in (856). The first black to be named the Most Valuable Player three times (1951, 1953, and 1955), Campanella was inducted into the Hall of Fame in Cooperstown, New York in 1969. A 1958 automobile accident left the Philadelphia, Pennsylvania, native confined to a wheelchair.

Sources: Jet 84 (12 July 1993), pp. 14–17; *Negro Almanac, 1989,* p. 1428; *Total Baseball,* pp. 318–19, 1005; Young, *Negro Firsts in Sports,* pp. 213–14.

1955 • Elston Gene "Ellie" Howard (1929–80) became the first black player for the New York Yankees. First an outfielder and later a catcher, he became the Yankee's first black coach—and the first in the American League—in 1969. He held this position until 1979. In the 1958 World Series

OPPOSITE PAGE: HALL-OF-FAMER SATCHEL PAIGE WAS THE FIRST BLACK TO PITCH IN THE AMERICAN LEAGUE.

he became the first black to win the Babe Ruth Award, and in 1963 he was named Most Valuable Player in the American League, the first black so honored.

Sources: Ashe, *A Hard Road to Glory,* vol. 2, p. 17; Jones and Washington, *Black Champions Challenge American Sports,* pp. 107, 149; *Total Baseball,* pp. 1193, 2155.

The first black to pitch a no-hitter, and the first pitcher to have a no-hit game in forty years, was Samuel "Toothpick Sam" Jones (1925–71), a player in the game between the Chicago Cubs and the Pittsburgh Pirates held in Chicago on May 12.

Sources: Clark, *Sports Firsts,* p. 28; *Ebony* 14 (October 1959), p. 46; *Total Baseball,* p. 495, 1769.

1959 • The first National League player to win the Most Valuable Player award two years in succession was Ernie (Ernest) Banks (1931–), of the Chicago Cubs. Also known as "Mr. Cub," he and second baseman Gene Baker formed the first black double-play combination in the major leagues. A "disaster on base," Banks produced four consecutive years of more than forty home runs between 1957 and 1960 (43-47-45-41).

Sources: Ashe, *A Hard Road to Glory,* vol. 2, pp. 19, 20, 25, 42, 271; *Encyclopedia of Black America,* p. 12; Jones and Washington, *Black Champions Challenge American Sports,* pp. 106-7, 149; *Total Baseball,* pp. 309–10, 946–47.

Pumpsie (Elijah Jerry) Green (1933–), of Oakland, California, infielder, was the first black player on the Boston Red Sox, the last major league team to sign a black player.

Sources: Ashe, *A Hard Road to Glory,* vol. 2, pp. 21, 32; *Total Baseball,* p. 1144; Young, *Negro Firsts in Sports,* p. 215.

1961 • "Gene" (Eugene Walter) Baker (1925–) was the first black to manage a club at any level in professional baseball. The Pittsburgh Pirates gave him the position at their Batavia, New York, Class D franchise. In 1953 he had been the first black on the Chicago Cubs.

Sources: Ashe, *A Hard Road to Glory,* vol. 3, pp. 19, 32; *Total Baseball,* pp. 561, 944; Young, *Negro Firsts in Sports,* pp. 208, 217.

1962 • The Chicago Cubs signed John "Buck" O'Neil (1911–) as coach, making him the first black coach on a major league baseball team. A notable first baseman in black baseball, he had served for several years as a scout.

Sources: Ashe, *A Hard Road to Glory,* vol. 1, p. 32; Bennett, *Before the Mayflower,* p. 637; Young, *Negro Firsts in Sports,* pp. 208-9.

1964 • The first black batting champion in the American League was Tony (Pedro) Oliva (Lopez) of the Minnesota Twins.

Sources: Alford, *Famous First Blacks,* p. 80; Jones and Washington, *Black Champions Challenge American Sports,* p. 148; *Total Baseball,* p. 1356.

1966 • Emmett Ashford (d. 1980) became the first black major league umpire, working in the American League. He had been the first black professional umpire in the minor leagues in 1951.

Sources: Ashe, *A Hard Road to Glory,* vol. 3, p. 32; Young, *Negro Firsts in Sports,* p. 209.

Frank Robinson (1935–), playing for the National League Cincinnati Reds in 1961 and for the American League Baltimore Orioles in 1966, was the first black named the Most Valuable Player in both leagues. In 1966 he was also was the first black to win the triple crown—the most home runs, most runs batted in, and the highest batting average. Robinson became the first black manager of a major league baseball team when he was hired by the Cleveland Indians in 1975.

Sources: Bennett, *Before the Mayflower,* p. 636; Clark, *Sports Firsts,* p. 32; *Encyclopedia of Black America,* p. 128; Jones and Washington, *Black Champions Challenge American Sports,* pp. 107, 137, 148, 149, 151; *Total Baseball,* p. 383, 1411, 2146.

1972 • The first person of any race to hit thirty or more home runs in fourteen seasons was Hank (Henry Louis) Aaron (1934–). "Hammering Hank" hit forty more in 1973. Playing for the Atlanta Braves, on April 8, 1974, he hit his 715th home run in a game with the Los Angeles Dodgers to beat Babe Ruth's major league record. He retired in 1976 after 755 home runs, and became vice-president of player personnel for the Braves.

Sources: Alford, *Famous First Blacks,* p. 80; Ashe, *A Hard Road to Glory,* vol. 3, pp. 18–19, 268; *Total Baseball,* pp. 306, 924.

Ferguson (Arthur) Jenkins (1943–), a Canadian, of the Chicago Cubs, was the first pitcher to win twenty games in six consecutive years.

Sources: Alford, *Famous First Blacks,* p. 85; Ashe, *A Hard Road to Glory,* vol. 3, pp. 6, 29; *Total Baseball,* pp. 353, 1763.

Art Williams (1934–79) was the first black umpire in the National League. He has been a pitcher in the mid 1950s and was the first black player with the Detroit Tigers. After serving as a minor league umpire for four seasons, he made his major league debut in San Diego, but was later fired from the position. His lawsuit with the Equal Employment Opportunity Commission was pending when he died in 1979.

Source: Jet 43 (5 October 1972), p. 48; *Jet* 55 (1 March 1979), p. 48.

1973 • Roberto Clemente (Walker) (1934–72), born in Puerto Rico of black and Hispanic heritage, was the first black to enter the Hall of Fame in a special election (before the five-year waiting period was met). He was the first Hispanic to enter the Hall of Fame and the second baseball player to be featured on a stamp, on August 17, 1984. He died in a 1972 airplane crash.

Sources: Current Biography 1973, p. 452; *I Have A Dream,* pp. 50–51; *Negro Almanac 1976,* pp. 696–97; *Total Baseball,* pp. 324, 1025–26.

1979 • Outfielder Dave (David Gene) Parker (1951–)was the first person of any race to become a million-dollar-a-year player when he signed a five-year, five-million-dollar contract with the Pittsburgh Pirates. A drug addiction problem led to poor performance, and he won the reputation of the most unpopular player ever to wear the Pittsburgh uniform. In 1984 Parker signed with the Cincinnati Reds as a free agent, having overcome his drug problem.
Sources: Ashe, *A Hard Road to Glory,* vol. 3, pp. 39–40, 41; *Jet* 70 (12 May 1968), p. 46; *Total Baseball,* pp. 377, 1367.

1980 • Sharon Richardson Jones was named director of outreach activities for the Oakland Athletics, becoming the first black woman in major league baseball administration.
Source: Jet 81 (2 March 1992), p. 20.

1989 • Eric Greg was the first black umpire to officiate in a World Series game. He appeared in the contest between the Oakland Athletics and the San Francisco Giants but was unable to work behind the plate since the series ended before his turn. In 1993, Charlie Williams became the second umpire to officiate in a World Series game. In his thirteen years as a National League umpire, Williams was also the first black to call balls and strikes in a World Series game—between the Toronto Blue Jays and the host Philadelphia Phillies.
Source: Jet 84 (8 November 1993), p. 57.

Bill (William De Kova) White (1934–), a Lakewood, Florida, native, was the first black president of a baseball league, the National League. He entered professional baseball in 1956 when he joined the New York Giants. White was named to the National League All-Star team six times and served as a play-by-play broadcaster in the 1979–80 seasons.
Sources: Contemporary Black Biography, vol. 1, pp. 243–45; *Total Baseball,* p. 1540.

1990 • The first black woman assistant general manager of the Boston Red Sox was Elaine C. Weddington.
Source: Jet 77 (26 February 1990), p. 52.

1991 • Rickey Henderson (1958–)was the first black to steal 939 bases in a career, surpassing Lou Brock. He already held the record for the most in one season, 939. The first person of any race to steal 130 bases in one season under the present-day way of counting was Maury (Maurice Morning) Wills (1932–), a Los Angeles Dodgers shortstop, who broke Ty Cobb's record of 96 stolen bases in a single season (1915) in 1962. His son Bump Wills was also a proficient base stealer during his six-year career (1977–82).

OPPOSITE PAGE:
HANK AARON HIT
755 HOME RUNS
DURING HIS CAREER
IN THE MAJORS.

Lou (Louis Clark) Brock (1939–) topped this record in 1974 with 118 and ended his career in 1976 with the all-time record of 938.

Sources: Ashe, *A Hard Road to Glory,* vol. 2, pp. 21, 26–27, 43; *A Hard Road to Glory,* vol. 3, pp. 27–28, 43–44, 269; *Current Biography 1975,* pp. 43–44 (Brock); *Encyclopedia of Black America,* p. 129; *Jet* 80 (20 May 1991), pp. 46–47; Jones and Washington, *Black Champions Challenge American Sports,* pp. 149–50, 151; *Total Baseball,* pp. 31, 316, 404, 1547.

1993 • Anthony Young of the New York Mets was the first pitcher of any race to lose twenty-seven consecutive decisions, the longest losing streak in major league baseball. The Mets lost to the Florida Marlins 5-4 at Shea Stadium on Wednesday, July 28. Young's previous win was April 19, 1992, at Montreal.

Source: (Nashville) *Tennessean* (29 July 1993).

BASKETBALL

1908 • The first intercity competition between black clubs was that between the Smart Set Club of Brooklyn, New York, and the Crescent Athletic Club, Washington, D.C. The Brooklyn club won at home and away.

Source: Young, *Negro Firsts in Sports,* p. 238.

1909 • Lincoln University (Pennsylvania), Hampton Institute (now University), and Wilberforce University fielded the first black college basketball teams in 1909 and 1910. YMCAs and YWCAs formed the first black teams and introduced the game on campuses through their student associations and the schools eventually embraced it.

Sources: Ashe, *A Hard Road to Glory,* vol. 1, pp. 104–5; Bennett, *Before the Mayflower,* p. 633; Young, *Negro Firsts in Sports,* p. 238.

1923 • The Rens, named after the team's home court, the Renaissance Casino in New York, was the first black professional basketball team. Founded and managed by Robert J. Douglas, the team ran up a record of 1,588 wins to 239 losses. They played from 1923 to 1939 and were the first black team in the Basketball Hall of Fame. On March 28, 1939 the Rens became the first black team on record to win a professional world's championship.

Sources: Chalk, *Pioneers of Black Sport,* pp. 83, 85–86, 88–89, 90–95; *Encyclopedia of Black America,* p. 129; Henderson, *The Black Athlete,* pp. 65–67; Young, *Negro Firsts in Sports,* pp. 80, 238.

1947 • Don (Donald Argee) Barksdale (1923–93) of UCLA was the first black selected for All-American basketball honors. He was also the first black player on, and the first black captain of, the United States Olympic basketball team in 1948. Barksdale won an Olympic Gold medal. He and R. Jackie Robinson were the two blacks in the London games. In 1947 Barksdale was the first black elected to the Helms All-Amateur Basketball

Hall of Fame, in Culver City, California. Elected to the National Basketball Association's all-star game in 1953, Barksdale was also the first black to participate in that event.

Sources: Bennett, *Before the Mayflower,* p. 634; Jones and Washington, *Black Champions Challenge American Sports,* p. 89; Page, *Black Olympian Medalists,* pp. 162; Young, *Negro Firsts in Sports,* pp. 240, 279.

1950 • Chuck (Charles) Cooper (?–1984?) of Duquesne University became the first black drafted by a National Basketball Association (NBA) team, the Boston Celtics, in April. The New York Knickerbockers purchased Nathaniel "Sweetwater" Clifton, of Xavier University, from the Harlem Globetrotters in 1950, making him the second black player signed by the NBA.

Sources: Bennett, *Before the Mayflower,* p. 634; *Detroit Free Press,* 14 January 1992; *Encyclopedia of Black America,* p. 130; *Jet* 65 (20 February 1984), p. 51; Lee, *Interesting People,* p. 131; Young, *Negro Firsts in Sports,* p. 239.

The first black to play in the NBA (October 21) was Earl Lloyd of West Virginia State College, a forward for the Washington Capitols. Although he was recruited later than Cooper and Clifton, he became the first to play (by one day) because of a quirk in NBA scheduling. Though Lloyd played ten seasons with Washington, Syracuse, and the Pistons, his NBA statistics were modest. He was also the first black assistant coach and the first black chief scout in the NBA.

Sources: Detroit Free Press, 14 January 1992; *Encyclopedia of Black America,* p.131; Jones and Washington, *Black Champions Challenge American Sports,* pp. 89, 100; Young, *Negro Firsts in Sports,* p. 239.

1952 • The Harlem Globetrotters team was founded, owned, and coached by Abe Saperstein of Chicago. Formed in Chicago, they were the first basketball club to make complete playing trips around the world, first in 1952 and again in winter 1960–61. They were the first professional basketball team to have its own fall training camp in October 1940. The best known and best loved team in the world, their finest decade was the 1950s. Mannie Jackson, a former Globetrotter, became the first black to own the team in 1993.

Sources: Henderson, *The Black Athlete,* pp. 61, 64-65; *Jet* 84 (9 August 1993), pp. 49–51; Jones and Washington, *Black Champions Challenge American Sports,* pp. 57–58, 82, 83, 87–89, 110–11; Young, *Negro Firsts in Sports,* pp. 230–38.

1955 • Missouri "Big Mo" Arledge of Philander Smith College in Arkansas was the first black woman All-American basketball player. The five-foot, ten-inch player averaged twenty-one points a game.

Source: Young, *Negro Firsts in Sports,* p. 241.

1961 • Johnny (John B.) "Coach Mac" McLendon was the first black coach of a predominantly white professional team in the modern era. In the 1961–62 season he coached the Cleveland Pipers of the American Basket-

WILT CHAMBERLAIN
SCORED MORE THAN
4,000 POINTS IN HIS
1961–62 SEASON WITH
THE PHILADELPHIA
76ERS.

ball League, and as a college coach his record of .825 in twenty was the second winning percentage behind that of Adolph Rupp of Kentucky. McLendon's Tennessee State teams won national small college championships in 1957, 1958, and 1959. He resigned from the Pipers in the second half of the 1961–62 season.

Sources: Ashe, *A Hard Road to Glory,* vol. 2, pp. 55, 56, 285; Bennett, *Before the Mayflower,* p. 636; Young, *Black Firsts in Sports,* pp. 90, 117, 239–40.

1962 • Wilt (Wilton Norman) "Wilt the Stilt" Chamberlain (1936–), then with the Philadelphia 76ers, was the first professional player to score more than 3,000 points in one season. In 1961–62 he scored 4,029 points and became the first player to score more than 4,000 points in a single season. Chamberlain was also the first black to score 100 points in a single game.

Sources: Ashe, *A Hard Road to Glory,* vol. 2, pp. 67, 70–71, 299–300, 303; Chalk, *Pioneers of Black Sports,* pp. 114, 115, 116, 117; *Current Biography 1960,* pp. 85–86; Young, *Negro Firsts in Sports,* pp. 78–79, 239, 265.

1966 • Bill (William Felton) "Mr. Basketball" Russell (1934–), while still a member of the Boston Celtics basketball team, was signed by the Celtics on April 18 to become the first black coach in the National Basketball Association, and the first to coach a major, predominantly white professional team. He immediately produced a world championship team, a record which continued from 1968–70. Called the greatest defensive player ever, Russell led the University of San Francisco to six straight wins and two NCAA championships, won a Gold Medal in the 1960 Olympics, and led the Celtics to eight consecutive world titles. As a college player, he played in one losing game, and at the end of 1955 the NCAA widened the foul lane from six to twelve feet because of his dominance at rebounds.

Sources: Ashe, *A Hard Road to Glory,* vol. 3, pp. 68–70; Bennett, *Before the Mayflower,* p. 636; *Encyclopedia of Black America,* pp. 130–31, 737; Jones and Washington, *Black Champions Challenge American Sports,* pp. 108–9, 137, 138; Page, *Black Olympian Medalists,* p. 132.

1967 • Clarence "Bighouse" Gaines (1923–) led the Winston-Salem Rams of Winston-Salem State University in North Carolina to national prominence when they became the first black college and the first in the entire South to win the NCAA College Division Basketball championship. Gaines never had a losing season and closed his coaching career with eight CIAA Conference victories, more than any other coach. He was celebrated more recently after winning his eight-hundredth basketball game on January 24, 1990—the most ever in basketball history. Gaines retired in 1993, having served the college for forty-seven years as head basketball coach, head football coach, chair of the department of physical education, and athletic director. The Paducah, Kentucky, native graduated from Morgan State College and Columbia University.

Sources: Ashe, *A Hard Road to Glory,* vol. 3, pp. 55, 56; *Ebony* 24 (February 1969), pp. 46, 50, 52; *Pittsburgh Courier* (4 March 1978).

1972 • The first black general manager in any sport was Wayne Embry (1937–), of the Milwaukee Bucks. He played as a center in the NBA for eleven years (eight of them with the Cincinnati Royals, then the Boston Celtics and finally the Milwaukee Bucks) and was a five-time NBA all-star. The Springfield, Ohio, native graduated from Miami University of Ohio.

Sources: Alford, *Famous First Blacks,* p. 87; *Ebony* 30 (January 1975), p. 97; 28 (February 1973), pp. 74–80; *Sepia* 23 (December 1974), p. 62.

Fred "The Fox" Snowden (1937–94) became the first black basketball coach at a major white institution, the University of Arizona. He was born in a sharecropper's shack in Brewton, Alabama, and grew up in Detroit. In his first year as coach, he brought the Arizona Wildcats to a winning season.

Sources: *Ebony* 32 (April 1977), pp. 44–50; *Jet* 76 (4 September 1989), p. 40; *Sepia* 27 (April 1979), pp. 48–54.

1973 • The first black vice-president of the NBA was Simon Peter Gourdine (1940–). He held this position until 1972 and served as deputy commissioner from 1974 to 1981. Gourdine received a law degree from Fordham University and is currently general counsel for the NBA Players Association.

Sources: Alford, *Famous First Blacks,* p. 87; *Who's Who Among Black Americans, 1992–93,* p. 543.

1982 • John Chaney became the first black basketball coach at Temple University in Philadelphia.

Source: Ashe, *A Hard Road to Glory,* vol. 3, p. 253.

1983 • George Henry Raveling became the first black head basketball coach at the University of Iowa. The following year he was an assistant coach for the 1984 Olympic squad.

Sources: Ashe, *A Hard Road to Glory,* vol. 3, pp. 54, 253; *Jet* 65 (20 February 1984), p. 40; *Who's Who Among Black Americans, 1992–93,* p. 1167.

1984 • Hubert Anderson was the first black coach at the 1985 World Games for the Deaf.

Source: Jet 66 (28 May 1984), p. 47.

On April 3 John Thompson (1919–) of Georgetown University became the first black coach to win the NCAA Division I championship. The squad, led by Patrick Ewing, won over Houston 84-75. A former Boston Celtics player, Thompson began his coaching career at St. Anthony's High School in Washington, D.C., and moved to the Georgetown Hoyas in 1972.

Sources: Ashe, *A Hard Road to Glory,* vol. 3, pp. 54, 63, 64, 80, 253; *Jet* 66 (16 April 1984), p. 52; *Time* (16 April 1984), p. 64.

Lynette Woodard (1959–) of the University of Kansas was the first woman to become a member of the Harlem Globetrotters.

Sources: Ashe, *A Hard Road to Glory,* vol. 3, pp. 64, 253; *Black Women in America,* vol. 2, p. 1282–83; *Jet* 73 (16 November 1987), p. 48; *Jet* 77 (12 February 1990), p. 50; Page, *Black Olympian Medalists,* pp. 126, 163.

1989 • The first black NBA team owners were Bertram Lee and Peter Bynoe, Chicago businessmen. On July 10, they purchased the Denver Nuggets for $65 million. (*See also* **Business: Manufacturing, 1990.**)

Sources: Hornsby, *Milestones in 20th-Century African-American History,* p. 409; *Jet* 76 (24 July 1989), p. 51; *Who's Who Among Black Americans, 1992–93,* p. 212 (Bynoe).

1991 • The first black commissioner of the Continental Basketball Association was Terdema L. Ussery. With this appointment he became the highest ranking black in professional sports.

Source: Who's Who Among Black Americans, 1992–93, p. 1427.

1992 • Rob Evans became the first black head coach at the University of Mississippi.

Source: (Nashville) *Tennessean* (31 March 1992).

BODYBUILDING

1970 • The first black Mr. America winner was Chris Dickerson.

Source: Negro Almanac, 1989, pp. 1430–31.

BOWLING

1939 • Wynston Brown was the first president of the National Negro Bowling Association, organized in Detroit on August 20. In the 1940s the organization dropped the word "Negro" from its title and included white members as well.

Sources: Negro Almanac, 1989, p. 952; Young, Negro Firsts in Sports, pp. 179–80, 183.

1951 • In April a team from Inkster, Michigan became the first to be entered in the ABC bowling championships. Team member William Rhodman (1916–62) rolled a 719 series in the tournament, becoming the first black bowler to win top rank in ABC competition.

Source: Young, Negro Firsts in Sports, p. 281.

1993 • George Branham III (1963–) became the first black bowler to win the Firestone Tournament of Champions. He won two championships in less than a month, including the Baltimore Open. The Detroit native learned to bowl when he was six years old and turned professional in 1984.

Source: Jet 84 (7 June 1993), p. 46.

BOXING

1791 • The first black fighter on record is Joe Lashley, who fought in England. His place of birth is unknown.

Source: Ashe, A Hard Road to Glory, vol. 1, p. 21.

1805 • Bill (William) Richmond (1763–1829), born on Staten Island, New York, was the first black to become a prominent boxer in England. He was active until 1810 and fought again in 1814 and 1818. He was the first black to seek his living as a boxer, and the first American boxer to achieve a substantial measure of success. As a fifteen-year-old soldier for the British Army during the American Revolution, Richmond was the hangman at Nathan Hale's execution. He accompanied the British troops when they withdrew to England after the American Revolution.

Sources: Ashe, A Hard Road to Glory, vol. 1, pp. 17–21, 30; Chalk, Pioneers of Black Sport, pp. 121–23; Encyclopedia of Boxing, p. 190; Negro Almanac, 1976, p. 580; Young, Negro Firsts in Sports, pp. 5, 18–20, 49.

1886 • On September 25 Peter "The Black Prince" Jackson (1861–1901) became the first black to win a national boxing crown, the Australian heavyweight title. A native of the Virgin Islands, he knocked out Frank Slavin in 1892 to gain the British Empire heavyweight title.

Sources: Ashe, A Hard Road to Glory, vol. 1, pp. 25–28; Chalk, Pioneers of Black Sport, pp. 141–43, 144, 145; Young, Negro Firsts in Sports, pp. 23–24.

1890 • George "Little Chocolate" Dixon, (1870–1909), born in Halifax, Nova Scotia, became the first black world champion in boxing when he defeated Nunc Wallace to win the bantamweight title on June 27. On March 31, 1891, he knocked out Cal McCarthy and became the first black man to hold an American title in any sport. Dixon was also the first to regain the title and the first to win the featherweight and the paperweight world championships.

Sources: Ashe, *A Hard Road to Glory,* vol. 1, pp. 22–24, 113; Bennett, *Before the Mayflower,* p. 634; *Encyclopedia of Boxing,* p. 40; Young, *Negro Firsts in Sports,* pp. 19, 24–26, 225.

1901 • Joe Walcott (1873–1935), the first black welterweight champion, defeated Rube Ferns and won the title at Fort Erie, Ontario, on December 18. He won the New England lightweight and middleweight wrestling titles in the same night. Born in Barbados, West Indies, Walcott was sometimes known as the "Barbados Demon."

Sources: Ashe, *A Hard Road to Glory,* vol. 1, pp. 24–25; Bennett, *Before the Mayflower,* p. 634; Chalk, *Pioneers of Black Sport,* pp. 130–34, 136–37; *Encyclopedia of Boxing,* p. 134.

1902 • Joe Gans (Joseph Gaines, 1874–1910) was the first American-born black to win a world crown (the lightweight), defeating Frank Erne in one round at the Fort Erie on May 12. Born in Knoxville, Tennessee, he was elected to the Hall of Fame in 1954. Gans retired in 1910 and died of tuberculosis the following year.

Sources: Ashe, *A Hard Road to Glory,* vol. 1, pp. 28–30; Bennett, *Before the Mayflower,* p. 634; *Encyclopedia of Black America,* p. 132; *Encyclopedia of Boxing,* p. 51; Young, *Negro Firsts in Sports,* p. 225.

JACK JOHNSON

1908 • Jack (John Arthur) Johnson (1878–1946) knocked out Tommy Burns on December 26 in Sydney, Australia, in the fourteenth round to become the first black heavyweight boxing champion. He lost only five of ninety-seven fights. Born in Galveston, Texas, Johnson was known as "Little Arthur" in his childhood. Because of his fearlessness, flamboyant style, and colorful life, he became one of the most reviled and hated men in America. Some experts called him the greatest fighter of of this weight ever. In 1954 Johnson was elected to the Hall of Fame.

Sources: Bennett, *Before the Mayflower,* p. 634; Chalk, *Pioneers of Black Sport,* 141, 144–48, 152–63; *Encyclopedia of Boxing,* pp. 65–66; Jones and Washington, *Black Champions Challenge American Sports,* pp. 25–27, 36–38.

1926 • Tiger (Theodore) Flowers (1895–1927) became the first black middleweight champion of the world, defeating Harry Greb to win the title in

New York City on February 26. A religious, honest, and clean-living man, he died during an eye operation.

Sources: Bennett, *Before the Mayflower,* p. 634; *Encyclopedia of Boxing,* p. 48; Jackson and Washington, *Black Champions Challenge American Sports,* pp. 48, 60; Young, *Negro Firsts in Sports,* pp. 20, 29, 31, 226.

1937 • The sole person to hold three championships and three world titles at once was Henry "Hammering Hank" Armstrong (1912–88). During a ten-month between period in 1937 and 1938 he won the featherweight, welter-weight, and lightweight titles and challenged for the middleweight, fighting to a draw. Armstrong, won twenty-seven fights in 1937 alone, twenty-six by knockout. He lost the last of his three titles, the welterweight, in 1940. Having saved little of his earning, he eventually became an ordained minister.

Sources: Encyclopedia of Black America, p. 134; *Encyclopedia of Boxing,* p. 12; Jones and Washington, *Black Champions Challenge American Sports,* pp. 71–73; Young, *Negro Firsts in Sports,* p. 226.

1938 • Joe Louis (Joseph Louis Barrow, 1914–61) became the first black of his rank to score a one-round knock-out when he defeated Max Schmelling on June 22, immediately becoming the first black national sports hero. He was the first black to hold a boxing title ten years or more, maintaining the title of world champion for almost twelve years. Universally loved, Louis fought Max Baer at New York on September 24, 1935, and became the first black fighter to draw a million-dollar gate. The following year he was the first black to win *Ring* maga-zine's fight-of-the year award. By 1949 Louis had become the first black to defend his title successfully twenty-five times, and in 1954 he became the first black heavyweight elected to Boxing's Hall of Fame. Born in Alabama, this son of a sharecropping cotton farmer fought often as a child. At the age of eight he knocked out four boyhood tormentors, and by 1934 he turned professional. Now a folk hero, his success broke down many barriers to black participation in ath-letics in other areas.

JOE LOUIS

Sources: Cantor, *Historic Landmarks of Black America,* pp. 24–25; *Encyclopedia of Black America,* p. 133; Young, *Negro Firsts in Sports,* pp. 98–114, 228–29.

1947 • The first televised heavyweight boxing championship bout was between Joe Louis and Jersey Joe Walcott (Arnold Raymond Cream, 1914–) on December 5 from Madison Square Garden. In 1951 Walcott and Ezzard "Quiet Tiger" Charles (1921–75) fought in the first heavyweight champi-onship prizefight telecast from coast-to-coast. In the fifteen-round bout held in Philadelphia's Municipal Stadium on June 5, Walcott outpointed Charles. Then thirty-seven years old, Walcott was the oldest person ever to win the heavyweight title. The first prizefight heavyweight championship bout tele-vised on large-screen was the Joe Louis match with Lee Savold. The

American Telephone and Telegraph Company telecast the event by microwave to the Empire State Building and then by coaxial cable closed-circuit to movie theaters in six cities. The fight was held in New York City on June 15; Louis won the scheduled 15-round fight in the 6th.

Sources: Ashe, *Hard Road to Glory,* vol. 2, p. 330; Chalk, *Pioneers in Sports,* pp. 191–93; *Encyclopedia of Black America,* p. 133; *Encyclopedia of Boxing,* p. 149; Kane, *Famous First Facts,* p. 652.

1958 • Sugar Ray (Walker Smith) Robinson, Jr., (1921–) became the first black fighter to hold the middleweight title on five separate occasions. Although he lived like a champion, drove flashy cars, and enjoyed fun and night life, he was always well prepared for his fights. In 202 professional fights Robinson lost only 19, and was never knocked out.

Sources: Current Biography, 1951, p. 526; *Encyclopedia of Black America,* pp. 111–12; Robinson, *Historical Negro Biographies,* p. 246.

1960 • Floyd Patterson (1935–) became the first black to regain the heavyweight title. Born to an extremely poor family in Waco, North Carolina, he developed his famous peek-a-boo defense as an amateur. Patterson lost his heavyweight title to Ingemar Johansson on June 26 and regained it nearly a year later when he knocked out Johansson in the fifth round. When he first won the championship, he was the youngest ever at twenty-one years of age. Patterson won an Olympic medal in 1952 and became the first black Olympic medalist to win a world title. Sonny Liston knocked him out in two minutes six seconds of the first round to win the title in 1962; in the rematch Patterson lasted four seconds longer.

Sources: Ashe, *A Hard Road to Glory,* vol. 2, pp. 90–92; Chalk, *Pioneers of Black Sports,* pp. 194–95, 198–99; *Encyclopedia of Black America,* p. 133; *Encyclopedia of Boxing,* p. 105.

1963 • The first and sole person to win five championships in boxing was Emile Griffith (1938–), of the Virgin Islands. First a welterweight champion, he later moved into the middleweight division.

Sources: Chalk, *Pioneers of Black Sports,* p. 189; *Encyclopedia of Boxing,* p. 55; Jones and Washington, *Black Champions Challenge American Sports,* pp. 130, 131, 132.

1971 • The first black boxers to draw a multimillion dollar gate were Joe Frazier and Muhammad Ali, in their fight at Madison Square Garden on March 8. After fifteen rounds, Frazier won the match on points. The bout grossed some $20 million, and each fighter received $2.5 million.

Sources: Ashe, *A Hard Road to Glory,* vol. 3, p. 345; Chalk, *Pioneers of Black Sports,* pp. 204–8; *Encyclopedia of Boxing,* pp. 49–50, 199; Jones and Washington, *Black Champions Challenge American Sports,* pp. 160–61.

1978 • The first black prizefight to gross more than a five-million dollar gate was the bout at the Louisiana Superdome in New Orleans on

September 15. Muhammad Ali won in a 13-round unanimous decision and became the first to win the heavyweight title three times.

Sources: Ashe, *A Hard Road to Glory,* vol. 3, p. 100; *Encyclopedia of Boxing,* pp. 7–10; Kane, *Famous First Facts,* p. 508.

1980 • The first black woman commissioner on the Michigan State Boxing Commission was Hiawatha Knight.

Source: Jet 57 (6 March 1980), p. 18.

1987 • The first black to win boxing titles in five different weight classes was Thomas "Hit Man" Hearns (1958–). In 1977 he was national NAA light welterweight champion and national Golden Gloves welterweight champion. His titles include the vacant USBA welterwight title (March 2, 1980); the WBA welterweight title (August 2, 1980); the WBC junior middleweight title (December 3, 1982); the world middlewight title (April 15, 1985); and the WBC light heavyweight title (February 1987).

Sources: Ashe, *A Hard Road to Glory,* vol. 3, pp. 347–50; *Negro Almanac, 1989,* pp. 980–81; *Who's Who Among Black Americans, 1992–93,* p. 633.

COMMITTEES

1992 • Anita Luceete DeFrantz (1952–), president of the Athletic Foundation of Los Angeles and elected to the International Olympic Committee in 1987, was the first black elected to its executive board. She won a bronze metal for Rowing Eights in the Montreal Olympics in 1976, where she was the first black American to compete for the United States in Olympic rowing. An outspoken critic of the Olympian movement during the 1980 boycott, DeFrantz became only the second American athlete to receive the International Olympic Committee's Bronze Medal of the Olympic Order.

Sources: Ashe, *A Hard Road to Glory,* vol. 3, pp. 215–16; *Jet* 71 (9 February 1987), p. 51; *Jet* 72 (27 July 1987), p. 48; *Jet* 82 (17 August 1992), p. 48; Page, *Black Olympian Medalists,* pp. 30–31.

Leroy Tashreau Walker (1918–) was the first black to hold the four-year post of president of the United States Olympic Committee. The retired coach, who in 1976 was head coach of the United States Track and Field team at the Olympic Games in Montreal, is chancellor emeritus of North Carolina Central University.

Sources: Ebony 47 (August 1992), p. 7; *Jet* 83 (26 October 1992), p. 46; *Who's Who Among Black Americans, 1992–93,* p. 1444.

CREW

1915 • Joseph E. Trigg manned the number seven oar at Syracuse University and became the first known black athlete on a varsity rowing team. Trigg was also an outstanding football player.

Sources: Ashe, *A Hard Road to Glory,* vol. 3, p. 215; Young, *Negro Firsts in Sports,* pp. 75, 176.

CYCLING

MARSHALL TAYLOR WAS KNOWN AS THE "FASTEST BICYCLE RIDER IN THE WORLD."

1898 • Marshall W. "Major" Taylor (1878– ?), of Indianapolis, Indiana, was the first native-born black American to win a major bicycle race. He began as a trick rider for a local cycling shop and participated in a few amateur events. Taylor won his first professional start, a half-mile handicap held at Madison Square Garden, in spite of racism in cycling; his 121-point-score made him the first black American champion in any sport. (Boxing champion George Dixon was Canadian. *See* **Sports: Boxing, 1890.**) Toward the end of the year, he compiled twenty-one first-place victories, thirteen second-place berths, and eleven third-place showings. Taylor was known as the "fastest bicycle rider in the world" until his 1910 retirement.

Sources: Alford, *Famous First Blacks,* p. 97; Ashe, *A Hard Road to Glory,* vol. 1, pp. 54–57; *Encyclopedia of Black America,* p. 143; Young, *Negro Firsts in Sports,* pp. 177–78.

DARTS

1972 • Adelle Nutter, the only black woman in dart championship play this year, became the first black U.S. dart champion. She was a founder and charter member of the American Dart Foundation.

Source: Black Sports (April 1973), pp. 26–27.

EDUCATION

1859 • On October 16 the first black director of physical culture at Harvard University was Abraham Molineaux Hewlitt.

Source: Ashe, *A Hard Road to Glory,* vol. 1, pp. 11–12.

FOOTBALL

1890 • William Henry Lewis (1868–1949) and teammate W. T. S. Jackson became the first recorded black players on a white college football team. Lewis was captain of the Amherst team in 1891–92 and the first black to win this distinction at an Ivy League school. He was the first black All-American and was selected as a center on Walter Camp's All-American teams of 1892 and 1893. Lewis completed his law degree at Harvard and became assistant district attorney in Boston. He wrote *How to Play Football* in 1896, becoming the first black athlete known to write a book. He became line coach at Harvard while he studied law, and later he became an Assistant United States Attorney General. (*See also* **Government—Federal Firsts: Federal Appointees, 1911.**) William Tecumseh Sherman Jackson was also the first black track star as a runner for Amherst; he set a school record of 2 minutes 5.4 seconds for 880 yards.

Sources: Ashe, *A Hard Road to Glory,* vol. 1, pp. 22, 90–91, 97; Bennett, *Before the Mayflower,* p. 635; *Dictionary of American Negro Biography,* pp. 396–97; Henderson, *The Black Athlete,* pp. 45–46; Jones and Washington, *Black Champions Challenge American Sports,* pp. 18, 19, 22, 43.

1892 • Biddle University (now Johnson C. Smith) in Charlotte, North Carolina, and Livingston College, Salisbury, North Carolina, played the first recorded black college football game on Thanksgiving day, winning by a 4-0 score. Two years later, Howard University, Lincoln University (Pennsylvania), and Atlanta University fielded football teams.

Sources: Ashe, *A Hard Road to Glory,* vol. 1, pp. 94–95; Bennett, *Before the Mayflower,* p. 634; Clark, *Sports Firsts,* p. 36.

1904 • Charles W. Follis (1879–?) became the first black professional football player, for the Blues of Shelby, Ohio. He was born in Cloverdale, Virginia, and moved to Wooster, Ohio, where he played at Wooster High. One of his high school teammates was Branch Rickey, later president of the Brooklyn Dodgers baseball team. The Blues were part of the American Professional Football League, formed in Ohio in this year, and a forerunner of the National Football League, which was formed in Canton, Ohio, in the summer of 1919, the year usually taken as the date of the beginning of modern professional football.

Sources: Ashe, *A Hard Road to Glory,* vol. 1, pp. 98, 99; Clark, *Sports Firsts,* p. 40; *Encyclopedia of Football,* pp. 18–23.

**"FRITZ"
POLLARD**

1916 • Frederick Douglas "Fritz" Pollard, Sr. (1890–), a diminutive back of Brown University became the first black to play in the Rose Bowl. Brown lost to Washington State 14-0. Pollard became the first black player-coach in professional football in 1919, when he joined the Akron Indians of the American Professional Football Association, which in 1921 became the National Football League. He coached the team to a championship in 1920. In 1921 Paul Robeson became one of Pollard's players. Pollard's career lasted through 1925. Blacks continued to play on professional teams until the end of the 1933 season and resumed play in 1946. His son Frederick Douglas Pollard, Jr., continued the family's athletic tradition by playing football for North Dakota and winning a bronze medal for the high hurdles in the 1936 Olympics.

Sources: Ashe, *A Hard Road to Glory,* vol. 1, pp. 100–2; Bennett, *Before the Mayflower,* p. 634, 636; Chalk, *Pioneers of Black Sport,* pp. 216–20, 222–23; Jones and Washington, *Black Champions Challenge American Sports,* pp. 40–41; Young, *Negro Firsts in Sports,* pp. 75–76, 146, 147, 250, 251.

1921 • The first black to receive the Most Valuable College Player Award was Frederick "Duke" Slater (1898–1966), tackle with the University of Iowa's undefeated team in 1921. He became a municipal court judge in Chicago in 1948. He was the first black elected to the College Football Hall of Fame at Rutgers in 1951.

Sources: Alford, *Famous First Blacks,* p. 92; Chalk, *Pioneers of Black Sport,* pp. 220–26, 253; Jones and Washington, *Black Champions Challenge American Sports,* pp. 49–50.

1929 • The Prairie View Bowl contest, played on January 1, was the first black college football bowl game. It was held in Houston, Texas, and Prairie View lost to Atlanta University by a 6-0 score. The bowl was discontinued in 1961.

Sources: Negro Almanac, 1989, p. 1426; Young, *Negro Firsts in Sports,* p. 254.

1947 • Buddy (Claude Henry Keystone) Young (1926–) became the first black to score a Rose Bowl touchdown, in the University of Illinois vs. UCLA New Year's Day game. Young joined the AAFC New York Yankees in 1947 and eventually played for the Cleveland Browns from 1953 to 1955. In 1964 he became the first director of player relations for the NFL, the first black to hold an executive position with the league. His football jersey was retired by the Baltimore Colts in 1965, a first for a team.

Sources: Ashe, *A Hard Road to Glory,* vol. 3, p. 129; *Encyclopedia of Football,* p. 607; *Jet* 65 (25 January 1984), p. 53; Young, *Negro Firsts in Sports,* p. 279.

Kenny Washington of UCLA became the first black professional player to break the color barrier in existence since 1933, when Joe Lillard of the Chicago Cardinals and Ray Kemp of the Pittsburgh Pirates were the last of the thirteen blacks who played in the National Football League between

1920 and 1933. It is surmised that the barrier in the NFL was broken only because the newly organized All-American Football Conference was signing black players. Washington signed with the Los Angeles Rams of the National Football League on March 21. Other blacks who signed in that year were Woody Strode, with the Rams on May 7; and in the All-American Conference, Bill Willis on August 6, and Marion Motley on August 9, both with the Cleveland Browns. Washington played for the Rams through 1948. The last NFL team to be integrated was the Washington Redskins, which signed Bobby Marshall in 1962.

Sources: Ashe, *A Hard Road to Glory,* vol. 2, pp. 108–9; vol. 3, pp. 128–30; Bennett, *Before the Mayflower,* p. 635; *Encyclopedia of Football,* p. 592; Jones and Washington, *Black Champions Challenge American Sports,* pp. 79, 91; Young, *Negro Firsts in Sports,* pp. 144–46.

The first black professional player from an all-black college was Paul "Tank" Younger (1920–), of Grambling University. He signed with the Los Angeles Rams. He played for the Rams until 1958, when he spent his final season with the Pittsburgh Steelers. Younger's success in professional ball established Grambling's reputation for nurturing future players.

Sources: Encyclopedia of Football, p. 608; Jones and Washington, *Black Champions Challenge American Sports,* p. 120; Young, *Negro Firsts in Sports,* p 131.

1948 • On January 1 in New Orleans, Wally Triplett and Dennie Hoggard, members of Pennsylvania State, became the first blacks to play in the Cotton Bowl. This was one sign of the very slow and reluctant acceptance of blacks on football teams by the South. Triplett later played for the Detroit Lions and the Chicago Cardinals.

Sources: Ashe, *A Hard Road to Glory,* vol. 3, p. 121; *Encyclopedia of Football,* p. 586; *Jet* 81 (30 December-January 1992), p. 32.

1953 • The first black professional quarterback was Willie Thrower, a Michigan State graduate who signed with the Chicago Bears. Since the position was viewed traditionally as "white," Thrower played only a few downs and was active only one season. The first black quarterback to play professionally with any regularity was Marlin Briscoe in 1968 for the Denver Broncos, then in the American Football League.

Sources: Ashe, *A Hard Road to Glory,* vol. 3, p. 125, 143; Chalk, *Pioneers of Black Sports,* pp. 239–40; Clark, *Sports Firsts,* p. 50; *Encyclopedia of Football,* p. 583.

1958 • Jim (James) Nathaniel Brown (1936–) was the first black athlete to win the Jim Thorpe Trophy. He is a football legend at his alma mater, Syracuse Univesity, and played nine years with the Cleveland Browns. In the 1960s he also became the first black to score 126 career touchdowns. He later became an actor, producer, sports commentator, and marketing executive.

Sources: Bontemps, *Famous Negro Athletes,* pp. 119–31; *Current Biography, 1964,* pp. 5–58; Henderson, *The Black Athlete,* pp. 200–4; *Historical Negro Biographies,* pp. 169–90; Toppin, *Biographical History of Blacks,* p. 259.

1961 • Ernie (Ernest) Davis (1939–62), a Syracuse University running back, was cited as the first black player of the year and winner of the Heisman Trophy. Other early black Heisman winners were Mike Garrett in 1965, and O. J. (Orenthal James) Simpson in 1968. Davis was the first draft pick in both the NFL and the AFL, but he never played a moment of professional football since he was diagnosed with leukemia a few days before the college all-star game against the Green Bay Packers.

Sources: Ashe, *A Hard Road to Glory,* vol. 2, p. 12; Bennett, *Before the Mayflower,* p. 635; Henderson, *The Black Athlete,* pp. 203–4; Young, *Negro Firsts in Sports,* p. 281.

1965 • Emlen "The Gremlin" Tunnel (1925–75) was the first black coach in the National Football League. Tunnel had played for the New York Giants from 1948 to 1958 and the Green Bay Packers from 1959 to 1961. During his career he played in nine Pro Bowls and was an All-Pro four times. He was signed as assistant defensive coach by the New York Giants on May 1. In 1967 he became the first black elected to the professional Hall of Fame.

Sources: Ashe, *A Hard Road to Glory,* vol. 3, pp. 130–31, 355–56; Bennett, *Before the Mayflower,* p. 635, 637; *Encyclopedia of Football,* p. 586.

1969 • Alonzo Smith "Jake" Gaither (1905–) of Florida A & M University, known as "the Papa Rattler" was the first black coach to win more than two hundred games. His career record was 203 victories in 25 seasons. He also won more conference titles than Eddie Robinson of Grambling—twelve to eight. He entered the Football Hall of Fame on January 30, 1975. The Dayton, Tennessee, native graduated from Knoxville College, Knoxville, Tennessee, and Ohio State University.

Sources: Ashe, *A Hard Road to Glory,* vol. 3, p. 118; Bennett, *Before the Mayflower,* p. 637; Robinson, *Historical Negro Biographies,* p. 193; *Who's Who Among Black Americans 1992–93,* p. 500; Young, *Negro Firsts in Sports,* pp. 89–90.

1971 • Alan Cedric Page (1924–) became the first defensive player in the history of the NFL to receive the Most Valuable Player Award. Known as the NFL's Marathon Man, he was the first player to complete a full 26.2 mile marathon. A former member of the Chicago Bears, he is a practicing attorney. On November 3, 1992, he was elected to the Minnesota Supreme Court. (*See also* **Government—County & State Pioneers: Minnesota, 1992.**)

Sources: Encyclopedia of Football, p. 529; Hornsby, *Milestones in Twentieth Century African-American History,* p. 502.

1973 • On September 16, O. J. Simpson (1947–) of the Buffalo Bills was the first black to rush for 250 yards in one game. In his years with the NFL he set records for running the most games in a season with 100 yards or more (11 in 1973), the most rushing attempts in a season (332 in 1975), and the most yards gained rushing in a single game (273 in 1976). Simpson played in the Pro Bowl in 1972, 1974, 1975, and 1976. The San Francisco native graduated

from the University of Southern California, where he ran for 3,295 yards, scored thirty-four touchdowns, and led the Trojans to a national championship. In 1968 he received the Heisman Trophy, was named Rose Bowl Football Player of the Year, and received the Walter Camp Award, the Maxwell Award, and the Sporting News college player of the year award. Simpson was named NFL Player of the Decade in 1979, and was named to the College Football Hall of Fame (1983) as well as the Pro Football Hall of Fame (1985). He became a sports commentator and actor.

O. J. SIMPSON, RIGHT, RUNS WITH THE BALL IN A 1975 GAME AGAINST THE NEW YORK JETS.

Sources: Great Athletes, vol. 16, pp. 2341–43; *Encyclopedia of Football,* p. 327; *Negro Almanac, 1989,* p. 970; *Who's Who Among Black Americans, 1992–93,* p. 1284.

1979 • Willie Jefferies (1939–) became the head coach at Wichita State, the first at a major white institution.

Source: Jet 56 (22 March 1979), p. 48.

1983 • The first major black player to sign with the United States Football League was Herschel Walker (1962–), who signed with the New Jersey Gremlins. When the USFL collapsed in 1986, Walker was signed by the Dallas Cowboys. In 1989 he went to the Minnesota Vikings. Walker was an outstanding player at the University of Georgia, where he set a NCAA freshman rushing record of 1,616 yards and was the first freshman to finish in the top ten in votes for the Heisman Trophy.

Source: Contemporary Black Biographies, vol. 1, pp. 235–36.

WALTER PAYTON

1986 • Walter Jerry Payton (1954–) was the first black player to gain more than 20,000 yards. The number-one draft choice of the Chicago Bears in 1974 set NFL records for the most rushing touchdowns (110), most all-purpose running yards (21,803), most rushing yards (16,726), most seasons with at least 1,000 rushing yards (10), and set a new NFL record for the most rushing yards in a game (275 in 1977). He led the NFC in rushing five times, and in two games rushed 200 or more yards. His career ended on January 10, 1988, with a total of 16,726 rushing yards. The Columbia, Mississippi, native graduated from Jackson State University, Jackson, Mississippi, where he set an all-time NCAA record of sixty-six touchdowns, scored 464 total points, and set nine school records. He was named College Player of the Year and an All-American. Payton's uniform number 34 was retired by the Bears.

Sources: Great Athletes, vol. 14, pp. 1968–71; *Jet* 71 (27 October 1986), p. 52; *Who's Who Among Black Americans, 1992–93,* p. 1101.

1988 • Johnny Grier was the first black referee in the National Football League.

Sources: Jet 74 (18 April 1988), p. 46; *Who's Who Among Black Americans, 1992–93,* p. 546.

Doug Williams was the first black quarterback to start a Super Bowl game, for the Washington Redskins in Super Bowl XXII. He joined the Redskins after playing for the Tampa Bay Buccaneers.

Source: Jet 81 (16 April 1990), p. 51.

1989 • Arthur "Art" Shell, Jr.,(1946–), became the first black head coach in modern NFL history when he was appointed coach of the Los Angeles Raiders. (The first was Fritz Pollard in 1923.) Shell was born in Charleston, South Carolina, and previously served as offensive line coach for the Raiders.

Sources: Contemporary Black Biography, vol. 1, pp. 219–20; *Sports Illustrated* (23 October 1989); *Jet* 77 (23 October 1989), p. 48; *Jet* (26 February 1990), p. 48.

1990 • Eddie Robinson (1919–) of Grambling University became the first college coach of any race to win 368 games in a career. In 1978 he was the first black coach to be considered seriously for the position of head coach of the Los Angeles Rams. Robinson has sent more players to the pros than any other black coach: sixty-nine as of 1988.

Sources: Alford, Famous First Blacks, p. 91; *Ashe, A Hard Road to Glory,* vol. 2, p. 119; vol. 3, p. 119; *Jones and Washington, Black Champions Challenge American Sports,* pp. 120–21.

1991 • The first black vice-president for labor relations of the National Football League was Harold Henderson. This was the league's third highest post, and Henderson became the highest ranking black in the history of the NFL.

Source: Jet 80 (6 May 1991), p. 48.

GOLF

1926 • The United Golf Association held its first national tournament. The winners were Harry Jackson, of Washington, D.C., and Marie Thompson, Chicago. Founded in the 1920s, national tournaments for black golfers continued for a number of years. A few black-owned country clubs existed in such cities as Westfield, New Jersey; Kankakee, Illinois; and Atlanta, Georgia. Tuskegee Institute sponsored the first black intercollegiate championship in 1938 on its nine-hole course.

Sources: Ashe, *A Hard Road to Glory,* vol. 2, pp. 66–68; *Encyclopedia of Black America,* p. 141; Young, *Black Firsts in Sports,* p. 164.

1957 • Charlie (Charles) Sifford (1922–) won the Long Beach Open on November 10 and became the first black to win a major professional golf tournament. He also became the first black to play in a major PGA tournament in the South at Greensboro, North Carolina, in 1961.

Sources: Ashe, *A Hard Road to Glory,* pp. 150–51, 154, 157; Bennett, *Before the Mayflower,* p. 635; *Encyclopedia of Black America,* p. 142; Jones and Washington, *Black Champions Challenge American Sports,* p. 116; Young, *Negro Firsts in Sports,* pp. 162–75, 281.

1967 • Renee Powell was the first black woman on the Ladies' Professional Golf Association (LPGA) tour. A native of Canton, Ohio, Powell had won the USGA women's title in 1964.

Sources: Ashe, *A Hard Road to Glory,* vol. 3, p. 152; *Spradling,* p. 780.

1971 • Lee Elder (1934–) became the first American to compete against whites in South Africa in the South African PGA Open. In 1974 he became the first black to qualify for the Masters Tournament and on April 10, 1975, teed off in Atlanta, Georgia, as the Master's first black entry. He became black America's first Ryder Cup Team member in 1979.

Sources: Alford, *Famous First Blacks,* p. 94; Ashe, *A Hard Road to Glory,* vol. 3, pp. 154, 156, 158; Bennett, *Before the Mayflower,* p. 635; Jones and Washington, *Black Champions Challenge American Sports,* pp. 147, 159.

1991 • At fifteen, Eldrick "Tiger" Woods, of Cypress, California was the first black and the youngest person ever to win the U.S. Junior Amateur championship. With his participation in the Los Angeles Open in March, 1992, he also became the youngest person ever to play in a Professional Golf Association tour event. He became the first two-time winner of the USGA Junior Amateur crown when he successfully defended his title in 1992 at the championship in Milton, Massachusetts. Woods won his third consecutive U.S. Junior Amateur Golf Championship title in 1993, at the Waverly Golf Course and Country Club, Portland, Oregon. He is the only golfer ever to win three straight titles.

Sources: Jet 82 (31 August 1992), p. 47; *Jet* 84 (30 August 1993), p. 46; *USA Weekend* (24-26 July 1992).

GYMNASTICS

1981 • The first black woman to win the United States Gymnastics Championships was Diane Durham, who won the title for two consecutive years. The first internationally ranked black American female gymnast, she seemed a sure medalist for the 1984 Olympics but injured herself just before the competition.

Sources: Ashe, *A Hard Road to Glory,* vol. 3, p. 221; *Jet* 65 (2 January 1984), p. 31.

1988 • Charles Lakes became the first black man to be a member of the United States Olympic team.

Source: Jet 75 (5 September 1988), p. 48.

1992 • The first black women gymnasts to complete on a United States Olympic team were Dominique Dawes and Elizabeth Okino, who were in the games in Barcelona, Spain.

Source: Jet 82 (17 August 1992), p. 48.

HOCKEY

1950 • Arthur Dorrington, a dentist, signed with the Atlantic City Seagulls of the Eastern Amateur League on November 15, becoming the first black to play in organized hockey. He played in the 1950–51 season and in 1952 with the Johnstown (Pennsylvania) Jets.

Sources: Kane, *Famous First Facts,* p. 301; *Negro Almanac, 1989,* p. 1428; Young, *Negro Firsts in Sports,* p. 281.

1958 • The first black professional hockey player was Willie (William) Eldon O'Rhee, of the National Hockey League's Boston Bruins. He played with the Bruins in their 3-0 win over the Montreal Canadiens in Montreal on January 18. He was born in Frederickton, New Brunswick and, like many Canadians, spent considerable time at the ice rink.

Sources: Ashe, *A Hard Road to Glory,* vol. 2, p. 222; Clark, *Sports Firsts,* p. 69; Kane, *Famous First Facts,* p. 301.

1981 • The National Hockey League drafted its first black player, Grant Fuhr. He was picked in the first round and became the goalie for the world champion Edmonton Oilers.

Source: Ashe, *A Hard Road to Glory,* vol. 3, p. 222.

HORSE RACING

C. 1806 • "Monkey" Simon was the first known black jockey. He has been called the best jockey of his day, and he commanded more than a hundred dollars per ride for himself and his master.
Source: Ashe, *A Hard Road to Glory,* vol. 1, p. 44–45.

1875 • The first jockey of any race to win the Kentucky Derby was Oliver Lewis, who rode three-year-old Aristides in the first race in record time. Thirteen of the fourteen jockeys in the first race were black. In 1911 Jess Conley was the last black jockey from the United States to ride in a Derby.

OLIVER LEWIS WON THE FIRST EVER KENTUCKY DERBY IN 1875.

WINNING KENTUCKY DERBY BLACK JOCKEYS

YEAR	NAME
1877	William "Billy" Walker
1880	George Lewis
1882	Babe Hurd
1884	Isaac Murphy
1885	Erskine Henderson
1887	Isaac Lewis
1890	Isaac Murphy
1891	Isaac Murphy
1892	Alonzo Clayton
1895	James Perkins
1896	Willie Sims
1898	Willie Sims
1901	Jimmie Winkfield
1902	Jimmie Winkfield

Sources: Ashe, *A Hard Road to Glory,* vol. 1, pp. 43–53, 129; Alford, *Famous First Blacks,* p. 95; Garrett, *Famous First Facts About Negroes,* pp. 77, 78–79, 185; *Encyclopedia of Black America,* pp. 138, 949.

ISAAC MURPHY

1890 • Isaac Murphy (Isaac Burns, 1861?–96), the first jockey of any race to win the Kentucky Derby three times, was considered one of the greatest race riders in American history: he won forty-four percent of all the races he rode. His Derby record held until 1930. Murphy won the first in 1884 and the second in 1890, which made him the first jockey to capture Derby titles two years in a row. In 1884 he became the only jockey to win the Derby, the Kentucky Oaks, and the Clark Stakes in the same Churchill Downs meeting. In 1955 Murphy was the first jockey voted into the Jockey Hall of Fame at the National Museum of Racing, Saratoga Springs, New York. Born on the David Tanner farm in Fayette County, Kentucky, he took the name Murphy to honor his grandfather, Green Murphy, a well-known auctioneer in Lexington. He learned to ride at age fourteen.

Sources: Ashe, *A Hard Road to Glory,* vol. 1, pp. 47–49; *Churchhill Downs News, 1980 Black Expo Edition,* p. 2; *Dictionary of American Negro Biography,* pp. 462–63; Young, *Negro Firsts in Sports,* pp. 49.

1899 • The Kentucky Derby distance was trimmed from one and one-half miles to one and one-quarter miles in 1896. Willie (Willy) Simms (1870–?) of Augusta, Georgia, was the first winner of the race at this distance. He won many of the best-known horse races in America, such as the Preakness Stakes (1898), Belmont Stakes (1893 and 1894) and the Champagne Stakes at Belmont in 1895. He was also the first American jockey on an American horse to win on the English track, and he became the first black American jockey to win international fame.

Sources: Ashe, *A Hard Road to Glory,* vol. 1, p. 49; Jones and Washington, *Black Champions Challenge American Sports,* p. 18; Young, *Negro Firsts in Sports,* pp. 52–53.

1971 • Cheryl White (1954–) became the first woman jockey on June 15.
Source: Encyclopedia of Black America, p. 138.

HORSE RIDING

1990 • Donna Cheek became the first black member of the U.S. Equestrian Team. She was the first and only equestrienne to be inducted into the Women's Sports Hall of Fame.
Source: Jet 79 (21 January 1991), p. 48.

OPPOSITE PAGE: DEBI THOMAS WAS THE FIRST BLACK U.S. ATHLETE TO WIN A MEDAL IN THE WINTER OLYMPICS.

ICE SKATING

1984 • Debi Thomas (1967–) was the first black skater on a World Team, and in 1985 she held United States and world figure skating championships.

Her 1988 silver medal was the first medal won by a black athlete in the Winter Olympics. She was born in Poughkeepsie, New York.

Sources: Ashe, *A Hard Road to Glory,* vol. 3, pp. 224, 257; *Jet* 67 (25 February 1985), p. 54; *Who's Who Among Black Americans, 1992–93,* p. 1381.

MARATHON WALKING

1879 • The first known black to set a United States record for marathon walking was Frank Hart, also known as "O'Leary's Smoked Irishman." (O'Leary, his trainer, was the former champion.) The contest was held in New York City; the contestants traveled as far as they could in three or six days, for a purse of several thousand dollars.

Source: Lane, *William Dorsey's Philadelphia and Ours,* p. 17.

OLYMPICS

1904 • George Coleman Poage (1880–1962) became the first black to represent the United States in the Olympic Games. He finished fourth in the 400 meters and third in the 400-meter hurdles at the St. Louis event. He was born in Hannibal, Missouri, and later became an orator and scholar.

Sources: Jones and Washington, *Black Champions Challenge American Sports,* p. 31; Page, *Black Olympian Medalists,* pp. 94–95, 149; Young, *Negro Firsts in Sports,* pp. 83–84.

1908 • John Baxter "Doc" Taylor, Jr., (1882–1908) became the first black winner of a gold medal in the Olympics won for the 4 x 400-meter relay in London. One of the first great black quarter-milers, Taylor was also the first black to win a gold medal as a United States team member. He died five months after winning the gold medal.

Sources: Ashe, *A Hard Road to Glory,* vol. 1, pp. 63–64, 65–66; Page, *Black Olympian Medalists,* pp. 111–12, 149; Young, *Negro Firsts in Sports,* pp. 83–84.

1920 • Harry Francis Vincent Edwards (1895–1973) was the first black Olympic medalist from Great Britain. He won a bronze medal at in the 100-meter run and the bronze for the 200-meter run at Antwerp. Italian coach Mussabini was his trainer.

Source: Black Olympian Medalists, pp. 35, 156.

1924 • William DeHart Hubbard (1903–76) became the first black in Olympic history to win an individual gold medal when he won the broad jump by leaping 24 feet 5½ inches on July 8. He set a new record on July 13, 1925, at Stagg Field in the NCAA championships where he leaped 25 feet 5⅛ inches. Although best known for his broad-jumps, he was also a sprinter, tying the world record of 9.6 seconds in the 100 yard dash. On his graduation from Ohio State, he was one of eight blacks in a class of 1,456.

Sources: Ashe, *A Hard Road to Glory,* vol. 2, p. 79; Bennett, *Before the Mayflower,* p. 636; Page, *Black Olympian Medalists,* pp. 54, 149.

1936 • Cornelius Johnson (1913–) won a gold medal in the 1936 Olympics for the high jump and became the first black high jumper to clear the bar at 6 feet, 9 inches. Born in Los Angeles, he attended Compton Junior College.

Sources: Jones and Washington, *Black Champions Challenge American Sports,* p. 70; Page, *Black Olympian Medalists,* pp. 58–59; Young, *Negro Firsts in Sports,* pp. 86–87, 104–5.

Jesse Owens (James Cleveland Owens, 1913–80), son of an Alabama sharecropper, ran with Ralph Metcalf and won the first gold medal for the 4 x 100-meter relay held in Berlin in 1936 and set both Olympic and world records. When he won a gold for the long jump, he set a record that remained unbroken for 24 years. He ran 200 meters in 20.7 seconds at the Berlin Olympics, then the fastest ever around a full turn. He tied the Olympic record for the 100-meter run at Berlin. Altogether he won four gold medals and set three records. Earlier, Owens ran in the Big Ten Championships in Ann Arbor, Michigan, on May 25, 1935, and set five world records and tied a sixth within 45 minutes. For his athletic achievement, his name was published in the record book for forty years, showing that at the pinnacle of his career he had won nine records in seven events and once held as many as eleven records. The world was stunned and his fame spread when Adolf Hitler refused to acknowledge Owens and the medals he had won in the Berlin Olympics. Later he was successful in business, as a speaker and youth worker. In 1976 he was the first black appointed by the Department of State as goodwill ambassador to the Olympic games. He was appointed to the United States Olympic Committee and in 1976 won the Presidential Medal of Freedom. Ohio State University, where he had studied, awarded him an honorary doctorate in 1972. In 1984 the Jesse Owens Memorial Monument was dedicated in his hometown, Oakville, Alabama.

JESSE OWENS

Sources: Negro Almanac, 1989, p. 964–65; Page, *Black Olympian Medalists,* pp. 91–92, 149; Young, *Negro Firsts in Sports,* p. 98–105, 280.

The first black to win the 400-meter race in the Olympics was Archie Williams (1915–93). His time was 46.1 seconds. The Oakland, California, native won a gold medal for the race at the Berlin Olympics. In 1939 he graduated from the University of California, Berkeley, with a degree in mechanical engineering.

Sources: Jet 84 (12 July 1993), p. 51; Jones and Washington, *Black Champions Challenge American Sports,* p. 70; Young, *Negro Firsts in Sports,* p. 86.

John Woodruff (1915–), first great American black middle-distance runner, was the first black to win the 800-meter race in the Olympics. Since his performance in 1936 and 1937, no athlete has equalled his dominance of the

800 meter and half-mile runs. He came to national attention in the 1936 Olympic sectional trials when he won this race. He won a gold medal in Berlin; that year he was also Amateur Athletic Union of the United States (AAU) champion. In addition to other titles, in 1940 he broke the American 800 record. Woodruff was born in Connellsville, Pennsylvania.

Sources: Alford, *Famous First Blacks,* p. 100; Jones and Washington, *Black Champions Challenge American Sports,* p. 70; Page, *Black Olympian Medalists,* pp. 126–27.

1948 · Alice Coachman (Davis) (1923–) was the first black woman Olympic gold medal winner and the only American woman to win a gold medal in the 1948 Olympics in London. She took the gold for the high jump and set an Olympic record that held until two Olympiads later. Born in Albany, Georgia, she received a trade degree from Tuskegee Institute (now Tuskegee University) and later received a bachelor's degree from Albany State College.

Sources: Encyclopedia of Black America, p. 143; *Notable Black American Women,* pp. 193–95; Page, *Black Olympian Medalists,* pp. 23–24.

ALICE COACHMAN WON A GOLD MEDAL FOR THE HIGH JUMP IN THE 1948 OLYMPICS.

The first black heavyweight lifting champion in the Olympics was John Davis, of Brooklyn. He had thoroughly established himself in the field in 1941 when he set a record of 1005 pounds for three lifts. Davis was Olympic champion again in 1952. Once called "the world's strongest man," he was the first weight-lifter known to hoist 400 pounds over his head, a feat he accomplished in the 1951 National AAU senior championship in Los Angeles.

Sources: Alford, *Famous First Blacks,* p. 98; Young, *Negro Firsts in Sports,* pp. 184–85.

1952 · The first black to win the 400-meter hurdles in the Olympics was Charles Moore, Jr., with a time of 50.8 seconds.

Sources: Alford, *Famous First Blacks,* p. 99; *Encyclopedia of Sports,* p. 741.

1956 · Lee Quincy Calhoun (1923–) won a gold medal in 1956 at the Melbourne Olympics and again in 1960 at the Rome Olympics, both for the 110-meter hurdles, and became the first athlete to win this event twice. Trained at North Carolina Central, he was also the first black from a black college to win an Olympic gold medal.

Sources: Ashe, *A Hard Road to Glory,* vol. 3, p. 184; Page, *Black Olympian Medalists,* p. 19.

Milt (Milton) Gray Campbell (1934–), one of the first great black decathletes, won 7,937 points and became the first black to win the Olympic decathlon. He first won a bronze medal for the event in 1952 as a high school student. Campbell concentrated on the hurdles and competed in the decathlon only five times in his career. Campbell has been called the best all-around athlete of the 1950s. During his professional football career, it is alleged that he suffered from serious prejudice on the part of the Cleveland

Browns for whom he played in the 1957 season, especially because he had married a white woman. Later, he worked with underprivileged youth in New Jersey, and also became a well-known lecturer.

Sources: Ashe, *A Hard Road to Glory,* vol. 3, pp. 152, 183, 184, 516; *Encyclopedia of Black America,* p. 141; Henderson, *The Black Athlete,* p. 245; Jones and Washington, *Black Champions Challenge American Sports,* p. 115; Page, *Black Olympian Medalists,* p. 19.

1960 • Rafer Lewis Johnson (1934–), winner of a silver medal for the decathlon at the 1956 Olympics and a gold medal for the same event at the 1960 Olympics, was the first black to carry the American flag at an Olympic event—the opening ceremony at Rome in 1960. In winning the decathlon, Johnson set a new Olympic record of 8,001 points. He retired from track and became involved in community activities in California. He was with presidential candidate Robert F. Kennedy in Los Angeles when he was assassinated in 1968. Born in Hillsboro, Texas, he graduated from UCLA. He has been national head coach for Special Olympics.

Sources: Ashe, *A Hard Road to Glory,* vol. 2, pp. 184, 186; Henderson, *The Black Athlete,* p. 244; Page, *Black Olympian Medalists,* pp. 59–60.

Wilma Glodean Rudolph (1940–), born with polio that left her paralyzed in the left leg and unable to walk well until age ten, was the first woman to win three track gold medals in the Olympics. While a student at Tennessee State University, Nashville, she was a member of the famed Tigerbelles and became well known for her running technique and scissoring stride. She ran in the 100-meter, 200-meter, and relay, becoming also the first black woman winner of the 200-meter. She won a bronze medal as a member of the women's 4 x 100-meter relay team at the Melbourne Olympics in 1956. Rudolph was the first black woman to win the Sullivan Award (1954) and she is the winner of numerous other awards as an outstanding athlete. Her autobiography, *Wilma,* was made into a television film in 1977. She became a well-known lecturer, talk-show host and good-will ambassador, and is now a vice president at Baptist Hospital in Nashville. Rudolph was one of five athletes and the only track star honored in June 1993 at the first annual National Sports Awards held in Washington, D.C.

WILMA RUDOLPH

Sources: Ashe, *A Hard Road to Glory,* vol. 2, pp. 182, 185, 187, 189, 201; *Jet* 84 (12 July 1993), pp. 56–58; Kane, *Famous First Facts,* p. 45; *Notable Black American Women,* pp. 958–61; Page, *Black Olympian Medalists,* pp. 102–3.

1964 • Wyomia Tyus (1945–) the most successful U.S. woman track and field Olympic athlete, was the first athlete, male or female, to win an Olympic sprint title twice. She won a gold medal for the 100-meter run at the 1964 Olympics in Tokyo and a silver medal for the 4 x 100-meter relay at the same event. In 1968 she won the gold medal for the 100-meter run and the 4 x 100-meter relay in Mexico City. She set an Olympic and world record in the 100-meter run (the second time she had set a world record in the event) and helped set an Olympic and world record of 42.8 seconds in the latter event. In 1974 she joined the first professional track and field association. The state of Georgia elected her to its Athletic Hall of Fame in 1976. The Los Angeles resident was born in Griffin, Georgia, and graduated from Tennessee State University, where she was a member of the Tigerbelles.

Sources: Ashe, *A Hard Road to Glory,* vol. 3, pp. 188, 197, 201, 205, 514, 515, 518; *Guiness Book of Olympic Records;* Henderson, *The Black Athlete,* pp. 263–65; Page, *Black Olympian Medalists,* p. 118.

1968 • On October 16 Tommie C. Smith (1944–), with John Wesley Carlos (1945–), were the first to refuse to recognize the American flag and national anthem at an Olympic event. During this event at the 1968 Olympics in Mexico City, they lowered their heads and raised a black glove-encased fist to make a black power salute reflecting the black power movement of the decade. Smith, who won a gold medal for the 200-meter run at the Olympics, and Carlos, who won a bronze medal for the 200-meter run, were expelled from the games. Vincent Matthews and Wayne Collett made a similar protest four years later in Munich when their attitude on the victory stand made clear their lack of respect for the American flag. They were banned from any future Olympic competition.

Sources: Ashe, *A Hard Road to Glory,* vol. 3, pp. 190–95, 199–200; Jones and Washington, *Black Champions Challenge American Sports,* pp. 134–36; Page, *Black Olympian Medalists,* pp. 20–21, 108.

Madeline Manning (1948–) was the first black woman to win a gold medal for the 800-meter race in the Olympics with an Olympic record time of 2 minutes 0.9 seconds. In the 1972 games in Munich she won a silver for the women's 4 x 400-meter relay. A Tennessee State track star, she won the 800-meters six times at the AAU.

Sources: Alford, *Famous First Blacks,* p. 102; Ashe, *A Hard Road to Glory,* vol. 3, pp. 197, 200.

1972 • Willye Brown White (Whyte) (1940–) became the first black woman to compete in five Olympic games. She won a silver medal for the long jump in 1956 and another silver for the 400-meter relay in 1964. White won the AAU long jump title ten times and the indoor, once. A native of Greenwood, Mississippi, she was the first black inducted into the Mississippi Hall of Fame in 1982.

Sources: Ashe, *A Hard Road to Glory,* vol. 3, p. 185; *Ebony* 18 (June 1963), pp. 115–20; *Ebony* 32 (August 1977), p. 62; Lee, *Interesting People,* p. 186.

1975 • Edwin Corley Moses (1955–) is the only athlete to perfect the technique of taking thirteen strides between the hurdles. This concentration on his event led to his being the first person to win 107 400-meter hurdles event in a row. His winning streak in the 400-meter intermediate hurdles began on September 2, 1977, in Dusseldorf, West Germany. The streak ended at the Madrid meet on June 4, 1987, when he was handed his first defeat in ten years. Moses won a gold medal at Montreal in 1976 for the 400-meter hurdles and set a world and Olympic record of 47.64 seconds, a time he lowered to 47.02 seconds when he set his fourth world record on August 31, 1983. He won a second gold medal in 1984 at Los Angeles for the 400-meter hurdle, and a bronze, also for the 400-meter hurdles, in Seoul in 1988. Born in Dayton, Ohio, he graduated from Morehouse College in Atlanta and became an aeronautical engineer.

Sources: Ashe, *A Hard Road to Glory,* vol. 3, pp. 201–2, 204; Page, *Black Olympian Medalists,* pp. 85–86, 153, 154.

1980 • The first blacks to participate in the Winter Olympics were Jeff Gadley and Willie Davenport, a bobsled team.

Sources: Clark, *Sports Firsts,* p. 222; *People* (25 February 1980), p. 35.

1984 • Carl (Frederick Carlton) Lewis (1961–) was the first athlete to win four gold medals in a single Olympics since Jesse Owens. Lewis was influenced by Owens, whom he met at a school awards ceremony while in high school and who told him, "Dedication will bring its rewards." At the Los Angeles meet in 1984 Lewis won a gold medal each for the 100-meter run, the 200-meter run, the long jump, and the 4 x 100-meter relay. He continued to win other honors and to set records. Born in Birmingham, Alabama, he attended the University of Houston.

Sources: Ashe, *A Hard Road to Glory,* vol. 3, pp. 204–86; *Ebony* 39 (October 1984), p. 172; Page, *Black Olympian Medalists,* pp. 72–73, 154–56; *Sports Illustrated* (August 20, 1984).

Valerie Brisco-Hooks won gold medals and set world records at the 1984 Olympics in Los Angeles for both the 200-meter run and the 400-meter run and became the first athlete to win at both distances. Running on the winning relay team that year, she tied Wilma Rudolph as winner of three gold medals in United States women's track and field events. She also received a silver medal for the 4 x 400-meter relay in the 1988 Olympics in Seoul. Born in Greenwood, Mississippi, she attended California State University at Northridge.

Source: Ashe, *A Hard Road to Glory,* vol. 3, pp. 189, 205.

Cheryl De Ann Miller (1964–) was the first player, male or female, to be named to the Parade All-American team for four consecutive years. She played in the 1984 Olympics in Los Angeles when the Americans won their first gold medal in women's basketball. Other black women on the United States team were Pam McGee, Lynette Woodard, Janice Lawrence, Cathy Boswell, and Teresa Edwards. She also led the United States team to gold medal victories in the World Championships and the Goodwill Games in Moscow, both in 1986.

Sources: Ashe, *A Hard Road to Glory,* vol. 3, pp. 54, 57, 64, 254; Page, *Black Olympian Medalists,* pp. 83–84, 163.

The first black referee and judge for the Olympic Games, one of four Americans, was Carmen Williamson.

Source: Jet 66 (30 July 1984), p. 33.

1988 • Jacqueline "Jackie" Joyner-Kersee (1962–) was the first U.S. woman to win the Olympic long jump and the first athlete in sixty-four years to win both a multi-event competition and an individual event in one Olympics. She won a silver medal for the heptathlon at the 1984 Olympics, and a gold medal in 1988 for the heptathlon, setting an Olympic and world record. This year she became the only woman to gain more than seven thousand points four times in the heptathlon. Again in 1988 she won the gold for the long jump and set an Olympic record. She became the first woman ever to repeat as Olympic heptathlon champion in 1992 when she won the two-day, seven-event marathon. She has been called the world's fastest woman and the greatest female athlete. Born in East St. Louis, she graduated from UCLA and in 1986 married Bob Kersee, her sprint coach. She was the first woman to receive The *Sporting News's* Waterford Trophy, a prestigious annual award.

Sources: Black Women in America, pp. 667–69; *Current Biography, 1987,* pp. 293–96; *Epic Lives,* pp. 305–11; *Sports Illustrated* (27 April 1987).

Anthony Nesty of Surninam was the first black swimming champion in Olympic games and the first swimming champion from South America. He won a gold medal at the Olympics in Seoul for the 100-meter butterfly in swimming to give Surinam its first Olympic medal. Nesty attended the University of Florida.

Sources: Page, *Black Olympian Medalists,* pp. 88, 167; *USA Today* (3 October 1988).

1992 • Robert Pipkins became the first black member of the Olympic luge team and the first black in international competition. He also won the junior world championship in Sapporo, Japan.

Source: Time (10 February 1991).

RODEOS

1876 • Nat Love (1844–?), former slave, frontiersman, and cowboy, was the only black claimant to the title Deadwood Dick and so claimed to be the first known black rodeo champion. His account of his life, as written in his autobiography, is sometimes unconvincing since none of the cowboys he worked with seemed to have ridden with other crews and records are lacking. Whatever its authenticity, the story does exist and makes interesting reading.

Sources: Durham and Jones, *The Negro Cowboys,* pp. 192–206; Katz, *Black People Who Made the Old West,* pp. 113–17; Katz, *The Black West, 1993,* pp. 150–52.

1887 • Pinto Jim and Bronco Jim Davis are the first known blacks to participate in a rodeo, in October in Denver, Colorado. Pinto Jim could rope, bridle, saddle, and mount his horse in thirteen minutes. Bronco Jim Davis's contest was abandoned after thirty minutes of struggle in which the man and the horse appeared every evenly matched.

Source: Durham and Jones, *The Negro Coyboys,* p. 207.

1890 • Early written accounts of rodeos are sparse, but the first black known to have set a record in steer roping was an unnamed man in Mobeetie, Texas, with a time of one minute and forty-five seconds.

Source: Durham and Jones, *The Negro Cowboys,* p. 206.

1905 • Bill Pickett (1860–1932), rodeo cowboy and former slave, is generally credited with being the first person to develop a way of bulldogging that made the act a spectacular performance. A black man named Andy bulldogged in the 1870s; Sam Johnson, a big and impressive man, did later. It was Pickett, however, who joined the 101 Ranch in 1900, who mastered his new technique by biting the upper lip of the steer after the throw and raising his hands to show that he was no longer holding. The 101 Ranch put on its first major rodeo in 1905 and continued until the outbreak of World War I in 1914. Pickett was presented to King George V and Queen Mary after a special performance in that year. Pickett lived out his days on the 101 Ranch. On December 9, 1971, he became the first black elected to the National Rodeo Cowboy Hall of Fame.

BILL PICKETT BECAME THE FIRST BLACK ELECTED TO THE NATIONAL RODEO COWBOY HALL OF FAME.

Sources: Alford, *Famous First Blacks,* p. 68; *Crisis* 77 (November 1970), p. 388; Durham and Jones, *Negro Cowboys,* pp. 209–19; *Ebony* 33 (May 1978), pp. 58–62; Katz, *The Black West, 1983,* pp. 160–62.

1982 • The first black World Rodeo champion was Charles Sampson of Los Angeles. The bullrider won the National Finals Rodeo in 1981, and the next year won the Winston Rodeo Series and was awarded the world title. He won the Sierra Circuit title in 1984, and for five consecutive years, 1981–85, qualified for the National Finals Rodeo. The popular rider appeared in magazine advertisements.

Sources: Ashe, *A Hard Road to Glory,* vol. 3, p. 234; *Jet* 65 (20 February 1984), p. 40.

SAILING

1992 • Martin Stephan and Art Prince became the first black Americans to sail in the America's Cup.

Source: Emerge 3 (October 1992), p. 38.

SQUASH

1988 • The first black member of the men's All-American squash team of the National Intercollegiate Squash Racquets Association was Wendell Chestnut.

Source: Jet 74 (23 May 1988), p. 20.

TENNIS

1899 • The first black to arrange an interstate tournament for black players was W. W. Walker of the Chautauqua Tennis Club. The Philadelphia event attracted competitors from several nearby states. Walker became the first of a long line of great black tennis coaches.

Sources: Ashe, *A Hard Road to Glory,* vol. 1, p. 59; *Encyclopedia of Black America,* p. 141; Jones and Washington, *Black Champions Challenge American Sports,* p. 21.

1917 • Tally Holmes of Washington, D.C., and Lucy Diggs Slowe (1885–1937) of Baltimore won the men's and women's singles respectively to become the first players to win the all-black American Tennis Association championships. The matches, the first ATA Nationals, were held in August this year at Druid Hill Park in Baltimore. Slowe also became the first black woman national champion in any sport.

Sources: Ashe, *A Hard Road to Glory,* pp. 60–61; Bennett, *Before the Mayflower,* p. 635; *Notable American Women,* pp. 1031–33 (Slowe); Young, *Negro Firsts in Sports,* pp. 183–84.

1935 • The first black woman to win seven consecutive titles in the American Tennis Association was Ora Washington (1898–1971). She began her career in 1924. During twelve undefeated years, she used her blazing pace to upset many of the American Tennis Association's top-seeded stars. She remained undefeated until 1936, when she became ill during play and lost the match but regained the championship in 1937.

Sources: Jones and Washington, *Black Champions Challenge American Sports,* pp. 54–56, 60, 80, 84; Young, *Black Firsts in Sports,* 183, 187, 194–96.

1948 • Reginald Weir (1912–), a physician of New York City, was the first black to participate in the United States Indoor Lawn Tennis Association championship. He won his first match at the New York City event on March 11 and was eliminated on March 13.

Sources: Ashe, *A Hard Road to Glory,* vol. 2, pp. 61, 62, 64; Kane, *Famous First Facts,* p. 662; Young, *Negro Firsts in Sports,* pp. 184, 188.

1953 • Lorraine Williams (1939–) became the first black to win a nationally recognized tennis title when she won the junior girl's championship this year.

Sources: Bennett, *Before the Mayflower,* p. 635; *Ebony* 9 (January 1954), p. 24; *Ebony* 7 (June 1952), pp. 41–45; Young, *Negro Firsts in Sports,* p. 280.

1956 • Althea Gibson (1927–) became the first black to win a major tennis title when she won the women's singles in the French Open on May 26. She won the Wimbledon championship on July 6, 1957, when she also captured the women's singles, becoming the first black to win these honors. She became the first black to win a major United States national championship on September 8, 1957, when she defeated Louise Brough at Forest Hills to win the women's singles. In 1991 she was the first black woman to receive the Theodore Roosevelt Award of the NCAA. In 1968 Gibson was the first black inducted into the International Tennis Hall of Fame.

Sources: Ashe, *A Hard Road to Glory,* pp. 58, 64, 100; Bennett, *Before the Mayflower,* pp. 635; *Encyclopedia of Black America,* p. 141; *Notable Black American Women,* pp. 397–402.

ALTHEA GIBSON

1963 • Arthur Ashe (1943–93) was the first black named to the American Davis Cup team. In 1961, the year he won the USLTA junior indoor title, another first, he had been named the first black on the United States Junior Davis Cup team. In 1968 he became the first black man to win a major tennis title, the national men's singles in the United States Lawn Tennis Association open tournament at Forest Hills. This was the first time the contest was open to professionals as well as amateurs. He became the first black man to win single titles at Wimbledon in 1975. In 1983 he received a contract to produce the first complete book on blacks in sports, *A Hard Road to Glory.* He was the first black man inducted into the International Tennis Hall of Fame in 1985. Ashe retired from active play after a mild heart attack on July 31, 1979. In 1993 Ashe died of AIDS acquired through a blood transfusion. In June 1993 President Bill Clinton honored him posthumously with the Presidential Medal of Freedom, awarded at the first annual National Sports Awards presentation in Washington, D.C.

ARTHUR ASHE

Sources: Encyclopedia of Black America, p. 142; *Jet* 84 (12 June 1993), pp. 56, 58; Jones and Washington, *Black Champions Challenge American Sports,* p. 146.

1988 • Zina Garrison (1963–) won a gold medal in doubles and a bronze in the singles, becoming the first black Olympic winner in tennis. She also was the first black to rank in the top ten on the women's professional tour.

Sources: Black Women in America, pp. 480–81; *Contemporary Black Biography,* vol 2, pp. 89–92; *Jet* 78 (23 July 1990), p. 51.

TRACK AND FIELD

1912 • The first black to hold the record for the 100-yard dash was Howard Porter Drew (1890–), of Lexington, Virginia. He was called the world's fastest human and won the National Amateur Athletic Union championship on September 12. In this year also he won the 220-yard dash championship. He never competed in the Olympics.

Sources: Ashe, *A Hard Road to Glory,* vol. 1, pp. 64–65, 67; *Encyclopedia of Black America,* p. 139; Jones and Washington, *Black Champions Challenge American Sports,* pp. 39–40, 44, 45, 48.

Theodore "Ted" Cable of Harvard University, a hammer-throw specialist, was the first black to win an intercollegiate weight championship.

Sources: Ashe, *A Hard Road to Glory,* vol. 1, p. 64; Jones and Washington, *Black Champions Challenge American Sports,* p. 31; Young, *Negro Firsts in Sports,* pp. 84, 87.

1921 • Edward Orval Gourdin (1897–1966) was the first person of any race to long-jump more than 25 feet, surpassing that distance by 3 inches in a college international meet at Cambridge, Massachusetts, on July 23, 1921. This year he also was the first black to win the pentathlon in the National Amateur Athletic Union championships. In 1924 he won a silver medal in the Paris Olympics. A graduate of Harvard, he was admitted to the Massachusetts Bar and the Federal Bar. He became United States District Attorney in 1936 and in 1958 became the first black on the Massachusetts Supreme Court.

Sources: Ashe, *A Hard Road to Glory,* vol. 2, pp. 79–80; *Dictionary of American Negro Biography,* pp. 264–65; *Negro Year Book, 1921–1922,* pp. 30–31; Page, *Black Olympian Medalists,* pp. 44, 149; Young, *Negro Firsts in Sports,* p. 86.

1930 • Thomas Edward "Little Eddie" Tolan (1908–67) ran in Evanston, Illinois, this year and was the first person officially credited with running 100 yards in 9.5 seconds. He set two Olympic records in the Los Angeles meet in 1932 and became the first black to win gold medals in both the 100- and 200-meter dash. In his career he won three hundred races and lost seven. A graduate of the University of Michigan, he became an elementary school teacher in 1935.

Sources: Alford, *Famous First Blacks,* p. 99; *Encyclopedia of Black America,* p. 139; Young, *Negro Firsts in Sports,* pp. 84–85; Page, *Black Olympian Medalists,* pp. 116–17, 149.

1932 • Ralph Metcalf (1910–78), while training for the Olympics, broke three world records on June 11—100 meters, 200 meters, and 220 yards. In 1934 he became the first man to win the NCAA doubles three times and the next year he became the only sprinter to win five times in a single event. In 1934–35 he was called the "world's fastest human." He and Jesse Owens were the first blacks to win a gold medal for the 400 x 100-meter relay, which they ran in Berlin in 1936. Metcalf studied at Marquette University and later was a coach and instructor of political science. He became well known as a member of the Chicago city council and later was a member of the United States House of Representatives.

Sources: Jones and Washington, *Black Champions Challenge American Sports,* pp. 67–68, 69, 70; Page, *Black Olympian Medalists,* pp. 82, 149; Young, *Negro Firsts in Sports,* pp. 84–85.

1937 • The women's track team of Tuskegee Institute (now University) was the first black team to win the National AAU women's track and field championship. Coached by Christine Evans Petty, Lulu Hymes sparked the team by winning the long jump, taking second place in the 50 meter dash, and helping the 400 meter relay team place second. The team continued winning the AAU title through 1942.

Sources: Ashe, *A Hard Road to Glory,* vol. 2, pp. 76–77; Young, *Negro Firsts in Sports,* p. 91.

1954 • Since 1930 the Amateur Athletic Union has presented annually the James E. Sullivan Memorial Trophy to the top amateur athletes in the United States. Track star Malvin Greston "Mal" Whitfield (1924–) of Ohio State was the first black man to win the award. From 1948 to 1954, Whitfield dominated the 800-meters; during this period he won sixty-nine races and lost three. He won five AAU titles and held five indoor and outdoor world records.

Sources: Ashe, *A Hard Road to Glory,* vol. 3, p. 182; Clark, *Sports Firsts,* p. 237; Kane, *Famous First Facts,* p. 45; Young, *Negro Firsts in Sports,* p. 86.

1956 • Charles Everett Dumas (1937–), who won a gold medal at the 1956 Olympics at Melbourne with an Olympic record leap of 6 feet 11$\frac{1}{4}$ inches, was the first man to break the 7-foot high jump barrier, clearing 7 feet $\frac{5}{8}$ inches at the Olympic finals trial at the Los Angeles Coliseum.

Sources: Ashe, *A Hard Road to Glory,* vol. 3, pp. 184, 516; Page, *Black Olympian Medalists,* p. 34; *Negro Almanac,* p. 1429.

1960 • The first black to clear 7 feet 3$\frac{3}{4}$ inches in the high jump was John Thomas, at the 1960 United States Olympics trials. A foul-up by officials at the 1959 Millrose Games deprived him of the indoor world record when he first cleared seven feet as a seventeen year old. At the Olympics, Thomas had to settle for a bronze medal.

Sources: Ashe, *A Hard Road to Glory,* vol. 2, pp. 187, 192, 201; *Encyclopedia of Black America,* p. 141; Henderson, *The Black Athlete,* pp. 249–50.

1987 • Karen Keith was the first woman of any race to coach men's and women's teams at a major institution, Boston College.

Sources: Jet 73 (23 November 1988), p. 46; *Who's Who Among Black Americans, 1992–93,* p. 810.

WRESTLING

1992 • The first black heavyweight wrestling champion was Ron Simmons, three-time All-American nose tackle at Florida State. He captured the World Championship Wrestling title for a first in the sixty-year history of the sport.

Source: Jet 82 (21 September 1992), p. 50.

WRITERS: PUBLISHED
AND PRIZEWINNING

AUTOBIOGRAPHY

1760 • Briton Hammon was the first black American writer of prose. The fourteen-page work, "A Narrative of the Uncommon Sufferings and Surprising Deliverance of BRITON HAMMON, A Negro Man—Servant to General Winslow, of Marshfield in New England; Who Returned to Boston, after Having Been Absent almost Thirteen Years," was published in Boston. This account tells of his providential escape from captivity by Indians, and then from his Spanish rescuers.

Sources: Dictionary of American Negro Biography, p. 281; Jackson, A History of Afro-American Literature, vol. 1, pp. 47–48.

1798 • A Narrative of the Life and Adventure of Venture, a Native of Africa But Resident Above Sixty Years in the United States of America was the first slave narrative written by a black American. There are precursors, but they were written down by whites, like Some Memoirs of the Life of Job (1734), by Thomas Bluett; difficult to credit fully, like A Narrative of the Lord's Dealings with John Marrant (1789); or complete fictions. The author of the very important The Interesting Narrative of the Life of Olaudah Equiano (1789) spent only a few days in the American Colonies. Venture [Broteer] [Smith] (1729–1805) recalls his royal descent in Africa, his slavery in Connecticut and Long Island, New York, and his prosperity after he was able to purchase his freedom by the age of forty-six.

Sources: Dictionary of American Negro Autobiography, pp. 617–18; Jackson, A History of Afro-American Literature, vol. 1, pp. 61–62.

HISTORY

1836 • Robert Benjamin Lewis was the first black to publish a history, Light and Truth. Practically nothing is known about Lewis, except that he was a native of Boston and had both black and Indian ancestors. Characterized by a remarkable disregard for any standard of evidence, the book tries among other things to create a black presence in history and to establish Native Americans as the descendents of the lost tribes of Israel.

Source: Jackson, *A History of Afro-American Literature,* vol. 1, pp. 200–01.

1841 • James William Charles Pennington (1807–70) was the author of the first history of black people written by an African-American for children, *The Origin and History of the Colored People.* A slave blacksmith in Maryland, Pennington escaped, and learned to read and write. He became a teacher, a Congregational minister, and a Presbyterian minister. He was an active and prominent abolitionist. He officiated at the wedding of Frederick Douglass and his wife.

Sources: Dictionary of American Negro Biography, pp. 488–90; Garrett, *Famous First Facts About Negroes,* p. 77; Jackson, *A History of Afro-American Literature,* vol. 1, p. 201.

1855 • The first black history founded on written documentation is *The Colored Patriots of the American Revolution* by William Cooper Nell (1816–74). Although deficient as history by modern standards, it nonetheless contains materials of lasting value. Nell's work began as a twenty-three page pamphlet in 1851. A native of Boston, Nell was a major leader in the ultimately successful fight to desegregate the Massachusetts public schools, as well as an associate of Garrison and Douglass in the abolition movement. (*See also* **Government—Federal Firsts: Federal Appointees, 1861.**)

Sources: Dictionary of American Negro Biography, pp. 472–73; Garrett, *Famous First Facts About Negroes,* p. 156; Jackson, *A History of Afro-American Literature,* vol. 1, pp. 201–02.

1882 • George Washington Williams (1849–91) was the author of the first major history of blacks in America. His *History of the Negro Race in America from 1619 to 1880,* in two volumes, was a major event and earned him respect for meeting the standards of professional historians. Born in Bedford Springs, Pennsylvania, he was an underage soldier in the Union Army. In 1875, he became an ordained Baptist minister, then turned to law and politics, serving a term in the Ohio legislature. His active life did not preclude the collection of materials for his histories. His other writings include the valuable *History of the Negro Troops in the War of the Rebellion* (1877). His last efforts were attacks on the inhumane government of the Congo Free State, following a 1890 visit there.

Sources: Dictionary of American Negro Biography, pp. 657–59; Garrett, *Famous First Facts About Negroes,* p. 77; Jackson, *A History of Afro-American Literature,* vol. 1, pp. 211–18.

1896 • William Edward Burghardt (W. E. B.) Du Bois (1868–1963) wrote the first scientific historical monograph by a black American, *The Suppression of the African Slave Trade, 1638–1870.* The book was published as the first volume in the Harvard University Historical Studies. *The Souls of Black Folk*

(1903) established Du Bois as a peerless essayist. His 1935 account of the Reconstruction era, *Black Reconstruction in America,* was the first account of the era from a black viewpoint. A founding member of the National Association for the Advancement of Colored People, Du Bois edited *The Crisis,* the magazine of the NAACP, taught at Atlanta University for a number of years, and was an ardent supporter of African liberation movements. He was the leading black intellectual of the first half of the twentieth century. (*See also* **Organizations: Academic and Intellectual Societies, 1897.**)

Sources: Garrett, *Famous First Facts About Negroes,* pp. 77, 79–80; *Dictionary of American Negro Biography,* pp. 193–99.

1916 • The *Journal of Negro History* was the first American black historical research journal. Carter Goodwin Woodson (1875–1950) was its founder and first editor. Born in New Canton, Virginia, his early education was limited due to his need to work for his family's support in the West Virginia coal fields. He completed his high school program in a year and a half, and began a college career that led to a Ph.D. from Harvard in 1912. He was a co-founder and the first executive director of the Association for the Study of Negro Life and History, established on September 9, 1915. In 1926, Woodson launched the first Negro History Week (now Black History Month). In 1937, he began publishing *The Negro History Bulletin.* Throughout his life he was devoted both to the establishment of black history on a sound footing, and to the dessemination of historical knowledge about black people. (*See also* **Organizations: Academic and Intellectual Societies, 1915.**)

Sources: Garrett, *Famous First Facts About Negroes,* p. 77; *Dictionary of American Negro Biography,* pp. 665–67.

LITERATURE

1845 • Armand Lanusse (1812–67) compiled the first collection of American black poets, *Les Cenelles,* devoted to poetry in French. Lanusse was a free man of color in New Orleans, and the leader of a local group of young poets. From 1852 to 1866, he was principal of the Bernard Couvent Institute for Indigent Catholic Orphans.

Sources: Dictionary of American Negro Biography, pp. 384–85; *Hughes and Bontemps, Poetry of the Negro 1746–1949,* p. 400; Jackson, *A History of Afro-American Literature,* vol. 1, pp. 225–34.

1893 • Paul Laurence Dunbar (1872–1906) was the first black poet to gain national fame. The Ohio-born writer was accepted whole-heartedly and widely recognized in the late nineteenth century. He used dialect and standard English in his work. His first book, *Oak and Ivy* appeared in 1893, and two years later his second book, *Majors and Minors,* attracted the attention of the celebrated critic William Dean Howells. His third book, *Lyrics of Lowly Life* (1896), gained him his national reputation.

Sources: Brown, Davis, and Lee, *The Negro Caravan,* p. 303; *Dictionary of American Negro Biography,* pp. 200–03; Hughes and Bontemps, *The Poetry of the Negro 1746–1949,* p. 395.

1986 • Wole Soyinka (1934–), Nigerian playwright, poet, and novelist, was the first African to win a Nobel Prize for literature. His works have been acclaimed for his portrayals of the human condition in emergent Africa.

Sources: Black Writers, pp. 529–34; *Encyclopedia Americana,* vol. 25, p. 351.

1992 • Derek Walcott (1930–), poet, educator, playwright, journalist, and painter, was the first African-Caribbean to be honored with the Nobel Prize in Literature. The prize was given for his "melodious and sensitive" style and "historic vision." His writings reflect the cultural diversity of his native Caribbean homeland, St. Lucia. A teacher at Boston University, Walcott also won a $250,000 John D. and Catherine T. MacArthur Foundation grant eleven years earlier. He has been regarded as one of the finest living poets in English.

Sources: Black Writers, pp. 567–71; *Jet* 83 (26 October 1992), p. 14; *Time* 140 (19 October 1992), pp. 24, 65.

**TONI
MORRISON
(1931–)**

1993 • Toni Morrison (1931–), novelist, educator, and editor, was the first black American to win the Nobel Prize in literature, which was awarded on October 7. The Swedish Academy called her "a literary artist of first rank," and one who "gives life to an essential aspect of American reality." Informed of the honor, Morrison said that her work was inspired by "huge silences in literature, things that had never been articulated, printed or imagined and they were the silences about black girls, black women." Her novel *Song of Solomon,* published in 1977, won the National Book Critics Award for fiction that year, and in 1988 she won the Pulitzer Prize for fiction for her work *Beloved.* Her other novels are *The Bluest Eye* (1970), *Sula* (1974), *Tar Baby* (1981), and *Jazz* (1992). Toni Morrison was born in Lorraine, Ohio, and graduated from Howard University in Washington, D.C., in 1953. She received a master's degree in English from Cornell University in 1955. In 1965 Morrison became a textbook editor for a subsidiary of Random House Publishing in Syracuse, New York, and three years later she moved to New York City as a senior editor in the trade department at Random House. She mixed her editorial work with a teaching career and taught at a number of colleges. She left the publishing field in 1984, and in 1989 became the Robert F. Goheen Professor of the Council of the Humanities at Princeton University.

Sources: Black Women in America, pp. 815–19; *Contemporary Biography,* vol. 2, pp. 167–72; (Nashville) *Tennessean* (8 October 1993); (Nashville) *Tennessean* (9 October 1993); *Notable Black American Women,* pp. 770–75; *Washington Post* (8 October 1993).

NONFICTION

1878 • James Monroe Trotter (1842–92) wrote the first important book on blacks in music, *Music and Some Highly Musical People.* The book contains valuable biographical material and an appendix reproducing the scores of thirteen black compositions. The book is a major source of information.

Sources: Dictionary of American Negro Biography, pp. 602–03; Garrett, *Famous First Facts About Negroes,* p. 126.

1881 • William Sanders Scarborough (1852–1926) was the first black American scholar to publish a Greek language textbook. A widely used textbook, *First Lessons in Greek,* won recognition for Scarborough. In 1886, his *Birds of Aristophanes* was published. An African Methodist Episcopal minister, he was active in black intellectual circles, and served as president of Wilberforce University (Ohio) from 1908 to 1920.

Sources: Dictionary of American Negro Biography, pp. 545–46; Garrett, *Famous First Facts About Negroes,* p. 102.

1918 • Benjamin Griffith Brawley (1882–1939), college professor, dean and author, edited the first book devoted exclusively to black art and literature, *The Negro in Literature and Art.* The book was reprinted in 1937 as *The*

Negro Genius. Born in Columbia, South Carolina, Brawley took an M.A. degree at Harvard University in 1908. He was a poet, and a prolific scholar, who had a distinguished teaching career at Atlanta Baptist Seminary (now Clark Atlanta University), Shaw, and Howard.

Sources: Brown, Davis, and Lee, *The Negro Caravan,* p. 757; Hughes and Bontemps, *The Poetry of the Negro 1746–1949,* p. 390; *Dictionary of American Negro Biography,* pp. 60–61.

NOVELS

WILLIAM WELLS BROWN (1814–84)

1853 • William Wells Brown (1814–84) was the first black novelist. His novel, *Clotel; Or, The President's Daughter: A Narrative of Slave Life in the United States,* was published in England. The son of a slave mother and plantation owner in Kentucky, he escaped in 1834. In 1843, he became an agent of abolitionist societies. He spent five years in Europe championing emancipation, and wrote the first novel, the first book of travel, *Three Years in Europe,* (1852), and the first dramatic work, *Experience; or How to Give a Northern Man a Backbone* (1856), by an American black. (*See also* **Arts and Entertainment: Theater, 1823.**) His second play, *Escape; or, A Leap for Freedom,* also written in 1856, was the first play published by an American black. Before the end of the Civil War, he became a physician and maintained a practice until his death; his interest also turned to writing the history of black achievement. Brown wrote more than a dozen books and pamphlets.

Sources: *Dictionary of American Negro Biography,* pp. 71–73; Garrett, *Famous First Facts About Negroes,* p. 100; Jackson, *A History of Afro-American Literature,* vol. 1, pp. 322–42.

1857 • Frank J. Webb published (in England) the first novel to deal with the problems of Northern free blacks, *The Garies and Their Friends.* Its innovative themes include the first in-depth treatment of a mixed marriage, the first presentation of a lynch mob, and the first use of passing for white as a major theme. Little is known of Webb, who is associated with Philadelphia.

Source: Jackson, *A History of Afro-American Literature,* vol. 1, pp. 343–50.

1859 • Harriet E. Adams Wilson (c. 1827–70), was the first black woman to publish a novel. *Our Nig; or, Sketches from the Life of a Free Black, In a Two Story White House North, Showing That Slavery's Shadows Fall Even There* was published in Boston, where she was living alone, after her husband had abandoned her and her son. She hoped to realize money from the book to reunite herself with her son, but he died before this was accomplished. The book was also the first novel published in the United States by a black man or woman; William Wells Brown's *Clotel,* and Frank J. Webb's *The Garies and Their Friends* were both published in England. *Our Nig* presents social, racial, and economic brutality suffered by a free mulatto woman in the antebellum North.

Sources: Jackson, *A History of Afro-American Literature,* vol. 1, p. 351–63; *Notable Black American Women,* p. 1266–68; Shockley, *Afro-American Women Writers 1746–1933,* p. 84.

1930 • Nella Marian Larsen (1893–1964) was the first black woman recipient of a Guggenheim Fellowship in creative writing. Her novels, *Quicksand* (1928) and *Passing* (1929), were highly acclaimed. Both deal with the tragic mulatto theme. She treated black women characters in urban settings, and was the foremother to African-American novelists to follow her. Larsen was one of the first black women novelists to grapple with female sexuality and sexual politics.

Sources: Black Women in America, pp. 695–97; *Notable Black American Women,* pp. 652–57; Shockley, *Afro-American Women Writers 1746–1933,* p. 432.

1932 • Rudolph Fisher (1897–1934) was the first black writer to write a detective novel, *The Conjure Man Dies,* which revealed Fisher's medical and scientific knowledge in the denouement of the crime. Fisher took a M.D. at Howard University Medical School in 1924, became a radiologist, and died of cancer. He wrote a number of very good short stories, and two novels, in addition to his detective novel. He was considered one of the wittiest of the Harlem Renaissance group.

Sources: Brown, Davis, and Lee, *The Negro Caravan,* p. 54; Garrett, *Famous First Facts About Negroes,* p. 102; *Dictionary of American Negro Biography,* pp. 222–23.

1940 • *Native Son* by Richard Wright (1908–60) was the first book by a black selected by the Book of the Month Club. The book was an outstanding critical and popular success, and became a significant milepost. Born in poverty in Mississippi, Wright sought to escape ignorance and poverty with a move to Chicago. He became a member of the Federal Writers Project (1935), moved with the project to New York (1937), and won a Guggenheim Fellowship (1939). His works include *Uncle Tom's Children* (1938), which established his reputation and won him a five hundred dollar prize, and *Black Boy* (1945), another Book of the Month Club selection. Wright established himself later in Paris, where he continued to write.

Sources: Dictionary of American Negro Biography, pp. 674–75; Hughes and Bontemps, *The Poetry of the Negro 1746–1949,* p. 408; *Negro Almanac, 1989,* pp. 1021–22.

1949 • Frank Garvin Yerby (1916–91) was the first black to write a series of best-selling novels. Beginning with *The Foxes of Harrow* in 1949, he concentrated on costume novels, producing an annual best seller. The general reading public was unaware of his racial identity, and there is little in the novels to suggest it. In 1952, he established himself in Europe, principally in Spain, where he died.

Sources: Hornsby, *Milestones in 20th-Century African-American History,* p. 484; *Negro Almanac, 1989,* p. 1022; Wilson and Ferris, *Encyclopedia of Southern Culture,* p. 1143.

1953 • Ralph Waldo Ellison (1914–) was the first black to win the National Book Award for his novel, *Invisible Man.* Written in 1952, the book deals with a black man's "place" in a white man's world. Born in Oklahoma, he studied at Tuskegee Institute before going to New York in 1936. His novel also won the Russworm Award. He has published a collection of essays, Shadow and Act (1964).

Sources: *Black Writers,* pp. 176–83; *Encyclopedia Americana,* vol. 10, p. 255; *Negro Almanac, 1989,* pp. 989–90.

ALICE WALKER
(1944–)

1983 • Alice Walker (1944–) was the first black woman writer to win a Pulitzer Prize for a work of fiction. The novel, *The Color Purple,* was popular but controversial. It also won the American Book Award. Her third novel, *The Color Purple* was made into an Oscar-nominated movie, which intensified discussion among black men and women over her presentation of black men. Walker is also a poet, essayist, and short fiction writer. The Georgia-born writer was labeled a rebel and forced to leave Spelman College; she graduated from the more liberal Sarah Lawrence College in 1965, and worked in the civil rights movement in Mississippi after graduation. An ardent feminist, Walker uses the term "womanist" to describe her work.

Sources: *Black Writers,* pp. 571–73; Lanker, *I Dream a World,* p. 24; *Notable Black American Women,* pp. 1178–82; Wilson and Ferris, *Encyclopedia of Southern Culture,* p. 898.

PAMPHLETS

1829 • David Walker (1785–1830) published the first pamphlet by an American black calling for a slave revolt, *David Walker's Appeal.* Walker was a free black who had wandered across the South, before settling in Boston, as the proprietor of shop buying and selling second-hand clothing. Despite efforts to suppress it, *The Appeal* became one of the most widely circulated pamphlets of the time. The circulation of the work became a crime in the South, and a bounty was placed on Walker's life. In 1848, *The Appeal* was published with Henry Highland Garnet's *Address* (1843), another call to revolt, in a volume financially supported by John Brown.

Sources: *Dictionary of American Negro Biography,* pp. 622–23; Hornsby, *Chronology of African-American History,* p. 16; Jackson, *A History of Afro-American Literature,* vol. 1, pp. 100–2.

1852 • Martin Robinson Delany (1812–85) wrote the first major appeal for emigration: *The Condition, Elevation, Emigration and Destiny of the Colored People of the United States, Politically Considered.* In 1859, Delany wrote Blake, the first black nationalist novel, which today exists only in an incomplete form, with the last six chapters missing. (*See also* **Military: United States Army, 1865; Miscellaneous: Exploration, 1859.**)

Sources: Dictionary of American Negro Biography, pp. 169–72; Jackson, *A History of Afro-American Literature,* vol. 1, pp. 364–69; Robinson, *Historical Negro Biographies,* p. 72; Simmons, *Men of Mark,* pp. 1007–15; Smythe, *Black American Reference Book,* pp. 660–61.

NATIONALIST NOVELIST, MARTIN ROBINSON DELANY

POETRY

1746 • Lucy Terry (Prince) (c. 1730–1821), a slave, was the first black American poet. "Bars Fight," written this year (her only known poem), was inspired by an Indian ambush of haymakers in the Bars, a small plateau near Deerfield, Massachusetts. It was not published until 1855, in Josiah Gilbert Holland's *History of Western Massachusetts.* Terry was kidnapped as an infant in Africa and brought to Rhode Island. In 1756, Terry married Abijah Prince and obtained her freedom. She is also noted for her determined, if unsuccessful, attempt to persuade Williams College (Massachusetts) to accept her son as a student—she is reported to have argued before the board of trustees for three hours.

Sources: Jackson, A History of Afro-American Literature, vol. 1, pp. 29–33; *Notable Black American Women,* pp. 881–82; Shockley, *Afro-American Women Writers 1746–1933,* p. 13.

1760 • Jupiter Hammon (1711–1806?) was the first black to publish a poem, as a separate work, in America. This poem was the eighty-eight lines of "An Evening Thought. Salvation by Christ, with Penitential Cries: Composed by Jupiter Hammon, a Negro belonging to Mr.[Henry] Lloyd of Queen's Village on Long Island, the 25th of December, 1760." Born a slave on Long Island, Hammon revealed an intensely religious conviction of the Methodist variety in this and his other publications.

Sources: Dictionary of American Negro Biography, pp. 281–82; Garrett, *Famous First Facts About Negroes,* p. 98; Jackson, *A History of Afro-American Literature,* vol. 1, pp. 33–37.

**PHILLIS
WHEATLEY
(C. 1753–84)**

1773 • Phillis Wheatley (c.1753–84), born on the west coast of Africa, published the first book of poetry by a black person in America (and the second published by a woman). *Poems on Various Subjects, Religious and Moral* was published in London, England. A Boston merchant, John Wheatley, had bought Phillis as a child of about seven or eight, and had allowed her to learn to read and write. Wheatley's first published poem, "On the Death of the Reverend George Whitefield," appeared in 1770 in a Boston broadside. In 1773, she traveled abroad with the Wheatleys' son, partially in the hope of restoring her health with exposure to sea air, and she attracted considerable attention in England as a poet. It was at about this time that she was freed. Deaths had ended the connection with the Wheatley family by 1788, when she married a freeman, John Peters. Her first two children died, and at the end of her life she worked as a maid in a boarding house to support herself. She died in December, followed the same day by her third child, an infant.

Sources: *Dictionary of American Negro Biography*, pp. 640–43; Jackson, *A History of Afro-American Literature*, vol. 1, pp. 38–46; *Notable Black American Women*, p. 1243–48.

1829 • George Moses Horton (1797–1883?) was the first Southern black to publish a collection of poetry. *The Hope of Liberty,* containing twenty-one poems, was published in Raleigh, North Carolina. He anticipated proceeds from this volume would pay his way to Liberia. As with all his attempts at gaining freedom before Emancipation, this did not succeed. Somehow Horton managed to educate himself and establish a connection with the University of North Carolina in Chapel Hill. He was able to purchase his own time from his owners at twenty-five cents a day, later fifty cents. A tolerated character at the university, he seems to have earned part of his money by writing poems for undergraduates.

Sources: *Dictionary of American Negro Autobiography*, pp. 327–28; Jackson, *A History of Afro-American Literature*, vol. 1, pp. 83–100.

OPPOSITE PAGE:
THE FIRST BLACK
WOMAN TO WRITE A
PUBLISHED SHORT
STORY, FRANCES
ELLEN WATKINS
HARPER GAINED
WIDESPREAD RECOG-
NITION FOR HER
POETRY AND HER
NOVEL, IOLA LEROY.

1877 • Albery Allson Whitman (1851–1902) was the first black American poet to publish a poem more than five thousand lines long, *Not a Man and Yet a Man.* Born a slave near Munfordville, Kentucky, Whitman began life as a laborer, and had only a few months' formal education. He nevertheless became a very effective African Methodist Episcopal preacher. Alcoholism contributed to the shortness of his life. Whitman is considered the finest black poet of the Reconstruction era. (Whitman's poem was surpassed in length by some 3,500 lines with the publication of Robert E. Ford's *Brown Chapel, A Story in Verse,* in 1903.)

Sources: Brown, Davis, and Lee, *The Negro Caravan*, p. 297; *Dictionary of American Negro Biography*, pp. 650–51; Jackson, *A History of Afro-American Literature*, vol. 1, pp. 272–92.

**GWENDOLYN
BROOKS
(1917–)**

1950 • Gwendolyn Brooks (1917–), poet and novelist, was the first black to win a Pulitzer Prize for poetry with *Annie Allen*. She became established as a major American poet, and in 1976, she was the first black woman inducted into the National Institute of Arts and Letters. A sensitive interpreter of Northern ghetto life, she began to write poetry at age seven; her first poems were published in the *Chicago Defender*. From 1969 on, she has promoted the idea that blacks must develop their own culture. She changed her writing style in an effort to become accessible to the ordinary black reader. She was poet laureate of Illinois for sixteen years, and is poetry consultant to the Library of Congress.

Sources: Garrett, *Famous First Facts About Negroes,* p. 103; Hughes and Bontemps, *The Poetry of the Negro 1746–1949,* p. 390; *Notable Black American Women,* pp. 105–09.

1993 • Maya Angelou was the first black inaugural poet, at the swearing in of President Bill Clinton on January 20. (*See also* **Arts: Dramatists, 1970.**) Her poem was published as *On the Pulse of Morning* soon after the ceremony. Robert Frost was the first poet to read at the inauguration of a president, John F. Kennedy.

Sources: Jet (8 February 1993), pp. 4–10; (Nashville) *Tennessean* (20 January 1993); *USA Today* (21 January 1993).

SHORT STORIES

1853 • Frederick Douglass (1817–95) wrote the first short story published by a black, "The Heroic Slave." It appeared in four installments in his newspaper, *The North Star.* This long short story, almost a novella, is based on the real-life exploit of Madison Washington, a recaptured fugitive slave, who took the lead in seizing the ship on which he was being sent to be sold from Virginia to Louisiana, and regained his freedom by sailing the vessel to Nassau. (*See also* **Government—Federal Firsts: Political Parties, 1866.**) for further information.)

Source: Blyden Jackson, *A History of Afro-American Literature,* vol. 1, pp. 118–20.

1859 • Frances Ellen Watkins Harper (1825–1911) wrote "The Two Offers," the first short story published by a black woman in the United States. It appeared in the *Anglo-African* magazine in 1859. Harper was born in Baltimore, Maryland, of free parents. She became a noted speaker in the abolition movement, and after the Civil War supported the suffrage and temperance movements. She was an extremely successful poet—*Poems on*

Miscellaneous Subjects is reported to have sold fifty thousand copies by 1878—and her novel *Iola Leroy* (1892) had three editions printed.

Sources: Brown, Davis, and Lee, *The Negro Caravan,* p. 293; *Dictionary of American Negro Biography,* pp. 289–90; Hughes and Bontemps, *The Poetry of the Negro 1746–1949,* p. 397; Jackson, *A History of Afro-American Literature,* vol. 1, pp. 265–72; 392–97; *Notable Black American Women,* pp. 457–62; Shockley, *Afro-American Women Writers 1746–1933,* p. 56.

INDEX BY YEAR

35
first person identified as a black convert to Christianity, 320

186
first pope identified as an African, 320

410
first saint whose black identity is well established, 321

622
first muezzin of Islam, 327

1536
first black to traverse the southern portion of the United States, 262

1539
first black to explore Arizona and New Mexico, 262

1565
first permanent dwelling place for blacks in present United States, 194

1619
first blacks arrive in Virginia to be sold as indentured servants, 77

1622
first known free blacks, 77

1623
first known black child baptized in the colonies, 319

1626
first blacks in New York City, 205

1630
Massachusetts passed the first law protecting slaves who fled brutal treatment, 131

1640
first known black slave, 77

1641
first baptism of a black in New England performed, 304

first colony to legalize slavery (Massachusetts), 77, 131

1642
first law against fugitive slaves, 77

1643
first intercolony agreement about fugitive slaves, 77

1644
first known attempt to decree by law that baptism did not lead to slaves' freedom, 78

1651
first black landowners in Virginia, 77

first black to enter Virginia as a free man, 77

1652
first law regulating black servitude was passed by the General Court of Election (Rhode Island), 146

1653
first black on record as a slave owner, 77

1663

first major consipracy between black slaves and indentured servants, 74

1664

act drafted declaring baptism of slaves does not lead to their freedom (Maryland), 304

1667

first trained black physician in New Amsterdam, 350

1688

first formal abolitionist document, 67

1693

first known example of ethnic religious association, 319

1704

first catechism school opened for blacks in New York City, 319

1706

first black to introduce inoculation against smallpox to the American Colonies, 350

1712

first major slave revolt in New York City, 74

1720

first insurrection of slaves in South Carolina, 75

1730

efforts undertaken to instruct black catholics, 312

1734

first known black to obtain a European medical doctorate, 87

1739

first major black insurrection in South Carolina, 75

1743

first known black Baptist, 304

first known school to train black missionaries, 319

1746

first black American poet, 417

1750

first free school for blacks, 105

1757

first organized activity of Presbyterians among blacks, 335

1758

first known black Baptist congregation 304

first two known black converts (one being a woman) to the Methodism movement, 328

1760

first black American writer of prose, 409

first black to publish a poem as a separate work, 417

1764

first black American to compose in the European tradition, 9

first Methodist society in the colonies, 328

1770s

first black classical composer of note, 9

1773

first black Baptist church under black leadership formed in Silver Bluff, South Carolina, 304

first book of poetry published by a black person in America, 418

first recognized black physician in the United States, 350

1774

first act passed forbidding the importation of black slaves, 132

1775

first abolition society, 289

first black Masons, 291

first black to win a battle commendation, 238

first blacks to participate in armed phase of American Revolution, 238

first known black Baptist missionary, 305

first regiment of slave soldiers promised freedom by the British forces, 238

1777
first state to abolish slavery, 67, 150

1778
first and only all-black regiment in Revolutionary War, 238

1780
first attested black mutual aid society, 283

first blacks protest the denial of suffrage by refusing to pay taxes, 132

1781
first major American City founded with a majority black population, 190

first sermon preached by a black to a congregation of Methodists, 328

1783
first black Baptist church in Nova Scotia established, 305

law suit filed that gave blacks civil equality in Massachusetts, 132

one of first black music teachers in United States, 9

1784
first black to sail as master of his own ship, 64

first sermon preached by a black to a white congregation, 328

1785
first black Congregational minister, 320

first black Methodist churches in Baltimore, 329

1786
first black corresponding member of the French Academy of Sciences, 271

first evidence of an underground railroad, 78

1787
Continental Congress prohibited slavery in the Northwest Territory, 142

first black organization of note, 284

first church to install a segregated gallery, 329

first free secular school in New York City, 105

Free African Society organized in Philadelphia, 329

1788
first black organization to advocate black emigration to Africa, 290

1790
first known black mutual aid soiety in South Carolina, 284

1791
African Baptist Church of Petersburg, Virginia, was officially recognized, 306

first black fighter on record, 379

first successful slave revolt in Haiti to result in liberation, 75

1792
first black known to be employed as a preacher by a racially mixed congregation, 306

first black man to issue an almanac, 359

first building built for the purpose of black worship in Savannah, Georgia, 306

1794
first all-black church for persons who eventually stayed in the Methodist Episcopal Church, 330

first black hymnal compiled, 299

first black Protestant Episcopal church, 321

first known Sunday catechism classes for blacks, 312

1796
first African Chapel for Methodists organized, 301

1797

first antislavery petition presented to Congress, 67

1798

first black portrait painter to win recognition in America, 30

first black to invent a novel sail-handling device, 343

first major black-owned sailmaking shop, 56

first slave narrative written by a black American, 409

1799

first black ordained deacon in the Methodist Episcopal Church, 330

1800

first camp meetings to inaugurate the Great Western Revival, 335

first Methodist church established in Fayetteville, North Carolina, 330

1801

Ezion Church established, 303

first African Methodist Episcopal Zion Church was incorporated, 302

first black hymnal compiled, 299

first black Presbyterian missionary in the South, 335

1803

first publication of a musical composition by a black American, 9

1804

first black to reach mouth of the Columbia River overland, 262

first black to receive an honorary degree in the United States, 104

1805

first black to become a prominent boxer in England, 379

1806

first black Baptist congregation in Boston, 306

first known black jockey, 393

first major building in Boston to be constructed entirely by blacks, 341

1807

first all-black Presbyterian church was organized in Philadelphia, 335

1810

first known black insurance company, 52

1811

first systematic attempt by a black to resettle blacks in Sierra Leone, 268

1812

first black Baptist church west of the Mississippi River organized, 306

1815

first black pastor of a Methodist church, 299

1816

first bishop of AME elected (but declined the position), 300

first bishop of AME, 300

first black English-speaking settler in California, 268

first black missionary to the Wyandotte Indians, 330

1817

first abolitionist newspaper, 219

first woman to preach in AME church, 300

1818

first black American musician to publish sheet music, 10

first slave in Tennessee to be licensed as a preacher by the Presbyterians, 336

first widely recognized black furniture maker in deep South, 56

1819

first African missionary associated with the AME, 300

first black Protestant Episcopal church in New York City, 321

1820

first all-black Congregational church, 320

first African Methodist Episcopal Conference started, 302

first and only open anti-slavery declaration by a Methodist church, 302

first antislavery magazine, 227

1821

first black Baptist missionary to Africa, 307

first black Presbyterian church established in New York City, 336

first black theatrical company, 42

first black to receive a patent, 343

1822

first bishop of the African Methodist Episcopal Zion Church, 302

first pastor of the African Baptist Church, Albany, New York, 307

first slave revolt leader of note, 75

1823

first known black to graduate from an American college, 88

first play written by a black performed in the United States, 42

1824

first attempt to build a community of black nuns, 312

1826

first black actor to attain international renown, 42

first black to reach California by overland travel, 268

1828

first black church to own an organ, 321

first black graduate of Princeton Theological Seminary, 336

first black women's charitable group, 284

1829

first black priest to do missionary work in the South, 321

first boarding school for black girls, 105

first pamphlet by an American black calling for a slave revolt, 416

first permanent order of black Catholic nuns, 312

first Southern black to publish a collection of poetry, 418

1830

first National Negro Convention, 71

1831

first black to establish a prominent shipbuilding firm, 64

first slave revolt of magnitude, 76

1832

first black women's antislavery society, 67

first hospital and asylum established for aged and afflicted blacks, 342

1833

first American-born woman to speak publicly on political themes, 67

first black woman to lecture in defense of women's rights, 68

first college in the United States founded with a mission to educate blacks, 98

1834

first all-black Baptist association of churches, 308

first known black bookseller, 62

1836

first black to be ordained by an American bishop, 313

first black to become an elder (priest) in the Mormon church, 333

first black to publish a history book, 409

1837

first black to obtain an M.D. degree, 351

1838

first black periodical, 227

first known black regular anti-slavery lecturer and first major black abolitionist, 68

1839
first slave revolt at sea that led to legal freedom, 76

1840s
first American musician of any race to take a musical group abroad to perform in Europe, 10

first black editor tried for libel, 219

first black to give formal band concerts, 10

first black to win wide acclaim as a musician in the United States and Europe, 10

1840
first known black to command an American whaling ship, 64

1841
first history of black people written for children by a black man, 410

first issue of the oldest continually published black periodical, 227

1842
first appearance in print of Frederick Douglass, 78

first black American landscape painter to win accalaim at home and abroad, 30

first highly publicized fugitive slave trial, 345

1843
first black Catholic association whose documentation has been preserved, 313

first black newspaper, 219

first black newspaper west of the Alleghenies, 219

first black Oddfellows lodge, 293

production of sugar revolutionized, 344

1844
first black to receive a bachelor's degree from Oberlin College, 88

1845
first black dance star, 3

first black formally admitted to the bar, 132

first black to hold a diplomatic post, 59

first collection of American black poets, 411

1846
first building constructed for hydropathic treatments in the United States, 351

first hotel in San Francisco, 59

first known black Baptist church in Canada, 308

first known organization in St. Louis dedicated to the overthrow of slavery, 68

1847
first AME church in Chicago, Illinois, 300

first black to graduate from an American medical school, 351

first blacks to settle in Salt Lake Valley, 268

first horse race in California, 59

first steamboat in California, 59

1848
first public school in California, 59

invention of an improved whaling harpoon, 344

1849
first black faculty member on a white college campus, 96

first petition filed to abolish segregated schools, 106

1850
first AME church in California, 300

first black woman to graduate from college, 88

first president of the American League of Colored Workers, 53

first to introduce potato chips, 264

1852
first black woman to obtain a degree from a four-year college, 88

first book of travel by a black, 414

first dramatic work written by an American black, 414

first major appeal for emigration by a black, 417

1853

first black singer to give a command performance before royalty, 10

first black woman journalist, editor, and publisher, 228

first black YMCA organized in Washington, DC, 284

first novel by a black American published in England, 414

first short story published by a black, 420

1854

first American black to be ordained in the Catholic church, 313

first black social organization south of the Ohio River, 293

first black to join a medical society, 295

first successful suit to end segregation on street cars, 70

incorporation of Lincoln University, 99

1855

first black candidate for New York state office, 138

first black history based on written documentation, 410

first black newspaper in California, 190, 219

first black to win an elective office, 176

first major city to eliminate segregated schools, 106

first substantial historical work published by a black man in America, 153

first woman admitted as corresponding member of black convention movement, 228

1856

Wilberforce University was incorporated, 99

1857

first clear declaration by Supreme Court that black were not citizens of the United States, 70

first novel by a black to deal with problems of Northern free blacks, 414

1858

first black Methodist Episcopal missionary bishop, 331

first black pianist to win national fame, 11

first black labor organization on record, 53

first college south of the Ohio river that was established specifically to educate blacks and whites together, 99

first play published by a black American, 414

first play written by a black American, 43

1859

first black American explorer in Africa, 262

first black director of physical culture at Harvard University, 384

first black nationalist novel, 417

first largely black Shaker family established in Philadelphia, 340

first published novel written by a black woman, 414

first short story published by black in the United States, 420

1860

first black Pony Express riders, 268

1861

first black organization chartered south of the Ohio River, 293

first black to fight with Union forces during Civil War, 241

first black to hold a federal position, 153

first black wounded in the Civil War, 237

first teacher supported by the American Missionary Association, 106

1862

first abolition of slavery in the District of Columbia, 68

first black troops to fight a skirmish in Civil War, 241

first black woman to earn a B.A. degree at Oberlin College, 88

first regiment of black soldiers raised in Civil War, 241

first seamen, 53

1863

first and only black to attain the rank of captain in the navy, 251 first battles to demonstrate the worth of black troops in combat, 242

first black army nurse in United States history, 358

first black chaplain in army, 243

first black commissioned army officer, 243

first black commissioned medial officer, 242

first black president of a black college, 80

first black regiment raised in North during Civil War, 242

first black surgeon in the United States Army, 351

first black to earn Medal of Honor in Civil War, 242

first black woman to be appointed principal in the New York public school system, 106

first exclusively black parish in the United States, 313

first major engagment seen by black troops in Civil War, 242

1864

first and only black correspondent for a major daily during the Civil War, 220

first black awarded the Naval Medal of Honor, 251

first black daily newspaper, 220

first black museum assistant at the Smithsonian Institution, 342

first black teacher in Fayette County, Pennsylvania, 142

first black woman awarded a medical degree, 352

1865

first black American to receive an earned doctorate, 88

first black appointed to Coast Guard, 249

first black commissioned field officer in the army, 243

first black Confederate troops, 237

first black elected to office in the United States, 142

first black man admitted to practice before the U.S. Supreme Court, 167

first black man to preach in the rotunda of the Capitol to the House of Representatives, 170

first black principal of Avery Normal Institute (South Carolina), 107

first black to head a U.S. hospital, 351

first black to receive an appointment from the federal government as inspector of customs for the Port of New Orleans, 153

first permanent black minstrel company, 43

1866

first black admitted to the Pennsylvania bar, 146

first black delegate to a national political convention, 170

first blacks elected to a state legislature, 132

first institution of higher learning for blacks in Florida, 99

first granting of citizenship to blacks by legislation, 70

first institution of higher learning for blacks in Mississippi, 99

Missouri's first tax-supported school for blacks, 154

first known black woman property owner in Los Angeles, 61

first major black shipfitting company, 64

1867

black men first granted the right to vote, 70

first black delegate to international convention of the YMCA, 284

first black units in regular army, 243

black baseball begins, 365

first black college founded in Tennessee, and still in existence, 99

first black graduate of the Female Medical College of Pennsylvania, 352

first black school to establish undergraduate, graduate, and professional schools, 99

first college open to blacks in Alabama, 100

first known intercity baseball contest, 365

first national organization of black Baptists, 308

1868

first black elected to Congress, 172

first black in Mississippi to be accused of the murder of a white man and acquitted by an all-white jury, 134 first black lieutenant governor of Louisiana, 129

first black South Carolina secretary of state, 146

first granting of citizenship and equal protection under the law for blacks, 71

first law department established at a black school, 105

first university open to all races, 102

first state legislative body with a black majority, 146

1869

first attempt to build a national black labor organization, 53

first black baseball team to play an all-white club, 365

first black commanding general of the South Carolina National Guard, 237

first black diplomat (minister resident to Haiti), 154

first black to graduate from Harvard Law School, 88

first black to receive an honorary degree from Howard University, 351

first black to serve as a United States postmaster, 154

first black woman to head a major educational institution for blacks, 107

first Presbyterian church to split from the white denomination in the South, 336

1870

first bishops of the Colored (now Christian) Methodist Episcopal Church, 331

first black admitted to West Point, 250

first black American barrister admitted to practice before English courts, 220

first black American sculptor to study abroad, 36

first black elected to Congress to represent South Carolina, 173

first black mayor of Natches and possibly first black mayor in the United States, 203

first black minister nominated for appointment to Liberia, 154

first black state supreme court justice in the United States, 146

first black teacher to be engaged by the Freedmen's Aid Society, 96

first black to earn the Medal of Honor in Indian campaigns, 243

first black to graduate from Harvard University, 88

first black to teach white college students in Kentucky, 96

first black U.S. senator, 174

first black votes as a result of the adoption of the Fifteenth Amendment, 71

first black woman to graduate from a New York state medical school, 352

first state school for blacks, 107

1871

first black artist to exhibit in Rome, 36

first black congressman ever elected from the state of Florida, 173

first black elected to any public office in Cook County, Illinois, 124

first black Masonic lodge recognized by white Masonry, 294

first black minister to Liberia, 154

first black president of a predominantly white university, 88

first black to found a large integrated city in the United States, 214

first black to hold a professional position at the Library of Congress, 154

first black to speak in the House of Representatives as a congressman, 175

first college founded as a land grant college for blacks, 100

1872

first African Methodist Episcopal church in Los Angeles, 61

first black appointed to municipal court, 190

first black appointed to Naval Academy, 251

first black fire company in Northern cities, 197

first black graduate of the Medical School of the University of Michigan, 352

first black police officer in Chicago, 197

first black state governor of Louisiana, 129

first black to be nominated as a vice presidential candidate, 170 first black woman admitted to practice before the Supreme Court (Washington, DC), 153

first black woman lawyer in the United States, 153

first black woman to establish a medical practice in Pennsylvania, 352

patenting of lubricator for steam engines, 344

1873

first black congressman from Mississippi, 175

first black elected municipal court judge, 190

first black member of the Tennessee state house of representatives, 147

first black opera troupe organized to present complete operas, 11

first black to preside over a national nominating convention, 175

first black woman doctor to be formally certified, 352

1874

first black bishop in any Episcopal church, 321

first black elected to a full term in the U.S. Senate, 175

first black to preside over the U.S. House of Representatives, 173

first black to receive a doctorate from an American university, 89

first state-supported institution in the United States to train black teachers, 100

1875

first black Catholic bishop of Portland, ME, 314

first black U.S. congressman for North Carolina, 176

first jockey of any race to win the Kentucky Derby, 393

1876

first black student branch of YMCA, 284

first black to achieve full recognition in America as a painter, 31

first black who claimed to be rodeo champion, 402

first medical school founded solely for the education of blacks, 349

first monument dedicated to a black by blacks, 259

1877

first black elected to Phi Beta Kappa, 271

first black graduate of West Point, 250

first black to graduate from Rogers High School in Newport, Rhode Island, 107

first black to publish a poem over five thousand lines long, 418

first normal school for blacks in North Carolina, 100

1878

first black man to play Uncle Tom on the stage, 6

first black newspaper in Chicago, 220

first black newspaper in Kansas, 220

first black to compose a song that became an official state song, 11

first black to preside over the U.S. Senate, 176

first important book on blacks in music, 413

first known black professional baseball player, 365

John Jasper preached for the first time his famous sermon "De Sun Do Move," 308

1879

first black American certified to teach in the public schools of Rhode Island, 107

first black graduate nurse in the United States, 358

first black to enter the college department of the University of Pennsylvania, 89

first known black to set a United States record for marathon walking, 396

1880

Baptist Foreign Mission Convention of the United States of America formed, 308

first and only all-black Coast Guard facility, 249

first black lawyer to argue a case before the Supreme Court, 186

1881

first black American scholar to publish a Greek language textbook, 413

first black college varsity baseball player, 365

first black doctor to serve the president of the United States, 342

first black elected to Indiana's house of representatives, 126

first black in minor league baseball, 365

first black surgeon-in-chief to head a civilian hospital, 342

first black to serve as recorder of deeds, 170

first building in Texas and west of the Mississippi built to educate blacks, 87

first institution of higher education established to educate black women, 100

first passage of "Jim Crow" legislation, 71, 147

first privately-run hospital in the United States exclusively for blacks, 343

1882

first black elected to state office outside the deep South (Kansas State auditor), 128

first black graduate of the University of Pennsylvania, 343

first major history of blacks in America, 410

patent on a paper bag manufacturing device, 345

patenting of the first cost-efficient method for producing carbon filaments for electric lights, 345

1883

first all-black incorporated town, 194

first black caucus in the Protestant Episcopal Church, 322

first black to graduate from the University of Pennsylvania with a B.A., 89

first black to patent an improved window ventilator for railroad cars, 345

patenting of the first successful shoe lasting machine, 345

1884

first black American to gain recognition as a photographer, 31

first black chaplain in the regular army, 243

first black editor of the *Southwestern Christian Advocate* of the Methodist Episcopal Church, 331

first black medical society, 295

telephone transmitter patent, 345

1885

first black admitted to the Philadelphia Medical Society, 343

first black represents a majority white constituency in a state, 142

first black to sit in the American House of Bishops, 322

first patent of the first known black woman inventor, 346

first publication of the oldest continually published non-church newspaper, 220

first steam saw and planing mill owned and operated entirely by blacks, 56

1886

first black holiness church, 326

first black officer in Coast Guard, 249

first black priest to be widely known and publicized celebrated his first mass in the United States, 314

first black to win a national boxing crown, 379

first meeting of the American National Baptist Convention, 309

first nursing school for black women, 358

1887

first black mayor of Mound Bayou, MS, 203

first gymnasium erected on a black college campus, 87

first known blacks to participate in a rodeo, 403

1888

first black newspaper to feature portraits and cartoons, 220

first black employed by YMCA, 285

first black to be nominated as a presidential candidate, 170

first black to graduate from the University of Pennsylvania Law School, 90 first black Virginian elected to the House of Representatives, 176

first black-created and black-run banks, 50

1889

first black bank in Tennessee, 50

first black elected to the Washington legislature, 151

first black graduate of Williams College, 206

first black on the Illinois State Board of Health, 353

first black physician to pass the California state boards, 353

first black professional baseball team, 365

first black to be appointed to a major Illinois state job, 125

first black to earn Ph.D. in biology, 89

first black to serve as U.S. minister to Haiti, 170

first known black range boss, 267

first lasting black opera company, 11

first black to graduate from the Spencerian College of Commerce (Philadelphia), 285

first meeting of the Catholic Afro-American Lay Congress, 314

1890

first black known to have set a record in steer roping, 403

first black man reputed to be a millionaire, 62

first black postmistress in the United States, 154

first black world champion in boxing, 380

first black-owned bank in Alabama, 50

first jockey of any race to win the Kentucky Derby three times, 394

first recorded black players on a white college football team, 384

1891

first American hospital operated by blacks, 343

first black assistant city prosecuting attorney in Chicago, 197

first black man to hold an American title in any sport, 380

first black priest ordained in the United States, 314

first black to form what may have been a real jazz band, 11

first minstrel show to introduce black women into the cast (and one of first in which black performers did not wear black face), 43

first schools of nursing for blacks attached to hospitals, 358

first theatrical presentation of the cake walk, 43

1892

first black All-American football player, 384

first black elected to the state legislature from Omaha, Nebraska, 136

first editor of the first black medical journal in the nation, 353

first hotel to provide needles, thread, buttons, and cologne in guest rooms, 267

first recorded black college football game, 385

1893

first Aunt Jemima and first living trademark, 49

first black branch of YWCA, 285

first black diplomat appointed to a white republic (Bolivia), 155

first black graduate of Oberlin Conservatory of Music, 89

first black poet to gain national fame, 411

first black secretary of International YMCA, 284

first black to earn Ph.D. in Latin, 92

first formal organization for black Presbyterians in the North, 336

world's first successful heart operation, 353

first life insurance company to reach one hundred million dollars in assets, 52

1894

first black to graduate from Iowa State College, 261

1895

first black member of the Chicago Women's Club, 198

first black to earn a Ph.D. from Harvard University and the first to receive a Ph.D. in history, 90

first black woman to serve on the Washington, DC, Board of Education, 107

first meeting of the National Conference of Colored Women, 290

first national black medical association, 295

first special exhibit of the inventions of blacks, 346

National Baptist Convention, USA, held its first meeting in Atlanta, 309

Philadelphia's first hospital primarily for blacks founded, 343

1896

first black athlete known to write a book, 385

first black on the medical staff in a nonsegregated hospital, 353

first black on the medical staff of Chicago's Cook County Hospital, 353

first black recipient of an honorary degree from Harvard University, 104

first black to earn a Ph.D. in Greek and Latin, 92

first scientific historical monography by a black American, 410

founding of the Church of God and Saints of Christ, 311

1897

first black show to play on Broadway and escape playing in burlesque theaters, 43

first black to graduate from Vassar College, 90

first black to patent a coupling device for railroad cars, 346

first black to serve on the District of Columbia's Board of Medical Examiners, 342

first national black learned society, 271

first piano rag by a black published, 12

1898

first and only black sailor to receive the Naval Medal of Honor, 252

first black chaplain in the United States Army in 1863, 301

first black musical comedy, 43

first black show to be organized, produced, and managed by blacks, 43

first blacks to earn Medal of Honor in Spanish-American War, 244

first Methodist woman to be ordained an elder, 302

first native-born black American to win a major bicycle race, 384

first prominent black churchman to declare that God is black, 301

first show to introduce syncopated ragtime music to New York City theatergoers, 44

1899

first black to arrange an interstate tennis tournament for black players, 404

first winner of the new one-and-one-quarter-mile Kentucky Derby, 394

first YMCA building built for blacks, 284

1900

first black woman to graduate from Smith College, 91

1901

first black player in the American League, 365

first black to record with Victor Talking Machine Company, 12

first black welterweight champion, 380

1902

first American-born black to win a world boxing crown, 380

first and only continuous written record of activities of black nurses, 358

first appearance of blacks in film, 6

first black judge in Washington, DC, and first at any level, 215

first black to sing the blues in a professional show, 13

1903

first black dance band to record, 13

first black woman to be a bank president, 50

1904

first black Greek letter organization, 294

first black military attaché in the United States, 244

first black professional football player, 385

first black to represent the United States in the Olympic Games, 396

first president of National Association of Teachers in Colored Schools, 274

railroad brake patent, 346

1905

first black appointed by a president to hold office north of the Mason-Dixon line, 155

first black to open Harlem to black residents, 62

first black-owned theater in the United States, 44

first issue of the *Chicago Defender,* 220

first known American film with an all-black cast, 6

first meeting of Niagara Movement, 290

first person to recognize bones of extinct bison near Folsom, New Mexico, 267

first singing band, first dancing conductor, and first drummer to perform stunts while drumming, 13

first syncopated music show, 13

1906

first black athletic association was organized, 363

first black repertory company in this century, 44

first black American to hold the rank of lieutenant colonel, 244

first black president of Gammon Theological Seminary, 81

first black to earn the Ph.D. in sociology, 92

first influential revival to emphasize the centrality of speaking in tongues, 334

first intercollegiate Greek letter fraternity, 294

1907

first black Rhodes scholar, 79

first secretary for black student affairs of YWCA, 285

1908

first black American architect registered in New York State, 1

first black Greek letter sorority, 294

first black heavyweight boxing champion, 380

first black teacher honored by the Jeanes Teacher Program, 108

first black-owned bank in Chicago, 50

first convention of Alpha Phi Alpha, 294

first intercity basketball competition between black clubs, 374

1909

first black American to receive a Ph.D. from a German University, 93

first black army bandmasters, 244

first black college basketball teams, 374

first black man to reach the North Pole, 262

first black national Catholic fraternal order, 294

first editor of the *Journal of the National Medical Association,* 359

first issue of the *New York Amsterdam News,* 221

first written blues composition and first popular song to use a jazz break, 14

organizational meeting of the NAACP held in New York City, 290

1910

first black to achieve fame as a syndicated cartoonist, 1

first black to receive feature billing in the Ziegfield Follies, 12

first black woman to become a millionaire, 56

first issue of *Crisis* magazine, 228

1911

first black appointed to a sub-Cabinet post, 155

first Ph.D. in sociology from an organized graduate school, 92

National Urban league formed, 291

1912

first black to hold the record for the 100-yard dash, 405

first black to patent a safety hood and smoke protector, 347 first black to win an intercollegiate weight championship, 406

first black woman to own and publish a newspaper, 222

first blues composition published, 14

1913

first and only black invited to become a charter member of the American College of Surgeons, 353

first black member of American College of Surgeons, 296

first chartered black bank in Georgia, 51

first separate list of black inventors published, 347

first step to the appearance, or the reappearance, of various forms of black Islam, 327

1914

Father Divine first proclaimed himself God, 334

first black justice of the peace in California, 244

first black mass movement organization, 72

first black to play the title role in a film, *Uncle Tom's Cabin,* 6

first black to star in a movie, 12

1915

first and only black Catholic college, 100

first black alderman in Chicago, 197

first black American woman to sing on radio, 7

first black stock company in New York in this century, 44

first black to receive the Spingarn Medal, 263

first black woman to organize a professional black stock dramatic company, 44

first executive director of the Association for the Study of Negro Life and History, 411

first known black athlete on a varsity rowing team, 384

first learned society dedicated to the professional study of black history, 271

first president of the National Baptist Convention, Unincorporated, 309

first published jazz arrangement, 14

first verifiable spiritual congregation, 339

1916

first American black historical research journal, 411

first black to earn a Ph.D. in physiology and zoology, 89

first black to manufacture cars, 49

first black to play in the Rose Bowl, 386

first issue of the *Journal of Negro History,* 272

first known play written by a black American and presented on stage by black actors in this century, 44

first military person to be honored with Spingarn Medal, 244

1917

first allied regiment to reach the Rhine in World War I, 245

first and only official black war correspondent during World War I, 228

first army camp for training black officers in World War I, 245

first black assistant attorney-general in Illinois, 125

first black bandleader in the U.S. Navy, 252

first black elected to the New York assembly, 138

first black officer in the New York National Guard, 238

first black to sing in Boston's Symphony Hall, 15

first black troops to arrive in France during World War I, 245

first book devoted exclusively to black art and literature, 413

first black soldiers awarded the French croix de guerre, 245

first black delegate seated at International Council of Women, 263

first black to earn a Ph.D. in German, 92

first black to earn a ship master's license, 267

first black to star in a major American play, 45

first black woman national champion in any sport, 404

first black woman to make a record, 35

first blues song ever recorded, 35

first players to win the all-black American Tennis Association, 404

first presentation by black actors of serious drama to a mainstream audience, 44

first settlement house for blacks with a black staff, 267

1918

first black suffragan bishops of the Protestant Episcopal Church, 322

first black woman admitted to the Iowa bar, 128

1919

African Orthodox Church was organized, 303

first black appointed to a New York City municipal hospital, 354

first black lawyer in charge of an important case for the NAACP, 117

first black player-coach in professional football, 386

first black to serve in the California legislature, 118

1920

claim that blacks were Ethiopians who would fulfill a Biblical prophecy to return to their homeland, 326

first black elected to the Missouri legislature in modern times, 136

first black elected to the New Jersey legislature, 137

first black Olympic medalist from Great Britain, 396

first black to obtain a degree in neurology, 354

first black ward committeeman in Chicago, 125

first black woman admitted to the Illinois bar, 125

first elected bishops by the United Methodist Church for service in the U.S., 331

first successful black professional baseball league organized, 366

1921

first black graduate of Hamline University, 207

first black member of the American Bankers Association, 275

first black owned and operated record company, 15

first black to earn a Ph.D. in economics, 92

first black to earn a Ph.D. in English, 92

first black to receive the Most Valuable College Player Award, 386

first black woman to earn a Ph.D. in German, 92

first black woman to gain a pilot's license, 255

first person of any race to long-jump more than 25 feet, 406

first three black American women to earn a Ph.D. degree, 93

1922

first black appointed to head a Veterans Administration hospital, 354

first black Democrat elected to any political office, 138

first black roentgenologist in New York City, 354

first black spiritual denomination, 339

first black woman member of the New York City Board of Education, 108

first black woman stunt pilot, 255

first black woman to receive the Spingarn medal, 263

first instrumental jazz recording, 15

first woman assistant prosecutor in Chicago, 125

1923

first black professional basketball team, 374

first black show to introduce the Charleston to nonblack audiences, 3

first black to participate in automobile racing, 363

first black to sing with a major symphony orchestra, 15

first male to record the blues guitar, 16

first nonmusical play by a serious black writer to reach Broadway, 45

first record by a black to sell over a million copies, 16

first separate and segregated seminary to train black priests, 314 three-way automatic traffic signal patent, 347

1924

first black American to pass the foreign service examination, 155

first black and first woman to serve on Chicago Library Board, 198

first black elected to the Illinois Senate, 125

first black in Olympic history to win an individual gold medal, 396

first black musician to perform on the Grand Ole Opry radio show, 17

first black to achieve recognition for performance on the soprano saxophone, 16

first black to give a recital at Carnegie Hall, 15

first man to achieve success as a recorded blues guitarist, 16

first world series between Negro league clubs, 367

1925

first black state-supported liberal arts college, 101

first black to earn a Ph.D. in French, 92

first black to earn a Ph.D. with a concentration in history, 92

first major nationwide black union, 53

first president of the National Bar Association, 275

1926

first black on-screen romance, 7

first black president of Howard University, 81

first black presidents of selected black colleges, 81

first black member of the Connecticut Society of the Sons of the American Revolution, 294

first black woman to achieve acclaim as the director of a professional choral group, 17

first black woman lawyer admitted to practice before the United States Supreme Court 125

first black woman to graduate from the University of Bellevue Medical Center, 355

first black woman to intern at Harlem Hospital, 355

first black middleweight champion of the world, 380

first Negro History Week (now Black History Month), 272, 411

1927

first black American to sing opera with an organized European opera company, 17

first black artist elected to full membership in the National Academy, 31

first black heard on nationwide radio, 17

first black talk show sponsored by a black newspaper, 230

first black radio talk show, 230

first black woman to enter the bar and practice law in Pennsylvania, 93

first black woman to receive a law degree from the School of Law at the University of Pennsylvania, 93

first black woman to receive the Harmon Award for her painting, 31

first regular black newscast, 33

first woman to receive law degree from Loyola University, 198

1928

first black member of the Twentieth Century Club (Boston), 80

first black sound film, 7

first black to have a recording session in Nashville, TN, 17

first black to patent a permanent waving machine, 347

1929

first and only black college consortium, 101

first black college football bowl game, 386

first black congressman elected from a northern state, 176

first black congressman elected in the twentieth century, 176

first black dean at the Howard University School of Medicine, 355

first black group to have commercial sponsorship on a national network, 33

first black to have a national and international radio audience, 326

first black radio venture, 33

first black-oriented all-talking, all-singing film from a major company, 7

first full-length films with all-black casts, 7

1930

first black woman recipient of a Guggenheim Fellowship in creative writing, 415

first major mainstream newspaper to capitalize Negro, 222

first major religious group to endorse gospel music, 18

first person officially credited with running 100 yards in 9.5 seconds, 406

first woman to lead an all-male band, 17

1931

first black to earn a Ph.D. in Spanish, 92

first black to earn the Ph.D. in anthropology, 92

first black to have a symphony performed by a major orchestra, 18

first black to receive a master's degree in nursing education, 97

first black-owned and black-controlled general insurance brokerage and risk management agency in the South, 52

first gospel choir founded, 18

1932

first black actuary in the United States, 52

first black daily newspaper in modern times, 222

first black dancer involved in ballet, 4

first black orchestra leader to have a sponsored radio series, 19

first black to choreograph a show of white dancers, 3

first detective novel by a black American, 415

first music publishing company dedicated only to gospel music, 18

first Nation of Islam temple to be established in Chicago, 334

first poet to teach creative writing at a black college, 97

first predominantly black New Thought church established, 304

1933

first annual East-West All-Star baseball game, 367

first black cartoonist to work for national publications, 2

first black hero to be heard on network radio, 33

first black pilots to make a round-trip transcontinental flight, 255

first black to sing with the Chicago Opera Company, 19

first black woman to compose a symphony performed by a major symphony orchestra, 19

first folk opera by a black to reach Broadway, 45

1934

first black Democratic congressman, 177

first black member of the National Association of Women Painters and Sculptors, 36

first black person to co-star with white players below the Mason-Dixon Line, 46

first black specialist in the field of digestive diseases and endoscopy, 355

first black to earn a Ph.D. in political science, 92, 264

first black woman in the U.S. to hold a commercial pilot's license, 255

first black-performed opera on Broadway, 19

first symphony on black folk themes by a black composer performed by a major orchestra, 19

1935

first account of Reconstruction from a black point of view, 411

first black fighter to draw a million-dollar gate, 381

first black foreign correspondent, 222

first black high school teacher in the Detroit public schools, 109

first black union to be official bargaining agent for black workers, 54

first black woman assistant district attorney in New York, 205

first black woman to win seven consecutive titles in the American Tennis Association, 404

first full-time paid special counsel for the NAACP, 72

first play by a black author to be a long-run Broadway hit, 45

first president of the National Council of Negro Women, 291

founding of the Rastafarian movement in Jamaica, 338

National Youth Administration (NYA) founded, 155

1936

first black director of nursing at City Hospital No. 2, 359

first black elected to the Kentucky state legislature, 128

first black high jumper to clear the bar at 6 feet, 9 inches, 396

first black to be hired as a director of research by a major chemical manufacturing co., 347

first black to conduct a major symphony orchestra, 18

first black to win *Ring* magazine's fight-of-the year award, 381

first black to win the 400-meter race in the Olympics, 397

first black to win the 800-meter race in the Olympics, 397

first black woman to have a full-time principalship in a desegregated New York City public school, 109

first black woman to head a federal office, 155

first blacks to win an Olympic gold medal for the 400 x 100-meter relay, 406

first gold medal for the 4 x 100-meter Olympic relay, 396

first united front organization of black workers, 54

first woman ordained a local elder in Methodist Episcopal Church, 331

1937

first black appointed to the federal bench, 168

first black president of Marogan State College, 81

first black team to win the National AAU women's track and field championship, 407

first black to sing with the Chicago Civic Opera Company during the regular season, 19

first black woman to earn a Ph.D. in sociology, 92

first president of the College Language Association, 272

only boxer to hold three championships and three world titles, 381

1938

first black intercollegiate golf championship, 391

first black named as one of the country's "Ten Outstanding Young Men," 61

first black national sports hero, 381

first black of his rank to score a one-round knock-out, 381

first black secretary of the Presbyterian Division of Work with Colored People, 338

first black to take gospel music into a secular setting, 20

first black vice president of National Maritime Union, 54

first black woman elected to a state legislature in the United States, 143

first black-owned flying school, 255

1939

first black lawyer with the U.S. Department of Labor, 156

first black team on record to win a professional world's basketball championship, 374

first black to serve as a member of the Chicago Board of Education, 109

first black woman judge in the United States, 206

first black woman to perform the leading role in a dramatic play on Broadway, 46

first president of the National Negro Bowling Association, 379

1940

first black American depicted on U.S. postage stamp, 259

first black general in the army, 245

first black to work for the American Red Cross in a professional and policy-making position, 341

first black woman to earn a Ph.D. in Zoology, 89

first gospel recording to sell more than a million copies, 20

first novel by a black to be a Book of the Month Club selection, 415

first person to set up a blood bank, 355

first professional basketball team to have its own fall training camp, 375

founding of the National Negro Newspapers Association, 275

invention of a practical refrigeration system for trucks and railroad cars, 347

Thirteenth Amendment stamp, 259

1941

first black electric guitarist to use single-string solos, 20

first black member of New York City Council, 206

first black to conduct the New York Philharmonic, 20

first black to earn a Ph.D. in political science and international relations, 92

first black to receive a Rosenwald Fellowship for photography, 229

first licensed certified public accountant in Michigan, 134

first national black hero during World War II, 252

1942

first and only training facility for black airmen in World War II, 241

first black air unit, 241

first black captain of a merchant ship, 54

first black captain of American merchant marine ship, 267

first black judge in Ohio, 210

first black researcher hired by Bell Telephone Systems, 360

first black to work for the U.S. Farm Security Administration, 229

first magazine devoted to summarizing and excerpting articles and news about blacks, 228

first president of the National Urban Urban League Guild, 286

1943

first black airman to shoot down an enemy plane, 241

first black consultant on the staff of a national nursing organization, 97

first black consultant on the staff of any national organization, 359

first black elected to the National Institue of Arts and Letters, 272

first black firefighter in Buffalo, NY, 206

first black medical army group sent overseas, 245

first black member of the National CIO Executive Board, 54

first black sculptor to design a U.S. coin, 36

first black to play Othello on an American stage with a white cast, 46

first black to work for the U.S. Office of War Information, 229

first black woman major in the WACS, 245

first live black country blues program, 33

first naval destroyer with a predominantly black crew, 253

first person to combine blues and amplified guitar to create modern urban blues, 21

first person to sing gospel at the Apollo Theater, 20

first submarine chaser with an all-black crew, 253

1944

first (and only) integrated units in World War II, 246

first black admiral in navy, 253

first black admitted to White House press conferences, 223

first black college cooperative fund-raising organization, 286

first black ensign commissioned during World War II, 253

first black governor of the Virgin Islands, 168

first black member of the House of Representatives from the East, 177

first black nondiplomatic official in the United States Department of State, 156

first black to become a regular high school teacher in Philadelphia, 109

first black warrant officer in the marines, 249

first black WAVES, 253

first black woman certified as a war correspondent, 223

first black woman deputy sheriff in the United States, 119

first issue of *Ebony* magazine, 228

first navy fighting ship named for a black, 253

first U.S. Army training film favorably depicting blacks, 8

United Negro College Fund established, 101

1945

first black elected to Louisville city council since Reconstruction, 200

first black elected to Ypsilanti City Council, 202

first black judge of a U.S. Customs Court, 168

first black to perform with a white southern symphony orchestra, 21

first black to sing with a major American opera company, 21

first black U.S. federal judge, 168

first black woman nurse in navy, 253

first black woman to sing with the New York City Opera, 21

first black sculptor elected to the National Academy of Arts and Letters, 37

first black-owned magazine to attract advertising from white-owned companies, 228

founding of the first and only school of veterinary medicine in a black college or university, 349

New York was the first state to establish a Fair Employment Practices Commission, 138

1946

first black American Mother of the Year, 263

first black deputy attorney general of California, 119

first black head of Phelps-Stokes Fund, 286

first black head of the Southern Sociological Society, 272

first black president of Fisk University, 82, 273

first black professor at the University of Chicago, 97

first black reference librarian in Chicago libraries, 198

first black president of Saint Augustine's College (NC), 82

first black to receive an honorary degree from a white college, 104

first black woman instructor in New York University's department of nursing education, 97

first coin honoring a black and designed by a black, 260

first person to bring gospel singing to the general public, 22

1947

first black elected to the Helms All-Amateur Basketball Hall of Fame, 374

first black elected to the Women's National Press Club, 224

first black in major league baseball, 367

first black pitcher in the major leagues, 367

first black player in the American League (major league), 367

first black players in a World Series, 367

first black police officer in Georgia, 196

first black professional player from an all-black college, 387

first black professional player to break the color barrier in the NFL since 1933, 386

first black reporter granted access to the congressional press galleries, 223

first black selected for All-American basketball honors, 374

first black to score a Rose Bowl touchdown, 386

first black woman accredited to the White House and the State Department, 224

first known freedom ride, 73

first televised heavyweight boxing championship bout, 381

1948

first all-black television show, 38

first black announcer and disc jockey on WOOK, 34

first black captain of a United States Olympic basketball team, 374

first black clerk in the Supreme Court, 186

first black diplomat to receive the designation of ambassador, 156

first black heavyweight lifting Olympic champion, 398

first black jazz group to have its own sponsored program on radio, 33

first black news correspondent to cover a presidential campaign, 224

first black nurse in the regular army, 246

first black performer to have her own network television program, 38

first black pitcher in the American League, 369

first black player on a United States Olympic basketball team, 374

first black president of the American Sociological Society, 273

first black scientist on postage stamp, 260

first black to co-organize an airline outside the United States, 64

first black to hit a run in the World Series, 367

first black to participate in the United States Indoor Lawn Tennis Association championship, 404

first black to pitch in a World Series game, 369

first black woman appointed to a residency as a general surgeon, 356

first black woman Olympic gold medal winner, 398

first blacks to play in the Cotton Bowl, 387

first recipient of an M.A. in nursing education from Teachers College of Columbia University, 359

first Southern medical association to admit blacks, 296

1949

first black American to have an opera performed by a major opera company, 18

first black batting champion, 367

first black boxer to defend his title successfully twenty-five times, 381

first black disk jockey in the South, 34

first black full-time reporter for the *Mirror-News,* 224

first black graduate of Naval Academy, 251

first black managing editor of *Stars and Stripes,* 230

first black photojournalist on the staff of *Life* magazine, 229

first black pilot in Naval Reserve, 254

first black president of Hampton Institute, 82

first black professor at Harvard Medical School, 356

first black to head a congressional standing committee in recent, 177

first black to preside over the New Orleans Mardi Gras, 6

first black to receive the National League's Most Valuable Player Award, 367

first black to win an Oscar, 7

first black to write a series of best-selling novels, 415

first black trained as a cancer surgeon at Sloan Kettering Hospital, 356

first black variety talent show series with an all-black cast, 38

first black woman elected to Cleveland City Council, 210

first black-owned radio station in Atlanta, 34

first radio station to have all black-oriented programming, 34

1950S

first black lyric soprano to achieve international diva status in our time, 25

1950

first black American to win the Nobel Peace Prize, 156

first black appointed to U.S. delegation to the United Nations, 198

first black drafted by a National Basketball Association team, 375

first black flier killed in the Korean War, 254

first black to play in organized hockey, 392

first black to play in the National Basketball Association, 375

first black to receive honorary LL.D. from New York University, 286

first black to serve in AMA House of Delegates, 297

first black to star in a scheduled comedy program on television, 46

first black to win a Pulitzer Prize for poetry, 420

first black to win Nobel Peace Prize, 263

first black war correspondents in the Korean conflict, 224

first black woman elected to the Michigan legislature, 133

first black woman to graduate from the University of Maryland law school, 93

first full-time black woman reporter on a mainstream newspaper, 224

first Negro Gospel and Religious Music Festival, 21

1951

first black bowler to win top rank in ABC competition, 379

first black elected to the College Football Hall of Fame, 386

first black pitcher to win twenty games in a major league, 369

first black prima ballerina at the Metropolitan Opera, 4

first black professional umpire, 371

first black runs-batted-in champion of the National League, 369

first black state senator in Michigan, 133

first black to perform in the Empire Room of New York's Waldorf Astoria, 8

first black to qualify as a Democratic Party primary candidate, 130

first black to win Medal of Honor in Korea, 246

1952

first basketball club to make complete playing trips around the world, 375

first black elected to the New York state senate, 138

first black enshrined in the Baseball Hall of Fame, 367

first black home run champion, 367

first black marine pilot, 249

first black pitcher to win a World Series game, 369

first black to graduate from the University of North Carolina Law School, 95

first black to win the 400-meter hurdles in the Olympics, 398

first black woman in the United States to be elected to a state senate (Michigan) 133

first black woman to run for vice president, 171

first black woman vice presidential candidate in a national election, 222

first full-time black reporter for the *Washington Post,* 224

1953

first black bishop consecrated in the United States, 315

first black bishop to ordain black priests in the United States, 315

first black catcher to hit twenty or more homers in five successive seasons, 369

first black city council member in California, 191

first black elected to a school board in the deep South since Reconstruction, 109

first black fellow of the American Institute of Architects, 1

first black licensed mortgage banker in the United States, 51

first black mortgage banking firm, 51

first black on the Chicago Cubs, 370

first black president of borough of Manhattan, 207

first black president of Spelman College, 82

first black president of the American Political Science Association, 273

first black professional quarterback, 387

first black student at Vanderbilt University, 103

first black to play in the National Basketball Association All-Star Game, 375

first black to sing a principal role at La Scala, 22

first black to sing at a presidential inauguration, 22

first black to win a nationally recognized tennis title, 404

first black to win National Book Award, 416

first chapter of Phi Beta Kappa at a black university, 273

1954

first black air force general, 239

first black assistant secretary of labor, 156

first black basketball All-American at Notre Dame, 198

first black federal legislator from Michigan, 177

first black graduate of Louisiana State University School, 200

first black heavyweight elected to Boxing's Hall of Fame, 381

first black man to win the James E. Sullivan Memorial Trophy, 407

first black pastor in the Reformed Dutch Church, 339

first black permanent member of the delegation to the United Nations, 156

first black radio network, 34

first black singer to appear on the stage of the Vienna State Opera, 21

first black Supreme Court page, 187

first black to enter the Pikes Peak Hill Climb automobile race, 363

first black to head a component organization of the AMA, 297

first black woman elected to the New York state legislature, 138

first black woman member of a mayoral cabinet, 207

first black woman registered architect, 1

first black woman to receive a doctorate in political science, 95

first black woman to win the Sullivan Award, 399

first rock and roll record, 23

1955

first black disc jockey trade organization, 35

first black man to join the Metropolitan Opera, 23

first black man to serve as White House aide, 157

first black player for the New York Yankees, 369

first black to appear in an opera on television, 25

first black to be named the Most Valuable Player three times, 369

first black to hold cabinet rank in Pennsylvania, 144

first black to hold cabinet rank in the New York, 138

first black to pitch a no-hitter, 370

first black to serve as captain of the basketball team of Columbia, 288

first black to sing a principal role at the Metropolitan Opera, 23

first black woman All-American basketball player, 375

first black woman named assistant U.S. attorney for northern Illinois, 157

first black woman nominated for an Oscar in a leading role, 8

first Methodist minister assigned to an all-white congregation, 331

1956

first black admitted to the National Press Club, 223

first black advertising agency in the United States, 49

first black elected to the Colorado state senate, 120

first black elected to the Milwaukee Common Council, 152

first black from a black college to win an Olympic gold medal, 398

first black licensed to teach African and African-American history in New York State public schools, 110

first black musician to make an overseas tour sponsored by the State Department, 23

first black orthopedic surgeon in California, 356

first black student admitted to the University of Alabama, 103

first black to hold federal government cabinet rank as secretary of housing and urban development, 140

first black to sing a romantic lead at the Metropolitan Opera, 22 first black to win a major tennis title, 405

first black to win the Olympic decathlon, 398

first black winner of the Cy Young Award, 369

first man to break the 7-foot high jump barrier, 407

1957

first black American to head the President's Committee on Government Employment Policy, 157

first black pilot of a scheduled passenger commercial airline, 256

first black president of the American Association of Physical Anthropologists, 273

first black producer of network television programs at NBC, 38

first black secretary, United States Mission to NATO, 157

first black to represent a major white-owned insurance company, 52

first black to win a major professional golf tournament, 391

first black to win a major United States national championship, 405

first black to win a Wimbledon championship, 405

first black vice president of AFL-CIO, 54

first black woman to serve in the New Jersey state assembly, 137

first exploration of the theme of interracial love in a Hollywood movie, 8

first gospel group to perform at the Newport Jazz Festival, 20

first Imhotep Conference, 273

first organization to coordinate groups devoted to racial integration, 73

1958

first black athlete to win the Jim Thorpe Trophy, 387

first black commercial airline stewardess, 256

first black congressman from Pennsylvania, 178

first black dancer in the United States to become a member of a classical ballet company, 4

first black elected to serve on the National Convention Committee of either party, 152

first black fighter to hold the middleweight boxing title on five separate occasions, 382

first black graduate from the Little Rock, Arkansas Central High School, 110

first black male nominated for an Academy Award for best actor, 8

first black on the Massachusetts Supreme Court, 406

first black pianist to give a jazz concert in Carnegie Hall, 24

first black professional hockey player, 392

first black televison newscaster, 231

first black to graduate and receive a Ph.D. from Vanderbilt, 103

first black to head a United States delegation to a European country, 155

first black to serve on New York City Board of Hospitals, 297

first black to win the Babe Ruth Award, 370

first black woman to vote in Miami, Florida, 196

first black women elected to the Maryland House of Delegates, 131

first gospel artist to sing at Newport Jazz Festival, 22

first major black television news correspondent, 231

first Methodist minister with two all-white churches, 331

first sit-ins in modern times to win concessions in the South, 73

first woman elected to the Illinois legislature, 125

1959

first black director of a straight play on Broadway, 47

first black man to win a Grammy, 24

first black player on the Boston Red Sox, 370

first black to have an hour-long special on television, 38

first black to win the New York Drama Critics Award, 46

first black woman to win a Grammy, 24

first National League player to win the Most Valuable Player award two years in succession, 370

first play on Broadway written by a black woman, 46

first serious black drama to have an impact on the dominant culture, 46

first woman judge in the Pennsylvania, 144

first woman to establish a successful booking and talent agency in New York City, 59

1960

first and only record to reach number one on the pops charts twice, 24

first athlete to win 110-meter hurdles twice, 398

first black brothers to hold simultaneously the presidencies of two large black universities, 82

first black cardinal in the Catholic church, 315

first black comedienne to have a best-selling record, 36

first black county court judge in New Jersey, 137

first black judge in Alameda County, CA, 192

first black memorialized by a federal monument, 261

first black presidential press secretary, 157

first black public defender in Cuyahoga County, 142

first black state legislator, 116

first black television news reporter in Washington, DC, 230

first black to be nominated to run for statewide office in Massachusetts, 132

first black to carry the American flag at an Olympic event, 399

first black to clear 7 feet, 3 3/4 inches in the high jump, 407

first black to regain the heavyweight title, 382

first black White House broadcast correspondent on radio, 230

first black woman to earn a Ph.D in sociology from Ohio State University, 97

first book series to present minority histories for the general and educational markets, 61

first city to integrate its lunch counters, 74

first national chair of Student Nonviolent Coordinating Committee (SNCC), 74, 291

first sit-in movement to achieve major results, 73

first woman to win three track gold medals in the Olympics, 399

1961

first black administrator of the Federal Housing and Home Finance Administration, 158

first black admitted to the University of Mississippi, 103

first black American ambassador to Nigeria, 157

first black appointed judge of a U.S. district court in the continental United States, 168

first black coach of a predominantly white professional team in the modern era, 375

first black college football player of the year, 388

first black guard at the Tomb of the Unknown Soldier, 246

first black municipal judge in California, 191

first black on the United States Junior Davis Cup team, 405

first black students to attend the University of Georgia, 232

first black students to enroll at the University of Georgia, 103

first black to chair the Education and Labor Committee, 177

first black to have a speaking part in a nationally televised commercial, 39

first black to manage a club at any level in professional baseball, 370

first black to perform at the Wagner Bayreuth Festival, 24

first black to play in a major PGA tournament in the South, 391

first black U.S. attorney in the continental United States, 158

first black vice president of a white record company, 24

first black winner of the Heisman Trophy, 388

first black-owned mortgage banking firm approved by the Federal Housing Administration and Veterans Administration, 51

first gospel group to appear in nightclubs, 20

1962

first black canonized a saint by the Catholic Church, 315

first black coach on a major league baseball team, 370

first black elected to a Southern legislature since Reconstruction, 122

first black elected to the House from California, 178

first black federal assistant district attorney in the South, 158

first black member of the Atlanta Chamber of Commerce, 275

first black member of the International Executive Board of the United Auto Workers, 54

first black moderator of the Presbyterian Church, 338

first black network news correspondent, 231

first black to be elected Massachusetts attorney general, 132

first black to command a ship in the modern navy, 253

first black to have cabinet rank in West Virginia government, 151

first black vice president of a leading national corporation, 57

first black woman elected municipal judge, 198

first black woman elected to the state senate of Maryland, 131

first black woman to be elected to state office in Missouri, 136

first person of any race to steal 130 bases in one season, 373

first president of the Progressive National Baptist Convention, USA, 310

first professional basketball player to score more than 3,000 points in one season, 376

first professional basketball player to score more than 4,000 points in one season, 376

first woman in the United States to head a state Mental Health Department, 151

1963

first and only black driver to win a NASCAR Winston Cup race, 364

first and only person to win five boxing championships, 382

first black astronaut candidate, 360

first black cabinet member in Ohio, 143

first black named to the American Davis Cup team, 405

first black postmaster to head a postal unit of a major city (Los Angeles, CA), 158

first black student admitted to Clemson University, 103

first black to serve on the National Labor Relations Board, 170

first black to win the Most Valuable Player award in the American League, 370

Emancipation Proclamation stamp, 260

first (and only) black in wholesale-retail fur manufacturing, 58

first black artist to design a postage stamp, 261

first black choreographer to work for Metropolitan Opera, 4

first black elected official in Los Angeles, 191

first black national correspondent for *Time* magazine, 228

first black to appear in a continuing key part on a television series, 38

first black to win an Oscar for a starring role, 8

first black winners of the Presidential Medal of Freedom, 264

first blacks to attend the Naval College, 253

first gospel group to sing at Radio City Music Hall, 20

first recipient of Hailie Selassie I prize, 264

first woman to head *Tan* magazine, 228

1964

first black full-time general assignment reporter for UPI, 225

first black judge in Georgia in modern times, 196

first black patrolman in Laurel, Mississippi, 203

first black to serve on the board of directors of a major nonblack corporation, 52

first black to win the *Downbeat* magazine award for jazz on the organ, 25

first blacks elected over whites in Alabama in this century, 189

first integrated comic strip by a black cartoonist, 2

first of the large riots of the 1960s in black urban areas, 74

first person to popularize the phrase "Black Power," 74

first athlete to win an Olympic sprint title twice, 399

first black batting champion in the American League, 370

first black bishops of the United Methodist Church appointed to predominantly white jurisdictions, 332

first black deputy assistant secretary of state for public affairs, 158

first black elected to the General Assembly in this century, 147

first black elected to the Oklahoma senate, 143

first black judge in Florida since Reconstruction, 122

first black moderator of the United Presbyterian Church, 338

first black to head the United States Information Agency, 159

first black to hold an executive position with the National Football League, 386

first black to serve in the Delaware senate, 121

first black woman to win a seat in the New York state senate, 140

first director of player relations for the National Football League, 386

first school in the state of New York founded to offer preprofessional training to mostly black and Latino children, 110

1965

first black American ambassador to the United Nations, 160

first black American U.S. Solicitor General, 160

first black appointed to a federal regional administrative post, 160

first black coach in the National Football League, 388

first black criminal court judge in Tennessee, 148

first black member of the governing body of the Federal Reserve, 159

first black president of the Council of Bishops, 332

first black student to graduate from the University of Alabama, 104

first black woman ambassador appointed to an overseas post, 159

first woman New York City borough head, 140

oldest man ever to pitch in the major leagues, 369

first black actress to play major parts at the American Shakespeare Festival, 47

first black in a nontraditional role in a network television series, 39

first black judge in Arizona, 190

first black lawyer to work in the U.S. Attorney's office in Louisiana, 200

first black Medal of Honor winner in the Vietnam War, 246

first black member of the National Academy of Sciences, 273

first black on the board of directors of the San Francisco Symphony Foundation and the San Francisco Symphony Association, 286

first black-chartered and black-operated bank in Harlem, 51

1966

first black actor to win an Emmy award for best actor in a running series, 39

first black alderman in Paterson, New Jersey, 205

first black bureau chief for Washington Broadcasting Network, 230

first black elected to town board of Fairmont, North Carolina, 210

first black faculty member at Naval Academy, 251

first black fire chief in a major city, 207

first black graduate of Coast Guard Academy, 249

first black mayor of an integrated Ohio city, 210

first black navy chaplain to attain the rank of captain, 254

first black on the board of Yale University, 83

first black showgirl with Ringling Brothers Circus, 3

first black to head a college in New York State, 83

first black to open a Metropolitan Opera season and first to sing title role at the new opera house, 25

first black to produce a major show for television, 38

first black woman president of the borough of Manhattan, 207

first black California assemblywoman, 181

first black Catholic bishop to serve in the United States in the twentieth century, 315

first black coach in the National Basketball Association, 376

first black elected to the South Carolina state house since Reconstruction, 146

first black major league umpire, 371

first black member of the Atomic Energy Commission, 341

first black named the Most Valuable Player in both major baseball leagues, 371

first black to be elected to the U.S. Senate since Reconstruction, 178

first black to coach a major, predominantly white professional sports team, 376

first black to serve in the cabinet of a president, 158

first black to win baseball's triple crown, 371

first black woman federal judge, 168

first proponent of Black Theology to attract national attention, 311

United Church and Science of Living Institute first founded, 340

1967

America's first black woman associate dean of a major medical school, 356

election of first black president of the Atlanta Public School Board, 111

first black associate justice of the Supreme Court, 160

first black astronaut, 360

first black college and the first in the entire South to win the NCAA College Division basketball championship, 377

first black elected to the professional Hall of Fame, 388

first black elected to the state legislature of Louisiana since Reconstruction, 130

first black elected to the state senate (Arizona), 117

first black medical student at Emory University (Georgia), 103

first black national secretary of the United Church of Christ, 318

first black Pennsylvania state senator, 144

first black president of the New York State Civil Service Commission, 140

first black sheriff in the South since Reconstruction, 115

first black to sit in the Texas senate since 1883, 149

first black woman elected to the state assembly, 119

first black woman in the Georgia state legislature, 122

first black woman on the Ladies' Professional Golf Association, 391

first black woman to serve in the Tennessee state legislature, 148

first black civil rights leader on postage stamp, 260

first black elected mayor of a major city, 210

first black marine to receive the Medal of Honor, 250

first black mayor of Flint, Michigan, 202

first black mayor of Washington, DC, 215

first black president of YWCA, 286

first black singer with the Grand Ole Opry, 25

first black to have an Oldsmobile dealership, 49

first black to have hand and foot prints placed in front of Grauman's Chinese Theater, 8 first full-time black news announcer for WINS radio (New York City), 225

first woman in the army awarded Expert Field Medical Badge, 246

1968

first black captain in U.S. Navy Medical Corps, 254

first black head of major jail, 198

first black president of the National Education Association, 275

first black principal conductor of a leading American Symphony Orchestra, 26

first black shopper-news publication in the Kansas and Missouri area, 225

first black to have her own television series in a nonstereotypical role, 39

first black to serve on the Democratic National Committee, 203

first black vice president of Macys, 62

first black woman president of the University of Missouri, 86

first black woman to host a television show in the South, 232

first black-produced community program on television, 39

first major black-sponsored shopping center, 62

first African-American woman elected to the House of Representatives, 180

first black American Jewish group to migrate to Israel, 312

first black elected to the Florida legislature in this century, 121

first black elected to the state legislature of Mississippi since Reconstruction, 135

first black in the Virginia House of Delegates in this century, 150

first black inducted into the International Tennis Hall of Fame, 405

first black man to win a major tennis title, 405

first black priest in Tennessee, 315

first black professional quarterback to play regularly, 387

first black woman elected to the Oklahoma state house of representatives, 143

first black woman to serve as an assistant secretary of state, 160

first black woman to win an Olympic gold medal for the 800-meter race, 400

first blacks proposed for president and vice president at the same convention, 171

first full-time black faculty member at Duke University Medical School, 97

first to refuse to recognize the American flag and national anthem at an Olympic event, 400

first woman of any race to preach at Saint Paul's Cathedral, 319

1969

first black coach in the American League, 369

first black dean in an Episcopal cathedral, 322

first black faculty member in the Vanderbilt University Divinity School, 98

first black football coach to win more than two hundred games, 388

first black law professor at Harvard Law School, 97

first black majority leader in the Pennsylvania house of representatives, 144

first black mayor of Fayette, Mississippi, 135

first black member of the New York state legislature in modern times, 141

first black state superintendent of public instruction since Reconstruction, 111

first black to become head of the predominantly white American Baptist Convention, 310

first black to chair the Foreign Relations Subcommittee on Africa, 177

first black to head a diocese in the Protestant Episcopal Church, 322

first black to patent an image converter for detecting electromagnetic radiation, 349

first black to speak on the floor of the House, 173

first black Virginia state senator since Reconstruction, 151

first black woman judge in Georgia, 122

first black, and the first woman, elected to the Kentucky state senate, 129

first blacks elected to the Tennessee state senate, 148

first chairperson of Harvard University's Department of Afro-American Studies, 97

first executive director of the Metro-Denver Urban Coalition, 120

first white church to give money in response to James Forman's demand for reparations from white churches, 332

first black actress to receive an Emmy award, 39

first black blues musician on postage stamp, 260

first black co-anchor on midday newscast WTOP-TV (Washington, DC), 233

first black elected mayor of predominantly white southern city, 210

first black elected to Boston City Council, 202

first black entertainer to sleep in the White House, 267

first black mayor of racially mixed Mississippi town, 203

first black on the board of Williams College, 83

first black president of the American Psychological Association, 273

first black to become a British peer, 267

first black to win a Pulitzer Prize for a feature photographer, 229

first black woman elected judge in Ohio, 211

first black woman television reporter to cover the White House, 232

first black woman to have a non-fiction work on the best-seller list, 5

first black woman to host a television variety show, 40

first integrated advertising agency with black principals, 231

first nuclear-powered submarine named in honor of a black, 261

1970

first black and first woman director of the Detroit Public Libraries, 277

first black artist to receive Spingarn Medal, 31

first black contestant in Miss America Pageant, 257

first black dramatist to win Pulitzer Prize for drama, 5

first black judge on New Orleans Juvenile Court, 200

first black man to have a weekly prime time comedy television show in his own name, 40

first black mayor of a major Eastern city, 205

first black member of New York Stock Exchange, 63

first black Miss World, 257

first black on Savannah city council, 196

first black pilot of a 740 jumbo jet, 257

first black president of a major American University in the twentieth century, 83

first black president of a major white firm, 58

first black president of the National Cooperative Education Association, 275

first black president of the Southern Historical Association, 273

first black public prosecutor in a major American city, 201

first black to head National Council of YMCA, 286

first black to serve on the board of a major bank not run by blacks, 51

first black to serve on the Federal Trade Commission, 83

first black vice president of the United Auto Workers, 54

first black winner of Constance Lindsay Skinner Award of the Women's National Book Association, 264

first black woman to have an original screenplay produced, 5

first national correspondent for WKBS-TV, 232

first popularly elected governor of Virgin Islands, 291

first black secretary of state in modern times, 134

first black elected to a statewide office in California, 111

first black elected to represent Missouri in Congress, 180

first black in the United States appointed to a governor's cabinet, 137

first black lieutenant colonel in the Salvation Army in the United States, 339

first black Mr. America winner, 378

first black nonvoting delegate to Congress from the District of Columbia, 180

first black since Reconstruction to hold office in Shreveport, LA, 111

first black superintendent of adult parole in Illinois, 125

first black to hold a major post in the Agency for International Development, 161

first black to serve as a general counsel to the United States Treasury Department, 160

first black woman in the Florida state legislature, 121

first blacks in the Alabama legislature, 115

first elected governor of the Virgin Islands, 150

first native-born governor of the Virgin Islands, 150

first civil rights lawyer for Martin Luther King, Jr., 115

1971

first American to compete against whites in South Africa, 391

first black appointed superintendent of schools in Baltimore, MD, 111

first black boxers to draw a multimillion dollar gate, 382

first black candidate for governor in modern times, 135

first black elected to the Baseball Hall of Fame, 369

first black elected to the National Rodeo Cowboy Hall of Fame, 403

first black governor in the nation since Reconstruction, 126

first black judge in North Carolina, 141

first black man in North Carolina legally married a white woman, 141

first black member of the Appropriations Committee, 180

first black member of the House Select Committee on Intelligence, 180

first black member of the Maine legislature, 130

first black superior court judge in the South in modern times, 141

first black tenured faculty member at Duke University Medical School, 97

first black tenured professor at Harvard Law School, 97

first black to attain the civil service rank of GS 16 while working for the army, 360

first black to head a chamber of a legislature since Reconstruction, 126

first black to head Church Women United, 332

first black to serve on the New Jersey Civil Service Commission, 137

first black woman cabinet member in Pennsylvania, 145

first black woman elected to the Louisiana legislature, 130

first black woman to hold the position of correctional programs administrator for the Illinois Department of Corrections, 125

first black, and the first woman, elected to the Wake County, NC, Board of Commissioners, 141

first concerted effort on the part of black representatives to influence congressional party politics, 180

first National Football League defensive player to receive the Most Valuable Player award, 388

first woman of any race to serve on the New York State Public Service Commission, 140

first woman jockey, 394

first black appointed to the United States Court of Military Appeals, 240

first black city editor on a mainstream paper, 225

first black company to become a member of the New York Stock Exchange, 63

first black director of the U.S. Chamber of Commerce, 276

first black elected to Birmingham city council, 189

first black elected to major Chicago office, 198

first black firm listed on a major stock exchange, 63

first black mayor of Berkeley, California, 191

first black mayor of East St. Louis, 199

first black mayor of Princeton Township, New Jersey, 205

first black member of the National Association of Radio and Television News Directors, 232

first black named Entertainer of the Year and Male Vocalist of the Year in the field of country music, 25

first black naval officer to have a frigate named for him, 254

first black police chief of Princeton, New Jersey, 205

first black private detective and super-hero in a motion picture, 8

first black selected to sit on board of General Motors, 62

first black to own a rubber recycling plant, 58

first black to seek governorship in Mississippi in this century, 203

first black top executive of a major airline, 64

first black woman alderman in Chicago, 199

first black woman to become an aircraft maintenance officer, 239

first woman co-anchor of WTVF-TV (Nashville, TN), 234

first black army officer to receive a brigadier general, 241

1972

first black commissioner of corrections in New York City, 208

first black director of the American Library Association, 276

first black elected mayor of Washington, DC, 215

first black elected to Louisiana Fourth Circuit Court of Appeals, 200

first black mayor in Georgia, 196

first black mayor in sizeable Alabama city, 189

first black mayor of Cincinnati, OH, 211

first black mayor of Englewood, NJ, 205

first black member of the board of the Ohio Council of Retail Merchants Association, 276

first black member of the Federal Aviation Agency's Women's Advisory Commission, 255

first black member of the Gridiron Club, 276

first black president of the National Council of Chuches in America, 295

first black television show sponsored by a black business, 40

first black to command a naval unit in the deep South, 254

first black to conduct opera for the Metropolitan Opera, 26

first black to own a radio station in Chicago, 35

first black to receive Henry Johnson Fisher Award of the Magazine Publishers Association, 61

first black to serve on the board of the New York Stock Exchange, 63

first black vice chair of the Southern Governors Conference, 291

first black woman elected to board of Yale University, 83

first black-controlled station of the National Federation of Community Broadcasters, 35

first building built by blacks in downtown Chicago since the eighteenth century, 59

first black candidate officially certified to run for the U.S. Senate, 115

first acting black governor of Texas, 149

first black assigned to serve in South Africa, 161

first black basketball coach at a major white institution, 377

first black candidate certified to run for a U.S. Senate seat, 115

first black commissioner of the Federal Communications Commission, 161

first black congresswoman from the West, 181

first black general manager in any sport, 377

first black member of the House from Georgia since 1870, 181

first black U.S. dart champion, 384

first black umpire in the National League, 371

first black woman judge in Wisconsin, 152

first black woman to preside over a legislative body in the United States, 149

first black woman to compete in five Olympic Games, 400

first black woman to seek nomination as the Democrats' presidential candidate, 180

first black woman vice-chair of the Democratic National Convention, 181

first person of any race to hit thirty or more home runs in fourteen seasons, 371

first pitcher to win twenty games in six consecutive years, 371

first southern black woman elected to the House, 181

Patterson was the first black to win a major party nomination for a congressional seat, 148

1973

first black congressman to head the Committee for the District of Columbia, 177

first black congresswoman from Illinois, 182

first black deputy assistant secretary of defense, 162

first black in the South to serve as a member of the Texas State Board of Pharmacy, 149

first black musician to receive an honorary degree for work in the blues, 104

first black president of the New York City Health and Hospital Corporation, 357

first black superintendent of schools in Atlanta, Georgia, 111

first black to enter the Hall of Fame in a special election, 371

first black to rush for 250 yards in one National Football League game, 388

first black vice president of the National Basketball Association, 377

first black woman deputy United States solicitor general, 157

first black woman in the United States to receive a doctorate from Massachusetts Institute of Technology, 95

first black woman member of the South Carolina Board of Education, 112

first Hispanic to enter the baseball Hall of Fame, 371

first member of Congress to give birth while serving in office, 181

first black elected mayor of Atlanta, 196

first black elected mayor of Detroit, 203

first black mayor of Los Angeles, 191

first black mayors of cities of over one million population, 203

first black painter on postage stamp, 260

first black president of Phi Beta Kappa, 273

first black woman mayor in the United States, 211

first black woman on National Business Committee for the Arts, 276

1974

first black deputy mayor of New York City, 208

first black president of Chicago Theological Seminary, 83

first black president of San Francisco Dental Society, 297

first black president of the National Association of Universities and Land Grant Colleges, 276

first black to head the AFL-CIO civil rights department in Washington, DC, 54

first black woman navy chaplain, 254

first black woman to appear on the cover of a major fashion magazine, 257

first statue of a black erected on public land, 261

first woman head of a nationally circulated black newspaper, 226

first black cabinet officer in Alabama, 115

first black congressman from the state of Tennessee, 182

first black elected lieutenant governor of Colorado, 120

first black elected to the Montana legislature, 136

first black elected to the state senate of Louisiana in this century, 130

first black member of the House Ways and Means Committee, 182

first black New Hampshire state representative, 137

first black to be elected lieutenant governor of California, 119

first black to qualify for the Masters Tournament, 391

first black to serve in the California legislature, 119

1975

first black man to win single Wimbledon titles, 406

first black manager of a major league baseball team, 371

first black to become moderator of the Presbyterian Church, 338

first black to chair the House Government Operations Subcommittee on Manpower and Housing, 182

first black to play in the Masters Tournament, 391

first black to serve as chief of a U.S. district court, 168

first black whip-at-large (U.S. Congress), 182

first person to win 107 400-meter hurdles events in a row, 400

first black elected to city council of New London, CT, 193

first black four-star general in the air force, 239

first black member of New Orleans City Council, 200

first black municipal traffic judge in Georgia, 196

first black municipal court solicitor in Georgia, 196

first black poet on postage stamp, 260

first black president of Girl Scouts of America, 286

first black show to run eleven seasons, 40

first black to open a cookie-only retail store, 62

first black woman appointed to District of Columbia Appellate Court, 215

first television station owned and operated by blacks, 40

1976

first appearance of Bronx-style rapping, 27

first black and first woman on the Mayor's Criminal Justice Commission (San Francisco), 286

first black and first woman vice president for consumer affairs of Potomac Electric Power Company, 217

first black national officer of Steel Workers Union, 54

first black president of the American Library Association, 277

first black president of the United States Conference of Mayors, 205

first black president of the Virginia Education Association, 277

first black tenured faculty member at West Point, 250

first black to head a federal Court of Appeals, 215

first black to head a police union in New York State, 277

first black vice president of the National Association of Intercollegiate Athletics Sports Information Directors, 276

first black woman and nurse to graduate with an M.A. from the U.S. Army Command and General Staff College, 246

first black woman inducted into the National Institute of Arts and Letters, 420

first black woman mayor in Mississippi, 204

first woman on Atlanta SWAT team, 197

first black American to compete for the United States in Olympic competition, 383

first black appointed by the Department of State as goodwill ambassador to the Olympic Games, 397

first black appointed to the Louisiana State Board of Pharmacy, 130

first black circuit court judge in South Carolina, 147

first black man to call the roll at a Republican Party national convention, 171

first black woman agent with the Federal Bureau of Investigations, 167

first black woman cabinet member, 159

first black woman moderator of the United Presbyterian Church, 338

first Episcopal suffragan bishop in Michigan, 322

1977

first black American treasurer of the United States, 162

first black assistant secretary for administration, U.S. Department of Agriculture, 162

first black bishop of the Episcopal Church in the diocese of Washington, 324 first black chair of the Maryland Republican party, 131

first black director of the United States Justice Department's Civil Rights Division, 162

first black member of the Boston School Committee, 112

first black member of the House Armed Services Committee, 186

first black member of the Pardon and Parole Board, 116

first black member of the Tenn-Tom Waterway Board of Directors, 116

first black named assistant secretary of state for Latin America, 162

first black Navy general counsel, 163

first black secretary of the army, 162

first black speaker of the house in any state house of representatives, 144

first black speaker of the house in Pennsylvania house of representatives, 144

first black state supreme court judge, 119

first black to become registrar of a major scientific museum, 357

first black to head 4-H home economics activities in Maryland, 131

first black to head a diocese in the Catholic Church in this century, 317

first black to serve as Republican state chairman in Maryland, 171

first black to serve on the Fulton County, Georgia, Superior Court, 122

first black woman assistant attorney general of Iowa, 128

first black woman elected to the Missouri state senate, 136

first black woman member of the Pennsylvania state Civil Service Commission, 145

first black woman to head the western region of the U.S. Department of Housing and Urban Development, 162

first female and the first black neurosurgical resident at the University of Minnesota, 357

first time an African American led the U.N. American delegation, 181

first woman ordained a priest in the Protestant Episcopal Church, 324

first black alderman of Tchula, MS, 204

first black captain on Greenville, MS, police force, 204

first black chair of University of Minnesota Board of Regents, 83

first black mayor of New Orleans, 200, 201

first black mayor of Oakland, CA, 192

first black mayor of Richmond, VA, 214

first black member of the Newport, RI, City Council, 212

first black Miss Universe, 259

first black police chief in Berkeley, CA, 192

first black president of Los Angeles Bar Association, 277

first black president of the American Chemical Association, 274

first black president of the Metropolitan St. Louis YWCA, 286

first black to record a best-selling album at the age of eighty-three, 27

first black to win a Pulitzer Prize for television, 41

first black vice president of Atlanta Press Club, 277

first black vice president at BBDO Advertising, 49

first black woman clown with Ringling Brothers, 3

first black woman deputy mayor of New York City, 208

first black woman to head a major public transportation network, 268

first black-owned company to sign a million-dollar contract with Consolidated Edison, 60

first known black member of the Daughters of the American Revolution, 295

first large hotel designed and built by blacks, 59

first major American black-owned commercial insurance brokerage firm on Wall Street, 53

first songs by blacks to be sent out of the solar system, 26

1978

first black and first woman president of Planned Parenthood, 286 first black chair of the Mayor's Criminal Justice Commission (San Francisco), 286

first black man to sing at the Bayreuth Festival, 27

first black mayor in New England, 193

first black mayor of Rock Island, IL, 199

first black member of Los Angeles County Board of Supervisors, 192

first black network news anchor, 233

first black police chief in Washington, DC, 215

first black president of the American Historical Association, 273

first black president of the Atlanta Chamber of Commerce, 277

first black president of the New York State School Boards Association, 277

first black woman and one of first two women to be commanding air officers, 239

first black woman engineer for the Burlington-Northern Railroad, 55

first black woman on postage stamp, 260

first black woman pilot on a major airline, 257

first black woman to anchor a national newscast, 232

first president of the National Association of Black Women Entrepreneurs, 277

first black elected to statewide office as comptroller of Illinois, 126

first black federal judge in the deep South in modern times, 169

first black Mormon priest (elder) in the twentieth century, 333

first black named to the Virginia state cabinet as secretary of the Department of Human Resources, 150

first black prizefight to gross more than a five-million dollar gate, 382

first black to run for statewide office in Maryland, 131

first black woman elected to the state senate, 119

first black woman trooper in the South Carolina state highway patrol, 147

first black, the first woman, and the first non-physician to head the California Board of Medical Quality, 119

first black elected to a statewide constitutional office, 152

first boxer to win the heavyweight title three times, 383

first woman and black to head the Peace Corps, 163

1979

first black American Ryder Cup Team member, 391

first black American to chair a federal regulatory commission, 163

first black American U.S. judge in the District of Massachusetts, 169

first black appointed circuit judge in Alabama in this century, 116

first black blues artist to perform in the USSR, 104

first black chairman of the South Carolina Commission on Aging, 147

first black Federal Bureau of Investigations field office chief, 163

first black federal judge in Florida, 183

first black head coach at a major white institution, 389

first black justice on the South Carolina state supreme court, 147

first black Michigan state treasurer, 134

first black secretary of labor in Florida, 121

first black superintendent of the Memphis City School System, 112

first black woman judge on the U.S. Court of Appeals, Second District of New York, 169

first person of any race to become a million-dollar-a-year baseball player, 373

first black and first woman president of the American Pharmaceutical Association, 297

first black captain and brigade commander of the Corps of Cadets, 250

first black chair of board of American National Red Cross, 297

first black director of the Chicago Child Care Society, 287

first black general in the marines, 249

first black mayor of Birmingham, AL, 189

first black president of the Georgia Association of Independent Juvenile Courts, 279

first black president of the Municipal Court Clerks Association, 279

first black president of the Texas Restaurant Association, 279

first black recipient of the AMC Cancer Research Center Humanitarian Award, 264

first black superintendent of Memphis public schools, 213

first black to direct the editorial operations of a major American daily newspaper, 226

first black to head a major foundation, 288

first black to win a Nobel Prize in economics, 264

first black woman on board of Gannett Company, 61

first minority-owned company to operate a railroad, 65

first person of any race to perform before the Georgia Assembly, 27

first two rap records, 27

first woman of any ethnic group to become a longshoreman on the Eastern seaboard, 55

1980

first black anchor at Cable News Network, 233

first black chair of the board of a predominantly white university in the South, 84

first black chair of the board of the Baseball Writers Association of America, 279

first black city manager of Little Rock, AR, 288

first black mayor of Seattle, 214

first black on Council on Medical Services of AMA, 297

first black president of the Federal Bar Association, 279

first black president of the Society for the Study of Sociological Problems, 273

first black to found and own a black-oriented cable television network, 41

first black to head Spelman College Board of Trustees, 83

first black woman fellow of American Institute of Architects, 1

first black woman graduate of Naval Academy, 251

first black American chief counsel of the Senate Judiciary Committee, 183

first black astronaut to participate in a mission, 360

first black federal judge in the state of Tennessee, 169

first black in the Kentucky state cabinet as secretary of the Department of Justice, 129

first black member of the United States Civil Aeronautics Board, 163

first black on the Tennessee Supreme Court, 148

first black president at a predominantly white college, 349

first black speaker of the California State Assembly, 120

first black to sit on a court of record, 117

first black woman commissioner on the Michigan State Boxing Commission, 383

first black woman elected to the Connecticut state legislature, 120

first black woman in major league baseball administration, 373

first black woman to serve in the Illinois state cabinet, 126

first blacks to participate in the Winter Olympics, 401

1981

first African American to chair the United States Civil Rights Commission, 163

first black and first woman to serve as superintendent of the Chicago school system, 112

first black assistant secretary of commerce, 164

first black chair of the Merit System Protection Board, 164

first black circuit court judge in Mississippi, 135

first black head of the Ecumenical Committee of the World Methodist Conference, 332

first black on the Alabama state Supreme Court, 116

first black player drafted by the National Hockey League, 392

first black to head the U.S. Commission on Aging, 164

first black national coordinator of the Junior Catholic Daughters of the Americas, 317

first black woman to earn the doctor of science (Sc.D.) in chemical engineering, 95

first black woman to head the New York State Department of Labor, 140

first black woman to win the United States Gymnastics Championship, 392

first nationally televised benefit for education, 101

first black brigade commander at Naval Academy, 251

first black city manager of Miami, 196

first black coeditor of "Sixty Minutes," 233

first black deputy chief in Los Angeles Police Department, 193

first black gospel star to receive a star on Hollywood's Walk of Fame, 27

first black mayor in Delaware, 194

first black mayor of Augusta, GA, 197

first black mayor of Newport, RI, 212

first black mayor of Spokane, WA, 214

first black president of the American Society of Internal Medicine, 297

first black president of the California State Bar, 277

first black president of the University of Zimbabwe, 84

first black rector of James Madison University, 84

first black to receive four Special Commendation Awards from BMI, 26

first black woman junior college president in Alabama, 84

first black woman member of the AFL-CIO Executive Council, 55

first black woman president in the California higher education system, 84

first black woman president of the Chicago Teachers Union, 55

establishment of the Black Tennis and Sports Foundation, 288

first popularly elected black mayor in New England, 193

first woman police precinct commander in Detroit, 203

first woman president of the National Bar Association, 279

1982

first black and first woman executive director of the Metropolitan Housing Authority (Akron, OH), 211

first black Army Nurse Corps officer to graduate from the Army War College, 246

first black cohost of the "Today" show, 233

first black director of the Cuyahoga Metropolitan Housing Authority (Cleveland, OH), 211

first black executive editor of the news department of the *Portland Oregonian*, 226

first black four-star general in the army, 246

first black male member of the American Occupational Therapy Association, 297

first black percussionist inducted into the Percussive Art Society, 28

first black police chief in Charleston, SC, 212

first black police chief in Houston, TX, 213

first black president of the Michigan Occupational Education Association, 279

first black president of the National Association of Power Engineers, 279

first black presiding judge in Nashville-Davidson County's courts (Tennessee), 213

first black to hold an executive position in the Cleveland police department, 211

first black to win the Fourth Estate Award of the National Press Club, Washington, DC, 224–225

first black vice president of Optimists International, 288

first black woman bank president in Pennsylvania, 51

first black woman firefighter in New York City, 208

first black woman member of board of Sears, Roebuck, and Company, 63

first black woman publisher of a mainstream paper, 226

first reputed all-black and all-woman city administration, 204

first woman mayor of a city of more than 100,000, 192

first African American to sit on the bench of the U.S. Claims Court, 169

first black auxiliary bishop in the Archdiocese of New York, 317

first black basketball coach at Temple University, 377

first black elected to public office in Alaska as a Republican, 117

first black episcopal vicar of Central Harlem, 317

first black female priest in the Diocese of Newark, NJ, 324

first black inducted into the Mississippi Hall of Fame, 400

first black member of the Georgia Board of Bar Examiners, 123

first black nominated by a major party (Democratic) as a candidate for governor, 120

first black priest ordained in the Archdiocese of Miami, 317

first black state senator of Florida since Reconstruction, 121

first black superintendent of the Philadelphia, Pennsylvania, public schools, 112

first black superior court judge in Montgomery County, Maryland, 131

first black woman elected to the Anchorage, Alaska, Board of Education, 112

first black woman judge in the state of Florida, 121

first black woman ordained in the Unitarian-Universalist Church, 339

first black woman state trooper, 121

first black World Rodeo champion, 403

first black, and the first female, priest in the Diocese of Southeast Florida, 324

first director of the Mineral Management Service, U.S. Department of the Interior, 164

first elected black woman judge in the state of Tennessee, 148

first female priest of the Protestant Episcopal Church in the New York City Archdiocese, 324

first woman president of the predominantly black National Convocation of the Christian Church (Disciples of Christ), 318

1983

first black American astronaut to make a space flight, 362

first black chair of the Arkansas state Game and Fish Commission, 118

first black chief of the southern district of the California Highway Patrol, 120

first black deputy whip in the House, 182

first black elected bishop of the Evangelical Lutheran Church in America, 328

first black head basketball coach at the University of Iowa, 378

first black in Missouri to hold the position of clerk of the Superior Court, 136

first black Iowa state senator, 128

first black member of the Virginia state supreme court, 150

first black on the New York state supreme court, 141

first black to address a joint session of the legislature in the twentieth century, 116

first black United States executive director for the African Development Bank and Fund, 164

first black woman assistant sergeant-at-arms of the Senate, 183

first black woman circuit court judge in Missouri, 136

first black woman to chair the United States Federal Labor Relations Authority, 164

first black and first female pastor in the American Baptist Churches in the USA, 310

first Catholic auxiliary bishop in the Archdiocese of Detroit, 317

first complete book on blacks in sports, 405

first major black player to sign with the United States Football Lelague, 389

first state organization to authorize the ordination of women, 310

first woman Baptist to be president of the Clergy Council of Cranford, NJ, 310

first album to produce five top singles, 28

first black anchor for WMAQ-TV (Chicago), 233

first black director of the Arkansas Finance and Administration Department, 289

first black district attorney in Denver, CO, 193

first black elected mayor of Charlotte, NC, 210

first black mayor of Chicago, 199

first black Miss America, 259

first black Miss New Jersey, 259

first black municipal judge in Baton Rouge, LA, 201

first black national chair of the National Workshop on Christian Unity, 295

first black police superintendent in Chicago, 199

first black president of the North Carolina Watchmakers Association, 280

first black president of the Washington Press Club, 280

first black president of Women in Municipal Government, 280

first black to become a majority shareholder in a major metropolitan daily newspaper, 226

first black woman to win a Pulitzer Prize for a work of fiction, 416

first black-owned soft drink company, 63

1984

first black chair of American Board of Surgery, 298

first black chief of nursing at Walter Reed Army Medical Center (Washington, DC), 246

first black elected to the State Street Council (Chicago), 52

first Black Family Summit, 74

first black from a predominantly black denomination to preside over the National Council of Churches, 295

first black instrumentalist to simultaneously receive Grammy Awards as best classical and best jazz soloist, 28

first black mayor of Atlantic City, 205

first black mayor of Philadelphia, 212

first black mayors of Union Springs, Hillsboro, and Hurtsboro, AL, 189

first black member of the Birmingham Rotary Club, 288

first black modern dance troupe to perform in the Metropolitan Opera House, 5

first black police chief in Baltimore, 201

first black police chief in New York City, 208

first black president of Washington, DC, Urological Society, 298

first black runner-up in the Miss America contest, 259

first black woman financial future specialist for Prudential-Bache Securities in Chicago, 64

first black woman president of Michigan State Employees Union, 55

first black woman still photographer admitted to International Photographers of the Motion Picture and Television Industries Union, 55

first Miss America to resign title, 259

first woman of any race to be executive director of Gary, Indiana, Chamber of Commerce, 280

first woman of any race to become president of Wilberforce University, 85

first athlete to win both the 200-meter run and the 400-meter run, 401

first athlete to win four gold medals in a single Olympics since Jesse Owens (1936), 401

first black American to be a nonsymbolic candidate for the presidential nomination, 172

first black bishop of his church in South Africa, 324

first black captain in the New York State Police, 141

first black coach at the 1985 World Games for the Deaf, 378

first black coach to win the NCAA Division I championship, 378

first black congressman to chair the House Budget Committee, 183

first black doctor to establish the surgical implantation of an automatic defibrillator in the human heart, 357

first black judge in Texas, 150

first black named to the Georgia state court of appeals, 123

first black Pennsylvania state supreme court justice, 145

first black referee and judge for the Olympic Games, 402

first black skater on a World Team, 394

first black to chair the rules committee for the Democratic National Convention, 171

first black to sit on a state Supreme Court bench since Reconstruction, 178

first black to win a seat on the Harris County, Texas, Commissioners Court, 149

first black woman appointed to the Securities and Exchange Commission, 164

first black woman Louisiana state judge, 130

first black woman member of the Virginia General Assembly, 151

first black woman neurosurgeon in the United States, 357

first black woman nominated to the federal bench in Chicago, 169

first black woman state registrar of vital records in the United States, 131

first black woman tax collector in Dallas County, 116

first judge and first black appointed to the newly created Texas County Court-at-Law, Number 3, 149

first player named to the Parade All-American team for four consecutive years, 401

first woman bishop of the United Methodist Church, 333

first woman to become a member of the Harlem Globetrotters, 378

1985

first black and first woman treasurer of the Democratic National Convention, 172

first black and first woman to chair the Georgia Campaign and Financial Disclosure Commission, 124

first black congressman to head the Program and Budget Authorization Subcommittee of the House Permanent Select Committee on Intelligence, 180

first black director of the Federal Emergency Management Agency, 164

first black man inducted into the International Tennis Hall of Fame, 405

first black superintendent of schools in the Boston public school system, 112

first black supreme court judge, 135

first black tenured professor at Harvard Business School, 98

first black to serve full-time on the New York state court of appeals, 141

first black to serve on the Georgia state supreme court in this century, 124

first black woman appointed judge in the State Court of Fulton County, Georgia, 124

first black woman member of the Mississippi state house of representatives, 135

first to pilot a space shuttle mission, 362

first black chancellor of California's community colleges, 85

first black mayor in the state of New York, 208

first black member of board of AMA, 297

first black member of the board of Norfolk Southern Railroad Company, 65

first black police chief of Miami, 196

first black police superintendent of New Orleans, 201

first black president of Pontiac Kiwanis Club (MI), 288

first black president of the South Carolina Bar Association, 280

first black to head an American Legion department in the deep South, 295

first black vice-chairperson of Board of Regents of the University System of Georgia, 85

first black woman deputy police chief in Washington, DC, 215

first black woman educator on postage stamp, 260

first black woman to head a major community foundation, 288

first black woman to obtain the rank of brigadier general in the regular army, 247

1986

first African to gain the Nobel Prize for literature, 412

first black and first woman mayor of Newport News, VA, 214

first black appointed conductor of the Royal Ballet Company, 29

first black assistant chief in Los Angeles Fire Department, 192 first black chair of Georgia University System Board of Regents, 85

first black city manager of Dallas, 213

first black commander of the Quantico, VA, marine facility, 250

first black explorer on postage stamp, 260

first black jazz musician on postage stamp, 260

first black police chief in Greenville, MS, 204

first black police chief in Pittsburgh, 212

first black police lieutenant in Birmingham, 190

first black president at any level in the National Academy of Television Arts and Sciences, 280

first black president of Boston City Council, 202

first black president of the Harvard Ripon Society, 274

first black president of the Trident Chamber of Commerce (SC), 280

first black sole owner of a major soft-drink bottling franchise, 58

first black sorority to have a sorority house on the campus of the University of Alabama, 295

first black to chair a session of the International Courtly Literature Society, 274

first black vice president/region manager in St. Louis, 63

first black weekday anchor KCBS-TV (Los Angeles), 234

first black woman city attorney in California, 192

first black woman mayor of major northeastern city, 193

first black woman president of Lincoln University (PA), 85

first black woman selected for induction into the Rock 'n' Roll Hall of Fame and Museum, 29

first black woman to Chair Oxfam America, 288

first black woman to host a nationally syndicated talk show, 234

first black-owned network affiliate televison station, 41

first elected black mayor of Baltimore, 202

first woman mayor of Little Rock, Arkansas, 190

first woman presiding judge in Los Angeles Municipal Court, 192

first black American ambassador to South Africa, 165

first black astronaut killed during a space mission, 362

first black chair of the Pennsylvania state Civil Service Commission, 145

first black congressman elected from Mississippi since Reconstruction, 183

first black FBI executive assistant director, 163

first black football player to gain more than 20,000 yards, 390

first black lieutenant governor of Virginia, 151

first black prosecutor for Essex County, NJ, 138

first black woman athletic director in the Southern Intercollegiate Athletic Conference, 363

first black woman elected to the Oklahoma state senate, 143

first black woman member of the state legislature from Charleston County, South Carolina, 147

first blacks elected to the Alabama Board of Education, 113

first councilwoman-at-large of New Orleans, 130

first female president of the New Jersey Council of Churches, 327

1987

first black and the first woman commissioner of Mississippi's Workers' Compensation Commission, 135

first black appointed to the state racing commission, 117

first black chair of the Georgia Board of Bar Examiners, 123

first black commissioner of the Pennsylvania state police, 145

first black elected in a Mississippi county-wide election since Reconstruction, 135

first black member of the Tennessee state court of appeals, 148 first black occupies a cabinet position in Oklahoma, 143

first black to command a space shuttle, 362

first black to head a predominantly white United Methodist church in the Central Texas Conference, 333

first black to head the Potomac Association Conference of the United Church of Christ, 340

first black to win boxing titles in five different weight classes, 383

first black trustee-elected professor at a Southern Baptist institution, 310

first black Virginia state judge in Fairfax County, 151

first black woman astronaut, 362

first black woman speaker pro tem of the Tennessee house, 149

first National Black Catholic Congress meeting since 1894, 318

first woman elected mayor of Little Rock, 118

first woman of any race to coach men's and women's teams at a major institution, 408

first black and first woman elected president of the Niagara Frontier Corporate Counsel Association, 280

first black and first woman to chair the Dallas/Fort Worth International Airport Board of Directors, 257

first black chair of the Arts, Communication, Entertainment, and Sports section of the Michigan State Bar Association, 281

first black chair of the National Pulitzer Prize Board, 226

first black chief of the U.S. Army Nurse Corps, 246

first black fraternity to have a house on fraternity row at the University of Mississippi, 295

first black frontiersman on postage stamp, 260

first black law school dean in the South, 85

first black member of the Junior League of Birmingham, AL, 288

first black national security advisor, 247

first black on executive board of the National Police Officers Association of America, 281

first black president of National Association of Boards of Pharmacy, 298

first black president of Professional Secretaries International, Illinois division, 280

first black president of Southern California Chapter of the American College of Surgeons, 298

first black president of the Georgia Municipal Association, 281

first black president of the Georgia School Boards Association, 281

first black president of Women's Advertising Club (Chicago), 280

first black to serve as mayor of Baltimore, 202

first black to direct a major national radio news network, 230

first black to head a division of Greyhound Lines, 65

first black to head Women in Real Estate (Chicago), 281

first black woman automobile dealer, 50

first black woman president of Spelman College, 85

first state historic site honoring a black in North Carolina, 261

first black president of the New York State Society of Certified Public Accountants, 280

1988

first black assistant chief in Los Angeles Police Department, 193

first black assistant corporate vice president of urban affairs at Turner Broadcasting System, 232

first black cultural group to tour the Soviet Union under the renewed cultural exchange program, 4

first black elected to Olympia, WA, City Council, and first black woman elected to any city post in the state, 214

first black general manager of Greater Macon Chamber of Commerce (Georgia), 281

first black head of a major mixed ethnic group of the AFL-CIO, 56

first black mayor in Augusta, ME, 201

first black member of Salesmanship Club, Dallas, 282

first black police chief in Natchez, MS, 204

first black police chief in Philadelphia, 212

first black vice president of the International Ladies' Garment Workers Union, 55

first black winner of ASCAP Duke Award, 29

first black woman commander on Chicago police force, 200

first monument to blacks in the Revolutionary War approved, 262

first National Black Arts Festival, 6

first president of Clark Atlanta University, 85

first woman vice president of YMCA of Greater New York, 288

first black woman judge in Pulaski County, 118

first African American and first woman to appear on the presidential ballot in all fifty states, 172

first black American woman to qualify for federal matching funds in a presidential election, 172

first black archbishop in the United States, 318

first black bishop of the Evangelical Lutheran Church in America, 328

first black chancellor of the New York City school system, 113

first black commissioner of the Department of Mental Health, 132

first black congressman elected from the state of New Jersey, 183

first black director of public safety in DeKalb County, Georgia, 124

first black executive director of the North Carolina state Democratic Party, 141

first black identical twins ordained priests in the Catholic Church, 318

first black in the First Judicial District, 118

first black judge in Fayette County, Kentucky, 129

first black male member of the United States Olympic gymnastics team, 392

first black member of the men's All-American squash team of the National Intercollegiate Squash Racquets Association, 405

first black Olympic winner in tennis, 405

first black priest in Arkansas, 318

first black quarterback to start a Super Bowl game, 390

first black referee in the National Football League, 390

first black swimming champion in Olympic games, 402

first black Texas Ranger, 149

first black to chair the state board of law examiners, 118

first black Virginia state supreme court justice, 151

first black woman to serve on a United States Bankruptcy Court, 148

first black woman to serve on state supreme court (Pennsylvania), 144

first blacks appointed to curcuit chancery judgeships to oversee the juvenile division , 117

first general superintendent of the Dallas, Texas, Independent School District, 113

first international development program sponsored by a black church, 301

first medal won by a black athlete in the Winter Olympics, 396

first swimming champion from South America, 402

first U.S. woman to win the Olympic long jump, 402

first head of Service and Development Agency, 301

1989

first all-black church in Vermont, 311

first black administrator of the Office of Personnel Management, 165

first black cabinet member in the Bush administration, 165

first black commissioner of the Continental Basketball Association, 378

first black female assistant secretary in the U.S. Health and Human Services Department, 165

first black head coach in modern National Football League history, 390

first black named chairman of the National Democratic Party, 183

first black National Basketball Association team owners, 378

first black president of a baseball league, 373

first black supreme court justice, 123

first black to serve as a majority whip in the House, 183

first black umpire to officiate in a World Series game, 373

first black woman moderator of the Presbytery of Baltimore, 338

first black woman to head the Presbyterian Church (USA), 338

first black woman to serve as Commissioner of Social Security, 165

first chief veterinary officer for the U.S. Public Health Service, 165

first female Anglican bishop in the world, 324

first black chair of board of United Way, 288

first black chairman of the Joint Chiefs of Staff, 247

first black chancellor of Los Angeles Community Colleges, 86

first black columnist to win a Pulitzer Prize, 226

first black congressman from New Jersey, 286

first black executive vice president of programming for Public Broadcasting Service, 41

first black first woman chair of the Board of Trustees of the Free Library of Philadelphia, 212

first black head of Rockefeller Foundation, 288

first black inspector general of the army, 247

first black mayor of Fairmont, NC, 210

first elected black mayor of New York City, 208

first black mayor of Tchula, MS, 204

first black president of Alabama Society of Pediatric Dentistry, 298

first black president of Business and Professional Women/USA, 282

first black president of the American Speech-Language-Hearing Association, 282

first black Rockette at Radio City Music Hall, 30

first black to head New York City Bar Association, 282

first black man to host a nationally broadcast weekly television talk show, 41

first black woman director of a full-length film for a major U.S. studio, 9

first black woman vice president of a major record company, 29

first memorial to the civil rights movement of the 1960s, 71

first person to receive an honorary degree from the Coast Guard Academy, 249

first woman warden of Manhattan House of Corrections, 209

1990

first black (and first woman) president of the University of Houston, 86

first black anchor team in a major metropolitan city, 234

first black chief of the *Detroit Free Press* City-County Bureau, 226

first black city editor of the *Times Picayune*, 227

first black director of Reebok International, 59

first black lobbyist for the Junior League, 289

first black Miss USA, 259

first black president of a Rotary Club in South Carolina, 288

first black president of American College of Obstetricians, 298

first black president of McDonald's Owners of Chicagoland and Northwest Indiana, 282

first black president of Middle Tennessee State University, 86

first black president of the International Association of Chiefs of Police, 282

first black to head a major utility company, 60

first black to head Kentucky Association of State Employees/FSE, 56

first black to head Tennessee university system, 86

first black to director of total quality management with Caltex Petroleum Corporation (TX), 282

first black to win the Democratic nomination for United States senator, 210

first black trustee of Kiwanis International, 289

first black undersecretary of the Smithsonian Institution, 268

first black vice president of Nissan Mortor Corporation in the United States, 50

first black woman brigadier general in the air force, 239

first black woman city attorney in Austin, TX, 213

first black woman journalist on postage stamp, 260

first black woman mayor of Washington, DC, 217

first black woman president of Chicago State University, 86

first black woman to edit a major daily newspaper, 227

first blackwoman press secretary for a United States senator, 230

first building named in honor of a black at Louisiana State University, Baton Rouge, 80

first person to receive the Nelson Mandela Courage Award, 38

first woman president of the National Conference of Black Mayors, 204

African-American Catholic Church established, 303

first black American to chair the United States Postal Rate Commission, 166

first black and first woman elected president of the Philadelphia Board of Education, 109

first black appointed to the Indiana Court of Appeals, 126

first black chair of the state Democratic Party, 118

first black chief judge of the Northern California U.S. District Court, 169

first black governor of Virginia, 151

first black member of the U. S. Equestrian Team, 394

first black state supreme court chief justice of Florida, 122

first black student to become editor of the *Harvard Law Review,* 105

first black to head any branch of government in Florida, 122

first black to head the National Science Foundation, 357

first black woman assistant general manager of the Boston Red Sox, 373

first black woman elected to the Allegheny County, Pennsylvania, bench, 145

first black woman president of the New York City Board of Education, 113

first college football coach of any race to win 368 games in a career, 390

1991

first black and the youngest golfer ever to win the U.S. Junior Amateur championship, 391

first black commander of the Connecticut State Police, 121

first black elected to a New York statewide position, 142

first black elected to the Minnesota state supreme court, 134

first black ever to qualify for the Indianapolis 500, 364

first Black Muslim to give the invocation in the House of Representatives, 334

first black named to the Colorado supreme court, 120

first black Protestant Episcopal bishop in the West, 325

first black speaker of the Arkansas state house of representatives, 118

first black to be elected Fulton County, Georgia solicitor, 124

first black to be one of the seven presidents of the World Council of Churches, 327

first black to receive the National Medal of Technology, 349

first black to steal 939 bases in a career, 373

first black vice president for labor relations of the National Football League, 390

first black woman chair of the Democratic Party of Maryland, 131

first black woman elected sheriff, 124

first black woman elected to the Tennessee state senate, 149

first black woman in the United States to be elected state attorney, 128

first black woman judge in Saint Clair County, Missouri, 136 first black woman to chair the Executive Council of the United Church of Christ, 340

first black woman to receive the Theodore Roosevelt Award of the NCAA, 406

first elected black woman judge in Kentucky, 129

first black and first woman co-chair of National Conference of Christians and Jews, 295

first black awarded Medal of Honor for World War I (posthumous), 248

first black inventor on postage stamp, 260

first black mayor of Denver, CO, 193

first black mayor of Kansas City, MO, 204

first black national president of the American Business Women's Association, 282

first black president of Andover Newton Theological School, Newton Centre, MA, 86

first black woman cartoonist nationally syndicated in the white press, 3

first black woman on Los Angeles City Council, 193

1992

first African-Caribbean writer to win the Nobel Prize in literature, 412

first black Americans to sail in the America's Cup, 403

first black and first Baptist to become university chaplain at Yale University, 311

first black and first woman general counsel of Pennsylvania Electric Association, 283

first black board member of National Association of the Deaf, 283

first black chancellor of the Philadelphia Bar Association, 283

first black church to be admitted to the Selma Baptist Association, 311

first black dean of Washington National Cathedral, 325

first black elected to International Olympic Committee executive board, 383

first black elected to national board of Sierra Club, 289

first black elected to represent Alabama in the House since Reconstruction, 185

first black film director nominated for an Acadamy Award, 9

first black group to have a record at top of pop chart for twelve consecutive weeks, 30

first black head coach at the University of Mississippi, 378

first black heavyweight wrestling champion, 407

first black husband and wife team on Superior Court of the District of Columbia, 217

first black in international luge competition, 402

first black in senior management post with the Red Cross, 341

first black mayor of Memphis, 112, 213

first black member of the Olympic luge team, 402

first black musical director of the "Tonight Show," 29

first black pianist to win the Naumburg Competition, 30

first black police chief in Cairo, IL, 200

first black police chief in Los Angeles, 212

first black police chief in St. Paul, MN, 203

first black popularly elected mayor of Cincinnati, 211

first black president of Academy of General Dentistry, 298

first black president of the Boston Society of Architects, 283

first black president of the Virginia Association of Broadcasters, 283

first black representatives from North Carolina in the twentieth century, 185

first black to hold the four-year post of president of the United States Olympic Committee, 383

first black U.S. Congressman from South Carolina in modern times, 186

first black woman editor of *Oakland Tribune,* 227

first black woman elected to the U.S. House from Georgia, 185

first black woman in space, 362

first black woman representative from North Carolina, 185

first black woman to head a public university in Michigan, 87 first black woman to represent Florida in Congress, 184

first black woman writer-director to have a feature-length film in national distribution, 9

first black women gymnasts to compete on a United States Olympic team, 392

first drag queen recording star, 30

first impeached federal officer to be elected to another federal post, 183

first non-American black elected to head the Board of Bishops of the AME Zion Church, 302

first U.S. black woman senator, 184

first woman chair of National Black Police Association, 283

first woman ever to repeat as Olympic heptathlon champion, 402

first woman president of Chicago Dental Scoeity, 298

first woman to head a major public utility, 60

recipient of largest gift ever given to a historically black college, 101

1993

first black American to win the Nobel Prize in literature, 413

first black and Democrat mayor of Evanston, IL, 200

first black and first woman Secretary of Energy, 167

first black and the first woman United States Surgeon General, 166

first black appointed director of the Centers for Disease Control, 350

first black bishop in the state of Tennessee, 318

first black bowler to win the Firestone Tournament of Champions, 379

first black boxer on postage stamp, 260

first black chair of the House Armed Services Committee, 186

first black chief academic and budget officer at Stanford University, 87

first black ever confirmed to the cabinet as head of Veterans Affairs, 166

first black fire chief in New Orleans, 201

first black head of Administrators and Teachers of English as a Second Language, 283

first black honored as American Business Woman of the Year, 60

first black inaugural poet, 420

first black inducted into the Walk of Western Stars, 9

first black mayor of St. Louis, MO, 204

first black named deputy secretary of state, 167

first black president of American Society of Newspaper Editors, 226

first black Secretary of Agriculture, 183

first black to call balls and strikes in a World Series game, 373

first black to head a major public broadcasting organization, 231

first black to head the Federal Highway Administration, 167

first black to hold the cabinet post of Secretary of Commerce, 183

first black to own the Harlem Globetrotters, 375

first black to head a medical school in the United States, 87

first black to serve as governor of Arkansas, 118

first black woman to serve as White House photographer, 167

first pitcher of any race to lose twenty-seven consecutive decisions, 374

KEYWORD INDEX

(ITALICIZED PAGE NUMBERS INDICATE PHOTOS)

A

Aaron, Hank, 371, 372, *372*

Abbot, Robert Sengstake. *See* Sengstake, Robert Abbott

ABC bowling championships, 379

ABC television, 46, 233

Abel, Elijah, 333

Abeta Hebrew Cultural Center, 312

Abolition, 150, 410

Abrams, Albert, 281

Abrams, Roslyn Maria (Roz), 277

Abyssinian Baptist Church, 39, 305

Academy Award, 9

Academy of General Dentistry, 298

Acme Colored Giants, 365

Actor's Equity Association, 47

Actors Playhouse, 39

Adair, Thelma Davidson, 338

Adam-Ender, Clara Leach, 246

Adams, Alton Augustus, 252

Adams, John Quincy, 76

Adams, Numa Pompilius Garfield, 355

Adams, Oscar W., Jr., 116

Addams, Jane, 290

Adger, William, 89

Administrators and Teachers of English as a Second Language, 283

Advertising, 49

AFL-CIO Executive Council, 55

AFL-CIO Steel Workers Union, 54, 56

African Baptist Church, 305, 306, 307

African Blood Brotherhood, 293

African Development Bank and Fund, 164

African Dorcas Society (New York), 284

African Free School, 105, *106,* 336, 351

African Free School No. 2, 42, 105

African Friendly Society (Philadelphia), 284

African Insurance Company, 52

African Legion, 72

African Meeting House, 306, 341

African Methodist Episcopal (AME) Church, 99, 142, 227, 243, 250, 299–301, 324, 327, 329, 330

African Methodist Episcopal (AME) Zion Church, 301–303

African Orthodox Church, 207, 303, 337

African Society (Boston), 284

African Society (New York), 284

African Theater Company, 42

African Union American Methodist Episcopal Church, 303

African Union Society (Newport, RI), 283, 290

African Zoar Church, 330

African-American Catholic Church, 303

Africana, 46

Afro-American Company, 223

Afro-American group, 224

Afro-American Symphony, 18

Afro-Presbyterian Council, 336

Agency for International Development, 161

Agins, Michelle V., 55

Agyeman, Jaramogi Abebe, 311

Aida, 19

Aiken, Loretta Mary. *See* Mabley, Moms

Ailey, Allen, 5

Air Corps' Central Instructors School, 64

"Airy Man Blues," 16

Akron Indians, 386

Akron, OH, 211

Alabama Center for Higher Education, 189

Alabama Penny Savings Bank, 50

Alabama Society of Pediatric Dentistry, 298

Alabama Southern Baptist Convention, 311

Alabama State University, 100

Alabama, municipal government in, 189

Alabama, 115–116

Alabama-Mississippi, 116

Alameda Newspaper Group, 226

Alaska, 116–117

Alcorn Agricultural and Mechanical College (Mississippi), 100

Alcorn College (Alcorn State University), 81, 135, 175

Alcorn, James I., 100

Aldrige, Ira Frederick, 42

Alexander and Company General Insurance Agency, 52

Alexander High School (Monrovia, Liberia), 220

Alexander Pierre Tureaud, Sr., Hall, 80

Alexander, Clifford, Jr., 162

Alexander, Fritz W., II, 141

Alexander, Joyce London, 169

Alexander, Michael, 313

Alexander, Sadie Tanner Mossell, 93, 95

Alexander, Theodore Martin, Sr., 52

Alexander, Walter Gilbert, 137

Alexis, Marcus, 163

Ali, Muhammad, 382, 383

Ali, Noble Drew, 327

Alice Freeman Palmer Institute, 80. See also Palmer Memorial Institute

Alienated American, 221

All American Women, 85

All-American Football Conference, 387

Allen & Son Super Market, 379

Allen, Aris, 131, 171

Allen, Elbert E., 111

Allen, Macon B., 132, 190

Allen, Milton B., 201

Allen, Richard, 72, 75, 259, 299, 299, 300, 329, 330

Allen, William G., 96

Allensworth, Allen, 244

Allensworth, California, 244

Alpha Kappa Alpha, 294, 295

Alpha Lodge of New Jersey, Number 116, Free and Accepted Masons, 294

Alpha Phi Alpha, 1, 294

Alpha Phi Omega, 347

Alvin Ailey Dance Theater, 5

"A.M. Chicago," 234

Amalgamated Meat Cutters and Butcher Workmen, 55

Amateur Athletic Union, 398, 407

AMC Cancer Research Center Humanitarian Award, 264

AME. See African Methodist Episcopal (AME) Church

AME Church Magazine, 227

AME Zion Church. See African Methodist Episcopal (AME) Zion Church

American Antislavery Society, 56

American Association, 365

American Association League, 367

American Association of Physical Anthropologists, 273

American Bankers Association, 275

American Baptist Churches in the USA, 310

American Baptist Missionary Convention, 307

American Baptist Publication Society, 309

American Baptist, 222

American Bar Association, 73

American Basketball League, 375

American Board of Surgery, 298

American Business Woman of the Year, 60

American Business Women, 282

American Business Women's Association, 60

American Chemical Association, 273

American College of Obstetricians and Gynecologists, 298

American College of Surgeons, 296

American Dart Foundation, 384

American Federation of Government Employees, 55, 56

American flag, 400

American Football League, 387

American Friends Service Committee, 143

American Hall of Fame (New York University), 37

American Historical Association, 273

American Institute of Architects, 1

American League of Colored Workers, 53

American Library Association, 276, 277

American Medical Association, 296

American Medical Society, 295, 297

American Methodism, 330

American Missionary Association, 99, 100, 107, 320

American Music Awards, 28

American National Baptist Convention, 309

American National Red Cross, 297

American Negro Academy, 271

American Occupational Therapy Association, 297

American Pharmaceutical Association, 297

American Political Science Association, 273

American Professional Football Association, 386

American Professional Football League, 385

American Psychological Association, 273

American Red Cross, 341, 355

American Revolution, 379

American Seamen's Protective Association, 53

American Shakespeare Festival (Stratford,CT), 47

American Society of Newspaper Editors, 226

American Sociological Society, 273

American Speech-Language-Hearing Association, 282

American Stock Exchange, 63

American Telephone and Telegraph Company, 382

American Tennis Association, 404

American Theatre Wing, 47

American University, 268

Amerson, Lucius D., 115

Amherst College, 88, 157

Amherstburg Association, 307

Amistad revolt, 76

Amo, Anthony William, 87

Amos, Wally, 62

Amsterdam News, 53, 221

Ancient Order of Gleaners, 293

Anderson, Charles Alfred, 255

Anderson, Charles W., 128, 155

Anderson, Edwyna, 283

Anderson, Hubert, 283, 378

Anderson, James, Jr., 250

Anderson, James H., 221

Anderson, Marian, 23, 24, 264

Anderson, Moses, 317

Anderson, Mother Leafy, 339

Anderson, Vinton R., 327

Anderson, Violette N., 125

Anderson, William, 303

Andover Newton Theological School, 86

Angelou, Maya (Marguerite Johnson), 5, *5, 420*

Anglo-African magazine, 221, 420

Anita Bush Players, 44

Annie Allen, 420

Anthony and Cleopatra, 25

Anti-Slavery Society, 170, 306

Antioch Association of Metaphysical Science, 304

Antioch College, 56

Antislavery laws, 69

Apollo Theater, 20, 24, 36, 40

Apostolic Overcoming Holy Church of God, 337

Appropriations Committee, 180

Arab-Israeli War, 156

Archibald, Julius A., 138

Architecture, 1

Ardennes offensive (WWII), 246

Aristides, 393

Arizona, 117

Arizona State University, 117

Arizona, municipal government in, 190

Arkansas, 117–118

Arkansas Finance and Administration Department, 288

Arkansas Regional Minority Council, 118

Arkansas riot of October 1919, 117

Arkansas State University Board of Trustees, 83

Arkansas, municipal government in, 190

Arledge, Missouri "Big Mo," 375

Arlene, Herbert, 144

Armstrong, (Daniel) Louis, 6

Armstrong, Henry "Hammering Hank," 381

Armstrong, Joan B., 130

Army War College, 246

Arnett, Benjamin William, 142, *142*

Arrington, Richard, Jr., 189

Art Institute of Chicago, 46

Arthur, Chester, 70

Arts, Communication, Entertainment, and Sports Section, Michigan State Bar Association, 281

As Thousands Cheer, 46

Asbury, 329

Asbury Methodist Church, 303

Asbury, Francis, 330

ASCAP, 17

ASCAP Duke Award, 29

Ashe, Arthur, *178,* 405, *405*

Ashford, Emmett, 371

Ashmun Institute, 99

Associated Actors and Artists of America, 47

Associated Negro Press, 224

Associated Press, 280

Association for the Study of Negro Life and History, 271, 411

Association of Black Caulkers, 53

Association of the Bar of the City of New York, 282

Athletic Foundation of Los Angeles, 383

Atkins, Hannah Diggs, 143

Atkins, Thomas I., 202

Atlanta Baptist Female Seminary, 100

Atlanta Baptist Seminary (now Clark Atlanta University), 414

Atlanta Braves, 371

Atlanta Chamber of Commerce, 275, 277

Atlanta Christian College, 320

Atlanta Committee for the Olympic Games, 181

Atlanta Constitution, 227

Atlanta Daily World, 222, 223

Atlanta Fire Bureau, 124

Atlanta, GA, 196, 197

Atlanta Life Insurance Company, 277

Atlanta Municipal Court, 124

Atlanta Press Club, 277

Atlanta State Savings Bank, 51

Atlanta University, 101, 140, 157, 186, 250, 263, 385, 386, 411

Atlanta University System, 101

Atlanta Urban League, 122

Atlantic City Seagulls, 392

Atlantic City, NJ, 205

Atlantic Records, 29

Atomic Energy Commission, 341

Augusta Opportunities Industrialization Center, 124

Augusta, Alexander T., 242, 351

Augusta, GA, 197

Augusta, ME, 201

Aunt Jemima Mills Company, 49

Aunt Jemima, 49

Austin, Richard H., 134

Austin, TX, 213

Autobiography: Benjamin O. Davis, Jr.: American, 239

Autobiography of a Fugitive Negro (Ward) 53, 170

Autobiography of Malcolm X, 41

Automobile industry, 49

Automobile racing, 363, 364

Avery Normal Institute, 107

Ayer, Gertrude Elise McDougald, 109

Azusa Street Mission, 334

B

"Baby Seals Blues," 14

"Backwater Blues," 16

Bacon, Alice M., 359

Baer, Max, 381

Baety, Edward L., 196

Bailey, DeFord, Sr., 17

Bailey, Frederick Augustus, 170

Baker, Evelyn Marie, 136

Baker, Gene, 370

Baker, Gwendolyn Calvert, 113

Baker, Henry Edwin, 347

Baker, James Estes, 161

Baker, Nelson T., Sr., 93

Bakersfield, CA, 191

Bakr, Abu, 327

Balas, Mary Frances, 312

Baldwin, Cynthia A., 145

Baldwin, John, 290

Baltimore Afro-American, 222, 223

Baltimore City Council, 131

Baltimore Colts, 386

Baltimore County Medical Society, 296

Baltimore Intelligencer, 30

Baltimore Open, 379

Baltimore Orioles, 366, 371

Baltimore, MD, 201, 202, 237

Bankhead, Dan, 367

Banks, Ernie, 370

Banks, Fred, 135

Banks, Jessie, 204

Banneker, Benjamin, 359, *359*

Bannister, Edward Mitchell, 31

Baptism, 304

Baptist Foreign Mission Convention of the United States of America, 308

Baptist Hospital, 399

Baptist Publishing Board, 310

Baptists, 304–311

Barack, Obama, 105

Barber, Samuel, 25

Barksdale, Don, 374

Barnard College, 160

Barnett, Ethel S., 145

Barnett, Marguerite Ross, 86

Barnett, Ross R., 103

Barrett, Jackie, 124

Barry, Marion S., Jr., 74, *74,* 291

"Bars Fight," 417

Barthé, Richmond, 37

Barthelemy, Sidney John, 130, *130*

Baseball, 365–374

Baseball Writers Association of America, 279

Basie, Count (William), 24

Basketball, 374–378

Bass, Charlotta A. Spears, 171, 222

Bass, Sam, 203

Bassett, Ebenezer Don Carlos, 154

Bates College, 165, 233

Bates, Daisy, 110

Baton Rouge, LA, 201

Baxter, Nathan D., 325

Bay of Pigs, 317

Bayreuth Festival. *See* Wagner Bayreuth Festival

BBDO Advertising, NY, 49

Beard, Andrew J., 346

Beard, Delawrence, 131

Bearden, Bessye Jeanne Banks, 108

Bearden, Romare, 108

"Beat It," 28

Bebop, 28. *See also* Bop

Bechet, Sidney, 16

Beckham, Ruth Howard, 93

Becton, Julius Wesley, Jr., 164

Belafonte, Harry (Harold George), Jr., 8, 38

Bell, Christine, 64

Bell, Dennis, 244

Bell, Derrick, 97

Bell, Jack, 279

Bell, James "Cool Papa," 366

Bell, Kathleen, 117

Bell, Mary, 204

Bell, Travers, Jr., 63

Belmont Stakes, 394

Beloved, 413

Benezet, Anthony, 105

Benham, Robert, 123

Benjamin Banneker Honor College, 95

Benjamin, Miriam E., 346

Bennett College, 163, 286

Bennett, Hyram S., 264

Benny Goodman's band, 20

Berea College (Kentucky), 96, 99, 272

Berkeley, CA, 191, 192

Berklee College of Music, 25

Bernard Couvent Institute for Indigent Catholic Orphans, 411

Berry, Chuck (Charles Edward Anderson), 26

Berry, Edwin C., 267

Berry, Leonidas H., 355

Berry, Theodore Moody, 211

Bertrand, Joseph G., 198

Bess, Reginald, 274

Bethel African Methodist Episcopal Church, 329

Bethel Church, 299, 300

Bethune, Mary McLeod, 104, 155, 184, 260, 261, 291

Bethune, Thomas Greene (Blind Tom), 11

Bethune-Cookman College, 184

"Beulah," 7, 46

Bible Church of Christ, 337

Bible Way Church of Our Lord Jesus Christ World Wide, 337

Bicycling, 384

Biddle University, 385

Biddle, Nicholas, 237

Big Sea, The, 45

Bilal, 327

Billboard's Hot One Hundred chart, 30

"Billie Jean," 28

Binga State Bank, 50

Binga, Jesse, 50

Birch, A. A., Jr., 148, 213

Birds of Aristophanes, 413

Birmingham Black Barons, 25

Birmingham Rotary Club, 288

Birmingham, AL, 189, 190

Birth of a Nation, 7

Bishop, Josiah, 306

Black Bottom, 3

Black Bourgeoisie, 273

Black Boy, 415

Black Christian Nationalism, 311

Black Christian Nationalist Church, 311

Black Cross Nurses, 72

Black Entertainment Television (BET), 41

Black History Month. *See* Negro History Week

Black Journal, 39

Black Judaism, 311–312

Black Man in the White House (Morrow), 157

Black Messiah, The, 311

Black Methodists for Church Renewal, 340

Black Militia, 237

Black nationalism, 311

Black Nationalist Church, 311

Black nuns, 312

"Black Power," 74

Black Presbyterians United, 336

Black Progressive Shopper-News, 225

Black Requiem, 25

Black Revolutionary War Patriots Memorial, 262

Black Star Shipping Line, 72

Black Stars, 228

Black Swan label, 15

Black Swan Opera Troupe, 10

Black Tennis and Sports Foundation, 288

Black Voices, 143

Black World, 228

Black, Joe, 369

Blackburn, Cleo W., 276

Blackiston, Harry S., 92

Blackman, Pomp, 238

Blacks Elected to The House of
Representatives in the Nineteenth
Century, 174

Blacks Elected to the Senate in the
Nineteenth Century, 175

Blackwell, David H., 273

Blackwell, James E., 273

Blackwell, Unita, 204

Blackwood, Ronald A., 208

Blair, Ezell, 73

Blair, Henry, 343

Blake, Robert, 251

Bland, James, 11

Blayton, J. B., 34

Blind Tom. *See* Bethune, Thomas Greene

Blue, Daniel Terry, Jr., 118

Blues of Shelby, Ohio, 385

Bluest Eye, The, 413

"Bluestone" African Baptist Church, 304

Bluett, Thomas, 409

Bluford, Guion S., 362, *362*

Bluitt, Juliann, 298

BMI, 17, 26

Board of Regents of the University System
of Georgia, 85

Bob (Juan Crisobal), 268

Bodybuilding, 378–179

Boegues, Rosine, 312

Bolden, Charles "Buddy" ("King Bolden"),
11

Bolin, Gaius C., 206

Bolin, Jane M., 206

Bolivia, 155

Bolle, Winnie McKenzie, 324

Bolling, Bruce C., 202

Bond, Horace Mann, 81

Bond, Julian, 171

Book of the Month Club, 415

Booker T. Washington Theater, 12

Booker, Joe, 276

Booker, Simeon S., 224

Booth, L. Venhael, 310

Bop, 20, 23. *See also* Bebop

Borromeo, Saint Charles, 317

Boseman, B. A., 102

Bosley, Freeman, Jr., 204

Bostic, Joe, 21

Boston Braves, 367

Boston Bruins, 392

Boston Celtics, 375, 376, 377, 378

Boston College, 407

Boston College of Law School, 186

Boston Foundation, 288

Boston Globe, 279

Boston Red Sox, 373

Boston Society of Architects, 283

Boston Symphony, 15

Boston University, 155, 165, 178, 234, 412

Boston University Law School, 181

Boston, A. F., 64

Boston, MA, 202

Boswell, Cathy, 401

Boswell, Leviticus Lee, 339

Bottoms, Lawrence Wendell, 338

Bouchet, Edward Alexander, 89, 271

Bousfield, Midian Othello, 109

Bowdoin College, 88, 157, 295

Bowen, Anthony, 284

Bowen, John Wesley E., Sr., 81, 102

Bowen, Ruth J., 59

Bowers, Joseph Oliver, 315

Bowling, 379

Boxing, 379

Boyd, R. F., 296

Boyd, William M., III, 83

Boys N the Hood, 9

Boyz II Men, 30

Bradford, Perry, 35

Bradley, Andrew M., 144

Bradley, Buddy (Clarence), 3

Bradley, Edward P. (Ed), 233, *233*

Bradley, Roberta Palm, 60

Bradley, Thomas, 120, 191, 203

Brady, Saint Elmo, 96

Branch, Ben F., 63

Brandon, Barbara, 3

Brandon, Brumsic, Jr., 3

Branham, George, III, 379

Braun, Carol E. Moseley, 184, *185*

Brawley, Benjamin Griffith, 413

Brewer, Jesse A., 193

Brewster, W. Herbert, Sr., 20

Brimmer, Andrew Felton, 159

Brisco-Hooks, Valerie, 401

Briscoe, Marlin, 387

Bristow, Lonnie R., 297

British Army, 379

Broadcast Music, Inc. *See* BMI

Brock, Lou, 373, 374

Bronx Community College, 83

Brooke, Edward William, 132, *133,* 178

Brooklyn College, 163, 180, 208

Brooklyn Dodgers, 367, 369, 385

Brooklyn Law School, 208

Brooklyn Uniques, 365

Brooks, Elmer D., 288

Brooks, Gwendolyn, 420, *420*

Brooks, Vincent K., 250

Brough, Louise, 405

Brown Chapel, A Story in Verse, 418

Brown Fellowship (Charleston, SC), 284

Brown University, 82, 157, 171, 386

Brown v. Board of Education, 72, 160

Brown, Ava L., 280

Brown, Caesar, 238

Brown, Charlotte Hawkins, 80, *80*

Brown, Cheryl Adrenne, 257

Brown, Cora M., 133, *133*

Brown, Dorothy Lavinia, 148, 356

Brown, Dwayne, 128

Brown, Gayleatha, 289

Brown, George, 148

Brown, George L., 120

Brown, Henry, 42

Brown, Jesse, 166

Brown, Jesse Leroy, 254

Brown, Jill, 257

Brown, Jim, 387

Brown, John, 31, 76, 416

Brown, Lee P., 213, 282

Brown, Morris, 75, 299

Brown, Robert J., 65

Brown, Ronald (Ron) H., 183, *183*

Brown, Solomon G., 342

Brown, Thomas Edison, Jr., 124

Brown, Vander, Jr., 65

Brown, Wesley A., 251

Brown, Willard Jessie, 367

Brown, William Wells, 43, 414, *414*

Brown, Willie Lewis, Jr., 120, *120*

Brown, Wynston, 379

Brown-Chappell, Willa, 255

Browne, Rose Butler, 95

Brownhelm, OH, 176

Bruce, Blanche Kelso, 175

Bryan, Andrew, 304, 306

Buchanan, Bessie Allison, 138, *139*

Buchanan, Charles P., 138

Buffalo Bills, 388

Buffalo Soldiers, 243

Buffalo, NY, 206

Buford, Kenneth L., 189

Bulkley, William L., 92

Bumbry, Grace Ann, 24

Bunche, Ralph Johnson, 92, 156, *156,* 263, 264, 273

Bunker Hill, battle of, 238

Bureau Control Division, WACS, 245

Bureau of Latin America, 161

Burgess, John M., 322

Burke, Lillian W., 211

Burke, Selma (Hortense), 36

Burke, Yvonne Braithwaite, 119, 181, 192

Burlington Industries, 58

Burlington-Northern Railroad, 55

Burney, William D., Jr., 201

Burns, Clarence Du, 202

Burns, Francis, 331

Burns, Isaac, 394

Burns, Tommy, 380

Burris, Roland W., 126, *127*

Bush administration, 165

Bush, Anita, 44

Bush, Charles Vernon, 187

Bush, George, 87, 126, 157

Bush, George Washington, 151

Bush, William Owen, 151

Business and Professional Women/USA,
    282

Butler University, 21

Butler, Gloria, 124

Bynoe, Peter, 59, 378

C

C and T Telephone Company, 231

Cab Calloway Show, 20

Cab Calloway's band, 23

Cabin in the Sky, 46

Cable, Theodore "Ted," 406

Cade, Henry, 298

Cadoria, Sherian Grace, 247

Caesar, Lois Towles, 286

Caesar, Richard, 297

Cain, Richard H., 174

Cairo, IL, 200

Cake walk (dance), 43

Caldwell, Charles, 134

Calhoun, Lee Quincy, 398

California Board of Medical Quality, 119

California Eagle, 171, 222

California Highway Patrol, 120

California Institute of the Arts, 9

California State Bar Association, 277

California State University at Fullerton, 84

California State University at Los Angeles,
    171, 288

California State University, Northridge, 87

California, 118–120

Caliver, Ambrose, 108

Call and Post, 143

Callender, Charles, 43

Callender's Georgia Minstrels, 43

Calloway, Blanche, 17, 196

Calloway, Cab (Cabell) III, 17, 29

Calloway, Deverne Lee, 136

Caltex Petroleum Corporation (Irving, TX),
    282

Calvin, Floyd Joseph, 230

Camp Barker, 351

Camp, Walter, 385

Campanella, Roy "Campy," 369

Campbell, Carlos Cardozo, 164

Campbell, Cloves C., 117

Campbell, E[lmer] Sims, 2, *2*

Campbell, Joan Salmon, 338

Campbell, Milt, 398

Campbell, Ralph, Jr., 142

Campbellites (Disciples of Christ), 335

Camphor, Alexander P., 331

Canada, Alexia Irene, 357

Canady, Blanton Thandreus, 282

Candace Award, 50, 226

Cape Fear, NC, Watchmakers Guild, 280

Capers, Jean Murrell, 210

Capital Savings Banks, 50

Capital Theater (New York City), 17

Capra, Frank, 8

Caravans, 27

Cardoza, Francis Louis, 102, 107, 146, *146,*
    320

Carey, Archibald J., Jr., 157

Carey, Lott, 307

Carlos, John Wesley, 400

Carmen Jones, 8

Carmen, 11

Carmichael, Stokely, 74

Carnegie Hall, 15, 21, 24

Carney, William Harvey, 242

Carrillo, Sergio, 317

Carroll, Diahann, 39

Carruthers, George R., 349

"Carry Me Back to Old Virginny," 11

Carter, Ammi, 312

Carter, Bonita, 189

Carter, Eunice Hunton, 205

Carter, Herbert, 288

Carter, Jimmy, 159, 170, 181

Carter, Pamela, 128

Cartoons, 1

"Carve dat 'Possum," 6

Carver, George Washington, 260, 261

Cary, W. Sterling, 295

Case Western Reserve University, 273

Case Western Reserve, 21

Cash, James Ireland, Jr., 98

Cashwell, G. B., 335

Casino Roof Garden, 44

Catechism classes, 312

Catholic Afro-American Lay Congress, 314

Catholic Church, 313, 315

Catholic University of America, 164

Catholic University of America School of Law, 151

Catholics, 312–318

Cato, 75

"CBS Evening News with Walter Cronkite," 233

CBS radio network, 33

"CBS Reports," 233

"CBS Sunday Night News," 233

CBS television, 38, 231, 233

Centennial Exhibition, 36

Central Christian Advocate, 331

Central College (McGrawville, NY), 88, 96

Central Michigan University, 239

Central News-Wave Publications, 224

Central State University (OH), 85, 289

Central Tennessee College, 349

Centralia, WA, 214

Challenger, 362

Chamberlain, Wilt, 376, *376*

Champagne Stakes, 394

Chaney, John, 377

Chanute Field (IL), 241

Chapel Hill, NC, 210

Chapel of Blessed Peter Claver, 314

Chapman College, 239

Chappelle, Yvonne Reed, 339

Charitable organizations, 341–342

Charles Drew University of Medicine and Science, 298

Charles, Ezzard "Quiet Tiger," 381

Charles, Ray (Ray Charles Robinson), 25, 27, 59

Charles, RuPaul Andre, 30

Charles, Suzette, 259

Charleston (dance), 3, 24

Charleston, Oscar, 366

Charleston, SC, 190, 212

Charlotte Hawkins Brown Memorial State Historic Site, 261

Charlotte, NC, 210

Charm-Tred-Monticello, 58

Chase Manhattan, 51

Chase National Bank, 159

Chase, James, 214

Chautauqua Tennis Club, 404

Chavis, John, 335

Cheatham, Henry P., 174

Checker, Chubby (Ernest Evans), 24

Cheek, Donna, 394

Cherry, F. S., 311

Cherry, Gwendolyn Sawyer, 121

Chesapeake Marine Railway and Drydock Company, 64

Cheshier, Isaac, 326

Chesnut, Morris, 9

Chess, Sammie, Jr., 141

Chester L. Washington Golf Course (Los Angeles), 224

Chestnut, Wendell, 404

Cheyney State College, 98, 233

Cheyney Training School for Teachers, 31

Chicago Bears, 387, 388, 390

Chicago Cardinals, 386, 387

Chicago Child Care Society, 287

Chicago City College, 166

Chicago Civic Opera Company, 19

Chicago Cubs, 370, 371

Chicago Defender, 220

Chicago Dental Society, 298

Chicago Giants, 366

Chicago Music College, 23

Chicago Symphony, 19

Chicago Teachers Union, 55

Chicago Theological Seminary, 83, 172

Chicago Tribune, 226

Chicago Urban League, 82

Chicago White Sox, 367

Chicago World Fair, 19

Chicago, IL, 197, 198, 199, 200

Chick Webb's band, 24

"Chico and the Man," 40

Children's Defense Fund, 83

Chinn, May Edward, 355

Chip Woman's Fortune, 45

Chisholm, Shirley, 180, *180*

Chisum, Gloria Twine, 212

Choice of Weapons, 229

Chow, Kenneth, 225

Christ's Sanctified Holy Church, 337

Christian Church (Disciples of Christ), 318

Christian Herald, 221, 227

Christian Recorder, 221, 222, 227

Christian Science, 304

Christian, Charlie, 20

Christianity, 311

Church of Christ, 318

Church of Christ Holiness, USA, 337

Church of England, 319

Church of God (Black Jews), 311

Church of God and Saints of Christ, 311, 337

Church of God in Christ, 148, 334, 337

Church of God, USA, 335

Church of the Living God, 337

Church of the Redemption, 339

Church Women United, 332

Church's Fried Chicken, 63

Cincinnati Reds, 371, 373

Cincinnati Royals, 377

Cincinnati, OH, 211

Cinque, 76, *76*

CIO, 46

Circus, 3

Citizenship, Intelligence, Affluence, Honor and Trust, 96

City Cable Television (St. Louis), 280

City College of New York, 247

Civic Communications Corporation, 41

Civil Air Patrol Squadron, 255

Civil Aviation Authority, 255

Civil rights, 129, 290

Civil Rights, Bill of 1866, 70

Civil Rights Division, U.S. Justice Department, 162

Civil Service Commission, 164

Civil War, 129, 147, 237

"Civil War, The," 42

Claflin College (South Carolina), 96

Claflin University, 221

Clair, Matthew W., Sr., 331

Clairmont College, 119

Clarion, 221

Clark Atlanta University, 85, 101

Clark College, 101

Clark Memorial, 329

Clark Stakes, 394

Clark, Charles Warfield, 298

Clark, Kenneth Bancroft, 273

Clark, Robert G., 135

Clarke, Alyce Griffin, 135

Clarke, John Henrik, 110

Clarke, Kenny, 20

Clay, William L., 180

Clayton, Alonzo, 393

Clayton, Eugene S., 200

Clayton, Eva, 185

Clayton, Mrs. Robert, 286

Clayton, Xerona, 232

Cleage, Albert B., Jr., 311

Cleaver, Emanuel III, 204

Clement, Clarissa (Williams), 263

Clement, Rufus Early, 109, 263

Clemente, Roberto, 371

Clements, Floy, 125

Clemson University (South Carolina), 103, 210

Clergy Council of Cranford, New Jersey, 310

Cleveland Browns, 386, 387, 398

Cleveland City Council, 143

Cleveland, Grover, 155

Cleveland Indians, 367, 371

Cleveland Institute of Music, 21

Cleveland, James, 27, 29

Cleveland Marshall Law School, 211

Cleveland, OH, 210, 211

Cleveland Pipers, 375

Clifford, Maurice C., 349

Clifton, Nathaniel "Sweetwater," 375

Clinton, Bill, 97, 118, 167, 213, 405, 420

Clinton Memorial African Methodist Episcopal Zion Church, 327

Clinton state administration, 167

Clorindy, 44

Clotel; Or, The President's Daughter, 414

Clyburn, Jim, 186

Coachman (Davis), Alice, 398, *398*

Coast Guard, 121

Coast Guard Academy, 249

Cobb, Jewel Plummer, 84

Cobb, Montague, 273

Cobb, Ty, 373

Coburg Theater, 42

Coburn, Titus, 238

Cochran, Thad, 230

Coffey School of Aeronautics, 255

Coffey, Cornelius R., 255

Coffey, Maryann, 295

Coffin, Alfred O., 89

Cofield, Elizabeth Bias, 141

Coker, Daniel, 300

Cole (Robinson), Johnetta Betsch, 85

Cole, Nat King (Nathaniel Coles), 33, 38

Cole, Rebecca J., 352

Cole, Robert, 43

Cole, Thomas W., 85

Coleman, Bessie, 255

Coleman, Valerie, 234

Coleman, William Thaddeus, Jr., 52, 186

Colgate Rochester Divinity School, 171

Collection of Spiritual Songs and Hymns, 299

College Administrators, 80–87

College buildings, 87

College degrees, 87–96

College faculty, 96–98

College Football Hall of Fame, 386, 388, 389

College foundings, 98–101

College fundraising, 101–102

College integration, 102–104

College Language Association, 272

College of Charleston, 147

College of New Jersey (Princeton), 335

College of New Rochelle, 164

Collett, Wayne, 400

Colley, W. W., 308

Collins, Bernice, 3

Collins, Cardiss Hortense Robertson, 182, *182*

Collins, Henry Holton, 191

Collins, Janet, 4

Collins, LaVerne Francis, 282

Collins, Robert Frederick, 169

Color Purple, The, 416

Colorado, 120

Colorado supreme court, 120

Colorado, municipal government in, 193

Colored (now Christian) Methodist
    Episcopal Church, 331

Colored American Opera Company, 11

Colored American, The, 96, 170, 221

Colored Baptist Society and Friends to
    Humanity, 307

Colored Brotherhood and Sisterhood of
    Honor, 293

Colored Cadet at West Point, 250

Colored Cumberland Presbyterian Church,
    336

Colored Industrial Fair (Richmond, VA), 31

Colored Man's Journal, 221

Colored Methodist Episcopal Church, 337

Colored Methodist Society, 328

Colored National Labor Union, 53

*Colored Patriots of the American Revolution,
    The*, 153, 410

Colored Prepatory High School, 107

Colored Primitive Baptists, 337

Colored Women's Democratic League, 108

Colored YMCA Building (Norfolk, VA),
    284

Colored YMCA, (Washington, DC), 284

Colston, James, 83

Columbia Giants, 366

Columbia Teachers College, 82

Columbia University, 21, 22, 38, 85, 163,
    164, 168, 171, 177, 180, 288

Columbia University Graduate School of
    Journalism, 230

Columbia University Law School, 46, 140

Columbia University Teachers College, 20

Columbian Exposition, 49

Columbus College, 163

Comedy of Errors, 45

Coming to America, 41

Commissiong, Janelle Penny, 259

Committee for Improving the Industrial
    Conditions of Negroes ..., 291

Committee for the District of Columbia, 177

Committee on Urban Conditions Among
    Negroes, 291

Concord Bridge, defense of, 238

*Condition, Elevation, Emigration and
    Destiny of the Colored People ...*, 417

Conference of Churchworkers Among
    Colored People, 322

Congo, Simon, 205

Congregationalists, 319–320

Congress of Racial Equality (CORE), 73, 95,
    172

Congressional Black Caucus, 177, 180

Conjure Man Dies, 415

Conley, Jess, 393

Connecticut, 120–121

Connecticut, municipal government in, 193

Connecticut Society of the Sons of the
    American Revolution, 294

Consolidated American Baptist Missionary
    Convention, 307, 308

Consolidated Edison, 60

Constantine, Learie (Lord Constantine),
    267

Consultation Church Union, Princeton, NJ,
    295

Constance Lindsay Skinner Award (now the
    WNBA Award), 264

Continental Basketball Association, 378

Continental Congress, 142

Convention of Free Men, 170

Conyers, James Henry, 251

Cook County (Illinois) Bar Association, 279

Cook County jail, 198

Cook, Celestine Strode, 276

Cook, Mercer, 157

Cook, Will Marion, 13, 44

Cooke, Marvel Jackson, 224

Cooleyhighharmony, 30

Cooper, Algernon J., 189

Cooper, Anna Haywood, 92

Cooper, Chuck, 375

Cooper, Clarence, 124

Cooper, Edward Elder, 220

Cooper, Jack L., 32

Cooper, Julia P., 215

Coppin State College, 202

Coppin, Fanny Jackson, 107, *107*

Cordery, Sara Brown, 338

Cornell University, 1, 63, 161, 294, 413

Cornish, James, 353

Cornish, Samuel E[li], 219, 336

Cortisone, 347

Cosby, Bill, 8, 39, 364

Cosmopolitan, 2

Cotter, James G., 125

Cotton Club, 20, 138

Cotton Comes to Harlem, 229

Cotton States and International Exposition, 295

Council of the North and West, 336

Council on African Affairs, 46

Council on Medical Services of the American Medical Association, 297

Cousin, Philip R., 295

Cowan, James Rankin, 137

Cox, Elbert, 96

Cox, Minnie, 154

Craft, Samuel, 238

Crane College, 29

"Crazy Blues," 35

Cream, Arnold Raymond, 381

Creighton University School of Medicine, 298

Crenshaw, Sallie A., 331

Creole Show, The, 43

Crescent Athletic Club, 374

Crew, 384

Crim, Alonzo A., 111

Crisis, 224, 228, 411

Crisobal, Juan (Bob), 268

Crockett, George W., Jr., 156

Crogman, William Henry, 96

Croix de guerre, 245

Cromwell, Otelia, 91

"Crooked Shanks," 9

Crosby Furniture Company, 276

Crosby, Fred M., 276

Crosby, Oscar, 268

Cross, Alexander, 318

Cross, Dolores E., 86

Crowdy, William S., 311

Crowther, Samuel, 322

Crum, George, 265

Crummell, Alexander, 271, 322

Crump, Edward H., 14

Cuban Giants, 365

Cuffe, John, 132

Cuffe, Paul (insurrectionist), 75

Cuffe, Paul (ship owner), 64, 132, 268

Cullers, Vincent T., 49

Cumberland Street Methodist Episcopal Church, 329

Curtis, Austin Maurice, 353

Cuyahoga Metropolitan Housing Authority (OH), 211

Cycling, 384

D

Dailey, Phyllis Mae, 253

Daily Compass, 224

Dallas Cowboys, 389

Dallas, TX, 213, 282

Dallas/Fort Worth International Airport, 257

Dalley, George Albert, 163

Dance Theatre of Harlem, 4

Dandrige, Dorothy, 8

Dandrige, Ray, 366

Daniels and Bell, 63

Daniels, Hayzel Burton, 190

Daniels, Willie L., 63

Dark of the Moon, The, 39

"Dark Was the Night, Cold Was the Ground," 26

Darktown Jubilee, 12

Dartmouth College, 141, 263

Darts, 384

Dash, Julie, 9

Daughters of the American Revolution, 23, 295

Daughters of the Dust, 9

Davenport, Willie, 401

David Walker's Appeal, 132, 416

Davidson, Ezra C., 3, 298

Davidson-Randall, Julia, 131

Davis, Abraham Lincoln, 200

Davis, Allison, 97

Davis, Benjamin Oliver, Jr., 239

Davis, Benjamin Oliver, Sr., 241, 245

Davis, Bettye, 112

Davis, Bronco Jim, 403

Davis, Ernie, 388

Davis, Errol B., Jr., 60

Davis, Jefferson, 174, 237

Davis, Jim, 199

Davis, John, 398

Davis, Marianna White, 112

Davis, Ossie, 47

Davis, Sammy, Jr., 59, 267

Davis, Samuel, 335

Davis-Hinton tests, 356

Dawes, Dominique, 392

Dawson, William Levi, 19, 177

Day, Thomas, 56

Days, Drew Saunders, III, 162

Dean, Dora, 43

De Baptiste, Richard, 220

Deberry, Lois Marie, 149

Decca, 20

Defiant Ones, The, 8

DeFrantz, Anita Luceete, 383

De Grasse, John V., 295

DeHart, Donald, 282

Delany, Henry B., 322

Delany, Martin Robinson, 219, 227, 243, 262, 417, *417*

Delarge, Robert C., *173,* 174

Delaware, 121

Delaware, municipal government in, 194

Delaware North Companies (Buffalo, NY), 280

Delaware State College, 63

Delille, Henriette, 313

Delinquent Girl, The, 126

"Della Reese Show," 40

Dellums, Ronald V., 186

Delta Sigma Theta, 294

Demby, Edward T., 322

Democrat and Chronicle, 280

Democratic National Committee, 159, 172

Democratic National Convention (1972), 181

Democratic National Convention (1976), 181

Democratic National Convention (1984), 171

Democratic Party, 131

Dennis, Andre L., 283

Dennison, Franklin A., 197

Denver Broncos, 387

Denver, CO, 193

Denver Nuggets, 59, 378

Department For Employment Services, Lexington, KY, 56

DePaul University (Chicago, IL), 161

De Porres, Martin, 315, *316*

DePriest, Oscar Stanton, 176, 197

Der Fliegende Hollander, 27

Des Moines Bystander (IA), 222

Desegregation, 118, 148

Desegregation of schools, 80, 109

Detroit College of Law, 177

Detroit Free Press, 3, 226

Detroit Lions, 387

Detroit, MI, 171, 203

Detroit Public Libraries, 277

Detroit Tigers, 371

Dewey, John, 290

Dewey, Thomas E., 206

DeWitt Wallace/Spelman College fund, 102

Dickerson, Chris, 378

Dickson, Clarence, 196

Dickson, Moses, 68

Diggs, Charles C., Jr., 133, *176,* 177, 181

Diggs, Charles C., Sr., 133
Diggs, R. L., 92
Dihigo, Martin, 366
Dillard College, 320
Dillard University, 135, 227
Dining Car Employees #582, 54
Dinkins, David, 208
Diocese of Little Rock, 318
Disabled American Veterans, 166
Discriminatory laws, abolition of, 142
District of Columbia Bar, 153
Divine Word Seminary, 315
Divinity School of the Pacific, 324
Dixie Hospital, 358
Dixon, Sharon Pratt. See Kelly, Sharon Pratt Dixon
Dixon, Dean Charles, 20
Dixon, George "Little Chocolate," 380, 384
Dixon, Irma, 131
Dixon, Julian, 171
Dixwell Congregational Church, 320
Dizzy Gillespie Quintet, 28
"Do Your Duty," 16
Dobbs, Mattiwilda, 22
Doby, Larry, 367
Doctor of Alcantara, 11
Doctor, Henry, Jr., 247
Doley, Harold E., Jr., 164
Donald, Bernice Bouie, 148
Dorrington, Arthur, 392
Dorsey, Edmund Stanley, 230
Dorsey, Thomas, 18
Doubleday, 61
Douglas, Robert J., 374
Douglass, Frederick Augustus, 53, 78, 138, 170, 170, 260, 374, 410, 420
Dover Association, 306
Dowdy, Lew Carnegie, 276
"Down Home Blues/Oh, Daddy," 15
Downbeat magazine, 25
"Downhearted Blues/Gulf Coast Blues," 16
Dr. Branch Products, 63

Drama Committee of the NAACP, 44
Drama of King Shotaway, 42
Dramatists, 5
Dred Scott v. Sanford, 70
Drew, Charles Richard, 355, 355, 362
Drew, Howard Porter, 405
Drew, Timothy, 327
Drexel, Katherine, 100
Drury, Theodore, 11
Dry cleaning, 343
Dry White Season, 9
Du Bois, William Edward Burghardt (W. E. B.) 90, 91, 224, 228, 271, 272, 290, 321, 343, 410
Dubuclet, Antoine, 129
Duchemin, Mary Theresa, 312
Dudley, Edward R., 156
Duke University, 84
Dumas, Charles Everett, 407
Dunbar, Paul Laurence, 44, 260, 411, 411
Duncan, Robert Morton, 240
Duncan, Robert Todd, 21
Duncanson, Robert Scott, 30
Dunham, Katherine, 4
Dunn, Oscar James, 129
Dunnigan, Alice, 224, 244
Duquesne Light Company, PA, 283
Duquesne University, 375
Duquesne University School of Law, 145
Durham, Diane, 392
Durham, James, 350
Du Sable, Jean Baptiste Point, 59, 260
Duse Award, 39
Dwight, Edward Joseph, Jr., 360
Dykes, Eva Beatrice, 92, 93, 93
Dymally, Mervyn M., 119, 120

E

E. G. Bowman Company, 53
Eads, Charlestown, 238

Eagleson, William Lewis, 220

Earl of Dunmore, 238

Early Christians, 320–321

Early, Norman S., Jr., 193

East Louisiana State Hospital, 12

"East Side, West Side" (television series), 38

East St. Louis, IL, 199

East-West Records America, 29

Eastern Airlines, 64

Eastern Amateur League, 392

Eastern Rubber Reclaiming Company, 58

Eastman School of Music, 338

Eato, Edward V. C., 284

Eatonville, FL, 194

Ebbets Field, 367

Ebenezer Baptist Church (Chicago), 18

Ebony, 8, 228

Ebony Fashion Fair, 8

Ecumenical Committee of the World Methodist Conference, 332

"Ed Sullivan Show," 22

Edelman, Marian Wright, 83, *83*

Edmonton Oilers, 392

Education, 384

Education and Labor Committee, 177

Education Awards and Honors, 79–80

Edward Waters College (Florida), 99

Edwards, Harry Francis Vincent, 396

Edwards, Marvin E., 113

Edwards, Nelso Jack, 54

Edwards, Teresa, 401

Eglin, Ellen F., 346

Eichberg, Julius, 11

Eighth Illinois Infantry, 197

Eighth United States Volunteers, 245

Eikerenkoetter, Frederick J., II, 340

Eisenhower, Dwight D., 22, 110, 133, 156, 157

Ekemam, Samuel Chuka, 302

Elaine, Arkansas riot of October 1919, 117

Elder, Lee, 391

Elder-Berry gastrobiopsy scope, 355

Elders, M. Joycelyn, 166

Elevator, The, 221

Ellicot, George, 359

Ellington, Duke, 260

Elliott, Robert Brown, *173,* 174, 237

Ellis, Harold, 354

Ellis, Harrison W., 336

Ellison, Ralph Waldo, 416

Emancipation Proclamation stamp, 261

Emancipation, dates of in Northern states, 68

Emancipator, The 227

Embree, Elihu, 227

Embry, Wayne, 377

Emmy Awards, 39, 233

Emory Institution School of Law, 124

Emory University, 124

Emperor Jones, 4, 45

Empire State Building, 382

End of the Road, 30

England, Bishop John, 313

Englewood, NJ, 205

Entertainer of the Year, 25

Epiphany Apostolic College, 317

Episcopal Missionary Diocese, 322

Episcopalians, 321–325

Equal Employment Opportunity Commission, 371

Erskine, George M., 336

Escape, The, 43

"Esky," 2

Espy, Alphonso Michael (Mike), 183, *184*

Esquire, 2

Estabrook, Prince, 238

Estes, Simon Lamont, 27

Estevanico (Estevan), 262

Eternal Life Spiritual Church, 339

Etheridge, Richard, 249

Ethicon division, Johnson and Johnson (Albuquerque, NM), 283

Ethiopian Art Players, 45

Ethiopians, 326, 327

Europe, James Reese, 245

Eva Jessye Choir, 17

Evangelical Lutheran Church, 328

Evans Chapel, 329, 330

Evans, Annie Lillian, 17

Evans, Henry, 330

Evans, Joseph H., 318

Evans, Leonard, Jr., 34

Evans, Melvin H., 150, 291

Evans, Rob, 378

Evanston, IL, 200

Evanti, Lillian, 17

"Evening Thought, An. Salvation by Christ, with Penitential Cries...," 417

Evergreen, 3

Evers, (James) Charles, 135, 203

Evers, Medgar, 135

Evolution of the Negro College, 82

Ewing, Patrick, 378

Excelsiors of Philadelphia, 365

Experience; or How to Give a Northern Man a Backbone, 414

Ezion Church, 303, 329

F

Facts of Reconstruction, The, 175

Fairmont, NC, 210

Famous Amos Chocolate Chip Cookies, 62

Fannings, Raymond W., 287

Fard, W. D., 327, 334

Farley, James Conway, 31

Farmer, James, 95

Farmer, Karen, 295

Farmer, Sharon, 167

Farrakhan, Louis, 334

Fatback Band, 27

Father Divine (George Baker), 334

Fauntroy, Walter E., 180

Fauset, Crystal Bird, 143, *143*

Fauset, Jessie, 17

Fayette, MS, 135, 203

Fayetteville State, 100

Federal Appointees, 153–167

Federal Aviation Administration, 282

Federal Aviation Agency's Women's Advisory Commission, 255

Federal Bar Association, 279

Federal Bureau of Investigations, 163, 167

Federal Communications Commission, 161

Federal Department of Housing and Urban Development, 159, 160, 162

Federal Emergency Management Agency, 164

Federal Employees, 167, 342

Federal Highway Administration, 167

Federal Housing Administration, 51

Federal Housing and Home Finance Administration, 158

Federal Reserve System, 159

Federal Trade Commission, 83

Federal Women's Program of the Agricultural Stabilization and Conservation Service, 60

Federal Writers Project, 415

Fellowship of Reconciliation, 73

Female Benevolent Society (Philadelphia), 284

Ferguson, Samuel David, 322

Ferndale Honda (Ferndale, MI), 50

Ferns, Rube, 380

Ferrit, Caesar John, 238

Festivals, 6

Fetchit, Stepin (Lincoln Theodore Monroe Andrew Perry), 7

Fielding, Herbert Ulysses, 146

Fifty-fourth Massachusetts Colored Infantry, 242

Finley, Clarence C., 58

Finney, Ernest A., Jr., 147

Finney, William K., 203

Fire Baptized Holiness Church, 337

First African Baptist Church, 305, 306

First African Church, 335

First and Second Kansas Colored Volunteers, 241

First Baptist Church, 307

First Baptist Church of Nashville, 308

First Colored Baptist Church, 305

First Colored Methodist, 329

First Colored Presbyterian Church, 336

First Fight Artillery of Ohio, 241

First Lessons in Greek, 413

First National Conference of Negro Methodists, 340

First Regiment Louisiana Native Guards, 241

First Regiment of the Louisiana National Guard, 154

First Rhode Island Regiment, 238

First South Carolina Volunteers, 241

Fishburne, Larry, 9

Fisher, Carl Anthony, 317

Fisher, Gail, 39

Fisher, Rudolph, 415

Fisk Jubilee Singers, 15

Fisk University, 15, 81, 82, 87, 99, 125, 133, 135, 151, 156, 167, 177, 184, 273, 320, 363

Fisk, General Clinton B., 99

Fitzbutler, Henry, 352

Fitzgerald, Ella, 24

Fitzsimons Army Medical Center, 297

503rd Infantry, 246

Flake, Green, 268

Fletcher School, 161

Flint, MI, 202

Flipper, Henry Ossian, 250

Flipper, Josephus, 250

Florida, 121–122, 173, 184

Florida Agricultural and Mechanical University, 63, 121, 184, 274, 388

Florida Education Association, 121

Florida Marlins, 374

Florida, muncipal government in, 194

Florida State Normal and Industrial College, 56

Florida State University, 234, 407

Flowers, Tiger (Theodore), 380

Floyd, Donald Joseph, 149

Floyd, James A., 205

Floyd, Otis L., 86

Foley, Lelia Smith, 211

Foley, Red, 25

Follis, Charles W., 385

Fontaine, Joan, 8

Football, 384

Foote, Julia A., 302

Ford, Bowles C., 196

Ford, Harold Eugene, 182

Ford, Madeline, 288

Ford, Robert E., 418

Foreign Relations Subcommittee on Africa, 177

Forman, James, 332

Forsyne, Ida, 13

Forsythe, Albert Ernest, 255

Fort Des Moines, Iowa, 245

Fort Wagner, attack on, 242

Forten daughters, 56

Forten, James, Sr., 56, 343

Foster, Andrew "Rube," 366, *366*

Foster, Laurence, 92

Four Saints in Three Acts, 19

Four Vagabonds, 38

Fourth Estate Award of the National Press Club, 225

Fowler, John W. "Bud," 365

Foxes of Harrow, The, 415

Foxx, Redd, 38

Frances, Henry Minton, 162

Francis, Patrick, 313

Francisco, John, 205

Frankfurter, Justice Felix, 187

Franklin, Aretha, 29, 59

Franklin, John Hope, 273

Frazier, E. Franklin, 273

Frazier, Joe, 382

Frederick Douglass Memorial Hospital, 89, 343

Frederick Douglass Museum, 263

Free African Society (Philadelphia), 283, 284, 290, 321, 329, 330

Free Christian Zion Church of Christ, 337

Free Library of Philadelphia, 212

Freedman's Commission of the Protestant Episcopal Church, 82

Freedmen's Aid Society, 99, 349

Freedmen's Bureau, 99, 100, 176, 244, 351

Freedmen's Hospital, 342, 351, 353, 354, 355, 356

Freedom and Citizenship (Langston), 176

Freedom Baptist Church, 311

Freedom National Bank, 51

Freedom's Journal, 219, 336

Freedomways: A Quarterly Review of the Negro Freedom Movement, 110

Freeman, Joseph, Jr., 333

Freeman, The, 220

French Academy of Sciences, 271

French Institute, 231

French Open, 405

From the Virginia Plantation to the National Capitol, 176

Frost, Robert, 420

Frye, Henry E., 141

Frye, Theodore, 18

Fuhr, Grant, 392

Fulani, Lenora, 172

Fuller, Oscar A., 102

Fulton County Superior Court (GA), 124

Fulton County Board of Education (GA), 280

Fund for Corporate Initiatives, 61

Furnace, Walt, 117

Futrell, Mary Hatwood, 277

G

Gadley, Jeff, 401

Gaines, Clarence "Bighouse," 377

Gaines, Joseph, 380

Gaines, Paul Laurence, 212

Gainey, Leroy, 310

Gaither, Alonzo Smith "Jake," 388

Gallaudet University, 283

Galpin, Jesse, 305

Gamble, Kenneth, 264

Gammon Theological Seminary, 81

Gannett Company, 61, 226

Gans, Joe, 380

Gantt, Harvey Bernard, 103, 210

Garden City Theater, 44

Gardner, Errol Louis, 24

Gardner, Newport (Occramer Marycoo), 9

Gardone, Charles, 5

Garies and Their Friends, The, 414

Garland, Hazel, 226

Garnet, Henry Highland, 106, 170, *170,* 416

Garnet, Sarah J. Smith Thompson, 106, *106*

Garrett, Mike, 388

Garrison, William Lloyd, 68, 306, 410

Garrison, Zina, 405

Garvey, Marcus (Mozian Manasseth), 72, *72,* 303, 327, 339

Gary, Howard, 196

Gary, IN, Chamber of Commerce, 280

Gasden, Marie, 288

Gaston, Gloria, 161

Gaudin, Juliette, 313

Gaufin, George, 305

General Electric, 58

General Motors, 50, 62, 134

Genius of Freedom, 221

George Foster Peabody Award, 232

George Hubbard Hospital, 356

George Washington Carver National Monument, 261

George Washington University, 247

George, David, 304, 305

George, J. Russell, 274

Georgetown Law School, 131

Georgetown University, 88, 313, 378

Georgia, 122–124

Georgia Assembly, 27

Georgia Association of Independent Juvenile Court Judges, 279

Georgia Athletic Hall of Fame, 400

Georgia, Georgia, 5

Georgia Infirmary (Savannah), 342

Georgia Minstrels, 43

Georgia Municipal Association, 280

Georgia, municipal government in, 196

"Georgia on My Mind," 27

Georgia School Boards Association, 280

Georgia state senate, 122

Ghandi, Mahatma, 73, 81

Gibbs, Marla, 40

Gibbs, Mifflin Wistar, 132, 190, 219, *219*

Gibson, Althea, 405, *405*

Gibson, Jack, 34

Gibson, Johnnie Mae M., 167

Gibson, Kenneth Allen, 205

Gibson, Paul, 208

Gibson, Reginald Walker, 169

Giles, Gwen B., 136

Gillespie, Dizzy, 11, 20, 23, 24

Gilmore, Buddy, 13

Gilpin, Charles Sidney, 45

Girl at the Fort, The, 44

"Girl Is Mine, The," 28

Girl Scouts of America, 286

Gist, Carole, 259

Gleason, Eliza Atkins, 102

Glenn, Mildred, 51

Glickman, Loretta Thompson, 192

Glidden Company (Chicago), 347

Gloster, Hugh Morris, 272

Gloucester County conspiracy (VA), 74

Gloucester, John, Sr., 335

Glover, John D., 163

Golden Gate Theological Seminary, 310

Golden Rule Foundation, 263

Golden West, The, 7

Golf, 391

Gone with the Wind, 7

Good Samaritan Hospital, 343

Goode, Malvin (Mal) Russell, 231, *231*

Goode, Sarah E., 346

Goode, W. Wilson, 212

Gooding, Cuba, Jr., 9

Gospel Music Workshop of America, 28

Gospel Spreading Church, 326

Gourdin, Edward Orval, 406

Gourdine, Simon Peter, 377

Gowan Prophet, 306

Graham, Billy, 46

Grambling University, 274, 387, 388, 390

Grammy Awards, 24, 28

Grand National race, 364

Grand Ole Opry, 17, 25

Grand Order of Galilean Fishermen, 293

Grand United Order of J. R. Gidding's and Jolliffe Union, 293

Grand United Order Sons and Daughters of Peace, 293

Grant, Charles, 365

Grant, Ray, 38

Grant, Ulysses S., 154, 176

Grauman's Chinese Theater, 8

Gravely, Samuel Lee, Jr., 253

Gray, Arthur D., 81

Gray, Fred Davis, 115

Gray, William H., III, 183

Greased Lightning, 364

Greater Macon Chamber of Commerce (GA), 281

Greb, Harry, 380

Green Bay Packers, 388

Green Pastures, 45

Green, Ernest Gideon, 110

Green, Nancy, 49

Green, Paul Stewart, 254

Green, Pumpsie, 370

Green, Richard R., 113

Greenberg, Reuben M., 212

Greener, Richard Theodore, 88, *88*

Greenfield, Elizabeth Taylor, 10

Greenfield-Patterson cars, 49

Greenlee, Gus, 367

Greenville, GA, 196

Greenville, MS, 204

Greg, Eric, 373

Gregory, Dick, 2, 38

Gregory, Frederick Drew, 362

Greyhound Corporation, 369

Greyhound Lines, 65

Gridiron Club (Washington, D.C.), 276

Grier, Johnny, 390

Griffith, D. W., 7

Griffith, Emile, 382

Grimké, Angelina 44

Grimké, Charlotte Forten, 56

Gross, Barbara Rudd, 280

Groves, Berton, 363

Gruenberg, Louis, 4

Grumman Corporation, 120

Guaranty Life Insurance Company, 196

Guggenheim Fellowship, 415

Guilmenot, Richard A., III, 49

Guinness Book of Records, 28

Guinier, Ewart, 97

Guinier, Lani, 97

Gumbel, Bryant Charles, 233, *233*

Gunn, Howard A., 116

Gymnastics, 392

H

Hailie Selassie I prize, 264

Haiti, 75, 154, 170

Hale, Cynthia L., 318

Hale, Nathan, 379

Haley, Alex, 41, 249

Haley, George Williford Boyce, 166

Hall, Arsenio, 41

Hall, Charles B., 241

Hall, Edgerton, 95

Hall, Ethel Harris, 113

Hall, Juanita, 35

Hall, Mary, 197

Hall, Prince, 291

Hall, Vera, 131

Hallelujah, 7, 17

Hamilton, Grace Towns, 122, *123*

Hamilton, Harriet, 363

Hamline University, 207

Hammon, Briton, 409

Hammon, Jupiter, 417

Hammond Business College (IN), 214

Hammond, Wade, 244

Hammons, George, 117

Hampton Institute, 23, 63, 82, 106, 221, 320

Hampton University, 59, 81, 164

Hampton, Wade, 89, 102

Handy, W[illiam] C[hristopher], 14, 15, 260

Hansberry, Lorraine, 46, 47

Hansberry, William Leo, 264

"Happy Pappy," 38

Haralson, Jeremiah, 174

Hard Road to Glory, A, 405

Harlem Broadcasting Corporation, 33

Harlem Globetrotters, 205, 375, 378

Harlem Hospital, 297, 354

Harlem Quarterly 110

Harlem Rag, 12

Harlem Renaissance, 82, 109, 415

Harlem School of the Arts, 23, 110

Harmon Award, 31

Harmon, Leonard Roy, 253

Harper, Conrad Kenneth, 282

Harper, Frances Ellen Watkins, *419,* 420

Harper, Thelma Marie, 149

Harpo Productions, 234

Harris, Barbara, 324, *325*

Harris, Charles F., 61

Harris, Gayle Elizabeth, 324

Harris, Jean Louise, 150

Harris, Marcelite, 239

Harris, Patricia Roberts, 159, *159*

Harris, Reggie, 234

Harris, Walter G., 288

Harrison Street Baptist Church, 305

Hart, Frank, 396

Hart, Gary, 172

Hartford Theological Seminary, 181

Hartford, CT, 193

Hartley, Sharon B., 280

Harvard Law Review, 105

Harvard Ripon Society, 274

Harvard University, 59, 62, 80, 88, 90, 92, 104, 151, 157, 158, 159, 164, 177, 186, 215, 231, 239, 264, 272, 406, 411, 414

Harvard University Law School, 82, 88, 202, 274

Harvey, Claire Collins, 332

Harvey, L. Warren, 318

Harvey, William R., 58

Hassell, Leroy Rountree, Sr., 151

Hastie, William Henry, 168

Hastings, Alcee Lamar, 183

Hatcher, Andrew T., 157

Hatcher, Richard G., 210

Hathaway, Isaac S., 260

Haverford College, 161

Hawkins, Augustus Freeman, 119, 178

Hawkins, Edler Garnet, 338

Hawkins, Erskine, 40

Hawkins, W. Lincoln, 360

Hayes, Dudley, 295

Hayes, George Edmund, 291

Hayes, Roland, 15

Hayes, Rutherford B., 102, 176

Haynes, Daniel, 7

Haynes, George Edmund, 291

Haynes, Lemuel, 104, 238, 320, *320*

Hayre, Ruth Wright, 109

Healy, James Augustine, 249, 313, 314, 315

Healy, Michael Augustine, 249

Healy, Patrick Francis, 88, 249

Hearns, Thomas "Hit Man," 383

Hearts in Dixie, 7

Hedgeman, Anna Arnold, 207

Heisman Trophy, 388, 389

Hemings, Sally, 118

Hemmings, Anita, 90

Hemsley, Sherman, 40

Henderson, Erskine, 393

Henderson, Fletcher, 15

Henderson, George Washington, 271

Henderson, Harold, 390

Henderson, Rickey, 373

Henderson, Thelton Eugene, 169

Hendricks, Caesar, 150

Hendricks, Karen, 289

Henry Johnson Fisher Award, 61

Henry, Robert Clayton, 210

Henson, Matthew Alexander, 260, 262

Herald of Freedom, 221

Herenton, Willie W., 112, 213

Heritage, John W., III, 141

Hernandez, Juano, 33

Heroic Slave, The, 420

Herriman, George, 1

Hewlett, James, 42

Hewlitt, Abraham Molineaux, 384

Hickman, Elnor B. G., 280

Hicks, Charles, 43

Hicks, James L., 223, 224

Hicks, Sherman G., 328

Hicks, William H., 205

Higginbotham, Leon A., Jr., 83

High School of Music and Art, 39

High School of Performing Art, 4

Highsmith, Charles Albert, 112

Hill, Henry Aaron, 273

Hill, Jesse, Jr., 277

Hill, Julius, 356

Hill, Oliver W., 213

Hill, Richmond, 196

Hilliard, Earl Frederick, 185

Hilliard, William A., 225

Hillsboro, AL, 189

Hines, Gregory, 268

Hinton, Albert L., 224

Hinton, James Sidney, 126

Hinton test for syphilis, 356

Hinton, William Augustus, 356

His Eye Is on the Sparrow, 46

History of the African Methodist Episcopal Church, 80

History of the Negro Race in America from 1619 to 1880, 410

History of the Negro Troops in the War of the Rebellion, 410

History of Western Massachusetts, 417

Hitler, Adolf, 397

Hobson, Charles, 39

Hockey, 392

Hogan, Beverly Wade, 135

Hogan, Ernest, 13

Hoggard, Dennie, 387

Holiness, 326

Holland, Cheryl, 136

Holland, Jerome Heartwell, 63

Holland, John Heartwell, 297

Holland, Josiah Gilbert, 417

Holley, Sandra Cavanaugh, 282

Holloman, John Lawrence Sullivan, 357

Holloway, Herman M., Sr., 121

Holloway, Ruth Burnett Love, 112

Holly, James T., 321, 322

Holmes, Dwight Oliver Wendell, 81

Holmes, Hamilton Earl, 103

Holmes, Tally, 404

Holy See, 313

Homes, Hamilton, 232

Honolulu Chamber of Commerce, 363

Honorary degrees, 104

Hood, Denise Page, 340

Hood, James, 104

Hood, William, 295

Hooks, Benjamin Lawson, 74, 148, 161, *161*

Hooks, Julia Britton, 96

Hope of Liberty, The 418

Hope, John, 101

Hopkins, Albert, Sr., 149

Horse racing, 393–394

Horse riding, 394

Horton, George Moses, 418

Horton, Odell, 169

Hosier, Harry, 328, *328*

Hospitals, 342–343

Host Club/Lions Club International (Cleveland), 288

Hosten, Jennifer Josephine, 257

House Armed Services Committee, 186

House Budget Committee, 183

House Expenditures Committee, 177

House Select Committee on Intelligence, 180

House Ways and Means Committee, 182

Housing Authority of Thurston County, WA, 214

Houston Informer, 222

Houston Symphony, 25

Houston, Charles Hamilton, 72, *72,* 102

Houston, TX, 213

How to Play Football, 385

Howard Inn, 59

Howard Law School, 116, 153

Howard School of Divinity, 339

Howard University, 17, 74, 99, 105, 111, 122, 146, 147, 156, 157, 159, 160, 161, 163, 164, 169, 171, 176, 178, 181, 182, 183, 184, 186, 294, 385

Howard University Cancer Research Center, 356

Howard University Law School, 11, 72, 116, 151, 153, 168, 215, 217, 279, 283

Howard University Medical School, 131, 150, 297, 298, 415

Howard University, Phi Beta Kappa Chapter at, 273

Howard University Press, 61

Howard University School of Dentistry, 56, 298

Howard University School of Medicine, 150, 297

Howard, Elston, 369

Howard, General Oliver O., 100

Howard, Paul L., Jr., 124

Howard, Robert B., Jr., 206

Howells, William Dean, 290, 412

Howlin' Wolf (Chester Burnett), 34

Howze, Joseph Lawson, 317

Hubbard, Arnette R., 279

Hubbard, Charlotte Moton, 158

Hubbard, George W., 349

Hubbard, Marilyn French, 277

Hubbard, William DeHart, 396

Huff, Leon, 264

Hughes, Langston, 45

"Human Nature," 28

Hunter College, 47, 231

Hunter, Alberta, 27

Hunter-Gault, Charlayne, 103, 232

Hunton, Addie, 285

Hunton, Benjamin L., 241

Hunton, William Alphaeus, 284

Hurd, Babe, 393

Hurtsboro, AL, 189

Huston-Tillotson College, 87, 162

Hutchinson, Barbara B., 55

Hydropathology, 351

Hyman, John A., 174, 176

Hymes, Lulu, 407

Hymnals, 299

Hyson, Roberta, 7

I

I Know Why the Caged Bird Sings, 5

I Pagliacci, 21

I Spy, 39

"I Wonder as I Wander," 45

I Wouldn't Take Nothin' for My Journey, 355

IBM. *See* International Business Machines

Ice Cube, 9

Ice skating, 394

"If You See My Savior," 18

Illinois, 182

Illinois College of Law, 125

Illinois Federation of Teachers, 55

Illinois, municipal government in, 197

Illinois State Police, 200

Illinois Wesleyan University, 89, 92

Imhotep Conference, 273

Impartial Citizen, 221

Improved Benevolent and Protective Order of Elks of the World, 293

In Dahomey, 12

In Old Kentucky, 7

In the Evening by the Moonlight, 11

Independent Order of Saint Luke, 293

Indiana University, 120, 233, 286

Indiana, 126–128

Indianapolis 500, 364

Indianapolis ABC, 366

Indianapolis Recorder, 222

Indianola, Mississippi, 154

Ingram-Grant, Edith Jacqueline, 122

Inoculation, 350

Inside Bedford-Stuyvesant, 39

Institute for Colored Youth, 88, 89, 96, 107, 154

Institute of Mathematical Statistics, 273

Inter-American Development Bank, 164

Interchurch Organizations, 327

Interdenominational Theological Seminary, 101

Interesting Narrative of the Life of Olaudah Equiano, 409

International Association of Chiefs of Police, 282

International Business Machines (IBM), 159, 277

International Council of Women, 263

International Ladies' Garment Workers Union, 55

International League of Independent Baseball Clubs, 366

International Olympic Committee, 383

International Tchaikovsky Vocal Competition, 27

International Tennis Hall of Fame, 405

Interscholastic Athletic Association, 363

Inventions and patents, 343–349

Invisible Man, 416

Iola Leroy, 421

Iowa, 128

Iowa Civil Rights Commission, 128

Iowa State College, 261

Irvin, Monfors "Monte," 366, 369

Irvis, K. Leroy, 144

Isham, John, 43

Islam, 327

Island in the Sun, 8

It's Right Here for You, 35

Ithaca College, 231

Ithaca, New York, Journal, 226

J

Jack Carey's Orchestra, 16

Jack, Hulan, 207

Jack, Rojo, 363, 364

Jackson, Charlie, 16

Jackson, Hal, 34

Jackson, Harry, 391

Jackson, Ira, 280

Jackson, Isaiah, 29

Jackson, J. H., 310

Jackson, Jacquelyne Johnson, 97

Jackson, Jesse Louis, 116, 172, *172*

Jackson, John W., 365

Jackson, Lee, 56

Jackson, Leo Edwin, 193

Jackson, Mahalia, 22, 40

Jackson, Mannie, 375

Jackson, Maynard Holbrook, 196

Jackson, Michael, 28

Jackson, Perry B., 210

Jackson, Peter "The Black Prince," 379

Jackson, Rebecca Cox, 340

Jackson, Shirley Ann, 95

Jackson State College, 135

Jackson State University, 390

Jackson, William Tecumseh Sherman, 384, 385

Jacobs, Francis, 302

Jacobs, JoAnn M., 208

James Cleveland Singers, 28

James E. Sullivan Memorial Trophy, 407

James Madison University (VA), 84

James, Daniel H., 239

James, George, 211

Jarboro (Yarboro), Caterina, 19

Jarvis Christian College, 276

Jasper, John, 308, *308*

Jazz, 413

Jeanes Teacher Program, 108

Jeanes, Anna T., 108

Jefferies, Willie, 389

Jefferson, Thomas, 118

"Jeffersons," 40

"Jelly Roll Blues," 14

Jemison, Mae C., *361, 362*

Jenkins, Augustus, 288

Jenkins, Ferguson, 371

Jenkins, Howard, Jr., 170

Jennings, Thomas L., 343

Jessye, Eva, 17

Jet, 228

Jewell, Jerry Donal, 118

Jim Crow laws, 147

Jim Russell Driving School, 364

Jim Thorpe Trophy, 387

Jockey Hall of Fame, 394

Johansson, Ingemar, 382

John D. and Catherine T. MacArthur Foundation grant, 412

John Gupton College, 182

John Henry Black River Giant, 33

John Marshall Law School, 157, 180, 279

John Murray Anderson's Almanac, 38

John Seigenthaler Chair of Excellence in First Amendment Studies, 229

John Street Methodist Episcopal Church, 301, 302

"Johnny B. Goode," 26

Johns Hopkins University, 165

Johnson, Albert William, 49

Johnson, Andrew, 70, 176

Johnson, Anthony, 319

Johnson, Anthony and Mary, 77

Johnson, Beverly, 257

Johnson, Blind Willie, 26

Johnson C. Smith University, 82, 156, 385

Johnson, Charles Spurgeon, 43, 81, 82, 82, 123, 272, 291

Johnson, Cornelius, 396

Johnson, Edward A., 138

Johnson, Erma Chansler, 257

Johnson, (Francis) Hall, 4, 45

Johnson, Frank (Francis), 10

Johnson, George Ellis, 63

Johnson, Henry, 245

Johnson, I. S. Leevy, 280

Johnson, Isabella, 319

Johnson, Jack, 380, 380

Johnson, James F., 249

Johnson, James Weldon, 96

Johnson, John, 77

Johnson, John H., 35, 228

Johnson, John, Sr., 77

Johnson, Johnny, 190

Johnson, Joseph A., Jr., 103

Johnson, Joy Joseph, 210

Johnson, Leroy Reginald, 122

Johnson, Lew, 43

Johnson, Lewis, 304

Johnson, Lyndon B., 158, 159, 160, 170

Johnson, Mal, 232

Johnson, Merle, 92

Johnson, Mordecai Wyatt, 81

Johnson, Pamela McAllister, 226

Johnson Products, 40

Johnson Publishing Company, 59, 60, 225, 228

Johnson Publishing House, 198

Johnson, Rafer Lewis, 399

Johnson, Raymond L., 120

Johnson, Richard, 77

Johnson, Robert L., 41

Johnson, Sam, 403

Johnson, Suzanne Denise, 310

Johnson, William "Judy," 319, 366

Johnston, Joshua, 30

Johnstown Jets, 392

Joint Chiefs of Staff, 247

Jonas, R. D., 326

Jones, Absalom, 299, 321, 329, 330

Jones, Anna F., 288

Jones, Bert, 365

Jones, E. P., 309

Jones, Eddie, 204

Jones, Edward A., 88

Jones, Eugene Kinckle, 291

Jones, Frederick McKinley, 347

Jones, George M., 102

Jones, Gilbert H., 93

Jones, Iris J., 213

Jones, Jennifer, 30

Jones, John, 124

Jones, Mordecai W., 288

Jones, Quincy (Delight), Jr., 24

Jones, Robert E., 331

Jones, Samuel "Toothpick Sam," 370

Jones, Scipio Africanus, 117

Jones, Sharon Richardson, 373

Jones, Sherman, 288

Jones, Theodore W., 125

Joplin, Scott, 13

Jordan, Barbara Charline, 149, 181, 181

Jordan, Jack, 277

Jordan, Leria Lowe, 288

Joubert, James, 312

Journal of Negro History, 272, 411

Journal of the National Medical Association
359

Joy Street Baptist Church, 305, 306

Joyner, Marjorie Stewart, 347

Juba (dance), 3

Judaism, 311–312

Judiciary, 167–169

Juilliard School of Music, 20, 25, 27, 38

Juilliard String Ensemble, 29

Julia, 39

Julian Laboratories, 347

Julian, Anna Johnson, 92

Julian, Percy Lavon, 347, *348*

Junior Catholic Daughters of the Americas, 317

Junior League, 288, 289

Just Between Me and You, 25

Just, Ernest E., 89, 263

Justin, John, 8

K

Kamba, Walter J., 84

Kansas, 128

Kansas City Athletics, 369

Kansas City Monarchs, 366

Kansas City, MO, 204

Kappa Alpha Psi, 294

KCBS-TV (Los Angeles), 234

Kearney, Jesse, 117

Kearse, Amalya Lyle, 169

Keeble, Sampson W., 147

Keith, Karen, 407

Kellee Communications Group, 59

Kelley, George B., 294

Kelly, Leontine T. C., 333, *333*

Kelly, Sharon Pratt Dixon, 172, 217

Kennedy, Cain James, 116

Kennedy, John F., 38, 157, 160, 170, 420

Kennedy, Robert F., 399

Kennedy, Yvonne, 84

Kent College of Law, 177, 221

Kent-Barry-Eaton Connection Railway Company, 65

Kentucky, 128–129

Kentucky Association of State Employees/FSE, 56

Kentucky Derby, 394

Kentucky, municipal government in, 200

Kentucky Oaks, 394

Kentucky State College (Frankfort), 224, 230

Kenwood Commercial Furniture, 60

Kersee, Bob, 402

Kershaw, Joe Lang, 121

KFFA (Helena, AR), 33

Kilgore, Thomas, Jr., 310

"King Biscuit Time," 33

King Bolden. *See* Bolden, Charles

King Cole Trio, 34

King George V, 403

King Lear, 47

King Oliver, 16

King Tim III (Personality Jock), 27

King, B. B., 104

King, Blues Boy, 34

King, Coretta Scott, 230, 319

King, Gwendolyn Stewart, 165

King, Martin Luther, Jr., 73, 81, 98, 111, 115, 130, 172, 180, 181, 230, 264, 310

Kinte, Kunte, 41

Kittrell, Flemmie P., 102

Kiwanis International, 289

Knight, Hiawatha, 383

Knight, Richard, Jr., 213, 282

Knights and Daughters of Tabor Society, 68, 293

Knights of Labor, 53

Knights of Liberty, 68

Knights of Peter Claver, 294

Knights of Pythias, 293

Knights of the Invisible Colored Kingdom, 293

Knox College (Illinois), 174

Knox, Clinton Everett, 157
Knoxville College, 83
Kodesh Church of Immanuel, 337
Koontz, Elizabeth Duncan, 275
KP00-FM (San Francisco), 35
Krazy Kat, 2
Ku Klux Klan, 237
KWEM (West Memphis, AR), 34

L

La Bohème, 26
Labor Relations, 170
Lafayette Players, 44
Lafayette Theater, 3, 44
Lafayette Theater Company, 45
Lafayette, Marquis de, 351
Lafon, Thomy, 62
Lafontant, Jewel Stradford, 157
LaGrange, Vickie Miles, 143
Lakes, Charles, 392
Lakmé, 17
Lambert, Samuel Fredrick, 279
Lane, William Henry (Master Juba), 3
Lange, Laura J., 331
Lange, Elizabeth, 312
Langston, John Mercer, 81, 105, 142, *142,* 174, 176
Langston University, 17
Lanusse, Armand, 411
Lapointe, Lafond, 322
Larsen, Nella Marian, 415
Lashley, Joe, 379
Latimer, George, 78, 345
Latimer, Lewis H., 78, 345, *345*
Latin America, 162
Laurel, MS, 203
Laurinburg Institute, 23
Lautier, Louis, 223
Law schools, 105
"Lawdy, Lawdy Blues," 16

Lawrence, Jacob, Jr., 31
Lawrence, Janice, 401
Lawrence, Robert H., Jr., 360
Lawson, Jennifer Karen, 41
Lawson State Community College, 116
Lay, Hank, 268
Le Moyne College (Syracuse, NY), 161
Le Moyne-Owen College, 169
Lead Me, Guide Me, 317
Learning Tree, The, 229
Lee, Bertram M., 59, 378
Lee, El Franco, 149
Lee, Fitz, 244
Lee, Gabriel S., Jr., 288
Lee, Howard N., 210
Lee, Jarena, 300, *300*
Lee, John Robert Edward, 274
Lee, M. Davis, 283
Lee, Maurice W., 102
Lee, Rebecca, 352
Lee, Robert E., 237
Lee Strasberg Actors Studio, 39
LeFlore, John L., 115
Leftenant, Nancy C., 246
Legal Aid Bureau (Illinois office), 157
Legal Foundation Assistance of Chicago, 280
Legal Rights Association, 343
Lehmann, Lotte, 24
Leidesdorff, William, 59
Leonard, Walter "Buck," 366
Les Cenelles, 411
Levingston, William, 321
Levinson, Stanley, 73
Lew, Barzillai, 238
Lewis and Clark Expedition, 262
Lewis, Arthur (W. Arthur), 264
Lewis, Carl, 401
Lewis, Delano Eugene, 230
Lewis, [Mary] Edmonia, 36
Lewis, Edward S., 275
Lewis, George, 393

Lewis, Henry, 26

Lewis, Isaac, 393

Lewis, James, 153

Lewis, Jesse J., 115

Lewis, Julian H., 102

Lewis, Oliver, 393, *393*

Lewis, Robert Benjamin, 409

Lewis, William Henry, 155, 156, 384

Liberia, 154, 156

Liberty Party, 138, 170

Library of Congress, 154

Liele, George, 304, 305

Life and Times of Frederick Douglass, The, 170

"Lift Every Voice and Sing" (sculpture), 36

Light and Truth, 409

Lilies of the Field, 8

Lillard, Joe, 386

Lincoln Hospital School for Nurses, 246

Lincoln Theater, 44

Lincoln University (NY), 178

Lincoln University (PA), 45, 64, 81, 85, 98, 160, 385

Lincoln University (PA) Hampton Institute, 374

Lislet-Geoffrey, Jean-Baptiste, 271

Liston, Sonny, 382

L'Italiana in Algieri, 22

Little Rock, AR, 190, 288

"Little Rock Nine," 110

Littlefield, George W., 267

Livingstone College, 302, 385

Lloyd, Earl, 375

Lloyd, John Henry "Pop," 366

Locke, Alain Leroy, 79, *79,* 109

Lockwood, Junior (Robert), 33

Lofton, William, Jr., 297

Lomac, Louis Emanuel, 231

Long Beach Open, 391

Long, Howard H., 95

Long, Jefferson Franklin, 174, 175

Long, Joseph H., *173*

Longford, Anna R., 199

Loper, 64

Los Angeles Angels, 25

Los Angeles Bar Association, 277

Los Angeles Board of Education, 119

Los Angeles, CA, 4, 158, 190, 191, 192, 193

Los Angeles City Fire Department, 192

Los Angeles Community Colleges, 86

Los Angeles County Housing Authority, 211

Los Angeles County Parks and Recreation Commission, 224

Los Angeles Dodgers, 371, 373

Los Angeles International Airport, 1

Los Angeles Municipal Court, 192

Los Angeles Open, 391

Los Angeles Philharmonic, 18

Los Angeles Raiders, 390

Los Angeles Rams, 387

Los Angeles Sentinel, 224

Los Angeles Times, 224

Los Angeles United School District, 119

Lost-Found Nation of Islam in the West (Black Muslims), 337

Lott Carey Foreign Mission Convention, 307

Louis Barrow, Joe, 260

Louis, Joe, 381, *381*

Louisiana, 129

Louisiana American Legion, 295

Louisiana Baptist Association, 307

Louisiana, municipal government in, 200

Louisiana State University, 80

Louisiana Superdome, 382

Louisville, KY, 200

Louisville National Medical College, 352

Louvain University (Belgium), 88

L'Ouverture, Toussaint, *75*

Love, Nat, 402

Loving, Alvin D., Sr., 109

Lowery, Robert O., 207

Lowery, Samuel R., 186

Loyola University School of Law, 130

Lucas, Sam (Samuel Milady), 6

Lucy Foster, Autherine Juanita, 103

"Luther," 3

Lutherans, 328

Luthuli,Albert J., 264

Luxembourg, 159

Lyke, James P., 315

Lyle, Ethel Hedgeman, 294

Lynch, John R., 174, 175

Lynch, Leon, 54

Lynk, Miles Vandahurst, 353

Lyrics of Lowly Life, 412

M

M Street High School, 107

"Mabelline," 26

Mabley, Moms (Jackie), 36

MacArthur Fellowship, 204

MacNeil/Lehrer Report, 232

Macon, GA, 154

MacVicar Hospital, 358

Madam Butterfly, 21

Madison, Frederick, 118

Madison Square Garden, 382

Magazine Photographer of the Year, 229

Magazine Publishers Association, 61

Mahone, Barbara J., 164

Mahoney, Charles H., 156

Mahoney, Mary Elizabeth, 358, *358*

Maine, 130–131

Maine Board of Education, 130

Maine, muncipal government in, 201

Maine State Housing Authority, 201

Majors and Minors, 411

Majors, Monroe Alpheus, 353

Malcolm, Benjamin J., 208

Malcolm X, 41, 225, 334

Male Vocalist of the Year, 25

Malone, Annie Turnbo, 56, *58*

Malone, Vivian, 104

Mamba's Daughters, 46

Man's Life, A, 226

Manhattan Borough Community College, 85

Manhattan House of Corrections, 209

Manley, Albert Edward, 81, 82

Manley, Audrey Forbes, 165

Mann, Thomas J., Jr., 128

Manning, Madeline, 400

Manuel, Wiley E., 119

Manumission Society, 105

"Maple Leaf Rag," 13

Mapps, Grace A., 88

Marathon walking, 396

March, Henry III, 214

March on Washington, 207

Maricopa County Superior Court, 117

Mariner's Temple Baptist Church, Manhattan, 310

Marino, Eugene Antonio, 318

Marr, Carmel Carrington, 140

Marsalis, Wynton, 28

Marshall, Bobby, 387

Marshall, Harriet (Hattie) Aletha Gibbs, 90

Marshall, Thurgood, 160, *160*

Martin, Dean, 268

Martin, Janice R., 129

Martin, Mahlon, 288

Martin, Montez Cornelius, Jr., 280

Mary Mahoney Medal, 358

Maryland, 131

Maryland, municipal government in, 201

Mashow, John, 64

Mason, Biddy, 61, *61*

Mason, C. H., 334, 335

Mason, James W., 154

Masons, 291

Massachusetts, 131–133, 169

Massachusetts Bar, 406

Massachusetts, first colony to legalize slavery, 77

Massachusetts Institute of Technology, 210

Massachusetts Medical Society, 295

Massachusetts, municipal government in, 202

Massey, Walter E., 357

Massie, Samuel P., 251

Mastin, Will, 268

Mather, Cotton, 319, 350

Matseliger, Jan E., 260

Matthews, Artie, 14

Matthews, Vincent, 400

Matzeliger, Jan, 345, *345*

Mauritius, 271

Maynard, Robert C., *225,* 226

Maynor, Dorothy, 22, 110

Mayors, 286

Mays, Benjamin Elijah, 111, *111*

Mayson, H. Irving, 322

McAfee, Walter, 360

McAlpin, Harry S., 223

McAnulty, William Eugene, 129

McCabe, Edward P., 128

McCain, Franklin, 73

McCarthy, Cal, 380

McCoo, Marilyn, 101

McCoy, Albert B., 338

McCoy, Elijah, 344, *344*

McCree, Floyd, 202

McCurdy, Merle M., 142

McDaniel, Hattie, 7, 46

McDaniels, Warren E., 201

McDonald, 282

McFadden, Vivian, 254

McFarlin, Emma Daniels, 162

McFerrin, Robert, 23

McGee, Benjamin Lelon, 83

McGee, Pam, 401

McGhee, Dolores G., 280

McGowan, John, 189

McGuire, George Alexander, 303

McIntyre, B. Barton, 339

McIntyre, Edward H., 197

McJunkin, George, 267

McKinley House, 267

McKinley, Ada S., 267

McKinley, William, Jr., 142

McKinney, Cynthia, 185

McKinney, Nina Mae, 7

McKissick, Floyd Bixler, 95

McLendon, Johnny "Coach Mac," 375

McMillan, Elridge, W., 85

McNair, Ronald, 362

McNeil, Joseph, 73

McSmith, Blanche Preston, 116

McSween, Cirilo A., 52

Mechanics Saving Bank, 275

Medal of Honor, 242, 243, 244, 246, 248

Medical Agencies and Schools, 349

Medical and Surgical Observer, 353

Medical College of Pennsylvania, 349

Medical College of Virginia, 150

Medico, 295

Medill, Joseph, 197

Medill School of Journalism (Northwestern University), 226

Medley, Tyrone E., 150

Meek, Carrie, 121, 184

Meharry Medical College, 137, 165, 298, 349

Melancholy Dame, 7

Melody Maker, 6

"Memphis Blues," 14

Memphis Red Sox, 25

Memphis State University, 86

Memphis State University School of Law, 148

Memphis Students, 13

Memphis, TN, 213

Menard, John Willis, 172

Mendez, Arnaldo Tamayo, 360

Mennonite Antislavery Resolution, 67

Mercury Records, 24

Meredith, James, 74, 103, 148, 168

Merit System Protection Board, 164

Merry, Nelson G., 308

Metcalf, Ralph, 396, 406

Methodist Episcopal church, 299, 300, 303, 328, 330, 331

Methodists, 328–333

Metro-Denver Urban Coalition, 120

Metropolitan Akron Housing Authority (OH), 211

Metropolitan Opera, 4, 5, 22, 23, 25, 26

Metropolitan Spiritual Churches of Christ, 339

Metropolitan St. Louis YWCA, 286

Meyersville, MS, 204

Miami, FL, 196

Michaux, Henry M., Jr., 158

Michaux, Solomon Lightfoot, 326, *326*

Michigan, 133–134, 177

Michigan, municipal government in, 202

Michigan Occupational Education Association, 279

Michigan State Employees Union, 55

Michigan State Supreme Court, 134

Michigan State University, 83, 164

Michigan State University College of Osteopathic Medicine, 87

Mid-Western Baseball League, 367

Middle States League, 365

Middle Temple (London, England), 220

Middle Tennessee State University, 86, 229

Middlebury College (VT), 88, 92, 104, 183, 320

Milam, Lorenzo, 35

Miles, Ben, 283

Miles, W. H., 331

Mill, John, Jr., 33

Miller, Cheryl, 401

Miller, Dorie, 252

Miller, Rice (Willie; Sonny Boy Williamson, No. 2), 33

Miller, Ross M., Jr., 298

Miller, Thomas E., 174

Miller, William, 301

Miller, Yvonne Bond, 151

Mills Brothers, 33

Mills, Lois Terrell, 282

Milner, Thirman L., 193

Milwaukee Bucks, 377

Milwaukee, WI, 163

Mines, Janie L., 251

Mingus, Nathan, 294

Ministerial Institute and College (West Point, MS), 116

Minnesota, 134

Minnesota, municipal government in, 203

Minnesota Twins, 370

Minnesota Vikings, 134, 389

Minton, Henry McKee, 294

Minton's Playhouse, 20

Mirror of Liberty, 227, 351

Mirror of the Times, 190, 219, 221

Mirror-News, 224

Miss America Pageant, 257

Miss Black Teenage America Pageant, 34

Mississippi, 134–135, 175, 183

Mississippi Freedom Democratic Party, 204

Mississippi Hall of Fame, 400

Mississippi, municipal government in, 203

Missouri, 136, 154, 180

Missouri, municipal government in, 204

Mitchell, Abbie, 13

Mitchell, Arthur W., 4, 177

Mitchell, Bert Norman, 280

Mitchell, Charles Lewis, 132

Mitchell, John R., Jr., 275

Mitchell, Juanita E. Jackson, 93

Mitchell, Sinora M., 217

Mitchell, Therese L., 145

Mitchell-Bateman, Mildred, 151

Moabites of the Bible, 327

Mobley, Sybil Collins, 63

Modern Modes, 38

Mohawk Airlines, 256

Mollison, Irving Charles, 168

"Mona Lisa," 34

Mondale, Walter, 172

Monroe Meadows (Yosemite National Park), 269

Monroe, George, 268

Monroe, Loren Eugene, 134

Montana, 136

Montgomery Bus Boycott, 73, 115, 178

Montgomery Civil Rights Monument, 71

Montgomery, Simon Peter, 331

Moon, Molly, 286

Moon's Clubhouse, 265

Moore v. Dempsey, 117

Moore, Charles, Jr., 398

Moore, Emerson J., Jr., 317

Moore, Fred, 246

Moore, Lewis B., 92

Moore, Roscoe Michael, Jr., 165

Moore, Walthall M., 136

Moore, Wenda Weekes, 83

Moore, William, 212

Moore, Winston, E., 198

Moorish Science Temple, 327

Moorish Zionist Temple, 311

Moral Reform, The, 221

Morehouse College, 83, 101, 111, 124, 156, 160, 165, 166, 169, 186, 197, 272

Morehouse School of Medicine, 166

Moret, Curtis J., 279

Morgan, Aletha, 147

Morgan, Garrett A., 347, *347*

Morgan State College (now University), 17, 81

Morial, Ernest Nathan, 130, 200, 201

Mormons, 333

Morón, Alonzo Graseano, 81, 82

Morrill Act of 1862, 100

Morris Brown College, 101

Morris, E. C., 309

Morris, Thomas Chester, 220, *220*

Morrison, George, 15

Morrison, Toni, 413, *413*

Morrison, Trudi Michelle, 183

Morrow, E. Frederic, 157

Morton, Azie B. Taylor, 162

Morton, Jelly Roll, 14

Morton, Lorraine H., 200

Moses, 306

Moses, Edwin Corley, 400

Mosley, Archibald, 288

Moss, Carlton, 8

Moss (Philips), Elizabeth B.Murphy, 223

Mossell, Aaron Albert, Jr., 89

Mossell, Nathan Francis, 89, 343

Mossell, Sadie Tanner, 89, 92

Moten, Lynette, 230

Mother Bethel Church, Philadelphia, 71

Motley, Constance Baker, 140, 168, *168,* 207

Motley, Marion, 387

Motley, Pealine, 60

Mott, Robert, 44

Mound Bayou, MS, 203

Mount Hope, 329

Mount Providence Junior College, 312

Mount Vernon, NY, 208

Mount Zion, 329

Move On Up a Little Higher, 22

MTV, 30

Muhammad, Elijah, 334

Muhammad, Wallace J., 334

Mulatto, 45

Mulzac, Hugh, 54, 267

Municipal Court Clerks Association of California, 279

Municipal Court of Atlanta, 124

Murphy, Eddie, 41

Murphy, Green, 394

Murphy, Isaac, 393, 394, *394*

Murray, Daniel Alexander Payne, 154

Murray, George Washington, 174

Murray, Jacqueline, 200

Murray, Joan, 231

Murray, John, Earl of Dunmore, 238

Murray, Pauli, 119, *323,* 324

Murray, Peter Marshall, 297

Muse, Clarence, 7

Museums, 357

Music and Some Highly Musical People, 413

Muslims, 334

Mutual Bank and Trust Company, 50

Myers, Isaac, 53, 64

Myrtilla Miner Normal School, 44

Mystery, The, 219, 221

N

NAACP, 54, 72, 115, 160, 161, 168, 290, 343, 354, 355, 411

NAACP Legal Defense Fund, 162, 189

NAACP Spingarn Medal, 160, 161. *See also* Spingarn Medal

NAACP Youth Council, 73

Nabrit, James Madison, Jr., 82, 160

Nabrit, Samuel Milton, 82, 341

Narrative of the Life and Adventure of Venture, 409

Narrative of the Lord's Dealings with John Marrant, 409

Narrative of the Uncommon Sufferings and Surprising Deliverance, 409

NARTA, 35

NASA (National Aeronautics and Space Agency), 349

NASCAR Winston Cup, 364

Nash, Charles E., 174

Nashville City Council, 149

Nashville, TN, 213

Natchez, MS, 204

Nation of Islam, 327, 334

National Academy, 31

National Academy of Arts and Letters, 37

National Academy of Sciences, 273

National Academy of Television Arts and Sciences, 280

National Airmen's Association of America, 255

National Alliance Party, 172

National Amateur Athletic Union, 406

National Association for Equal Opportunity in Higher Education, 288

National Association for the Advancement of Colored People. *See* NAACP

National Association of Black Journalists, 227

National Association of Black Women Entrepreneurs, 277

National Association of Boards of Pharmacy, 298

National Association of Broadcasters' Hall of Fame, 34

National Association of Colored Women, 107, 290, 291

National Association of Colored Women, Suffrage Department, 107

National Association of Power Engineers, 279

National Association of Professional Baseball Clubs, 366

National Association of Radio and Television News Directors, 232

National Association of Radio Announcers, 34, 35

National Association of Teachers in Colored Schools, 274

National Association of the Deaf, 283

National Association of Universities and Land Grant Colleges, 276

National Association of Women Judges, 191

National Association of Women Painters and Sculptors, 36

National Association of Intercollegiate Athletics Sports Information Directors, 276

National Baptist Convention of America, 309

National Baptist Convention, Inc., 310

National Baptist Convention, USA, 18, 307, 309

National Baptist Convention, Unincorporated, 309

National Baptist Evangelical Life and Soul Saving Assembly of USA, 337

National Bar Association, 279

National Basketball Association, 376, 378

National Black Arts Festival, 6

National Black Catholic Congress, 318

National Black Police Association, 283

National Book Award, 41, 416

National Book Critics Award, 413

National Business Committee for the Arts, 276

National Coalition of 100 Black Women, 226

National Colored Spiritualist Association of Churches, 339

National Conference of Black Mayors, 204

National Conference of Christians and Jews, 295

National Conference of Colored Women, 290

National Convocation of the Christian Church, 318

National Cooperative Education Association, 275

National Council of Churches, 295

National Council of Churches in America, 295

National Council of Negro Women, 291

National Council of YMCA, 286

National David Spiritual Temple of Christ Church Union (Inc.), 337

National Education Association, 275, 277

National Educational Television, 39

National Federation of Afro-American Women, 290

National Federation of Community Broadcasters, 35

National Football League, 385, 386

National Football League Hall of Fame, 134

National Institute of Arts and Letters, 272, 420

National Intercollegiate Squash Racquets Association, 404

National Labor Relations Board, 170

National Labor Union, 53

National League for the Protection of Colored Women, 291

National Loyalists' Union party, 170

National Maritime Union, 54

National Medical Association, 295

National Museum of Racing, 394

National Negro Baseball League, 366, 367

National Negro Congress, 46, 54

National Negro Convention, 71

National Negro Music Center, 89

National Negro Network, 35

National Negro Newspapers Association, 275

National Negro Opera, 23

National Negro Press Association, 223

National Newspapers Association, 275

National Order of Mosaic Templers of America, 293

National Organization of Black Law Enforcement Executives, 202

National Police Officers, 280

National Press Club, 225

National Primitive Baptist Convention of the USA, 337

National Public Radio (NPR), 230

National Pulitzer Prize Board, 226

National Radio Pulpit of the National Council of Churches, 333

National Science Foundation, 357

National Security Council, 87, 159

National Spiritualist Association, 339

National Sports Awards, 405

National Urban League, 163, 291

National Urban League Guild, 286

National War College, 165, 247

National Watchman, 221

National Workshop on Christian Unity, 295

National Youth Administration (NYA), 155

National Youth Administration's Division of Negro Affairs, 261

Native Son, 415

"Nature Boy," 34

Naumburg Competition, 30

Naval College, 253

Naval Medal of Honor, 251, 252

NBA Players Association, 377

NBC television, 38

NBC-TV Opera Workshop, 25

Neal, Audrey, 55

Neau, Elias, 319

Nebraska, 136–137

Negro American Baseball League, 25

Negro Art Theater Dance Group, 4

Negro Digest, 228

Negro Ensemble Company, 8

Negro Folk Symphony, 19

Negro Genius, 414

Negro Gospel and Religious Music Festival, 21

Negro History Bulletin, 411

Negro History Week, 272

"Negro Hour, The," 32

Negro in Literature and Art, 413

Negro International League, 367

Negro Inventor, 347

Negro National Labor Union, 176

Negro National League, 366

Negro Newspaper Association, 224

Negro Newspapers Publishers Association, 223, 224

Negro Opera Company (Washington, DC), 17

Negro Soldier, The, 8

Negro Urchin, 36

Negro Waifs Home for Boys, 6

Negro World, 72

Nell, William Cooper, 153, 410

Nelson, Harold E., 200

Nelson Mandela Courage Award, 38

Nelson, Mary Ann, 289

Nesty, Anthony, 402

New Age, 119

New Alpha Missionary Baptist Church, 311

New England Anti-Slavery Society, 68

New England Confederation, 77

New England Conservatory of Music, 18, 19

New England Law School, 169

New Hampshire, 137

New Jersey, 137–138, 183

New Jersey Council of Churches, 327

New Jersey Gremlins, 389

New Jersey Jaycees, 282

New Jersey, municipal government in, 205

New Jersey Symphony, 26

New London, CT, 193

New Negro, The, 109

New Orleans, LA, 130, 200, 201

New Orleans Mardi Gras, 6

New Orleans Symphony, 21

New Orleans World Exposition, 31

New School for Social Research, 38, 231

New Theatre School, 47

New Thought church, 304

New World National Bank, 51

New York, 138–141

New York Airways, 256

New York Amsterdam News, 354

New York City, 168, 205–208

New York City Ballet, 4

New York City Board of Education, 279

New York City Board of Hospitals, 297

New York City Housing Patrolmen, 277

New York City Opera, 18, 21

New York County Medical Society, 297

New York Drama Critics Award, 46

New York Giants, 369, 373, 388

New York Knickerbockers, 375

New York Law School, 160

New York Life Insurance Company, 52

New York Mets, 374

New York National Guard, 238

New York Philharmonic, 20

New York, Second District of, 155

New York Silurians Award, 225

New York Society for the Promotion of Education Among Colored Children, 170

New York State Legislature, 138

New York State School Boards Association, 277

New York State Senate, 168

New York State Society of Certified Public Accountants, 280

New York Stock Exchange, 63

New York Times, 222

New York University, 52, 83, 84, 168, 182, 230, 272, 276, 286

New York University College of Medicine, 297

New York University School of Law, 141, 147, 189

New York World's Fair 193940, 36

New York Yankees, 367, 369, 386

New Yorker, 2

Newark College of Engineering, 205

Newark Housing Authority, 205

Newark, NJ, 205

Newcomb, Don "Newk," 369

Newman, Constance Berry, 165

Newman, Theodore Roosevelt, Jr., 215

Newnan Station, 329

Newport Jazz Festival, 20, 22

Newport News, VA, 214

Newport, RI, 212

Niagara Frontier Corporate Counsel Association, 280

Niagara Movement, 290, 343

Nigeria, 157

"Nigger Add" ("Old Add," "Old Negro Ad"), 267

Ninety-ninth Pursuit Squadron, 241

Ninety-third Division, 109

Ninth and Tenth Cavalry Regiments, U.S. Colored Troops, 243

Ninth Cavalry, 243, 245

Ninth Ohio Regiment, 244

Ninty-ninth Pursuit Squadron, 241

Nissan Motor Corporation, 50

Nixon, Richard M., 170, 181

Nix, Robert N. C., Jr., 145, *145,* 178–179

Nix, Robert N. C., Sr., *178*

No Place to Be Somebody, 5

Nobel Peace Prize, 156, 264

Nobles, Walter, 251

Nonfiction, 413

Nordskog label, 15

Norfolk Southern Railroad Company, 65

Norfolk State University, 151

Norford, George E., 38

North Atlantic Treaty Organization (NATO), 157

North Carolina, 141–142, 158, 176, 185

North Carolina Agricultural and Technical College, 73, 172

North Carolina Agricultural and Technical State University, 276

North Carolina Aquarium, 249

North Carolina Central University, 101, 141, 158, 251, 383

North Carolina College for Negroes, 101

North Carolina, municipal government in, 210

North Carolina Mutual Life Insurance Company, 52

North Carolina Watchmakers Association, 280

North Central College, 59

North Star, 221, 420

Northeastern University, 259

Northern California U.S. District Court, 169

Northern Pacific Railroad, 214

Northern States Power Company, 167

Northwest and Southern Baptist Convention, 307

Northwest Territory, 142

Northwestern University, 4, 21, 24, 85, 122, 160, 177

Northwestern University School of Dentistry, 298

Not a Man and Yet a Man, 418

Noted Negro Women: Their Triumphs and Activities, 353

Notre Dame University, 134, 169

Nursing, 358–359

Nutter, Adelle, 384

O

Oak and Ivy, 411

Oakland Athletics, 373

Oakland, CA, 192

Oakland Tribune, 226, 227

Oberlin College, 36, 88, 98, 157, 168, 176, , 190, 233, 365

Oberlin Conservatory of Music, 18, 89

Oblate Sisters of Providence, 105, 312

O'Bryant, John D., 112

Oddfellows, 293

Off to Bloomingdale Asylum, 6

Office of Highway Traffic Safety, 115

Office of National Drug Policy, 213

Office of Personnel Management, 165

Ogden, Peter, 293

"Oh, Dem Golden Slippers," 11

O'Hara, James E., 174

Ohio, 142–143

Ohio Council of Retail Merchants Association, 276

Ohio, municipal government in, 210

Ohio State University, 158, 164, 240, 407

Ohio University College of Osteopathic Medicine, 87

Ohio University School of Nursing, 286

O'Jays, 264

OKeh Records, 35

Okino, Elizabeth, 392

Oklahoma, 143

Oklahoma, municipal government in, 211

Olden, Georg (George), 261

Oldham, Todd, 30

O'Leary, Hazel, 167, *167*

Oliva, Tony, 370

Olive, Milton L. III, 246

Oliver, King (Joseph), 11, 15

Olympia, WA, 214

Olympic Games, 233, 396

Omega Psi Phi, 294

O'Neal, Frederick Douglass, 47

O'Neil, John "Buck," 370

O'Neil, Valerie Hanis, 55

O'Neill, Eugene, 45

Onesimus, 350

Onley, Watson, 56

Operation Breadbasket, 172

Operation PUSH (People United to Serve Humanity), 172

Opportunity, 2, 82, 273, 291

"Oprah Winfrey Show," 234

Orduna, Paul A., 192

Organ, Claude H., Jr., 298

O'Rhee, Willie Eldon, 392

Origin and History of the Colored People, 410

Original Hebrew Israelite Nation, 312

Original Race Records, 35

Ornstein School of Music, 25

Orr, Wallace E., 121

Ory, Kid (Edward), 15

Osborn, Charles, 219

Osborne, Estelle Massey Riddle, 97, 359

Oscar, 7, 8

Osei, Kwame, 340

Otis-Lewis, Alexis, 136

Our Nig, 414

Our World, 223

Over, Oscar, 244

Owens, Jesse, 396, *396,* 401, 406

Oxfam, America, 288

Oxford University, 79

P

Pace, Henry, 15

Pace Phonograph Company, 15

Pace-Handy Company, 15

Paddington, George, 313

Page, Alan Cedric, 134, 388

Page, Clarence, 226

Pagedale, MO, 204

Paige, Josh, 366

Paige, Satchel, 366, *368,* 369

Paine College, 231

Palcy, Euzham, 9

Palmer Memorial Institute, 80, 262

Parade of Stars, Lou Rawls', 101

Paramount Records, 15

Parham, Thomas David, Jr., 254

Park, Robert E., 82

Parker, Charlie, 23

Parker, Dave, 373

Parker, Kermit, 130

Parks, Gordon A., Sr., 229, *229*

Parks, Rosa, 115

Parsons, James Benton, 168, *168*

Partee, Cecil A., 126

Pasadena, CA, 192

Passaic County Probation Department, NJ, 282

Passing, 415

Paterson, NJ, 205

Patrick-Yeboah, Jennie, 95

Patterson, Cecil Booker, Jr., 117

Patterson, Floyd, 382

Patterson, Frederick Douglass, 49, 102, 286, 349

Patterson, J. O., Jr., 148

Patterson, Lloyd, 211

Patterson, Mary Jane, 88

Patterson, Moses, 105

Patterson, Rodney S., 311

Patterson, Roland Nathaniel, 111

Paul, Nathan, 307

Paul, Thomas, Sr., 306, 307

Paul, Willie, 113

Payne, Claudia H., 131

Payne, Daniel A., 80, *80,* 81

Payne, Donald M., 183, 286

Payne, Gary D., 129

Payton, Carolyn Robertson, 163

Payton, Phillip A., Jr., 62

Payton, Walter, 390, *390*

Pea Island, North Carolina, Lifesaving Station, 249

Peabody Institute, 30

Peace Corps, 163

Peace Mission, 334

Peake, Mary Smith Kelsick, 106

"Peanuts," 2

Peary, Robert E., 262

Peck, David J., 351

Pekin Stock Company, 44, 45

Pekin Theater, 44

Pendergrass, Teddy, 264

Pendleton, Clarence M., Jr., 163

Penn, Robert, 252

Pennington, James William Charles, 410

Pennsylvania, 178

Pennsylvania Academy of the Fine Arts, 31

Pennsylvania Electric Association, 283

Pennsylvania Iron and Oil League, 365

Pennsylvania, municipal government in, 212

Pennsylvania Society for the Abolition of Slavery, 289

Pennsylvania State College, 133

Pennsylvania State University, 86, 387

Pennsylvania Supreme Court, 144, 178

Pentecostals, 334–345

Peoples Involvement Corporation, 59

People's Press, 221

People's Voice, 224

Pepsico Company, 57

Percussive Art Society, 28

Perdreau, Connie, 283

Perkins, Edward Joseph, 165

Perkins, James, 393

Perry, Carrie Saxon, 120, 193

Perry, Elso, 63

Perry, Harold Robert, 315, *315*

Perry, Joseph, Jr., 121

Peters, Aulana Louise, 164

Peters, John, 418

Peterson, Alan Herbert, 280

Peterson, Frank E., Jr., 249

Peterson (Peterson-Mundy), Thomas Mundy, 71

Pettiford, Oscar, 23

Petty, Christine Evans, 407

Phelps, Donald Gayton, 86

Phelps-Stokes Fund, 286, 288

Phi Beta Kappa, 46, 82, 271, 273

Phi Beta Sigma, 294
    Eta Beta chapter, 295

Philadelphia Bar Association, 283

Philadelphia Centennial Exhibition of 1876,
    31

Philadelphia City Items, 365

Philadelphia International Records, 264

Philadelphia Municipal Court, 144

Philadelphia, PA, 212

Philadelphia Phillies, 373

Philadelphia Press, 220

Philadelphia Pythons, 365

Philadelphia Quakers, 105

Philadelphia 76ers, 376

Philadelphia Tribune, 145, 220, 222

Philander Smith College, 117, 162, 167, 375

Philanthropist, 219

Phillips, Channing E., 171

Phillips, J. D., 333

Phillips, Vel R., 152

Philomethian Lodge No. 646, 293

Phoenix, AZ, 190

Photography, 31

Physostigmine, 347

Pickett, Bill, 403, *403*

Pierce, Samuel Riley, Jr., 160

Pikes Peak Hill Climb, 363

Pinchback, Pinckney Benton Stewart, *129*

Pinson, Cora, 214

Pinto Jim, 404

Pipkins, Robert, 402

Pitcher, Freddie, 201

Pitts, Robert B., 160

Pittsburgh Courier, 222, 223, 226, 230

Pittsburgh, PA, 212

Pittsburgh Pirates, 370, 373, 386

Pittsburgh Steelers, 387

Planned Parenthood Federation, 286

Plantation Minstrel Company, 43

Planter, The, 251

Playboy magazine, 25, 41

Plessy v. Ferguson, 71, 147

Plinton, James O., Jr., 64, *64*

Plummer, Henry Vinson, 243

Poage, George Coleman, 396

Poems on Miscellaneous Subjects, 421

*Poems on Various Subjects, Religious and
    Moral,* 418

Poitier, Sidney, 8

Political Parties, 170

Polk, Anthony Joseph, 341

Polk, William, 244

Pollard, Frederick Douglas "Fritz," Sr., 386,
    386

Pollard, Frederick Douglas, Jr., 386

Pollard, Fritz, 390

Pollard, William E., 54

Pontiac, MI, Kiwanis Club, 3, 288

Pontiac, MI, School District, 280

Pony Express, 268

Poole, Cecil Francis, 158

Poor People's Campaign of 1968, 180

Poor People's Radio, 35

Poor, Salem, 238

Pope John Paul, 317

Porgy and Bess, 17, 21, 29

Port Hudson, battle for, 154

Port Hudson, Louisiana, siege of, 242

Port of New Orleans, 153

Porter, Carey, 52

Porter, E. Melvin, 143

Porter, Frederick M., 205

Porter, Jennie, 108

Porter, John T., 116

Porter, John W., 111

Porterfield's Marina Village (Detroit), 50

Portland Oregonian, 225

Portuguese, Anthony, 205

Posse, 9

Postage stamps, blacks commemorated on, 260

Poston, Ersa Hines, 140, *140*

Potato chips, 264

Potomac Association Conference of the United Church, 340

Potomac Electric Power Company, 217

Powell, Adam Clayton, 224

Powell, Adam Clayton, Jr., 177, *177,* 206

Powell, Adam Clayton III, 230

Powell, Clilan Bethany, 354

Powell, Colin, 247

Powell, Renee, 391

Powell, William M., 53

Powers, Georgia M. Davis, 129

Poynter, Jonathan, 330

Prairie View Agricultural and Mechanical University, 165, 267, 276, 386

Prairie View Bowl, 386

Prater, Constance C., 226

Pratt, Awadagin, 30

Prattis, Percival L., 223

Preakness Stakes, 394

Preer, Evelyn, 7

Presbyterian Division of Work with Colored People, 338

Presbyterians, 335–338

Presbytery of Baltimore, 338

President's Committee on Government Employment Policy, 157

Presidential Medal of Freedom, 264, 405

Presley, Elvis, 30

Press secretary, 230

Prestage, Jewel Limar, 95

Price, Florence, 19

Price, Leontyne (Mary Violet Leontine), 25

Prichard, AL, 189

Pride, Charley, 25

Prince Hall Masons, 291

Prince, Abijah, 417

Prince, Art, 403

Princeton, NJ, 205

Princeton Theological Seminary, 336

Princeton University, 413

Pro Football Hall of Fame, 389

Procope, Ernesta G., 53

Progress of a Race, 96

Progress Plaza, 62

Progressive National Baptist Convention, USA, 309, 310

Progressive Party, 46, 171

Promise Anthem, 9

Prosser, Gabriel, 76

Protestant Episcopal Church, 321, 328

Providence Art Club, 31

Providence Association, 308

Provident Hospital (Chicago), 198, 343, 352

Provident Hospital Training School, 359

Provincial Freeman, 228

Prudential-Bache Securities, 64

Pryor, Richard, 364

Public Broadcasting Service, 41

Public school segregation, 160

Publications, 359

Pulitzer Prize, 41, 226, 229, 413, 416, 420

Pulitzer Prize for poetry, 5

Pullman Palace Car Company, 54

Punch, John, 77

Purlie Victorious, 47

Purnell, Janet, 211

Purvis, Charles Burleigh, 342

Purvis, Robert, 342

Purvis, W. B., 345

Q

Quakers, 78. *See also* Society of Friends

Quassey, 304

Queen Mary, 403

Queens College, 310, 338

Quicksand, 415

Quisqueya Lte., 64

Quonset Point, Rhode Island, Naval Air Station, 254

R

Rabbit Foot Minstrels, 13, 16

Rachel, 44

Radcliffe College, 92

Radio City Music Hall, 20, 30

Rainey, Joseph Hayne, 173, *173*, 174

Rainey, Ma (Gertrude), 13, 16

Raisin in the Sun, 46, 47

Raisin, 46

Ram's Horn, 221

Randolph, A. Philip, 53, 54, *54*

Randolph, Joseph, 52

Randolph, Virginia Estelle, 108, *108*

Random House Publishing, 61, 413

Rangel, Charles Bernard, 163, 182

Ranier National Bank, 214

Rankin, Michael L., 217

Ranne (Ranee), Peter, 268

Ransier, Alonzo J., 174

Rap music, 27

Rapier, James T., 174

"Rapper's Delight," 27

Rastafarians, 338

Rattley, Jessie M., 214

Raveling, George, 378

Rawls, Lou, 101, 264

Ray Kemp, 386

Ray, Charles Bennett, 153, 170

Ray, Charlotte E., 153

Ray, Florence T., 153

RCA Records, 25

Reagan administration, 160, 165

Reagan, Ronald, 160, 164, 165

Reason, Charles Lewis, 88, 96, *96*

Recollections of Seventy Years, 80

Reconstruction, 126, 146, 175

Recording, 35

Redbook, 2

Redding, Grover Cleveland, 326

Redman, Don (Donald Matthew), 19

Reebok International, 59

Reed, Gregory J., 281

Reed, Thomas J., 115

Reese, Cynthia, 121

Reese, Della, 40

Reformed Dutch Church, 339

Reformed Zion Union Apostolic Church, 337

Reid, William Ferguson, 150

Reminiscences of My Life in Camp, 358

Remond, Charles Lenox, 68

Renaissance Casino, 374

Rens (team), 374

Republican Party, 175

Republican Party national convention, 171

Revelations (dance), 5

Revels, Hiram Rhoades (Rhodes), 5, 81, 100, *173,* 174, 175

Reynolds, Humpfrey H., 345

Reynolds, Milton L., 277

Rhea, La Julia, 19

Rhode Island, 146

Rhode Island School of Design, 31

Rhode Island, battle of, 238

Rhode Island, municipal government in, 212

Rhodes scholar, 79

Rhodman, William, 379

Rhone, Sylvia, 29

Ribbs, Willy (Willie) T., 364, *364*

Rice, Condoleeza, 87

Rice, Fred, 199

Rice, Norman Blann, 214

Richards, Lloyd, 47

Richardson, Henry B., 137

Richardson, Willis, 45

Richmond, Bill, 379

Richmond, David, 73

Richmond Planet, 275

Richmond, VA, 213, 214

Ricketts, Matthew O., 136

Rickey, Branch, 385

Rights of All, 221

Rigoletto, 22

Riles, Wilson Camanza, 111

Rillieux, Norbert, 344, *344*

Ringling Brothers Circus, 3

Rio, James Del, 51

Roach, Max (Maxwell Lemuel), 28

Robert F. Goheen Professor of the Council of the Humanities, 413

Roberta Martin Singers, 27

Roberts, Adelbert H., 125

Roberts, Benjamin, 106

Roberts, Frederick Madison, 118

Roberts, John W., 331

Roberts, Lillian, 140

Roberts, Needham, 245

Roberts v. Boston, 106

Robeson, Paul, 46, 343, 386

Robinson, Dillard, 322

Robinson, Eddie, 388, 390

Robinson, Frank, 371

Robinson, Jackie, 367

Robinson, Max, 233

Robinson, R. Jackie, 374

Robinson, Roscoe, Jr., 246

Robinson, Sugar Ray, Jr., 382

Robinson, William, 268

Roche, Alvin A., Sr., 295

Rochester Philharmonic Orchestra, 18

Rock 'n' Roll Hall of Fame and Museum, 29

Rock Island, IL, 199

Rock, John Sweat, 167, 186

Rockefeller Foundation, 288

Rockefeller, John D., 100

Rodeos, 402

Rogers, Timmie, 38

Rogers, Will, 7

Rogosin, Donn, 366

"Roll Over Beethoven," 26

Rollins College (Florida), 104

Rollins, Charlemae Hill, 264

Roman, Charles Victor, 359

Romney, Edgar O., 55

Rooks, Charles Shelby, 83

Roosevelt, Franklin D., 36, 155

Roosevelt University, 28, 55

Roots, 41

Rose Bowl Parade, 233

Rose, Lucille Mason, 208

Rosenwald Fellowship, 229

Ross, Diana, 87

Ross-Lee, Barbara, 87

Rotary Club of Cheraw, SC, 288

Rotary Club of Tanzania, 289

Roundtree, Richard, 8

Rowan, Carl Thomas, 159, 276

Royal Ballet Company, 29

Royal Circle of Friends of the World, 293

"Royal Family, The," 40

Royal Knights of King David, 293

Rucker, Robert D., Jr., 126

Rudolph, Wilma, 399, *399,* 401

Ruffin, George Lewis, 88

Ruffin, Josephine St. Pierre, 88, 290

Rugambwa, Laurian, 315

Ruggles, David, 62, 227, 351

"Rules for the Society of Negroes," 319

Rumania, 155

Run, Little Children, (Run Little Chillun), 4, 45

Runge, Mary, 297

Running Wild, 3, 19

Rupp, Adolph, 376

Rush, Gertrude E. Durden, 128

Rush Medical College, 351

Russell, Bill, 376

Russell, Harvey Clarence, Jr., 57

Russell, Herman Jerome, 275

Russell, Nipsey, 2, 38

Russwurm, John Brown, 88, 219, 336

Russwurm Award for Excellence in Radio News Reporting, 225, 416

Rust College (Mississippi), 99, 207

Rust, Richard, 99

Rustin, Bayard, 73

Rutgers University, 46, 157, 158

Rutgers University School of Law, 138, 167

Ruth, Babe, 371

S

S. D. State Junior College (now Bishop State Community College), 84

Sailing, 403

Saint Andrew's AME Church, 300

Saint Andrew's United Methodist Church, 333

St. Augustine, Florida, 194

Saint Augustine's College, 81, 82, 141

Saint Augustine's Seminary, 314, 315

Saint Bonaventure University, 317

Saint Edmond Seminary, 317

Saint Francis Academy (Baltimore), 105

Saint Francis Xavier Church, 313, 314, 317

Saint Gelasius I, 320

Saint-Georges, Chevalier de (Joseph Boulogne), 9

Saint George's Methodist Episcopal Church, 328–330

Saint James United Methodist Church (Kansas City, MO), 204

Saint James' Church (Baltimore, MD), 321

St. John's University (Brooklyn), 156

St. John's University Law School, 182, 183

Saint Joseph's Seminary, 318

Saint Joseph's Society, 317

Saint Louis Blues (also known as *Best of the Blues*), 16

St. Louis, MO, 204

Saint Louis University, 180, 204

Saint Luke Penny Savings Bank, 50

Saint Luke's Church (New Haven, CT), 321

Saint Miltiades, 320

Saint Moses the Black, 321

St. Paul, MN, 203

Saint Paul's Cathedral, 319

Saint Phillip's African Church, 321

Saint Thomas' African Episcopal Church, 321

Saint Victor I, 320

Salem, Peter, 238

Salome, 45

Salvation Army, 339

Sam Huston College, 87

Sampson, Charles, 403

Sampson, Edith Spurlock, 198

San Francisco Dental Society, 297

San Francisco Giants, 373

San Francisco Symphony Foundation and Association, 286

Sanders, Joseph Stanley, 79

Sanford, Isabel, 40

Santa Clara Law School, 183

Santiago, Margaret, 357

Santomee, Lucas, 350

Saperstein, Abe, 375

Sarah Lawrence College, 416

Sarandon, Susan, 9

Satanism, 281

Satcher, David, 350, *350*

Saunders, Doris Evans, 198

Savage, Augusta [Fells], 36

Savannah, GA, 196

Savold, Lee, 381

Scales, Jerome C., 298

Scarborough, Williams Sanders, 413

Schmelling, Max, 381

Schmoke, Kurt Lidell, 202

School History of the Negro Race in America from 1619 to 1890, 138

School of American Ballet, 4

Schools, 105–113

Schultz, Charles, 2

Science & Medicine, 341–362

SCLC-Operation Breadbox Orchestra, 63

Scott, Dred, 70

Scott, Gloria Dean Randle, 286

Scott, Gregory K., 120

Scott, Hazel Dorothy, 38

Scott, Isaiah B., 331

Scott, Marshall Logan, 338

Scott, Robert C. (Bobby), 186

Scott, Stanley S., 225

Scott, Wendell Oliver, 364, *364*

Scott, William A., III, 222

Searles, Joseph L., 63

Sears, Roebuck and Company, 63

Seattle City Light, 60

Seattle, WA, 214

Second Baptist Church, Los Angeles, California, 310

Second Cumberland Presbyterian Church, 336, 337

Secretary of Energy, 167

Secretary of Housing and Urban Development, 158

Securities and Exchange Commission, 164

Segregation, 147

Selassie, Haile, 338

Seligman, Edwin R. A., 291

Sellers, Walter G., 289

Senate Rules Committee, 223

Sendaba, Sheleme S., 50

Sengstake, Robert Abbott, 220

Sergeant Rutledge, 9

Service and Development Agency, 301

Sessions, Mrs. Levi N. *See* Stanton, Lucy Ann

Seton Hall University, 183

Sewell, Mack, 279

Seymore, Leslie, 283

Seymour and Lundy Associates, 202

Seymour, Frank M., 202

Seymour, Frederick Williams, 294

Seymour, William J., 334

Sh-Boom, 23

Shackelford, Lottie H., 118, 190

Shadd (Cary), Mary Ann, 228

Shadow and Act, 416

Shadow and Light (Autobiography), 190

Shaft, 8

Shakespeare, William, 45

Shanks, Simon, Jr., 203

Shannon, David T., 86

Sharecroppers, 117

Sharp Street, 329

Sharp Street Church, 329

Sharpe, Ronald M., 145

Shaw, Bernard, *232,* 233

Shaw, Leander J., Jr., 122

Shaw, Leslie N., 158

Shaw, Robert Gould, 242

Shaw University, 141, 414

Shaw v. Reno, 185

Shell, Arthur "Art," Jr., 390

Shepard, James E., 101

Sherwood, Alexander, 313

Sherwood, Kenneth N., 60

Shields, Henry W., 138

Short stories, 420

Shrine of the Black Madonna, 311

Shrines of the Black Madonna Pan-African Orthodox Christian Church, 311

Shuffle Along, 19, 34

Sierra Club, 289

Sifford, Charlie, 391

Sigma Pi Phi, 294

Simmons College, 80

Simmons, Leonard (Bud), 137

Simmons, Ron, 407

Simmons, Rosie S., 135

Simmons, William J., 309, *309*

Simms, Leah, 121

Simms, Willie (Willy), 394

Simon, "Monkey," 393

Simple Speaks His Mind, 45

Simple Stakes a Claim, 45

Simpson, Georgianna Rose, 92, 93, *94*

Simpson, O. J., 388, *388*

Simpson, Thacher, and Bartlett, 282

Sims, Willie, 393

Sinatra, Frank, 268

Singleton, John, 9

Siraj Wahaj, 334

Sissle, Noble, 245

Sisters of Loretto, 312

Sisters of the Blessed Sacrament, 101

Sisters of the Holy Family, 313

Sivart Mortgage Company, 51

Sixth Avenue Baptist Church, 116

"Sixty Minutes," 233

Sklarek, Norma Merrick, 1

Slater, Frederick "Duke," 386

Slater, Rodney, 167

Slave revolt in New York City, 74

Slave revolt in South Carolina, 75

Slave, first known, 77

Slavery, 132, 142
          abolition of, 150
          freedom from, 132

Slavin, Frank, 379

Sleet, Moneta J., 229

Slowe, Lucy Diggs, 294, 404

Small, Bishop John B., 302

Small, Mary J., 302

Smalls, Robert, 174, 251

Smart Set Club, 374

Smith, Bessie, 16

Smith, Charles R., 280, 318

Smith, Chester, 318

Smith College, 91

Smith, Ferdinand C., 54

Smith, J. Clay, Jr., 279

Smith, James McCune, 351, *351*

Smith, James Webster, 250

Smith, Jimmy (James Oscar), 25

Smith, Joshua L., 85

Smith, Kelly Miller, Sr., 98

Smith, Mamie, 35

Smith, Merle J., Jr., 249

Smith, Otis M., 134

Smith, Stanley Hugh, 189

Smith, Tommie C., 400

Smith, William H., 314

Smith, William M., 332

Smithsonian Institution, 268, 342

Smyrna, DE, 194

Snowden, Carolynne, 7

Snowden, Fred "The Fox," 377

Snowden School (Virginia), 107

Society for the Propagation of the Gospel in
     Foreign Parts, 319

Society for the Study of Social Problems, 273

Society of Colored People of Baltimore, 313

Society of Friends, 67, 107

Society of the Divine Word, 314

Society of the Sons of New York, 284

Some Memoirs of the Life of Job, 409

Somerville, Dora B., 125

Song of Solomon, 413

Sonny Boy Williamson, 33

Sorbonne, 157

Soul City, 95

"Soul Train," 40

Souls of Black Folk, 410

Sounder, 39, 229

South Africa, 161, 165

South African PGA Open, 391

South Carolina, 146–147, 173

South Carolina Baptist Educational and
     Missionary Convention, 310

South Carolina Bar Association, 280

South Carolina, municipal government in,
     212

South Carolina National Guard, 237

South Carolina State College, 186

South Carolina State College, 247

South Carolina Volunteers, 358

Southern Baptist Convention, 308

Southern California Chapter of the American
     College of Surgeons, 298

Southern California Community Choir, 28

Southern Christian Leadership Conference
     (SCLC), 73, 172, 200

Southern Christian Leadership Council, 161

Southern Connecticut State University, 282

Southern Education Foundation, 85

Southern Governors, Conference, 291

Southern Historical Association, 273

Southern Illinois University, 8

Southern Intercollegiate Athletic Conference, 363

Southern Sociological Society, 272

Southside Settlement House, 267

Southwestern Christian Advocate, 331

Southwestern University, 171

Soyinko, Wole, 412

Space, 360–362

Spaulding, Asa T., 52

Spaulding, Charles, 52

Spears, Doris E., 119

Special Commendation Awards, 26

Special Olympics, 399

Spelman College, 22, 81-83, 85, 100, 101, 165, 217, 239, 277, 358, 416

Spelman Seminary, 358

Spencer, Peter, 303

Spencer, Vaino Hassen, 191

Spingarn Medal, 31, 45, 110, 160, 161, 244, 263, 273, 354, 355

Spiritual, 339

Spivey, Victoria, 7

Spofford, Ainsworth R., 154

Spokane, WA, 214

Sports Administration, 363

Spratlin, Valaurez B., 92

Springfield, OH, 210

Sproles, Tommy, 118

Squash, 405

Srong, Ariel Perry, 228

Stallings, George Augustus, 303

Stanford University, 82, 87, 282

Stanley, Frank L., Sr., 275

Stanton, Clara Jones, 277

Stanton, Lucy Ann (Mrs. Levi N. Sessions), 88

Star of Liberia, 220

Star of Zion, 222

State Normal School (Salem, MA), 80

State Normal School and University for Colored Students and Teachers, 100

State Street Council (Chicago), 52

State University of Iowa, 92

State University of New York, 83

Steele, Shirley Creenard, 128

Steib, J. Terry, 318

Stephan, Martin, 403

Stephens, Paul, 298

Steward, Susan McKinney, 107, 352, *352*

Steward, Theophylus G., 271, 352

Stewart, John, 330

Stewart, Maria W., 67

Stewart, Pearl, 227

Still, William Grant, 15, 18

Stith, James H., 250

Stock, Frederick, 19

Stokes, Carl, 210

Stokes, Louis, 180

Stone, I. F., 224

Stone, James, 241

Story of Ruby Valentine, 35

Story, Moorfield, 290

Stout, Juanita Kidd, 144, *144*

Stoval, Mary, 189

Stowers, Freddie, 248

Straighten Up and Fly Right, 34

Street, Shirley, 281

Streets, Frederick J., 311

Strode, Woody, 9, 387

Stroud, Florence, 119

Student Nonviolent Coordinating Committee (SNCC), 74, 171, 291, 332

Sturdivant, John Nathan, 56

Sudarkasa, Niara, 85

Sugar Hill Gang, 27

Sugar Hill Times, 38

Sul-Tee-Wan, Madame, 7

Sula, 413

Sullivan, Leon Howard, 62, *62*

Sullivan, Louis Wade, 165, *166*

Sulton-Campbell and Associates, 59

Sumner, Francis Cecil, 93

Sunshine Orchestra, 15

Super Bowl XI, 233

Supermodel (You Better Work!), 30

Supreme Camp of American Woodmen, 293

Supression of the African Slave Trade, 1638–1970, 410

Surely God Is Able, 20

Sutherland, Donald, 9

Suthern, Orrin Clayton, 21

Sweatman, Wilbur, 13

Sweitzer, Anne, 328

Sylverster, Odell H., Jr., 192

Symphony Hall (Boston), 15

Symphony in E Minor, 19

Syphilis and Its Treatment 356

Syracuse University, 92, 162, 384, 387, 388

T

Taft, OK, 211

Taft, William Howard, 155

Talbert, Mary Burnett, 263

Talbot, Gerald Edgerton, 130

Talladega College, 81, 100, 147

Talmadge, Herman, 196

Talton, Chester Lovelle, 325

Taming of the Shrew, 47

Tampa Bay Buccaneers, 390

"Tan Town Jamboree," 34

Tan, 228

Tandy, Vertner W., 238

Tandy, Vertner W, Sr., 1

Tango, 3

Tanner, Henry Ossawa, 31, 260

Tannhäuser, 24

Tapsico, Jacob, 299

Tar Baby, 413

Tate, Herbert Holmes, Jr., 138

Tate, Merze, 92

TAW International Leasing, 51

Taylor, C. H. J., 155

Taylor, Dorothy Mae, 130

Taylor, James H., 84

Taylor, John Baxter "Doc," Jr., 396

Taylor, Marshall W. "Major," 331, 384, *384*

Taylor, Prince A., 332

Taylor, Ruth Carol, 256

Taylor, Sampson, 238

Taylor, Susie King, 358, *358*

Taylor, Walter Scott, 205

Taylor, William Frank, 339

Tchula, MS, 204

Teague, Colin, 307

Temple University, 39, 377

Temple, Lewis, 344

Temple, Shirley, 7

Tennessee, 147–149, 169, 182

Tennessee Board of Regents, 86

Tennessee, municipal goverment in, 213

Tennessee State University, 86, 149, 182, 376, 399, 400

Tennis, 405–406

Tenth Cavalry, 244, 250

Terre Haute Federal Penitentiary, 225

Terrell, Mary Church, 107, *109,* 290

Terrell, Robert H., 215

Terry (Prince), Lucy, 417

Terry, Wallace Houston, II, 228

Texas, 149

Texas, municipal government in, 213

Texas Restaurant Association, 279

Texas Southern University, 83, 181

Tharpe, "Sister" Rosetta, 20

Theodore Drury Colored Opera Company, 11

Thetford Academy (Vermont), 220

"This Thing Called Love," 35

Thomas, Alfred Jack, 244

Thomas, Debi, 394, *395*

Thomas, Franklin A., 288

Thomas, James Joshua, 339

Thomas, James S., Jr., 332

Thomas, Jesse O., 341

Thomas, John, 408

Thomas, John Charles, 150

Thomas, Maxine F., 192

Thompkins, William H., 244

Thompson, Betty Lou, 280
Thompson, Charles H., 108
Thompson, Edward, 7
Thompson, Egbert, 244
Thompson, Frank P., 365
Thompson, George I., 253
Thompson, Hank, 367
Thompson, John, 378
Thompson, Marie, 391
Thompson, Vergil, 19
Thompson, William Henry, 246
Thornburgh, Governor Dick, 145
Three Years in Europe, 414
369th Infantry Regiment, 245
"Thriller," 28
Thrower, Willie, 387
Thurgood Marshall School of Law, Texas
    Southern University, 213
Tigerbelles, 399, 400
Tillery, Dwight, 211
Tillman, Juliann Jane, 300
Times Picayune, 227
"Tisket-A-Tasket," 24
Tobias, Channing Heggie, 286
"Today," 233
Todman, Terence A., 162
Tokahama, Charles, 365
Tolan, Thomas Edward "Little Eddie," 406
Tolliver, Lennie Marie Pickens, 164
Tolton, Augustus, 314
Tomb of the Unknown Soldier, 246
Tomes, Henry, Jr., 132
Tomkins, George, H., 244
"Tonight Show," 29
Tony Award, 5, 38, 46
"Too Young," 34
Toote, Gloria E. A., 164
Torian, Nathanial, 189
Toronto Blue Jays, 373
Torrence, Ridley, 44
Tosca, 25
Tougaloo College (Mississippi), 104, 230, 320

Townsel, Ronald, 125
Track and field, 363, 405
Trans World Airlines, 64
TransAfrica Forum, 38
Travis, Dempsey J., 51
Travis, Geraldine, 136
Tribune de la Nouvelle Orléans, 220
Trident Chamber of Commerce (NC), 280
Trigg, Christine E., 327
Trigg, Harold L., 81, 82
Trigg, Joseph E., 384
Trinity Lutheran Seminary, 328
Trip to Coontown, 6, 43
Triplett, Wally, 387
Triumph the Church and Kingdom of God
    in Christ, 337
Trotter, James Monroe, 413
Trotter, William Monroe, 290
Troubled Island, 18
Trout, Nelson W., 328
True Reformers' Bank, 50
Truman, Harry S., 224
Tubman, Harriet, 31, 78, 260
Tucker, [Cynthia] Dolores Nottage, 145, 227
Tucker, Governor Jim Guy, 118
Tucker, Joyce, 126
Tuesday, 34
Tulane University, 227
Tunnel, Emlen "The Gremlin," 388
Tureaud, Alexander Pierre, Sr., 80
Turner, Alfred B., 102
Turner, Benjamin S., *173,* 174
Turner Broadcasting System, 232
Turner, Carmen Elizabeth, 268
Turner, Henry McNeal, 154, 243, 301, *301*
Turner, James Milton, 154
Turner, Morrie (Morris), 2
Turner, Nat, 76, *76,* 335
Turpin, Thomas Million, 12
Tuskegee, AL, 189
Tuskegee Choir, 19

Tuskegee Institute,   115, 177, 189, 259, 260, 261, 274, 286, 349, 391, 407, 416

Tuskegee University,   84, 124, 135, 165, 239

Tutu, Desmond,   264, 324

"Twelve Clouds of Joy,"   18

Twentieth Century Club (Boston),   80

Twenty-first Congressional District of Illinois,   176

Twenty-fourth Infantry Regiment,   246

Twilight, Alexander Lucius,   88

"Twist, The,"   24

"Two Offers, The,"   420

Tyler, Dana,   234

Tyler, Ralph Waldo,   228, 234

Tyson, Cicely,   38

Tyus, Wyomia,   399

U

UCLA,   374, 386

Ugly Club (New York),   284

Un Ballo in Maschera,   23

Uncle Tom's Cabin,   6

Uncle Tom's Children,   415

Uncles, Charles Randolph,   314

Under the Oaks,   31

Underground Railroad,   78

Union Association,   307

Union Benevolent Society (Lexington, KY),   294

Union Church of Africans,   303

Union Memorial,   329

Union of Black Episcopalians,   322

Union Springs, AL,   189

Union Theological Seminary,   338

Unitarian-Universalist Church,   339

United Auto Workers,   54

United Beauty School Owners and Teachers Association,   347

United Brothers of Friendship and Sisters of the Mysterious Ten, 293

United Church and Science of Living Institute,   340

United Church Board for Homeland Ministries,   83

United Church of Christ,   318, 340

United Free Will Baptist Church,   337

United Golf Association,   391

United Holy Church,   326

United Holy Church of America,   337

United Methodist Africa University,   101

United Methodist Church,   101, 331, 332, 333, 340

United Nations,   140, 156, 160

United Nations Security Council,   160

United Negro College Fund,   101, 183, 286

United Negro Improvement Association (UNIA),   72, 303

United Order of Brothers and Sisters, Sons and Daughters of Moses,   293

United Order of True Reformers,   293

United Presbyterian Church,   338

United Press International,   225

United Society of Believers in Christ's Second Coming (Shakers), 340

United States Army,   137

United States Army Air Corps,   64, 241

United States Army Command and General Staff College,   246

United States Army Nurse Corps,   246

United States Chamber of Commerce,   276

United States Circuit Court of the Southern District of New York, 168

United States Civil Aeronautics Board,   163

United States Civil Rights Commission,   163

United States Claims Court,   169

United States Coast Guard,   313

United States Commission on Aging,   164

United States Conference of Mayors,   205

United States Court of Appeals,   126

United States Court of Appeals, Second District of New York,   169

United States Court of Military Appeals,   240

United States Customs Court,   168

United States Department of Agriculture, 131, 162

United States Department of Health and Human Services, 165

United States Department of Labor, 156

United States Department of State, 23

United States Department of the Interior, 164

United States District Court, 122

United States District Court of Northern Illinois, 168

United States Equal Employment Opportunity Commission, 126

United States Federal Labor Relations Authority, 164

United States Foreign Service, 155

United States Health and Human Services Department, 165

United States House of Representatives, 119, 129, 149, 172–174

United States Indoor Lawn Tennis Association, 404

United States Information Agency, 159

United States Interstate Commerce Commission, 163

United States Junior Amateur Championship, 391

United States Junior Chamber of Commerce, 61

United States Lawn Tennis Association, 405

United States Marines, 249

United States Merit Systems Protection Board, 140

United States Military Academy, 162

United States Military Academy, 247

United States Navy Medical Corps, 254

United States Olympic Committee, 383, 397

United States Patent Office, 346

United States Post Office Department, 133

United States Postal Rate Commission, 166

United States Public Health Service, 165

United States Revenue Service, 249

United States Senate, 129, 155, 174–186, 223

United States State Department, 46

United States Supreme Court, 117, 147, 160, 167, 186

United States Surgeon General, 166

United States Treasury Department, 160

United Way, 288

Universal Press Syndicate, 3

University City, MO, 280

University of Alabama, 84, 295

University of Alabama at Birmingham, 104, 298

University of Arizona, 190, 377

University of Arkansas at Little Rock, 118, 166, 167

University of Arkansas Medical School, 167

University of Berlin, 79

University of California, 171

University of California, Berkeley, 83, 158, 169, 213

University of California, Hastings College of Law, 192

University of California, Los Angeles, 85, 158

University of California, Los Angeles, Medical School, 298

University of Carolina Law, 141

University of Chicago, 4, 82, 86, 89, 92, 125, 156, 157, 164, 168, 184, 263, 264, 272, 273, 276

University of Chicago Graduate Library School, 143

University of Denver, 120

University of Georgetown Law School, 217

University of Georgia, 124, 232, 389

University of Glasgow, 42

University of Houston, 86

University of Illinois, 52, 63, 126, 172, 233, 273, 282, 386

University of Iowa, 27, 386

University of Iowa Law School, 128

University of Kansas, 230, 378

University of Kentucky, 129

University of Legion, Ghana, 317

University of Louisville Law School, 129

University of Maine, 201

University of Maryland, 131, 165, 239

University of Maryland Law School, 201

University of Miami Law School, 121

University of Michigan, 51, 52, 86, 122, 156, 158, 163, 164, 169

University of Michigan, Dearborn, 87

University of Michigan Law School, 169

University of Minnesota, 165

University of Minnesota Board of Regents, 83

University of Minnesota Law School, 134

University of Mississippi, 103, 148, 168, 295

University of Mississippi Law School, 135

University of Nebraska College of Medicine, 137

University of North Carolina, Chapel Hill, 185, 418

University of Notre Dame, 198

University of Ohio, Athens, 283

University of Oklahoma, 189

University of Paris, 92

University of Pennsylvania, 63, 89, 92, 162, 169, 186

University of Pennsylvania Law School, 89, 145, 178

University of Pittsburgh, 247

University of Pittsburgh Law School, 145

University of San Francisco, 376

University of South Carolina, 88, 102

University of Southern California, 164, 185, 389

University of Tennessee, 85

University of Texas at Austin, 149, 181

University of Utah Law School, 150

University of Vermont, 271

University of Washington, 159, 160, 214

University of Wisconsin, 46, 152, 162, 163

University of Wittenberg, 87

University of Zimbabwe, 84

Urban League of Greater Little Rock, 118

Ursuline nuns, 312

Usry, James Leroy, 205

USS Arizona, 253

USS Falgout, 253

USS Harmon, 253

USS Iowa, 252

USS Liscome Bay, 253

USS Marblehead, 251

USS Mason, 253

Ussery, Terdema L., 378

Utah, 150

V

Valparaiso University School of Law, 126

Van Vechten Gallery of Art, 87

Vanderbilt School of Law, 143

Vanderbilt Theatre, 45

Vanderhorst, Richard H., 331

Varick, James, 302

Vashon, George Boyer, 88, 96

Vassar College, 90

Vaughan, Sarah, 38

Vaughn, Jacqueline Barbara, 55

Venture [Broteer] [Smith], 409

Vermont, 67, 150

Vesey, Denmark, 75, 300

Veterans Administration, 51

Veterans Hospital (Tuskegee), 354

Victor Talking Machine Company, 12

Vienna State Opera, 21

Villa Lewaro, 1, 238

Villard, Oswald Garrison, 290

Virgin Islands, 150, 168

Virginia, 150–151

Virginia Association of Broadcasters, 283

Virginia Education Association, 277

Virginia, first black landowners in, 77

Virginia, first black to enter as a free man, 77

Virginia, municipal government in, 213

Virginia Normal and Collegiate Institute (Virginia State College), 176

Virginia State College, 21, 61, 81

Virginia State University, 85

Virginia Theological Seminary, 324

Virginia Union University, 82, 151, 169, 171, 224, 233

Voice of the Negro, The, 81

Voyager I, 26

W

W. T. Grant Company, 52

Wade in the Water, 4

Wade, Melvin R., 58

Wagner Bayreuth Festival, 24, 27

Wagner, Robert F., 207

Wagner, Wieland, 24

Wahaj, Siraj, 334

Walcott, Derek, 412

Walcott, Jersey Joe, 380, 381

Walden, Austin T., 122, 196

Walgreen Company, 298

Walk of Fame (Hollywood), 27

Walk of Western Stars, 9

Walker, Alice, 416, *416*

Walker and Williams, 12

Walker, D. Ormond, 85

Walker, David, 416

Walker, Edward Garrison, 132

Walker, George Nash, 12, 44

Walker, Herschel, 389

Walker, Jackie, 116

Walker, James, 86

Walker, John T., 324

Walker, Leroy Tashreau, 383

Walker, Madame C. J., 1, 56, *57,* 238, 347

Walker, Maggie Lena, 50, *50*

Walker, Moses Fleetwood, 365, *365*

Walker, W. W., 404

Walker, William "Billy," 393

Walker, William O., 143

Walker-Taylor, Yvonne, 85

Wallace, George, 104, 115

Wallace, Joan Scott, 162

Wallace, Nunc, 380

Waller, Fats, 24

Walls, Josiah Thomas, 173, 174

Walter Heller Graduate School of Business, 50

Walter Reed Army Medical Center, 246

Walters, Rita, 193

"Wanna Be Startin' Somethin'," 28

Wanton, George H., 244

Ward, Benjamin, 208

Ward, Clara Mae, 20

Ward, Everett Blair, 141

Ward, Gertrude, 20

Ward, Horace T., 122

Ward, Joseph H., 354

Ward, Samuel Ringgold, 53, 170, 320

Ward Singers, 20

Waring, Laura Wheeler, 31

Warmoth, Governor Henry Clay, 129

Warren, Joyce Williams, 117

Washburn School of Law, 231

Washington Academy, 335

Washington, Althea, 108

Washington and Lee University, 335

Washington, Booker T., 37, 104, 259, 260

Washington Capitols, 375

Washington, Chester Lloyd, 224

Washington Conservatory of Music, 89

Washington, Dinah, 59

Washington, D.C., Metropolitan Area Transit Authority, 268

Washington, D.C., Urological Society, 298

Washington, George, 214

Washington, Harold, 55, 199

Washington, Joseph Reed, 331

Washington, Kenny, 386

Washington, Madison, 420

Washington, Mildred, 7

Washington, municipal government in, 214

Washington National Cathedral, 325

Washington, Ora, 404

Washington Post, 224, 226

Washington Press Club, 280

Washington Redskins, 387, 390

Washington Square United Methodist Church, 332

Washington State University, 274

Washington University, 159

Washington University School of Law, 136

Washington, Walter, 215

Waterford Trophy, 402

Waters, Ethel, 15, 46

Waters, Muddy (McKinley Morganfield), 21

Watkins, Levi, Jr., 357

Watkins, S. A. T., 197

Watley, William, 295

Watson, Barbara M., 160

Watson, Diane Edith, 119

Watt, Melvin, 185

Wattleton, Faye, 286

WAVES, 253

Wayne State University, 40, 55, 169, 177

WCBS-TV (New York City), 234

WCDX (Richmond, VA), 283

WDIA (Memphis, TN), 34

Weaver, Jonathan L., 301

Weaver, Robert Clifton, 138, 158

Weaver, Sylvester, 16

Webb, Frank J., 414

Webb, Wellington E., 193

Weddington, Elaine C., 373

Wedgeworth, Robert, Jr., 276

"Wee Pals," 2

Weir, Reginald, 404

Welcome, Mary, 196

Welcome, Verda Freeman, 131

Wellesley College, 169

Wells (Barnett), Ida B., 107, 260

Wells, Josiah T., 173, *173*

WENR-TV (Chicago), 38

WERD (Atlanta), 34

Wesley Chapel, 329

Wesley, Carter Walder, 275

Wesley, Charles H., 92

Wesley, John, 328

West Kentucky Industrial College, 224

West Virginia, 151

West Virginia Board of Regents, 86

West Virginia State College, 147, 203, 375

West, Harriet M., 245

West, Togo Dennis, Jr., 163

Westbrook, Scott C. III, 279

Western Colored Baptist Convention, 307

Western Reserve University, 273

Western University, 17

WGBS radio (Pittsburgh), 230

WGPR-TV (Detroit), 40

WGRT (Chicago), 35

Wharton, Clifton Reginald, Jr., 83, 155, 167

Wharton, Dolores, 61

Wharton School of Finance and Commerce, 30

Wheatley, John, 418

Wheatley, Phillis, 109, 418, *418*

Where I'm Coming From, 3

Whipper, Lucille Simmons, 147

White, Bill, 373

White, Charline, 133

White, Cheryl, 394

White, George H., 174

White, Jack E., 356

White, Janice, 209

White, John, 196

White, Slappy, 38

White (Whyte), Willye Brown, 400

Whiteside, Larry W., 279

Whitfield, Malvin Greston "Mal," 407

Whitman, Albery Allson, 418

Whittemore, Cuff, 238

Wichita State University, 389

Wicks, Catherine A., 265

Widener, Warren Hamilton, 191

Wilberforce University, 18, 80, 81, 85, 98, 143, 374, 413

Wilde, Oscar, 45

Wilkins, James Ernest, Jr., 156

Wilkins, James Ernest, Sr., 156

Wilkins, Roger Wood, 226

Wilkins, Roy, 226

Wilkinson, John A., 141

Willamette University Law School, 121

William Byrd plantation, 304

William Morris Agency, 62

William Penn High School, 109

Williams, Althea, 55

Williams, Ann Claire, 169

Williams, Archie, 397

Williams, Art, 371

Williams, Avon Nyanza, Jr., 148

Williams, Bert (Egbert Austin), 12, 32

Williams, Betty Anne, 280

Williams, Camilla, 21

Williams, Charlie, 373

Williams, Clarence, 35

Williams College (MA), 83, 157, 206, 417

Williams, Daniel Hale, 198, 296, 343, 353, 353

Williams, Doug, 390

Williams, Fannie Barrier, 198

Williams, George Washington, 410

Williams, James E., Sr., 199

Williams, Jayne, 192

Williams, Lorraine, 404

Williams, Madaline A., 137

Williams, Marcus Doyle, 151

Williams, Marguerite Thomas, 96

Williams, Nat D., 34

Williams, Paul Revere, 1

Williams, Peter, Jr., 301, 321

Williams, Peter, Sr., 301, 302

Williams, Richard E., 254

Williams, Samuel L., 277

Williams, Toni, 3

Williams, Vanessa Lynn, 259

Williams, Willie L., 212

Williams-Warren, Joyce, 118

Williamson, Carmen, 402

Williamson, Spencer, 7

Willis, A. W., Jr., 147

Willis, Bill, 387

Willis, Billie Ann, 203

Willis, Joseph, 306

Wills, Bump, 373

Wills, Maury, 373

Wilma, 399

Wilson, Barbara J., 50

Wilson, Blenda J., 87

Wilson, Flip (Clerow), 40

Wilson, Frederick D., 62

Wilson, Harriet E. Adams, 414

Wilson, James D., 130

Wilson, Laval S., 112

Wilson, Lionel J., 192

Wilson, Sandra Antoinette, 324

Wimbledon Championship, 405

WIND (Washington, D.C.), 230

Winfield, Hemsley, 4

Winfrey, Oprah, 234

Winkfield, Jimmie, 393

Winston-Salem State University Rams, 377

Wisconsin, 151

Wisconsin Power and Light, 60

Witherspoon, Fredda, 286

WKBS-TV, 232

WLBT-TV (Jackson, MS), 41

WLW (Chicago), 33

WMAQ-TV (Chicago), 233

WNEW-TV (New York), 39

WNTA-TV (New York City), 231

Wolfe, Deborah Partridge, 310

Woman Suffrage Association Convention, 170

Women in Muncipal Government, 280

Women in Real Estate (Chicago), 281

Women's Auxiliary of the National Baptist Convention, 128

Women's Hospital and Dispensary, 352

Women's Loyal Union of New York and Brooklyn, 352

Wood, Robert H., 203

Wood, Thomas A., 51

Woodard, Lynette, 378, 401

Woodfork, Warren G., Sr., 201

Woodruff, John, 397

Woods, Eldrick "Tiger," 391

Woods Electric Company, 346

Woods, Granville T., 345, 346

Woods, Keith, 227

Woods, Lyates, 346

Woodson, Carter Goodwin, 271, 411

Woodson, George H., 275

Wooing and Wedding of a Coon, 6

WOOK (Washington, DC), 34

WOOK radio-television (Washington, D.C.), 230

Woolworth, F. W., store, 73

Works Progress Administration (WPA), 143

World Council of Churches, 327

World Games for the Deaf (1985), 283

Wrestling, 407

Wright, E. H., 125

Wright, George C., 194

Wright, Jane Cooke, 356

Wright, Jonathan Jasper, 146

Wright, Louis Tompkins, 354, *354*

Wright, R. R., Sr., 109

Wright, Richard Robert, Jr., 92

Wright, Richard, 415

Wright, Robert Richard, Jr., 109

Wright, Theodore Sedgewick, 336

WRNY (New York), 33

WTOP-TV (Washington, D.C.), 233

WTVF-TV (Nashville, TN), 234

WWDC radio (Washington, D.C.), 230

WXIA-TV (Atlanta), 277

Wyandotte Indians, 330

Wyatt, Addie, 55

Wyatt-Cummings, Thelma Laverne, 124

X

Xavier University (New Orleans), 100, 130, 164, 375

Xavier University College of Pharmacy, 130

Y

Yale University, 83, 89, 162, 202, 302, 311

Yale University Divinity School, 180

Yale University Law School, 83, 84, 162, 185

Yale University, Phi Beta chapter of, 271

Yale University School of Drama, 47

Yancey, Roger M., 137

Yank magazine, 38

Yarbrough, Marilyn, 85

Yates, Josephine Silone, 107, *107*

Yellow Tavern, 56

Yerby, Frank Garvin, 415

YMCA, 284, 286, 374

YMCA of Greater New York, 288

York, 262

"You Can't Keep a Good Man Down," 35

Young, Andrew Jackson, Jr., 181

Young, Anthony, 374

Young, Buddy, 386

Young, Charles, 244

Young, Coleman, 203

Young, Lee Roy, 149

Young, Maxine, 280

Young, Otis B., Jr., 257

Young, Perry H., 256

Young, Roger Arliner, 89

Younger, Paul "Tank," 387

Youngstown Sheet and Tube Company, 55

Ypsilanti, MI, 202

YWCA, 207, 284, 285, 286, 374

Z

Zebra Associates, 231

Zenith Books, 61

Zeta Phi Beta, 294

Zimbabwe, 101